Ford Fiesta
Service and Repair Manual

Steve Rendle, Mark Coombs and A K Legg LAE MIMI

Models covered

(3397-8AJ6-384)

All Ford Fiesta models with petrol and diesel engines, including Van, Courier and Combi models, and special/limited editions

1242 cc, 1298 cc, 1388 cc and 1596 cc petrol engines
1753 cc diesel engine

Does NOT cover Fiesta Classic

T0385074

© Haynes Group Limited 2005

A book in the **Haynes Service and Repair Manual Series**

ISBN **978 1 78521 287 1**

British Library Cataloguing in Publication Data
A catalogue record for this book is available from the British Library.

Haynes Group Limited
Haynes North America, Inc

www.haynes.com

Contents

LIVING WITH YOUR FORD FIESTA

Safety first!   Page   0•5
Introduction   Page   0•6

Roadside Repairs
If your car won't start   Page   0•7
Jump starting   Page   0•8
Identifying leaks   Page   0•9
Towing   Page   0•9
Wheel changing   Page   0•10

Weekly Checks
Introduction   Page   0•12
Underbonnet check points   Page   0•12
Engine oil level   Page   0•13
Brake and clutch fluid level   Page   0•14
Coolant level   Page   0•15
Power steering fluid level   Page   0•15
Tyre condition and pressure   Page   0•16
Washer fluid level   Page   0•17
Wiper blades   Page   0•17
Battery   Page   0•18
Electrical systems   Page   0•18

Lubricants and fluids   Page   0•19

Tyre pressures   Page   0•20

MAINTENANCE

Routine Maintenance and Servicing

Ford Fiesta petrol models   Page   1A•1
   Servicing specifications   Page   1A•2
   Maintenance schedule   Page   1A•4
   Maintenance procedures   Page   1A•6
Ford Fiesta diesel models   Page   1B•1
   Servicing specifications   Page   1B•2
   Maintenance schedule   Page   1B•3
   Maintenance procedures   Page   1B•6

Contents

REPAIRS & OVERHAUL

Engine and associated systems

Endura-E petrol engine in-car repair procedures	Page **2A•1**
Zetec-SE petrol engine in-car repair procedures	Page **2B•1**
Endura-DE diesel engine in-car repair procedures	Page **2C•1**
Endura-DI diesel engine in-car repair procedures	Page **2D•1**
Engine removal and overhaul procedures	Page **2E•1**
Cooling, heating and air conditioning systems	Page **3•1**
Fuel and exhaust systems – petrol engine models	Page **4A•1**
Fuel and exhaust systems – Endura-DE diesel engine models	Page **4B•1**
Fuel and exhaust systems – Endura-DI diesel engine models	Page **4C•1**
Emission control systems	Page **4D•1**
Starting and charging systems	Page **5A•1**
Ignition system – petrol engine models	Page **5B•1**
Preheating system – diesel engine models	Page **5C•1**

Transmission

Clutch	Page **6•1**
Manual transmission	Page **7A•1**
Automatic transmission	Page **7B•1**
Driveshafts	Page **8•1**

Brakes and suspension

Braking system	Page **9•1**
Suspension and steering	Page **10•1**

Body equipment

Bodywork and fittings	Page **11•1**
Body electrical system	Page **12•1**

Wiring diagrams

	Page **12•20**

REFERENCE

Dimensions and weights	Page **REF•1**
Conversion factors	Page **REF•2**
Buying spare parts	Page **REF•3**
Vehicle identification numbers	Page **REF•3**
General repair procedures	Page **REF•4**
Jacking and vehicle support	Page **REF•5**
Tools and working facilities	Page **REF•6**
MOT test checks	Page **REF•8**
Fault finding	Page **REF•12**
Glossary of technical terms	Page **REF•21**

Index

	Page **REF•26**

Advanced driving

Many people see the words 'advanced driving' and believe that it won't interest them or that it is a style of driving beyond their own abilities. Nothing could be further from the truth. Advanced driving is straightforward safe, sensible driving - the sort of driving we should all do every time we get behind the wheel.

An average of 10 people are killed every day on UK roads and 870 more are injured, some seriously. Lives are ruined daily, usually because somebody did something stupid. Something like 95% of all accidents are due to human error, mostly driver failure. Sometimes we make genuine mistakes - everyone does. Sometimes we have lapses of concentration. Sometimes we deliberately take risks.

For many people, the process of 'learning to drive' doesn't go much further than learning how to pass the driving test because of a common belief that good drivers are made by 'experience'.

Learning to drive by 'experience' teaches three driving skills:

☐ Quick reactions. (Whoops, that was close!)
☐ Good handling skills. (Horn, swerve, brake, horn).
☐ Reliance on vehicle technology. (Great stuff this ABS, stop in no distance even in the wet...)

Drivers whose skills are 'experience based' generally have a lot of near misses and the odd accident. The results can be seen every day in our courts and our hospital casualty departments.

Advanced drivers have learnt to control the risks by controlling the position and speed of their vehicle. They avoid accidents and near misses, even if the drivers around them make mistakes.

The key skills of advanced driving are **concentration,** effective all-round **observation, anticipation** and **planning.** When **good vehicle handling** is added to

these skills, all driving situations can be approached and negotiated in a safe, methodical way, leaving nothing to chance.

Concentration means applying your mind to safe driving, completely excluding anything that's not relevant. Driving is usually the most dangerous activity that most of us undertake in our daily routines. It deserves our full attention.

Observation means not just looking, but seeing and seeking out the information found in the driving environment.

Anticipation means asking yourself what is happening, what you can reasonably expect to happen and what could happen unexpectedly. (One of the commonest words used in compiling accident reports is 'suddenly'.)

Planning is the link between seeing something and taking the appropriate action. For many drivers, planning is the missing link.

If you want to become a safer and more skilful driver and you want to enjoy your driving more, contact the Institute of Advanced Motorists at www.iam.org.uk, phone 0208 996 9600, or write to IAM House, 510 Chiswick High Road, London W4 5RG for an information pack.

Working on your car can be dangerous. This page shows just some of the potential risks and hazards, with the aim of creating a safety-conscious attitude.

General hazards

Scalding

• Don't remove the radiator or expansion tank cap while the engine is hot.
• Engine oil, automatic transmission fluid or power steering fluid may also be dangerously hot if the engine has recently been running.

Burning

• Beware of burns from the exhaust system and from any part of the engine. Brake discs and drums can also be extremely hot immediately after use.

Crushing

• When working under or near a raised vehicle, always supplement the jack with axle stands, or use drive-on ramps. **Never venture under a car which is only supported by a jack.**
• Take care if loosening or tightening high-torque nuts when the vehicle is on stands. Initial loosening and final tightening should be done with the wheels on the ground.

Fire

• Fuel is highly flammable; fuel vapour is explosive.
• Don't let fuel spill onto a hot engine.
• Do not smoke or allow naked lights (including pilot lights) anywhere near a vehicle being worked on. Also beware of creating sparks (electrically or by use of tools).
• Fuel vapour is heavier than air, so don't work on the fuel system with the vehicle over an inspection pit.
• Another cause of fire is an electrical overload or short-circuit. Take care when repairing or modifying the vehicle wiring.
• Keep a fire extinguisher handy, of a type suitable for use on fuel and electrical fires.

Electric shock

• Ignition HT voltage can be dangerous, especially to people with heart problems or a pacemaker. Don't work on or near the ignition system with the engine running or the ignition switched on.

• Mains voltage is also dangerous. Make sure that any mains-operated equipment is correctly earthed. Mains power points should be protected by a residual current device (RCD) circuit breaker.

Fume or gas intoxication

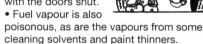

• Exhaust fumes are poisonous; they often contain carbon monoxide, which is rapidly fatal if inhaled. Never run the engine in a confined space such as a garage with the doors shut.
• Fuel vapour is also poisonous, as are the vapours from some cleaning solvents and paint thinners.

Poisonous or irritant substances

• Avoid skin contact with battery acid and with any fuel, fluid or lubricant, especially antifreeze, brake hydraulic fluid and Diesel fuel. Don't syphon them by mouth. If such a substance is swallowed or gets into the eyes, seek medical advice.
• Prolonged contact with used engine oil can cause skin cancer. Wear gloves or use a barrier cream if necessary. Change out of oil-soaked clothes and do not keep oily rags in your pocket.
• Air conditioning refrigerant forms a poisonous gas if exposed to a naked flame (including a cigarette). It can also cause skin burns on contact.

Asbestos

• Asbestos dust can cause cancer if inhaled or swallowed. Asbestos may be found in gaskets and in brake and clutch linings. When dealing with such components it is safest to assume that they contain asbestos.

Special hazards

Hydrofluoric acid

• This extremely corrosive acid is formed when certain types of synthetic rubber, found in some O-rings, oil seals, fuel hoses etc, are exposed to temperatures above 400°C. The rubber changes into a charred or sticky substance containing the acid. *Once formed, the acid remains dangerous for years. If it gets onto the skin, it may be necessary to amputate the limb concerned.*
• When dealing with a vehicle which has suffered a fire, or with components salvaged from such a vehicle, wear protective gloves and discard them after use.

The battery

• Batteries contain sulphuric acid, which attacks clothing, eyes and skin. Take care when topping-up or carrying the battery.
• The hydrogen gas given off by the battery is highly explosive. Never cause a spark or allow a naked light nearby. Be careful when connecting and disconnecting battery chargers or jump leads.

Air bags

• Air bags can cause injury if they go off accidentally. Take care when removing the steering wheel and/or facia. Special storage instructions may apply.

Diesel injection equipment

• Diesel injection pumps supply fuel at very high pressure. Take care when working on the fuel injectors and fuel pipes.

⚠ *Warning: Never expose the hands, face or any other part of the body to injector spray; the fuel can penetrate the skin with potentially fatal results.*

Remember...

DO

• Do use eye protection when using power tools, and when working under the vehicle.

• Do wear gloves or use barrier cream to protect your hands when necessary.

• Do get someone to check periodically that all is well when working alone on the vehicle.

• Do keep loose clothing and long hair well out of the way of moving mechanical parts.

• Do remove rings, wristwatch etc, before working on the vehicle – especially the electrical system.

• Do ensure that any lifting or jacking equipment has a safe working load rating adequate for the job.

DON'T

• Don't attempt to lift a heavy component which may be beyond your capability – get assistance.

• Don't rush to finish a job, or take unverified short cuts.

• Don't use ill-fitting tools which may slip and cause injury.

• Don't leave tools or parts lying around where someone can trip over them. Mop up oil and fuel spills at once.

• Don't allow children or pets to play in or near a vehicle being worked on.

The Ford Fiesta model range covered by this manual was introduced into the UK in October 1995 to supersede the previous Fiesta range. 3-door and 5-door Hatchback models are available, along with 3-door Van, and Courier and Combi light commercial variants (the Combi model is basically a Courier light commercial fitted with rear passenger seats and windows).

1.25, 1.4 and 1.6 litre 16-valve, and 1.3 litre 8-valve petrol engines are available, as well as two 1.8 litre diesel engines. All engines are mounted transversely at the front of the vehicle.

Models may be fitted with five-speed manual, or CTX continuously variable automatic transmissions, mounted at the left-hand side of the engine.

All models have front-wheel-drive with fully-independent front and semi-independent rear suspension. The front suspension is of conventional McPherson strut type, incorporating lower arms, and an anti-roll bar. Hatchback and Van models use a rear beam axle with trailing arms and McPherson struts, whereas the Courier and Combi models use a torsion bar rear suspension to provide a more spacious load area.

All models have a high trim level, which is very comprehensive in the upper model range. Driver's and passenger's airbag systems, central locking, electric windows, an electric sunroof, anti-lock brakes, and air conditioning are all available.

For the home mechanic, the Ford Fiesta is a relatively straightforward vehicle to maintain and repair since design features have been incorporated to reduce the actual cost of ownership to a minimum, and most of the items requiring frequent attention are easily accessible.

Your Ford Fiesta Manual

The aim of this manual is to help you get the best value from your vehicle. It can do so in several ways. It can help you decide what work must be done (even should you choose to get it done by a garage), provide information on routine maintenance and servicing, and give a logical course of action and diagnosis when random faults occur. However, it is hoped that you will use the manual by tackling the work yourself. On simpler jobs, it may even be quicker than booking the car into a garage and going there twice, to leave and collect it. Perhaps most important, a lot of money can be saved by avoiding the costs a garage must charge to cover its labour and overheads.

The manual has drawings and descriptions to show the function of the various components, so that their layout can be understood. Then the tasks are described and photographed in a clear step-by-step sequence.

References to the 'left' or 'right' of the vehicle are in the sense of a person in the driving seat, facing forwards.

Acknowledgements

Certain illustrations are the copyright of the Ford Motor Company, and are used with their permission. Thanks are also due to Draper Tools Limited, who provided some of the workshop tools, and to all those people at Sparkford who helped in the production of this manual.

We take great pride in the accuracy of information given in this manual, but vehicle manufacturers make alterations and design changes during the production run of a particular vehicle of which they do not inform us. No liability can be accepted by the authors or publishers for loss, damage or injury caused by any errors in, or omissions from, the information given.

The following pages are intended to help in dealing with common roadside emergencies and breakdowns. You will find more detailed fault finding information at the back of the manual, and repair information in the main chapters.

If your car won't start and the starter motor doesn't turn

☐ If it's a model with automatic transmission, make sure the selector is in P or N.
☐ Open the bonnet and make sure that the battery terminals are clean and tight.
☐ Switch on the headlights and try to start the engine. If the headlights go very dim when you're trying to start, the battery is probably flat. Get out of trouble by jump starting (see next page) using a friend's car.

If your car won't start even though the starter motor turns as normal

☐ Is there fuel in the tank?
☐ Is there moisture on electrical components under the bonnet? Switch off the ignition, then wipe off any obvious dampness with a dry cloth. Spray a water-repellent aerosol product (WD-40 or equivalent) on ignition and fuel system electrical connectors like those shown in the photos. Pay special attention to the ignition coil, wiring connector and HT leads. (Note that diesel engines don't normally suffer from damp.)

A Check the condition and security of the battery connections.

B Check that the spark plug HT leads are securely connected by pushing them onto the ignition coil (petrol models).

C Check that the wiring connectors are securely connected to the ignition coil (petrol models).

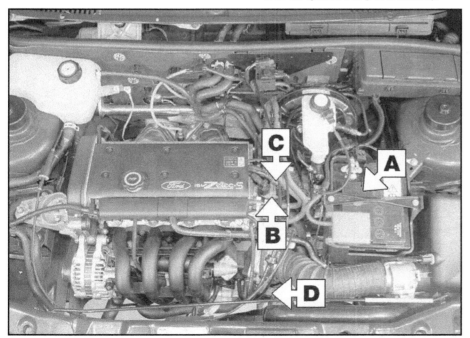

Check that electrical connections are secure (with the ignition switched off) and spray them with a water dispersant spray like WD-40 if you suspect a problem due to damp.

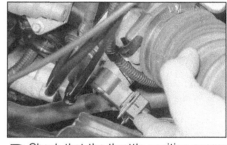

D Check that the throttle position sensor wiring plug is securely connected (petrol models).

E Check that the fuel cut-off switch has not been activated (petrol models).

HAYNES HINT

Jump starting will get you out of trouble, but you must correct whatever made the battery go flat in the first place. There are three possibilities:

1 *The battery has been drained by repeated attempts to start, or by leaving the lights on.*

2 *The charging system is not working properly (alternator drivebelt slack or broken, alternator wiring fault or alternator itself faulty).*

3 *The battery itself is at fault (electrolyte low, or battery worn out).*

When jump-starting a car using a booster battery, observe the following precautions:

✔ Before connecting the booster battery, make sure that the ignition is switched off.

✔ Ensure that all electrical equipment (lights, heater, wipers, etc) is switched off.

✔ Take note of any special precautions printed on the battery case.

✔ Make sure that the booster battery is the same voltage as the discharged one in the vehicle.

✔ If the battery is being jump-started from the battery in another vehicle, the two vehicles MUST NOT TOUCH each other.

✔ Make sure that the transmission is in neutral (or PARK, in the case of automatic transmission).

1 Connect one end of the red jump lead to the positive (+) terminal of the flat battery

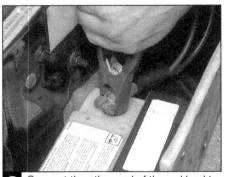

2 Connect the other end of the red lead to the positive (+) terminal of the booster battery.

3 Connect one end of the black jump lead to the negative (-) terminal of the booster battery

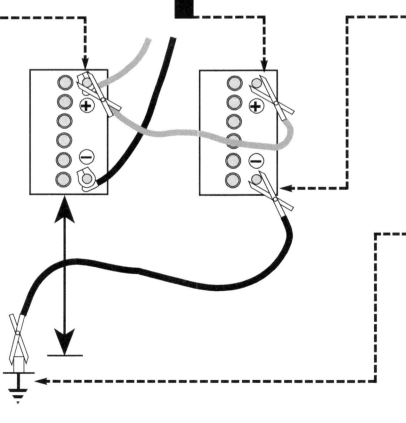

4 Connect the other end of the black jump lead to a bolt or bracket on the engine block, well away from the battery, on the vehicle to be started.

5 Make sure that the jump leads will not come into contact with the fan, drive-belts or other moving parts of the engine.

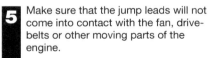

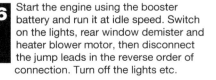

6 Start the engine using the booster battery and run it at idle speed. Switch on the lights, rear window demister and heater blower motor, then disconnect the jump leads in the reverse order of connection. Turn off the lights etc.

Identifying leaks

Puddles on the garage floor or drive, or obvious wetness under the bonnet or underneath the car, suggest a leak that needs investigating. It can sometimes be difficult to decide where the leak is coming from, especially if the engine bay is very dirty already. Leaking oil or fluid can also be blown rearwards by the passage of air under the car, giving a false impression of where the problem lies.

Warning: Most automotive oils and fluids are poisonous. Wash them off skin, and change out of contaminated clothing, without delay.

 The smell of a fluid leaking from the car may provide a clue to what's leaking. Some fluids are distinctively coloured. It may help to clean the car carefully and to park it over some clean paper overnight as an aid to locating the source of the leak.
Remember that some leaks may only occur while the engine is running.

Sump oil

Engine oil may leak from the drain plug...

Oil from filter

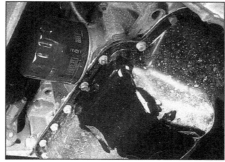

...or from the base of the oil filter.

Gearbox oil

Gearbox oil can leak from the seals at the inboard ends of the driveshafts.

Antifreeze

Leaking antifreeze often leaves a crystalline deposit like this.

Brake fluid

A leak occurring at a wheel is almost certainly brake fluid.

Power steering fluid

Power steering fluid may leak from the pipe connectors on the steering rack.

Towing

When all else fails, you may find yourself having to get a tow home – or of course you may be helping somebody else. Long-distance recovery should only be done by a garage or breakdown service. For shorter distances, DIY towing using another car is easy enough, but observe the following points:

☐ Use a proper tow-rope – they are not expensive. The vehicle being towed must display an ON TOW sign in its rear window.
☐ Always turn the ignition key to the 'on' position when the vehicle is being towed, so that the steering lock is released, and that the direction indicator and brake lights will work.

☐ Before being towed, release the handbrake and select neutral on the transmission.
☐ On models with automatic transmission, special precautions apply. If in doubt, do not tow, or transmission damage may result.
☐ Note that greater-than-usual pedal pressure will be required to operate the brakes, since the vacuum servo unit is only operational with the engine running.
☐ On models with power steering, greater-than-usual steering effort will also be required.
☐ The driver of the car being towed must keep the tow-rope taut at all times to avoid snatching.
☐ Make sure that both drivers know the route before setting off.

☐ Only drive at moderate speeds and keep the distance towed to a minimum. Drive smoothly and allow plenty of time for slowing down at junctions.
☐ A towing eye is supplied as part of the vehicle tool kit. The towing eye is located with the jack and wheelbrace in the luggage compartment (see *Wheel changing*).
☐ To fit the towing eye, prise the cover from the relevant bumper, then screw in the towing eye, anti-clockwise as far as it will go. **Note that the towing eye has a left-hand thread.** Tighten the towing eye with the wheelbrace. On Courier and Combi models, a fixed rear towing eye is welded to the rear of the chassis.

Wheel changing

Some of the details shown here will vary according to model. For instance, the location of the spare wheel and jack is not the same on all cars. However, the basic principles apply to all vehicles.

Warning: Do not change a wheel in a situation where you risk being hit by other traffic. On busy roads, try to stop in a lay-by or a gateway. Be wary of passing traffic while changing the wheel – it is easy to become distracted by the job in hand.

Preparation

☐ When a puncture occurs, stop as soon as it is safe to do so.
☐ Park on firm level ground, if possible, and well out of the way of other traffic.

☐ Use hazard warning lights if necessary.
☐ If you have one, use a warning triangle to alert other drivers of your presence.
☐ Apply the handbrake and engage first or reverse gear (or Park on models with automatic transmission).

☐ Chock the wheel diagonally opposite the one being removed – a couple of large stones will do for this.
☐ If the ground is soft, use a flat piece of wood to spread the load under the jack.

Changing the wheel

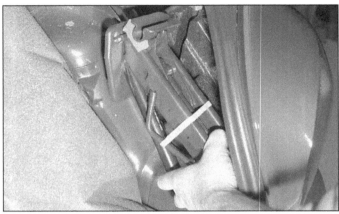

1 On Hatchback and Van models, the jack and wheelbrace are behind the trim panel on the right-hand side of the luggage compartment. Release the securing clip and fold back the trim panel from the side of the luggage compartment, then unhook the securing strap, and lift out the jack and wheelbrace. The wheelbrace is clipped to the jack.

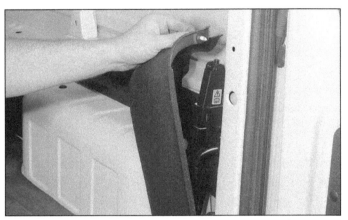

2 On Courier/Combi models, the jack, wheelbrace and jack handle are located behind the trim panel in front of the right-hand rear light assembly. Release the securing clip at the top of the trim panel, then lift the panel out. Unscrew the wing nut securing the jack retaining bracket, then swivel the bracket round until the jack and wheelbrace can be removed. Pull the jack handle from the retaining clips.

3 The spare wheel is in a cradle under the rear of the vehicle. Pull up the cover in the luggage compartment for access to the spare wheel cradle securing screw. Using the wheelbrace, loosen the screw then unhook the spare wheel cradle from the securing bracket under the back of the vehicle, and lower the cradle until it is resting on the floor.

4 On some models, it may be necessary to unclip a safety cord from the cradle before it can be fully lowered. Lift the spare wheel from the cradle.

5 Where applicable, prise off the wheel trim from the punctured wheel, using the end of the wheelbrace, then loosen each wheel nut by half a turn.

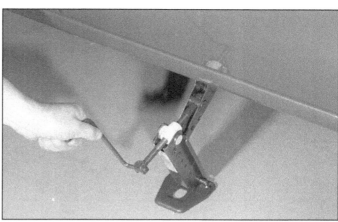

6 Locate the jack head below the reinforced jacking point nearest the wheel to be changed, and on firm ground. Ensure that the lug on the jack head engages with the cut-out in the jacking point.

7 Turn the jack handle clockwise (on Courier and Combi models, engage the end of the jack handle with the jack) until the wheel is raised clear of the ground. Remove the nuts and lift the wheel clear, then fit the spare wheel. Refit the wheel nuts and tighten moderately with the wheelbrace.

8 Lower the car to the ground, then finally tighten the wheel nuts in a diagonal sequence, and where applicable, fit the wheel trim. Note that the wheel nuts should be slackened and retightened to the specified torque at the earliest opportunity (see Chapter 1A or 1B).

Finally . . .

☐ Remove the wheel chocks.

☐ Stow the jack and tools in the correct locations in the car.

☐ Check the tyre pressure on the wheel just fitted. If it is low, or if you don't have a pressure gauge with you, drive slowly to the nearest garage and inflate the tyre to the correct pressure.

☐ Have the damaged tyre or wheel repaired, or renew it, as soon as possible.

Introduction

There are some very simple checks which need only take a few minutes to carry out, but which could save you a lot of inconvenience and expense.

These *Weekly checks* require no great skill or special tools, and the small amount of time they take to perform could prove to be very well spent, for example;

□ Keeping an eye on tyre condition and pressures, will not only help to stop them wearing out prematurely, but could also save your life.

□ Many breakdowns are caused by electrical problems. Battery-related faults are particularly common, and a quick check on a regular basis will often prevent the majority of these.

□ If your car develops a brake fluid leak, the first time you might know about it is when your brakes don't work properly. Checking the level regularly will give advance warning of this kind of problem.

□ If the oil or coolant levels run low, the cost of repairing any engine damage will be far greater than fixing the leak, for example.

Underbonnet check points

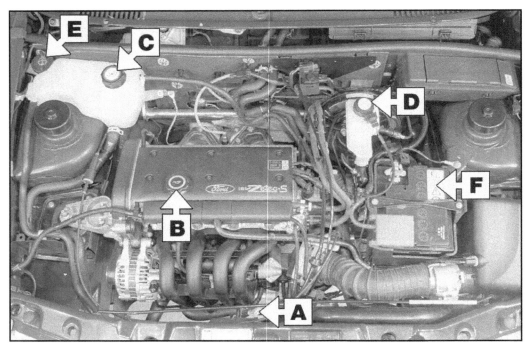

◄ **1.25 litre Zetec SE petrol**

A *Engine oil level dipstick*

B *Engine oil filler cap*

C *Coolant reservoir (expansion tank)*

D *Brake and clutch fluid reservoir*

E *Washer fluid reservoir*

F *Battery*

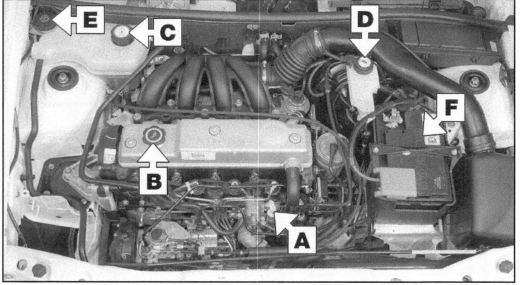

◄ **1.8 litre Endura-DE diesel**

A *Engine oil level dipstick*

B *Engine oil filler cap*

C *Coolant reservoir (expansion tank)*

D *Brake and clutch fluid reservoir*

E *Washer fluid reservoir*

F *Battery*

Engine oil level

Before you start

✔ Make sure that your car is on level ground.
✔ Check the oil level before the car is driven, or at least 5 minutes after the engine has been switched off.

The correct oil

Modern engines place great demands on their oil. It is very important that the correct oil for your car is used (See 'Lubricants and fluids').

Car Care

● If you have to add oil frequently, you should check whether you have any oil leaks. Place some clean paper under the car overnight, and check for stains in the morning. If there are no leaks, the engine may be burning oil.

● Always maintain the level between the upper and lower dipstick marks (see illustration 3). If the level is too low, severe engine damage may occur. Oil seal failure may result if the engine is overfilled by adding too much oil.

 HAYNES HiNT *If the oil level is checked immediately after driving the vehicle, some of the oil will remain in the upper engine components, resulting in an inaccurate reading on the dipstick.*

1 The dipstick is located in a tube at the front of the engine on Zetec-SE petrol engines and diesel engines, or at the rear of the engine on Endura-E petrol engines (see *Underbonnet check points* for exact location). Withdraw the dipstick.

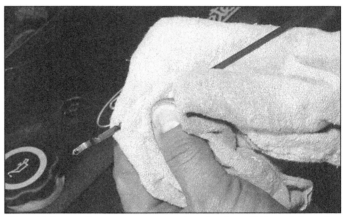

2 Using a clean rag or paper towel, wipe all the oil from the dipstick. Insert the clean dipstick into the tube as far as it will go, then withdraw it again.

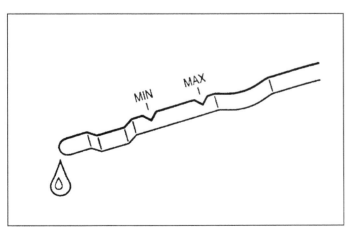

3 Note the oil level on the end of the dipstick, which should be between the upper (MAX) mark and the lower (MIN) mark. The dipstick will vary according to the type of engine fitted.

4 Oil is added through the filler cap. Unscrew the filler cap, then top-up the level. A funnel may help to reduce spillage. Add the oil slowly, checking the level on the dipstick often. Don't overfill.

Brake and clutch fluid level

All models have a hydraulically-operated clutch, which uses the same fluid as the braking system

Warning:
● Brake fluid can harm your eyes and damage painted surfaces, so use extreme caution when handling and pouring it.
● Do not use fluid that has been standing open for some time, as it absorbs moisture from the air, which can cause a dangerous loss of braking effectiveness.

● Make sure that your car is on level ground.
● The fluid level in the reservoir will drop slightly as the brake pads wear down, but the fluid level must never be allowed to drop below the MIN mark.

Safety First!

● If the reservoir requires repeated topping-up this is an indication of a fluid leak somewhere in the system, which should be investigated immediately.

● If a leak is suspected, the car should not be driven until the braking system has been checked. Never take any risks where brakes are concerned.

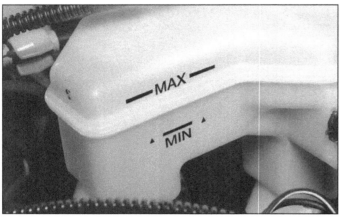

1 The MAX and MIN marks are indicated on the side of the reservoir, which is located at the rear left-hand side of the engine compartment. The fluid level must be kept between these two marks.

2 If topping-up is necessary, first wipe the area around the filler cap with a clean rag, then hold the fluid level sensor wiring plug as the cap is unscrewed. When adding fluid, it's a good idea to inspect the reservoir. The fluid should be changed if dirt is visible.

3 Carefully add fluid, avoiding spilling it on surrounding paintwork. Use only the specified hydraulic fluid; mixing different types of fluid can cause damage to the system and/or a loss of braking effectiveness. Bear in mind that the level in the reservoir will rise slightly when the cap/float assembly is refitted. After filling to the correct level, refit the cap securely. Wipe off any spilt fluid.

4 When checking the fluid level, also check the operation of the low fluid level warning light. Switch on the ignition and ask an assistant to press the button on top of the reservoir cap. The brake fluid level/handbrake 'on' warning light should come on – if not, the level switch, wiring or bulb may be faulty. If the warning light comes on and the fluid level is not low, check that the handbrake is not on. Switch off the ignition after testing.

Coolant level

Warning: DO NOT attempt to remove the expansion tank pressure cap when the engine is hot, as there is a very great risk of scalding. Do not leave open containers of coolant about, as it is poisonous.

Car Care
● Adding coolant should not be necessary on a regular basis. If frequent topping-up is required, it is likely there is a leak. Check the radiator, all hoses and joint faces for signs of staining or wetness, and rectify as necessary.

● It is important that antifreeze is used in the cooling system all year round, not just during the winter months. Don't top-up with water alone, as the antifreeze will become too diluted.
● Use the correct antifreeze – see *Lubricants and fluids* and the relevant part of Chapter 1.

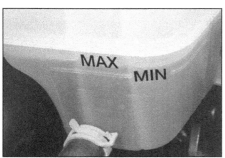

1 The coolant level varies with the temperature of the engine. The expansion tank has MAX and MIN level markings. When cold, the level should be between the two marks. When the engine is hot, the level may rise slightly above the MAX mark.

2 If topping-up is necessary, wait until the engine is cold, then turn the pressure cap on the expansion tank slowly anti-clockwise, and pause until any pressure remaining in the system is released. Unscrew the cap and lift off.

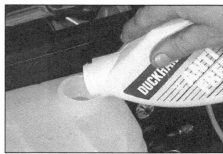

3 Add a mixture of water and antifreeze to the expansion tank, until the coolant is up to the MAX mark. Refit the cap, turning it clockwise as far as it will go until it is secure. Re-check that the cap is securely tightened once the engine is warm.

Power steering fluid level

Before you start
✔ Park the vehicle on level ground.
✔ Set the steering wheel straight-ahead.
✔ The engine should be turned off.

HAYNES HiNT *For the check to be accurate, the steering must not be turned once the engine has been stopped.*

Safety First!
● The need for frequent topping-up indicates a leak, which should be investigated immediately.

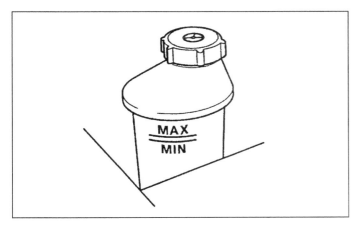

1 The power steering fluid reservoir is located at the front right-hand corner of the engine compartment. The fluid level should be checked with the engine stopped. A translucent reservoir is fitted, with MAX and MIN markings on the side of the reservoir.

2 The fluid level should be between the MAX and MIN marks. If topping-up is necessary, and before removing the cap, wipe the surrounding area so that dirt does not enter the reservoir.

3 Unscrew the cap, allowing the fluid to drain from the bottom of the cap as it is removed. Top-up the fluid level to the MAX mark, using the specified type of fluid (do not overfill the reservoir), then refit and tighten the filler cap.

Tyre condition and pressure

It is very important that tyres are in good condition, and at the correct pressure - having a tyre failure at any speed is highly dangerous. Tyre wear is influenced by driving style - harsh braking and acceleration, or fast cornering, will all produce more rapid tyre wear. As a general rule, the front tyres wear out faster than the rears. Interchanging the tyres from front to rear ("rotating" the tyres) may result in more even wear. However, if this is completely effective, you may have the expense of replacing all four tyres at once!

Remove any nails or stones embedded in the tread before they penetrate the tyre to cause deflation. If removal of a nail does reveal that the tyre has been punctured, refit the nail so that its point of penetration is marked. Then immediately change the wheel, and have the tyre repaired by a tyre dealer.

Regularly check the tyres for damage in the form of cuts or bulges, especially in the sidewalls. Periodically remove the wheels, and clean any dirt or mud from the inside and outside surfaces. Examine the wheel rims for signs of rusting, corrosion or other damage. Light alloy wheels are easily damaged by "kerbing" whilst parking; steel wheels may also become dented or buckled. A new wheel is very often the only way to overcome severe damage.

New tyres should be balanced when they are fitted, but it may become necessary to re-balance them as they wear, or if the balance weights fitted to the wheel rim should fall off. Unbalanced tyres will wear more quickly, as will the steering and suspension components. Wheel imbalance is normally signified by vibration, particularly at a certain speed (typically around 50 mph). If this vibration is felt only through the steering, then it is likely that just the front wheels need balancing. If, however, the vibration is felt through the whole car, the rear wheels could be out of balance. Wheel balancing should be carried out by a tyre dealer or garage.

1 Tread Depth - visual check
The original tyres have tread wear safety bands (B), which will appear when the tread depth reaches approximately 1.6 mm. The band positions are indicated by a triangular mark on the tyre sidewall (A).

2 Tread Depth - manual check
Alternatively, tread wear can be monitored with a simple, inexpensive device known as a tread depth indicator gauge.

3 Tyre Pressure Check
Check the tyre pressures regularly with the tyres cold. Do not adjust the tyre pressures immediately after the vehicle has been used, or an inaccurate setting will result.

Tyre tread wear patterns

Shoulder Wear

Underinflation (wear on both sides)
Under-inflation will cause overheating of the tyre, because the tyre will flex too much, and the tread will not sit correctly on the road surface. This will cause a loss of grip and excessive wear, not to mention the danger of sudden tyre failure due to heat build-up.
Check and adjust pressures
Incorrect wheel camber (wear on one side)
Repair or renew suspension parts
Hard cornering
Reduce speed!

Centre Wear

Overinflation
Over-inflation will cause rapid wear of the centre part of the tyre tread, coupled with reduced grip, harsher ride, and the danger of shock damage occurring in the tyre casing.
Check and adjust pressures

If you sometimes have to inflate your car's tyres to the higher pressures specified for maximum load or sustained high speed, don't forget to reduce the pressures to normal afterwards.

Uneven Wear

Front tyres may wear unevenly as a result of wheel misalignment. Most tyre dealers and garages can check and adjust the wheel alignment (or "tracking") for a modest charge.
Incorrect camber or castor
Repair or renew suspension parts
Malfunctioning suspension
Repair or renew suspension parts
Unbalanced wheel
Balance tyres
Incorrect toe setting
Adjust front wheel alignment
Note: *The feathered edge of the tread which typifies toe wear is best checked by feel.*

Washer fluid level

Screenwash additives not only keep the windscreen clean during foul weather, they also prevent the washer system freezing in cold weather – which is when you are likely to need it most. Don't top-up using plain water as the screenwash will become too diluted, and will freeze during cold weather.

Warning: On no account use coolant antifreeze in the washer system - this could discolour or damage paintwork.

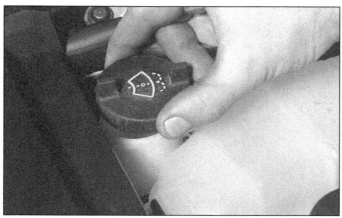

1 The windscreen/tailgate/headlight washer fluid reservoir is located at the rear right-hand corner of the engine compartment. If topping-up is necessary, open the cap.

2 When topping-up the reservoir a screenwash additive should be added in the quantities recommended on the bottle.

Wiper blades

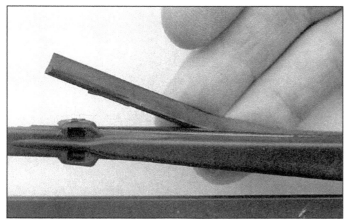

1 Check the condition of the wiper blades; if they are cracked or show any signs of deterioration, or if the glass swept area is smeared, renew them. For maximum clarity of vision, wiper blades should be renewed annually, as a matter of course.

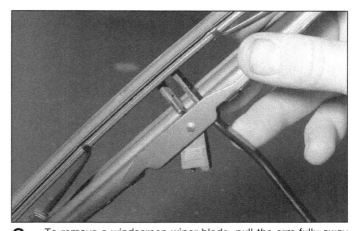

2 To remove a windscreen wiper blade, pull the arm fully away from the screen until it locks. Swivel the blade through 90°, then depress the locking clip at the base of the mounting block, and slide the blade out of the hooked end of the arm. Where applicable, don't forget to check the tailgate wiper blade as well. The blade can be removed by swivelling the blade through 90°, then sliding the blade from the arm.

Battery

Caution: Before carrying out any work on the vehicle battery, read the precautions given in 'Safety first!' at the start of this manual.

✔ Periodically (approximately every three months), check the charge condition of the battery as described in Chapter 5A.

✔ If the battery is flat, and you need to jump start your vehicle, see *Roadside Repairs*.

✔ Make sure that the battery tray is in good condition, and that the clamp is tight. Corrosion on the tray, retaining clamp and the battery itself can be removed with a solution of water and baking soda. Thoroughly rinse all cleaned areas with water. Any metal parts damaged by corrosion should be covered with a zinc-based primer, then painted.

HAYNES HiNT

Battery corrosion can be kept to a minimum by applying a layer of petroleum jelly to the clamps and terminals after they are reconnected

1 The battery is located on the left-hand side of the engine compartment. The exterior of the battery should be inspected periodically for damage such as a cracked case or cover.

2 Check the tightness of the battery cable clamps to ensure good electrical connections. You should not be able to move them. Also check each cable for cracks and frayed conductors.

3 If corrosion (white, fluffy deposits) is evident, remove the cables from the battery terminals, clean them with a small wire brush, then refit them. Automotive stores sell a tool for cleaning the battery post . . .

4 . . . as well as the battery cable clamps.

Electrical systems

✔ Check all external lights and the horn. Refer to the appropriate Sections of Chapter 12 for details if any of the circuits are found to be inoperative.

✔ Visually check all accessible wiring connectors, harnesses and retaining clips for security, and for signs of chafing or damage.

 HAYNES HiNT *If you need to check your brake lights and indicators unaided, back up to a wall or garage door and operate the lights. The reflected light should show if they are working properly.*

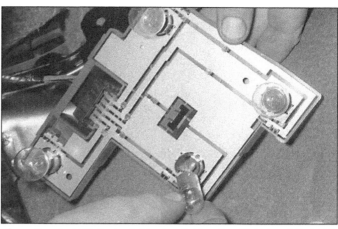

1 If a single indicator light, stop-light or headlight has failed, it is likely that a bulb has blown and will need to be replaced. Refer to Chapter 12 for details. If both stop-lights have failed, it is possible that the stop-light switch operated by the brake pedal has failed. Refer to Chapter 9 for details.

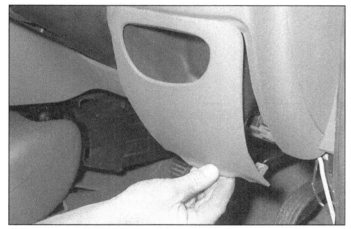

2 If more than one indicator light or headlight has failed, it is likely that either a fuse has blown or that there is a fault in the circuit (see Chapter 12). The main fuses are mounted in a panel located at the lower driver's side of the facia under a cover. Pull the cover to release it from the facia. Additional fuses are located in the auxiliary fusebox at the rear left-hand corner of the engine compartment.

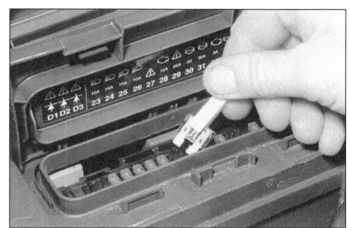

3 To renew a blown fuse, remove it, where applicable, using the plastic tool provided. Fit a new fuse of the same rating, available from car accessory shops. It is important that you find the reason that the fuse blew (see *Electrical fault finding* in Chapter 12).

Engine

Pre-July 1998 models:

Recommended oil . . . . Multigrade engine oil, viscosity SAE 5W/30, to Ford specification WSS-M2C913-A or WSS-M2C912-A1

Alternative oil . . . . Multigrade engine oil, viscosity SAE 5W/40 to 10W/40, to ACEA-A3/B3 or A1/B1

July 1998 models onwards* . . . . Multigrade engine oil, viscosity SAE 5W/30, to Ford specification WSS-M2C913-A or WSS-M2C912-A1

Cooling system

Pre-September 1998 models (blue/green coolant)** . . . . Ethylene glycol-based antifreeze to Ford specification ESD-M97B49-A

September 1998 models onward (orange coolant)** . . . . Monoethylene glycol-based antifreeze to Ford specification WSS-M97B44-D

Manual transmission . . . . SAE 75W/90 synthetic gear oil, to Ford specification WSD-M2C200-B

Automatic transmission . . . . Transmission fluid to Ford specification ESP-M2C166-H

Braking system . . . . Hydraulic fluid to DOT 4 and Ford specification SAM-6C9103-A

Power steering . . . . Transmission fluid to Ford Specification ESP-M2C166-H

Wheel bearing grease . . . . Grease to Ford specification SAM-1C9111-A

* Multigrade engine oil, viscosity SAE 5W/40 to 10W/40, to ACEA-A3/B3 or A1/B1 may be used for topping-up only.
** Do not mix the two coolant types.

Choosing your engine oil

Engines need oil, not only to lubricate moving parts and minimise wear, but also to maximise power output and to improve fuel economy.

HOW ENGINE OIL WORKS

• *Beating friction*

Without oil, the moving surfaces inside your engine will rub together, heat up and melt, quickly causing the engine to seize. Engine oil creates a film which separates these moving parts, preventing wear and heat build-up.

• *Cooling hot-spots*

Temperatures inside the engine can exceed 1000° C. The engine oil circulates and acts as a coolant, transferring heat from the hot-spots to the sump.

• *Cleaning the engine internally*

Good quality engine oils clean the inside of your engine, collecting and dispersing combustion deposits and controlling them until they are trapped by the oil filter or flushed out at oil change.

OIL CARE - FOLLOW THE CODE

To handle and dispose of used engine oil safely, always:

0800 66 33 66
www.oilbankline.org.uk

- • *Avoid skin contact with used engine oil. Repeated or prolonged contact can be harmful.*
- • *Dispose of used oil and empty packs in a responsible manner in an authorised disposal site. Call 0800 663366 to find the one nearest to you. Never tip oil down drains or onto the ground.*

Note: *Pressures given here are a guide only, and apply to original-equipment tyres – the recommended pressures may vary if any other make or type of tyre is fitted; check with the vehicle handbook, or the tyre manufacturer or supplier for latest recommendations.*

Normal load (up to 3 people)

	Front	Rear
155/70 R 13 tyres:		
Hatchback models	2.4 bar (35 psi)	1.8 bar (26 psi)
Van models	2.1 bar (30 psi)	1.8 bar (26 psi)
165/60 R 14 tyres:		
All models except 1.4 litre Zetec-SE petrol engine models	2.1 bar (30 psi)	1.8 bar (26 psi)
1.4 litre Zetec-SE petrol engine models	2.2 bar (32 psi)	2.0 bar (29 psi)
165/65 R 14 tyres:		
All models except 1.4 litre Zetec-SE petrol engine models	2.2 bar (32 psi)	1.8 bar (26 psi)
1.4 litre Zetec-SE petrol engine models	2.2 bar (32 psi)	2.0 bar (29 psi)
165/70 R 13 tyres:		
All models except Courier and Combi	2.1 bar (30 psi)	1.8 bar (26 psi)
Courier and Combi models	2.0 bar (29 psi)	1.8 bar (26 psi)
175/65 R 14 tyres:		
All petrol engine models except 1.4 litre Zetec-SE	2.2 bar (32 psi)	1.8 bar (26 psi)
1.4 litre Zetec-SE petrol engine models	2.2 bar (32 psi)	2.0 bar (29 psi)
All diesel engine models	2.4 bar (35 psi)	1.8 bar (26 psi)
185/55 R 14 tyres	2.2 bar (32 psi)	2.0 bar (29 psi)
195/50 R 15 tyres	2.0 bar (29 psi)	1.9 bar (28 psi)

Full load (more than 3 people)

	Front	Rear
155/70 R 13 tyres:		
Hatchback models	2.5 bar (36 psi)	2.8 bar (41psi)
Van models	2.3 bar (33 psi)	2.8 bar (41 psi)
165/60 R 14 tyres	2.5 bar (36 psi)	2.8 bar (41 psi)
165/65 R 14 tyres	2.4 bar (35 psi)	2.8 bar (41 psi)
165/70 R 13 tyres:		
All models except Van (diesel engine), Courier and Combi models . .	2.5 bar (36 psi)	2.8 bar (41 psi)
Van (diesel engine), Courier and Combi models	2.3 bar (33 psi)	2.8 bar (41 psi)
175/65 R 14 tyres:		
All petrol engine models except 1.4 litre Zetec-SE	2.5 bar (36 psi)	2.8 bar (41 psi)
1.4 litre Zetec-SE petrol engine models	2.5 bar (36 psi)	2.8 bar (41 psi)
All diesel engine models	2.5 bar (36 psi)	2.8 bar (41 psi)
185/55 R 14 tyres:		
All models except Van (diesel engine) models	2.5 bar (36 psi)	2.8 bar (41 psi)
Van (diesel engine) models	2.3 bar (33 psi)	2.8 bar (41 psi)
195/50 R 15 tyres	2.5 bar (36 psi)	2.8 bar (41 psi)

Chapter 1 Part A:
Routine maintenance and servicing – petrol engine models

Contents

Air filter element renewal 17	Manual transmission oil level check 21
Automatic transmission fluid and strainer renewal 18	Oil filler cap check – models with Endura-E engine 20
Automatic transmission fluid level check 11	Pollen filter renewal 15
Auxiliary drivebelt check and renewal 6	Regular maintenance 2
Brake fluid renewal 26	Road test 14
Brake pad and disc wear check 8	Roadwheel nut tightness check 13
Brake shoe and drum wear check 9	Selector cable check and adjustment – models with automatic
Coolant renewal and pressure cap check 27	transmission 5
Crankcase ventilation system check – Endura-E engine 19	Spark plug renewal and ignition system check – Endura-E engine . 16
Engine oil and filter renewal 3	Spark plug renewal and ignition system check – Zetec-SE engine . 22
Fuel filter renewal 24	Steering, suspension and driveshaft gaiters check 10
General information 1	Timing belt renewal – Zetec-SE engine 23
Hinge and lock lubrication 12	Valve clearance check and adjustment – Endura-E engine 4
Hose and fluid leak check 7	Valve clearance check and adjustment – Zetec-SE engine 25

Degrees of difficulty

Easy, suitable for novice with little experience	**Fairly easy,** suitable for beginner with some experience	**Fairly difficult,** suitable for competent DIY mechanic 	**Difficult,** suitable for experienced DIY mechanic	**Very difficult,** suitable for expert DIY or professional

Lubricants and fluids .... Refer to the end of *Weekly checks*

Capacities

Engine oil
Including oil filter:
    1.3 litre Endura-E engine (approximate) .... 3.25 litres
    1.25 and 1.4 litre Zetec-SE engine (approximate) .... 3.75 litres
    1.6 litre Zetec-SE engine (approximate) .... 4.25 litres
Excluding oil filter:
    1.3 litre Endura-E engine (approximate) .... 2.75 litres
    1.25 and 1.4 litre Zetec-SE engine (approximate) .... 3.50 litres
    1.6 litre Zetec-SE engine (approximate) .... 3.75 litres

Cooling system
1.3 litre Endura-E engine (approximate) .... 7.1 litres
1.25 and 1.4 litre Zetec-SE engine (approximate) .... 6.0 litres
1.6 litre Zetec-SE engine (approximate) .... 5.0 litres

Transmission
Manual transmission (approximate) .... 2.8 litres
Automatic transmission (approximate):
    From dry .... 5.6 litres
    At fluid change .... 3.5 litres

Washer fluid reservoir
Without headlight washers .... 4.0 litres
With headlight washers .... 8.0 litres

Fuel tank
All models .... 40.0 litres

Cooling system
Antifreeze mixture:
    50% antifreeze .... Protection down to –37°C
    55% antifreeze .... Protection down to –45°C
Note: *Refer to antifreeze manufacturer for latest recommendations.*

Ignition system

Spark plugs:	Type	Electrode gap
1.25 litre Zetec-SE engine	Bosch HR 8 MEV	1.3 mm
1.3 litre Endura-E engine	Bosch HR 7 DCX	1.1 mm
1.4 litre Zetec-SE engine	Bosch HR 8 MEV	1.3 mm
1.6 litre Zetec-SE engine	Bosch HR 8 MEV	1.3 mm

Brakes
Friction material minimum thickness:
    Front brake pads .... 1.5 mm
    Rear brake shoes .... 1.0 mm

Torque wrench settings

	Nm	lbf ft
Automatic transmission:		
Fluid strainer	8	6
Sump	8	6
Drain plug	33	24
Manual transmission filler/level plug	35	26
Roadwheel nuts	85	63
Spark plugs:		
Endura-E engine	17	13
Zetec-SE engine	15	11

Underbonnet view of a 1.25 litre Zetec-SE engine model

1 Engine oil filler cap
2 Suspension strut top cover
3 Windscreen washer fluid reservoir
4 Coolant reservoir (expansion tank)
5 Windscreen wiper motor
6 MAP sensor
7 Brake fluid reservoir
8 Auxiliary fuse/relay box
9 Air cleaner casing
10 Battery
11 Ignition coil
12 Engine oil level dipstick
13 Alternator

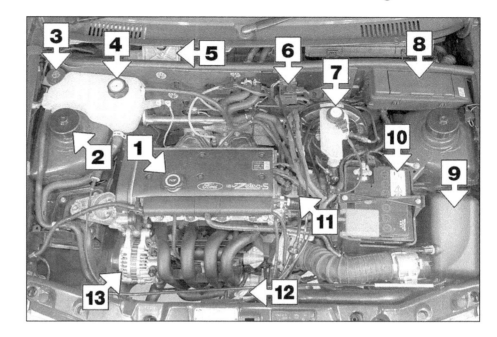

Front underbody view of a 1.25 litre Zetec-SE engine model

1 Brake caliper
2 Engine oil drain plug
3 Engine oil filter
4 Cooling fan
5 Horn
6 Track-rod end
7 Suspension lower arm
8 Gearchange rod
9 Exhaust system
10 Suspension subframe
11 Driveshaft

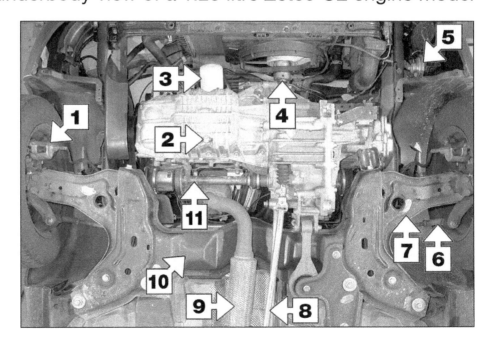

The maintenance intervals in this manual are provided with the assumption that you, not the dealer, will be carrying out the work. These are the minimum maintenance intervals recommended by us for vehicles driven daily. If you wish to keep your vehicle in peak condition at all times, you may wish to perform some of these procedures more often. We encourage frequent maintenance, because it enhances the efficiency, performance and resale value of your vehicle.

If the vehicle is driven in dusty areas, used to tow a trailer, or driven frequently at slow speeds (idling in traffic) or on short journeys, more frequent maintenance intervals are recommended.

When the vehicle is new, it should be serviced by a factory-authorised dealer service department, in order to preserve the factory warranty.

Every 250 miles or weekly

☐☐Refer to *Weekly checks*

Every 5000 miles or 6 months, whichever comes first

☐ Renew the engine oil and filter (Section 3)

Note: *Frequent oil and filter changes are good for the engine. We recommend changing the oil at the mileage specified here, or at least twice a year if the mileage covered is a less.*

Every 10 000 miles or 12 months, whichever comes first

☐ Check and, if necessary, adjust the valve clearances – models with Endura-E engine (Section 4)
☐ Check and, if necessary, adjust the selector cable – models with automatic transmission (Section 5)
☐ Check the condition and tension of the auxiliary drivebelt(s) (Section 6)
☐ Check all components, pipes and hoses for fluid leaks (Section 7)
☐ Check the brake pads and discs for wear (Section 8)
☐ Check the brake shoes and drums for wear (Section 9)
☐ Check the steering, suspension and driveshaft gaiters for condition and security (Section 10)
☐ Check the automatic transmission fluid level (Section 11)
☐ Lubricate all hinges and locks (Section 12)
☐ Check the roadwheel nuts are tightened to the specified torque (Section 13)
☐ Carry out a road test (Section 14)

Every 20 000 miles

☐ Renew the pollen filter (Section 15)

Note: *If the vehicle is used in dusty conditions, the pollen filter should be renewed more frequently.*

Every 30 000 miles

☐ Renew the spark plugs – models with Endura-E engine (Section 16)
☐ Renew the air filter (Section 17)
☐ Renew the automatic transmission fluid and strainer (Section 18)
☐ Check the crankcase ventilation system – models with Endura-E engine (Section 19)
☐ Check the oil filler cap – models with Endura-E engine (Section 20)
☐ Check the manual transmission oil level (Section 21)

Every 40 000 miles

☐ Renew the spark plugs – models with Zetec-SE engine (Section 22)
☐ Renew the timing belt – models with Zetec-SE engine (Section 23)

Note: *The Ford interval for belt renewal is actually at a much higher mileage than this. It is strongly recommended, however, that the interval is reduced to 40 000 miles, particularly on vehicles which are subjected to intensive use, ie, mainly short journeys or a lot of stop-start driving. The actual belt renewal interval is therefore very much up to the individual owner, but bear in mind that severe engine damage will result if the belt breaks.*

Every 60 000 miles

☐ Renew the fuel filter (Section 24)

Every 100 000 miles

☐ Check and, if necessary, adjust the valve clearances – models with Zetec-SE engine (Section 25)

Every 3 years, regardless of mileage

☐ Renew the brake fluid (Section 26)

Every 4 years, regardless of mileage

☐ Renew the coolant and check the condition of the expansion tank pressure cap (Section 27)

Rear underbody view – Hatchback and Van models

1   Suspension trailing arm
2   Shock absorber
3   Spare wheel cradle
4   Exhaust rear silencer
5   Suspension beam
6   Fuel tank

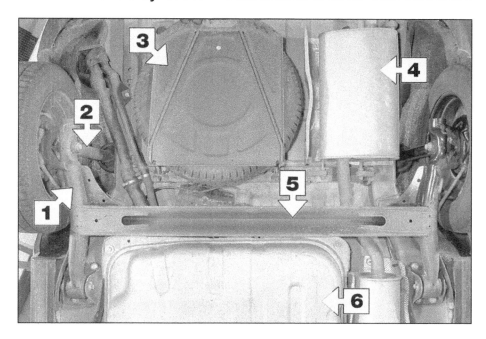

Rear underbody view – Courier and Combi models

1   Suspension torsion beam
2   Shock absorber
3   Exhaust rear silencer
4   Spare wheel cradle
5   Brake pressure proportioning valve
6   Suspension beam
7   Fuel tank

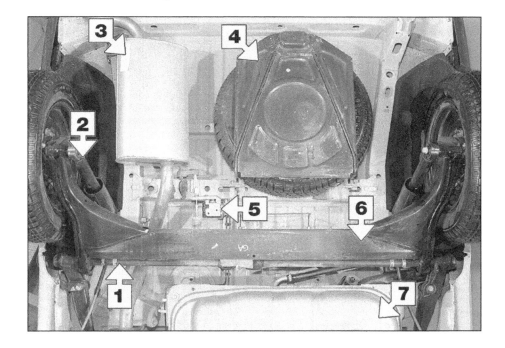

Maintenance procedures

1 General information

1 This Chapter is designed to help the home mechanic maintain his/her vehicle for safety, economy, long life and peak performance.

2 The Chapter contains a master maintenance schedule, followed by Sections dealing specifically with each task in the schedule. Visual checks, adjustments, component renewal and other helpful items are included. Refer to the accompanying illustrations of the engine compartment and the underside of the vehicle for the locations of the various components.

3 Servicing your vehicle in accordance with the mileage/time maintenance schedule and the following Sections will provide a planned maintenance programme, which should result in a long and reliable service life. This is a comprehensive plan, so maintaining some items but not others at the specified service intervals, will not produce the same results.

4 As you service your vehicle, you will discover that many of the procedures can – and should – be grouped together, because of the particular procedure being performed, or because of the proximity of two otherwise-unrelated components to one another. For example, if the vehicle is raised for any reason, the exhaust can be inspected at the same time as the suspension and steering components.

5 The first step in this maintenance programme is to prepare yourself before the actual work begins. Read through all the Sections relevant to the work to be carried out, then make a list and gather all the parts and tools required. If a problem is encountered, seek advice from a parts specialist, or a dealer service department.

2 Regular maintenance

1 If, from the time the vehicle is new, the routine maintenance schedule is followed closely, and frequent checks are made of fluid levels and high-wear items, as suggested throughout this manual, the engine will be kept in relatively good running condition, and the need for additional work will be minimised.

2 It is possible that there will be times when the engine is running poorly due to the lack of regular maintenance. This is even more likely if a used vehicle, which has not received regular and frequent maintenance checks, is purchased. In such cases, additional work may need to be carried out, outside of the regular maintenance intervals.

3 If engine wear is suspected, a compression test (refer to Chapter 2A or 2B, as applicable) will provide valuable information regarding the overall performance of the main internal components. Such a test can be used as a basis to decide on the extent of the work to be carried out. If, for example, a compression test indicates serious internal engine wear, conventional maintenance as described in this Chapter will not greatly improve the performance of the engine, and may prove a waste of time and money, unless extensive overhaul work is carried out first.

4 The following series of operations are those most often required to improve the performance of a generally poor-running engine:

Primary operations

a) Clean, inspect and test the battery (refer to 'Weekly checks').
b) Check all the engine-related fluids (refer to 'Weekly checks').
c) Check the condition and tension of the auxiliary drivebelt (Section 6).
d) Renew the spark plugs (Sections 16 or 22).
e) Check the condition of the air filter, and renew if necessary (Section 17).
f) Renew the fuel filter (Section 23).
g) Check the condition of all hoses, and check for fluid leaks (Section 7).

5 If the above operations do not prove fully effective, carry out the following secondary operations:

Secondary operations

All items listed under Primary operations, plus the following:
a) Check the charging system (refer to Chapter 5A).
b) Check the ignition system (refer to Chapter 5B).
c) Check the fuel system (refer to Chapter 4A).

3.4 Removing the oil filler cap

3.9 Using an oil filter removal tool to loosen the filter

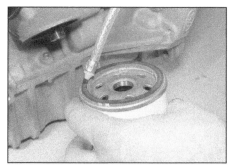

3.11 Apply a light coating of engine oil to the sealing ring on the new filter

Every 5000 miles or 6 months, whichever comes first

3 Engine oil and filter renewal

1 Frequent oil and filter changes are the most important preventative maintenance procedures which can be undertaken by the DIY owner. As engine oil ages, it becomes diluted and contaminated, which leads to premature engine wear.

2 Before starting this procedure, gather together all the necessary tools and materials. Also make sure that you have plenty of clean rags and newspapers handy, to mop up any spills. Ideally, the engine oil should be warm, as it will drain more easily, and more built-up sludge will be removed with it. Take care not to touch the exhaust or any other hot parts of the engine when working under the vehicle. To avoid any possibility of scalding, and to protect yourself from possible skin irritants and other harmful contaminants in used engine oils, it is advisable to wear gloves when carrying out this work.

3 Firmly apply the handbrake then jack up the front of the vehicle and support it on axle stands (see *Jacking and vehicle support*).

4 Remove the oil filler cap **(see illustration)**.

5 Using a spanner, or preferably a socket and bar, slacken the drain plug about half a turn. Position the draining container under the drain plug, then remove the plug completely.

> **HAYNES HiNT** *As the plug releases from the threads, move it away sharply, so that the stream of oil from the sump runs into the container, not up your sleeve.*

6 Allow some time for the oil to drain, noting that it may be necessary to reposition the container as the oil flow slows to a trickle.

7 After all the oil has drained, wipe the drain plug and the sealing washer with a clean rag. Examine the condition of the sealing washer, and renew it if it shows signs of scoring or other damage which may prevent an oil-tight seal. Clean the area around the drain plug opening, and refit the plug complete with the washer and tighten it securely.

8 Move the container into position under the oil filter which is located on the rear of the cylinder block on the Endura-E engine and on the front of the cylinder block on the Zetec-SE engine.

9 Use an oil filter removal tool to slacken the filter initially, then unscrew it by hand the rest of the way **(see illustration)**. Empty the oil from the old filter into the container.

10 Use a clean rag to remove all oil, dirt and sludge from the filter sealing area on the engine.

11 Apply a light coating of clean engine oil to the sealing ring on the new filter, then screw the filter into position on the engine **(see illustration)**. Tighten the filter firmly by hand only – **do not** use any tools.

12 Remove the old oil and all tools from under the vehicle then lower the vehicle to the ground.

13 Fill the engine through the filler hole, using the correct grade and type of oil (refer to *Weekly checks* for details of topping-up). Pour in half the specified quantity of oil first, then wait a few minutes for the oil to drain into the sump. Continue to add oil, a small quantity at a time, until the level is up to the lower mark on the dipstick. Adding approximately a further 0.5 litre will bring the level up to the upper mark on the dipstick.

14 Start the engine and run it for a few minutes, while checking for leaks around the oil filter seal and the sump drain plug. Note that there may be a delay of a few seconds before the low oil pressure warning light goes out when the engine is first started, as the oil circulates through the new oil filter and the engine oil galleries before the pressure builds up.

15 Stop the engine, and wait a few minutes for the oil to settle in the sump once more. With the new oil circulated and the filter now completely full, recheck the level on the dipstick, and add more oil as necessary.

16 Dispose of the used engine oil safely with reference to *General repair procedures*.

Every 10 000 miles or 12 months, whichever comes first

4 Valve clearance check and adjustment – Endura-E engine

This procedure is described in Chapter 2A.

5 Selector cable check and adjustment – models with automatic transmission

This procedure is described in Chapter 7B.

6 Auxiliary drivebelt check and renewal

Checking

1 A single auxiliary drivebelt is fitted at the right-hand side of the engine. The length and type of the drivebelt varies according to

6.6 Using a spanner, turn the tensioner anti-clockwise to release the tension then remove the belt from the pulleys

whether air conditioning and/or power steering is fitted. Depending on engine type and year of production, the belt may have an automatic tensioner, or it may have to be tensioned manually.

2 Due to their function and material makeup, drivebelts are prone to failure after a long period of time and should therefore be inspected regularly.

3 Since the drivebelt is located very close to the right-hand side of the engine compartment, it is possible to gain better access by raising the front of the vehicle and removing the right-hand wheel, then unbolting the crankshaft pulley lower cover from the underbody.

4 With the engine stopped, inspect the full length of the drivebelt for cracks and separation of the belt plies. It will be necessary to turn the engine (using a spanner or socket and bar on the crankshaft pulley bolt) in order to move the belt from the pulleys so that the belt can be inspected thoroughly. Twist the belt between the pulleys so that both sides can be viewed. Also check for fraying, and glazing which gives the belt a shiny appearance. Check the pulleys for nicks, cracks, distortion and corrosion.

Renewal

5 To remove the drivebelt, first raise the front of the vehicle and support on axle stands (see *Jacking and vehicle support*). Unbolt and remove the crankshaft pulley cover.

6 Where an automatic tensioner is fitted, using a spanner on the tensioner centre bolt, turn the tensioner anti-clockwise to release the drivebelt tension. Note how the drivebelt is routed, then remove the belt from the pulleys **(see illustration)**.

7 Where an automatic tensioner is not used, slacken the alternator upper mounting/adjustment bolt and the two lower mounting nuts and bolts and move the alternator toward the engine to release the drivebelt tension. Note how the drivebelt is routed, then remove the belt from the pulleys.

8 Fit the new drivebelt onto the crankshaft, alternator, power steering pump, and air conditioning compressor pulleys as applicable, ensuring that it is correctly located.

9 Where an automatic tensioner is used, turn the tensioner anti-clockwise, locate the drivebelt on the pulley, then release the tensioner.

10 On engines without an automatic tensioner, tighten the alternator upper mounting/adjustment bolt slightly so that the alternator is gripped, but can still be moved. Tension the drivebelt by moving the alternator away from the engine until the total deflection of the belt on its longest span is approximately 10 mm. Hold the alternator in this position and securely tighten the upper mounting/adjustment bolt, followed by the lower mounting nuts/bolts.

11 Refit the crankshaft pulley cover and lower the vehicle to the ground.

7 Hose and fluid leak check

1 Visually inspect the engine joint faces, gaskets and seals for any signs of water or oil leaks. Pay particular attention to the areas around the cylinder head cover, cylinder head, oil filter and sump joint faces. Bear in mind that, over a period of time, some very slight seepage from these areas is to be expected – what you are really looking for is any indication of a serious leak. Should a leak be found, renew the offending gasket or oil seal by referring to the appropriate Chapters in this manual.

2 Also check the security and condition of all the engine-related pipes and hoses, and all braking system pipes and hoses. Ensure that all cable ties or securing clips are in place, and in good condition. Clips which are broken or missing can lead to chafing of the hoses, pipes or wiring, which could cause more serious problems in the future.

3 Carefully check the radiator hoses and heater hoses along their entire length. Renew any hose which is cracked, swollen or deteriorated. Cracks will show up better if the hose is squeezed. Pay close attention to the hose clips that secure the hoses to the cooling system components. Hose clips can pinch and puncture hoses, resulting in cooling system leaks. If the crimped-type hose clips are used, it may be a good idea to replace them with standard worm-drive clips.

4 Inspect all the cooling system components (hoses, joint faces, etc) for leaks.

>
> *A leak in the cooling system will usually show up as white- or rust-coloured deposits on the area adjoining the leak.*

5 Where any problems are found on system components, renew the component or gasket with reference to Chapter 3.

6 With the vehicle raised, inspect the fuel tank and filler neck for punctures, cracks and other damage. The connection between the filler neck and tank is especially critical. Sometimes a rubber filler neck or connecting hose will leak due to loose retaining clamps or deteriorated rubber.

7 Carefully check all rubber hoses and metal fuel lines leading away from the fuel tank. Check for loose connections, deteriorated hoses, crimped lines, and other damage. Pay particular attention to the vent pipes and hoses, which often loop up around the filler neck and can become blocked or crimped. Follow the lines to the front of the vehicle, carefully inspecting them all the way. Renew damaged sections as necessary. Similarly, whilst the vehicle is raised, take the opportunity to inspect all underbody brake fluid pipes and hoses.

8 From within the engine compartment, check the security of all fuel, vacuum and brake hose attachments and pipe unions, and inspect all hoses for kinks, chafing and deterioration.

9 Where applicable, check the condition of the power steering and automatic transmission fluid pipes and hoses.

8 Brake pad and disc wear check

1 Apply the handbrake, then jack up the front of the car and support it securely on axle stands (see *Jacking and vehicle support*). Remove the front roadwheels.

2 For a comprehensive check, the brake pads should be removed and cleaned. The operation of the caliper can then also be checked, and the condition of the brake disc itself can be fully examined on both sides. Refer to Chapter 9 for further information.

3 On completion refit the roadwheels and lower the car to the ground.

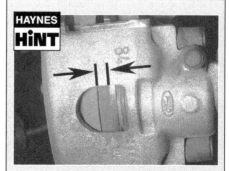

For a quick check, the thickness of friction material remaining on the inner brake pad can be measured through the aperture in the caliper body.

9 Brake shoe and drum wear check

Remove the brake drums, and check the brake shoes for signs of wear or contamination. At the same time, also inspect the wheel cylinders for signs of leakage, and the brake drum for signs of wear. Refer to the relevant Sections of Chapter 9 for further information.

10 Steering, suspension and driveshaft gaiters check

Front suspension/steering check

1 Raise the front of the vehicle, and securely support it on axle stands (see *Jacking and vehicle support*).
2 Visually inspect the balljoint dust covers and the steering rack-and-pinion gaiters for splits, chafing or deterioration. Any wear of these components will cause loss of lubricant, together with dirt and water entry, resulting in rapid deterioration of the balljoints or steering gear.
3 On vehicles with power steering, check the fluid hoses for chafing or deterioration, and the pipe and hose unions for fluid leaks. Also check for signs of fluid leakage under pressure from the steering gear rubber gaiters, which would indicate failed fluid seals within the steering gear.
4 Grasp the roadwheel at the 12 o'clock and 6 o'clock positions, and try to rock it (see illustration). Very slight free play may be felt, but if the movement is appreciable, further investigation is necessary to determine the source. Continue rocking the wheel while an assistant depresses the footbrake. If the movement is now eliminated or significantly reduced, it is likely that the hub bearings are at fault. If the free play is still evident with the footbrake depressed, then there is wear in the suspension joints or mountings.
5 Now grasp the wheel at the 9 o'clock and 3 o'clock positions, and try to rock it as before. Any movement felt now may again be

caused by wear in the hub bearings or the steering track rod balljoints. If the outer balljoint is worn, the visual movement will be obvious. If the inner joint is suspect, it can be felt by placing a hand over the rack-and-pinion rubber gaiter and gripping the track rod. If the wheel is now rocked, movement will be felt at the inner joint if wear has taken place.
6 Using a large screwdriver or flat bar, check for wear in the suspension mounting bushes by levering between the relevant suspension component and its attachment point. Some movement is to be expected, as the mountings are made of rubber, but excessive wear should be obvious. Also check the condition of any visible rubber bushes, looking for splits, cracks or contamination of the rubber.
7 With the car standing on its wheels, have an assistant turn the steering wheel back-and-forth, about an eighth of a turn each way. There should be very little, if any, lost movement between the steering wheel and roadwheels. If this is not the case, closely observe the joints and mountings previously described. In addition, check the steering column universal joints for wear, and also check the rack-and-pinion steering gear itself.

Rear suspension check

8 Chock the front wheels, then jack up the rear of the vehicle and support securely on axle stands (see *Jacking and vehicle support*).
9 Working as described previously for the front suspension, check the rear hub bearings, the suspension bushes and the strut or shock absorber mountings (as applicable) for wear.

Shock absorber check

10 Check for any signs of fluid leakage around the shock absorber body, or from the rubber gaiter around the piston rod. Should any fluid be noticed, the shock absorber is defective internally, and should be renewed. Note: *Shock absorbers should always be renewed in pairs on the same axle.*
11 The efficiency of the shock absorber may be checked by bouncing the vehicle at each corner. Generally speaking, the body will return to its normal position and stop after being depressed. If it rises and returns on a

rebound, the shock absorber is probably suspect. Also examine the shock absorber upper and lower mountings for any signs of wear.

Driveshaft gaiters check

12 With the vehicle raised and securely supported on stands, turn the steering onto full lock then slowly rotate the roadwheel. Inspect the condition of the outer constant velocity (CV) joint rubber gaiters while squeezing the gaiters to open out the folds (see illustration). Check for signs of cracking, splits or deterioration of the rubber which may allow the grease to escape and lead to water and grit entry into the joint. Also check the security and condition of the retaining clips. Repeat these checks on the inner CV joints. If any damage or deterioration is found, the gaiters should be renewed as described in Chapter 8.
13 At the same time check the general condition of the CV joints themselves by first holding the driveshaft and attempting to rotate the wheel. Repeat this check by holding the inner joint and attempting to rotate the driveshaft. Any appreciable movement indicates wear in the joints, wear in the driveshaft splines or loose driveshaft retaining nut.

11 Automatic transmission fluid level check

1 The level of the automatic transmission fluid should be carefully maintained. Low fluid level can lead to slipping or loss of drive, while overfilling can cause foaming, loss of fluid and transmission damage.
2 The transmission fluid level should only be checked when the transmission is hot (at its normal operating temperature). If the vehicle has just been driven over 10 miles (15 miles in a cold climate), and the fluid temperature is 160 to 175°F, the transmission is hot.
Caution: If the vehicle has just been driven for a long time at high speed, in city traffic in hot weather, or if it has been pulling a trailer, an accurate fluid level reading cannot be obtained. In these circumstances, allow the fluid to cool down for about 30 minutes.
3 Park on level ground, apply the handbrake, and start the engine. With the engine idling, depress the brake pedal and move the selector lever through all the gear positions three times, beginning and ending in P.
4 Allow the engine to idle for one minute, then (with the engine still idling) remove the dipstick from its tube. Note the condition and colour of the fluid on the dipstick.
5 Wipe the fluid from the dipstick with a clean rag, and re-insert it into the filler tube until the cap seats.
6 Pull the dipstick out again, and note the fluid level. The level should be between the

10.4 Check for wear in the hub bearings by grasping the wheel and trying to rock it

10.12 Check the condition of the driveshaft gaiters

12.2 Lubricate the bonnet lock with grease

MIN and MAX marks. If the level is on the MIN mark, stop the engine, and add the specified automatic transmission fluid (see *Lubricants and fluids*) through the dipstick tube, using a clean funnel if necessary. It is important not to introduce dirt into the transmission when topping-up.

7 Add the fluid a little at a time, and keep checking the level as previously described until it is correct.

8 The need for regular topping-up of the transmission fluid indicates a leak, which should be found and rectified without delay.

9 The condition of the fluid should also be checked along with the level. If the fluid on the dipstick is black or a dark reddish-brown colour, or if it has a burned smell, the fluid should be changed. If you are in doubt about the condition of the fluid, buy some new fluid, and compare the two for colour and smell.

12 Hinge and lock lubrication

1 Work around the vehicle and lubricate the hinges of the bonnet, doors and tailgate with a light machine oil.

2 Lightly lubricate the bonnet release mechanism and exposed section of inner cable with a smear of grease **(see illustration)**.

3 Check carefully the security and operation of all hinges, latches and locks, adjusting them where required. Check the operation of the central locking system (if fitted).

4 Check the condition and operation of the tailgate struts, renewing them if either is leaking or no longer able to support the tailgate securely when raised.

13 Roadwheel nut tightness check

1 Where applicable, remove the wheel trims, and slacken the roadwheel nuts slightly.

2 Tighten the nuts to the specified torque, using a torque wrench.

14 Road test

Instruments/electrical equipment

1 Check the operation of all instruments and electrical equipment.

2 Make sure that all instruments read correctly, and switch on all electrical equipment in turn, to check that it functions properly.

Steering and suspension

3 Check for any abnormalities in the steering, suspension, handling or road 'feel'.

4 Drive the vehicle, and check that there are no unusual vibrations or noises.

5 Check that the steering feels positive, with no excessive 'sloppiness', or roughness, and check for any suspension noises when cornering and driving over bumps.

Drivetrain

6 Check the performance of the engine, clutch, transmission and driveshafts.

7 Listen for any unusual noises from the engine, clutch and transmission.

8 Make sure that the engine runs smoothly when idling, and that there is no hesitation when accelerating.

9 Check that, where applicable, the clutch action is smooth and progressive, that the drive is taken up smoothly, and that the pedal travel is not excessive. Also listen for any noises when the clutch pedal is depressed.

10 Check that all gears can be engaged smoothly without noise, and that the gear lever action is smooth and not abnormally vague or 'notchy'.

11 On automatic transmission models, make sure that the drive seems smooth without jerks or engine speed 'flare-ups'. Check that all of the gear positions can be selected with the vehicle at rest. If any problems are found, they should be referred to a Ford dealer.

12 Listen for a metallic clicking sound from the front of the vehicle, as the vehicle is driven slowly in a circle with the steering on full lock. Carry out this check in both directions. If a clicking noise is heard, this indicates wear in a driveshaft joint (see Chapter 8).

Check the braking system

13 Make sure that the vehicle does not pull to one side when braking, and that the wheels do not lock prematurely when braking hard.

14 Check that there is no vibration through the steering when braking.

15 Check that the handbrake operates correctly, without excessive movement of the lever, and that it holds the vehicle stationary on a slope.

16 Test the operation of the brake servo unit as follows. Depress the footbrake four or five times to exhaust the vacuum, then start the engine. As the engine starts, there should be a noticeable 'give' in the brake pedal as vacuum builds up. Allow the engine to run for at least two minutes, and then switch it off. If the brake pedal is now depressed again, it should be possible to detect a hiss from the servo as the pedal is depressed. After about four or five applications, no further hissing should be heard, and the pedal should feel considerably harder.

Every 20 000 miles

15 Pollen filter renewal

1 Open the bonnet, and locate the pollen filter housing, at the left-hand corner of the scuttle at the rear of the engine compartment.

2 Release the two clips, and open the pollen filter cover **(see illustration)**.

3 Pull the filter from the housing, using the tab provided **(see illustration)**.

4 Fit the new filter using a reversal of the removal procedure. Make sure that the filter is fitted with the removal tab and the TOP/OBEN marking visible.

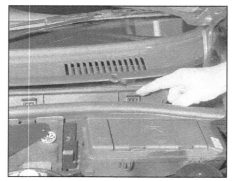

15.2 Releasing a pollen filter cover securing clip

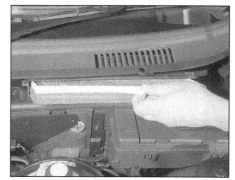

15.3 Pulling out the pollen filter

Every 30 000 miles

16 Spark plug renewal and ignition system check – Endura-E engine

Spark plug renewal

1 The correct functioning of the spark plugs is vital for the correct running and efficiency of the engine. It is essential that the plugs fitted are appropriate for the engine; suitable types are specified at the beginning of this Chapter, on the Vehicle Emissions Control Information (VECI) label located on the underside of the bonnet (only on models sold in some areas) or in the vehicle's Owner's Handbook. If the correct type is used and the engine is in good condition, the spark plugs should not need attention between scheduled replacement intervals. Spark plug cleaning is rarely necessary, and should not be attempted unless specialised equipment is available, as damage can easily be caused to the firing ends.

2 If the marks on the original-equipment spark plug (HT) leads cannot be seen, mark the leads to correspond to the cylinder the lead serves. Pull the leads from the plugs by gripping the end fitting, not the lead, otherwise the lead connection may be fractured.

3 It is advisable to remove the dirt from the spark plug recesses using a clean brush, vacuum cleaner or compressed air before removing the plugs, to prevent dirt dropping into the cylinders.

4 Unscrew the plugs from the front of the cylinder head using a spark plug spanner, suitable box spanner or a deep socket and extension bar (see illustration). Keep the socket aligned with the spark plug – if it is forcibly moved to one side, the ceramic insulator may be broken off. As each plug is removed, examine it as follows.

5 Examination of the spark plugs will give a good indication of the condition of the engine. If the insulator nose of the spark plug is clean and white, with no deposits, this is indicative of a weak mixture or too hot a plug (a hot plug transfers heat away from the electrode slowly, a cold plug transfers heat away quickly).

6 If the tip and insulator nose are covered with hard black-looking deposits, then this is indicative that the mixture is too rich. Should the plug be black and oily, then it is likely that the engine is fairly worn, as well as the mixture being too rich.

7 If the insulator nose is covered with light tan to greyish-brown deposits, then the mixture is correct and it is likely that the engine is in good condition.

8 The spark plug electrode gap is of considerable importance as, if it is too large or too small, the size of the spark and its efficiency will be seriously impaired. The gap should be set to the value given in the Specifications at the beginning of this Chapter.

9 To set the gap, measure it with a feeler blade and then bend open, or closed, the outer plug electrode until the correct gap is achieved. The centre electrode should never be bent, as this may crack the insulator and cause plug failure, if nothing worse. If using feeler blades, the gap is correct when the appropriate-size blade is a firm sliding fit (see illustrations).

10 Special spark plug electrode gap adjusting tools are available from most motor accessory shops, or from some spark plug manufacturers.

11 Before fitting the spark plugs, check that the threaded connector sleeves are tight, and that the plug exterior surfaces and threads are clean (see Haynes Hint).

12 Remove the rubber hose (if used), and tighten the plug to the specified torque using the spark plug socket and a torque wrench. Refit the remaining spark plugs in the same manner.

13 Connect the HT leads in their correct order.

Ignition system check

⚠️ **Warning: Voltages produced by an electronic ignition system are considerably higher than those produced by conventional ignition systems. Extreme care must be taken when working on the system with the ignition switched on. Persons with surgically-implanted cardiac pacemaker devices should keep well clear of the ignition circuits, components and test equipment.**

14 The spark plug (HT) leads should be checked whenever new spark plugs are fitted.

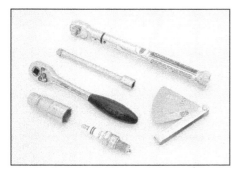

16.4 Tools required for changing spark plugs

16.9a Using a wire-type gauge when checking the gap

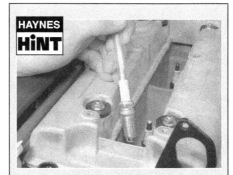

HAYNES HINT

It's often difficult to insert spark plugs into their holes without cross-threading them. To avoid this possibility, fit a short length of rubber or plastic hose over the end of the spark plug. The flexible hose acts as a universal joint, to help align the plug with the plug hole. Should the plug begin to cross thread, the hose will slip on the spark plug, preventing thread damage to the aluminium cylinder head.

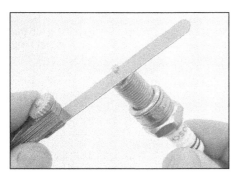

16.9b Measuring a spark plug gap with a feeler blade

16.9c To change the gap, bend the outer electrode only

15 Ensure that the leads are numbered before removing them, to avoid confusion when refitting. Pull the leads from the plugs by gripping the end fitting, not the lead, otherwise the lead connection may be fractured.

16 Check inside the end fitting for signs of corrosion, which will look like a white crusty powder. Push the end fitting back onto the spark plug, ensuring that it is a tight fit on the plug. If not, remove the lead again and use pliers to carefully crimp the metal connector inside the end fitting until it fits securely on the end of the spark plug.

17 Using a clean rag, wipe the entire length of the lead to remove any built-up dirt and grease. Once the lead is clean, check for burns, cracks and other damage. Do not bend the lead excessively, nor pull the lead lengthwise – the conductor inside might break.

18 Disconnect the other end of the lead from the ignition coil by squeezing the clips. Check for corrosion and a tight fit. If an ohmmeter is available, check the resistance of the lead by connecting the meter between each end of the lead. Refit the lead securely on completion.

19 Check the remaining leads one at a time, in the same way.

20 If new spark plug (HT) leads are required, purchase a set for your specific car and engine.

21 Even with the ignition system in first-class condition, some engines may still occasionally experience poor starting attributable to damp ignition components. To disperse moisture, a water-dispersant aerosol can be very effective.

17 Air filter element renewal

1 The air cleaner is located in the left-hand front corner of the engine compartment, or over the top of the engine on later 1.25 litre Zetec-SE engines. First release the clips (Endura-E engine) or unscrew the screws (Zetec-SE engine) securing the cover to the air cleaner housing **(see illustration)**.

2 Lift the cover and remove the filter element from the base **(see illustration)**. Note which way round it is fitted.

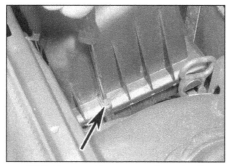

17.1 Remove the screws from both sides . . .

3 Wipe clean the interior surfaces of the cover and base.

4 Insert the new element making sure that it is seated correctly in the base.

5 Refit the cover and secure with the clips or retaining screws.

18 Automatic transmission fluid and strainer renewal

1 The transmission fluid should only be changed when the transmission is cold.

2 Position the vehicle over an inspection pit, on vehicle ramps, or jack it up, but make sure that it is level.

3 Place a suitable container beneath the drain plug on the transmission sump pan. Remove the transmission fluid dipstick to speed up the draining operation.

4 Thoroughly clean the area around the drain plug in the transmission sump pan then unscrew the plug and allow the fluid to drain into the container.

5 When all the fluid has drained (this may take some time) clean the drain plug, then refit it together with a new seal and tighten to the specified torque.

6 Unscrew the mounting bolts and lower the sump from the bottom of the automatic transmission. If it is stuck, use a screwdriver to free it taking care not to damage the mating surfaces of the sump and transmission.

7 Recover the gasket, and clean the mating surfaces of the sump and transmission.

8 With the sump removed, clean the magnet of any accumulation of metallic particles. The inside of the sump will give an indication of the condition of the transmission, also if the fluid is discoloured or burnt this indicates problems which should be diagnosed by an automatic transmission specialist. Clean out the inside of the sump with rags.

9 Unscrew the retaining bolt and lower the strainer from the transmission. Recover the sealing ring and discard it; a new one must be fitted on reassembly.

10 Fit the new strainer together with a new sealing ring and tighten the retaining bolt to the specified torque.

11 Refit the sump together with a new gasket

17.2 . . . then lift the cover and remove the filter element – Zetec-SE engine

and tighten the retaining bolts to the specified torque.

12 Place a funnel with a fine mesh screen in the transmission dipstick tube, and fill the transmission with the specified type of fluid. It is essential that no dirt is introduced into the transmission during this operation.

13 Depending on the extent to which the fluid was allowed to drain, it is possible that the amount of fluid required when filling the transmission may be less than the specified amount. Add about half the specified amount, then with Park (P) engaged run the engine up to its normal operating temperature and check the level on the dipstick (with the engine idling). Add fluid through the transmission dipstick tube until the level is up to the MAX mark, then refit the dipstick and switch off the engine.

19 Crankcase ventilation system check – Endura-E engine

Refer to Chapter 4D, and check that all crankcase ventilation hoses are clear and unblocked.

20 Oil filler cap check – models with Endura-E engine

1 Remove and inspect the oil filler cap to ensure that it is in good condition, and not blocked up with sludge.

2 Disconnect the hoses at the cap, and clean the cap if necessary by brushing the inner mesh filter with petrol, and blowing through with light pressure from an air line. Renew the cap if it is badly congested.

3 Refit the hoses and cap.

21 Manual transmission oil level check

1 Position the vehicle over an inspection pit, on vehicle ramps, or jack it up, but make sure that it is level.

2 Remove all traces of dirt then unscrew the filler/level plug from the front face of the transmission. Note it is the plug furthest from the engine – do not confuse it with the blanking plug near the bellhousing.

3 The level must be between 5 and 10 mm below the bottom edge of the filler/level plug hole (use a cranked tool such as an Allen key to check the level). If necessary, top up the level with the specified grade of oil (see *Lubricants and fluids*).

4 When the level is correct, clean and refit the filler level plug and tighten it to the specified torque.

5 Lower the car to the ground.

Every 40 000 miles

22 Spark plug renewal and ignition system check – Zetec-SE engine

Spark plug renewal

1 The correct functioning of the spark plugs is vital for the correct running and efficiency of the engine. It is essential that the plugs fitted are appropriate for the engine; suitable types are specified at the beginning of this Chapter, on the Vehicle Emissions Control Information (VECI) label located on the underside of the bonnet (only on models sold in some areas) or in the vehicle's Owner's Handbook. If the correct type is used and the engine is in good condition, the spark plugs should not need attention between scheduled replacement intervals. Spark plug cleaning is rarely necessary, and should not be attempted unless specialised equipment is available, as damage can easily be caused to the firing ends.

2 Remove the oil filler cap then unscrew the bolts and remove the plastic cover from the top of the cylinder head cover. Temporarily refit the filler cap.

3 If the marks on the original-equipment spark plug (HT) leads cannot be seen, mark the leads to correspond to the cylinder the lead serves. Pull the leads from the plugs by gripping the end fitting, not the lead, otherwise the lead connection may be fractured (see illustration).

4 It is advisable to remove any dirt from the spark plug recesses using a clean brush, vacuum cleaner or compressed air before removing the plugs, to prevent dirt dropping into the cylinders.

5 Unscrew the plugs from the cylinder head using a spark plug spanner, suitable box spanner or a deep socket and extension bar (see illustrations). Keep the socket aligned with the spark plug – if it is forcibly moved to one side, the ceramic insulator may be broken off. As each plug is removed, examine it as follows.

6 Examination of the spark plugs will give a good indication of the condition of the engine. If the insulator nose of the spark plug is clean and white, with no deposits, this is indicative of a weak mixture or too hot a plug (a hot plug transfers heat away from the electrode slowly, a cold plug transfers heat away quickly).

7 If the tip and insulator nose are covered with hard black-looking deposits, then this is indicative that the mixture is too rich. Should

the plug be black and oily, then it is likely that the engine is fairly worn, as well as the mixture being too rich.

8 If the insulator nose is covered with light tan to greyish-brown deposits, then the mixture is correct and it is likely that the engine is in good condition.

9 The spark plug electrode gap is of considerable importance as, if it is too large or too small, the size of the spark and its efficiency will be seriously impaired. The gap should be set to the value given in the Specifications at the beginning of this Chapter.

10 To set the gap, measure it with a feeler blade and then bend open, or closed, the outer plug electrode until the correct gap is achieved. The centre electrode should never be bent, as this may crack the insulator and cause plug failure, if nothing worse. If using feeler blades, the gap is correct when the appropriate-size blade is a firm sliding fit (see illustrations).

11 Special spark plug electrode gap adjusting tools are available from most motor accessory shops, or from some spark plug manufacturers.

12 Before fitting the spark plugs, check that the threaded connector sleeves are tight, and

22.3 Disconnecting the HT leads from the spark plugs (plastic cover removed) – Zetec-SE engine

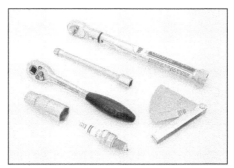

22.5a Tools required for changing spark plugs

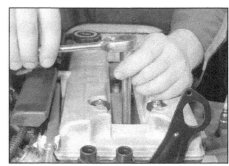

22.5b Unscrewing the spark plugs from the cylinder head

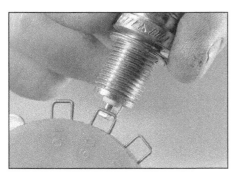

22.10a Using a wire-type gauge when checking the gap

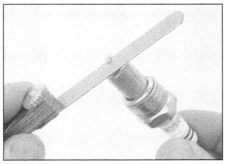

22.10b Measuring a spark plug gap with a feeler blade

22.10c To change the gap, bend the outer electrode only

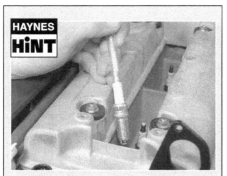

It's often difficult to insert spark plugs into their holes without cross-threading them. To avoid this possibility, fit a short length of rubber or plastic hose over the end of the spark plug. The flexible hose acts as a universal joint, to help align the plug with the plug hole. Should the plug begin to cross thread, the hose will slip on the spark plug, preventing thread damage to the aluminium cylinder head.

22.20 Squeeze the clips to disconnect the HT leads from the ignition coil

Ignition system check

 Warning: Voltages produced by an electronic ignition system are considerably higher than those produced by conventional ignition systems. Extreme care must be taken when working on the system with the ignition switched on. Persons with surgically-implanted cardiac pacemaker devices should keep well clear of the ignition circuits, components and test equipment.

16 The spark plug (HT) leads should be checked whenever new spark plugs are fitted.
17 Ensure that the leads are numbered before removing them, to avoid confusion when refitting. With the plastic top cover removed, pull the leads from the plugs by gripping the end fitting, not the lead, otherwise the lead connection may be fractured.
18 Check inside the end fitting for signs of

corrosion, which will look like a white crusty powder. Push the end fitting back onto the spark plug, ensuring that it is a tight fit on the plug. If not, remove the lead again and use pliers to carefully crimp the metal connector inside the end fitting until it fits securely on the end of the spark plug.
19 Using a clean rag, wipe the entire length of the lead to remove any built-up dirt and grease. Once the lead is clean, check for burns, cracks and other damage. Do not bend the lead excessively, nor pull the lead lengthwise – the conductor inside might break.
20 Disconnect the other end of the lead from the ignition coil by squeezing the clips **(see illustration)**. Check for corrosion and a tight fit. If an ohmmeter is available, check the resistance of the lead by connecting the meter between each end of the lead. Refit the lead securely on completion.
21 Check the remaining leads one at a time, in the same way.
22 If new spark plug (HT) leads are required, purchase a set for your specific car and engine.
23 Even with the ignition system in first-class condition, some engines may still occasionally experience poor starting attributable to damp ignition components. To disperse moisture, a water-dispersant aerosol can be very effective.

23 Timing belt renewal – Zetec-SE engine

The procedure is described in Chapter 2B.

that the plug exterior surfaces and threads are clean **(see Haynes Hint)**.
13 Remove the rubber/plastic hose (if used), and tighten the plug to the specified torque using the spark plug socket and a torque wrench. Refit the remaining spark plugs in the same manner.
14 Connect the HT leads in their correct order.
15 Refit the plastic cover and tighten the retaining bolts. Refit the oil filler cap.

Every 60 000 miles

24 Fuel filter renewal

1 The fuel filter is located on the front left-hand corner of the fuel tank. First, chock the front roadwheels, then jack up the rear of the

vehicle and support on axle stands.
2 Squeeze the tabs and disconnect the quick-release fittings from each end of the filter. Plug the fuel lines to prevent loss of fuel.
3 Note the fuel flow arrow on the filter, then unscrew and remove the clamp bolt and remove the filter from the mounting bracket which is riveted to the fuel tank flange.

4 Fit the new filter using a reversal of the removal procedure. Make sure the quick-release fittings are pushed fully onto the inlet and outlet stubs, and tighten the clamp bolt securely. Also make sure the filter is fitted the correct way around with the directional arrow pointing towards the fuel line leading to the engine compartment.

Every 100 000 miles

25 Valve clearance check and adjustment – Zetec-SE engine

The procedure is described in Chapter 2B.

Every 3 years, regardless of mileage

26 Brake fluid renewal

 Warning: Brake hydraulic fluid can harm your eyes and damage painted surfaces, so use extreme caution when handling and pouring it. Do not use fluid that has been standing open for some time, as it absorbs moisture from the air. Excess moisture can cause a dangerous loss of braking effectiveness.

1 The procedure is similar to that for the bleeding of the hydraulic system as described in Chapter 9 except that, on models with a conventional braking system, the brake fluid reservoir can be fully emptied by syphoning, using a clean poultry baster or similar before starting, and allowance should be made for the old fluid to be expelled when bleeding a section of the circuit. On models fitted with ABS, reduce the fluid level in the reservoir (by syphoning or using a poultry baster), but do not allow the fluid level to drop far enough to allow air into the system – if air enters the ABS hydraulic unit, the unit must be bled using special Ford test equipment (see Chapter 9).

2 Working as described in Chapter 9, open the first bleed screw in the sequence, and pump the brake pedal gently until nearly all the old fluid has been emptied from the master cylinder reservoir. Top-up to the MAX level with new fluid, and continue pumping until only the new fluid remains in the reservoir, and new fluid can be seen emerging from the bleed screw. Tighten the screw, and top the reservoir level up to the MAX level line.

3 Work through all the remaining bleed screws in the sequence until new fluid can be seen at all of them. Be careful to keep the master

> **HAYNES HiNT** *Old hydraulic fluid is invariably much darker in colour than the new, making it easy to distinguish the two.*

cylinder reservoir topped-up to above the MIN level at all times, or air may enter the system and greatly increase the length of the task.

4 When the operation is complete, check that all bleed screws are securely tightened, and that their dust caps are refitted. Wash off all traces of spilt fluid, and re-check the master cylinder reservoir fluid level.

5 Check the operation of the brakes before taking the car on the road.

6 Finally, check the operation of the clutch. Since the clutch shares the same fluid reservoir as the braking system, it may also be necessary to bleed the clutch as described in Chapter 6.

Every 4 years, regardless of mileage

27 Coolant renewal and pressure cap check

Cooling system draining

Note: *If the antifreeze used is Ford's own brand, or of similar quality, the coolant renewal interval may be extended. If the vehicle's history is unknown, if antifreeze of lesser quality is known to be in the system, or simply if you prefer to follow conventional servicing intervals, the coolant should be changed periodically (typically, every 4 years) as described here. Refer also to 'Antifreeze – notes on renewal' in this Section.*

 Warning: Wait until the engine is cold before starting this procedure. Do not allow antifreeze to come in contact with your skin, or with the painted surfaces of the vehicle. Rinse off spills

immediately with plenty of water. Never leave antifreeze lying around in an open container, or in a puddle in the driveway or on the garage floor. Children and pets are attracted by its sweet smell, but antifreeze can be fatal if ingested.

1 With the engine completely cold, remove the expansion tank filler cap. Turn the cap anti-clockwise, wait until any pressure remaining in the system is released, then unscrew it and lift it off.

2 Where applicable, remove the engine undershield, then position a suitable container beneath the radiator drain screw, at the bottom left-hand corner of the radiator.

3 Slacken the drain screw, and allow the coolant to drain into the container **(see illustration)**.

4 When the flow of coolant stops, tighten the radiator drain screw.

5 If the coolant has been drained for a reason other than renewal, then provided it is clean and less than two years old, it can be re-used, though this is not recommended.

Cooling system flushing

6 If coolant renewal has been neglected, or if the antifreeze mixture has become diluted, then in time, the cooling system may gradually lose efficiency, as the coolant passages become restricted due to rust, scale deposits, and other sediment (refer also to *Antifreeze – notes on renewal* later in this Section). The cooling system efficiency can be restored by flushing the system clean.

7 The radiator should be flushed independently of the engine, to avoid unnecessary contamination.

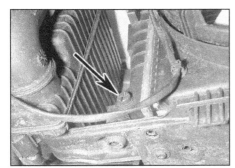

27.3 Radiator drain screw (arrowed)

Radiator flushing

8 Disconnect the top and bottom hoses and any other relevant hoses from the radiator, with reference to Chapter 3.

9 Insert a garden hose into the radiator top inlet. Direct a flow of clean water through the radiator, and continue flushing until clean water emerges from the radiator bottom outlet.

10 If after a reasonable period, the water still does not run clear, the radiator can be flushed with a good proprietary cleaning agent. It is important that their manufacturer's instructions are followed carefully. If the contamination is particularly bad, insert the hose in the radiator bottom outlet, and reverse-flush the radiator.

Engine flushing

11 Remove the thermostat as described in Chapter 3 then, if the radiator top hose has been disconnected from the engine, temporarily reconnect the hose.

12 With the top and bottom hoses disconnected from the radiator, insert a garden hose into the top hose. Direct a clean flow of water through the engine, and continue flushing until clean water emerges from the bottom hose.

13 On completion of flushing, refit the thermostat and reconnect the hoses with reference to Chapter 3.

Cooling system filling

14 Before attempting to fill the cooling system, make sure that all hoses and clips are in good condition, and that the clips are tight. Note that an antifreeze mixture must be used all year round, to prevent corrosion of the

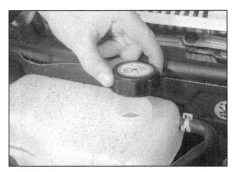

27.15 Removing the expansion tank filler cap

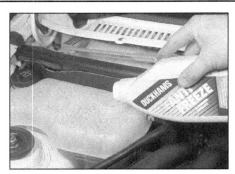

27.17 Fill the cooling system through the expansion tank

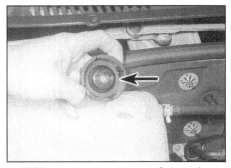

27.30 Inspect the pressure (expansion tank) cap seal (arrowed)

engine components. Also check that the cylinder block drain plug is in place and tight.

15 Prepare a sufficient quantity of the specified coolant mixture (see below), then remove the expansion tank filler cap **(see illustration)**.

16 Place a container under the vehicle, below the expansion tank, to catch any coolant which may be spilt during the topping-up procedure. Also place a wad of rags around the expansion tank.

17 Slowly fill the system until the coolant level reaches the MAX mark on the side of the expansion tank **(see illustration)**.

18 Refit and tighten the expansion tank filler cap.

19 Start the engine, and allow it to run until it reaches normal operating temperature (until the cooling fan cuts in and out).

20 Stop the engine, and allow it to cool, then re-check the coolant level with reference to *Weekly checks*. Top-up the level if necessary and refit the expansion tank filler cap. Where applicable, refit the engine undershield.

Antifreeze mixture

21 The antifreeze should always be renewed at the specified intervals. This is necessary not only to maintain the antifreeze properties, but also to prevent corrosion which would otherwise occur as the corrosion inhibitors become progressively less effective.

22 Always use an antifreeze which is suitable for use in mixed-metal cooling systems (see *Antifreeze – notes on renewal* below). The quantity of antifreeze and levels of protection are given in the Specifications.

23 Before adding antifreeze, the cooling system should be completely drained, preferably flushed, and all hoses checked for condition and security.

24 After filling with antifreeze, a label should be attached to the expansion tank, stating the type and concentration of antifreeze used, and the date installed. Any subsequent topping-up should be made with the same type and concentration of antifreeze.

25 Do not use engine antifreeze in the windscreen/tailgate washer system, as it will cause damage to the vehicle paintwork. A screenwash additive should be added to the washer system in the quantities stated on the bottle.

Antifreeze – notes on renewal

26 From approximately September 1998 onwards, all new Fiesta models were factory filled with an entirely new antifreeze type. This new antifreeze (which is orange in colour) is a concentration of monoethylene glycol and organic additives and is claimed to be greatly superior in comparison with the traditional ethylene glycol type antifreeze (blue/green in colour). Because of the different properties of the two types, they *must not* be mixed together in the same cooling system. If it is wished to change from one type to the other, the cooling system must be drained and thoroughly reverse-flushed before refilling with fresh coolant mixture.

27 Ford state that, where ethylene glycol antifreeze (blue/green) to Ford specification ESD-M97B-49-A is used, it will last approximately six years, whereas the monoethylene glycol type (orange) to Ford specification WSS-M97B44-D will last approximately ten years. Both these recommendations are subject to the antifreeze being used in the recommended concentration, unmixed with any other type of antifreeze or additive, and topped-up when necessary using only that antifreeze mixed 50/50 with clean water.

28 If the vehicle's history (and therefore the type and quality of the antifreeze in it) is unknown, owners who wish to follow Ford's recommendations are advised to drain and thoroughly reverse-flush the system before refilling with fresh coolant mixture. If the appropriate quality of antifreeze is used, the stated renewal intervals will apply.

29 If any antifreeze other than Ford's is to be used, the coolant must be renewed at regular intervals to provide an equivalent degree of protection; the conventional recommendation is to renew the coolant every three to four years.

Pressure (expansion tank) cap check

30 Clean the pressure cap, and inspect the seal inside the cap for damage or deterioration. If there is any sign of damage or deterioration to the seal, fit a new pressure cap **(see illustration)**.

Chapter 1 Part B:
Routine maintenance and servicing – diesel engine models

Contents

Air filter element renewal 17
Auxiliary drivebelt check and renewal 5
Brake fluid renewal 20
Coolant renewal and pressure cap check 21
Brake pad and disc wear check 7
Brake shoe and drum wear check 8
Driveshaft gaiter check 10
Engine oil and filter renewal 3
Fuel filter renewal 14
Fuel filter water draining – Endura-DE engine 4
General information 1

Hinge and lock lubrication 11
Hose and fluid leak check 6
Manual transmission oil level check 18
Pollen filter renewal 15
Regular maintenance 2
Road test 13
Roadwheel nut tightness check 12
Steering and suspension check 9
Timing belt and injection pump belt renewal 19
Valve clearance check and adjustment 16

Degrees of difficulty

| **Easy,** suitable for novice with little experience | | **Fairly easy,** suitable for beginner with some experience | | **Fairly difficult,** suitable for competent DIY mechanic |  | **Difficult,** suitable for experienced DIY mechanic | | **Very difficult,** suitable for expert DIY or professional | 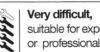 |

Lubricants and fluids . . . .   Refer to the end of *Weekly checks*

Capacities

Engine oil
Including oil filter:
   Endura-DE engine . . . .   5.0 litres
   Endura-DI engine . . . .   6.1 litres
Excluding oil filter:
   Endura-DE engine . . . .   4.5 litres
   Endura-DI engine . . . .   5.5 litres

Cooling system
All models (approximate) . . . .   9.3 litres

Transmission
Manual transmission (approximate) . . . .   2.8 litres

Washer fluid reservoir
Without headlight washers . . . .   4.0 litres
With headlight washers . . . .   8.0 litres

Fuel tank
Endura-DE engine models . . . .   40.0 litres
Endura-DI engine models . . . .   38.0 litres

Cooling system

Antifreeze mixture:
   50% antifreeze . . . .   Protection down to –37°C
   55% antifreeze . . . .   Protection down to –45°C
Note: *Refer to antifreeze manufacturer for latest recommendations.*

Brakes

Friction material minimum thickness:
   Front brake pads . . . .   1.5 mm
   Rear brake shoes . . . .   1.0 mm

Torque wrench settings

	Nm	lbf ft
Engine oil drain plug	25	18
Manual transmission filler/level plug	35	26
Roadwheel nuts	85	63

The maintenance intervals in this manual are provided with the assumption that you, not the dealer, will be carrying out the work. These are the minimum maintenance intervals recommended by us for vehicles driven daily. If you wish to keep your vehicle in peak condition at all times, you may wish to perform some of these procedures more often. We encourage frequent maintenance, because it enhances the efficiency, performance and resale value of your vehicle.

If the vehicle is driven in dusty areas, used to tow a trailer, or driven frequently at slow speeds (idling in traffic) or on short journeys, more frequent maintenance intervals are recommended.

When the vehicle is new, it should be serviced by a factory-authorised dealer service department, in order to preserve the factory warranty.

Every 250 miles or weekly
☐ Refer to *Weekly checks*

Every 5000 miles or 6 months, whichever comes first
☐ Renew the engine oil and filter (Section 3)
Note: *Frequent oil and filter changes are good for the engine. We recommend changing the oil at the mileage specified here, or at least twice a year if the mileage covered is a less.*

Every 10 000 miles or 12 months, whichever comes first
☐ Drain water from the fuel filter – Endura-DE engine (Section 4)
☐ Check the condition and tension of the auxiliary drivebelt(s) (Section 5)
☐ Check all components, pipes and hoses for fluid leaks (Section 6)
☐ Check the brake pads and discs for wear (Section 7)
☐ Check the brake shoes and drums for wear (Section 8)
☐ Check the steering and suspension components for condition and security (Section 9)
☐ Check the condition of the driveshaft gaiters (Section 10)
☐ Lubricate all hinges and locks (Section 11)
☐ Check the roadwheel nuts are tightened to the specified torque (Section 12)
☐ Carry out a road test (Section 13)

Every 20 000 miles
☐ Renew the fuel filter (Section 14)
☐ Renew the pollen filter (Section 15)
Note: *If the vehicle is used in dusty conditions, the pollen filter should be renewed more frequently.*

Every 30 000 miles
☐ Check and, if necessary, adjust the valve clearances (Section 16)
☐ Renew the air filter (Section 17)
☐ Check the manual transmission oil level (Section 18)

Every 40 000 miles
☐ Renew the timing belt and injection pump belt (Section 19)
Note: *The Ford interval for belt renewal is actually at a much higher mileage than this. It is strongly recommended, however, that the interval is reduced to 40 000 miles, particularly on vehicles which are subjected to intensive use, ie, mainly short journeys or a lot of stop-start driving. The actual belt renewal interval is therefore very much up to the individual owner, but bear in mind that severe engine damage will result if the belt breaks.*

Every 3 years, regardless of mileage
☐ Renew the brake fluid (Section 20)

Every 4 years, regardless of mileage
☐ Renew the coolant and check the condition of the expansion tank pressure cap (Section 21)

Underbonnet view of a 1.8 litre Endura-DE engine model

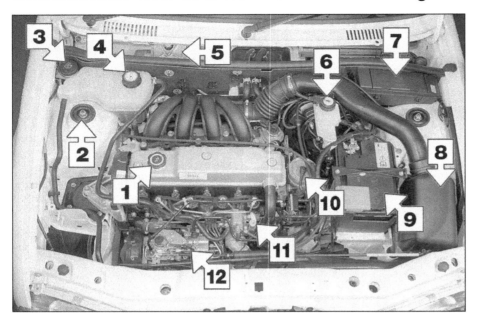

1 Engine oil filler cap
2 Suspension strut top mounting
3 Windscreen washer fluid reservoir
4 Coolant reservoir (expansion tank)
5 Windscreen wiper motor
6 Brake fluid reservoir
7 Auxiliary fuse/relay box
8 Air cleaner casing
9 Battery
10 Fuel filter
11 Engine oil level dipstick
12 Fuel injection pump

Front underbody view of a 1.8 litre Endura-DE engine model

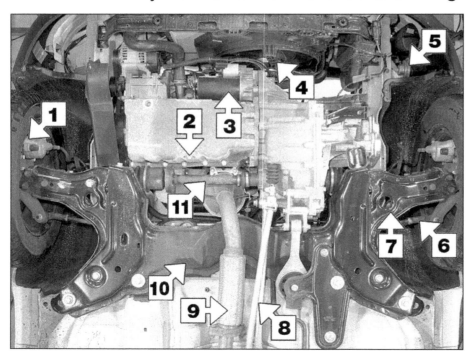

1 Brake caliper
2 Engine oil drain plug
3 Starter motor
4 Cooling fan
5 Horn
6 Track-rod end
7 Suspension lower arm
8 Gearchange rod
9 Exhaust system
10 Suspension subframe
11 Driveshaft

Rear underbody view – Hatchback and Van models

1 Suspension trailing arm
2 Shock absorber
3 Spare wheel cradle
4 Exhaust rear silencer
5 Suspension beam
6 Fuel tank

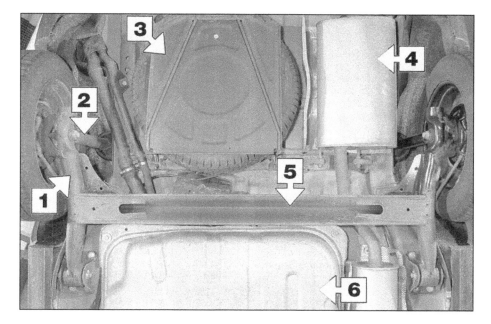

Rear underbody view – Courier and Combi models

1 Suspension torsion beam
2 Shock absorber
3 Exhaust rear silencer
4 Spare wheel cradle
5 Brake pressure proportioning valve
6 Suspension beam
7 Fuel tank

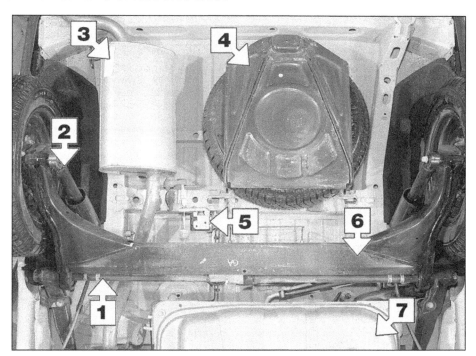

1 General information

1 This Chapter is designed to help the home mechanic maintain his/her vehicle for safety, economy, long life and peak performance.

2 The Chapter contains a master maintenance schedule, followed by Sections dealing specifically with each task in the schedule. Visual checks, adjustments, component renewal and other helpful items are included. Refer to the accompanying illustrations of the engine compartment and the underside of the vehicle for the locations of the various components.

3 Servicing your vehicle in accordance with the mileage/time maintenance schedule and the following Sections will provide a planned maintenance programme, which should result in a long and reliable service life. This is a comprehensive plan, so maintaining some items but not others at the specified service intervals, will not produce the same results.

4 As you service your vehicle, you will discover that many of the procedures can – and should – be grouped together, because of the particular procedure being performed, or because of the proximity of two otherwise-unrelated components to one another. For example, if the vehicle is raised for any reason, the exhaust can be inspected at the same time as the suspension and steering components.

5 The first step in this maintenance programme is to prepare yourself before the actual work begins. Read through all the Sections relevant to the work to be carried out, then make a list and gather all the parts and tools required. If a problem is encountered, seek advice from a parts specialist, or a dealer service department.

2 Regular maintenance

1 If, from the time the vehicle is new, the routine maintenance schedule is followed closely, and frequent checks are made of fluid levels and high-wear items, as suggested throughout this manual, the engine will be kept in relatively good running condition, and the need for additional work will be minimised.

2 It is possible that there will be times when the engine is running poorly due to the lack of regular maintenance. This is even more likely if a used vehicle, which has not received regular and frequent maintenance checks, is purchased. In such cases, additional work may need to be carried out, outside of the regular maintenance intervals.

3 If engine wear is suspected, a compression test or leakdown test (refer to Chapter 2C) will provide valuable information regarding the overall performance of the main internal components. Such a test can be used as a basis to decide on the extent of the work to be carried out. If, for example, a compression or leakdown test indicates serious internal engine wear, conventional maintenance as described in this Chapter will not greatly improve the performance of the engine, and may prove a waste of time and money, unless extensive overhaul work is carried out first.

4 The following series of operations are those most often required to improve the performance of a generally poor-running engine:

Primary operations

a) Clean, inspect and test the battery (refer to 'Weekly checks').
b) Check all the engine-related fluids (refer to 'Weekly checks').
c) Check the condition and tension of the auxiliary drivebelt (Section 5).
d) Check the condition of the air filter, and renew if necessary (Section 17).
e) Renew the fuel filter (Section 14).
f) Check the condition of all hoses, and check for fluid leaks (Section 6).

5 If the above operations do not prove fully effective, carry out the following secondary operations:

Secondary operations

All items listed under *Primary operations*, plus the following:

a) Check the charging system (refer to Chapter 5A).
b) Check the pre-heating system (refer to Chapter 5C).
c) Check the fuel system (refer to Chapter 4B or 4C).

Every 5000 miles or 6 months, whichever comes first

3 Engine oil and filter renewal

1 Frequent oil and filter changes are the most important preventative maintenance procedures which can be undertaken by the DIY owner. As engine oil ages, it becomes diluted and contaminated, which leads to premature engine wear.

2 Before starting this procedure, gather together all the necessary tools and materials. Also make sure that you have plenty of clean rags and newspapers handy, to mop up any spills. Ideally, the engine oil should be warm, as it will drain more easily, and more built-up sludge will be removed with it. Take care not to touch the exhaust or any other hot parts of the engine when working under the vehicle. To avoid any possibility of scalding, and to protect yourself from possible skin irritants and other harmful contaminants in used engine oils, it is advisable to wear gloves when carrying out this work.

3 Firmly apply the handbrake then jack up the front of the vehicle and support it on axle stands (see *Jacking and vehicle support*).

4 Remove the oil filler cap.

5 Using a spanner, or preferably a suitable socket and bar, slacken the drain plug about half a turn (see illustration). Position the draining container under the drain plug, then remove the plug completely.

6 Allow some time for the oil to drain, noting that it may be necessary to reposition the container as the oil flow slows to a trickle.

7 After all the oil has drained, wipe the drain plug and the sealing washer with a clean rag. Examine the condition of the sealing washer, and renew it if it shows signs of scoring or other damage which may prevent an oil-tight seal. Clean the area around the drain plug opening, and refit the plug complete with the washer and tighten it securely.

8 Move the container into position under the oil filter which is located on the rear of the cylinder block (see illustration).

9 Use an oil filter removal tool to slacken the filter initially, then unscrew it by hand the rest of the way. Empty the oil from the old filter into the container.

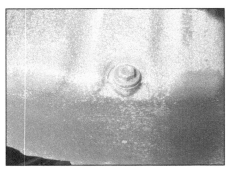

3.5 Engine oil drain plug on the sump

3.8 View of the oil filter from under the rear of the engine

10 Use a clean rag to remove all oil, dirt and sludge from the filter sealing area on the engine.

11 Apply a light coating of clean engine oil to the sealing ring on the new filter, then screw the filter into position on the engine. Tighten the filter firmly by hand only – **do not** use any tools.

12 Remove the old oil and all tools from under the vehicle then lower the vehicle to the ground.

13 Fill the engine through the filler hole, using the correct grade and type of oil (refer to *Weekly checks* for details of topping-up). Pour in half the specified quantity of oil first, then wait a few minutes for the oil to drain into the sump. Continue to add oil, a small quantity at a time, until the level is up to the lower mark on the dipstick. Adding approximately a further 0.5 litre will bring the level up to the upper mark on the dipstick.

14 Start the engine and run it for a few minutes, while checking for leaks around the oil filter seal and the sump drain plug. Note that there may be a delay of a few seconds before the low oil pressure warning light goes out when the engine is first started, as the oil circulates through the new oil filter and the engine oil galleries before the pressure builds-up.

15 Stop the engine, and wait a few minutes for the oil to settle in the sump once more. With the new oil circulated and the filter now completely full, recheck the level on the dipstick, and add more oil as necessary.

16 Dispose of the used engine oil safely with reference to *General repair procedures*.

Every 10 000 miles or 12 months, whichever comes first

4 Fuel filter water draining – Endura-DE engine

Caution: Before starting any work on the fuel filter, wipe clean the filter assembly and the area around it; it is essential that no dirt or other foreign matter is allowed into the system. Obtain a suitable container into which the filter can be drained and place rags or similar material under the filter assembly to catch any spillages. Do not allow diesel fuel to leak into the clutch bellhousing or it will contaminate the clutch driven plate friction material; this will cause severe clutch slip which can be cured only by the renewal of the clutch plate and the degreasing of all fouled surfaces. Similarly, diesel fuel should never be allowed to contaminate components such as the alternator and starter motor, the coolant hoses and engine mountings, and any wiring.

1 In addition to taking the precautions noted above to catch any fuel spillages, connect a tube to the drain spigot on the base of the fuel filter. Place the other end of the tube in a clean jar or can.

2 Open the drain cock by unscrewing the knurled wheel.

3 Allow the filter to drain until clean fuel, free of dirt or water, emerges from the tube (approximately 100 cc is usually sufficient). Close the drain cock and remove the tube, containers and rag, mopping up any spilt fuel.

4 If, as often happens, no fuel emerges on opening the drain cock, slacken the vent screw on the filter head to allow sufficient air into the filter for fuel to flow. If this does not work, remove the filter cartridge and check it carefully until the reason for the lack of flow can be identified and is cured. It is unwise simply to probe the drain cock with a piece of wire in an attempt to clear the obstruction; the small seals in the drain cock may be damaged or dislodged. Note that the system may require bleeding if the vent screw is disturbed or the filter unscrewed (refer to Chapter 4B or 4C).

5 On completion, dispose safely of the drained fuel. Check carefully all disturbed components to ensure that there are no leaks (of air or fuel) when the engine is restarted.

5 Auxiliary drivebelt check and renewal

Checking

1 The auxiliary drivebelt is fitted at the right-hand side of the engine and drives the alternator, air conditioning compressor and power steering pump (as applicable).

2 Due to their function and material makeup, drivebelts are prone to failure after a long period of time and should therefore be inspected regularly.

3 Since the drivebelt is located very close to the right-hand side of the engine compartment, it is possible to gain better access by raising the front of the vehicle and removing the right-hand wheel, then unbolting the crankshaft pulley lower cover from the underbody.

4 With the engine stopped, inspect the full length of the drivebelt for cracks and separation of the belt plies. It will be necessary to turn the engine (using a spanner or socket and bar on the crankshaft pulley bolt) in order to move the belt away from the pulleys so that the belt can be inspected thoroughly. Twist the belt between the pulleys so that both sides can be viewed. Also check

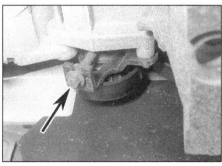

5.7 Auxiliary drivebelt tension adjustment bolt

for fraying, and glazing which gives the belt a shiny appearance. Check the pulleys for nicks, cracks, distortion and corrosion.

Renewal

Endura-DE engine

5 To remove the drivebelt, raise the front of the vehicle (if not already done) and support on axle stands (see *Jacking and vehicle support*). Unbolt and remove the crankshaft pulley cover.

6 Slacken the adjustment clamping bolt located in the centre of the tensioner pulley.

7 Back off the adjustment bolt **(see illustration)** to release the tension on the belt, then release it from the crankshaft, alternator, power steering pump, and air conditioning compressor pulleys (as applicable) and remove it from under the vehicle.

8 Locate the new drivebelt on the pulleys and around the tensioner. Make sure that the drivebelt is correctly seated in all of the pulley grooves.

9 Tighten the adjustment bolt until it is possible to deflect the drivebelt midway between the pulleys on the longest run approximately 3 mm under firm thumb pressure.

10 Tighten the adjustment clamping bolt securely, then refit the crankshaft pulley cover and lower the vehicle to the ground.

Endura-DI engine

11 To remove the drivebelt, raise the front of the vehicle (if not already done) and support on axle stands (see *Jacking and vehicle support*). Unbolt and remove the crankshaft pulley cover.

12 Using a spanner on the tensioner centre bolt, turn the tensioner clockwise to release the drivebelt tension. Note how the drivebelt is routed, then remove the belt from the pulleys.

13 Fit the new drivebelt onto the crankshaft, alternator, power steering pump, and air conditioning compressor pulleys, as applicable, then turn the tensioner anti-clockwise and locate the drivebelt on the pulley. Make sure that the drivebelt is correctly seated in all of the pulley grooves, then release the tensioner.

14 Refit the drivebelt lower cover and lower the vehicle to the ground.

6 Hose and fluid leak check

1 Visually inspect the engine joint faces, gaskets and seals for any signs of water or oil leaks. Pay particular attention to the areas around the cylinder head cover, cylinder head, oil filter and sump joint faces. Bear in mind that, over a period of time, some very slight seepage from these areas is to be expected – what you are really looking for is any indication of a serious leak. Should a leak be found, renew the offending gasket or oil seal by referring to the appropriate Chapters in this manual.

2 Also check the security and condition of all the engine-related pipes and hoses, and all braking system pipes and hoses. Ensure that all cable ties or securing clips are in place, and in good condition. Clips which are broken or missing can lead to chafing of the hoses, pipes or wiring, which could cause more serious problems in the future.

3 Carefully check the radiator hoses and heater hoses along their entire length. Renew any hose which is cracked, swollen or deteriorated. Cracks will show up better if the hose is squeezed. Pay close attention to the hose clips that secure the hoses to the cooling system components. Hose clips can pinch and puncture hoses, resulting in cooling system leaks. If the crimped-type hose clips are used, it may be a good idea to replace them with standard worm-drive clips.

4 Inspect all the cooling system components (hoses, joint faces, etc) for leaks.

A leak in the cooling system will usually show up as white- or rust-coloured deposits on the area adjoining the leak.

5 Where any problems are found on system components, renew the component or gasket with reference to Chapter 3.

6 With the vehicle raised, inspect the fuel tank and filler neck for punctures, cracks and other damage. The connection between the filler neck and tank is especially critical. Sometimes a rubber filler neck or connecting hose will leak due to loose retaining clamps or deteriorated rubber.

7 Carefully check all rubber hoses and metal fuel lines leading away from the fuel tank. Check for loose connections, deteriorated hoses, crimped lines, and other damage. Pay particular attention to the vent pipes and hoses, which often loop up around the filler neck and can become blocked or crimped. Follow the lines to the front of the vehicle, carefully inspecting them all the way. Renew damaged sections as necessary. Similarly, whilst the vehicle is raised, take the opportunity to inspect all underbody brake fluid pipes and hoses.

8 From within the engine compartment, check the security of all fuel, vacuum and brake hose attachments and pipe unions, and inspect all hoses for kinks, chafing and deterioration.

9 Where applicable, check the condition of the power steering fluid pipes and hoses.

7 Brake pad and disc wear check

1 Apply the handbrake, then jack up the front of the car and support it securely on axle stands (see *Jacking and vehicle support*). Remove the front roadwheels.

2 For a comprehensive check, the brake pads should be removed and cleaned. The operation of the caliper can then also be checked, and the condition of the brake disc itself can be fully examined on both sides. Refer to Chapter 9 for further information.

3 On completion refit the roadwheels and lower the car to the ground.

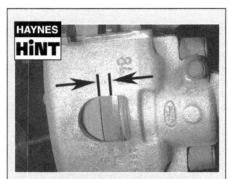

For a quick check, the thickness of friction material remaining on each brake pad can be measured through the aperture in the caliper body.

8 Brake shoe and drum wear check

Remove the rear brake drums, and check the brake shoes for signs of wear or contamination. At the same time, also inspect the wheel cylinders for signs of leakage, and the brake drum for signs of wear. Refer to the relevant Sections of Chapter 9 for further information.

9 Steering and suspension check

Front suspension/steering check

1 Raise the front of the vehicle, and securely support it on axle stands (see *Jacking and vehicle support*).

2 Visually inspect the balljoint dust covers and the steering rack-and-pinion gaiters for splits, chafing or deterioration. Any wear of these components will cause loss of lubricant, together with dirt and water entry, resulting in rapid deterioration of the balljoints or steering gear.

3 On vehicles with power steering, check the fluid hoses for chafing or deterioration, and the pipe and hose unions for fluid leaks. Also check for signs of fluid leakage under pressure from the steering gear rubber gaiters, which would indicate failed fluid seals within the steering gear.

4 Grasp the roadwheel at the 12 o'clock and 6 o'clock positions, and try to rock it **(see illustration)**. Very slight free play may be felt, but if the movement is appreciable, further investigation is necessary to determine the source. Continue rocking the wheel while an assistant depresses the footbrake. If the movement is now eliminated or significantly reduced, it is likely that the hub bearings are at fault. If the free play is still evident with the footbrake depressed, then there is wear in the suspension joints or mountings.

5 Now grasp the wheel at the 9 o'clock and 3 o'clock positions, and try to rock it as before. Any movement felt now may again be caused by wear in the hub bearings or the steering track rod balljoints. If the outer balljoint is worn, the visual movement will be obvious. If the inner joint is suspect, it can be felt by placing a hand over the rack-and-pinion rubber gaiter and gripping the track rod. If the wheel is now rocked, movement will be felt at the inner joint if wear has taken place.

6 Using a large screwdriver or flat bar, check for wear in the suspension mounting bushes by levering between the relevant suspension component and its attachment point. Some movement is to be expected, as the mountings are made of rubber, but excessive wear should be obvious. Also check the condition of any visible rubber bushes, looking for splits, cracks or contamination of the rubber.

7 With the car standing on its wheels, have an assistant turn the steering wheel back-and-forth, about an eighth of a turn each way. There should be very little, if any, lost

9.4 Check for wear in the hub bearings by grasping the wheel and trying to rock it

movement between the steering wheel and roadwheels. If this is not the case, closely observe the joints and mountings previously described. In addition, check the steering column universal joints for wear, and also check the rack-and-pinion steering gear itself.

Rear suspension check

8 Chock the front wheels, then jack up the rear of the vehicle and support securely on axle stands (see *Jacking and vehicle support*).
9 Working as described previously for the front suspension, check the rear hub bearings, the suspension bushes and the strut or shock absorber mountings (as applicable) for wear.

Shock absorber check

10 Check for any signs of fluid leakage around the shock absorber body, or from the rubber gaiter around the piston rod. Should any fluid be noticed, the shock absorber is defective internally, and should be renewed. **Note:** *Shock absorbers should always be renewed in pairs on the same axle.*
11 The efficiency of the shock absorber may be checked by bouncing the vehicle at each corner. Generally speaking, the body will return to its normal position and stop after being depressed. If it rises and returns on a rebound, the shock absorber is probably suspect. Also examine the shock absorber upper and lower mountings for any signs of wear.

10 Driveshaft gaiter check

1 With the vehicle raised and securely supported on stands, turn the steering onto full lock then slowly rotate the roadwheel. Inspect the condition of the outer constant velocity (CV) joint rubber gaiters while squeezing the gaiters to open out the folds **(see illustration)**. Check for signs of cracking, splits or deterioration of the rubber which may allow the grease to escape and lead to water and grit entry into the joint. Also check the security and condition of the retaining clips. Repeat these checks on the inner CV joints. If any damage or deterioration is found, the gaiters should be renewed as described in Chapter 8.
2 At the same time check the general condition of the CV joints themselves by first holding the driveshaft and attempting to rotate the wheel. Repeat this check by holding the inner joint and attempting to rotate the driveshaft. Any appreciable movement indicates wear in the joints, wear in the driveshaft splines or loose driveshaft retaining nut.

11 Hinge and lock lubrication

1 Work around the vehicle and lubricate the hinges of the bonnet, doors and tailgate with a light machine oil.
2 Lightly lubricate the bonnet release mechanism and exposed section of inner cable with a smear of grease **(see illustration)**.
3 Check carefully the security and operation of all hinges, latches and locks, adjusting them where required. Check the operation of the central locking system (if fitted).
4 Check the condition and operation of the tailgate struts, renewing them if either is leaking or no longer able to support the tailgate securely when raised.

12 Roadwheel nut tightness check

1 Where applicable, remove the wheel trims, and slacken the roadwheel nuts slightly.
2 Tighten the nuts to the specified torque, using a torque wrench.

13 Road test

Instruments/electrical equipment

1 Check the operation of all instruments and electrical equipment.
2 Make sure that all instruments read correctly, and switch on all electrical equipment in turn, to check that it functions properly.

Steering and suspension

3 Check for any abnormalities in the steering, suspension, handling or road 'feel'.
4 Drive the vehicle, and check that there are no unusual vibrations or noises.
5 Check that the steering feels positive, with no excessive 'sloppiness', or roughness, and check for any suspension noises when cornering and driving over bumps.

Drivetrain

6 Check the performance of the engine, clutch, transmission and driveshafts.
7 Listen for any unusual noises from the engine, clutch and transmission.
8 Make sure that the engine runs smoothly when idling, and that there is no hesitation when accelerating.
9 Check that the clutch action is smooth and progressive, that the drive is taken up smoothly, and that the pedal travel is not excessive. Also listen for any noises when the clutch pedal is depressed.
10 Check that all gears can be engaged smoothly without noise, and that the gear lever action is smooth and not abnormally vague or 'notchy'.
11 Listen for a metallic clicking sound from the front of the vehicle, as the vehicle is driven slowly in a circle with the steering on full lock. Carry out this check in both directions. If a clicking noise is heard, this indicates wear in a driveshaft joint (see Chapter 8).

Check the braking system

12 Make sure that the vehicle does not pull to one side when braking, and that the wheels do not lock prematurely when braking hard.
13 Check that there is no vibration through the steering when braking.
14 Check that the handbrake operates correctly, without excessive movement of the lever, and that it holds the vehicle stationary on a slope.
15 Test the operation of the brake servo unit as follows. Depress the footbrake four or five times to exhaust the vacuum, then start the engine. As the engine starts, there should be a noticeable 'give' in the brake pedal as vacuum builds up. Allow the engine to run for at least two minutes, and then switch it off. If the brake pedal is now depressed again, it should be possible to detect a hiss from the servo as the pedal is depressed. After about four or five applications, no further hissing should be heard, and the pedal should feel considerably harder.

10.1 Check the condition of the driveshaft gaiters

11.2 Lubricate the bonnet lock with grease

14.1 The fuel filter is located on a bracket at the left-hand end of the cylinder head – Endura-DE engine

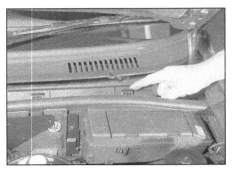

15.2 Releasing a pollen filter cover securing clip

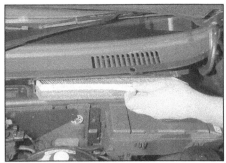

15.3 Pulling out the pollen filter

Every 20 000 miles

14 Fuel filter renewal

Caution: Before starting any work on the fuel filter, wipe clean the filter assembly and the area around it; it is essential that no dirt or other foreign matter is allowed into the system. Obtain a suitable container into which the filter can be drained and place rags or similar material under the filter assembly to catch any spillages. Do not allow diesel fuel to leak into the clutch bellhousing or it will contaminate the clutch driven plate friction material; this will cause severe clutch slip which can be cured only by the renewal of the clutch plate and the degreasing of all fouled surfaces. Similarly, diesel fuel should never be allowed to contaminate components such as the alternator and starter motor, the coolant hoses and engine mountings, and any wiring.

Endura-DE engine

1 The fuel filter is located on a bracket on the left-hand end of the cylinder head **(see illustration)**.
2 Drain the fuel filter with reference to Section 4.
3 Loosen the clamp bolt retaining the filter to the mounting bracket.
4 Note the location of the fuel lines then squeeze the tabs and disconnect the quick-release fittings from the inlet and outlet stubs on the filter. The inlet fuel line is the line from

the fuel heater, and the outlet fuel line is the line leading to the injection pump.
5 Remove the filter from the retaining bracket and withdraw from the engine compartment.
6 Fit the new filter using a reversal of the removal procedure. Make sure the quick-release fittings are pushed fully onto the inlet and outlet stubs, and tighten the clamp bolt securely. The direction of fuel flow is indicated on the top of the filter by arrows.

Endura-DI engine

7 The fuel filter is located at the rear of the engine compartment, on the right-hand side. Depending on equipment fitted, it may be necessary to move additional components aside for improved access.
8 Note the positions of the fuel pipes on top of the filter carefully, so that they can be refitted correctly. The filter supply pipe and the outlet pipe (to the injection pump) have a white band, while the return pipe has a red band. Have some clean rags ready, to soak up any fuel spillage.
9 Pull out the spring clip retaining the return pipes and control valve to the top of the filter, and lift the assembly off without disconnecting the pipes.
10 Squeeze together the lugs on the quick-release pipe fittings, and disconnect the fuel supply and filter outlet pipes from the top of the filter – be prepared for some fuel spillage. It is most important not to introduce any dirt into the fuel pipes while they are disconnected, and as little fuel as possible should be lost from the pipes, to make starting the engine easier on completion. If the pipes are to be left disconnected for long, they should be capped or plugged.

11 To remove the filter, loosen the clamp screw, and remove the filter from its holder, noting the alignment arrows on the holder and filter
12 Refitting is a reversal of removal, noting the following points:
a) *Line up the arrows on the filter and its holder.*
b) *Tighten the filter clamp screw securely, but without crushing the filter body.*
c) *Before fitting the pipes, the filter should be filled with clean fuel – use a small, clean funnel, and have plenty of clean rags available, to soak up any spillage.*
d) *Make sure that the pipe connections are correctly and securely remade.*
e) *Start the engine, noting that it may be necessary to crank the engine for longer than normal. With the engine running, check for fuel leaks from the disturbed pipes.*

15 Pollen filter renewal

1 Open the bonnet, and locate the pollen filter, at the left-hand corner of the scuttle at the rear of the engine compartment.
2 Release the two clips, and open the pollen filter cover **(see illustration)**.
3 Pull the filter from the housing, using the tab provided **(see illustration)**.
4 Fit the new filter using a reversal of the removal procedure. Make sure that the filter is fitted with the removal tab and the TOP/OBEN marking visible.

Every 30 000 miles

16 Valve clearance check and adjustment

This procedure is described in Chapter 2C or 2D according to engine type.

17 Air filter element renewal

1 The air cleaner is located in the left-hand front corner of the engine compartment.

First unscrew the screws securing the cover to the air cleaner housing. Disconnect the air inlet duct from the cover and, where applicable, disconnect the wiring from the inlet air temperature sensor.
2 Lift the cover and remove the filter element

17.2 Removing the element from the base of the air cleaner

from the base **(see illustration)**. Note which way round it is fitted. Due to the position of the battery, the element is best removed from the rear of the base.

3 Wipe clean the interior surfaces of the cover and base.

4 Insert the new element making sure that it is seated correctly in the base.

5 Refit the cover and secure with the retaining screws. Reconnect the air inlet duct and, where applicable, the temperature sensor wiring.

18 Manual transmission oil level check

1 Position the vehicle over an inspection pit, on vehicle ramps, or jack it up, but make sure that it is level.

2 Remove all traces of dirt then unscrew the filler/level plug from the front face of the transmission. Note it is the plug furthest from the engine – do not confuse it with the blanking plug near the bellhousing.

3 The level must be between 5 mm and 10 mm below the bottom edge of the filler/level plug hole (use a cranked tool such as an Allen key to check the level). If necessary, top up the level with the specified grade of oil (see *Lubricants and fluids*).

4 When the level is correct, clean and refit the filler level plug and tighten it to the specified torque.

5 Lower the car to the ground.

Every 40 000 miles

19 Timing belt and injection pump belt renewal

This procedure is described in Chapter 2C or 2D according to engine type.

Every 3 years, regardless of mileage

20 Brake fluid renewal

⚠️ **Warning: Brake hydraulic fluid can harm your eyes and damage painted surfaces, so use extreme caution when handling and pouring it. Do not use fluid that has been standing open for some time, as it absorbs moisture from the air. Excess moisture can cause a dangerous loss of braking effectiveness.**

1 The procedure is similar to that for the bleeding of the hydraulic system as described in Chapter 9 except that, on models with a conventional braking system, the brake fluid reservoir can be fully emptied by syphoning, using a clean poultry baster or similar before starting, and allowance should be made for the old fluid to be expelled when bleeding a section of the circuit. On models fitted with ABS, reduce the fluid level in the reservoir (by syphoning or using a poultry baster), but do not allow the fluid level to drop far enough to allow air into the system – if air enters the ABS hydraulic unit, the unit must be bled using special Ford test equipment (see Chapter 9).

2 Working as described in Chapter 9, open the first bleed screw in the sequence, and pump the brake pedal gently until nearly all the old fluid has been emptied from the master cylinder reservoir. Top-up to the MAX level with new fluid, and continue pumping until only the new fluid remains in the

HAYNES HiNT *Old hydraulic fluid is invariably much darker in colour than the new, making it easy to distinguish the two.*

reservoir, and new fluid can be seen emerging from the bleed screw. Tighten the screw, and top the reservoir level up to the MAX level line.

3 Work through all the remaining bleed screws in the sequence until new fluid can be seen at all of them. Be careful to keep the master cylinder reservoir topped-up to above the MIN level at all times, or air may enter the system and greatly increase the length of the task.

4 When the operation is complete, check that all bleed screws are securely tightened, and that their dust caps are refitted. Wash off all traces of spilt fluid, and recheck the master cylinder reservoir fluid level.

5 Check the operation of the brakes before taking the car on the road.

6 Finally, check the operation of the clutch. Since the clutch shares the same fluid reservoir as the braking system, it may also be necessary to bleed the clutch as described in Chapter 6.

Every 4 years, regardless of mileage

21 Coolant renewal and pressure cap check

Cooling system draining

Note: *If the antifreeze used is Ford's own* brand, or of similar quality, the coolant renewal interval may be extended. If the vehicle's history is unknown, if antifreeze of lesser quality is known to be in the system, or simply if you prefer to follow conventional servicing intervals, the coolant should be changed periodically (typically, every 4 years) as described here. Refer also to 'Antifreeze – notes on renewal' in this Section.

⚠️ **Warning: Wait until the engine is cold before starting this procedure. Do not allow antifreeze to come in contact with your skin, or with the painted surfaces of the vehicle. Rinse off spills immediately with plenty of water. Never leave antifreeze lying around in an open container, or in a puddle in the driveway or**

21.3 Radiator drain screw (arrowed)

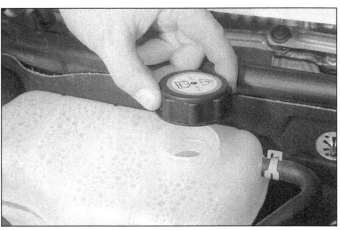

21.15 Removing the expansion tank filler cap

on the garage floor. Children and pets are attracted by its sweet smell, but antifreeze can be fatal if ingested.

1 With the engine completely cold, remove the expansion tank filler cap. Turn the cap anti-clockwise, wait until any pressure remaining in the system is released, then unscrew it and lift it off.

2 Where applicable, remove the engine undershield, then position a suitable container beneath the radiator drain screw, at the bottom left-hand corner of the radiator.

3 Slacken the drain screw, and allow the coolant to drain into the container (see illustration).

4 When the flow of coolant stops, tighten the radiator drain screw.

5 If the coolant has been drained for a reason other than renewal, then provided it is clean and less than two years old, it can be re-used, though this is not recommended.

Cooling system flushing

6 If coolant renewal has been neglected, or if the antifreeze mixture has become diluted, then in time, the cooling system may gradually lose efficiency, as the coolant passages become restricted due to rust, scale deposits, and other sediment. The cooling system efficiency can be restored by flushing the system clean.

7 The radiator should be flushed independently of the engine, to avoid unnecessary contamination.

Radiator flushing

8 Disconnect the top and bottom hoses and any other relevant hoses from the radiator, with reference to Chapter 3.

9 Insert a garden hose into the radiator top inlet. Direct a flow of clean water through the radiator, and continue flushing until clean water emerges from the radiator bottom outlet.

10 If after a reasonable period, the water still does not run clear, the radiator can be flushed with a good proprietary cleaning agent. It is important that their manufacturer's instructions are followed carefully. If the contamination is particularly bad, insert the hose in the radiator bottom outlet, and reverse-flush the radiator.

Engine flushing

11 Remove the thermostat as described in Chapter 3 then, if the radiator top hose has been disconnected from the engine, temporarily reconnect the hose.

12 With the top and bottom hoses disconnected from the radiator, insert a garden hose into the top hose. Direct a clean flow of water through the engine, and continue flushing until clean water emerges from the bottom hose.

13 On completion of flushing, refit the thermostat and reconnect the hoses with reference to Chapter 3.

Cooling system filling

14 Before attempting to fill the cooling system, make sure that all hoses and clips are in good condition, and that the clips are tight. Note that an antifreeze mixture must be used all year round, to prevent corrosion of the engine components. Also check that the cylinder block drain plug is in place and tight. Proceed as described in the following sub-Sections, according to engine type.

Endura-DE engine models

15 Remove the expansion tank filler cap (see illustration).

16 Place a container under the vehicle, below the expansion tank, to catch any coolant which may be spilt during the topping-up procedure. Also place a wad of rags around the expansion tank.

17 Slowly fill the system until the coolant level reaches the MAX mark on the side of the expansion tank (see illustration).

18 Refit and tighten the expansion tank filler cap.

19 Start the engine, and allow it to run until it reaches normal operating temperature (until the cooling fan cuts in and out).

20 Stop the engine, and allow it to cool, then re-check the coolant level. If necessary, top-up the level to the MAX mark, then refit the expansion tank filler cap. Where applicable, refit the engine undershield.

Endura-DI engine models

21 Open the upper air bleed valve (where fitted) located in the expansion tank hose adjacent to the right-hand front suspension strut tower.

22 Similarly, open the lower air bleed valve located in the radiator bottom hose.

23 Release the clip and disconnect the small coolant hose from the thermostat housing.

24 Remove the expansion tank filler cap and slowly fill the system until the coolant level reaches the MAX mark on the side of the expansion tank.

25 As soon as coolant free from air bubbles emerges from the lower bleed valve, close the valve. Add further coolant to the expansion tank, if necessary, to keep the level up to the MAX mark.

26 When coolant free from air bubbles emerges from the outlet on the thermostat housing, reconnect the coolant hose.

27 Top-up the coolant in the expansion tank once more, to the MAX mark, then refit and tighten the expansion tank filler cap.

28 Start the engine, and run it at approximately 3000 rpm until the cooling fan cuts in. Allow the engine to idle for a further 30 minutes then switch it off.

21.17 Fill the cooling system through the expansion tank

21.39 Inspect the pressure (expansion tank) cap seal (arrowed)

29 Close the upper bleed valve (where fitted) and allow the engine to cool. Re-check the coolant level, top-up to the MAX mark if necessary, then refit the expansion tank filler cap. Where applicable, refit the engine undershield.

Antifreeze mixture

30 The antifreeze should always be renewed at the specified intervals. This is necessary not only to maintain the antifreeze properties, but also to prevent corrosion which would otherwise occur as the corrosion inhibitors become progressively less effective.

31 Always use an antifreeze which is suitable for use in mixed-metal cooling systems (see *Antifreeze – notes on renewal* below). The quantity of antifreeze and levels of protection are given in the Specifications.

32 Before adding antifreeze, the cooling system should be completely drained, preferably flushed, and all hoses checked for condition and security.

33 After filling with antifreeze, a label should be attached to the expansion tank, stating the type and concentration of antifreeze used, and the date installed. Any subsequent topping-up should be made with the same type and concentration of antifreeze.

34 Do not use engine antifreeze in the windscreen/tailgate washer system, as it will cause damage to the vehicle paintwork. A screenwash additive should be added to the washer system in the quantities stated on the bottle.

Antifreeze – notes on renewal

35 From approximately September 1998 onwards, all new Fiesta models were factory filled with an entirely new antifreeze type. This new antifreeze (which is orange in colour) is a concentration of monoethylene glycol and organic additives and is claimed to be greatly superior in comparison with the traditional ethylene glycol type antifreeze (blue/green in colour). Because of the different properties of the two types, they *must not* be mixed together in the same cooling system. If it is wished to change from one type to the other, the cooling system must be drained and thoroughly reverse-flushed before refilling with fresh coolant mixture.

36 Ford state that, where ethylene glycol antifreeze (blue/green) to Ford specification ESD-M97B-49-A is used, it will last approximately six years, whereas the monoethylene glycol type (orange) to Ford specification WSS-M97B44-D will last approximately ten years. Both these recommendations are subject to the antifreeze being used in the recommended concentration, unmixed with any other type of antifreeze or additive, and topped-up when necessary using only that antifreeze mixed 50/50 with clean water.

37 If the vehicle's history (and therefore the type and quality of the antifreeze in it) is unknown, owners who wish to follow Ford's recommendations are advised to drain and thoroughly reverse-flush the system before refilling with fresh antifreeze. If the appropriate quality of antifreeze is used, the stated renewal intervals will apply.

38 If any antifreeze other than Ford's is to be used, the coolant must be renewed at regular intervals to provide an equivalent degree of protection; the conventional recommendation is to renew the coolant every three to four years.

Pressure (expansion tank) cap check

39 Clean the pressure cap, and inspect the seal inside the cap for damage or deterioration **(see illustration)**. If there is any sign of damage or deterioration to the seal, fit a new pressure cap.

Chapter 2 Part A:
Endura-E petrol engine in-car repair procedures

Contents

Compression test – description and interpretation 2
Crankshaft oil seals – renewal 14
Crankshaft pulley – removal and refitting 8
Cylinder head – dismantling and overhaul . . . . .See Chapter 2E
Cylinder head – removal and refitting 7
Cylinder head rocker cover – removal and refitting 4
Cylinder head rocker gear – removal, inspection and refitting 6
Engine oil and filter renewal .See Chapter 1A
Engine oil level check .See Weekly checks
Engine/transmission mountings – inspection and renewal 16
Flywheel – removal, inspection and refitting 15
General information 1
Oil pump – removal and refitting 12
Oil pump – dismantling, inspection and reassembly 13
Sump – removal and refitting 11
Timing chain cover – removal and refitting 9
Timing chain, sprockets and tensioner – removal, inspection and
    refitting 10
Top Dead Centre (TDC) for No 1 piston – locating 3
Valve clearances – checking and adjustment 5

Degrees of difficulty

Easy, suitable for novice with little experience	**Fairly easy,** suitable for beginner with some experience	**Fairly difficult,** suitable for competent DIY mechanic	**Difficult,** suitable for experienced DIY mechanic	**Very difficult,** suitable for expert DIY or professional

Specifications

General

Engine type	Four-cylinder, in-line overhead valve
Designation	Endura-E
Engine code:	
50PS engine	JJA, JJC, JJE, JJJ, JJK or JJM
60PS engine	J4C, J4J, J4L, J4Q, J4R or J4T
Capacity	1298 cc
Bore	73.96 mm
Stroke	75.48 mm
Compression ratio	9.5:1
Firing order	1-2-4-3 (No 1 cylinder at timing chain end)
Direction of crankshaft rotation	Clockwise (seen from right-hand side of vehicle)

Valves

	Inlet	Exhaust
Valve clearance (cold):		
Up to 20/11/96	0.20 mm	0.30 mm
21/11/96 onward*	0.20 mm	0.50 mm
Valve length	103.70 to 104.40 mm	104.02 to 104.72 mm
Valve head diameter	34.40 to 34.60 mm	28.90 to 29.10 mm
Valve stem diameter:		
Standard	7.025 to 7.043 mm	6.999 to 7.017 mm
Oversize 0.2 mm	7.225 to 7.243 mm	7.199 to 7.217 mm
Oversize 0.4 mm	7.425 to 7.443 mm	7.399 to 7.417 mm
Valve stem-to-guide clearance	0.020 to 0.069 mm	0.046 to 0.095 mm

*Note: Later engines can be identified by a label on the cylinder head rocker cover, indicating the revised valve clearances

Valve springs

Free length	41.0 mm

Cylinder head

Maximum permissible gasket surface distortion (measured over full length)	0.25 mm
Valve seat angle (inlet and exhaust)	45°
Valve seat width (inlet and exhaust)	1.18 to 1.75 mm

Note: The inlet and exhaust valves have special inserts which cannot be recut using conventional tools.

Camshaft

Camshaft bearing diameter . . . . 39.615 to 39.635 mm
Bearing bush inside diameter:
    Standard . . . . 39.662 to 39.682 mm
    Oversize . . . . 39.662 to 39.713 mm
Camshaft thrust plate thickness . . . . 4.457 to 4.508 mm
Endfloat . . . . 0.02 to 0.19 mm

Cylinder block

Cylinder bore diameter:
    Standard 1 . . . . 73.94 to 73.95 mm
    Standard 2 . . . . 73.95 to 73.96 mm
    Standard 3 . . . . 73.96 to 73.97 mm
    Oversize 0.5 mm . . . . 75.00 to 75.01 mm
Valve tappet diameter . . . . 13.081 to 13.094 mm
Valve tappet clearance in cylinder block . . . . 0.016 to 0.062 mm

Pistons and piston rings

Piston diameter:
    Standard 1 . . . . 73.91 to 73.92 mm
    Standard 2 . . . . 73.92 to 73.93 mm
    Standard 3 . . . . 73.93 to 73.94 mm
    Oversize 0.5 mm . . . . 74.46 to 74.49 mm
    Oversize 1.0 mm . . . . 74.96 to 74.99 mm
Piston-to-cylinder bore clearance . . . . 0.015 to 0.050 mm
Piston ring end gap – installed:
    Top compression ring . . . . 0.25 to 0.45 mm
    Second compression ring . . . . 0.45 to 0.75 mm
    Oil control ring . . . . 0.20 to 0.50 mm
Piston ring-to-groove clearance:
    Compression rings . . . . 0.20 mm (maximum)
    Oil control ring . . . . 0.10 mm (maximum)
Ring gap position:
    Top compression ring . . . . Offset 180° from oil control ring gap
    Second compression ring . . . . Offset 90° from oil control ring gap
    Oil control ring . . . . Aligned with gudgeon pin

Gudgeon pin

Length . . . . 63.6 to 64.4 mm
Diameter:
    White colour code . . . . 18.026 to 18.029 mm
    Red colour code . . . . 18.029 to 18.032 mm
    Blue colour code . . . . 18.032 to 18.035 mm
    Yellow colour code . . . . 18.035 to 18.038 mm
Clearance in piston . . . . 0.008 to 0.014 mm
Interference fit in connecting rod . . . . 0.016 to 0.048 mm

Crankshaft and bearings

Main bearings 5
Main bearing journal diameter:
    Standard . . . . 56.980 to 57.000 mm
    0.254 mm undersize (green) . . . . 56.726 to 56.746 mm
Main bearing journal-to-shell running clearance . . . . 0.009 to 0.056 mm
Crankpin (big-end) bearing journal diameter:
    Standard . . . . 40.99 to 41.01 mm
    0.254 mm undersize (green) . . . . 40.74 to 40.76 mm
    0.508 mm undersize . . . . 40.49 to 40.51 mm
    0.762 mm undersize . . . . 40.24 to 40.26 mm
Crankpin (big-end) bearing journal-to-shell running clearance . . . . 0.006 to 0.060 mm
Crankpin (big-end) bearing side clearance . . . . 0.100 to 0.25 mm
Crankshaft endfloat . . . . 0.05 to 0.26 mm
Thrustwasher thickness:
    Standard . . . . 2.80 to 2.85 mm
    Oversize . . . . 2.99 to 3.04 mm

Lubrication

Oil pressure:

At idle speed	0.60 bar
At 2000 rpm	1.50 bar
Oil pump clearances:	
Outer rotor to body	0.14 to 0.26 mm
Inner rotor to outer rotor	0.051 to 0.127 mm
Rotor endfloat	0.025 to 0.06 mm

Torque wrench settings

	Nm	lbf ft
Big-end bearing cap bolts*:		
Stage 1	4	3
Stage 2	Angle-tighten a further 90°	
Camshaft thrust plate bolts	11	8
Camshaft sprocket bolt	28	21
Crankshaft pulley bolt	115	85
Crankshaft left-hand oil seal housing	18	13
Cylinder head bolts (may be re-used once only):		
Stage 1	30	22
Stage 2	Angle-tighten a further 90°	
Stage 3	Angle-tighten a further 90°	
Engine/transmission mountings:		
Front engine mounting bracket to cylinder head	69	51
Left-hand front mounting bracket brace	49	36
Left-hand front mounting bracket to mounting	68	50
Left-hand rear mounting bracket to mounting	68	50
Left-hand rear mounting bracket to transmission	50	37
Right-hand mounting brace	69	51
Right-hand mounting bracket to cylinder block	69	51
Right-hand mounting to body	84	62
Right-hand mounting to cylinder block bracket	120	89
Flywheel bolts	67	49
Main bearing cap	95	70
Oil dipstick tube to inlet manifold	2	1
Oil pressure switch	14	10
Oil pump	18	13
Oil pump cover	10	7
Rocker cover bolts	6	4
Rocker shaft pedestal bolts	43	32
Timing chain tensioner	8	6
Timing chain cover	9	7
Sump:		
Stage 1	7	5
Stage 2	10	7
Stage 3 (with engine warm)	10	7

New bolts must be used

1 General information

How to use this Chapter

This Part of Chapter 2 is devoted to in-car repair procedures on the Endura-E petrol engine. All procedures concerning engine removal and refitting, and engine block/cylinder head overhaul can be found in Chapter 2E.

Refer to *Vehicle identification numbers* in the Reference Section at the end of this manual for details of engine code locations.

Most of the operations included in this chapter are based on the assumption that the engine is still installed in the car. Therefore, if this information is being used during a complete engine overhaul, with the engine already removed, many of the steps included here will not apply.

Engine description

The engine is an overhead valve, water-cooled, four cylinder in-line design, designated Endura-E. The Endura-E engine replaces the HCS engine fitted to earlier Fiesta models and, apart from an aluminium sump and modifications to the inlet manifold and inlet system, is virtually identical. The engine is mounted transversely at the front of the vehicle, together with the transmission, to form a combined power unit.

The crankshaft is supported in five shell-type main bearings. The connecting rod big-end bearings are also split shell-type, and are attached to the pistons by interference-fit gudgeon pins. Each piston is fitted with two compression rings and one oil control ring.

The camshaft, which runs on bearings within the cylinder block, is chain-driven from the crankshaft, and operates the valves via pushrods and rocker arms. The valves are each closed by a single valve spring, and operate in guides integral in the cylinder head.

The oil pump is mounted externally on the crankcase, incorporates a full-flow oil filter, and is driven by a skew gear on the camshaft.

Repair operations possible with the engine in the car

The following work can be carried out with the engine in the car:

a) Rocker shaft assembly – removal, inspection and refitting.

b) Cylinder head – removal and refitting

c) Crankshaft pulley – removal and refitting.

d) Crankshaft oil seals – renewal.

e) Timing chain, sprockets and tensioner – removal, inspection and refitting.

f) Oil pump – removal and refitting.

g) Sump – removal and refitting.

h) Connecting rods and pistons – removal and refitting*.

i) Flywheel – removal, inspection and refitting.

j) Engine/transmission mountings – inspection and renewal.

*Although the operation marked with an asterisk can be carried out with the engine in the car after removal of the sump, it is better for the engine to be removed in the interests of cleanliness and improved access. For this reason, the procedure is described in Part E of this Chapter.

2 Compression test – description and interpretation

1 When engine performance is down, or if misfiring occurs which cannot be attributed to the ignition or fuel systems, a compression test can provide diagnostic clues as to the engine's condition. If the test is performed regularly, it can give warning of trouble before any other symptoms become apparent.

2 The engine must be fully warmed-up to operating temperature, the oil level must be correct and the battery must be fully charged. The help of an assistant will also be required.

3 Refer to Chapter 12 and remove the fuel pump fuse from the fusebox. Now start the engine and allow it to run until it stalls.

4 Disable the ignition system by disconnecting the 3-pin multi-plug from the DIS ignition coil. Remove all the spark plugs with reference to Chapter 1A.

5 Fit a compression tester to the No 1 cylinder spark plug hole – the type of tester which screws into the spark plug thread is to be preferred.

6 Arrange for an assistant to hold the accelerator pedal fully depressed to the floor, while at the same time cranking the engine over for several seconds on the starter motor. Observe the compression gauge reading. The compression will build-up fairly quickly in a healthy engine. Low compression on the first stroke, followed by gradually-increasing pressure on successive strokes, indicates worn piston rings. A low compression on the first stroke which does not rise on successive strokes, indicates leaking valves or a blown head gasket (a cracked cylinder head could also be the cause). Deposits on the underside of the valve heads can also cause low compression. Record the highest gauge reading obtained, then repeat the procedure for the remaining cylinders.

7 Due to the variety of testers available, and the fluctuation in starter motor speed when cranking the engine, different readings are often obtained when carrying out the compression test. For this reason, compression pressure figures are not quoted by Ford. However, the most important factor is that the compression pressures are uniform in all cylinders, and that is what this test is mainly concerned with.

8 Add some engine oil (about three squirts from a plunger type oil can) to each cylinder through the spark plug holes, and then repeat the test.

9 If the compression increases after the oil is added, the piston rings are probably worn. If the compression does not increase significantly, the leakage is occurring at the valves or the head gasket. Leakage past the valves may be caused by burned valve seats and/or faces, or warped, cracked or bent valves.

10 If two adjacent cylinders have equally low compressions, it is most likely that the head gasket has blown between them. The appearance of coolant in the combustion chambers or on the engine oil dipstick would verify this condition.

11 If one cylinder is about 20 percent lower than the other, and the engine has a slightly rough idle, a worn lobe on the camshaft could be the cause.

12 On completion of the checks, refit the spark plugs and reconnect the HT leads and the DIS ignition coil plug. Refit the fuel pump fuse to the fusebox.

3 Top Dead Centre (TDC) for No 1 piston – locating

1 Top dead centre (TDC) is the highest point of the cylinder that each piston reaches as the crankshaft turns. Each piston reaches its TDC position at the end of its compression stroke, and then again at the end of its exhaust stroke. For the purpose of engine timing, TDC at the end of the compression stroke for No 1 piston is used. On the Endura-E engine, No 1 cylinder is at the crankshaft pulley/ timing chain end of the engine. Proceed as follows.

2 Ensure that the ignition is switched off. Disconnect the HT leads from the spark plugs, then unscrew and remove the plugs as described in Chapter 1A.

3 Unbolt and remove the auxiliary drivebelt lower cover for access to the crankshaft pulley, and unclip the coolant hose from the

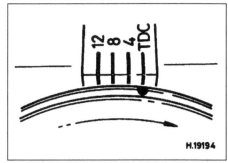

3.4 Timing mark on the crankshaft pulley aligned with the TDC (0) mark on the timing cover

cover. If necessary for improved access, apply the handbrake, then jack up the front of the vehicle and support it on axle stands (see *Jacking and vehicle support*).

4 Turn the engine over by hand (using a spanner on the crankshaft pulley) to the point where the timing mark on the crankshaft pulley aligns with the TDC (0) mark on the timing cover **(see illustration)**. As the pulley mark nears the timing mark, the No 1 piston is simultaneously approaching the top of its cylinder. To ensure that it is on its compression stroke, place a finger over the No 1 cylinder plug hole, and feel to ensure that air pressure exits from the cylinder as the piston reaches the top of its stroke.

5 A further check to ensure that the piston is on its compression stroke can be made by removing the rocker cover (see Section 4), so that the movement of the valves and rockers can be observed.

6 With the TDC timing marks on the crankshaft pulley and timing cover in alignment, rock the crankshaft back and forth a few degrees each side of this position, and observe the action of the valves and rockers for No 1 cylinder. When No 1 piston is at the TDC firing position, the inlet and exhaust valve of No 1 cylinder will be fully closed, but the corresponding valves of No 4 cylinder will be seen to rock open and closed.

7 If the inlet and exhaust valves of No 1 cylinder are seen to rock whilst those of No 4 cylinder are shut, the crankshaft will need to be turned one full rotation to bring No 1 piston up to the top of its cylinder on the compression stroke.

8 Once No 1 cylinder has been positioned at TDC on the compression stroke, TDC for any of the other cylinders can then be located by rotating the crankshaft clockwise (in its normal direction of rotation), 180° at a time, and following the firing order (see *Specifications*).

9 On completion, clip the coolant hose to the auxiliary drivebelt lower cover then refit the cover and tighten the mounting bolts. Where applicable, lower the vehicle to the ground.

10 Refit the spark plugs (see Chapter 1A) and reconnect the HT leads.

4 Cylinder head rocker cover – removal and refitting

Removal

1 Remove the air inlet duct from between the air cleaner and throttle housing (see Chapter 4A).

2 Detach the HT leads from the spark plugs and position them clear of the rocker cover. Pull on the connector of each lead (not the lead itself), and note the order of fitting.

3 Remove the engine oil filler cap, and disconnect the crankcase ventilation hose from the Tee-piece. Position the filler cap to one side.

4 Unscrew the four retaining bolts, and lift the rocker cover clear of the cylinder head. Remove the gasket.

Refitting

5 Thoroughly clean the rocker cover, and scrape away any traces of old gasket remaining on the cover and cylinder head mating surfaces.

6 Fit a new gasket to the rocker cover, then refit the rocker cover **(see illustrations)**. Tighten the cover retaining bolts to the specified torque wrench setting, in a diagonal sequence.

7 Refit the engine oil filler cap.

8 Reconnect the HT leads, and refit the air inlet duct (see Chapter 4A).

5 Valve clearances – checking and adjustment

Note: *The valve clearances must be checked and adjusted only when the engine is cold.*

1 The importance of having the valve clearances correctly adjusted cannot be overstressed, as they vitally affect the performance of the engine. If the clearances are too great, the engine will be noisy (characteristic rattling or tapping noises) and engine efficiency will be reduced, as the valves open too late and close too early. A more serious problem arises if the clearances are too small, however. If this is the case, the

5.6 Adjusting the valve clearances

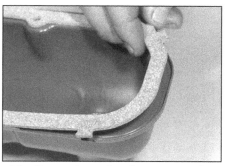
4.6a Engage tags of rocker cover gasket into the cut-outs in the cover

valves may not close fully when the engine is hot, resulting in serious damage to the engine (eg, burnt valve seats and/or cylinder head warping/cracking). The clearances are checked and adjusted as follows.

2 Set the engine to TDC for No 1 piston, as described in Section 3. It is not essential to remove the spark plugs, although if they are removed the engine will be easier to turn when adjusting the valve clearances.

3 Remove the cylinder head rocker cover as described in Section 4.

4 Starting from the thermostat end of the cylinder head, the valves are numbered as follows:

Valve No	Cylinder No
1 – Exhaust	1
2 – Inlet	1
3 – Exhaust	2
4 – Inlet	2
5 – Inlet	3
6 – Exhaust	3
7 – Inlet	4
8 – Exhaust	4

5 Adjust the valve clearances following the sequence given in the following table. Turn the crankshaft pulley 180° (half a turn) after adjusting each pair of valve clearances.

Valves 'rocking'	Valves to adjust
7 and 8	1 (exhaust), 2 (inlet)
5 and 6	3 (exhaust), 4 (inlet)
1 and 2	8 (exhaust), 7 (inlet)
3 and 4	6 (exhaust), 5 (inlet)

6 The clearances for the inlet and exhaust valves differ (refer to the Specifications). Use a feeler blade of the appropriate thickness to check each clearance between the end of the

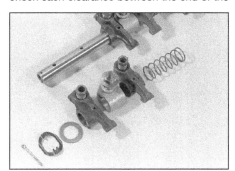
6.4 Rocker shaft partially dismantled for inspection

4.6b Refitting the rocker cover

valve stem and the rocker arm **(see illustration)**. The blade should be a firm sliding fit between the valve and rocker arm. Where adjustment is necessary, turn the adjuster bolt as required with a ring spanner to set the clearance to that specified. The adjuster bolts are of stiff-thread type, and require no locking nut.

7 On completion, refit the rocker cover as described in Section 4.

6 Cylinder head rocker gear – removal, inspection and refitting

Removal

1 Remove the rocker cover as described in Section 4.

2 Unscrew the four retaining bolts, and lift the rocker gear assembly from the cylinder head. As the assembly is withdrawn, ensure that the pushrods remain seated in their positions in the engine. **Note:** *Pushrod removal is described in Section 7.*

Inspection

3 To dismantle the rocker shaft assembly, extract the split pin from one end of the shaft, then withdraw the spring- and plain-washers from the shaft.

4 Slide off the rocker arms, the support pedestals and coil springs from the shaft, but take care to keep them in their original order of fitting **(see illustration)**.

5 Clean the respective components, and inspect them for signs of excessive wear or damage. Check that the oil lubrication holes in the shaft are clear.

6 Check the rocker shaft and arm pads which bear on the valve stem end faces for wear and scoring, and check each rocker arm on the shaft for excessive wear. Renew any components as necessary.

Refitting

7 Apply clean engine oil to the rocker shaft prior to reassembling.

8 Reassemble in the reverse order of dismantling. Make sure that the 'flat' on the left-hand end of the rocker shaft is to the same side as the rocker arm adjusting screws

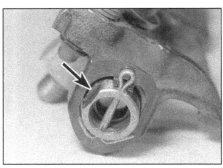

6.8 Flat on the rocker shaft (arrowed) to same side as rocker arm adjusting screws

(closest to the thermostat end of the cylinder head when fitted) **(see illustration)**. This is essential for the correct lubrication of the cylinder head components.

9 Refit the rocker shaft assembly. As it is fitted, ensure that the rocker adjuster screws engage with their corresponding pushrods.

10 Refit the rocker shaft pedestal bolts, hand-tighten them and then tighten them to the specified torque wrench setting. As they are tightened, some of the rocker arms will apply pressure to the ends of the valve stems, and some of the rocker pedestals will not initially be in contact with the cylinder head – these should pull down as the bolts are tightened to their specified torque. If for any reason they do not, avoid the temptation to overtighten in order to pull them into position; loosen off the bolts, and check the cause of the problem.

11 Adjust the valve clearances as described in Section 5.

7 Cylinder head – removal and refitting

Removal

Note: *The following procedure describes removal and refitting of the cylinder head complete with inlet and exhaust manifolds. If wished, the manifolds may be removed first, as described in the relevant Part of Chapter 4, and the cylinder head then removed on its own.*

1 Depressurise the fuel system as described in Chapter 4A.

2 Disconnect the battery negative (earth) lead (see Chapter 5A).

3 Refer to Chapter 1A and drain the cooling system.

4 Remove the air inlet duct from the throttle housing and air cleaner as described in Chapter 4A.

5 Refer to Section 6 and remove the rocker cover and rocker shaft complete with rocker gear.

6 Disconnect the 3-pin multi-plug from the DIS ignition coil.

7 Disconnect the accelerator cable from the

throttle housing and supports (see Chapter 4A).

8 Loosen the clip and disconnect the coolant top hose from the thermostat housing. At the same time release the wiring loom from the support clips then remove the clips from the hose.

9 Disconnect the oxygen sensor wiring at the multi-plug.

10 Disconnect the two engine wiring loom multi-plugs at the rear of the engine.

11 Disconnect the brake servo vacuum pipe from the rear of the inlet manifold.

12 Disconnect the evaporative canister purge valve vacuum pipe from the inlet manifold.

13 Unclip and remove the wiring loom support bracket.

14 Disconnect the wiring from the camshaft position sensor, oil pressure switch and engine coolant temperature sensor.

15 Disconnect the heater hose by releasing the quick-release fitting.

> **HAYNES HINT** *Whenever you disconnect any vacuum lines, coolant or emissions hoses, wiring connectors and fuel lines, always label them clearly, so that they can be correctly reassembled. Masking tape and/or a touch-up paint applicator work well for marking the locations of components and brackets.*

16 Unscrew the support bolt then withdraw the oil level dipstick tube.

17 Identify the fuel feed and return lines for position, then disconnect them from the fuel rail by squeezing the lugs on the quick-release couplings. Be prepared for some loss of fuel by placing cloth rags beneath the couplings.

18 Remove the spark plugs from the cylinder head as described in Chapter 1A.

19 Remove the pushrods by twisting them to release them from the tappets in the cylinder block. Keep them in order of fitting by labelling them 1 to 8, starting from the thermostat end of the cylinder head. Alternatively, push them through a piece of card in their fitted sequence.

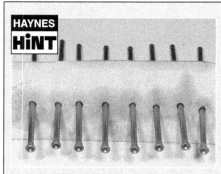

Keep the pushrods in the correct order of fitting by labelling them 1 to 8, or locate them in a card

20 Unbolt and remove the heatshield from the top of the exhaust manifold.

21 Undo the screws securing the exhaust downpipe to the exhaust manifold.

22 Unbolt and remove the cover from the crankshaft position sensor on the front of the cylinder block. Disconnect the wiring from the sensor.

23 Unbolt the wiring loom guide from the left-hand end of the cylinder head.

24 Using a trolley jack and block of wood, support the weight of the engine. Alternatively, use a hoist attached to a lifting eye bolted to the right-hand side of the cylinder block. Note that the lifting eye on the inlet manifold cannot be used since it will be removed together with the cylinder head.

25 Undo the screws and remove the right-hand front engine mounting upper bracket.

26 Progressively unscrew and loosen off the cylinder head retaining bolts in the reverse sequence to that shown for tightening **(see illustration 7.36a)**. When they are all loosened off, remove the bolts, then lift the cylinder head clear and remove the gasket. The gasket must always be renewed; it should be noted that the cylinder head retaining bolts may be re-used, but only once. They should be marked accordingly with a punch or paint mark. If there is any doubt as to how many times the bolts have been used, they must be renewed.

27 If necessary, remove the two dowel pins from the cylinder block.

28 To dismantle/overhaul the cylinder head, refer to Part E of this Chapter. It is normal for the cylinder head to be decarbonised and the valves to be reground whenever the head is removed.

Preparation for refitting

29 The mating faces of the cylinder head and cylinder block must be perfectly clean before refitting the head. Use a hard plastic or wood scraper to remove all traces of gasket and carbon; also clean the piston crowns. Take particular care during the cleaning operations, as aluminium alloy is easily damaged. Also, make sure that the carbon is not allowed to enter the oil and water passages – this is particularly important for the lubrication system, as carbon could block the oil supply to the engine's components. Using adhesive tape and paper, seal the water, oil and bolt holes in the cylinder block.

> **HAYNES HINT** *To prevent carbon entering the gap between the pistons and bores, smear a little grease in the gap. After cleaning each piston, use a small brush to remove all traces of grease and carbon from the gap, then wipe away the remainder with a clean rag.*

7.34 Cylinder head gasket top-face marking (OBEN)

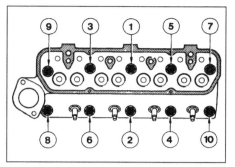

7.36a Cylinder head bolt tightening sequence

30 Check the mating surfaces of the cylinder block and the cylinder head for nicks, deep scratches and other damage. If slight, they may be removed carefully with a file, but if excessive, machining may be the only alternative to renewal.

31 If warpage of the cylinder head gasket surface is suspected, use a straight-edge to check it for distortion. Refer to Part E of this Chapter if necessary.

32 Clean the threads of the cylinder head bolts or use new ones (as applicable) and clean out the bolt holes in the block. Screwing a bolt into an oil-filled hole can (in extreme cases) cause the block to fracture, due to the hydraulic pressure created.

Refitting

33 Make sure that the two dowel pins are correctly located in the cylinder block.

34 Check that the new cylinder head gasket is the same type as the original, and that the TOP (or OBEN) marking is facing upwards. Locate the new cylinder head gasket onto the top face of the cylinder block and over the dowels. Ensure that it is correctly aligned with the coolant passages and oilways **(see illustration)**.

35 Lower the cylinder head carefully into position, then insert the retaining bolts and hand-tighten them.

36 Tightening of the cylinder head bolts must be done in three stages, and in the correct sequence. First tighten all of the bolts in the sequence shown to the Stage 1 torque setting. When all of the bolts are tightened to the Stage 1 setting, further tighten each bolt

(in sequence) through the Stage 2 specified angle of rotation. When the second stage tightening is completed on all of the bolts, further tighten them to the Stage 3 angle setting (in sequence) to complete. Where possible, use an angle-tightening setting gauge attachment tool for accurate tightening of Stages two and three **(see illustrations)**.

37 Lubricate the pushrods with clean engine oil, and then insert them into their original locations.

38 Refit the rocker shaft assembly. As it is fitted, ensure that the rocker adjuster screws engage with their corresponding pushrods.

39 Refit the rocker shaft pedestal bolts, hand-tighten them and then tighten them to the specified torque wrench setting. As they are tightened, some of the rocker arms will apply pressure to the ends of the valve stems, and some of the rocker pedestals will not initially be in contact with the cylinder head – these should pull down as the bolts are tightened. If for any reason they do not, avoid the temptation to overtighten in order to pull them into position; loosen off the bolts, and check the cause of the problem.

40 Adjust the valve clearances as described in Section 5.

41 Refit the rocker cover as described in Section 4.

42 The remainder of the refitting procedure is a reversal of the removal process. Tighten all fastenings to their specified torque setting (where given). Refer to Chapters 4A and 4D for details on reconnecting the fuel system and exhaust system components. Ensure that

all coolant, fuel, vacuum and electrical connections are securely made.

43 On completion, refill the cooling system and top-up the engine oil (see Chapter 1A and *Weekly checks*). When the engine is restarted, check for any sign of fuel, oil and/or coolant leakage from the various cylinder head joints.

8 Crankshaft pulley – removal and refitting

Removal

1 Disconnect the battery negative (earth) lead (see Chapter 5A).

2 Apply the handbrake, then jack up the front of the vehicle and support it on axle stands (see *Jacking and vehicle support*). Remove the right-hand front roadwheel.

3 Working beneath the vehicle, unbolt and remove the drivebelt lower cover, and unclip the coolant hose from the bracket.

4 Remove the auxiliary drivebelt as described in Chapter 1A.

5 Loosen off the crankshaft pulley retaining bolt. To prevent the crankshaft from turning, remove the starter motor (Chapter 5A) and lock the ring gear through the starter motor aperture using a large screwdriver or similar tool.

6 Fully unscrew the crankshaft pulley bolt, and withdraw the pulley from the right-hand end of the crankshaft. If it does not pull off by hand, lever it free using a pair of suitable levers positioned diagonally opposite each other behind the pulley.

7 If required, the crankshaft right-hand oil seal can be renewed at this stage, as described in Section 14.

Refitting

8 Refitting is a reversal of the removal procedure ensuring that the pulley retaining bolt is tightened to the specified torque setting.

9 Refit the auxiliary drivebelt (see Chapter 1A), and lower the vehicle to the ground.

9 Timing chain cover – removal and refitting

Removal

1 Remove the sump as described in Section 11.

2 Remove the crankshaft pulley as described in Section 8.

3 Disconnect the camshaft position sensor wiring multi-plug.

4 Unscrew the retaining bolts, and carefully prise free the timing chain cover. Note that one of the bolt holes is split and the bolt also secures the water pump.

5 A combined timing cover and water pump

7.36b Tightening the cylinder head bolts (Stage 1)

7.36c Cylinder head bolt tightening (Stages 2 and 3) using an angle gauge

gasket is fitted during production; if this is still fitted, it will be necessary to cut away the old gasket using a sharp knife keeping as close as possible to the water pump. If the timing cover has been removed at any time, the single gasket used originally will have been replaced by an individual gasket.

6 Clean the mating faces of the timing chain cover and cylinder block.

7 If necessary, renew the crankshaft right-hand oil seal in the timing cover prior to refitting the cover (see Section 14).

Refitting

8 Lightly lubricate the right-hand end of the crankshaft and the radial lip of the timing chain cover oil seal (already installed in the cover). Using a new gasket, fit the timing chain cover, centring it with the aid of the crankshaft pulley – lubricate the seal contact surfaces beforehand. Refit the retaining bolts and tighten to the specified torque. Note that the sump mating faces of the cover and cylinder block must be level with each other.

9 Refit the crankshaft pulley (see Section 8).

10 Reconnect the camshaft position sensor multi-plug.

11 Refit the sump as described in Section 11.

10 Timing chain, sprockets and tensioner – removal, inspection and refitting

Removal

1 Remove the timing chain cover as described in Section 9.

2 Remove the oil slinger from the right-hand end of the crankshaft, noting its orientation **(see illustration)**.

3 Retract the chain tensioner cam back against its spring pressure, then slide the chain tensioner arm from its pivot pin on the main bearing cap **(see illustration)**.

4 Unbolt and remove the chain tensioner.

5 Note the fitted position of the camshaft position sender plate, then unscrew and remove the camshaft sprocket bolts and remove the plate. Hold the sprocket stationary using a suitable tool engaged with the holes in the sprocket.

6 Withdraw the camshaft sprocket and unhook the timing chain from the crankshaft sprocket.

7 Slide the sprocket from the key on the nose of the crankshaft. If it is tight use, a suitable puller. If necessary, remove the Woodruff key from the groove in the crankshaft.

Inspection

8 Examine the teeth on the timing sprockets for any signs of excessive wear or damage.

9 The timing chain should always be renewed during a major engine overhaul. Slack links and pins are indicative of a worn chain. Unless the chain is known to be relatively new, it should be renewed.

10.2 Oil slinger removal from crankshaft

10 Examine the rubber cushion on the tensioner spring leaf. If grooved or deteriorated, it must be renewed.

Refitting

11 Commence reassembly by locating the Woodruff key in the crankshaft groove, making sure that it is parallel to the surface of the crankshaft.

12 Slide on the crankshaft sprocket and engage it with the Woodruff key. If it is tight, use the pulley together with its bolt to press on the sprocket. Make sure the timing mark is on the outer face of the sprocket.

13 Fit the timing chain tensioner and tighten the mounting bolts to the specified torque. Check that the face of the tensioner cam is parallel with the face of the cylinder block, ideally using a dial gauge. The maximum permissible error between two measuring points 20 mm apart is 0.16 mm. If necessary, loosen the mounting bolts, turn the tensioner as required, then tighten the bolts and re-check.

14 Turn the crankshaft so that the timing mark on the crankshaft sprocket is directly in line with the centre of the camshaft sprocket mounting flange.

15 Engage the camshaft sprocket with the timing chain, then engage the chain around the teeth of the crankshaft sprocket. Push the camshaft sprocket onto its mounting flange, and check that the sprocket retaining bolt holes are in alignment. Also check that the timing marks of both sprockets face each other. If required, turn the camshaft/sprocket

10.15a Fit the timing chain to the crankshaft and camshaft sprockets . . .

10.3 Chain tensioner arm removal from the pivot pin. Note tensioner retaining bolts (arrowed)

as required to achieve this. It may also be necessary to remove the camshaft sprocket from the chain in order to reposition it in the required location in the chain to align the timing marks. This is a 'trial and error' procedure, which must be continued until the exact alignment of the bolt holes and timing marks is made **(see illustrations)**.

16 Locate the camshaft position sender plate on the sprocket in its previously noted position, then insert the sprocket bolts and tighten them to the specified torque.

17 Retract the timing chain tensioner cam, and then slide the tensioner arm onto its pivot pin. Release the cam so that it bears on the arm.

18 Refit the oil slinger to the front of the crankshaft sprocket so that its convex side faces the sprocket.

19 Refit the timing chain cover as described in Section 9.

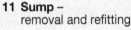

11 Sump – removal and refitting

Removal

1 Disconnect the battery negative (earth) lead (see Chapter 5A). Apply the handbrake, then jack up the front of the vehicle and support it on axle stands (see *Jacking and vehicle support*). Where applicable, remove the engine undershield.

10.15b . . . and check that the timing marks on the sprockets are in alignment

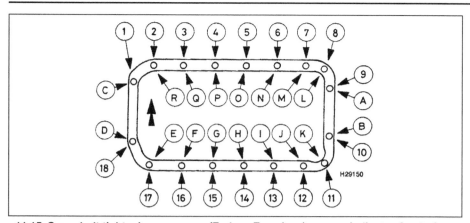

11.15 Sump bolt tightening sequence (Endura-E engines) – arrow indicates front of car
Refer to Specifications for torque wrench settings
Stage 1 – Tighten in alphabetical order
Stage 2 – Tighten in numerical order
Stage 3 – Tighten in alphabetical order

2 Refer to Chapter 1A and drain the engine oil. Refit the sump drain plug.
3 Trace the wiring back from the oxygen sensor on the downpipe and disconnect it at the wiring connector. Unbolt and remove the heatshields from the exhaust manifold, then unscrew the nuts securing the downpipe to the exhaust manifold, separate the downpipe and remove the ring gasket. Release the exhaust mounting rubber and lower the downpipe from the engine.
4 Remove the starter motor (see Chapter 5A).
5 Working beneath the vehicle, unbolt and remove the auxiliary drivebelt lower cover, and unclip the coolant hose from the bracket.
6 On models with air conditioning, remove the auxiliary drivebelt (Chapter 1A), unbolt the compressor from the sump mounting and position the compressor to one side. Do not disconnect any refrigerant hoses.
7 Unscrew the bolts securing the sump flange to the transmission.
8 Undo the eighteen bolts securing the sump to the base of the engine crankcase, then prise free and lower the sump. If the sump is stuck tight to the engine, cut around the flange gasket with a sharp knife, then lightly tap and prise it free. Keep the sump upright as it is lowered, to prevent spillage of any remaining oil in it. Also be prepared for oil drips from the crankcase when the sump is removed.
9 Remove the one-piece sump gasket.
10 Remove any dirt and old gasket from the contact faces of the sump and crankcase, and wash the sump out thoroughly before refitting. Check that the mating faces of the sump are not distorted. Check that the oil pick-up strainer is clear, cleaning it if necessary.

Refitting

11 Thoroughly clean the sump and cylinder block mating faces.
12 Apply sealing compound (available from Ford dealers) to the cylinder block mating face in the area of the joint between the timing

chain cover and cylinder block, and the left-hand oil seal housing and cylinder block. Also apply sealer into the corners of the semi-circular areas on the timing chain cover and left-hand oil seal housing.
13 Locate the one-piece gasket on the sump, then fit the sump to the crankcase. Fit the retaining bolts and tighten them initially finger-tight.
14 Using a straight-edge, check that the sump flange is level with the surface of the cylinder block. If necessary reposition the sump.
15 Tighten the bolts in the sequence shown through Stages 1 and 2, to the torques specified **(see illustration)**. Note that different tightening sequences are specified for the tightening stages. Final (Stage 3) tightening is carried out after the engine has been started and warmed-up.
16 Refit and tighten the bolts securing the sump flange to the transmission.
17 Where applicable, refit the air conditioning compressor, then refit and adjust the auxiliary drivebelt as described in Chapter 1A.
18 Refit the auxiliary drivebelt lower cover and clip the coolant hose into position.
19 Refit the starter motor.
20 Check that the downpipe and manifold mating faces are clean, then locate a new ring

gasket and reconnect the exhaust downpipe to the manifold. Where applicable, use new self-locking nuts, and tighten securely. Refit the rubber mounting, and reconnect the oxygen sensor wiring.
21 Check that the sump drain plug is fitted and tightened securely, then refill the engine with oil as described in Chapter 1A.
22 Reconnect the battery, then start the engine and run it up to its normal operating temperature. Check that no oil leaks are evident around the sump joint.
23 After the engine has warmed-up for approximately 15 minutes, switch it off. Tighten the sump bolts to the Stage 3 torque wrench setting given in the Specifications, in the correct sequence **(see illustration 11.15)**.
24 Refit the undershield and lower the vehicle to the ground.

12 Oil pump –
removing and refitting

Removal

1 The oil pump is externally-mounted, on the rear-facing side of the crankcase.
2 Apply the handbrake, then jack up the front of the vehicle and support it on axle stands (see *Jacking and vehicle support*).
3 Unscrew and remove the oil filter cartridge. It should unscrew by hand, but will probably be tight. Use a strap wrench to loosen it off, if required. Catch any oil spillage in a suitable container.
4 Undo the three retaining bolts and withdraw the oil pump from the engine **(see illustration)**.
5 Clean all traces of the old gasket from the mating surfaces of the pump and engine.

Refitting

6 The oil pump must first be primed with engine oil prior to fitting. To do this, turn its driveshaft and simultaneously inject clean engine oil into it.
7 Locate a new gasket into position on the pump mounting flange, then insert the pump, engaging the drivegear as it is fitted **(see illustration)**. Fit the retaining bolts, and tighten to the specified torque wrench setting.

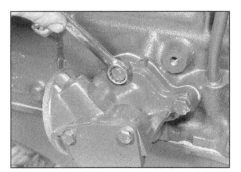

12.4 Unscrewing the oil pump retaining bolts

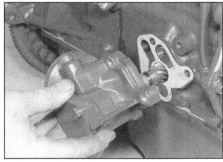

12.7 Refitting the oil pump. Note the new gasket

13.1 Extract the O-ring from the groove in the oil pump

8 Fit a new oil filter into position on the oil pump body, as described in Chapter 1A.
9 Lower the vehicle to the ground, and top-up the engine oil as described in *Weekly checks*.

13 Oil pump – dismantling, inspection and reassembly

Dismantling

1 To inspect the oil pump components for excessive wear, undo the retaining bolts and remove the cover plate from the pump body. Remove the O-ring seal from the cover face **(see illustration)**.
2 Wipe the exterior of the pump housing clean housing.

Inspection

3 Noting their orientation, extract and clean the rotors and the inner body of the pump housing. Inspect them for signs of severe scoring or excessive wear, which if evident will necessitate renewal of the complete pump.
4 Using feeler blades, check the clearances between the pump body and the outer rotor, the inner-to-outer rotor clearance, and the amount of rotor endfloat **(see illustrations)**.
5 Check the drivegear for signs of excessive wear or damage.
6 If the clearances measured are outside the specified maximum clearances and/or the drivegear is in poor condition, the complete pump unit must be renewed.

Reassembly

7 Refit the rotors into the pump (in their original orientation), lubricate the rotors and the new O-ring seal with clean engine oil, and refit the cover. Tighten the retaining bolts to the specified torque wrench setting.

14 Crankshaft oil seals – renewal

Timing chain end oil seal

1 Remove the crankshaft pulley as described in Section 8.
2 Using a suitable claw tool, extract the oil seal from the timing chain cover, but take care not to damage the seal housing. As it is removed, note the fitted orientation of the seal in the cover.

> **HAYNES HiNT**
> *If a claw tool is not available, screw two self-tapping screws into the seal, and pull on the screws to remove the seal.*

3 Clean the oil seal housing in the timing chain cover. Lubricate the sealing lips of the new seal and the crankshaft nose with clean engine oil.
4 Locate the new seal into position so that it is squarely located on the crankshaft stub and in the housing, and is correctly orientated. Drift it into position using a large socket, another suitable tool, or the old seal, until the new seal is flush with the edge of the timing chain cover.
5 Lightly lubricate the oil seal contact surface of the crankshaft pulley, then refit the pulley as described in Section 8.

Flywheel end oil seal

6 Remove the flywheel as described in Section 15.
7 Note the orientation and fitted depth of the oil seal to ensure correct fitting of the new seal.
8 Using a suitable claw tool, lever the seal from the left-hand seal housing (taking care not to damage the housing) – see Haynes Hint above.

9 Clean the seal housing, the crankshaft left-hand flange face and the flywheel mating surface.
10 Lubricate the crankshaft flange and the oil seal inner lip with clean engine oil.
11 If Ford service tool No 21-011F is available, position the seal on the service tool (ensuring correct orientation), then press the seal into its housing using two diagonally opposite flywheel bolts. Tighten the bolts progressively to ensure that the oil seal enters correctly. Remove the tool on completion.
12 If the service tool is not available, start the oil seal in its housing using finger pressure initially then carefully tap it into the housing to its previously noted position making sure it is kept square. If a suitable length of metal tube is available use this to drive in the seal.
13 Check that the crankshaft left-hand flange and the flywheel mating faces are clean, then refit the flywheel as described in Section 15.

15 Flywheel – removal, inspection and refitting

Removal

1 Remove the transmission as described in Chapter 7A, then remove the clutch as described in Chapter 6.
2 Unscrew the six retaining bolts, and remove the flywheel from the left-hand flange of the crankshaft – take care not to drop the flywheel, as it is heavy. A tool similar to that shown in illustration 15.5 can be fitted to prevent the flywheel/crankshaft from rotating as the bolts are removed. If on removal, the retaining bolts are found to be in poor condition (stretched threads, etc) they must be renewed.

Inspection

3 Inspect the starter ring gear on the flywheel for any broken or excessively worn teeth. If evident, the ring gear must be renewed; this is a task best entrusted to a Ford dealer or a competent garage. Alternatively, obtain a complete new flywheel.
4 The clutch friction surface on the flywheel must be carefully inspected for grooving or hairline cracks (caused by overheating). If

13.4a Checking the outer body-to-rotor clearance

13.4b Checking the inner rotor-to-outer rotor clearance

13.4c Checking the rotor endfloat

these conditions are evident, it may be possible to have the flywheel surface-ground, however this work must be carried out by an engine overhaul specialist. If surface-grinding is not possible, the flywheel must be renewed.

Refitting

5 Check that the mating faces of the flywheel and crankshaft are clean before refitting. Lubricate the threads of the retaining bolts with engine oil before they are screwed into position. Locate the flywheel onto the crankshaft so that the hole engages with the dowel, then insert the bolts. Hand-tighten them initially, then tighten them in a progressive sequence to the specified torque **(see illustration)**.

6 Refit the clutch as described in Chapter 6 and the transmission as described in Chapter 7A.

16 Engine/transmission mountings – inspection and renewal

Inspection

1 The engine/transmission mountings seldom require attention, but broken or deteriorated mountings should be renewed immediately, or the added strain placed on the driveline components may cause damage or wear.

2 During the check, the engine/transmission must be raised slightly, to remove its weight from the mountings.

3 Apply the handbrake, then jack up the front of the vehicle and support it on axle stands (see *Jacking and vehicle support*). Position a jack under the sump, with a large block of wood between the jack head and the sump, then carefully raise the engine/transmission just enough to take the weight off the mountings.

15.5 Tightening the flywheel retaining bolts to the specified torque

Note the 'peg' tool locking the ring gear teeth to prevent rotation as the bolts are tightened

4 Check the mountings to see if the rubber is cracked, hardened or separated from the metal components. Sometimes, the rubber will split right down the centre.

5 Check for relative movement between each mounting's brackets and the engine/transmission or body (use a large screwdriver or lever to attempt to move the mountings). If movement is noted, lower the engine and check the mounting nuts and bolts for tightness.

Renewal

6 The engine mountings can be removed if the weight of the engine/transmission is supported by one of the following alternative methods.

7 Either support the weight of the assembly from underneath using a jack and a suitable piece of wood between the jack and the sump (to prevent damage), or from above by attaching a hoist to the engine. A third method is to use a suitable support bar with end pieces which will engage in the water channel

each side of the bonnet lid aperture. Using an adjustable hook and chain connected to the engine, the weight of the engine and transmission can then be taken from the mountings.

8 Once the weight of the engine and transmission is suitably supported, any of the mountings can be unbolted and removed.

9 To remove the right-hand engine mounting, unscrew the nuts and remove the upper bracket, then unscrew the bolts and remove the lower bracket from the cylinder head. Unbolt the insulator from the right-hand side of the engine compartment.

10 To remove the left-hand mounting first remove the battery and battery tray as described in Chapter 5A, then loosen the clips and remove the air inlet duct from between the air mass air flow sensor on the air cleaner and the throttle housing. Unscrew the mounting nuts from the left-hand engine mounting, then unscrew the bolts and remove the upper bracket. Unscrew the bolts and remove the insulator from the left-hand side of the engine compartment.

11 To remove the rear engine mounting/link, apply the handbrake, then jack up the front of the vehicle and support it on axle stands (see *Jacking and vehicle support*). Unscrew the through-bolts and remove the rear engine mounting link from the bracket on the transmission and from the bracket on the underbody. Hold the engine stationary while the bolts are being removed since the link will be under tension.

12 Refitting of all mountings is a reversal of the removal procedure. Do not fully tighten the mounting nuts/bolts until all of the mountings are in position. Check that the mounting rubbers do not twist or distort as the mounting bolts and nuts are tightened to their specified torques.

Notes

Chapter 2 Part B:
Zetec-SE petrol engine in-car repair procedures

Contents

Camshaft oil seals – renewal 10
Camshafts and tappets – removal, inspection and refitting 11
Compression test – description and interpretation 2
Crankshaft oil seals – renewal 15
Crankshaft pulley/vibration damper – removal and refitting 6
Cylinder head – dismantling and overhaul . . . . See Chapter 2E
Cylinder head – removal, inspection and refitting 12
Cylinder head cover – removal and refitting 4
Engine oil and filter renewal . . . . See Chapter 1A
Engine oil level check . . . . See Weekly checks
Engine/transmission mountings – inspection and renewal 17

Flywheel/driveplate – removal, inspection and refitting 16
General information 1
Oil pump – removal, inspection and refitting 14
Sump – removal and refitting 13
Timing belt – removal and refitting 8
Timing belt covers – removal and refitting 7
Timing belt tensioner and sprockets – removal, inspection
    and refitting 9
Top Dead Centre (TDC) for No 1 piston – locating 3
Valve clearances – checking and adjustment 5

Degrees of difficulty

| **Easy,** suitable for novice with little experience | | **Fairly easy,** suitable for beginner with some experience | | **Fairly difficult,** suitable for competent DIY mechanic | | **Difficult,** suitable for experienced DIY mechanic | | **Very difficult,** suitable for expert DIY or professional |

Specifications

General

Engine type	Four-cylinder, in-line, double overhead camshafts
Designation	Zetec-SE
Engine code:	
1.25 litre	DHA, DHB, DHC or DHD
1.4 litre	FHA or FHE
1.6 litre	FYDA, FYDC, FYDG, L1T or L1V
Capacity:	
1.25 litre	1242 cc
1.4 litre	1388 cc
1.6 litre	1596 cc
Bore:	
1.25 litre	71.8 mm
1.4 litre	75.9 mm
1.6 litre	79.0 mm

General (continued)

Stroke:
- 1.25 and 1.4 litre .... 76.5 mm
- 1.6 litre .... 81.4 mm

Compression ratio:
- 1.25 litre 10.0:1
- 1.4 litre 10.3:1
- 1.6 litre 11.0:1

Firing order .... 1-3-4-2 (No 1 cylinder at timing belt end)

Direction of crankshaft rotation .... Clockwise (seen from right-hand side of vehicle)

Valves

	Inlet	Exhaust
Valve clearance (cold):		
1.25 and 1.4 litre	0.17 to 0.23 mm	0.27 to 0.33 mm
1.6 litre	0.17 to 0.23 mm	0.31 to 0.37 mm
Valve length:		
1.25 litre	97.65 mm	99.70 mm
1.4 litre	97.35 mm	99.40 mm
1.6 litre	96.95 mm	99.40 mm

Valve springs

Free length .... 53.2 mm

Cylinder head

Maximum permissible gasket surface distortion .... 0.05 mm

Cylinder block

Cylinder bore diameter:
- 1.25 litre engine:
  - Class 1 .... 71.900 to 71.910 mm
  - Class 2 .... 71.910 to 71.920 mm
  - Class 3 .... 71.920 to 71.930 mm
- 1.4 litre engine:
  - Class 1 .... 76.000 to 76.010 mm
  - Class 2 .... 76.010 to 76.020 mm
  - Class 3 .... 76.020 to 76.030 mm
- 1.6 litre engine:
  - Class 1 .... 79.000 to 79.010 mm
  - Class 2 .... 79.010 to 79.020 mm
  - Class 3 .... 79.020 to 79.030 mm

Pistons and piston rings

Piston diameter:
- 1.25 litre engine:
  - Class 1 .... 71.875 to 71.885 mm
  - Class 2 .... 71.885 to 71.895 mm
  - Class 3 .... 71.895 to 71.905 mm
- 1.4 litre engine:
  - Class 1 .... 75.960 to 75.970 mm
  - Class 2 .... 75.970 to 75.980 mm
  - Class 3 .... 75.980 to 75.990 mm
- 1.6 litre engine:
  - Class 1 .... 78.975 to 79.005 mm
  - Class 2 .... 78.985 to 79.015 mm
  - Class 3 .... 78.995 to 79.025 mm

Oversizes – all engines .... None available

Piston-to-cylinder bore clearance .... Not specified

Piston ring end gaps – installed:
- 1.25 litre:
  - Top compression ring .... 0.2 to 0.3 mm
  - Second compression ring .... 0.3 to 0.7 mm
  - Oil control ring .... 0.3 to 0.7 mm
- 1.4 and 1.6 litre:
  - Top compression ring .... 0.2 to 0.3 mm
  - Second compression ring .... 0.3 to 0.7 mm
  - Oil control ring .... 0.15 to 0.65 mm

Crankshaft

Note: *The crankshaft cannot be removed from the cylinder block (see text).*

Crankshaft endfloat .... 0.220 to 0.430 mm

Camshafts

Camshaft bearing journal diameter	Unavailable at time of writing
Camshaft bearing journal-to-cylinder head running clearance	Unavailable at time of writing
Camshaft endfloat (typical)	0.05 to 0.13 mm

Lubrication

Oil pressure (warm engine):	
Idling (800 rpm)	1.0 bars
At 2000 rpm	2.5 bars
Pressure relief valve opens at	5.0 bars
Oil pump clearances	Not specified

Torque wrench settings

	Nm	lbf ft
Battery box	25	18
Big-end bearing cap:		
Stage 1	8	6
Stage 2	Angle-tighten a further 90°	
Camshaft bearing cap:		
Stage 1	6	4
Stage 2	15	11
Camshaft sprocket bolt	60	44
Coolant outlet to cylinder head	19	14
Cover on cylinder head cover	6	4
Crankcase breather to cylinder block	9	7
Crankshaft left-hand oil seal housing	9	7
Crankshaft pulley/vibration damper*:		
Stage 1	40	30
Stage 2	Angle-tighten a further 90°	
Crankshaft sprocket/timing belt retainer plate to cylinder block	9	7
Cylinder head*:		
Stage 1	15	11
Stage 2	30	22
Stage 3	Angle-tighten a further 90°	
Cylinder head cover	10	7
Earth lead to alternator	11	8
Earth lead to transmission	30	22
Engine/transmission mountings:		
Left-hand engine mounting bracket bolts	49	36
Left-hand engine mounting bracket nuts	69	51
Rear engine mounting link to crossmember	70	52
Rear engine mounting link to engine	50	37
Right-hand engine mounting bracket to engine	55	41
Right-hand engine mounting bracket to mounting	69	51
Fluid pipes to transmission	21	15
Flywheel/driveplate:		
Stage 1	30	22
Stage 2	Angle-tighten a further 80°	
Lifting eye to cylinder head	19	14
Oil baffle to cylinder block	9	7
Oil dipstick tube	9	7
Oil drain plug	37	27
Oil filter connector	45	33
Oil intake pipe to oil baffle	9	7
Oil pressure switch	15	11
Oil pump to cylinder block	9	7
Sump:		
To crankcase (see text)	20	15
To transmission	44	32
TDC pin blanking hole	25	18
Thermostat housing to cylinder block	9	7
Timing belt tensioner	20	15
Timing belt tensioning pulley	35	26
Timing belt lower cover	9	7
Timing belt upper cover	9	7

* Use new fasteners

1 General information

How to use this Chapter

This Part of Chapter 2 is devoted to in-car repair procedures on the Zetec-SE petrol engine. All procedures concerning engine removal and refitting, and engine block/cylinder head overhaul can be found in Chapter 2E.

Refer to *Vehicle identification numbers* in the Reference Section at the end of this manual for details of engine code locations.

Most of the operations included in this chapter are based on the assumption that the engine is still installed in the car. Therefore, if this information is being used during a complete engine overhaul, with the engine already removed, many of the steps included here will not apply.

Engine description

The Zetec-SE engine (formerly Zeta) is of sixteen-valve, double overhead camshaft (DOHC), four-cylinder, in-line type, mounted transversely at the front of the vehicle, with the transmission on its left-hand end. It is available in 1.25 litre, 1.4 litre and 1.6 litre versions.

Apart from the plastic timing belt covers and plastic inlet manifold, and the cast iron cylinder liners, the engine (including the sump) is manufactured entirely of aluminium alloy.

Caution: When tightening bolts into aluminium castings, it is important to adhere to the specified torque wrench settings, to avoid stripping threads with the resultant time-consuming consequences.

The crankshaft runs in five main bearings, the centre main bearing's upper half incorporating thrustwashers to control crankshaft endfloat. Due to the very fine bearing clearances and bearing shell tolerances incorporated during manufacture, it is not possible to renew the crankshaft separate to the cylinder block; in fact it is not possible to remove and refit the crankshaft accurately using conventional tooling. This means that if the crankshaft is worn excessively, it must be renewed together with the cylinder block.

Caution: Do not unbolt the main bearing cap/ladder from the cylinder block, as it is not possible to refit it accurately using conventional tooling. Additionally, the manufacturers do not supply torque settings for the main bearing cap/ladder retaining bolts.

The connecting rods rotate on horizontally-split bearing shells at their big-ends, however the big-ends are of unusual design in that the caps are sheared from the rods during manufacture thus making each cap individually matched to its own connecting rod. The big-end bearing shells are also unusual in that they do not have any locating tabs and must be accurately positioned during refitting. The pistons are attached to the connecting rods by gudgeon pins which are an interference fit in the connecting rod small-end eyes. The aluminium alloy pistons are fitted with three piston rings: two compression rings and an oil control ring. After manufacture, the cylinder bores and pistons are measured and classified into three grades, which must be carefully matched together, to ensure the correct piston/cylinder clearance; no oversizes are available to permit reboring.

The inlet and exhaust valves are each closed by coil springs; they operate in guides which are shrink-fitted into the cylinder head, as are the valve seat inserts.

Both camshafts are driven by the same toothed timing belt, each operating eight valves via bucket tappets and shims. Each camshaft rotates in five bearings that are line-bored directly in the cylinder head and the (bolted-on) bearing caps; this means that the bearing caps are not available separately from the cylinder head, and must not be interchanged with caps from another engine.

The water pump is bolted to the right-hand end of the cylinder block, beneath the front run of the timing belt, and is driven by the auxiliary drivebelt from the crankshaft pulley.

Lubrication is by means of an eccentric-rotor trochoidal pump, which is mounted on the crankshaft right-hand end, and draws oil through a strainer located in the sump. The pump forces oil through an externally-mounted full-flow cartridge-type filter.

Repair operations possible with the engine in the car

The following work can be carried out with the engine in the car:

a) Cylinder head cover – removal and refitting.
b) Timing belt – renewal.
c) Timing belt tensioner and sprockets – removal and refitting.
d) Camshaft oil seals – renewal.
e) Camshafts, tappets and shims – removal and refitting.
f) Cylinder head – removal and refitting.
g) Sump – removal and refitting.
h) Crankshaft oil seals – renewal.
i) Oil pump – removal and refitting.
j) Flywheel/driveplate – removal and refitting.
k) Engine/transmission mountings – removal and refitting.

Note: *It is possible to remove the pistons and connecting rods (after removing the cylinder head and sump) without removing the engine. However, this is not recommended. Work of this nature is more easily and thoroughly completed with the engine on the bench, as described in Chapter 2E.*

2 Compression test – description and interpretation

1 When engine performance is down, or if misfiring occurs which cannot be attributed to the ignition or fuel systems, a compression test can provide diagnostic clues as to the engine's condition. If the test is performed regularly, it can give warning of trouble before any other symptoms become apparent.

2 The engine must be fully warmed-up to operating temperature, the oil level must be correct and the battery must be fully charged. The help of an assistant will also be required.

3 Refer to Chapter 12 and remove the fuel pump fuse from the fusebox. Now start the engine and allow it to run until it stalls.

4 Unscrew and remove the oil filler cap, then unbolt the plastic cover for access to the spark plugs. Refit the oil filler cap.

5 Disable the ignition system by disconnecting the 3-pin multi-plug from the DIS ignition coil. Remove all the spark plugs with reference to Chapter 1A.

6 Fit a compression tester to the No 1 cylinder spark plug hole – the type of tester which screws into the spark plug thread is to be preferred.

7 Arrange for an assistant to hold the accelerator pedal fully depressed to the floor, while at the same time cranking the engine over for several seconds on the starter motor. Observe the compression gauge reading. The compression will build-up fairly quickly in a healthy engine. Low compression on the first stroke, followed by gradually-increasing pressure on successive strokes, indicates worn piston rings. A low compression on the first stroke which does not rise on successive strokes, indicates leaking valves or a blown head gasket (a cracked cylinder head could also be the cause). Deposits on the underside of the valve heads can also cause low compression. Record the highest gauge reading obtained, then repeat the procedure for the remaining cylinders.

8 Due to the variety of testers available, and the fluctuation in starter motor speed when cranking the engine, different readings are often obtained when carrying out the compression test. For this reason, actual compression pressure figures are not quoted by Ford. However, the most important factor is that the compression pressures are uniform in all cylinders, and that is what this test is mainly concerned with.

9 Add some engine oil (about three squirts from a plunger type oil can) to each cylinder through the spark plug holes, and then repeat the test.

10 If the compression increases after the oil is added, the piston rings are probably worn. If the compression does not increase significantly, the leakage is occurring at the valves or the head gasket. Leakage past the valves may be caused by burned valve seats

3.7a Unscrewing the blanking plug from the right-hand rear side of the cylinder block

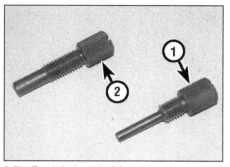

3.7b Ford timing pin (1) and locking tool (2)

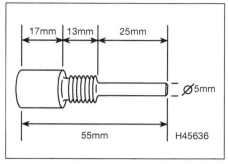

3.7c Timing pin dimensions

and/or faces, or warped, cracked or bent valves.

11 If two adjacent cylinders have equally low compressions, it is most likely that the head gasket has blown between them. The appearance of coolant in the combustion chambers or on the engine oil dipstick would verify this condition.

12 If one cylinder is about 20 percent lower than the other, and the engine has a slightly rough idle, a worn lobe on the camshaft could be the cause.

13 On completion of the checks, refit the spark plugs and reconnect the HT leads and the DIS ignition coil plug. Refit the plastic cover and oil filler cap. Refit the fuel pump fuse to the fusebox.

3 Top Dead Centre (TDC) for No 1 piston – locating

Note: *A timing pin and camshaft setting bar are required for this procedure (see text).*

1 Top dead centre (TDC) is the highest point of the cylinder that each piston reaches as the crankshaft turns. Each piston reaches its TDC position at the end of its compression stroke, and then again at the end of its exhaust stroke. For the purpose of engine timing, TDC on the compression stroke for No 1 piston is used. No 1 cylinder is at the timing belt end of the engine. Proceed as follows.

2 Disconnect the battery negative (earth) lead (refer to Chapter 5A). Remove the spark plugs as described in Chapter 1A.

3 Apply the handbrake, then jack up the front of the vehicle and support it on axle stands (see *Jacking and vehicle support*). If the engine is to be turned using the right-hand front roadwheel with 4th gear engaged (manual transmission models only), it is only necessary to raise the right-hand front roadwheel off the ground.

4 Where necessary, remove the engine undershield, then remove the auxiliary drivebelt lower cover for access to the crankshaft pulley and bolt.

5 Remove the cylinder head cover as described in Section 4.

6 The piston of No 1 cylinder must now be

positioned just before top dead centre (TDC). To do this, have an assistant turn the crankshaft until the slots in the left-hand ends of the camshafts are parallel with the upper surface of the cylinder head. Note that the slots are slightly offset so make sure that the lower edges of the slots are aligned with the cylinder head. Turn the crankshaft slightly anti-clockwise (viewed from the right-hand end of the engine).

7 Unscrew the blanking plug from the right-hand rear side of the engine cylinder block **(see illustration)**. A TDC timing pin must now be inserted and tightened into the hole. It is highly recommended that the special Ford timing pin 303-507 (21-210) is obtained, or alternatively, a timing pin from a reputable tool manufacturer such as Draper. **Note**: *Ford also supply a locking pin 303-748 (21-259) in addition to the timing pin, for use when tightening the crankshaft pulley bolt - do not use the timing pin as a locking tool, as it is easily broken.* The dimensions of the **timing** pin are as shown **(see illustrations)**. The diameter of the pin is critical as it determines the TDC point where the machined flat on the crankshaft web contacts the *shank* of the tool - note that the web does **not** contact the *end* of the tool.

8 With the timing pin in position, turn the crankshaft *slowly* clockwise until the specially machined surface on the crank web just touches the timing pin. No 1 piston is now at TDC on its compression stroke. To confirm this, check that the camshaft lobes for No 4 cylinder are 'rocking' (ie, exhaust valves closing and inlet valves opening).

9 It should now be possible to insert the camshaft setting bar into the slots in the left-

hand ends of the camshafts. If the Ford setting tool 303-376 (21-162B) is unavailable, a home-made tool can be fabricated out of a length of flat metal bar 5.00 mm thick. The bar must be a good fit in the slots and should be approximately 180 to 230 mm long by 20 to 30 mm wide **(see illustration)**.

10 If the bar cannot be inserted in the slots with the crankshaft at TDC, the valve timing must be adjusted as described in Section 8 of this Chapter.

11 Once the work requiring the TDC setting has been completed, remove the metal bar from the camshaft slots then unscrew the timing pin and refit the blanking plug. Refit the spark plugs (Chapter 1A), cylinder head cover (Section 4), auxiliary drivebelt lower cover, and where necessary the engine undershield. Lower the vehicle to the ground and reconnect the battery negative lead.

4 Cylinder head cover – removal and refitting

Removal

1 Disconnect the battery negative (earth) lead (see Chapter 5A).

2 Lift the flap over the centre of the fuel rail at the front of the cylinder head cover, then disconnect the crankcase breather hose **(see illustration)**.

3 Unscrew and remove the oil filler cap, then undo the screws and lift off the plastic cover for access to the spark plug HT leads **(see illustrations)**.

3.9 Home-made camshaft setting bar located in the camshaft slots

4.2 Lift the flap and disconnect the crankcase breather hose

4.3a Undo the screws . . .

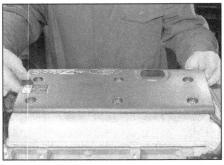

4.3b . . . and remove the plastic cover from the cylinder head cover

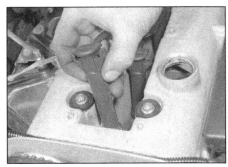

4.4a Disconnect the HT leads from the spark plugs . . .

4 Disconnect the HT leads from the spark plugs and ignition coil, suitably marking them for identification and position them to the left-hand side of the engine compartment. Also disconnect the camshaft position sensor wiring and remove it from the channel in the cylinder head cover **(see illustrations)**. On later engines release and move aside any additional wiring, vacuum or coolant pipes that may interfere with removal of the cylinder head cover.

5 On engines with a magnesium cylinder head cover, unscrew the four nuts securing the cylinder head cover to the top of the cylinder head **(see illustration)**. On later engines with a plastic cylinder head cover, unscrew the twelve bolts securing the cover to the cylinder head. On all engines, undo the screw securing the upper timing cover to the cylinder head cover

6 Carefully lift the cover from the top of the

cylinder head **(see illustration)**. Note that on engines with a magnesium cylinder head cover, the gasket is vulcanised to the cover and cannot be renewed separately. Take care not to damage the gasket, otherwise it will be necessary to obtain a new cover. Where a plastic cylinder head cover is fitted, the gasket can be renewed separately

7 Check the condition of the cylinder head cover gasket. If it is damaged or deteriorated in any way, then the gasket, or the complete cylinder head cover, as applicable, should be renewed. On engines with a magnesium cylinder head cover, also check the condition of the rubber plugs which locate over the cover mounting studs. If necessary, renew the plugs. The new plugs come together with a special plastic installer which is located on the lower lip of the plug. After pressing the plug into the cover, remove the installer **(see illustrations)**.

Refitting

8 Clean the surface of the cylinder head and the gasket on the cover. Where a separate gasket is used, position the gasket on the cover.

9 Lower the cover onto the cylinder head and over the location studs (where applicable). Refit and tighten the securing nuts/bolts to the specified torque progressively and in a diagonal or spiral pattern.

10 Insert and tighten the screw securing the upper timing cover to the cylinder head cover.

11 Reconnect the HT leads to the spark plugs.

12 Refit the plastic cover and tighten the securing screws, then refit the oil filler cap.

13 Reconnect the crankcase breather hose and refit the covering flap. Refit any additional wiring or hoses moved clear for access.

14 Reconnect the battery negative lead.

4.4b . . . and from the ignition coil

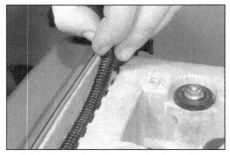

4.4c Removing the camshaft position sensor wiring from the channel in the cylinder head cover

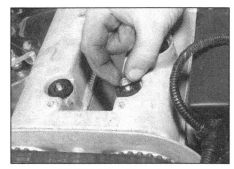

4.5 Unscrew the nuts . . .

4.6 . . . and remove the cylinder head cover

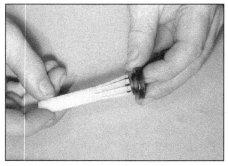

4.7a Locate the plastic installer on the rubber plug . . .

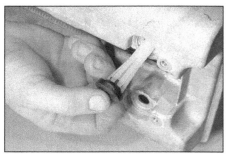

4.7b . . . then press the plug into the cylinder head cover, and remove the installer

5 Valve clearances – checking and adjustment

Checking

1 Remove the cylinder head cover as described in Section 4.

2 Remove the spark plugs (Chapter 1A) in order to make turning the engine easier. The engine may be turned using a spanner on the crankshaft pulley bolt or by raising the front right-hand roadwheel clear of the ground, engaging 4th gear (manual transmission models only) and turning the wheel. If the former method is used, jack up and support the front of the vehicle (see *Jacking and vehicle support*) then unbolt the lower cover for access to the pulley bolt; if the latter method is used, apply the handbrake then jack up the front right-hand side of the vehicle until the roadwheel is clear of the ground and support with an axle stand.

3 Draw the valve positions on a piece of paper, numbering them 1 to 8 inlet and exhaust, from the timing belt (right-hand) end of the engine (ie, 1E, 1I, 2E, 2I and so on). As there are two inlet and two exhaust valves for each cylinder, draw the cylinders as large circles and the four valves as smaller circles. The inlet valves are at the front of the cylinder head, and the exhaust valves are at the rear.

4 Turn the engine in a clockwise direction until both inlet valves of No 1 cylinder are fully shut and the apex of the camshaft lobes are pointing upwards away from the valve positions.

5 Use feeler blade(s) to measure the exact clearance between the heel of the camshaft lobe and the shim on the tappet; the feeler blades should be a firm sliding fit. Record the measured clearance on the drawing. From this clearance it will be possible to calculate the thickness of the new shim to be fitted, where necessary.

6 Measure the clearance of the second inlet valve for No 1 cylinder, and record it on the drawing.

7 Now turn the engine until the inlet valves of No 2 cylinder are fully shut and the camshaft lobes pointing away from the valve positions. Measure the clearances as described previously. After measuring all of the inlet valve clearances, measure the exhaust valve clearances in the same way.

8 Compare the measured clearances with the values given in the Specifications – any which fall within the range do not require adjustment. Note that the clearances for inlet and exhaust valves are different.

Adjustment

9 Where adjustment is required, the procedure is to remove the shim from the top of the tappet and fit a new shim to provide the

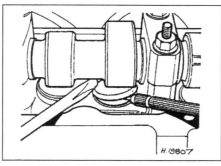

5.9 Depressing a tappet with a screwdriver and removing a shim

correct clearance. Ford technicians use a special tool (21-218) consisting of a bar bolted to the camshaft bearing caps. A sliding lever on the bar is used, together with a pushrod, to depress the relevant tappet in order to remove the old shim and fit the new one. Use of this tool, a similar tool or, with care, a screwdriver **(see illustration)** will save a considerable amount of time, as the alternative is to remove the camshafts with the additional time of disconnecting the timing belt and resetting the valve timing. However, if TDC setting tools are available (see Section 3) removal of the camshafts is to be preferred to using an ill-fitting tool to depress the tappets.

10 If the recorded clearance was too small, a thinner shim must be fitted, and conversely if the clearance was too large, a thicker shim must be fitted. To calculate the thickness of the new shim, first use a micrometer to measure the thickness of the existing shim (C) and add this to the measured clearance (B). Deduct the desired clearance (A) to provide the thickness (D) of the new shim. The thickness of the shim should be etched on the downward facing surface, but use the micrometer to verify this. The formula is as follows.

$$D = C + B - A$$

Where:
A = Required clearance
B = Measured clearance
C = Existing shim thickness
D = New shim thickness
All measurements in mm

Sample calculation – clearance too small

Required clearance (A)	*= 0.20*
Measured clearance (B)	*= 0.15*
Existing shim thickness (C)	*= 2.725*
Shim thickness required (D)	*= C+B–A*
	= 2.675

Sample calculation – clearance too large

Required clearance (A)	*= 0.30*
Measured clearance (B)	*= 0.40*
Existing shim thickness (C)	*= 2.550*
Shim thickness required (D)	*= C+B–A*
	= 2.650

11 The shims are available in thicknesses from 2.000 mm to 3.300 mm in increments of 0.025 mm **(see illustration)**. If the Ford tool (or similar) is being used to remove the shims

5.11 Valve clearance adjustment shim

without removing the camshafts, turn the tappets so that the slot is facing towards the centre of the engine. It will then be possible to use a small screwdriver to lift out the old shim. Fit the new shim then release the tool.

12 When fitting the new shim, make sure that the etched thickness is facing downwards onto the tappet.

13 It will be helpful for future adjustment if a record is kept of the thickness of shim fitted at each position. The shims required can be purchased in advance once the clearances and the existing shim thicknesses are known. It is permissible to interchange shims between tappets to achieve the correct clearances, but it is not advisable to turn the camshaft with any shims removed, since there is a risk that the cam lobe will jam in the empty tappet.

14 When all the clearances have been checked and adjusted, refit the lower cover (where removed), lower the vehicle to the ground and refit the cylinder head cover as described in Section 4.

6 Crankshaft pulley/vibration damper – removal and refitting

Caution: Removal of the crankshaft pulley effectively loses the valve timing setting, and it will be necessary to reset the timing using the procedure and tools described in Section 3.

Note: *The vibration damper retaining bolt may only be used once. Obtain a new bolt for the refitting procedure.*

Removal

1 Disconnect the battery negative (earth) lead (see Chapter 5A).

2 Apply the handbrake, then jack up the front of the vehicle and support it on axle stands (see *Jacking and vehicle support*). Remove the engine undershield if fitted.

3 Remove the right-hand front roadwheel, then where necessary undo the retaining screws and remove the wheelarch liner.

4 Unbolt and remove the auxiliary drivebelt

6.4 Removing the auxiliary drivebelt lower cover

6.7 Loosening the crankshaft pulley bolt while holding the pulley with a home-made tool

6.8a Use a puller to free the crankshaft pulley from the crankshaft taper . . .

lower cover for access to the crankshaft pulley **(see illustration)**.

5 Remove the auxiliary drivebelt as described in Chapter 1A.

6 Set the engine to the top dead centre (TDC) position as described in Section 3, then remove the camshaft position bar and the crankshaft timing pin. Do not leave the tools in position while the crankshaft pulley bolt is being loosened.

7 Hold the crankshaft pulley stationary using a home-made tool like the one shown **(see illustration)**. The bolt ends locate in the pulley holes and an extension bar and socket can then be used to loosen the bolt. Do not turn the crankshaft otherwise it will be more difficult to reset the valve timing, and also with the bolt loose the crankshaft sprocket may not turn with the crankshaft and the pistons may touch the valves.

6.8b . . . then withdraw the pulley from the end of the crankshaft

8 With the bolt loosened several turns, use a suitable puller to free the pulley from the taper on the end of the crankshaft. Fully unscrew the bolt and withdraw the pulley **(see illustrations)**.

9 Clean the end of the crankshaft and the pulley.

Refitting

10 The procedure in this paragraph is necessary in order to be able to set the valve timing after the crankshaft/vibration pulley has been refitted. Unbolt and remove the upper timing cover (see Section 7). While holding each of the camshaft sprockets stationary in turn using the home-made tool described in paragraph 7, loosen the sprocket retaining bolts until they are just finger-tight to enable the sprockets to turn on the camshafts. Alternatively the camshafts can be held stationary using a spanner on the special hexagon flats.

11 Locate the pulley on the end of the crankshaft and press it onto the taper as far as it will go. This procedure must always be carried out before inserting and tightening the new bolt. Do not simply insert and tighten the new bolt, as in certain circumstances the torque will not be sufficient to press the pulley fully onto the end of the taper on the crankshaft. Ford technicians use a special installer which consists of a threaded rod screwed into the crankshaft together with a spacer which locates on the pulley. In the absence of this tool, use a long bolt or threaded rod together with washers and a nut **(see**

illustration). As a last resort use the removed (old) bolt, however this is not recommended as the threads may be stretched (see Note at the beginning of this Section).

12 Remove the tool, then insert the new bolt and tighten it to the specified Stage 1 torque setting while holding the pulley stationary with the special tool **(see illustration)**.

13 Now angle-tighten the bolt through the specified Stage 2 angle.

14 The valve timing must now be set and the camshaft sprocket bolts tightened as described in Section 8.

15 Refit the upper timing cover.

16 Refit and tension the auxiliary drivebelt as described in Chapter 1A.

17 Refit the auxiliary drivebelt lower cover and tighten the retaining bolts.

18 Refit the wheelarch liner and where fitted the engine undershield, then refit the wheel and lower the vehicle to the ground.

19 Reconnect the battery negative lead.

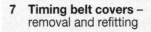

7   Timing belt covers – removal and refitting

Upper cover
Removal

1 Remove the auxiliary drivebelt as described in Chapter 1A.

2 Unbolt and remove the upper idler pulley **(see illustration)**. Unbolt and remove the coolant pump pulley.

6.11 Use a long bolt threaded into the crankshaft to draw the pulley onto the taper

6.12 Inserting the new crankshaft pulley retaining bolt

7.2 Removing the upper idler pulley

3 Unscrew the single upper bolt securing the upper timing cover to the cylinder head cover **(see illustration)**. **Note:** *On models with air conditioning, it will be necessary to slacken the power steering pump bracket bolts and move the pump about 10 mm to allow access.*
4 Unscrew the remaining retaining screws – there are three near the top, two half-way down and two at the bottom.
5 Manoeuvre the timing cover rearwards from behind the right-hand engine mounting brackets, and withdraw it from the engine compartment **(see illustration)**.

Refitting

6 Refitting is a reversal of removal, but tighten the retaining bolts to the specified torque.

Lower cover

Removal

7 The timing belt lower cover is located around the crankshaft. First remove the crankshaft pulley/vibration damper as described in Section 6.
8 Working beneath the right-hand wheelarch, unscrew the retaining bolts and withdraw the timing cover **(see illustrations)**.

Refitting

9 Refitting is a reversal of removal, but tighten the retaining bolts to the specified torque.

---

8   Timing belt – removal and refitting

Removal

1 Remove the crankshaft pulley/vibration damper as described in Section 6. This work includes removing the cylinder head cover and upper timing belt cover, and setting the engine at top dead centre (TDC).
2 With the camshaft timing bar removed, loosen the camshaft sprocket bolts several turns while holding the sprockets with a suitable tool **(see illustration)**. Using a soft-metal drift from behind the sprockets,

release the sprockets from the tapers on the ends of the camshafts so that they are free to rotate.
3 Remove the timing belt lower cover as described in Section 7. On later models it may be beneficial to remove the alternator as described in Chapter 5A to provide additional working clearance.
4 Remove the timing belt guide disc from the end of the crankshaft. Note which way round the disc is fitted – the concave side faces inwards **(see illustration)**.
5 Using a trolley jack and wooden block, support the weight of the engine beneath the right-hand side of the engine **(see illustration)**.
6 Unscrew the nuts and remove the upper

7.3 Unscrewing the timing cover upper retaining bolt

7.5 Removing the upper timing cover

7.8a Undo the bolts . . .

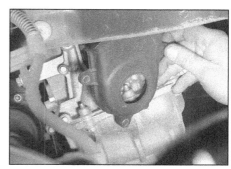

7.8b . . . and remove the lower timing cover

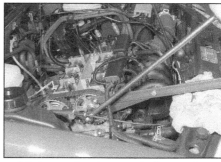

8.2 Loosening the camshaft sprocket retaining bolts while holding the sprockets with a home-made tool

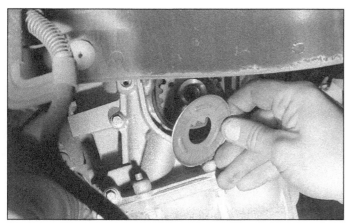

8.4 Removing the timing belt guide disc

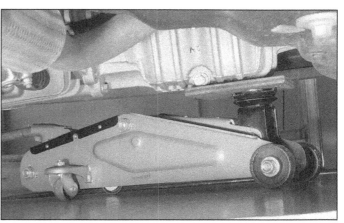

8.5 Support the engine with a trolley jack and block of wood

8.6 Removing the right-hand engine mounting upper bracket

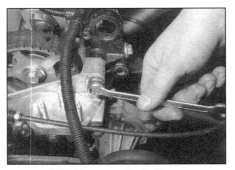

8.7a Unscrew the bolts . . .

8.7b . . . and remove the right-hand engine mounting lower bracket

bracket from the right-hand engine mounting (see illustration).

7 Unbolt the right-hand engine mounting lower bracket from the cylinder head (see illustrations).

8 One of three different types of timing belt tensioner may be fitted:

Type 1   The tensioner body incorporates a spring and pushrod to apply tension to the tensioner pulley.

Type 2   The tensioner pulley is mounted on an eccentric.

Type 3   The tensioner has a fixed pulley, with the belt being tensioned by pivoting the tensioner mounting bracket.

For clarity, in the remainder of this Chapter, these will be referred to as Type 1, Type 2 and Type 3 tensioners.

9 If the Type 1 tensioner is fitted, the timing belt tensioner spring and pushrod must now be compressed to release the tension on the timing belt. A home-made compressor tool can be made out of a long bolt fitted with two short lengths of metal and four nuts. Fit the tool over the tensioner spring body and compress the spring pushrod until a 1.5 mm diameter drill can be inserted through the upper end of the body through the pushrod. The drill will hold the tension spring in its compressed position and the tool can then be removed (see illustrations).

10 If working on the Type 2 or Type 3 tensioners, loosen the tensioner centre bolt (Type 2), or the two tensioner mounting bolts (Type 3), then move the tensioner away from the belt, and tighten the bolt (or

bolts) to hold the tensioner temporarily in this position.

11 If the timing belt is to be re-used, use white paint or similar to mark its direction of rotation, and note from the manufacturer's markings which way round it is fitted. Withdraw the belt from the sprockets and from over the tensioner (see illustrations). Do not attempt to turn the crankshaft or camshafts until the timing belt is refitted.

12 If the belt is being removed for reasons other than renewal, check it carefully for any signs of uneven wear, splitting, cracks (especially at the roots of the belt teeth) or contamination with oil or coolant. Renew the belt if there is the slightest doubt about its condition. As a safety measure, the belt should be renewed irrespective of its apparent

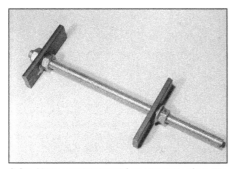

8.9a Home-made tool for compressing the timing belt tensioner spring on the Type 1 timing belt tensioner

8.9b With the spring compressed, insert a 1.5 mm diameter drill through the body and through the pushrod of the Type 1 timing belt tensioner

8.11a Showing the manufacturer's markings on the timing belt

8.11b Removing the timing belt from the camshaft sprockets . . .

8.11c . . . tensioner pulley . . .

8.11d . . . and crankshaft sprocket

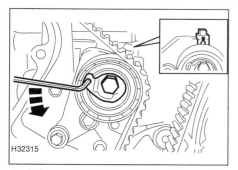

8.16 Setting the timing belt tension on the Type 2 timing belt tensioner

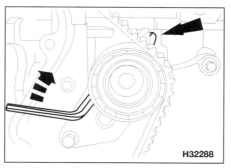

8.17 Setting the timing belt tension on the Type 3 timing belt tensioner

8.25 Tightening the camshaft sprocket retaining bolts

condition whenever the engine is overhauled. Check also the sprockets for signs of wear or damage, and ensure that the tensioner pulley rotates smoothly on its bearings; renew any worn or damaged components. If signs of oil or coolant contamination are found, trace the source of the leak and rectify it, then wash down the engine timing belt area and related components, to remove all traces of oil or coolant. If the tensioner spring and pushrod are thought to be worn, renew the tensioner as an assembly.

Refitting

13 Locate the timing belt on the crankshaft sprocket, then feed it over the tensioner pulley and finally over the two camshaft sprockets. If the original belt is being refitted, make sure that it is the correct way round as noted during removal.

14 Refit the crankcase sprocket/belt retainer plate to the cylinder block and tighten the bolt to the specified torque.

15 If working on the Type 1 timing belt tensioner, fit the compressor tool to the tensioner body and compress the pushrod until the drill can be removed. Carefully release the compressor to tension the timing belt, then remove the tool.

16 If working on the Type 2 tensioner, loosen the centre bolt, then using a 6 mm Allen key in the hole provided, turn the tensioner roller anti-clockwise to tension the belt. The correct tension is indicated by the pointer being exactly central in the rectangular window above and behind the tensioner roller **(see illustration)**. Hold the tensioner in this position, and tighten the centre bolt to the specified torque.

17 If working on the Type 3 tensioner, loosen the two bolts so that the tensioner is free to pivot. Using an 8 mm Allen key in the hole provided, turn the tensioner and bracket clockwise to tension the belt. The correct tension is indicated by the pointer being exactly central between the two marks behind the tensioner roller **(see illustration)**. Hold the tensioner in this position, and tighten the two bolts to the specified torque.

18 Refit the timing belt guide disc on the end of the crankshaft, making sure that the concave side faces inwards.

19 Refit the timing belt lower cover and tighten the bolts to the specified torque.

20 Locate the crankshaft pulley/vibration damper on the end of the crankshaft and press it onto the taper as far as it will go. This procedure must always be carried out before inserting and tightening the new bolt – it is not sufficient to press on the pulley by hand only. Ford technicians use a special installer which consists of a threaded rod screwed into the crankshaft together with a metal ring which locates on the pulley. In the absence of this tool, use the old pulley bolt together with a suitable metal ring to press the pulley squarely onto the crankshaft as far as it will go. Do not use the new bolt for this initial operation.

21 Insert the new bolt and tighten it to the specified Stage 1 torque setting while holding the pulley stationary with the special tool (see Section 6).

22 Now tighten the bolt through the specified angle. The crankshaft sprocket is now effectively clamped to the crankshaft.

23 Position No 1 piston at TDC as described in Section 3. The procedure is to insert and tighten the timing pin then turn the crankshaft clockwise until the machined surface on the crank web just touches the timing pin.

24 Set the camshafts at TDC as described in Section 3 and insert the setting bar in the slots.

25 Moderately tighten the bolts retaining the camshaft sprockets to the camshafts, then remove the setting bar and timing pin and fully tighten the bolts while holding the sprockets using the tool described in Section 6 or using a spanner on the hexagon flats provided **(see illustration)**.

26 Refit the right-hand engine mounting lower bracket and tighten the bolts to the specified torque.

27 Refit the upper mounting bracket and tighten the nuts to the specified torque. Withdraw the trolley jack from under the vehicle.

28 Check the accuracy of the valve timing by first turning the crankshaft two complete turns. Refit the TDC timing pin and position the crankshaft at TDC, then insert the setting bar in the camshaft slots. On completion remove the timing pin and bar and refit the blanking plug.

29 Refit the timing belt upper cover, and the alternator, if removed.

30 Refit and tension the auxiliary drivebelt as described in Chapter 1A.

31 Refit the auxiliary drivebelt lower cover and tighten the retaining bolts.

32 Refit the wheelarch liner and where fitted the engine undershield, then lower the vehicle to the ground.

33 Reconnect the battery negative lead.

---

9 Timing belt tensioner and sprockets – removal, inspection and refitting

Tensioner and tensioner pulley

Removal

1 Disconnect the battery negative (earth) lead (see Chapter 5A).

2 Apply the handbrake, then jack up the front of the vehicle and support it on axle stands (see *Jacking and vehicle support*). Remove the engine undershield if fitted.

3 Remove the right-hand front roadwheel, then undo the retaining screws and remove the wheelarch liner.

4 Unbolt and remove the auxiliary drivebelt lower cover for access to the crankshaft pulley.

5 Remove the auxiliary drivebelt as described in Chapter 1A.

6 Remove the timing belt upper cover as described in Section 7.

7 As a precaution against losing the valve timing, use string to tie the front and rear runs of the timing belt together. This will ensure that the belt remains engaged with the camshaft sprockets while the tensioner and pulley are removed.

8 Refer to Section 8 for descriptions and identification of the three types of timing belt tensioner that may be fitted.

9 If the Type 1 tensioner is fitted, the tensioner spring and pushrod must now be compressed to release the tension on the timing belt, and a 1.5 mm drill must be inserted through the upper end of the body and through the pushrod. The procedure is described in Section 8.

9.10a Removing the Type 1 timing belt tensioner body . . .

9.10b . . . and the timing backplate

9.11 Removing the Type 1 timing belt tensioner pulley

10 With the tensioner spring and pushrod held in their compressed position with the drill, unscrew the retaining bolts and remove the tensioner body from the cylinder block. If required, unbolt and remove the timing backplate **(see illustrations)**.

11 Unscrew the pivot bolt and remove the tensioner pulley from the cylinder block **(see illustration)**.

12 On the Type 2 and Type 3 tensioners, loosen the timing belt tensioner centre bolt (Type 2) or the two tensioner mounting bolts (Type 3). Move the tensioner away from the belt, and on Type 2 tensioners, tighten the centre bolt to hold it in the retracted position.

13 Loosen and/or completely remove the two tensioner mounting bracket bolts, and withdraw the tensioner from the engine.

14 While the tensioner and pulley are removed, make sure that the timing belt remains fully engaged with the camshaft and crankshaft sprockets.

Inspection

15 Spin the tensioner pulley and check that it turns freely without any roughness or tightness. Do not attempt to clean the pulley by immersing in any cleaning fluid.

16 If necessary, on the Type 1 tensioner, use the compressor tool to release the tension of the tensioner spring and remove it from the body. Clean the spring and body and inspect them for wear and damage.

17 Renew the components as required and, on the Type 1 tensioner, reassemble the tensioner spring to the body using the tool to compress it. Retain with the drill bit.

Refitting

18 Clean the cylinder block in the area of the tensioner.

19 If the Type 1 tensioner is being refitted, proceed as follows:

a) Locate the tensioner pulley on the block, insert the pivot bolt and tighten to the specified torque. Make sure that the back of the timing belt is located over the pulley.

b) Refit the tensioner body (with fitted spring) and tighten the retaining bolts to the specified torque. Ensure that the

pushrod of the tensioner locates correctly on the pulley contact surface.

c) Fit the compressor tool to the timing belt tensioner body and compress the pushrod until the drill can be removed. Carefully release the compressor to tension the timing belt, then remove the tool.

20 If the Type 2 or Type 3 tensioner is being refitted, proceed as follows:

a) Locate the tensioner pulley on the block, and insert the two mounting bolts.

b) On the Type 2 tensioner, tighten the two mounting bolts to the specified torque.

c) Tension the timing belt using the information in Section 8.

21 Provided that the timing belt has remained fully engaged with the camshaft and crankshaft sprockets, it should not be necessary to check the valve timing. However, if there is any doubt, check the valve timing as described in Section 3.

22 Refit the timing belt upper cover as described in Section 7.

23 Refit the auxiliary drivebelt as described in Chapter 1A.

24 Refit the auxiliary drivebelt lower cover and tighten the bolts.

25 Refit the wheelarch liner and the right-hand front roadwheel.

26 Refit the engine undershield (if fitted) and lower the vehicle to the ground.

27 Reconnect the battery negative lead.

Camshaft sprockets

Removal

28 Disconnect the battery negative (earth) lead (see Chapter 5A).

29 Apply the handbrake, then jack up the front of the vehicle and support it on axle stands (see *Jacking and vehicle support*). Remove the engine undershield if fitted.

30 Remove the right-hand front roadwheel, then undo the retaining screws and remove the wheelarch liner.

31 Unbolt and remove the auxiliary drivebelt lower cover.

32 Remove the auxiliary drivebelt as described in Chapter 1A.

33 Remove the timing belt upper cover as described in Section 7.

34 Set the No 1 piston and camshafts to top dead centre (TDC) as described in Section 3. This procedure includes removal of the cylinder head cover.

35 Using a trolley jack and wooden block, support the weight of the engine beneath the right-hand side of the engine.

36 Unscrew the nuts and remove the upper bracket from the right-hand engine mounting.

37 Unbolt the right-hand engine mounting lower bracket from the cylinder head.

38 Refer to Section 8 for descriptions and identification of the three types of timing belt tensioner that may be fitted, then release the tension on the timing belt accordingly.

39 Disengage the timing belt from the camshaft sprockets and position it to one side, taking care not to bend it sharply. The belt will remain engaged with the crankshaft sprocket by means of the retainer plate bolted to the cylinder block. However, as a precaution keep a little upward pressure on the belt by tying it to the side of the engine compartment.

40 Hold each of the camshaft sprockets stationary in turn using a home-made tool (see Section 6), then loosen the sprocket retaining bolts. Alternatively the camshafts can be held stationary using a spanner on the special hexagon flats **(see illustration)**. The TDC setting bar must not be used to hold the camshafts stationary.

41 Unscrew the bolts and remove the sprockets from the camshafts. If necessary, use a soft-metal drift to release the sprockets

9.40 Using a spanner to hold the camshafts stationary

9.41a Unscrew the bolt . . .

9.41b . . . and remove the camshaft sprocket

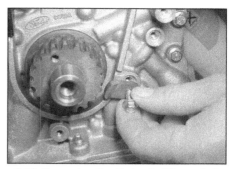

9.59 Removing the timing belt/sprocket holder plate

from the taper on the camshafts **(see illustrations)**.

Inspection

42 Examine the teeth of the sprockets for wear and damage, and renew them if necessary.

Refitting

43 Locate the sprockets on the camshafts and screw in the retaining bolts loosely.
44 Engage the timing belt with the camshaft sprockets.
45 If the Type 1 tensioner is being refitted, proceed as follows:
  a) *Locate the tensioner pulley on the block, insert the pivot bolt and tighten to the specified torque. Make sure that the back of the timing belt is located over the pulley.*
  b) *Refit the tensioner body (with fitted spring) and tighten the retaining bolts to the specified torque. Ensure that the pushrod of the tensioner locates correctly on the pulley contact surface.*
  c) *Fit the compressor tool to the timing belt tensioner body and compress the pushrod until the drill can be removed. Carefully release the compressor to tension the timing belt, then remove the tool.*
46 If the Type 2 or Type 3 tensioner is being refitted, proceed as follows:
  a) *Locate the tensioner pulley on the block, and insert the two mounting bolts.*
  b) *On the Type 2 tensioner, tighten the two mounting bolts to the specified torque.*
  c) *Tension the timing belt using the information in Section 8.*
47 Refit the right-hand engine mounting lower bracket and tighten the bolts to the specified torque.
48 Refit the upper mounting bracket and tighten the nuts to the specified torque. Withdraw the trolley jack from under the vehicle.
49 Position No 1 piston at TDC as described in Section 3. The procedure is to insert and tighten the timing pin then turn the crankshaft clockwise until the machined surface on the crank web just touches the timing pin.
50 Set the camshafts at TDC as described in Section 3 and insert the setting bar in the slots.
51 Moderately tighten the bolts retaining the camshaft sprockets to the camshafts, then remove the setting bar and timing pin and fully

tighten the bolts while holding the sprockets using the tool described in Section 6.
52 Check the accuracy of the valve timing by first turning the crankshaft two complete turns. Refit the TDC timing pin and position the crankshaft at TDC, then insert the setting bar in the camshaft slots. On completion remove the timing pin and bar and refit the blanking plug.
53 Refit the timing belt upper cover as described in Section 7.
54 Refit and tension the auxiliary drivebelt as described in Chapter 1A.
55 Refit the auxiliary drivebelt lower cover and tighten the retaining bolts.
56 Refit the wheelarch liner and where fitted the engine undershield, then refit the wheel and lower the vehicle to the ground.
57 Reconnect the battery negative lead.

Crankshaft sprocket

Removal

58 Remove the timing belt as described in Section 8.
59 Unbolt the belt/sprocket holder plate **(see illustration)**.
60 Slide the sprocket off the end of the crankshaft **(see illustration)**.

Inspection

61 Examine the teeth of the sprocket for wear and damage, and renew if necessary.

Refitting

62 Wipe clean the end of the crankshaft, then slide on the sprocket.
63 Refit the belt/sprocket holder plate and tighten the bolt.

10.3a Drill a small hole and insert a self-tapping screw . . .

9.60 Slide the sprocket from the end of the crankshaft

64 Refit the timing belt as described in Section 8.

10 Camshaft oil seals – renewal

1 Remove the camshaft sprockets as described in Section 9.
2 Note the fitted depths of the oil seals as a guide for fitting the new ones.
3 Using a screwdriver or similar tool, carefully prise the oil seals from the cylinder head/camshaft bearing caps. Take care not to damage the oil seal contact surfaces on the ends of the camshafts or the oil seal seatings. An alternative method of removing the seals is to drill a small hole then insert a self-tapping screw and use pliers to pull out the seal **(see illustrations)**.

10.3b . . . then pull out the oil seal using a pair of pliers

10.5 Locating the new oil seal into the cylinder head/camshaft bearing cap

10.6 Driving the new oil seal into position with a socket

11.3a No 3 inlet camshaft bearing cap

4 Wipe clean the oil seal seatings and also the ends of the camshafts.

5 Working on the first camshaft, dip the new oil seal in fresh oil, then locate it over the camshaft and into the cylinder head/camshaft bearing cap. Make sure that the closed end of the oil seal faces outwards **(see illustration)**.

6 Using a socket or length of metal tubing, drive the oil seals squarely into position to the previously noted depths. Wipe away any excess oil **(see illustration)**.

7 Refit the camshaft sprockets as described in Section 9.

11 Camshafts and tappets – removal, inspection and refitting

Removal

1 Before removing the camshafts it may be useful to check and record the valve clearances as described in Section 5. If any clearance is not within limits, new shims can be obtained and fitted.

2 Remove the camshaft sprockets as described in Section 9.

3 The camshaft bearing caps are marked for position – the inlet caps have the letter I and exhaust caps have the letter E. On the project vehicle these were not very clear, and if this is the case mark them using paint or a marker pen. Make sure they are identified for inlet and exhaust camshafts **(see illustrations)**.

4 Position the crankshaft so that No 1 piston is approximately 25 mm before TDC.

5 Position the camshafts so that none of the valves are at full lift. To do this turn each camshaft using a spanner on the hexagon flats provided.

6 Progressively loosen the camshaft bearing cap retaining bolts, noting the location of the extended bolts which secure the cylinder head

cover (engines with a magnesium cylinder head cover only). Work only as described to release gradually and evenly the pressure of the valve springs on the caps **(see illustration)**.

7 Withdraw the caps, keeping them in order to aid refitting, then lift the camshafts from the cylinder head and withdraw their oil seals. The exhaust camshaft can be identified by the reference lobe for the camshaft position sensor; therefore, there is no need to mark the camshafts **(see illustrations)**.

8 Obtain sixteen small, clean containers, and number them 1 to 8 for both the inlet and exhaust camshafts. Lift the tappets one by one from the cylinder head keeping the shims with the respective tappets **(see illustration)**.

Inspection

9 With the camshafts and tappets removed, check each for signs of obvious wear (scoring, pitting, etc) and for ovality, and renew if necessary.

11.3b No 3 exhaust camshaft bearing cap

11.3c Number the camshaft bearing caps with paint if they are not marked

11.6 Unscrew the camshaft bearing cap bolts . . .

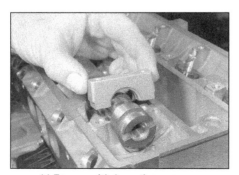

11.7a . . . withdraw the caps . . .

11.7b . . . then remove the camshafts

11.8 Removing the bucket tappets

10 If possible, use a micrometer to measure the outside diameter of each tappet – take measurements at the top and bottom of each tappet, then a second set at right-angles to the first; if any measurement is significantly different from the others, the tappet is tapered or oval (as applicable) and must be renewed. If the tappets or the cylinder head bores are excessively worn, new tappets and/or a new cylinder head will be required.

11 Visually examine the camshaft lobes for score marks, pitting, and evidence of overheating (blue, discoloured areas). Look for flaking away of the hardened surface layer of each lobe. If any such signs are evident, renew the component concerned.

12 Examine the camshaft bearing journals and the cylinder head bearing surfaces for signs of obvious wear or pitting. If any such signs are evident, renew the component concerned.

13 To check camshaft endfloat, remove the tappets, clean the bearing surfaces carefully, and refit the camshafts and bearing caps. Tighten the bearing cap bolts to the specified torque wrench setting, then measure the endfloat using a dial gauge mounted on the cylinder head so that its tip bears on the camshaft right-hand end.

14 Tap the camshaft fully towards the gauge, zero the gauge, then tap the camshaft fully away from the gauge, and note the gauge reading. If the endfloat measured is found to be more than the typical value given, fit a new camshaft and repeat the check; if the clearance is still excessive, the cylinder head must be renewed.

Refitting

15 Commence reassembly by lubricating the cylinder head tappet bores and the tappets with engine oil. Carefully refit the tappets (together with their respective shims) to the cylinder head, ensuring that each tappet is refitted to its original bore. Some care will be required to enter the tappets squarely into their bores.

16 Liberally oil the camshaft bearings and lobes. Ensuring that each camshaft is in its original location, refit the camshafts, locating each so that the slot in its left-hand end is approximately parallel to, and just above, the cylinder head mating surface. At this stage position the camshafts so that none of the valves are at full lift **(see illustration)**.

17 Clean the mating faces of the cylinder head and camshaft bearing caps, and ensure that the locating dowels are firmly in place.

18 Apply a 2 to 3 mm diameter bead of suitable sealant (Ford recommend WSK-M2G348-A5) to the No 1 camshaft bearing caps at the oil seal ends only **(see illustration)**. If preferred, the oil seals can be located at this stage, otherwise fit them later.

19 Oil the bearing surfaces, then locate the camshaft bearing caps on the camshafts and insert the retaining bolts loosely. Make sure that each cap is located in its previously noted position **(see illustrations)**.

11.16 Locating the camshafts in the cylinder head

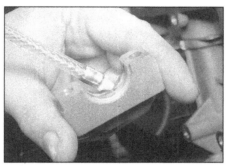

11.19a Oil the bearing surfaces . . .

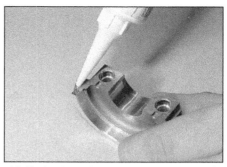

11.18 Apply sealant to the No 1 camshaft bearing caps

11.19b . . . then refit the camshaft bearing caps

20 Ensuring that each cap is kept square to the cylinder head as it is tightened down, and working in the sequence shown **(see illustration)**, tighten the camshaft bearing cap bolts slowly and by one turn at a time, until each cap touches the cylinder head. Next, go round again in the same sequence, tightening the bolts to the first stage torque wrench setting specified, then once more, tightening them to the second stage setting. Work only in the sequence shown so that pressure is gradually applied to the valve springs.

21 Wipe off all surplus sealant, and if not already done fit the new oil seals with reference to Section 10.

22 Refit the camshaft sprockets (Section 9).

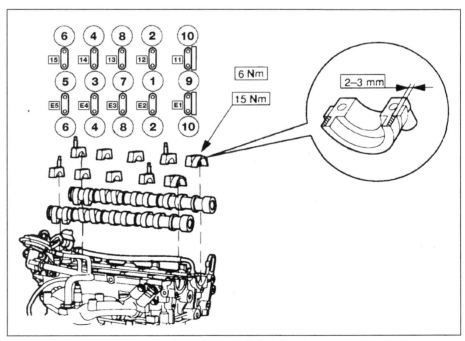

11.20 Camshaft bearing cap bolt tightening sequence

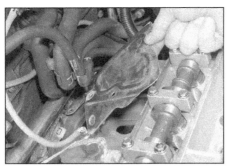

12.5 Removing the heatshield from the top of the exhaust manifold

12.7 Removing the battery box

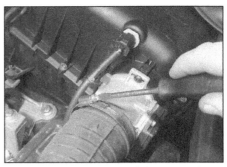

12.8 Disconnecting the air inlet duct from the mass airflow sensor on the air cleaner

12 Cylinder head – removal, inspection and refitting

Removal

Note: *The following paragraphs assume that the cylinder head will be removed together with the inlet and exhaust manifolds attached. This simplifies the procedure, but makes it a bulky and heavy assembly to handle – ideally an engine hoist will be required, to prevent the risk of injury, and to prevent damage to any delicate components as the assembly is removed and refitted. If it is wished first to remove the manifolds, refer to Chapter 4A, then amend the following procedure accordingly.*

1 Depressurise the fuel system (Chapter 4A).
2 Set the engine to TDC compression on piston No 1 as described in Section 3. This procedure includes disconnecting the battery and removing the cylinder head cover, then setting the engine to TDC using a timing pin and camshaft setting bar.
3 Remove the right-hand front roadwheel, then undo the retaining screws and remove the wheelarch liner.
4 Remove the auxiliary drivebelt as described in Chapter 1A.
5 Unscrew and remove the bolts securing the heatshield assembly to the catalytic converter and exhaust manifold at the rear of the engine. Access to the lower bolt is best from under the vehicle **(see illustration)**.
6 Drain the cooling system (see Chapter 1A).
7 Remove the battery as described in

Chapter 5A, then disconnect the wiring bracket and unbolt the battery box from the body **(see illustration)**.
8 Loosen the clips and remove the air inlet duct from between the mass airflow sensor and throttle body housing **(see illustration)**.
9 Unclip the fuel feed and return hoses from their supports, then squeeze together the quick-release fittings and disconnect the hoses from the fuel rail.
10 Lift the flap over the centre of the fuel rail at the front of the cylinder head cover, then disconnect the crankcase breather hose.
11 Disconnect the inner accelerator cable from the throttle body housing (refer to Chapter 4A). Also unbolt and remove the throttle body housing support bracket **(see illustrations)**.
12 Unscrew and remove the oil filler cap, then undo the screws and lift the plastic cover for access to the spark plug HT leads.
13 Disconnect the HT leads from the spark plugs and position them to the left-hand side of the engine compartment.
14 Disconnect the wiring from the following components:
a) *The throttle position sensor on the throttle body housing **(see illustration)**.*
b) *The DIS ignition coil **(see illustration)**.*
c) *The engine coolant temperature sensor on the left-hand end of the cylinder head **(see illustration)**.*
d) *The engine wiring loom plug on the left-hand end of the cylinder head.*
e) *The camshaft position sensor on the right-hand rear of the cylinder head.*

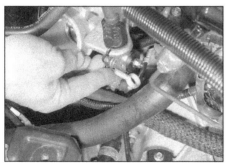

12.11a Disconnecting the accelerator cable from the throttle body housing

12.11b Unbolting the throttle body housing support bracket

12.14a Disconnecting the wiring from the throttle position sensor . . .

12.14b . . . DIS ignition coil . . .

12.14c . . . engine coolant temperature sensor . . .

12.14d . . . oxygen sensor . . .

12.14e . . . and the earth wire on the back of the cylinder head

12.18 Unscrewing the nuts securing the catalytic converter to the exhaust manifold

f) *The oxygen sensor wiring on the bulkhead* **(see illustration).**

g) *The earth wire from the rear of the cylinder head* **(see illustration).**

h) *Any additional wiring connectors, according to model.*

15 Loosen the clips, and disconnect the following coolant hoses:

a) *The top hose at the thermostat housing.*

b) *The expansion tank vent and heater hoses at the thermostat housing.*

16 Disconnect the vacuum hoses from the throttle body housing.

17 Where applicable, disconnect the vacuum hose from the EGR valve.

18 Unscrew the nuts securing the catalytic converter to the exhaust manifold **(see illustration).**

19 Remove the alternator as described in Chapter 5A.

20 Unscrew the bolt securing the oil level dipstick tube to the inlet manifold, then withdraw the tube from the cylinder block. Remove the O-ring and discard it **(see illustrations).**

21 Unscrew and remove the inlet manifold mounting bolts securing the manifold to the cylinder block **(see illustration).**

22 With reference to Section 4, unscrew the nuts or bolts securing the cylinder head cover to the top of the cylinder head. Also unscrew the bolts securing the rear timing cover to the cylinder head cover **(see illustrations).**

23 Carefully lift the cover from the top of the cylinder head. Note that engines with a magnesium cylinder head cover, the gasket is vulcanised to the cover and cannot be renewed separately. Take care not to damage the gasket otherwise it will be necessary to obtain a new cover. Note also that the four rubber plugs in the cover locate on extensions on the camshaft bearing caps.

24 Using a trolley jack and wooden block, support the weight of the engine beneath the right-hand side of the engine.

25 Unscrew the nuts and remove the upper bracket from the right-hand engine mounting.

26 Unbolt the right-hand engine mounting lower bracket from the cylinder head.

27 Hold the coolant pump pulley stationary

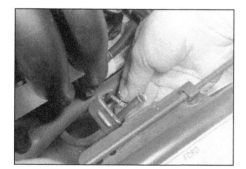

12.20a Unscrew the upper mounting bolt . . .

12.20b . . . remove the dipstick tube from the cylinder block . . .

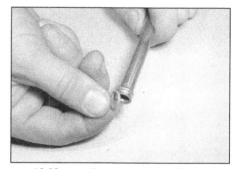

12.20c . . . then remove the O-ring

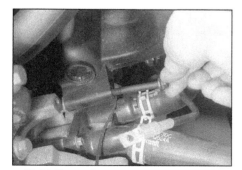

12.21 Removing the bolts securing the inlet manifold to the cylinder block

12.22a Unscrew the upper bolt securing the rear timing cover to the cylinder head . . .

12.22b . . . and the lower bolt

12.27 Removing the coolant pump drive pulley

12.32a Slacken the cylinder head bolts . . .

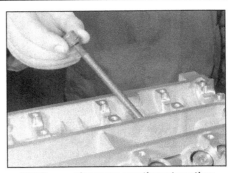

12.32b . . . then remove them together with their washers

using a strap wrench or oil filter removal tool, then unscrew the bolts and remove the pulley from the coolant pump drive flange **(see illustration)**.

28 Unbolt and remove the auxiliary drivebelt idler pulley.

29 Remove the upper timing belt cover as described in Section 7.

30 Remove the camshafts and tappets with reference to Section 11.

31 Unscrew and remove the two bolts securing the timing belt cover support bracket to the cylinder head.

32 Working in the reverse of the sequence shown in **illustration 12.43a**, slacken the ten cylinder head bolts progressively and by one turn at a time; a Torx key (TX 55 size) will be required. Remove all the bolts **(see illustrations)**.

33 Lift the cylinder head away; use assistance if possible, as it is a heavy assembly **(see illustration)**. Remove the gasket, noting the two dowels, and discard it. The gasket is manufactured from laminated steel and cannot be re-used.

Inspection

34 The mating faces of the cylinder head and cylinder block must be perfectly clean before refitting the head. Use a hard plastic or wood scraper to remove all traces of gasket and carbon; also clean the piston crowns. Take particular care during the cleaning operations, as aluminium alloy is easily damaged. Also, make sure that the carbon is not allowed to enter the oil and water passages – this is

particularly important for the lubrication system, as carbon could block the oil supply to the engine's components. Using adhesive tape and paper, seal the water, oil and bolt holes in the cylinder block. To prevent carbon entering the gap between the pistons and bores, smear a little grease in the gap. After cleaning each piston, use a small brush to remove all traces of grease and carbon from the gap, then wipe away the remainder with a clean rag.

35 Check the mating surfaces of the cylinder block and the cylinder head for nicks, deep scratches and other damage. If slight, they may be removed carefully with a file, but if excessive, renewal is necessary as it is not permissible to machine the surfaces.

36 If warpage of the cylinder head gasket surface is suspected, use a straight-edge to check it for distortion. Refer to Part E of this Chapter if necessary.

Refitting

37 Wipe clean the mating surfaces of the cylinder head and cylinder block. Check that the two locating dowels are in position in the cylinder block, and that all cylinder head bolt holes are free from oil. This is most important, as a hydraulic lock in a cylinder head bolt hole as the bolt is tightened can cause a fracture of the block casting.

38 Turn the crankshaft anti-clockwise so that pistons 1 and 4 are approximately 25 mm before TDC, in order to avoid the risk of valve/piston contact. Turn the crankshaft using a spanner on the pulley bolt.

39 Position a new gasket over the dowels on the cylinder block surface – it can only be fitted one way round **(see illustration)**.

40 As the cylinder head is such a heavy and awkward assembly to refit with manifolds, it is helpful to make up a pair of guide studs from two 10 mm (thread size) studs approximately 90 mm long, with a screwdriver slot cut in one end – two old cylinder head bolts with their heads cut off would make a good starting point. Screw these guide studs, screwdriver slot upwards to permit removal, into the bolt holes at diagonally-opposite corners of the cylinder block surface (or into those where the locating dowels are fitted); ensure that approximately 70 mm of stud protrudes above the gasket.

41 Refit the cylinder head, sliding it down the guide studs (if used) and locating it on the dowels. Unscrew the guide studs (if used) when the head is in place.

42 Fit the new cylinder head bolts carefully and screw them in by hand only until finger-tight.

43 Working progressively and in the sequence shown **(see illustrations)**, use first

12.33 Lifting the cylinder head complete with manifolds from the top of the cylinder block

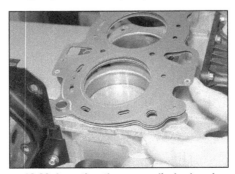

12.39 Locating the new cylinder head gasket on the cylinder block dowels

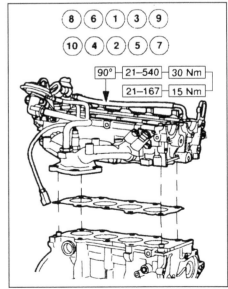

12.43a Cylinder head bolt tightening sequence

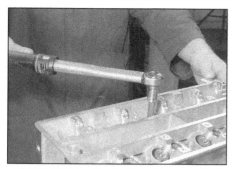

12.43b Tighten the bolts to the specified torques . . .

12.43c . . . then angle-tighten them

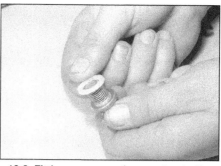

13.2 Fitting a new sealing washer to the engine oil drain plug

a torque wrench, then an ordinary socket extension bar and an angle gauge, to tighten the cylinder head bolts in the stages given in the Specifications of this Chapter. **Note:** *Once tightened correctly, following this procedure, the cylinder head bolts do not require re-checking.*

44 The remainder of refitting is a reversal of removal, noting the following points:

a) *Refit the camshafts as described in Section 11, and the timing belt as described in Section 8.*

b) *Tighten all fasteners to the specified torque, where given.*

c) *Ensure that all hoses and wiring are correctly routed, and that hose clips and wiring connectors are securely refitted.*

d) *Refill the cooling system as described in Chapter 1A.*

e) *Check all disturbed joints for signs of oil or coolant leakage once the engine has been restarted and warmed-up to normal operating temperature.*

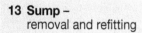

13 Sump –
removal and refitting

Removal

1 Apply the handbrake, then jack up the front of the vehicle and support it on axle stands (see *Jacking and vehicle support*).

2 Drain the engine oil, then check the drain

plug sealing washer and renew if necessary **(see illustration)**. Clean and refit the engine oil drain plug together with the washer, and tighten it to the specified torque wrench setting. Although not strictly necessary as part of the dismantling procedure, owners are advised to remove and discard the oil filter, so that it can be renewed with the oil (see Chapter 1A).

3 Unscrew the bolts securing the transmission to the sump.

4 Progressively unscrew the sump retaining bolts **(see illustration)**.

Models up to November 1999

5 Lower the sump from the crankcase, and withdraw it from under the vehicle.

6 Recover the sump gasket. Due to its laminated steel and vulcanised rubber construction, this gasket is expensive, therefore if it is in good condition it is possible to re-use it. Unlike more conventional gaskets, this gasket should release from the crankcase and sump surfaces easily.

7 While the sump is removed, take the opportunity to remove the oil pump pick-up/strainer pipe and clean it with reference to Section 14.

Models from December 1999

8 On later models, a sump gasket is not used, and sealant is used instead.

9 Unfortunately, the use of sealant makes removal of the sump more difficult. If care is taken not to damage the surfaces, the sealant can be cut around using a sharp knife.

10 On no account lever between the mating faces, as this will almost certainly damage them, resulting in leaks when finished. Ford technicians have a tool comprising a metal rod which is inserted through the sump drain hole, and a handle to pull the sump downwards.

11 While the sump is removed, take the opportunity to remove the oil pump pick-up/strainer pipe and clean it with reference to Section 14.

Refitting

12 Thoroughly clean the contact surfaces of the sump and crankcase. If necessary, use a cloth rag to clean the interior of the sump and crankcase. If the oil pump pick-up/strainer pipe was removed, fit a new gasket and refit the pipe with reference to Section 14.

Models up to November 1999

13 Apply a smear of sealant (Ford recommend WSE M4G323-A4, or equivalent) to the bottom face of the crankshaft left-hand oil seal housing. Also apply the sealant over the joints between the crankshaft left-hand oil seal and crankcase, and oil pump housing and crankcase **(see illustration)**. The sump bolts must be fitted and tightened within 10 minutes of applying the sealant.

14 Locate the gasket on the sump or crankcase **(see illustration)**, then offer the sump onto the crankcase and insert the retaining bolts finger-tight.

15 Before tightening the bolts, the sump must be accurately aligned with the end face

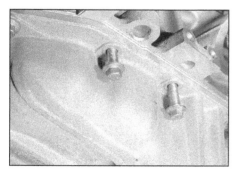

13.4 Removing the sump retaining bolts

13.13 Apply sealant to the joints between the crankcase and left-hand oil seal/oil pump housing – pre-November 1999 models

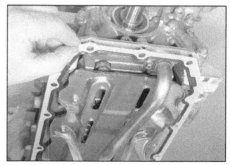

13.14 Locate the gasket on the crankcase or sump – pre-November 1999 models

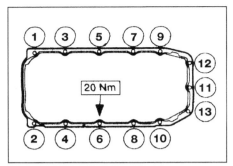

13.17 Sump bolt tightening sequence

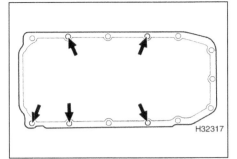

13.18 Sump alignment stud positions (arrowed) – December 1999 models onward

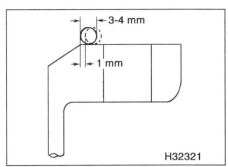

13.19 Showing how the bead of sealant is to be applied to the sump mating surface – December 1999 models onward

of the cylinder block. If the transmission is still attached to the engine, this presents no problem, provided that the sump-to-transmission bolts are tightened before the sump bolts. However, if the engine is detached from the transmission (eg, for overhaul), a straight-edge must be used for alignment.

16 Where possible, insert the sump-to-transmission bolts and tighten them to the specified torque.

17 Once the sump is correctly aligned, progressively tighten the sump-to-crankcase bolts to the specified torque using the specified sequence **(see illustration)**.

Models from December 1999

18 Ford state that, to refit the sump, five M8x20 studs must be screwed into the base of the engine, in the specified positions **(see**

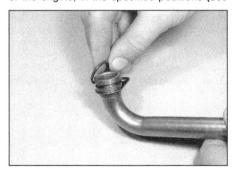

14.6 Removing the O-ring from the oil pump pick-up/strainer pipe

illustration). This not only helps to align the sump, ensuring that the bead of sealant is not displaced as the sump is fitted, but also ensures that the sealant does not enter the blind holes. Cut a slot across the end of each stud, to make removal easier when the sump is in place.

19 Apply a 3 to 4 mm diameter bead of sealant (Ford recommend WSE M4G323-A4, or equivalent) to the sump pan, to the inside of the bolt holes **(see illustration)**. The sump bolts must be fitted and tightened within 10 minutes of applying the sealant.

20 Offer the sump up into position over the studs, and fully refit the remaining bolts by hand. Unscrew the studs, and refit the sump bolts in their place.

21 Insert the sump-to-transmission bolts and tighten them to the specified torque.

22 The sump-to-crankcase bolts are tightened in the same sequence as for earlier models **(refer to illustration 13.17)**, but in two stages. First, following the sequence, tighten all the sump bolts to half the specified torque, then go around again in sequence, and tighten them fully to the specified torque.

All models

23 Lower the car to the ground, and where necessary, fit a new oil filter. To be on the safe side, wait a further 30 minutes for the sealant to cure before filling the sump with fresh oil, as described in Chapter 1A.

24 Finally start the engine and check for signs of oil leaks.

14 Oil pump – removal, inspection and refitting

Removal

1 Remove the timing belt as described in Section 8.

2 Remove the crankshaft sprocket as described in Section 9.

3 Refit the right-hand engine mounting lower and upper brackets and tighten the mounting bolts/nuts to their specified torques. Remove the trolley jack from under the sump.

4 Remove the sump and gasket as described in Section 13.

5 Unscrew the bolts securing the oil pump pick-up/strainer pipe to the baffle plate/main bearing cap.

6 Unscrew the bolt securing the oil pump pick-up/strainer pipe to the oil pump, then withdraw the pipe and recover the sealing O-ring **(see illustration)**. Discard the O-ring.

7 Unscrew the bolts securing the oil pump to the cylinder block/crankcase **(see illustration)**. Withdraw the pump over the nose of the crankshaft.

8 Recover then discard the gasket **(see illustration)**.

9 Support the oil pump on wooden blocks, then use a screwdriver to hook or drive out the crankshaft right-hand oil seal.

10 If necessary, unbolt and remove the baffle plate from the main bearing cap/ladder **(see illustration)**. Thoroughly clean all

14.7 Removing the oil pump mounting bolts

14.8 Removing the oil pump gasket

14.10 Unbolting the baffle plate from the main bearing cap/ladder

components, particularly the mating surfaces of the pump, the sump, and the cylinder block/crankcase.

Inspection

11 It is not possible to obtain individual components of the oil pump, furthermore, there are no torque settings available for tightening the pump cover plate bolts. However, the following procedure is provided for owners wishing to dismantle the oil pump for examination.

12 Unscrew the screws, and remove the pump cover plate; noting any identification marks on the rotors, withdraw the rotors.

13 Inspect the rotors for obvious signs of wear or damage, and renew if necessary; if either rotor, the pump body, or its cover plate are scored or damaged, the complete oil pump assembly must be renewed.

14 The oil pressure relief valve can be dismantled as follows.

15 Unscrew the threaded plug, and recover the valve spring and plunger. If the plug's sealing O-ring is worn or damaged, a new one must be obtained, to be fitted on reassembly.

16 Reassembly is the reverse of the dismantling procedure; ensure the spring and valve are refitted the correct way round, and tighten the threaded plug securely.

Refitting

17 If removed, refit the oil baffle plate to the crankcase and tighten the bolts.

18 The oil pump must be primed on installation, by pouring clean engine oil into it, and rotating its inner rotor a few turns.

19 Use a little grease to stick the new gasket in place on the cylinder block/crankcase.

20 Offer the oil pump over the nose of the crankshaft and turn the inner rotor as necessary to align its flats with the flats on the crankshaft. Locate the pump on the dowels, then insert the retaining bolts and progressively tighten them to the specified torque.

21 Fit a new crankshaft right-hand oil seal (see Section 15).

22 Locate a new O-ring (dipped in oil) on the pick-up/strainer pipe, then locate the pipe in

the oil pump and insert the retaining bolts. Insert the bolts retaining the pipe on the baffle plate/main bearing cap. Tighten the bolts to the specified torque.

23 Refit the sump as described in Section 13.

24 Support the weight of the engine with a trolley jack and wood block beneath the sump, then unscrew the nuts and bolts and remove the right-hand engine mounting upper and lower brackets.

25 Refit the crankshaft sprocket with reference to Section 9.

26 Refit the timing belt with reference to Section 8.

---

15 Crankshaft oil seals – renewal

Oil pump housing oil seal

1 Remove the timing belt as described in Section 8.

2 Remove the crankshaft sprocket as described in Section 9.

3 As a safety precaution, refit the right-hand engine mounting lower and upper brackets and tighten the mounting bolts/nuts.

4 Note the fitted depth of the oil seal as a guide for fitting the new one.

5 Using a screwdriver, prise the old oil seal from the oil pump housing. Take care not to damage the seal contact surface on the nose of the crankshaft or the seating in the housing.

6 Wipe clean the seating and the nose of the crankshaft.

7 Dip the new oil seal in fresh oil, then locate it over the crankshaft and into the oil pump housing. Make sure that the closed end of the oil seal faces outwards **(see illustration)**.

8 Using a socket or length of metal tubing, drive the oil seal squarely into position to the previously noted depth. The Ford installation tool (21-171) is used together with an old crankshaft pulley bolt to press the oil seal into position. The same idea may be used with metal tubing and a large washer – do not use a new crankshaft pulley bolt, as it is only

permissible to use the bolt once. With the oil seal in position, wipe away any excess oil.

9 Support the weight of the engine with a trolley jack and wood block beneath the sump, then unscrew the nuts and bolts and remove the right-hand engine mounting upper and lower brackets.

10 Refit the crankshaft sprocket with reference to Section 9.

11 Refit the timing belt with reference to Section 8.

Flywheel end oil seal

12 Remove the transmission (see the relevant Part of Chapter 7).

13 On manual transmission models remove the clutch as described in Chapter 6.

14 Remove the flywheel/driveplate as described in Section 16.

15 Unscrew the retaining bolts and withdraw the left-hand oil seal housing over the end of the crankshaft. Note that the seal and housing are manufactured as one unit incorporating a vulcanised gasket. It is not possible to obtain the seal separately.

16 Clean the housing contact surface on the cylinder block and the end of the crankshaft.

17 The new oil seal housing is supplied complete with a fitting ring which ensures that the oil seal lips are correctly located on the crankshaft.

18 Smear the end of the crankshaft with fresh engine oil, then locate the oil seal housing with fitting ring over the end of the crankshaft. Press the housing into position noting that the centre bolt holes are formed into locating dowels **(see illustration)**.

19 Insert the retaining bolts and progressively tighten them to the specified torque. Wipe away any surplus oil.

20 Remove the fitting ring and check that the oil seal lips are correctly located **(see illustration)**.

21 Refit the flywheel/driveplate as described in Section 16.

22 On manual transmission models refit the clutch as described in Chapter 6.

23 Refit the transmission (see the relevant Part of Chapter 7).

15.7 Locating the new right-hand oil seal over the crankshaft

15.18 Locating the new left-hand oil seal housing (complete with fitting ring) over the rear of the crankshaft

15.20 With the oil seal housing bolted in position, remove the fitting ring

16.3 Home-made tool for holding the flywheel stationary while loosening the bolts

16.4 Removing the flywheel retaining bolts (note the location dowel in the crankshaft)

16.7 Crankshaft speed/position sensor mounting and retaining bolt

16 Flywheel/driveplate – removal, inspection and refitting

Removal

1 Remove the transmission (see the relevant Part of Chapter 7).
2 On manual transmission models remove the clutch as described in Chapter 6.
3 Hold the flywheel/driveplate stationary using one of the following methods. If an assistant is available, insert one of the transmission mounting bolts into the cylinder block and have the assistant engage a wide-bladed screwdriver with the starter ring gear teeth while the bolts are loosened. Alternatively, a piece of angle-iron can be engaged with the ring gear and located against the transmission mounting bolt. A further method is to fabricate a piece of flat metal bar with a pointed end to engage the ring gear – fit the tool to the transmission bolt and use washers and packing to align it with the ring gear, then tighten the bolt to hold it in position (see illustration).
4 Unscrew and remove the retaining bolts, then lift the flywheel/driveplate off of the locating dowel on the crankshaft (see illustration).

Inspection

5 Clean the flywheel/driveplate to remove grease and oil. Inspect the surface for cracks, rivet grooves, burned areas and score marks. Light scoring can be removed with emery cloth. Check for cracked and broken ring gear teeth. Lay the flywheel/driveplate on a flat surface, and use a straight-edge to check for warpage.
6 Clean and inspect the mating surfaces of the flywheel/driveplate and the crankshaft. If the crankshaft left-hand oil seal is leaking, renew it (see Section 15) before refitting the flywheel/driveplate.
7 While the flywheel/driveplate is removed, clean carefully its inner face, particularly the recesses which serve as the reference points for the crankshaft speed/position sensor. Clean the sensor's tip, and check that the

sensor is securely fastened. The sensor mounting may be removed if necessary by first removing the sensor, then unscrewing the bolt and withdrawing the mounting from the cylinder block (see illustration).

Refitting

8 Make sure that the mating faces of the flywheel/driveplate and crankshaft are clean, then locate the flywheel/driveplate on the crankshaft and engage it with the locating dowel.
9 Insert the retaining bolts finger-tight.
10 Lock the flywheel/driveplate (see paragraph 3), then tighten the bolts in a diagonal sequence in the two Stages given in the Specifications.
11 On manual transmission models refit the clutch with reference to Chapter 6.
12 Refit the transmission (see the relevant Part of Chapter 7).

17 Engine/transmission mountings – inspection and renewal

Inspection

1 The engine/transmission mountings seldom require attention, but broken or deteriorated mountings should be renewed immediately, or the added strain placed on the driveline components may cause damage or wear.
2 During the check, the engine/transmission must be raised slightly, to remove its weight from the mountings.
3 Apply the handbrake, then jack up the front of the vehicle and support it on axle stands (see *Jacking and vehicle support*). Remove the engine undershield where fitted. Position a jack under the sump, with a large block of wood between the jack head and the sump, then carefully raise the engine/transmission just enough to take the weight off the mountings.
4 Check the mountings to see if the rubber is cracked, hardened or separated from the metal components. Sometimes, the rubber will split right down the centre.
5 Check for relative movement between each

mounting's brackets and the engine/transmission or body (use a large screwdriver or lever to attempt to move the mountings). If movement is noted, lower the engine and check the mounting nuts and bolts for tightness.

Renewal

6 The engine mountings can be removed if the weight of the engine/transmission is supported by one of the following alternative methods.
7 Either support the weight of the assembly from underneath using a jack and a suitable piece of wood between the jack and the sump (to prevent damage), or from above by attaching a hoist to the engine. A third method is to use a suitable support bar with end pieces which will engage in the water channel each side of the bonnet lid aperture. Using an adjustable hook and chain connected to the engine, the weight of the engine and transmission can then be taken from the mountings.
8 Once the weight of the engine and transmission is suitably supported, any of the mountings can be unbolted and removed.
9 To remove the right-hand engine mounting, unscrew the nuts and remove the upper bracket, then unscrew the bolts and remove the lower bracket from the cylinder head. Unbolt the insulator from the right-hand side of the engine compartment (see illustration).
10 To remove the left-hand mounting first remove the battery and battery tray as described in Chapter 5A, then loosen the clips

17.9 Right-hand engine mounting insulator on the inner wing panel

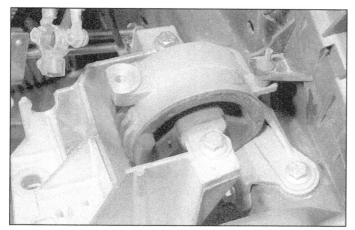

17.10 Left-hand engine/transmission mounting

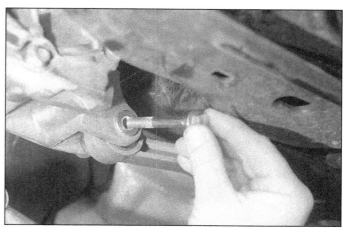

17.11 Removing a through-bolt from the rear engine mounting/link

and remove the air inlet duct from between the air mass air flow sensor on the air cleaner and the throttle body housing. Unscrew the mounting nuts from the left-hand engine mounting, then unscrew the bolts and remove the upper bracket. Unscrew the bolts and remove the insulator from the left-hand side of the engine compartment **(see illustration)**.

11 To remove the rear engine mounting/link, apply the handbrake, then jack up the front of the vehicle and support it on axle stands (see *Jacking and vehicle support*). Unscrew the through-bolts and remove the rear engine mounting link from the bracket on the transmission and from the bracket on the underbody **(see illustration)**. Hold the engine stationary while the bolts are being removed since the link will be under tension.

12 Refitting of all mountings is a reversal of the removal procedure. Do not fully tighten the mounting nuts/bolts until all of the mountings are in position. Check that the mounting rubbers do not twist or distort as the mounting bolts and nuts are tightened to their specified torques.

Notes

Chapter 2 Part C:
Endura-DE diesel engine in-car repair procedures

Contents

Auxiliary shaft oil seal – renewal 10
Camshaft and tappets – removal, inspection and refitting 11
Camshaft oil seal – renewal 9
Compression and leakdown tests – description and interpretation . 2
Crankshaft oil seals – renewal 15
Crankshaft pulley/vibration damper – removal and refitting 5
Cylinder head – dismantling and overhaul ....See Chapter 2E
Cylinder head – removal, inspection and refitting 12
Engine oil and filter renewal ....See Chapter 1B
Engine oil level check ....See Weekly Checks
Engine/transmission mountings – inspection and renewal 17

Flywheel – removal, inspection and refitting 16
General information 1
Oil pump – removal, inspection and refitting 14
Sump – removal and refitting 13
Timing belt and injection pump drivebelt –
　removal, inspection and refitting 7
Timing belt covers – removal and refitting 6
Timing belt/drivebelt tensioners and sprockets –
　removal, inspection and refitting 8
Top Dead Centre (TDC) for No 1 piston – locating 3
Valve clearances – checking and adjustment 4

Degrees of difficulty

Easy, suitable for novice with little experience	**Fairly easy,** suitable for beginner with some experience	**Fairly difficult,** suitable for competent DIY mechanic	**Difficult,** suitable for experienced DIY mechanic	**Very difficult,** suitable for expert DIY or professional

Specifications

General

Engine type	Four-cylinder in-line, four-stroke, overhead camshaft, compression ignition, normally-aspirated
Designation	Endura-DE
Engine code	RTK or RTJ
Capacity	1753 cc
Bore	82.5 mm
Stroke	82.0 mm
Compression ratio	21.5:1
Firing order	1-3-4-2 (No 1 cylinder at timing belt end)
Direction of crankshaft rotation	Clockwise (seen from right-hand side of vehicle)
Compression pressure (at starter motor cranking speed)	28 to 34 bar
Maximum power (DIN)	44 kW (60 PS) @ 4800 rpm
Maximum torque (DIN)	105 Nm (78 lbf ft) @ 2500 rpm

Cylinder block

Cylinder bore diameter:

Class A	82.500 to 82.515 mm
Class B	82.515 to 82.530 mm
Class C	82.660 to 82.675 mm
Class D	82.675 to 82.690 mm
Class E (first rebore)	83.000 to 83.015 mm
Class F (second rebore)	83.500 to 83.515 mm

Crankshaft

Main bearing journal diameter:	
Standard	53.970 to 53.990 mm
Undersize (0.25 mm)	53.720 to 53.740 mm
Undersize (0.50 mm)	53.470 to 53.490 mm
Main bearing running clearance	0.025 to 0.085 mm
Big-end bearing journal diameter:	
Standard	48.970 to 48.990 mm
Undersize (0.25 mm)	48.720 to 48.740 mm
Undersize (0.50 mm)	48.470 to 48.490 mm
Big-end bearing running clearance	0.025 to 0.085 mm
Crankshaft endfloat	0.1436 to 0.3688 mm
Connecting rod to crank web axial clearance	0.125 to 0.325 mm
Torque to rotate fitted crankshaft (without connecting rods or pistons)	10 Nm (7 lbf ft) max

Connecting rods

Big-end bore diameter	52.000 to 52.020 mm
Small-end bore diameter (with bush)	26.012 to 26.020 mm

Pistons

Diameter (measured at 90° to gudgeon pin bore):	
Class A	82.460 to 82.475 mm
Class B	82.475 to 82.490 mm
Class C	82.621 to 82.639 mm
Class D	82.636 to 82.654 mm
Class E (first rebore)	82.961 to 82.979 mm
Class F (second rebore)	83.461 to 83.479 mm
Clearance in bore (new)	0.025 to 0.055 mm
Piston protrusion at TDC	0.500 to 0.840 mm
Gudgeon pin diameter	25.96 to 26.00 mm

Piston rings

Clearance in groove:	
Top compression	0.090 to 0.122 mm
Second compression	0.050 to 0.082 mm
Oil control	0.030 to 0.062 mm
End gap (fitted):	
Top compression	0.30 to 0.32 mm
Second compression	0.30 to 0.32 mm
Oil control	0.250 to 0.580 mm

Camshaft

Endfloat	0.100 to 0.240 mm
Bearing journal diameter	27.960 to 27.980 mm
Bearing running clearance	0.020 to 0.079 mm

Valve timing

Inlet opens	6° BTDC
Inlet closes	32° ABDC
Exhaust opens	57° BBDC
Exhaust closes	7° ATDC

Valves

Valve clearances (cold):	
Inlet	0.285 to 0.415 mm
Exhaust	0.435 to 0.565 mm
Tappet shim thicknesses available	3.00 to 4.75 mm in increments of 0.05 mm
Valve spring free length	43 mm approx.

Cylinder head gasket

Selection according to piston protrusion:	
0.500 to 0.680 mm	1.36 mm thick (2 tooth marks)
0.681 to 0.740 mm	1.42 mm thick (3 tooth marks)
0.741 to 0.840 mm	1.52 mm thick (4 tooth marks)

Cylinder head

Distortion limit	0.08 mm overall
Swirl chamber protrusion	0.000 to 0.061 mm
Valve tappet bore diameter:	
Standard	35.000 to 35.030 mm
Oversize	35.500 to 35.530 mm
Valve guide bore diameter:	
Standard	8.000 to 8.025 mm
First oversize	8.263 to 8.288 mm
Second oversize	8.463 to 8.488 mm

Lubrication system

Oil pressure:	
At 750 rpm	0.75 bar
At 2000 rpm	1.50 bars
Oil pressure relief valve setting	2.0 to 4.0 bars
Oil pump inner-to-outer rotor maximum clearance	0.174 mm

Torque wrench settings

	Nm	lbf ft
Auxiliary drivebelt tensioner clamp bolt	6	4
Auxiliary shaft oil seal housing	23	17
Auxiliary shaft sprocket	45	33
Auxiliary shaft thrustplate bolts	9	7
Big-end bearing cap bolts:		
Stage 1	25	18
Stage 2	Angle-tighten a further 60°	
Stage 3	Angle-tighten a further 20°	
Camshaft bearing caps	20	15
Camshaft sprocket (engines with standard timing belt tensioner):		
Sprocket to flange	9	7
Flange to camshaft	30	22
Camshaft sprocket (engines with automatic timing belt tensioner):		
M8 bolt	35	26
M10 bolt	48	35
Crankshaft left-hand oil seal housing	20	15
Crankshaft position sensor bracket	14	10
Crankshaft pulley/vibration damper to sprocket flange	35	26
Crankshaft sprocket flange bolt (oiled)*:		
Stage 1	150	111
Stage 2	**Loosen** by 90°	
Stage 3	120	88
Stage 4	Angle-tighten a further 60°	
Cylinder head bolts (M12 and Torx T70 head)*:		
Stage 1	10	7
Stage 2	100	74
Stage 3 (after waiting 3 minutes):		
a)	**Loosen** No 1 bolt 180°	
b)	Tighten No 1 bolt to:	
	70	52
c)	Angle tighten No 1 bolt a further 120°	
Stage 4	Repeat stage three with each of the remaining bolts in sequence	
Cylinder head cover	5	4
Engine lifting eye	23	17
Engine/transmission mountings:		
Engine mounting bracket-to-cylinder block	33	24
Front engine mounting bracket:		
Outer nut	120	89
Inner nut	70	52
Front engine mounting reinforcement bracket	50	37
Rear engine mounting bracket bolts	50	37
Rear engine mounting bracket nuts	70	52
Rear engine mounting link to cylinder block	50	37
Rear engine mounting link to front subframe	70	52
Right-hand engine mounting bracket	45	33
Flywheel bolts*:		
Stage 1	18	13
Stage 2	Angle-tighten a further 45°	
Stage 3	Angle-tighten a further 45°	

Torque wrench settings (continued)	Nm	lbf ft
Front plate	24	18
Main bearing cap bolts:		
Stage 1	27	20
Stage 2	Angle-tighten a further 75°	
Oil baffle	20	15
Oil dipstick tube bracket	10	7
Oil inlet pipe bracket	22	16
Oil pressure switch	20	15
Oil pump	23	17
Retaining plate for oil separator, fuel filter, and fuel heater	20	15
Sump	11	8
TDC pin blanking plug	24	18
Timing belt adjusting eccentric (engines with automatic tensioner)	45	33
Timing belt covers:		
Rear cover	24	18
Side timing cover	8	6
Upper and lower covers	7	5
Timing belt idler sprocket (engines with standard tensioner)	45	33
Timing belt tensioner pulley	50	37
Timing belt tensioner to cylinder head	9	7

* Use new fasteners

1 General information

How to use this Chapter

This Part of Chapter 2 is devoted to in-car repair procedures. All procedures concerning engine removal and refitting, and engine block/cylinder head overhaul can be found in Chapter 2E.

Refer to the *Vehicle identification numbers* Section at the end of this manual for details of engine code locations.

Most of the operations included in Chapter 2C are based on the assumption that the engine is still installed in the car. Therefore, if this information is being used during a complete engine overhaul, with the engine already removed, many of the steps included here will not apply.

Engine description

The Endura-DE 1.8 litre diesel engine is of four-cylinder overhead camshaft design. The engine is mounted transversely, in line with the transmission. Both the cylinder block and the cylinder head are of cast iron.

The oil pump is mounted externally, and is driven by the auxiliary shaft.

The crankshaft runs in five main bearings, of the usual shell type. Endfloat is controlled by separate thrustwashers at the centre bearing. The crankshaft sprocket incorporates a flange for the crankshaft pulley/vibration damper which drives the alternator, power steering pump and air conditioning compressor.

Pistons, gudgeon pins and connecting rods are carefully selected to be of matching weight. The connecting rods are also graded by length. The gudgeon pins are fully floating in the pistons and rods and are retained by circlips. The big-ends of the rods are horizontally split and carry shell bearings.

Crankcase ventilation is by means of a hose which connects the camshaft cover to the inlet manifold. A non-return valve prevents crankcase pressurisation taking place. Another hose connects the camshaft cover to the lower crankcase.

Two toothed drivebelts (timing belts) are fitted, one to drive the fuel injection pump and the other to drive the camshaft, the oil pump auxiliary shaft and the coolant pump. The valves are operated by bucket tappets. Valve clearance adjustment is by means of selective shims. The cam lobes bear directly on the shims and tappets, which in turn bear directly on the valves. The camshaft runs in five renewable shell bearings.

Timing belt tensioner

Two different camshaft timing belt tensioner arrangements are used on the Endura-DE engine. On early models, a spring-loaded automatic tensioner is used in conjunction with a fixed idler sprocket. On later models, a modified automatic tensioner is used together with an adjustment eccentric. For identification purposes, the early arrangement is referred to as a standard timing belt tensioner and the later arrangement as an automatic timing belt tensioner.

Repair operations possible with the engine in the vehicle

The following operations can be carried out without having to remove the engine from the vehicle:

a) *Timing belt and injection pump drivebelt – renewal.*
b) *Timing belt/drivebelt tensioners and sprockets – removal and refitting.*
c) *Camshaft oil seal – renewal.*
d) *Camshafts and tappets – removal and refitting.*
e) *Auxiliary shaft oil seal – renewal*
f) *Cylinder head – removal and refitting.*
g) *Sump – removal and refitting.*
h) *Crankshaft oil seals – renewal.*
i) *Oil pump – removal and refitting.*
j) *Flywheel – removal and refitting.*
k) *Engine/transmission mountings – removal and refitting.*

Note: *It is possible to remove the pistons and connecting rods (after removing the cylinder head and sump) without removing the engine. However, this is not recommended. Work of this nature is more easily and thoroughly completed with the engine on the bench, as described in Chapter 2E.*

2 Compression and leakdown tests – description and interpretation

Compression test

Note: *A compression tester specifically designed for diesel engines must be used for this test.*

1 When engine performance is down, or if misfiring occurs which cannot be attributed to a fault in the fuel system, a compression test can provide diagnostic clues as to the engine's condition. If the test is performed regularly it can give warning of trouble before any other symptoms become apparent.

2 A compression tester specifically intended for diesel engines must be used, because of the higher pressures involved. The tester is connected to an adapter which screws into the glow plug or injector hole. It is unlikely to be worthwhile buying such a tester for occasional use, but it may be possible to borrow or hire one – if not, have the test performed by a garage.

3 Unless specific instructions to the contrary are supplied with the tester, observe the following points:

  a) *The battery must be in a good state of charge, the air filter must be clean and the engine should be at normal operating temperature.*

  b) *All the injectors or glow plugs should be removed before starting the test. If removing the injectors, also remove the fire seal washers (which must be renewed when the injectors are refitted – see Chapter 4B), otherwise they may be blown out.*

  c) *It is advisable to disconnect the stop solenoid on the pump to reduce the amount of fuel discharged as the engine is cranked.*

4 There is no need to hold the accelerator pedal down during the test because the diesel engine air inlet is not throttled.

5 The actual compression pressures measured are not so important as the balance between cylinders. Values are given in the Specifications.

6 The cause of poor compression is less easy to establish on a diesel engine than on a petrol one. The effect of introducing oil into the cylinders ('wet' testing) is not conclusive, because there is a risk that the oil will sit in the swirl chamber or in the recess on the piston crown instead of passing to the rings. However, the following can be used as a rough guide to diagnosis.

7 All cylinders should produce very similar pressures. Note that the compression should build-up quickly in a healthy engine; low compression on the first stroke, followed by gradually increasing pressure on successive strokes, indicates worn piston rings. A low compression reading on the first stroke, which does not build-up during successive strokes, indicates leaking valves or a blown head gasket (a cracked head could also be the cause).

8 A low reading from two adjacent cylinders is almost certainly due to the head gasket having blown between them.

Leakdown test

9 A leakdown test measures the rate at which compressed air fed into the cylinder is lost. It is an alternative to a compression test and in many ways it is better, since the escaping air provides easy identification of where pressure loss is occurring (piston rings, valves or head gasket).

10 The equipment needed for leakdown testing is unlikely to be available to the home mechanic. If poor compression is suspected, have the test performed by a suitably-equipped garage.

3 Top Dead Centre (TDC) for No 1 piston – locating

Note: *A timing pin and, on engines with an automatic tensioner, a camshaft setting bar are required for this procedure (see text).*

Note: *Refer to Section 1 to identify the standard/automatic timing belt tensioner.*

1 Top dead centre (TDC) is the highest point of the cylinder that each piston reaches as the crankshaft turns. Each piston reaches its TDC position at the end of its compression stroke, and then again at the end of its exhaust stroke. For the purpose of engine timing, TDC on the compression stroke for No 1 piston is used. No 1 cylinder is at the timing belt end of the engine. Proceed as follows.

2 Disconnect the battery negative (earth) lead (refer to Chapter 5A).

3 Apply the handbrake, then jack up the front of the vehicle and support it on axle stands (see *Jacking and vehicle support*). If the engine is to be turned using the right-hand front roadwheel with 4th gear engaged, it is only necessary to raise the right-hand front roadwheel off the ground.

4 Where necessary, remove the engine undershield, then remove the auxiliary drivebelt lower cover for access to the crankshaft pulley and bolt.

5 Remove the upper timing belt cover as described in Section 6.

6 Remove the glow plugs as described in Chapter 5C. This will enable the engine to be turned easily.

Automatic belt tensioner

7 Disconnect the crankcase ventilation hoses.

8 Unbolt and remove the cylinder head cover, and remove the gasket.

3.9 Camshaft rear offset slot (arrowed)

9 The piston of No 1 cylinder must now be positioned just before top dead centre (TDC). To do this, have an assistant turn the crankshaft until the slot in the left-hand end of the camshaft is parallel with the upper surface of the cylinder head. Note that the slot is slightly offset so make sure that the lower edges of the slots are aligned with the cylinder head. Turn the crankshaft slightly anti-clockwise from this position (viewed from the right-hand end of the engine) **(see illustration)**.

Standard belt tensioner

10 The piston of No 1 cylinder must now be positioned just before top dead centre (TDC). To do this, have an assistant turn the crankshaft until the timing hole in the camshaft sprocket is aligned with the corresponding hole in the cylinder head. Turn the crankshaft slightly anti-clockwise from this position (viewed from the right-hand end of the engine).

All engines

11 Remove the alternator as described in Chapter 5A, then unscrew the blanking plug from the right-hand front side of the engine cylinder block. Ford timing pin 21-104 must now be inserted and tightened into the hole. If necessary, a home-made pin can be made from an M10 bolt with a dimension of 47.5 mm from beneath its head to the tip, however it will be necessary to grind and slot the head to allow it to be inserted **(see illustrations)**.

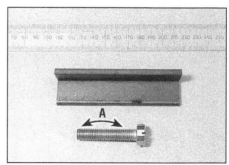

3.11c Home-made tools for setting the valve timing

A Head of bolt and area indicated will need grinding to allow the timing pin to be inserted

3.11a Remove the blanking plug from the cylinder block . . .

3.11b . . . and insert the TDC timing pin (arrowed)

12 With the timing pin in position, turn the crankshaft slowly clockwise until the specially machined surface on the crank web just touches the timing pin. No 1 piston is now at TDC on its compression stroke.

13 On engines with an automatic tensioner, it should now be possible to insert the camshaft setting bar into the slot in the left-hand end of the camshaft.

14 On engines with a standard tensioner, it should now be possible to insert Ford timing pin 23-019 through the camshaft sprocket and into the cylinder head hole.

15 Insert Ford timing pin 23-029 (or suitable drill bit) through the injection pump sprocket timing hole into the housing hole **(see illustration)**.

16 If any of the timing pins cannot be fitted, reset the valve timing as described in Section 7.

17 Once the work requiring the TDC setting has been completed, remove the timing pins and where applicable the camshaft setting bar, then refit the blanking plug. Refit all removed components referring to the relevant Chapters.

4 Valve clearances – checking and adjustment

Checking

1 Disconnect the two crankcase ventilation hoses from the left-hand end of the cylinder head cover.

2 Unscrew the mounting bolts and withdraw the cylinder head cover. Check the gasket and if necessary remove it for renewal **(see illustrations)**.

3 Unscrew the nuts and remove the baffle plate from the camshaft bearing caps **(see illustration)**. Temporarily refit and tighten the removed nuts to their specified torque.

4 During the following procedure, the crankshaft must be turned in order to position

3.15 Drill bit used as a timing pin inserted through the injection pump sprocket

the peaks of the camshaft lobes away from the valves. To do this, either turn the crankshaft on the pulley bolt or alternatively raise the front right-hand corner of the vehicle, engage 4th gear, and turn the front roadwheel. Access to the pulley bolt is gained by jacking up the front of the vehicle and supporting on axle stands, then removing the pulley lower cover.

5 If desired, to enable the crankshaft to be turned more easily, remove the glow plugs (Chapter 5C) or the fuel injectors (Chapter 4B).

6 Draw the valve positions on a piece of paper, numbering them 1 to 8 from the timing end of the engine. Identify them as inlet or exhaust (ie, 1I, 2E, 3I, 4E, 5I, 6E, 7I, 8E).

7 Turn the crankshaft until the valves of No 4 cylinder (flywheel end) are 'rocking'. The exhaust valve will be closing and the inlet valve will be opening. The piston of No 1 cylinder will be at the top of its compression stroke, with both valves fully closed. The clearances for both valves of No 1 cylinder may be checked at the same time.

8 Insert a feeler blade of the correct thickness (see Specifications) between the cam lobe and the shim on the top of the tappet bucket, and check that it is a firm sliding fit **(see illustration)**. If it is not, use the feeler blades to ascertain the exact clearance, and record this for use when calculating the new shim thickness required. Note that the inlet and

4.2a Removing the cylinder head cover . . .

4.2b . . . and gasket

exhaust valve clearances are different, so it is important that you know which valve clearance you are checking.

9 With No 1 cylinder valve clearances checked, turn the engine through half a turn so that No 2 valves are 'rocking', then check the valve clearances of No 3 cylinder in the same way. Similarly check the valve clearances of No 4 cylinder with No 1 valves 'rocking' and No 2 cylinder with No 3 valves 'rocking'.

Adjustment

10 If adjustment is required, turn the engine in the normal direction of rotation through approximately 90°, to bring the pistons to

4.3 Unscrew the four nuts (arrowed) and remove the oil baffle plate

4.8 Measuring a valve clearance with a feeler blade

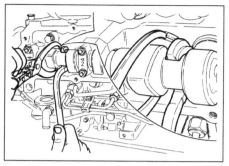

4.10a Maker's tools for tappet depression and shim extraction

mid-stroke. If this is not done, the pistons at TDC will prevent the tappets being depressed, and damage may result. Depress the tappets and then either shim can be withdrawn if the peak of the cam does not prevent access. The Ford tools for this operation are Nos 21-106 and 21-107, but with care and patience a C-spanner or screwdriver can be used to depress the tappet and the shim can be flicked out with a small screwdriver **(see illustrations)**.

11 If the valve clearance was too small, a thinner shim must be fitted. If the clearance was too large, a thicker shim must be fitted. The thickness of the shim (in mm) is engraved on the side facing away from the camshaft **(see illustration)**. If the marking is missing or illegible, a micrometer will be needed to establish shim thickness.

12 When the shim thickness and the valve clearance are known, the required thickness of the new shim can be calculated as follows: *All measurements in mm.*

Sample calculation – clearance too small

Desired clearance (A)	$= 0.50$
Measured clearance (B)	$= 0.35$
Shim thickness found (C)	$= 3.95$
Shim thickness reqd. (D)	$= C+B-A$
	$= 3.80$

Sample calculation – clearance too large

Desired clearance (A)	$= 0.35$
Measured clearance (B)	$= 0.40$
Shim thickness found (C)	$= 4.05$
Shim thickness reqd. (D)	$= C+B-A$
	$= 4.10$

13 With the correct shim fitted, release the tappet depressing tool. Turn the engine back so that the cam lobes are again pointing

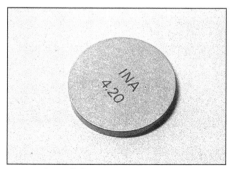

4.11 Shim thickness marking

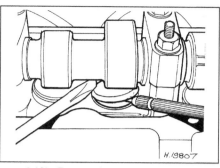

4.10b Depressing a tappet with a screwdriver and removing a shim

upwards and check that the clearance is now correct.

14 Repeat the process for the remaining valves, turning the engine each time to bring a pair of cam lobes upwards.

15 It will be helpful for future adjustment if a record is kept of the thickness of shim fitted at each position. The shims required can be purchased in advance once the clearances and the existing shim thicknesses are known.

16 It is permissible to interchange shims between tappets to achieve the correct clearances but it is not advisable to turn the camshaft with any shims removed, since there is a risk that the cam lobe will jam in the empty tappet.

17 When all the clearances are correct, refit the fuel injectors or glow plugs (Chapter 4B or 5C), then refit the oil baffle plate and tighten the nuts to the specified torque. Refit the cylinder head cover together with a new gasket and tighten the bolts to the specified torque.

18 Reconnect the crankcase ventilation hoses to the cylinder head cover.

5 Crankshaft pulley/vibration damper – removal and refitting

Removal

1 Disconnect the battery negative (earth) lead (see Chapter 5A).

2 Apply the handbrake, then jack up the front of the vehicle and support it on axle stands (see *Jacking and vehicle support*). Remove the engine undershield if fitted.

3 Remove the right-hand front roadwheel, then where necessary, undo the retaining screws and remove the wheelarch liner.

4 Unbolt and remove the auxiliary drivebelt lower cover for access to the crankshaft pulley.

5 Remove the auxiliary drivebelt as described in Chapter 1B.

6 Unscrew the bolts and remove the crankshaft pulley/vibration damper from the end of the crankshaft. To hold the crankshaft stationary while loosening the bolts, have an assistant engage 4th gear and depress the footbrake pedal, or alternatively remove the starter motor and have an assistant insert a

wide-bladed screwdriver in the teeth of the starter ring gear.

Refitting

7 Refitting is a reversal of removal, but tighten the mounting bolts to the specified torque.

6 Timing belt covers – removal and refitting

Removal

1 Apply the handbrake, then jack up the front of the vehicle and support it on axle stands (see *Jacking and vehicle support*). Where fitted, remove the engine undershield. Remove the right-hand front roadwheel.

2 The right-hand engine mounting brackets must now be removed for access to the timing belt covers. First support the weight of the engine using a trolley jack and block of wood beneath the sump. Alternatively, use a support bar across the top of the engine resting in the front wing water drain channels. With the engine supported, unscrew the bolts and remove the reinforcement bracket, then unscrew the nuts and remove the upper bracket. Make sure the engine is adequately supported.

3 Unscrew the single retaining bolt and release the clip then remove the upper timing belt cover.

4 Unscrew the bolts retaining the top of the lower timing belt cover. If necessary, slightly raise the engine for access to the bolts.

5 Unbolt and remove the auxiliary drivebelt lower cover for access to the crankshaft pulley.

6 Remove the auxiliary drivebelt as described in Chapter 1B.

7 Unscrew the bolts and remove the crankshaft pulley/vibration damper from the end of the crankshaft. To hold the crankshaft stationary while loosening the bolts, have an assistant engage 4th gear and depress the footbrake pedal, or alternatively remove the starter motor and have an assistant insert a wide-bladed screwdriver in the teeth of the starter ring gear.

8 Unscrew the lower bolts and remove the lower timing belt cover.

9 Unscrew the bolts and remove the cover from over the injection pump pulley.

Refitting

10 Refitting is a reversal of removal, but tighten the bolts to the specified torque.

7 Timing belt and injection pump drivebelt – removal, inspection and refitting

⚠ *Warning: Never re-use or retension a timing/injection pump drivebelt which has already been used. This could lead to the belt becoming over-tensioned, leading to its failure and resulting in serious engine damage.*

7.7 Home-made camshaft setting bar inserted in the offset slot

7.12 Drill bit used as a timing pin inserted through the camshaft sprocket

7.27 Screwing in the crankshaft timing pin

Note: *Refer to Section 1 to identify the standard/automatic timing belt tensioner.*

Removal

1 Disconnect the battery negative (earth) lead (see Chapter 5A).
2 Apply the handbrake, then jack up the front of the vehicle and support it on axle stands (see *Jacking and vehicle support*). Where fitted, remove the engine undershield. Remove the right-hand roadwheel and where necessary the wheelarch liner.
3 Remove the timing belt covers as described in Section 6.
4 Unbolt and remove the auxiliary drivebelt tensioner.
5 Remove the alternator as described in Chapter 5A.
6 Set Piston No 1 to TDC on its compression stroke as described in Section 3.

Automatic belt tensioner

7 With the cylinder head cover removed, fit Ford special tool 21-162B into the slot at the left-hand end of the camshaft. If the Ford tool is not available, a home-made version may be fabricated out of metal bar, making sure that it is a good fit in the slot **(see illustration)**.
8 Loosen the centre bolt of the timing belt adjusting eccentric then, using a suitable Allen key, turn the adjusting eccentric anti-clockwise to the 6 o'clock position to release the belt tension.
9 Loosen the camshaft sprocket retaining bolt two or three turns. To prevent the sprocket from turning as its retaining bolt is slackened, make up a sprocket holding tool. Obtain two lengths of steel strip (one long, the other short), and three nuts and bolts; one nut and bolt forms the pivot of the forked tool, with the remaining two nuts and bolts at the tips of the 'forks' to engage between the sprocket spokes.
10 Insert a screwdriver between the rear timing cover and the camshaft sprocket and apply light pressure to the sprocket. Insert a soft-metal drift through the hole in the rear cover and tap lightly on the sprocket to release it from the taper on the camshaft.
11 Remove the camshaft sprocket retaining bolt then withdraw the sprocket, together

with the timing belt, from the camshaft. Slip the timing belt off the remaining sprockets and pulleys and remove it from the engine.

Standard belt tensioner

12 Insert Ford timing pin 23-019 (or suitable drill bit) through the camshaft sprocket and into the special hole in the cylinder head **(see illustration)**.
13 Loosen the bolts securing the sprocket to the camshaft.
14 Loosen the tensioner bolt, then compress the tensioner spring and move the tensioner to release the belt tension. Tighten the tensioner bolt to hold it away from the belt.
15 Slip the timing belt from the sprockets and pulleys and remove it from the engine.

All engines

16 To remove the injection pump drivebelt, loosen the tensioner bolt then lever the tensioner to release the tension and retighten the bolt to hold the tensioner in its retracted position. Remove the belt from the crankshaft and injection pump sprockets and from the tensioner pulley.

Inspection

17 Clean the sprockets, idler and tensioner pulleys and wipe them dry, however do not apply excessive amounts of solvent to the idler and tensioners otherwise the bearing lubricant may be contaminated. Also clean the rear timing belt cover, and the cylinder head and block.
18 Examine the timing belt carefully for any signs of oil or coolant – the presence of either would indicate a leak, which must be cured before fitting the new belt. A new timing belt **must** be fitted once the old one has been removed – **never** refit a used timing belt.

Refitting

Caution: The engine must be cold, having been switched off for at least 4 hours before fitting the new timing belt(s).
19 Check that the No 1 piston is still positioned at TDC with the crankshaft web in contact with the timing pin. Check also that

the timing pin (or suitable drill bit) is still inserted through the injection pump sprocket timing hole into the housing hole.
20 Locate the new injection pump drivebelt on the crankshaft and injection pump sprockets so that it is taut between the two sprockets, and the directional arrows are pointing the correct way.
21 Slacken the injection pump sprocket bolts half a turn, and also slacken the belt tensioner bolt half a turn. Allow the belt tensioner to snap against the belt. Retighten all the slackened bolts and make sure that the bolts are centralised in the elongated holes.

Standard belt tensioner

22 Check that the timing pin (or suitable drill bit) is still inserted through the camshaft sprocket and into the special hole in the cylinder head.
23 Fit the new timing belt, with the directional arrows correct for normal crankshaft rotation. The belt should be slack on the tensioner side and taut between sprockets.
24 Slacken the camshaft sprocket bolts and the tensioner bolts half a turn. Allow the tensioner to snap against the belt.
25 Retighten all slackened bolts, and make sure that the bolts are centralised in the elongated holes. Remove all the timing pins and turn the crankshaft through two revolutions in the normal direction of rotation until the slot in the injection pump sprocket is again at the highest point (12 o'clock).
26 Now turn the crankshaft anti-clockwise until the slot in the injection pump sprocket is at the 11 o'clock position.
27 Refit the crankshaft timing pin **(see illustration)**.
28 Slowly turn the crankshaft clockwise until the crankshaft web contacts the timing pin.
29 Insert the timing pins in the camshaft and the injection pump sprockets.
30 Slacken the bolts (through half a turn) that secure the camshaft and injection pump sprockets and the belt tensioners.
31 Depress both drivebelts on the taut side opposite to the tensioners, and then release them.
32 Retighten all slackened bolts and remove

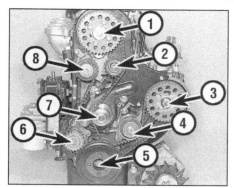

7.32 Timing belt and injection pump belt 'timed' and ready for fitting of the timing covers

1 Camshaft sprocket
2 Idler sprocket
3 Injection pump sprocket
4 Injection pump drivebelt tensioner
5 Crankshaft pulley vibration damper
6 Auxiliary shaft sprocket
7 Coolant pump sprocket
8 Timing belt tensioner

the timing pins. The valve timing is now set correctly **(see illustration)**.

Automatic belt tensioner

33 Check that the No 1 piston is still positioned at TDC with the crankshaft web in contact with the timing pin. Check also that the camshaft setting bar is in place in the slot in the camshaft.
34 Fit the new timing belt, with the directional arrows correct for normal crankshaft rotation. Locate it first on the crankshaft sprocket, then over the auxiliary shaft sprocket, coolant pump pulley, automatic tensioner pulley and adjusting eccentric sprocket. Keep the belt tight and feed it over the camshaft sprocket, then fit the sprocket to the camshaft.
35 Apply engine oil to the camshaft sprocket retaining bolt head contact face. Screw in the bolt finger-tight then back it off a quarter turn. Make sure that the sprocket is free to turn on the camshaft.
36 The timing belt tension must now be initially set by means of the adjusting eccentric. Once this is done, the correct tension will be maintained by the automatic tensioner.
37 Loosen the centre bolt of the adjusting eccentric then, using an Allen key, turn the adjusting eccentric clockwise to the 9 o'clock position to pre-tension the timing belt. Tighten the centre bolt to hold the adjusting eccentric in this position.
38 Tighten the camshaft sprocket retaining bolt to the specified torque while holding the sprocket stationary with the forked tool.
39 Remove all timing pins and the camshaft setting bar, and turn the crankshaft through six revolutions in the normal direction of rotation until the slot in the injection pump sprocket is at the 11 o'clock position.
40 Screw in the crankshaft timing pin.

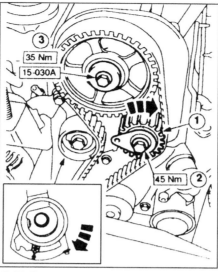

7.47 Turn the adjusting eccentric (1) until the arrows on the automatic tensioner (inset) are aligned, then tighten the centre bolt (2)

41 Slowly turn the crankshaft clockwise until the crankshaft web contacts the timing pin.
42 Loosen the centre bolt of the adjusting eccentric half a turn.
43 Insert the camshaft setting bar in the slot in the camshaft. If necessary, turn the camshaft using grips to align the slot.
44 Loosen the camshaft sprocket retaining bolt two or three turns while holding the sprocket stationary with the forked tool.
45 Insert a screwdriver between the rear timing cover and the camshaft sprocket and apply light pressure to the sprocket. Insert a soft-metal drift through the hole in the rear cover and tap lightly on the sprocket to release it from the taper on the camshaft.
46 Tighten the camshaft sprocket retaining bolt finger-tight then back it off half a turn. Make sure that the sprocket is still free to turn on the camshaft.
47 Observe the position of the two arrows on the automatic timing belt tensioner. The arrows are located below the tensioner pulley and it will be necessary to use a mirror to accurately view their position. Using an Allen key, turn the adjusting eccentric to apply tension to the belt, until the two arrows are aligned **(see illustration)**.
48 With the arrows on the tensioner aligned, hold the adjusting eccentric in this position and tighten the retaining bolt to the specified torque.
49 Tighten the camshaft sprocket retaining bolt to the specified torque while holding the sprocket stationary with the forked tool.
50 Remove the crankshaft timing pin and camshaft setting bar, and turn the crankshaft through six revolutions in the normal direction of rotation until the slot in the injection pump sprocket is at the 11 o'clock position.
51 Screw in the crankshaft timing pin.

7.56 Refitting the timing pin blanking plug

52 Slowly turn the crankshaft clockwise until the crankshaft web contacts the timing pin.
53 Check that the camshaft setting bar can be inserted into the slot in the camshaft, and that the arrows on the timing belt tensioner are still aligned. If this is not the case, repeat the procedure from paragraph 42 onward.
54 If all is satisfactory, remove the timing pin and the camshaft setting bar, then refit the cylinder head cover together with a new gasket and tighten the bolts.
55 Reconnect the crankcase ventilation hoses.

All engines

56 Refit and tighten the timing pin blanking plug **(see illustration)**.
57 Refit the alternator with reference to Chapter 5A.
58 Refit the auxiliary drivebelt tensioner and tighten the bolt to the specified torque.
59 Refit the timing belt covers with reference to Section 6.
60 Refit the undershield (where fitted) then refit the roadwheel and lower the vehicle to the ground.
61 Reconnect the battery negative (earth) lead (see Chapter 5A).

8 Timing belt/drivebelt tensioners and sprockets – removal, inspection and refitting

Note: *A new timing belt must always be fitted.*

Crankshaft sprockets

Removal

1 Remove the timing belt and injection pump drivebelt as described in Section 7. This procedure includes removal of the crankshaft pulley/vibration damper.
2 Hold the crankshaft stationary using a length of metal bar bolted to the sprocket flange, then unscrew and remove the retaining bolt. **Note:** *The bolt is very tight. Discard the bolt – a new one must be obtained for refitting.*

8.3 Removing the outer (timing belt) crankshaft sprocket

8.4a Removing the inner (injection pump) crankshaft sprocket

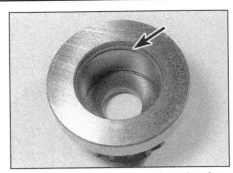

8.4b Inner crankshaft sprocket, showing O-ring seal (arrowed)

3 Remove the outer sprocket, using a suitable puller if necessary **(see illustration)**.
4 Remove the inner sprocket from the end of the crankshaft and recover the O-ring from the sprocket **(see illustrations)**. To remove the sprocket, use Ford tool 21-200 or a similar tool which engages the inside of the sprocket. If necessary, remove the locating pin from the end of the crankshaft.

Inspection

5 Examine the sprockets for wear and damage and renew them if necessary. Wipe clean the oil seal surface on the inner sprocket.
6 If there is any sign of oil leakage from the crankshaft right-hand oil seal, renew it with reference to Section 15. Note that the support ring on the new oil seal must remain in position until just before the inner crankshaft sprocket is fitted.

Refitting

7 Make sure the locating pin is fitted to the end of the crankshaft.
8 Fit the new O-ring to the inner sprocket, then lubricate the crankshaft with engine oil. Remove the oil seal support ring, then slide on the sprocket making sure that the hole is aligned with the locating pin. Press the sprocket fully onto the crankshaft.
9 Fit the outer sprocket onto the inner sprocket making sure that the vee engages with the cut-out. Lubricate the head of the new bolt with oil, then insert it and tighten it while holding the sprocket stationary. Observe the four stages as given in the

Specifications, and use an angle gauge where required.
10 Fit the new timing belt and injection pump drivebelt as described in Section 7.

Camshaft sprocket

Removal

11 Remove the timing belt as described in Section 7 – there is no need to remove the injection pump drivebelt. Note that if a support bar is located over the engine, it must be positioned to allow sufficient room to remove the camshaft sprocket.
12 On engines with a standard timing belt tensioner, hold the sprocket stationary using a tool engaged with the holes in the sprocket, then loosen the centre flange bolt and the four sprocket retaining bolts **(see illustration)**. Remove the sprocket from the flange, then pull the flange from the end of the camshaft using a suitable puller. Remove the Woodruff key from the groove in the camshaft.
13 On engines with an automatic timing belt tensioner, the sprocket is removed as part of the timing belt removal and refitting procedure described in Section 7.

Inspection

14 Inspect the sprocket for wear and damage and renew it if necessary.

Refitting

15 On engines with an automatic timing belt tensioner, the sprocket is refitted as part of the timing belt removal and refitting procedure described in Section 7.

16 On engines with a standard tensioner, refit the sprocket to the camshaft using a reversal of the removal procedure. Fully tighten the flange bolt but leave the sprocket bolts finger-tight.
17 Fit the new timing belt with reference to Section 7.

Auxiliary shaft sprocket

Removal

18 Remove the timing belt as described in Section 7 – there is no need to remove the injection pump drivebelt.
19 The auxiliary shaft sprocket must now be held stationary while the bolt is loosened. To do this, engage the old timing belt with the sprocket and locate both runs of the belt over the crankshaft sprocket. Using a lever, pull down on the belt to hold the auxiliary shaft stationary then loosen the bolt.
20 Unscrew the bolt and remove the sprocket from the locating dowel on the auxiliary shaft **(see illustration)**.

Inspection

21 Inspect the sprocket for wear and damage and renew it if necessary.

Refitting

22 Refitting is a reversal of removal, but tighten all nuts and bolts to the specified torque.
23 Fit the new timing belt as described in Section 7.

Injection pump sprocket

Removal

24 Remove the timing belt and injection pump drivebelt as described in Section 7.
25 Mark the sprocket in relation to the injection pump flange, then hold the sprocket stationary using a suitable tool engaged with the sprocket holes.
26 Unscrew the retaining bolts and remove the sprocket from the flange.

Inspection

27 Inspect the sprocket for wear and damage and renew it if necessary.

Refitting

28 Locate the sprocket on the flange making

8.12 Unscrewing the camshaft sprocket retaining bolts

8.20 Removing the auxiliary shaft sprocket

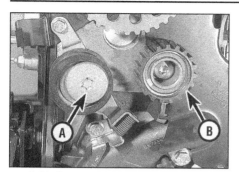

8.31 Standard timing belt tensioner pulley (A) and idler sprocket (B)

sure that the previously made marks are aligned with each other.
29 Fit the new timing belt as described in Section 7.

Standard tensioners

Removal

30 Remove the timing belt and, where applicable, the injection pump drivebelt as described in Section 7.
31 Unscrew the bolt and remove the relevant tensioner pulley and tension spring **(see illustration)**.

Inspection

32 Spin the pulley by hand and check for roughness and resistance. If evident, renew the tensioner.

Refitting

33 Clean the tensioner and the face of the cylinder head/block.
34 Refit the tensioner and spring and tighten the mounting bolt to the specified torque.
35 Fit the new timing belt and, where applicable, injection pump drivebelt as described in Section 7.

Automatic belt tensioner and adjusting eccentric

Removal

36 Remove the timing belt as described in Section 7 – there is no need to remove the injection pump drivebelt.
37 Unscrew the bolt from the centre of the adjusting eccentric sprocket and remove the sprocket.

38 Unscrew the bolts and remove the automatic tensioner assembly.

Inspection

39 Check the tensioner components for wear and damage and renew as necessary.

Refitting

40 Refit the adjusting eccentric sprocket and automatic tensioner assembly and tighten the bolts to the specified torque.
41 Fit the new timing belt as described in Section 7.

Idler

Removal

42 Remove the timing belt as described in Section 7 – there is no need to remove the injection pump drivebelt.
43 Unbolt and remove the idler.

Inspection

44 Spin the idler sprocket by hand and check for roughness and resistance. If evident, renew.

Refitting

45 Refit the idler and tighten the mounting bolt to the specified torque.
46 Fit the new timing belt as described in Section 7.

9 Camshaft oil seal – renewal

1 Remove the camshaft sprocket as described in Section 8.
2 Note the fitted depth of the oil seal before removing it, as a guide to fitting the new one.
3 Using a screwdriver or suitable hooked instrument, pull the oil seal from the cylinder head. If the seal is tight, drill two or three small holes in its outer face, then screw in self-tapping screws. Pull on the screws with a pair of pliers to remove the oil seal.
4 Wipe clean the seating and end of the camshaft.
5 Dip the new seal in oil, then locate it over the camshaft and initially press it in by hand making sure that it enters the cylinder head squarely.

6 Using a piece of metal tubing or a socket, carefully drive the oil seal into the cylinder head to the previously noted depth.
7 Wipe any excess oil from the oil seal and surrounding area.
8 Refit the camshaft sprocket and fit the new timing belt with reference to Section 8.

10 Auxiliary shaft oil seal – renewal

1 Remove the auxiliary shaft sprocket as described in Section 8.
2 Unbolt and remove the timing belt side cover.
3 Unscrew the bolts and remove the oil seal housing from the cylinder block **(see illustration)**. The oil seal is integral with the housing.
4 Clean the cylinder block and end of the auxiliary shaft.
5 Smear fresh engine oil on the auxiliary shaft and on the sealing lips of the new oil seal. Before fitting the new seal, locate the special fitting ring inside the sealing lips.
6 Locate the new oil seal over the end of the auxiliary shaft, then insert the bolts and tighten to the specified torque **(see illustrations)**.
7 Carefully remove the special ring and make sure that the seal lips are located on the shaft correctly.
8 Refit the timing belt side cover and tighten the bolts to the specified torque.
9 Refit the auxiliary shaft sprocket as described in Section 8.

11 Camshaft and tappets – removal, inspection and refitting

Removal

1 Remove the camshaft sprocket as described in Section 8.
2 Disconnect the crankcase ventilation hose from the right-hand rear of the cylinder head.
3 Disconnect the crankcase ventilation hose from the left-hand front of the cylinder head

10.3 Auxiliary shaft oil seal housing on the cylinder block

10.6a Auxiliary shaft oil seal retainer with plastic fitting ring

10.6b Tightening the auxiliary shaft oil seal housing bolts

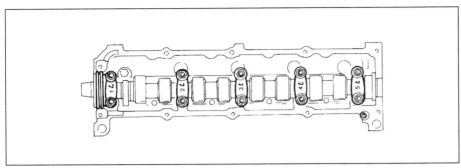

11.5 Camshaft bearing caps – note numbers and arrows

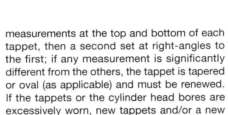

11.17 Fitting a camshaft lower bearing shell

cover, then unscrew the bolts and remove the cover.

4 Unscrew the nuts and remove the baffle plate.

5 Undo the nuts of bearing caps Nos 2 and 4. Remove these caps and their shells. Keep the shells with their caps if they are to be re-used. Note that the caps are numbered and carry an arrow pointing to the pulley end of the engine **(see illustration)**.

6 Slacken the nuts of bearing caps Nos 1, 3 and 5 one turn at a time, working from end-to-end so that the camshaft is released gradually. Remove the bearing caps and shells, again keeping the shells with their caps if necessary.

7 Lift out the camshaft with its oil seal. Recover the lower half bearing shells, keeping them in order if necessary.

8 If purchasing new bearing shells, note that either standard or oversize outside diameter shells may have been fitted in production. Oversize shells are identified by a green mark.

9 Obtain eight small, clean containers, and number them 1 to 8 from the timing end. Lift the tappets one by one from the cylinder head keeping the shims with their respective tappets.

Inspection

10 With the camshaft and tappets removed, check for signs of obvious wear (scoring, pitting, etc) and for ovality, and renew if necessary.

11 If possible, use a micrometer to measure the outside diameter of each tappet – take

measurements at the top and bottom of each tappet, then a second set at right-angles to the first; if any measurement is significantly different from the others, the tappet is tapered or oval (as applicable) and must be renewed. If the tappets or the cylinder head bores are excessively worn, new tappets and/or a new cylinder head will be required.

12 Visually examine the camshaft lobes for score marks, pitting, and evidence of overheating (blue, discoloured areas). Look for flaking away of the hardened surface layer of each lobe. If any such signs are evident, renew the component concerned.

13 Examine the camshaft bearing journals and the bearing shells for signs of obvious wear or pitting. If any such signs are evident, renew the camshaft and/or obtain a set of bearing shells.

14 To check camshaft endfloat, remove the tappets, clean the bearing surfaces carefully, and refit the camshaft and bearing caps with shells. Tighten the bearing cap nuts to the specified torque wrench setting, then measure the endfloat using a dial gauge mounted on the cylinder head so that its tip bears on the camshaft right-hand end.

15 Tap the camshaft fully towards the gauge, zero the gauge, then tap the camshaft fully away from the gauge, and note the gauge reading. If the endfloat measured is found to be more than the value given in the Specifications, fit a new camshaft and repeat the check; if the clearance is still excessive, the cylinder head must be renewed.

Refitting

16 Commence reassembly by lubricating the cylinder head tappet bores and the tappets with engine oil. Carefully refit the tappets (together with their respective shims – lettering facing downwards) to the cylinder head, ensuring that each tappet is refitted to its original bore. Some care will be required to enter the tappets squarely into their bores.

17 Place the lower half bearing shells (the ones with the oil holes) in position **(see illustration)**. Lubricate the shells.

18 Make sure that all tappets, shims and the vacuum pump plunger are in place. Remove the old oil seal, if not already done, and place the camshaft on the lower half bearings **(see illustration)**. Position the camshaft with the timing setting slot parallel with the head top face and the larger semi-circular segment uppermost.

19 Clean any old sealant from No 1 bearing cap. Fit the upper bearing shells to their caps and lubricate them. Coat the mating surfaces of No 1 cap with sealant (to Ford spec SPM-41G-9112 F/G) in the areas shown **(see illustrations)**.

20 Fit bearing caps and shells Nos 1, 3 and 5, making sure that they are the right way round (the arrows point to the timing belt end). Tighten the cap nuts, half a turn at a time, in the sequence No 3 – No 1 – No 5. Carry on until the caps are seated.

21 Fit caps and shells Nos 2 and 4, tapping them down with a mallet if necessary to seat them. Fit their nuts.

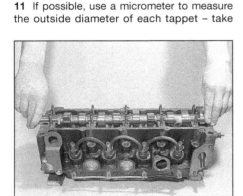

11.18 Fitting the camshaft

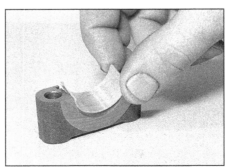

11.19a Fitting a camshaft upper bearing shell to its cap

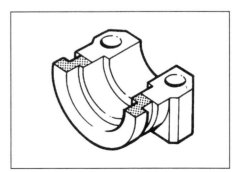

11.19b Camshaft No 1 bearing cap – coat shaded area with sealant

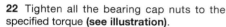

11.22 Tightening the camshaft bearing cap nuts

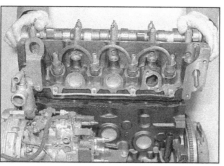

12.27 Removing the cylinder head

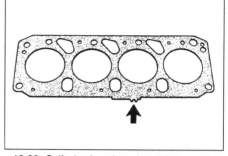

12.28 Cylinder head gasket thickness is indicated by the number of teeth (arrowed)

22 Tighten all the bearing cap nuts to the specified torque **(see illustration)**.
23 Insert the camshaft setting tool into the slot so that it is a snug fit.
24 Fit a new oil seal to the camshaft nose as described in Section 9.
25 Lubricate the cam lobes liberally with engine oil, or with special cam lube if supplied with a new camshaft.
26 Refit the baffle plate and tighten the nuts to the specified torque.
27 Refit the camshaft sprocket and flange as described in Section 8. Remember the timing belt has to be renewed.
28 Refit the cylinder head cover together with a new gasket and tighten the bolts to the specified torque.
29 Reconnect the crankcase ventilation hoses.

12 Cylinder head – removal, inspection and refitting

Removal

1 Disconnect the battery negative (earth) lead (see Chapter 5A).
2 Apply the handbrake, then jack up the front of the vehicle and support it on axle stands (see *Jacking and vehicle support*). Remove the engine undershield if fitted.
3 Drain the cooling system as described in Chapter 1B. Save the coolant in a clean container if it is fit for re-use.
4 Remove the timing belt as described in Section 7. There is no need to remove the injection pump drivebelt.
5 If a support bar was used to support the engine in paragraph 4, locate a trolley jack and block of wood beneath the sump then remove the support bar.
6 Remove the camshaft sprocket and timing belt tensioner with reference to Section 8.
7 Disconnect the crankcase ventilation hose from the right-hand rear end of the cylinder head.
8 Loosen the clips and remove the air inlet duct from the inlet manifold and air cleaner.
9 Unscrew the bolts and remove the upper inlet manifold from the lower manifold. Seal

the lower manifold using cloth rags or masking tape.
10 Loosen the clips and disconnect the coolant hoses from the thermostat housing.
11 Disconnect the wiring from the glow plugs, engine coolant temperature sensor, temperature gauge sender, and oil pressure switch.
12 Disconnect the brake servo vacuum line at the front left-hand side of the engine.
13 Disconnect the fuel feed line at the top of the filter.
14 Disconnect the fuel line to the fuel heater at the left-hand side of the engine.
15 Disconnect the fuel heater wiring.
16 Disconnect the vacuum hose and the wiring from the exhaust gas recirculation valve.
17 Disconnect the coolant hose from the fuel heater.
18 Disconnect the fuel leak-off pipes from the injectors.
19 Unscrew the union nuts and remove the injection pipes from the injectors and injection pump. Be prepared for some loss of fuel.
20 Unbolt the glow plug wiring bracket, then unbolt the oil dipstick tube bracket.
21 Unscrew the nuts securing the catalytic converter to the exhaust manifold.
22 If not already done, disconnect the crankcase ventilation hose from the front of the cylinder head cover. Unscrew the bolts and remove the cylinder head cover and gasket.
23 Remove the oil baffle plate.
24 Remove the injectors and heat shields as described in Chapter 4B.
25 Check that No 1 piston is still set to TDC as described in Section 3.
26 Unscrew the cylinder head bolts in the reverse order to tightening **(see illustration 12.37b)**. As new bolts will be required when refitting the cylinder head, note that the bolts have an M12 thread and a Torx T70 head.
27 With the help of an assistant, lift the cylinder head from the block together with the manifolds **(see illustration)**.
28 Remove the cylinder head gasket, but retain it for comparison with the new gasket. Three possible thicknesses of gasket are available according to the piston protrusion,

the details of which are given in the Specifications at the start of this Chapter **(see illustration)**. Refer to Chapter 2D, Section 11, for details of how to measure piston protrusion.

Inspection

29 The mating faces of the cylinder head and block must be perfectly clean before refitting the head. Use a scraper to remove all traces of gasket and carbon, and also clean the tops of the pistons. Take particular care with the aluminium cylinder head, as the soft metal is damaged easily. Also, make sure that debris is not allowed to enter the oil and water channels – this is particularly important for the oil circuit, as carbon could block the oil supply to the camshaft or crankshaft bearings. Using adhesive tape and paper, seal the water, oil and bolt holes in the cylinder block. Clean the piston crowns in the same way.

> **HAYNES HINT** *To prevent carbon entering the gap between the pistons and bores, smear a little grease in the gap. After cleaning the piston, rotate the crankshaft so that the piston moves down the bore, then wipe out the grease and carbon with a cloth rag.*

30 Check the block and head for nicks, deep scratches and other damage. If slight, they may be removed carefully with a file. More serious damage may be repaired by machining, but this is a specialist job.
31 If warpage of the cylinder head is suspected, use a straight-edge to check it for distortion. Refer to Chapter 2E if necessary.
32 Clean out the bolt holes in the block using a pipe cleaner, or a rag and screwdriver. Make sure that all oil is removed, otherwise there is a possibility of the block being cracked by hydraulic pressure when the bolts are tightened.
33 Examine the bolt threads and the threads in the cylinder block for damage. If necessary, use the correct-size tap to chase out the threads in the block.
34 If necessary, the valve clearances may be checked and adjusted with the cylinder head on the bench. Refer to Section 4.

12.37a Lowering the cylinder head onto the cylinder block – note the injectors protected against dirt

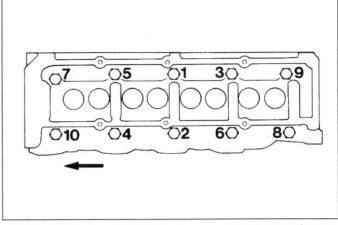

12.37b Cylinder head bolt tightening sequence. Arrow points to timing end of the engine

Refitting

35 Before fitting the cylinder head, make sure that the groove on the camshaft rear eccentric is parallel with the upper surface of the cylinder head, and the larger segment is uppermost. Also make sure that the crankshaft is at TDC.

36 Fit the new selected gasket and use new cylinder head bolts. Make sure that the centralising dowel sleeves are located at bolt holes 8 and 10, and the word TOP/OBEN is visible.

37 Fit the cylinder head, screw in the new bolts (**do not** oil the bolts), and tighten in the stages indicated in the Specifications and in the sequence shown **(see illustrations)**.

38 Refit the injectors and heat shields as described in Chapter 4B.

39 Refit the oil baffle plate and tighten the nuts to the specified torque.

40 On engines with a standard timing belt tensioner, refit the cylinder head cover together with a new gasket, and tighten the bolts.

41 Reconnect the crankcase ventilation hose.

42 Refit the catalytic converter to the exhaust manifold, then tighten the retaining nuts.

43 Refit the oil dipstick tube bracket and tighten the bolt.

44 Refit the glow plug wiring bracket.

45 Refit the injection pipes and tighten the union nuts. Reconnect the leak-off pipes.

46 Reconnect the coolant hose to the fuel heater.

47 Reconnect the exhaust gas recirculation vacuum valve hose and wiring.

48 Reconnect the fuel heater wiring and fuel line.

49 Reconnect the fuel feed line to the top of the filter, then reconnect the brake servo vacuum line.

50 Reconnect the wiring to the oil pressure switch, temperature gauge sender, engine coolant temperature sensor, and glow plugs.

51 Reconnect the hoses to the thermostat housing and tighten the clips.

52 Remove the cloth rags or masking tape, then refit the upper inlet manifold to the lower manifold and tighten the bolts.

53 Refit the air inlet duct between the inlet manifold and air cleaner and tighten the clips.

54 Reconnect the crankcase ventilation hose to the right-hand rear end of the cylinder head.

55 Refit the timing belt tensioner and camshaft sprocket as described in Section 8.

56 Where applicable, attach the support bar to the engine and remove the trolley jack.

57 Fit a new timing belt with reference to Section 7.

58 Refill the cooling system as described in Chapter 1B.

59 Refit the engine undershield, then lower the vehicle to the ground.

60 Reconnect the battery earth lead (see Chapter 5A).

61 The fuel system can now be primed, with reference to Chapter 4B.

62 Start the engine and run it to normal operating temperature. Check for leaks of oil and coolant.

13 Sump – removal and refitting

Removal

1 Note that the crankshaft left-hand oil seal housing is bolted directly onto the sump and cylinder block, making it necessary to remove the flywheel in order to unbolt the rear oil seal housing.

2 Apply the handbrake, then jack up the front of the vehicle and support it on axle stands (see *Jacking and vehicle support*).

3 Drain the engine oil, then check the sealing washer and renew if necessary. Clean and refit the engine oil drain plug together with the washer, and tighten it to the specified torque wrench setting (see Chapter 1B). Although not strictly necessary as part of the dismantling procedure, owners are advised to remove and discard the oil filter, so that it can be renewed with the oil (see Chapter 1B).

4 Remove the transmission as described in Chapter 7A. Make sure the engine is adequately and safely supported.

5 Remove the flywheel as described in Section 16.

6 Unbolt the oil seal housing and withdraw it over the end of the crankshaft (refer to Section 15).

7 If necessary, remove the crankshaft position sensor and unbolt its bracket from the sump.

8 Progressively unscrew the sump retaining bolts, then lower the sump from the crankcase and withdraw it from under the vehicle.

9 Recover the sump gasket **(see illustration)**.

10 While the sump is removed, take the opportunity to remove the oil pump pick-up/strainer pipe and clean it with reference to Section 14.

Refitting

11 Thoroughly clean the contact surfaces of the sump and crankcase. If necessary, use a cloth rag to clean the interior of the sump and crankcase. If the oil pump pick-up/strainer pipe was removed, fit a new O-ring and refit the pipe with reference to Section 14.

13.9 Removing the sump gasket from the crankcase

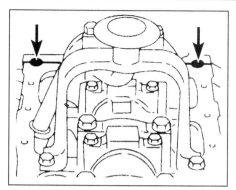

13.12 Apply suitable sealant to the cylinder block/sump mating surfaces at the points arrowed

12 Apply suitable sealant (Ford recommend SPM-4G-9112-F/G) to the joint (on each side) between the front timing housing and crankcase **(see illustration)**.

13 Locate the gasket on the sump, then offer the sump onto the crankcase and insert the retaining bolts finger-tight.

14 Before tightening the bolts, the sump must be accurately aligned with the end face of the cylinder block using a straight-edge.

15 Once the sump is correctly aligned, progressively tighten the sump-to-crankcase bolts to the specified torque.

16 If removed, refit the crankshaft position sensor and bracket.

17 Refit the crankshaft left-hand oil seal housing and tighten the bolts to the specified torque (refer to Section 15).

18 Refit the flywheel with reference to Section 16.

19 Refit the transmission as described in Chapter 7A.

20 Lower the vehicle to the ground, then fit a new oil filter (if necessary) and refill the engine with oil with reference to Chapter 1B.

21 Finally start the engine and check for signs of oil or coolant leaks.

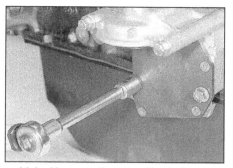

14.4a Unscrew the mounting bolts . . .

14 Oil pump – removal, inspection and refitting

Note: *The following procedure includes removal of the oil filter, and it is recommended that the filter be renewed rather than refitting the old unit. The engine oil should also be changed at the same time.*

Removal

1 Apply the handbrake, then jack up the front of the vehicle and support it on axle stands (see *Jacking and vehicle support*).

2 Where necessary, drain the engine oil with reference to Chapter 1B.

3 Place a suitable container beneath the rear of the engine, then unscrew and remove the oil filter (see Chapter 1B).

4 Unscrew the mounting bolts and remove the oil pump from the cylinder block. Recover the gasket **(see illustrations)**.

Inspection

5 Unscrew the crosshead screws and remove the cover from the oil pump.

6 Clean all parts and inspect them for wear or damage. Using a feeler blade, measure the

14.4b . . . remove the oil pump from the cylinder block . . .

14.4c . . . and recover the gasket

inner-to-outer rotor clearance. If the clearance exceeds that specified then the pump must be renewed as pump components are not available individually. It is wise to renew the pump on a precautionary basis at time of major overhaul, especially if there is evidence of oil starvation elsewhere.

7 If there are any signs of metallic debris inside the oil pump, it is recommended that the sump be removed and the pick-up pipe and strainer cleaned thoroughly. Renew the pick-up tube O-ring and the sump gasket on refitting and tighten the bolts securely **(see illustrations)**.

14.7a Removing the oil pump pick-up tube from the crankcase – note the O-ring which must be renewed

14.7b Tightening the oil pump pick-up tube mounting bolts

Refitting

8 Before refitting the oil pump, pour approximately 10 cc of engine oil into the pump to prime it, and oil the pump drive gear and driven gear.

9 Clean the mating faces of the pump and cylinder block, then refit the oil pump together with a new gasket, and tighten the mounting bolts progressively to the specified torque.

10 Fit a new oil filter and fill the engine with fresh oil as described in Chapter 1B.

11 Lower the vehicle to the ground.

15 Crankshaft oil seals – renewal

Timing belt end oil seal

1 Remove the crankshaft sprockets as described in Section 8.

2 Note the fitted depth of the oil seal in the engine.

3 Using a screwdriver or other suitable instrument, prise the oil seal from the engine plate. An alternative method is to drill two small holes in the oil seal, then screw in self-tapping screws and use grips to pull out the oil seal. If this method is used, make sure that all swarf is removed.

4 Inspect the seal rubbing surface on the inner crankshaft sprocket, and if necessary, renew the sprocket.

5 Wipe clean the oil seal seating in the engine.

6 Note that the new oil seal is supplied with a support ring which must remain in position until just before the inner crankshaft sprocket is fitted. The oil seal must be fitted dry.

7 Using a length of metal tube or a socket, drive the new oil seal into the engine to the previously noted depth. Leave the support ring in place at this stage.

8 Refit the crankshaft sprockets and timing belt with reference to Section 8.

Flywheel end oil seal

9 Remove the flywheel as described in Section 16.

10 Unbolt the oil seal housing from the sump and cylinder block and withdraw it over the end of the crankshaft. Note that the housing incorporates an integral oil seal and a vulcanised gasket.

11 Wipe clean the mating faces of the sump and cylinder block. Also wipe all oil from the end of the crankshaft. Note that the oil seal must be fitted dry.

12 Make sure that the support ring is located inside the oil seal, then locate the housing over the crankshaft. Screw in the retaining bolts finger-tight.

13 Make sure that the oil seal is centred on the end of the crankshaft, then progressively tighten the mounting bolts to the specified torque **(see illustration)**.

14 Carefully remove the support ring so that the lips of the oil seal rest on the crankshaft. If the ring is tight, it is likely that the faces of the sump and cylinder block are not accurately aligned with each other. To rectify this situation, loosen all of the sump bolts, reposition the sump, and retighten the bolts to the specified torque.

15 With the housing bolts tightened, refit the flywheel and transmission with reference to Section 16.

16 Flywheel – removal, inspection and refitting

Removal

1 Remove the transmission as described in Chapter 7A.

2 Remove the clutch components with reference to Chapter 6.

3 Make alignment marks on the flywheel and crankshaft to ensure correct refitting.

4 Hold the flywheel stationary using a locking tool engaged with the starter ring gear. A suitable home-made tool bolted to one of the transmission mounting bolt holes and engaged with the ring gear can be fabricated

out of metal bar.

5 Unscrew the mounting bolts and lift the flywheel from the end of the crankshaft. Take care not to drop the flywheel as it is very heavy. Discard the bolts and obtain new ones for the refitting procedure.

Inspection

6 Examine the clutch mating surface of the flywheel for scoring or cracks. Light grooving or scoring may be ignored. Surface cracks or deep grooving can sometimes be removed by specialist machining, provided not too much metal is taken off; otherwise the flywheel must be renewed.

7 Inspect the starter ring gear for damaged or missing teeth. A damaged ring gear can be renewed separately. The average DIY mechanic may prefer to leave the job to a Ford dealer or other competent workshop; for the enthusiast the procedure is as follows.

8 Drill two adjacent holes, 7 or 8 mm in diameter, through the ring gear. Take care not to drill into the flywheel.

9 Knock the ring gear off the flywheel with a hammer. Use light blows, evenly spaced around the ring.

10 Heat the new ring gear evenly to between 260° and 280°C (500° and 536°F). This is just about within the capability of most domestic ovens. Take care not to overheat the ring gear or its temper will be lost.

11 Using tongs or asbestos gloves, place the ring gear on the flywheel and tap it into place. Allow it to cool naturally. If the teeth have a bevelled lead-in for the starter motor pinion, make sure this is facing outwards (ie, towards the clutch face).

12 If renewing the flywheel, transfer the clutch locating dowels to the new unit.

Refitting

13 Commence refitting by placing the flywheel on the end of the crankshaft. Observe the alignment marks if refitting the original unit.

14 Insert the new bolts, and tighten them to the torque and angles given in the Specifications **(see illustration)**.

15.13 Tightening the oil seal housing mounting bolts

16.14 Angle-tightening the flywheel bolts

15 Refit the clutch components with reference to Chapter 6.
16 Refit the transmission with reference to Chapter 7A.

17 Engine/transmission mountings – inspection and renewal

Inspection

1 The engine/transmission mountings seldom require attention, but broken or deteriorated mountings should be renewed immediately, or the added strain placed on the driveline components may cause damage or wear.
2 During the check, the engine/transmission must be raised slightly, to remove its weight from the mountings.
3 Apply the handbrake, then jack up the front of the vehicle and support it on axle stands (see *Jacking and vehicle support*). Remove the engine undershield where fitted. Position a jack under the sump, with a large block of wood between the jack head and the sump, then carefully raise the engine/transmission just enough to take the weight off the mountings.
4 Check the mountings to see if the rubber is cracked, hardened or separated from the metal components. Sometimes, the rubber will split right down the centre.
5 Check for relative movement between each mounting's brackets and the engine/ transmission or body (use a large screwdriver or lever to attempt to move the mountings). If movement is noted, lower the engine and check the mounting nuts and bolts for tightness.

Renewal

6 The engine mountings can be removed if the weight of the engine/transmission is supported by one of the following alternative methods.
7 Either support the weight of the assembly from underneath using a jack and a suitable piece of wood between the jack and the sump (to prevent damage), or from above by attaching a hoist to the engine. A third method is to use a suitable support bar with end pieces which will engage in the water channel each side of the bonnet lid aperture. Using an adjustable hook and chain connected to the engine, the weight of the engine and transmission can then be taken from the mountings.
8 Once the weight of the engine and transmission is suitably supported, any of the mountings can be unbolted and removed.
9 To remove the right-hand engine mounting, first unbolt the reinforcement bracket then unscrew the nuts and remove the upper bracket. Unscrew the bolts and remove the lower bracket from the cylinder head. Unbolt the insulator from the right-hand side of the engine compartment.
10 To remove the left-hand mounting first remove the battery and battery tray as described in Chapter 5A, then loosen the clips and remove the air inlet duct from between the air mass air flow sensor on the air cleaner and the throttle housing. Unscrew the mounting nuts from the left-hand engine mounting, then unscrew the bolts and remove the upper bracket. Unscrew the bolts and remove the insulator from the left-hand side of the engine compartment.
11 To remove the rear engine mounting/link, apply the handbrake, then jack up the front of the vehicle and support it on axle stands (see *Jacking and vehicle support*). Unscrew the through-bolts and remove the rear engine mounting link from the bracket on the transmission and from the bracket on the underbody. Hold the engine stationary while the bolts are being removed since the link will be under tension.
12 Refitting of all mountings is a reversal of the removal procedure. Do not fully tighten the mounting nuts/bolts until all of the mountings are in position. Check that the mounting rubbers do not twist or distort as the mounting bolts and nuts are tightened to their specified torques.

Notes

Chapter 2 Part D:
Endura-DI diesel engine in-car repair procedures

Contents

Auxiliary drivebelt check and renewal . . . . .See Chapter 1B
Camshaft and tappets – removal, inspection and refitting 9
Camshaft oil seal – renewal 10
Compression and leakdown tests – description and interpretation . 2
Crankshaft oil seals – renewal 16
Crankshaft pulley – removal and refitting 6
Cylinder head – dismantling and overhaul . . . . .See Chapter 2E
Cylinder head – removal, inspection and refitting 11
Cylinder head cover – removal and refitting 4
Engine oil and filter change . . . . .See Chapter 1B
Engine oil level check .See Weekly checks
Engine/transmission – removal and refittin . . . . .See Chapter 2E
Engine/transmission mountings – inspection and renewal 18
Flywheel – removal, inspection and refitting 17
General information 1
Oil cooler – removal and refitting 15
Oil pressure warning light switch – removal and refitting 14
Oil pump – removal, inspection and refitting 13
Sump – removal and refitting 12
Timing belt – removal and refitting 7
Timing belt tensioner and sprockets – removal, inspection
   and refitting 8
Top dead centre (TDC) for No 1 cylinder – locating 3
Valve clearances – checking and adjustment 5

Degrees of difficulty

| **Easy,** suitable for novice with little experience | | **Fairly easy,** suitable for beginner with some experience | | **Fairly difficult,** suitable for competent DIY mechanic | | **Difficult,** suitable for experienced DIY mechanic | | **Very difficult,** suitable for expert DIY or professional | |

Specifications

General

Engine type	Four-cylinder, in-line, single overhead camshaft, cast-iron cylinder head and engine block
Designation	Endura-DI
Engine code	C9DC, RTP, RTN or RTQ
Capacity	1753 cc
Bore	82.5 mm
Stroke	82.0 mm
Compression ratio	19.4:1
Firing order	1-3-4-2 (No 1 cylinder at timing belt end)
Direction of crankshaft rotation	Clockwise (seen from right-hand side of vehicle)

Cylinder block

Cylinder bore diameter:

Class A	82.500 to 82.515 mm
Class B	82.515 to 82.530 mm

Crankshaft

Main bearing journal diameter:

Standard	53.970 to 53.990 mm
1st undersize	53.720 to 53.740 mm
2nd undersize	53.470 to 53.490 mm
Main bearing running clearance	0.015 to 0.062 mm
Crankshaft endfloat	0.11 to 0.37 mm

Big-end bearing journal diameter:

Standard	48.970 to 48.990 mm
1st undersize	48.720 to 48.740 mm
2nd undersize	48.470 to 48.490 mm
Big-end bearing running clearance	0.025 to 0.085 mm

Pistons

Piston diameter:	
Class A	82.410 to 82.425 mm
Class B	82.425 to 82.440 mm
Oversizes	None available
Piston-to-cylinder bore clearance	0.105 to 0.075 mm
Piston protrusion at TDC	0.500 to 0.840 mm
Gudgeon pin diameter	28.004 to 28.010 mm

Piston rings

End gaps (fitted):	
Top compression	0.31 to 0.50 mm
Second compression	0.31 to 0.50 mm
Oil control	0.25 to 0.58 mm
End gap spacing	120°
Clearance in groove:	
Top compression	0.090 to 0.122 mm
Second compression	0.070 to 0.102 mm
Oil control	0.050 to 0.082 mm

Camshaft

Bearing journal diameter	27.96 to 27.98 mm
Bearing running clearance	0.010 to 0.045 mm
Endfloat	0.100 to 0.240 mm

Valve clearances (cold)

Valve clearances (cold):	
Inlet	0.30 to 0.40 mm
Exhaust	0.45 to 0.55 mm
Tappet/shim thicknesses available	3.00 to 4.75 mm in varying increments

Cylinder head

Camshaft bearing diameter:	
Standard	30.500 to 30.525 mm
Oversize	30.575 to 30.600 mm
Maximum permissible gasket surface distortion	0.6 mm

Lubrication

Oil pressure – minimum (engine at operating temperature):	
At idle	0.75 bars
At 2000 rpm	1.50 bars
Oil pump clearance (inner-to-outer rotors)	0.23 mm

Torque wrench settings

	Nm	lbf ft
Auxiliary shaft oil seal carrier	23	17
Big-end bearing cap bolts:		
Stage 1	25	18
Stage 2	Angle-tighten a further 60°	
Stage 3	Angle-tighten a further 20°	
Camshaft bearing cap	23	17
Camshaft oil baffle	20	15
Camshaft sprocket bolt	50	37
Coolant pipe bracket	25	18
Crankcase ventilation oil separator	25	18
Crankshaft oil seal carrier	20	15
Crankshaft position sensor bracket	20	15
Crankshaft pulley bolt:		
Stage 1	90	66
Stage 2	Angle-tighten a further 90°	
Crankshaft rear oil seal carrier	20	15
Cylinder head bolts*:		
Stage 1	20	15
Stage 2	45	33
Stage 3	110	81
Stage 4:		
Short bolts	Angle-tighten a further 100°	
Long bolts	Angle-tighten a further 130°	
Driveshaft centre bearing to block	48	35

Torque wrench settings (continued)

	Nm	lbf ft
Engine/transmission mountings:		
Left-hand engine/transmission mounting	60	44
Rear engine mounting link to cylinder block	50	37
Rear engine mounting link to front subframe	70	52
Right-hand engine mounting bracket:		
Bolts	50	37
Mounting nut	60	44
Flywheel bolts:		
Stage 1	20	15
Stage 2	Angle-tighten a further 45°	
Stage 3	Angle-tighten a further 45°	
Front plate to cylinder block	24	18
Lower crankcase to cylinder block	11	8
Main bearing cap bolts:		
Stage 1	27	20
Stage 2	Angle-tighten a further 75°	
Oil baffle plate nuts	23	17
Oil intake pipe bracket to block	22	16
Oil pressure switch	20	15
Oil pump bolts/studs:		
Stage 1	10	7
Stage 2	18	13
Roadwheel nuts	85	63
Sump bolts	11	8
TDC setting plug cover	24	18
Timing belt adjuster cam to cylinder head	45	33
Timing belt inner cover bolts	24	18
Timing belt outer covers	8	6
Timing belt tensioner bolt	50	37
Timing chain guide retaining bolts	23	17
Timing chain tensioner	63	46

* Use new fasteners

1 General information

How to use this Chapter

This Part of Chapter 2 is devoted to in-car repair procedures. All procedures concerning engine removal and refitting, and engine block/cylinder head overhaul can be found in Chapter 2E.

Refer to the *Vehicle identification numbers* Section at the end of this manual for details of engine code locations.

Most of the operations included in Chapter 2D are based on the assumption that the engine is still installed in the car. Therefore, if this information is being used during a complete engine overhaul, with the engine already removed, many of the steps included here will not apply.

Engine description

The Endura-DI 1.8 litre diesel engine is derived from the previous Endura-DE engine, modified in line with the switch from indirect to direct fuel injection. The engine is an eight-valve, single overhead camshaft (SOHC), four-cylinder, in-line type, mounted transversely at the front of the vehicle, with the transmission on its left-hand end.

All major engine castings are of cast-iron, and there is a lower crankcase which is bolted to the underside of the cylinder block/crankcase, with a pressed-steel sump bolted under that. This arrangement offers greater rigidity than the normal sump arrangement, and helps to reduce engine vibration.

The crankshaft runs in five main bearings, the centre main bearing's upper half incorporating thrustwashers to control crankshaft endfloat. The connecting rods rotate on horizontally-split bearing shells at their big-ends. The pistons are attached to the connecting rods by gudgeon pins which are a floating fit in the connecting rod small-end eyes, secured by circlips. The aluminium alloy pistons are fitted with three piston rings: two compression rings and an oil control ring. After manufacture, the cylinder bores and piston skirts are measured and classified into two grades, which must be carefully matched together to ensure the correct piston/cylinder clearance; no oversizes are available to permit reboring.

The inlet and exhaust valves are each closed by coil springs; they operate in guides which are shrink-fitted into the cylinder head, as are the valve seat inserts.

The Endura-DI engine is unusual in that the fuel injection pump is driven by an offset double-row ('gemini') chain from a sprocket on the crankshaft, with the camshaft being driven from the injection pump sprocket by a conventional toothed timing belt.

The camshaft operates the eight valves via conventional tappets with shims. The camshaft rotates in five bearings that are line-bored directly in the cylinder head and the (bolted-on) bearing caps; this means that the bearing caps are not available separately from the cylinder head, and must not be interchanged with caps from another engine.

The vacuum pump (used for the brake servo and other vacuum actuators) is driven by a pushrod operated directly by a special lobe on the camshaft.

The coolant pump is bolted to the right-hand end of the cylinder block, and is driven with the power steering pump and alternator by a multi-ribbed auxiliary drivebelt from the crankshaft pulley.

Lubrication is by means of a G-rotor pump, which is mounted on the crankshaft right-hand end, and draws oil through a strainer located in the sump. The pump forces oil through an externally-mounted full-flow cartridge-type filter. From the filter, the oil is pumped into a main gallery in the cylinder block/crankcase, from where it is distributed to the crankshaft (main bearings) and cylinder head. An oil cooler is fitted next to the oil filter, at the rear of the block. The cooler is supplied with coolant from the engine cooling system.

While the crankshaft and camshaft bearings receive a pressurised supply, the camshaft lobes and valves are lubricated by splash, as are all other engine components. The undersides of the pistons are cooled by oil, sprayed from nozzles fitted above the upper main bearing shells. The turbocharger receives its own pressurised oil supply.

Repair operations possible with the engine in the vehicle

The following operations can theoretically be accomplished without removing the engine from the vehicle. However, it must be noted that working clearance in the engine compartment is extremely limited, particularly at the timing belt end of the engine. Depending on the experience of the person carrying out the work and the tools and working facilities available, some of the following operations may not be possible with the engine in the car. In all cases read through the relevant procedure carefully before starting and make an assessment of the feasibility of carrying out the work with the engine installed.

a) Compression pressure – testing.
b) Cylinder head cover – removal and refitting.
c) Timing belt cover – removal and refitting.
d) Timing belt – renewal.
e) Timing belt tensioner and sprockets – removal and refitting.
f) Camshaft oil seals – renewal.
g) Camshaft and tappets – removal and refitting.
h) Cylinder head – removal, overhaul and refitting.
i) Cylinder head and pistons – decarbonising.
j) Sump – removal and refitting.
k) Crankshaft oil seals – renewal.
l) Oil pump – removal and refitting.
m) Piston/connecting rod assemblies – removal and refitting (but see note below).
n) Flywheel – removal and refitting.
o) Engine/transmission mountings – removal and refitting.

Note: *It is possible to remove the pistons and connecting rods (after removing the cylinder head and sump) without removing the engine, however, this is not recommended. Work of this nature is more easily and thoroughly completed with the engine on the bench, as described in Chapter 2E.*

2 Compression and leakdown tests – description and interpretation

Compression test

Note: *A compression tester suitable for use with diesel engines will be required for this test.*
1 When engine performance is down, or if misfiring occurs which cannot be attributed to the fuel or emissions systems, a compression test can provide diagnostic clues as to the engine's condition. If the test is performed

regularly, it can give warning of trouble before any other symptoms become apparent.
2 The engine must be fully warmed-up to normal operating temperature, the battery must be fully charged and the glow plugs must be removed. The aid of an assistant will be required.
3 Make sure that the ignition is switched off (take out the key). Disconnect the wiring plug at the top of the fuel injection pump, and place the wiring to one side. While the plug is disconnected, cover each half of the plug to keep the pins clean, and to prevent any static discharge, which may damage the pump electronic control unit.
4 Remove the glow plugs as described in Chapter 5C.
5 Fit a compression tester to the No 1 cylinder glow plug hole. The type of tester which screws into the plug thread is preferred.
6 Crank the engine for several seconds on the starter motor. After one or two revolutions, the compression pressure should build up to a maximum figure and then stabilise. Record the highest reading obtained.
7 Repeat the test on the remaining cylinders, recording the pressure in each.
8 The cause of poor compression is less easy to establish on a diesel engine than on a petrol engine. The effect of introducing oil into the cylinders (wet testing) is not conclusive, because there is a risk that the oil will sit in the recess on the piston crown, instead of passing to the rings. However, the following can be used as a rough guide to diagnosis.
9 All cylinders should produce very similar pressures. Note that the compression should build-up quickly in a healthy engine. Low compression on the first stroke, followed by gradually increasing pressure on successive strokes, indicates worn piston rings. A low compression reading on the first stroke, which does not build-up during successive strokes, indicates leaking valves or a blown head gasket (a cracked head could also be the cause).
10 A low reading from two adjacent cylinders is almost certainly due to the head gasket having blown between them and the presence of coolant in the engine oil will confirm this.
11 On completion, remove the compression tester, and refit the glow plugs, with reference to Chapter 5C.
12 Take out the ignition key, then reconnect the injection pump wiring connector.

Leakdown test

13 A leakdown test measures the rate at which compressed air fed into the cylinder is lost. It is an alternative to a compression test, and in many ways it is better, since the escaping air provides easy identification of where pressure loss is occurring (piston rings, valves or head gasket).
14 The equipment required for leakdown testing is unlikely to be available to the home mechanic. If poor compression is suspected, have the test performed by a suitably-equipped garage.

3 Top Dead Centre (TDC) for No 1 cylinder – locating

General information

1 TDC is the highest point in the cylinder that each piston reaches as it travels up and down when the crankshaft turns. Each piston reaches TDC at the end of the compression stroke and again at the end of the exhaust stroke, but TDC generally refers to piston position on the compression stroke. No 1 piston is at the timing belt end of the engine.
2 Positioning No 1 piston at TDC is an essential part of many procedures, such as timing belt removal and camshaft removal.
3 The design of the engine is such that piston-to-valve contact may occur if the camshaft or crankshaft is turned with the timing belt removed. For this reason, it is important to ensure that the camshaft and crankshaft do not move in relation to each other once the timing belt has been removed from the engine.

Setting TDC on No 1 cylinder

Note: *Suitable tools will be required to lock the camshaft and the fuel injection pump sprocket in position during this procedure – see text.*
4 Disconnect the battery negative (earth) lead (refer to Chapter 5A).
5 Remove the cylinder head cover as described in Section 4.
6 Loosen the right-hand front wheel nuts, then firmly apply the handbrake. Jack up the front of the car, and support on axle stands (see *Jacking and vehicle support*). Remove the right-hand front wheel.
7 Loosen and remove the retaining screws and remove the engine undershield.
8 When No 1 cylinder is set to TDC on compression, an offset slot in the left-hand end of the camshaft (left as seen from the driver's seat) should align with the top surface of the cylinder head, to allow a special tool (Ford No 303-376) to be fitted. This tool can be substituted by a suitable piece of flat bar **(see illustrations)**. There is no need to fit this tool at this stage, but check that the slot

3.8a Offset slot in camshaft aligned with cylinder head

3.8b Flat bar engaged in camshaft slot

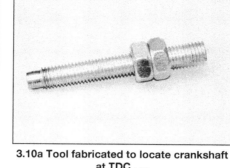

3.10a Tool fabricated to locate crankshaft at TDC . . .

3.10b . . . screw the tool into the cylinder block to locate with the crankshaft

3.12a Unscrew the blanking plug . . .

3.12b . . . and insert the timing pin

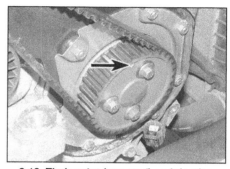

3.13 Timing dot (arrowed) on injection pump sprocket at 12 o'clock position

comes into the required alignment while setting TDC – if the slot is above the level of the head, No 1 cylinder could be on the exhaust stroke.

9 If required, further confirmation that No 1 cylinder is on the compression stroke can be inferred from the positions of the camshaft lobes for No 1 cylinder. When the cylinder is on compression, the inlet and exhaust lobes should be pointing upwards (ie, not depressing the tappets). The camshaft lobes are only visible once the oil baffle plate is removed, and the securing nuts also retain two of the camshaft bearing caps – for more information, refer to Section 9.

10 A TDC timing hole is provided on the front of the cylinder block, to permit the crankshaft to be located more accurately at TDC. A timing pin (Ford service tool 303-193, obtainable from Ford dealers or a tool supplier) screws into the hole, and the crankshaft is then turned so that it contacts the end of the tool. A tool can be fabricated to set the timing at TDC, using a piece of threaded rod **(see illustrations)**.

11 To gain access to the blanking plug fitted over the timing pin hole, remove the auxiliary drivebelt as described in Chapter 1B, then unbolt and remove the alternator coupling, as described in the alternator removal procedure in Chapter 5A.

12 Remove the camshaft setting tool from the slot, and turn the engine back slightly from the TDC position. Unscrew the timing pin blanking plug (which is located in a deeply-recessed hole), and screw in the timing pin **(see illustrations)**. Now carefully turn the

crankshaft forwards until it contacts the timing pin (it should be possible to feel this point – the crankshaft cannot then be turned any further forward).

13 If the engine is being set to TDC as part of the timing belt removal/renewal procedure, further confirmation of the TDC position can be gained once the timing belt outer cover has been removed. At TDC, a punched dot on the injection pump sprocket will be in the 12 o'clock position **(see illustration)**. However, removing the timing belt outer cover involves unbolting the engine right-hand mounting, so this is not included as part of this procedure. It is recommended at this point that the right-hand front wheel is refitted, and the car lowered to the ground before proceeding.

14 Once No 1 cylinder has been positioned at TDC on the compression stroke, TDC for any of the other cylinders can then be located by rotating the crankshaft clockwise 180° at a

time and following the firing order (see Specifications).

15 Before rotating the crankshaft again, make sure that the timing pin and camshaft setting bar are removed. When operations are complete, do not forget to refit the timing pin blanking plug.

4 Cylinder head cover – removal and refitting

Removal

1 Disconnect the battery negative (earth) lead (see Chapter 5A).

2 Noting their positions carefully for refitting, release the hose clips and detach the crankcase ventilation hoses from the cylinder head cover **(see illustrations)**. There are two

4.2a Two crankcase ventilation hoses at the front (rear hose not visible here)

4.2b Release the hose clips and pull the hoses off their stubs

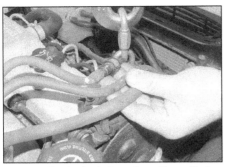

4.3 Unclip the fuel pipes from the cylinder head cover

4.4a Unscrew the securing bolts . . .

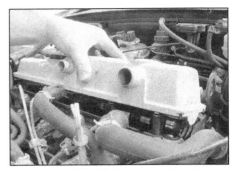

4.4b . . . and lift off the cylinder head cover

hoses at the front, and one at the rear. Move the hoses aside as far as possible.

3 Noting how they are located, unclip the fuel pipes from the cylinder head cover, without disconnecting them **(see illustration)**. Unbolt the power steering pipe bracket from the rear of the cover, and move it clear. Make sure, in moving all the pipes aside, that they are not put under undue strain.

4 Unscrew the three securing bolts, and lift the cylinder head cover off the engine **(see illustrations)**. Recover the gasket carefully – it can be re-used several times, but check its condition before doing so.

5 If required, the baffle plate fitted below the cover can be removed by unscrewing the nuts and taking off the spacer plates and sleeves – note, however, that these nuts also secure

Nos 2 and 4 camshaft bearing caps. Note the positions of all components carefully for refitting **(see illustration)**.

Refitting

6 Clean the sealing surfaces of the cover and the head, and check the condition of the rubber seals fitted to the cover bolts.

7 Before refitting the cover, check that the crankcase ventilation holes are clear. The connection at the rear of the cover leads to the ventilation valve – if this appears to be blocked, use a suitable degreaser to wash out the valve (it is not advisable to use petrol, as this may damage the valve itself).

8 Lightly lubricate the surfaces of the gasket with fresh oil, then fit the gasket to the cover, making sure it is correctly located.

9 Lower the cover into position, ensuring that the gasket is not disturbed, then fit the three bolts and tighten them a little at a time, so that the cover is drawn down evenly to make a good seal.

10 Further refitting is a reversal of removal. Ensure that the pipes are routed as noted on removal, and that the ventilation hoses are correctly and securely reconnected.

11 When the engine has been run for some time, check for signs of oil leakage from the gasket joint.

5 Valve clearances – checking and adjustment

Checking

1 Remove the cylinder head cover as described in Section 4.

2 Remove the baffle plate fitted below the cover by unscrewing the four nuts and taking off the spacer plates and sleeves. Note, however, that these nuts also secure Nos 2 and 4 camshaft bearing caps – it is advisable to refit the nuts temporarily, once the baffle plate has been removed **(see illustrations)**. Note the positions of all components carefully for refitting.

3 During the following procedure, the crankshaft must be turned in order to position the peaks of the camshaft lobes away from the valves. To do this, either turn the crankshaft on the pulley bolt or alternatively raise the front right-hand corner of the vehicle, engage 4th gear, and turn the front

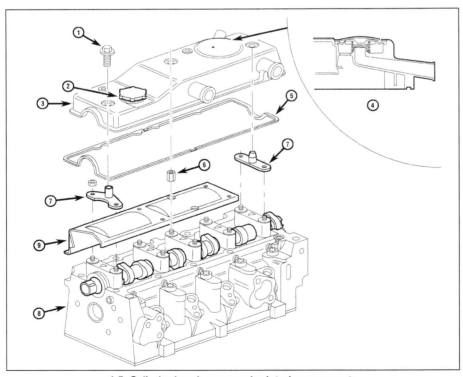

4.5 Cylinder head cover and related components

1 Cover bolt	4 Crankcase ventilation valve	7 Spacer plate
2 Engine oil filler cap	5 Gasket	8 Cylinder head
3 Cylinder head cover	6 Spacer sleeve	9 Baffle plate

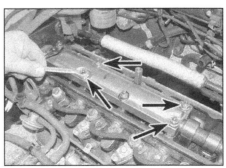

5.2a Unscrew the four nuts . . .

5.2b . . . and lift off the baffle plate . . .

5.2c . . . refit the camshaft bearing cap
nuts temporarily

roadwheel. Access to the pulley bolt is gained by jacking up the front of the vehicle and supporting on axle stands, then removing the auxiliary drivebelt lower cover.

4 If desired, to enable the crankshaft to be turned more easily, remove the glow plugs as described in Chapter 5C.

5 Draw the valve positions on a piece of paper, numbering them 1 to 8 from the timing belt end of the engine. Identify them as inlet or exhaust (ie, 1I, 2E, 3I, 4E, 5I, 6E, 7I, 8E).

6 Turn the crankshaft until the valves of No 4 cylinder (flywheel end) are 'rocking' – the exhaust valve will be closing and the inlet valve will be opening. The piston of No 1 cylinder will be at the top of its compression stroke, with both valves fully closed. The clearances for both valves of No 1 cylinder may be checked at the same time.

7 Use feeler blade(s) to measure the exact clearance between the heel of the camshaft lobe and the shim on the tappet; the feeler blades should be a firm sliding fit. Record the measured clearance on the drawing. From this clearance it will be possible to calculate the thickness of the new shim to be fitted, where necessary. Note that the inlet and exhaust valve clearances are different, so it is important that you know which valve clearance you are checking.

8 With No 1 cylinder valve clearances checked, turn the engine through half a turn so that No 2 valves are 'rocking', then measure the valve clearances of No 3 cylinder in the same way. Similarly check the valve clearances of No 4 cylinder with No 1 valves 'rocking' and No 2 cylinder with No 3 valves 'rocking'. Compare the measured clearances with the values give in the Specifications – any which fall within the range do not require adjustment.

Adjustment

9 If adjustment is required, turn the engine in the normal direction of rotation through approximately 90°, to bring the pistons to mid-stroke. If this is not done, the pistons at TDC will prevent the tappets being depressed, and damage may result. Depress the tappets and then either shim can be withdrawn if the peak of the cam does not prevent access. The Ford tools for this

operation are Nos 21-106 and 21-107, but with care and patience a C-spanner or screwdriver can be used to depress the tappet and the shim can be flicked out with a small screwdriver.

10 If the valve clearance was too small, a thinner shim must be fitted. If the clearance was too large, a thicker shim must be fitted. The thickness of the shim (in mm) is engraved on the side facing away from the camshaft. If the marking is missing or illegible, a micrometer will be needed to establish shim thickness.

11 When the shim thickness and the valve clearance are known, the required thickness of the new shim can be calculated as follows (all measurements in mm):

Sample calculation – clearance too small

Desired clearance (A)	= 0.50
Measured clearance (B)	= 0.35
Shim thickness found (C)	= 3.95
Shim thickness reqd. (D)	= C+B–A = 3.80

Sample calculation – clearance too large

Desired clearance (A)	= 0.35
Measured clearance (B)	= 0.40
Shim thickness found (C)	= 4.05
Shim thickness reqd. (D)	= C+B–A = 4.10

12 With the correct shim fitted, release the tappet depressing tool. Turn the engine back so that the cam lobes are again pointing upwards and check that the clearance is now correct.

13 Repeat the process for the remaining valves, turning the engine each time to bring a pair of cam lobes upwards.

14 It will be helpful for future adjustment if a record is kept of the thickness of shim fitted at each position. The shims required can be purchased in advance once the clearances and the existing shim thicknesses are known.

15 It is permissible to interchange shims between tappets to achieve the correct clearances but it is not advisable to turn the camshaft with any shims removed, since there is a risk that the cam lobe will jam in the empty tappet.

16 When all the clearances are correct, refit the glow plugs (Chapter 5C), then refit the oil baffle plate and tighten the nuts to the specified torque. Refit the cylinder head cover as described in Section 4.

6 Crankshaft pulley –
removal and refitting

Removal

1 Disconnect the battery negative (earth) lead (see Chapter 5A).

2 Loosen the right-hand front roadwheel nuts, then raise the front of the vehicle, and support securely on axle stands (see *Jacking and vehicle support*). Remove the roadwheel.

3 Remove the engine undershield.

4 Remove the two fasteners securing the auxiliary drivebelt lower cover, and remove the cover from under the car.

5 Remove the auxiliary drivebelt, as described in Chapter 1B.

6 The centre bolt which secures the crankshaft pulley must now be slackened. This bolt is tightened to a very high torque, and it is first of all essential to ensure that the car is adequately supported, as considerable effort will be needed.

7 Ford technicians use a special holding tool (205-072) which locates in the outer holes of the pulley and prevents it from turning. If this, or a suitable alternative is not available, select a gear, and have an assistant firmly apply the handbrake and footbrake as the bolt is loosened. If this method is unsuccessful, remove the starter motor as described in Chapter 5A, and jam the flywheel ring gear, using a suitable tool, to prevent the crankshaft from rotating.

8 Unscrew the bolt securing the pulley to the crankshaft, and remove the pulley. It is advisable to obtain a new bolt for reassembly.

9 With the pulley removed, it is advisable to check the crankshaft right-hand oil seal for signs of oil leakage. If necessary, fit a new seal as described in Section 16.

Refitting

10 Refit the pulley to the crankshaft sprocket, then fit the new pulley securing bolt and tighten it as far as possible before the crankshaft starts to rotate.

11 Holding the pulley against rotation as for removal, first tighten the bolt to the specified Stage 1 torque.

12 Stage 2 involves tightening the bolt though an angle, rather than to a torque. The bolt must be rotated through the specified angle – special angle gauges are available from tool outlets. As a guide, a 90° angle is equivalent to a quarter-turn, and this is easily judged by assessing the start and end positions of the socket handle or torque wrench.

13 Refit and tension the auxiliary drivebelt as described in Chapter 1B.

14 Refit the auxiliary drivebelt lower cover, and where removed, the engine undershield(s) and wheelarch liner panels.

15 Refit the roadwheel, lower the vehicle to the ground, and reconnect the battery negative lead. Tighten the wheel nuts to the specified torque.

7.13a Slacken the tensioner bolt . . .

7.13b . . . and remove the tensioner completely

7 Timing belt – removal and refitting

Note 1: *Vehicles manufactured before August 2000 were fitted with a manual timing belt tensioner which entailed the use of a special tool to correctly adjust the timing belt tension. From August 2000, an automatic timing belt tensioner was fitted which automatically maintains the correct timing belt tension after an initial setting up procedure has been carried out. If an early type manual tensioner is encountered (as shown in the photos accompanying this Section), the later type automatic tensioner should be used when the timing belt is fitted.*

Note 2: *Due to the very limited working clearance at the timing belt end of the engine, this is an awkward procedure to carry out with the engine in the car. It will be necessary to raise and lower the right-hand end of the engine to gain sufficient clearance for access to the various components. Read through the entire procedure while viewing the engine, and ascertain whether you have the necessary tools, skill and patience to undertake the work with the engine in the car. Alternatively, remove the engine/transmission as described in Chapter 2E. If the work is to be carried out with the engine in the car, take great care not*

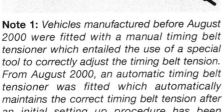

7.13c Slip the timing belt from its sprockets

to strain any attached components as the engine is being raised and lowered. It may be beneficial to remove the driveshafts (Chapter 8) and disconnect the exhaust system at the front pipe flange, if the engine is to be raised and lowered significantly.

Removal

1 Disconnect the battery negative (earth) lead (see Chapter 5A).

2 Apply the handbrake, then jack up the front of the vehicle and support it on axle stands (see *Jacking and vehicle support*).

3 Remove the coolant expansion tank mounting bolt, unclip it at the rear, and move the tank to one side without disconnecting the hoses.

4 Referring to the information in Section 3, set the engine to TDC on No 1 cylinder. The timing pin described must be used, to ensure accuracy.

5 Ford recommend that the engine is further prevented from turning by fitting another special tool, to lock the flywheel ring gear (this prevents the injection pump sprocket from moving). This tool (Ford No 303-393) is also available from Ford dealers, and is quite simple. With the starter motor removed as described in Chapter 5A, the tool bolts across the starter motor aperture in the bellhousing, and a peg on the back of the tool engages and locks the flywheel ring gear. A substitute for this tool could be made, or the ring gear jammed using another suitable tool.

6 Before unbolting the engine mounting, it is recommended that the right-hand wheel is refitted, and the car lowered to the ground (assuming the car has been raised as part of setting the engine to TDC).

7 The engine must now be supported before the right-hand mounting is removed. Ford technicians use an engine support bar, which locates in the channels at the top of each inner wing, and a further beam attached to this, which rests on the front crossmember. If such an arrangement is not available, use an engine crane; either way, use a suitable length

of chain and hooks to attach the lifting gear to the engine lifting eye. If the engine must be supported from below (and this is not recommended), use a large piece of wood on a trolley jack to spread the load and reduce the chance of damage to the sump.

8 With the weight of the engine supported, unscrew the nut and three bolts securing the engine right-hand mounting bracket, and lift off the bracket.

9 With the mounting removed, the engine can be raised and lowered at the right-hand end slightly to improve working clearance.

10 At the rear of the timing belt cover, unbolt the support bracket for the power steering fluid pipe. Unscrew the three bolts (and one stud/bolt at the top), and remove the timing belt outer cover.

11 If the timing belt is not being fitted straight away (or if the belt is being removed as part of another procedure, such as cylinder head removal), temporarily refit the engine right-hand mounting and tighten the bolts securely.

12 Before proceeding further, check once more that the engine is positioned at TDC on No 1 cylinder, as described in Section 3. The position of the injection pump sprocket can now be confirmed – a dot marking on the sprocket should be at the 12 o'clock position.

13 Slacken the timing belt tensioner bolt, and remove the tensioner completely. Slip the timing belt from the sprockets, and remove it **(see illustrations)**.

14 The camshaft sprocket must be removed – this is necessary as part of setting up the new timing belt, to ensure that the correct valve timing is preserved. Not only will a method for holding the sprocket stationary be required, but the sprocket itself is mounted on a taper, so a puller will be needed to free it from the camshaft. Due to its design, the sprocket cannot readily be removed using an ordinary puller, so either the Ford tool (303-651) must be obtained, or a suitable alternative fabricated.

15 Holding the camshaft sprocket using a suitable tool, loosen the sprocket bolt. **Note:** *Do not rely on the TDC setting bar engaged in*

7.21 Refit the camshaft sprocket bolt, hand tight at first

7.23 Tool fitted to slot in the end of the camshaft

the slot at the opposite end of the camshaft to hold it stationary – not only is this dangerous, it could well result in damage to the camshaft.

16 Using a suitable puller, release the camshaft sprocket from the taper, and remove it.

17 Do **not** be tempted to re-use the old timing belt under any circumstances – even if it is known to have covered less mileage than the renewal interval indicated in Chapter 1B. Ford state that, once a new timing belt has been run on the engine, it is considered worn, and should be discarded. In any case, given the potential expense involved should the belt fail in service, re-using an old belt would be a false economy.

18 Before disposing of the old belt, however, examine it for evidence of contamination by coolant or lubricant. If there are any signs of contamination, find the source of the contamination before progressing any further. If an oil leak is evident, this will most likely be from the camshaft seal. Cure the problem, then wash down the whole area (including the sprockets) with degreaser and allow to dry before fitting the new belt.

19 Obtain a new timing belt and the later type automatic tensioner assembly. If genuine Ford parts are being used, the automatic tensioner is supplied with the new timing belt as part of a repair kit.

Refitting

20 Ensure that the crankshaft and camshaft are still set to TDC on No 1 cylinder, as described in Section 3.

21 Refit the camshaft sprocket to the camshaft, tightening the bolt by hand only **(see illustration)**.

22 Fit the timing belt tensioner into position, noting that the adjustment plate (containing the hexagonal slot) must be set pointing to the 3 o'clock position. Fit the retaining bolt, tightening it finger-tight only at this stage.

23 Fit the timing belt over the sprockets and above the tensioner pulley, ensuring that the injection pump sprocket does not move (the

camshaft sprocket must be free to turn – remember that the camshaft itself is locked by the tool fitted to its slotted end) **(see illustration)**.

24 Using an Allen key inserted into the hexagonal slot on the adjustment plate, tension the timing belt by turning the adjustment plate anti-clockwise to approximately the 9 o'clock position. Check that the moving pointer on the tensioner body is now centralised within the slot on the adjustment plate. Hold the adjustment plate in this position and tighten the tensioner retaining bolt to the specified torque.

25 Hold the camshaft sprocket using the home-made tool, and tighten the sprocket bolt to the specified torque.

26 Remove the locking tools from the engine, so that it can be turned; these may include the timing pin, the plate fitted into the camshaft slot, and the tool used to lock the flywheel.

27 Mark the TDC position of the crankshaft pulley, using paint or typist's correction fluid, to give a rough indication of TDC, and so that the number of turns can be counted.

28 Using a spanner or socket on the crankshaft pulley centre bolt, turn the engine forwards (clockwise, viewed from the timing belt end) through six full turns, bringing the engine almost up to the TDC position on completion.

29 Using the information in Section 3, insert the crankshaft timing pin and continue turning the crankshaft until it once again contacts the timing pin. With the crankshaft now at TDC, check that it is possible to insert the camshaft locking tool.

30 Observe the timing belt tensioner and check that the moving pointer on the tensioner body is still centralised within the slot on the adjustment plate. The moving pointer may have moved upward slightly in relation to the slot, but this is acceptable.

31 If it was not possible to insert the camshaft locking tool with the crankshaft positioned at TDC, or if the tensioner pointer is not in the correct position, repeat the

procedure from paragraph 20 onward. If all is satisfactory so far, continue as follows.

32 Remove the camshaft locking tool and crankshaft timing pin from the engine. Refit the blanking plug to the timing pin hole, then refit the alternator coupling (Chapter 5A).

33 If the engine right-hand mounting had been temporarily refitted as described in paragraph 11, support the engine once more, and remove the mounting.

34 Refit the timing belt outer cover, and tighten the retaining bolts securely.

35 Refit the engine right-hand mounting bracket, and tighten the nuts and bolts to the specified torque.

36 With the engine securely supported by its mounting once more, the engine supporting tools can be carefully removed.

37 Refit the cylinder head cover as described in Section 4 and the auxiliary drivebelt as described in Chapter 1B.

38 Refit the coolant expansion tank.

39 Refit all other components removed for access, then reconnect the battery negative lead.

8   Timing belt tensioner and sprockets – removal, inspection and refitting

Timing belt tensioner

1 The timing belt tensioner is removed as part of the timing belt renewal procedure, in Section 7.

Camshaft sprocket

2 The camshaft sprocket is removed as part of the timing belt renewal procedure, in Section 7.

Fuel injection pump sprocket

3 Removal of the injection pump sprocket is described as part of the injection pump removal procedure, in Chapter 4C. Note that the sprocket is sealed to the pump using two types of sealant/locking compound.

9 Camshaft and tappets – removal, inspection and refitting

Note: *A new camshaft oil seal will be required on refitting.*

Removal

1 Remove the timing belt and camshaft sprocket as described in Section 7.

2 Remove the camshaft oil seal. The seal is quite deeply recessed – Ford dealers have a special seal extractor for this (tool No 303-293). In the absence of this tool, do not use any removal method which might damage the sealing surfaces, or a leak will result when the new seal is fitted **(see Haynes Hint)**.

 One of the best ways to remove an oil seal is to carefully drill or punch two holes through the seal, opposite each other (taking care not to damage the surface behind the seal as this is done). Two self-tapping screws are then screwed into the holes; by pulling on the screw heads alternately with a pair of pliers, the seal can be extracted.

3 Unscrew and remove the nuts securing the oil baffle plate to the top of the engine, noting that these nuts also secure Nos 2 and 4 camshaft bearing caps. Lift off the baffle plate, and recover the bearing caps – if no identification numbers are evident on the caps, mark them for position, as they must be refitted to the correct locations.

4 Progressively unscrew (by half a turn at a time) the nuts securing the remaining (Nos 1, 3 and 5) bearing caps until the camshaft is free.

5 Lift off each bearing cap and bearing shell in turn, and mark it for position if necessary – all the caps must be refitted in their original positions.

6 Carefully lift out the camshaft, and place it somewhere safe – the lobes must not be scratched. Remove the lower part of the bearing shells in turn, and mark them for position **(see illustration)**.

9.6 Remove the camshaft bearing shells

7 Before lifting out the tappets and shims, give some thought to how they will be stored while they are removed. Unless new components are being fitted, the tappets and shims must be identified for position. The best way to do this is to take a box, and divide it into eight compartments, each with a clearly-marked number; taking No 1 tappet and shim as being that nearest the timing belt end of the engine, lift out each tappet and shim, and place it in the box. Alternatively, keep the tappet/shim assemblies in line, in fitted order, as they are removed – mark No 1 to avoid confusion.

Inspection

8 With the camshaft removed, examine the bearing caps and the bearing locations in the cylinder head for signs of obvious wear or pitting. If evident, a new cylinder head will probably be required. Also check that the oil supply holes in the cylinder head are free from obstructions. (New bearing shells should be used on reassembly.)

9 Visually inspect the camshaft for evidence of wear on the surfaces of the lobes and journals. Normally their surfaces should be smooth and have a dull shine; look for scoring, erosion or pitting and areas that appear highly polished, indicating excessive wear. Accelerated wear will occur once the hardened exterior of the camshaft has been damaged, so always renew worn items. **Note:** *If these symptoms are visible on the tips of the camshaft lobes, check the corresponding tappet/shim, as it will probably be worn as well.*

10 If suitable precision measuring equipment (such as a micrometer) is available, the camshaft bearing journals can be checked for wear, by comparing the values measured with those specified.

11 If the machined surfaces of the camshaft appear discoloured or blued, it is likely that it has been overheated at some point, probably due to inadequate lubrication. This may have distorted the shaft, in which case the runout should be checked; Ford do not quote a runout tolerance, so if this kind of damage is suspected, an engine reconditioning specialist should be consulted. In the case of inadequate lubrication, distortion is unlikely to be the only damage which has occurred, and a new camshaft will probably be needed.

12 To measure the camshaft endfloat, temporarily refit the camshaft to the cylinder head, then fit Nos 1 and 5 bearing caps and tighten the retaining nuts to the specified torque setting. Anchor a DTI gauge to the timing belt end of the cylinder head. Push the camshaft to one end of the cylinder head as far as it will travel, then rest the DTI gauge probe on the end face of the camshaft, and zero the gauge. Push the camshaft as far as it will go to the other end of the cylinder head, and record the gauge reading. Verify the reading by pushing the camshaft back to its original position and checking that the gauge indicates zero again. **Note:** *The tappets must*

not be fitted whilst this measurement is being taken.

13 Check that the camshaft endfloat measurement is within the limit listed in the Specifications. If the measurement is outside the specified limit, wear is unlikely to be confined to any one component, so renewal of the camshaft, cylinder head and bearing caps must be considered.

14 The camshaft bearing running clearance should now be measured. One method (which will be difficult to achieve without a range of micrometers or internal/external expanding calipers) is to measure the outside diameters of the camshaft bearing surfaces and the internal diameters formed by the bearing caps and the bearing locations in the cylinder head. The difference between these two measurements is the running clearance.

15 Another, more accurate, method of measuring the running clearance involves the use of Plastigauge. This consists of a fine thread of perfectly-round plastic which is compressed between the bearing cap and the journal. When the cap is removed, the plastic is deformed, and can be measured with a special card gauge supplied with the kit. The running clearance is determined from this gauge. Plastigauge is sometimes difficult to obtain, but enquiries at one of the larger specialist quality motor factors should produce the name of a stockist in your area. The procedure for using Plastigauge is as follows.

16 Ensure that the cylinder head, bearing cap, bearing shell and camshaft bearing surfaces are completely clean and dry. Lay the lower bearing shells and camshaft in position in the cylinder head.

17 Lay a length of Plastigauge on top of each of the camshaft bearing journals.

18 Place the bearing caps/shells in position over the camshaft, and progressively tighten the retaining nuts to the specified torque. **Note:** *Do not rotate the camshaft whilst the bearing caps are in place, as the measurements will be affected.*

19 Unscrew the nuts and carefully remove the bearing caps again, lifting them vertically away from the camshaft to avoid disturbing the Plastigauge. The Plastigauge should remain on the camshaft bearing surface.

20 Hold the scale card supplied with the kit against each bearing journal, and measure the width of the crushed Plastigauge, using the graduated markings on the card. The width of the crushed Plastigauge corresponds to the bearing running clearance.

21 Compare the camshaft running clearance measurements with the figure given in the Specifications; if any are outside the specified tolerance, then check with Ford for new bearing shells. If no other size of shells are available, the camshaft, cylinder head and bearing caps should be renewed.

22 On completion, remove the bearing caps/shells and camshaft, and clean off all remaining traces of Plastigauge.

9.25 Lubricate the tappets before refitting

9.26 Refit the brake vacuum pump pushrod before refitting the camshaft

23 Inspect the tappets and shims for obvious signs of wear or damage, and renew if necessary.

Refitting

24 Make sure that the top surfaces of the cylinder head, and in particular the camshaft bearings and the mating surfaces for the camshaft bearing caps, are completely clean.
25 Smear some clean engine oil onto the sides of the tappets, and offer each one into position in their original bores in the cylinder head, together with its respective shim **(see illustration)**. Push them down until they contact the valves, then lubricate the top surface of each shim.
26 Lubricate the camshaft and cylinder head bearing journals with clean engine oil. If the

pushrod which operates the brake vacuum pump has been removed from the cylinder head **(see illustration)**, refit it now – once the camshaft is in position, the pushrod cannot be refitted.
27 Carefully lower the camshaft into position in the cylinder head, making sure that the cam lobes for No 1 cylinder are pointing upwards. Also use the position of the locking tool slot at the end of the camshaft as a guide to correct alignment when refitting – the slot should be flush to the top surface of the cylinder head (the larger 'semi-circle' created by the offset slot should be uppermost).
28 Prior to refitting the No 1 camshaft bearing cap, the front halves of the flat sealing surface must be coated with a smear of suitable sealant, as shown **(see illustration)**.

29 Lubricate Nos 1, 3 and 5 bearing caps and shells with clean oil (taking care not to get any on the sealant-coated surfaces of No 1 cap), then place them into their correct positions. Refit the bearing cap nuts, and tighten them progressively to the specified torque wrench setting.
30 The outer edges of No 1 bearing cap must now be sealed to the cylinder head surface with a thin bead of suitable sealant.
31 Clean out the oil seal housing and the sealing surface of the camshaft by wiping it with a lint-free cloth. Remove any swarf or burrs that may cause the seal to leak.
32 Apply a little oil to the new camshaft oil seal, and fit it over the end of the camshaft, lips facing inwards. To avoid damaging the seal lips, wrap a little tape over the end of the camshaft. Ford dealers have a special tool (No 303-199) for fitting the seal, but if this is not available, a deep socket of suitable size can be used. It is important that the seal is fitted square to the shaft, and is fully seated.
33 Refit the camshaft sprocket and timing belt as described in Section 7.
34 Check the valve clearances as described in Section 5.
35 Oil the bearing surfaces of Nos 2 and 4 bearing caps, then refit them and the oil baffle plate to the engine. Tighten the bearing cap nuts to the specified torque.
36 Refit the cylinder head cover as described in Section 4.
37 Further refitting is a reversal of removal.

10 Camshaft oil seal – renewal

1 Remove the timing belt and camshaft sprocket as described in Section 7. Access to the seal is hampered by the presence of the timing belt backplate, but this can only be removed after taking off the injection pump sprocket; it should not prove necessary to remove the backplate in practice.
2 Remove the camshaft oil seal. The seal is quite deeply recessed – Ford dealers have a special seal extractor for this (tool No 303-293). In the absence of this tool, do not use any removal method which might damage the sealing surfaces, or a leak will result when the new seal is fitted **(see Haynes Hint)**.

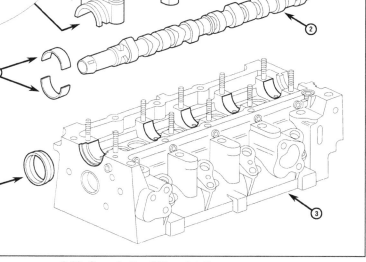

9.28 Camshaft refitting details

1 *Bearing caps (1 to 5)*
2 *Camshaft*
3 *Cylinder head*
4 *Camshaft oil seal*
5 *Bearing shells*
A *Sealant application areas on No 1 bearing cap*

> **HAYNES HINT** *One of the best ways to remove an oil seal is to carefully drill or punch two holes through the seal, opposite each other (taking care not to damage the surface behind the seal as this is done). Two self-tapping screws are then screwed into the holes; by pulling on the screw heads alternately with a pair of pliers, the seal can be extracted.*

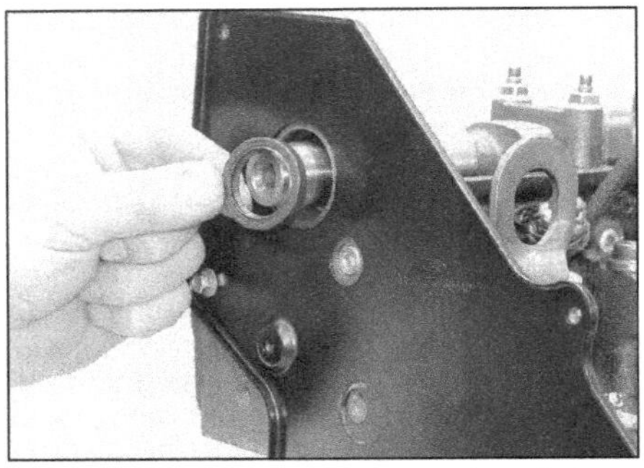

10.4a Lubricate the oil seal before fitting over the camshaft . . .

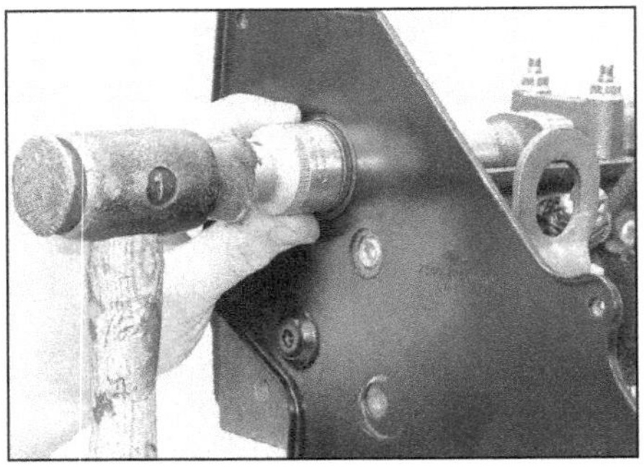

10.4b . . . and use a suitable socket to tap seal in squarely

3 Clean out the seal housing and the sealing surface of the camshaft by wiping it with a lint-free cloth. Remove any swarf or burrs that may cause the seal to leak.

4 Apply a little oil to the new camshaft oil seal, and fit it over the end of the camshaft, lips facing inwards. To avoid damaging the seal lips, wrap a little tape over the end of the camshaft. Ford dealers have a special tool (No 303-199) for fitting the seal, but if this is not available, a deep socket of suitable size can be used. **Note:** *Select a socket that bears only on the hard outer surface of the seal, not the inner lip which can easily be damaged.* It is important that the seal is fitted square to the shaft, and is fully seated **(see illustrations)**.

5 Refit the camshaft sprocket and timing belt as described in Section 7.

11 Cylinder head – removal, inspection and refitting

Note: *Ford technicians remove the cylinder head complete with the inlet and exhaust manifolds. Whilst this may reduce the overall time spent, it makes the cylinder head assembly incredibly heavy and awkward to lift clear (the head is of cast iron, and is quite heavy enough on its own). We felt that, for the DIY mechanic at least, removing the manifolds would be the more sensible option.*

Removal

1 Remove the battery as described in Chapter 5A, then unscrew the bolts and remove the tray from the engine compartment.

2 Remove the air cleaner housing as described in Chapter 4C.

3 Remove the cylinder head cover as described in Section 4.

4 Using the information in Section 3, bring the engine round to just before the TDC position on No 1 cylinder. Do not insert any of the locking tools at this stage.

5 Apply the handbrake, then jack up the front of the car and support it on axle stands (see *Jacking and vehicle support*).

6 Drain the cooling system as described in Chapter 1B.

7 Remove the turbocharger/exhaust manifold and the inlet manifold as described in Chapter 4C.

8 Remove the timing belt as described in Section 7.

9 Remove the bolt securing the timing belt backplate to the cylinder head, and the seven nuts around the injection pump sprocket. While this does not allow the backplate to be removed, it makes it possible to bend the plate enough for the camshaft's tapered end to pass as the head is lifted. If the backplate is to be removed completely, this requires that the injection pump sprocket and its oil seal housing are also removed, as described in Chapter 4C.

10 Disconnect the glow plug supply lead in front of the dipstick tube, and move the wiring harness to one side.

11 Release the clips from the crankcase ventilation hoses as necessary, and disconnect the wiring plug from the oil pressure switch, then unbolt and remove the oil separator from the left-hand end of the cylinder head **(see illustrations)**.

12 Unclip and disconnect the large wiring plug for the cylinder head temperature sensor, next to the brake vacuum pump **(see illustration)**.

13 Disconnect the vacuum hose and the oil return pipe from the vacuum pump at the left-hand end of the cylinder head (left as seen from the driver's seat). Unscrew the top mounting bolt, and loosen the lower bolt – the lower mounting is slotted, to make removal easier – and lift off the pump. Recover the

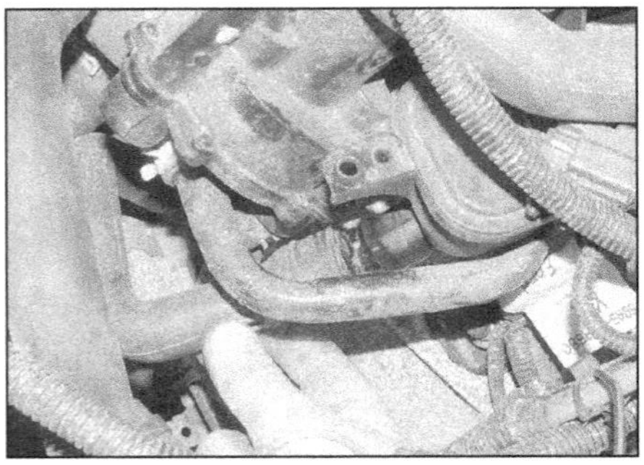

11.11a Disconnect the breather hoses . . .

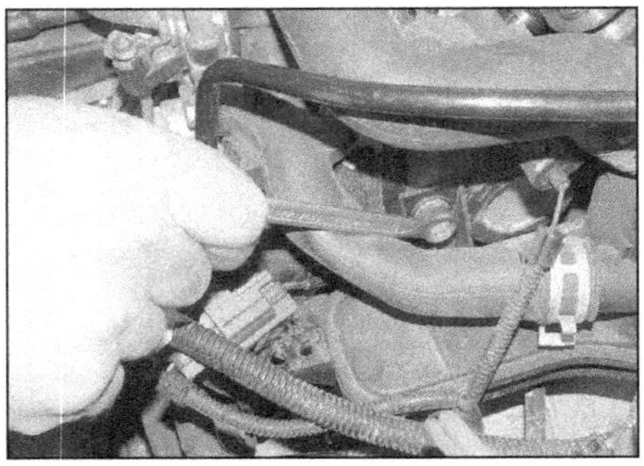

11.11b . . . unscrew the mounting bolt . . .

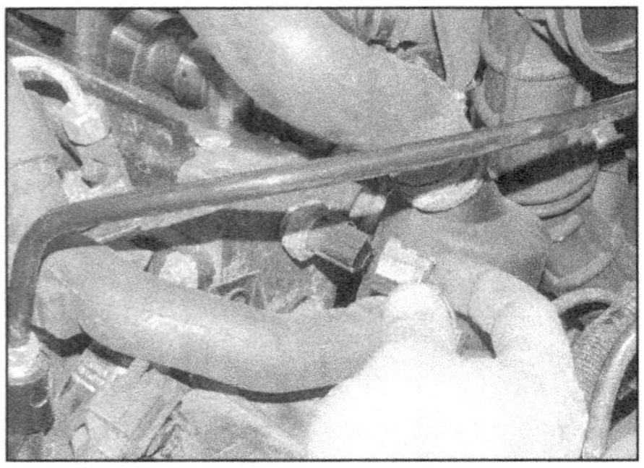

11.11c . . . disconnect the oil pressure warning light switch . . .

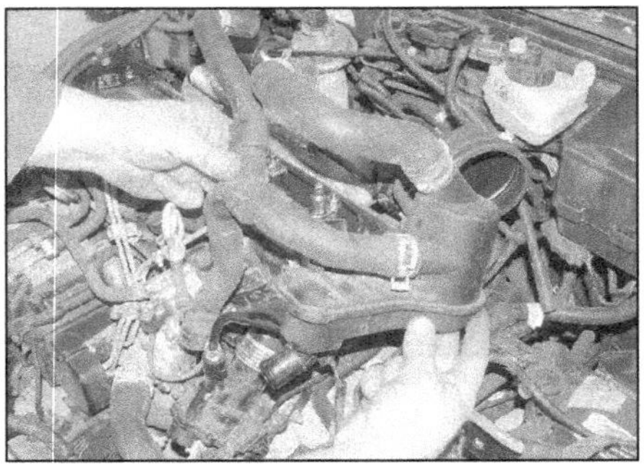

11.11d . . . and remove the oil separator from the end of the cylinder head

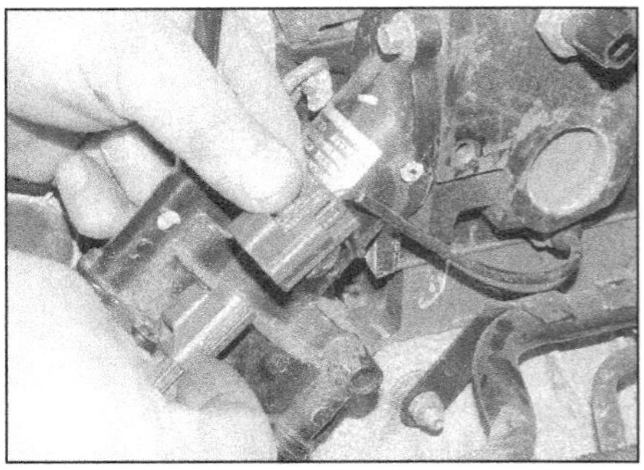

11.12 Disconnecting the cylinder head temperature sensor wiring plug

11.13a Unscrew the vacuum hose union . . .

11.13b . . . release the hose clip and disconnect the oil return pipe . . .

11.13c . . . then unbolt the vacuum pump . . .

11.13d . . . and remove the vacuum pump – recover the O-ring

11.14a Remove the glow plug supply lead securing screw

11.14b Unscrew the thermostat housing bolts

large O-ring seal – a new one must be used on reassembly **(see illustrations)**.

14 Remove the screw securing the glow plug supply lead to the thermostat housing. Remove the two bolts securing the thermostat housing to the front of the head, then pull the housing forwards and rest it clear of the head without disconnecting any further pipework **(see illustrations)**. Note that a new thermostat housing gasket will be needed for reassembly.

15 Disconnect the injection pump wiring connector, by pulling the securing clip towards the front, then pulling the wiring plug out to the side **(see illustrations)**.

16 Where fitted, cut the cable-ties securing the insulation cover fitted over the pump, and remove the cover. Clean around the pipe unions at the injectors and at the pump.

17 Unscrew the union nuts and disconnect the leak-off pipes, and remove each pair of fuel injection pipes. When unscrewing the unions at the pump end, counterhold the pump adapters with one spanner, and loosen the unions with another. Cover over the end fittings on the injection pump and on the injectors, to keep the dirt out **(see illustrations)**.

18 Unbolt the power steering pipe bracket from the left-hand side of the cylinder head.

19 Remove the four nuts securing the oil baffle plate, and carefully lift the plate off the

11.15a Pull the locking clip out towards the front . . .

11.15b . . . then separate the wiring plug from the injection pump

11.17a Unscrew the union nuts . . .

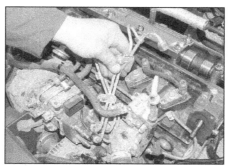

11.17b . . . then remove each pair of injection pipes

11.17c Plastic bag taped over the injector pipe unions

11.17d Fingers cut from rubber gloves, secured over the injector unions

11.21a Working in the reverse of the tightening sequence, unscrew . . .

11.21b . . . and remove the cylinder head bolts

engine. Note that these nuts are also used to secure Nos 2 and 4 camshaft bearing caps, which will then be loose. Once the plate is removed, refit the nuts by hand, to keep the caps in place.

20 Check around the head and the engine bay that there is nothing still attached to the cylinder head, nor anything which would prevent it from being lifted away.

21 Working in the reverse order of the tightening sequence **(refer to illustration 11.46)**, loosen the cylinder head bolts by half a turn at a time, until they are all loose. Remove the head bolts, and discard them – Ford state that they must not be re-used, even if they appear to be serviceable **(see illustrations)**. Note the fitted positions of the two shorter bolts, which should be the two nearest the timing belt end of the engine.

22 Bend the timing belt backplate gently away from the head sufficiently for the camshaft stub to clear it. Lift the cylinder head away; use assistance if possible, as it is a very heavy assembly.

23 If the head is stuck (as is possible), be careful how you choose to free it. Striking the head with tools carries the risk of damage, and the head is located on two dowels, so its movement will be limited. Do not, under any circumstances, lever the head between the mating surfaces, as this will certainly damage the sealing surfaces for the gasket, leading to leaks.

24 Once the head has been removed, recover the gasket from the two dowels. The gasket is manufactured from laminated steel, and cannot be re-used, but see paragraph 26.

11.29 Measuring piston protrusion with a dial test indicator (DTI)

Inspection

25 If required, dismantling and inspection of the cylinder head is covered in Part E of this Chapter.

Cylinder head gasket selection

26 Examine the old cylinder head gasket for manufacturer's identification markings. These will be in the form of notches (two to seven) on the front edge of the gasket, which indicate the gasket's thickness **(refer to illustration 11.42)**.

27 Unless new components have been fitted, or the cylinder head has been machined (skimmed), the new cylinder head gasket must be of the same type as the old one. Purchase the required gasket, and proceed to paragraph 33.

28 If the head has been machined, or if new pistons have been fitted, it is likely that a head gasket of different thickness to the original will be needed. Gasket selection is made on the basis of the measured piston protrusion above the cylinder head gasket surface (the protrusion must fall within the range given in the Specifications.

29 To measure the piston protrusion, anchor a dial test indicator (DTI) to the top face (cylinder head gasket mating face) of the cylinder block, and zero the gauge on the gasket mating face **(see illustration)**.

30 Rest the gauge probe above No 1 piston crown, and turn the crankshaft slowly by hand until the piston reaches TDC (its maximum height). Measure and record the maximum piston projection at TDC.

31 Repeat the measurement for the remaining pistons, and record the results.

32 If the measurements differ from piston to piston, take the highest figure, and use this to determine the thickness of the head gasket required. At the time of writing, details of the gasket selection (ie, which gasket to use for amount of protrusion) were not published by Ford; however, if the measured protrusion is taken to a Ford dealer, it should be possible for them to suggest the required gasket.

Preparation for refitting

33 The mating faces of the cylinder head and cylinder block must be perfectly clean before refitting the head. Use a hard plastic or

wooden scraper to remove all traces of gasket and carbon; also clean the piston crowns. **Note:** The new head gasket has rubber-coated surfaces, which could be damaged from sharp edges or debris left by a metal scraper.

34 Take particular care when cleaning the piston crowns, as the soft aluminium alloy is easily damaged.

35 Make sure that the carbon is not allowed to enter the oil and water passages – this is particularly important for the lubrication system, as carbon could block the oil supply to the engine's components. Using adhesive tape and paper, seal the water, oil and bolt holes in the cylinder block.

36 To prevent carbon entering the gap between the pistons and bores, smear a little grease in the gap. After cleaning each piston, use a small brush to remove all traces of grease and carbon from the gap, then wipe away the remainder with a clean rag. Clean all the pistons in the same way.

37 Check the mating surfaces of the cylinder block and the cylinder head for nicks, deep scratches and other damage (refer to the Note in paragraph 33). If slight, they may be removed carefully with a file, but if excessive, machining may be the only alternative to renewal.

38 If warpage of the cylinder head gasket surface is suspected, use a straight-edge to check it for distortion. Refer to Part E of this Chapter if necessary.

39 Ensure that the cylinder head bolt holes in the crankcase are clean and free of oil. Syringe or soak up any oil left in the bolt holes. This is most important in order that the correct bolt tightening torque can be applied, and to prevent the possibility of the block being cracked by hydraulic pressure when the bolts are tightened.

Refitting

40 Turn the crankshaft anti-clockwise all the pistons at an equal height, approximately halfway down their bores from the TDC position (see Section 3). This will eliminate any risk of piston-to-valve contact as the cylinder head is refitted.

41 To guide the cylinder head into position, screw two long studs (or old cylinder head

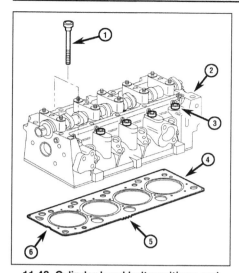

11.42 Cylinder head bolt positions and gasket details

1   *Shorter bolts (two, 137 mm long)*
2   *Cylinder head*
3   *Longer bolts (eight, 177 mm long)*
4   *Cylinder head gasket*
5   *Thickness marking (notches)*
6   *Position marking (cut-out)*

bolts with the heads cut off, and slots cut in the ends to enable the bolts to be unscrewed) into the end cylinder head bolt locations on the manifold side of the cylinder block.

42 Ensure that the cylinder head locating dowels are in place at the front corners of the cylinder block, then fit the new cylinder head gasket over the dowels, ensuring that the OBEN/TOP marking is uppermost, and the notches are at the front (there is a further cut-out at the timing belt end of the gasket) **(see illustration)**. Take care to avoid damaging the gasket's rubber coating.

43 Lower the cylinder head into position on the gasket, ensuring that it engages correctly over the guide studs and dowels.

44 Fit the new cylinder head bolts to the eight remaining bolt locations (remember that the two shorter bolts are fitted at the timing belt end of the engine) and screw them in as far as possible by hand.

45 Unscrew the two guide studs from the exhaust side of the cylinder block, then screw in the two remaining new cylinder head bolts as far as possible by hand.

46 Working in the sequence shown **(see illustration)**, tighten all the cylinder head bolts to the specified Stage 1 torque.

47 Again working in the sequence shown, tighten all the cylinder head bolts to the specified Stage 2 torque.

48 When all the bolts have been tightened to the Stage 2 torque, go around again in the tightening sequence, and tighten all the cylinder head bolts to the specified Stage 3 torque.

49 Stage 4 involves tightening the bolts

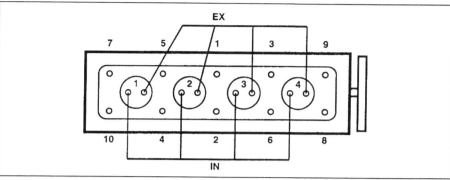

11.46 Cylinder head bolt tightening sequence

though an angle, rather than to a torque. Each bolt in sequence must be rotated through the specified angle – special angle gauges are available from tool outlets. As a guide, a 90° angle is equivalent to a quarter-turn, and this is easily judged by assessing the start and end positions of the socket handle or torque wrench. **Note:** *The two shorter bolts at the timing belt end of the engine are tightened through a smaller angle than the remaining eight bolts – do not get confused when following the tightening sequence.*

50 After finally tightening the cylinder head bolts, turn the crankshaft forwards to bring No 1 piston up to TDC, so that the crankshaft contacts the timing pin (see Section 3).

51 The remainder of the refitting procedure is a reversal of the removal procedure, bearing in mind the following points:

a) *Refit the timing belt with reference to Section 7.*
b) *Reconnect the exhaust front section to the exhaust manifold with reference to Chapter 4C.*
c) *Refit the cylinder head cover with reference to Section 4.*
d) *Refit the air cleaner as described in Chapter 4C.*
e) *Refill the cooling system as described in Chapter 1B.*
f) *Check and if necessary top up the engine oil level as described in 'Weekly checks'.*

12 Sump – removal and refitting

Removal

Note: *The full procedure outlined below must be followed so that the mating surfaces can be cleaned and prepared to achieve an oil-tight joint on reassembly.*

1 Apply the handbrake, then jack up the front of the vehicle and support it on axle stands (see *Jacking and vehicle support*).

2 Referring to Chapter 1B if necessary, drain the engine oil, then clean and refit the engine oil drain plug, tightening it to the specified torque wrench setting. Although not strictly

necessary as part of the dismantling procedure, owners are advised to remove and discard the oil filter, so that it can be renewed with the oil.

3 A conventional sump gasket is not used, and sealant is used instead.

4 Progressively unscrew the twelve sump retaining bolts, and the two retaining nuts (the bolts are of different lengths, but it will be obvious where they fit on reassembly). Break the joint by striking the sump with the palm of the hand, then lower the sump away, turning it as necessary.

5 Unfortunately, the use of sealant can make removal of the sump more difficult. If care is taken not to damage the surfaces, the sealant can be cut around using a sharp knife. On no account lever between the mating faces, as this will almost certainly damage them, resulting in leaks when finished. Ford technicians have a tool comprising a metal rod which is inserted through the sump drain hole, and a handle to pull the sump downwards.

>
> *If the sump is particularly difficult to remove, extracting the two studs may prove useful – thread two nuts onto the stud, tightening them against each other, then use a spanner on the inner nut to unscrew the stud. Note the locations of the studs for refitting.*

Refitting

6 On reassembly, thoroughly clean and degrease the mating surfaces of the cylinder block/crankcase and sump, removing all traces of sealant, then use a clean rag to wipe out the sump and the engine's interior.

7 If the two studs have been removed, they must be refitted before the sump is offered up, to ensure that it is aligned correctly. If this is not done, some of the sealant may enter the blind holes for the sump bolts, preventing the bolts from being fully fitted.

8 Referring to the accompanying illustration, apply sealant to the sump flange, making sure the bead is around the inside edge of the bolt

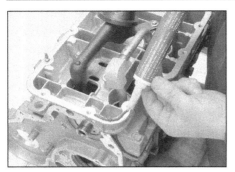

12.8a Apply the sealant to the crankcase

holes. Ford specify that the sealant must be applied in two different thicknesses, but this may be difficult to achieve in practice **(see illustrations)**. **Note:** *The sump must be refitted within 10 minutes of applying the sealant.*

9 Fit the sump over the studs, and insert the sump bolts and two nuts, tightening them by hand only at this stage.

10 Tighten all the bolts and nuts in the sequence shown **(refer to illustration 12.8b)**.

11 Lower the car to the ground. Wait at least 1 hour for the sealant to cure (or whatever time is indicated by the sealant manufacturer) before refilling the engine with oil. If removed, fit a new oil filter with reference to Chapter 1B.

13 Oil pump – removal, inspection and refitting

Removal

1 Remove the crankshaft pulley as described in Section 6.

2 Unbolt the auxiliary drivebelt idler pulley in front of the crank pulley location.

3 Remove the timing belt and camshaft sprocket as described in Section 7.

4 Remove the injection pump sprocket and oil seal housing as described in Chapter 4C.

5 Unbolt and remove the timing belt backplate from the engine.

6 The oil pump is secured by seven studs and twelve bolts – note their positions carefully for refitting. The studs can be unscrewed using a spanner on the hex provided.

7 Once all the fasteners have been removed, carefully lift the pump from its location. Recover the main gasket, and the smaller spacer ring from below the injection pump. Neither gasket may be re-used – obtain new ones for reassembly.

Inspection

8 Undo the retaining screws and remove the cover from the oil pump **(see illustration)**. Note the location of the identification marks on the inner and outer rotors for refitting.

9 Unscrew the plug and remove the pressure relief valve, spring and plunger, clean out and

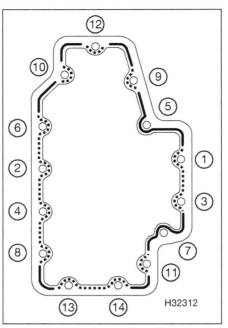

12.8b Sump bolt tightening sequence and sealant application details

Solid line – 3.5 mm diameter bead of sealant
Dotted line – 2.5 mm diameter bead of sealant

check condition of components **(see illustration)**.

10 The clearance between the inner and

13.8 Undo the retaining screws and remove the rotor cover

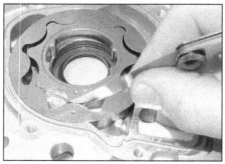

13.10 Checking the clearance between the inner and outer rotor

outer rotors can be checked using feeler blades, and compared with the value given in the Specifications **(see illustration)**.

11 Check the general condition of the oil pump, and in particular, its mating face to the cylinder block. If the mating face is damaged significantly, this may lead to oil loss (and a resulting drop in available oil pressure).

12 Inspect the rotors for obvious signs of wear or damage; it is not clear at the time of writing whether individual components are available separately. Lubricate the rotors with fresh engine oil and refit them into the body, making sure that the identification marks are positioned as noted on removal **(see illustration)**.

13 If the oil pump has been removed as part of a major engine overhaul, it is assumed that the engine will have completed a substantial mileage. In this case, it is often considered good practice to fit a new (or reconditioned) pump as a matter of course. In other words, if the rest of the engine is being rebuilt, the engine has completed a large mileage, or there is any question as to the old pump's condition, it is preferable to fit a new oil pump.

Refitting

14 Before fitting the oil pump, ensure that the mating faces on the pump and the engine block are completely clean.

15 Lay the main metal gasket and a new spacer ring in position on the engine – in the case of the spacer ring, 'stick' it in position

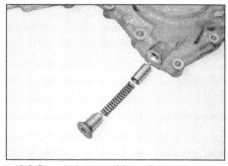

13.9 Check the condition of the pressure relief valve and clean out the oilways

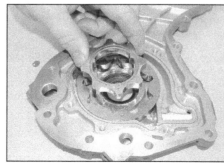

13.12 Check and lubricate the rotors when refitting

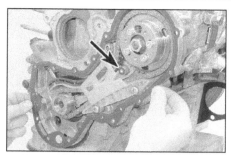

13.15 Fitting the new metal gasket and spacer ring (arrowed) in position

with a little oil or grease if required **(see illustration)**.

16 Offer the pump into position, and secure it with the studs and bolts, tightened only loosely at this stage **(see illustration)**.

17 Ford technicians use a special tool (303-652) to align the oil pump as it is being fitted and tightened **(see illustration)**. The tool is basically a circular socket, which fits over the end of the crankshaft, and ensures that the corresponding hole in the oil pump is centrally located over the end of the crankshaft. In the absence of the tool, this alignment could be confirmed visually, or a large socket/piece of tubing (perhaps wrapped with tape) could be used instead.

18 Ensuring that the correct alignment of the pump is maintained, tighten the pump securing studs and bolts to the specified Stage 1 torque, in the sequence shown **(refer to illustration 13.16)**.

19 When all the fasteners have been tightened to the Stage 1 torque, go around again in the sequence, and tighten them all to the specified Stage 2 torque.

20 Refit the timing belt backplate to the engine.

21 Refit the injection pump sprocket and oil seal housing as described in Chapter 4C.

22 Refit the timing belt and camshaft sprocket as described in Section 7.

23 Refit the auxiliary drivebelt idler pulley, and tighten the bolt securely.

24 Refit the crankshaft pulley as described in Section 6.

25 When the engine is next started, check for correct oil pump operation (at least, as indicated by the oil pressure warning light going out).

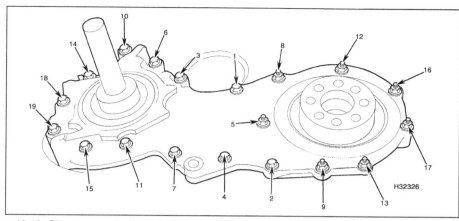

13.16 Oil pump nut/bolt tightening sequence – note special tool 303-652 used to align pump

14 Oil pressure warning light switch – removal and refitting

Removal

1 The switch is screwed into the left-hand (flywheel) end of the cylinder head, behind the vacuum pump.

2 Disconnect the battery negative (earth) lead (see Chapter 5A).

3 To improve access to the switch, it will be necessary to remove (or partially remove) the air cleaner inlet duct. It will also be helpful to release the hoses and remove the crankcase ventilation system oil separator from the left-hand end of the cylinder head.

4 Unplug the wiring from the switch and unscrew it; be prepared for some oil loss **(see illustration)**.

Refitting

5 Refitting is the reverse of the removal procedure; apply a thin smear of suitable sealant to the switch threads, and tighten it to the specified torque wrench setting.

6 Refit all components removed for access to the switch.

7 Check the engine oil level and top-up as necessary (see *Weekly checks*).

8 Check for correct warning light operation, and for signs of oil leaks, once the engine has

been restarted and warmed-up to normal operating temperature.

15 Oil cooler – removal and refitting

Removal

Note: *New sealing rings will be required on refitting.*

1 The oil cooler is mounted next to the oil filter on the rear of the cylinder block. Access to the oil cooler is best obtained from below – apply the handbrake, then jack up the front of the car and support it on axle stands.

2 Position a container beneath the oil filter to catch escaping oil and coolant. To improve access to the coolant hoses, unscrew and remove the oil filter, making sure that the filter sealing ring is removed with the filter cartridge – anticipate a small loss of engine oil as the filter is removed. Provided the filter is not due for renewal, it can be refitted on completion.

3 Clamp the oil cooler coolant hoses to minimise spillage, then remove the clips, and disconnect the hoses from the oil cooler. Be prepared for coolant spillage.

4 Loosen the turbocharger oil supply union bolt at the top of the cooler **(see illustration)**, and separate the pipe (be prepared for oil spillage). Recover the copper washers from

13.17 Tool used to align the oil pump, before tightening the retaining bolts fully

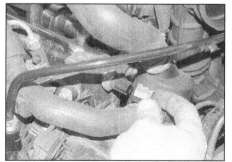

14.4 Disconnect the wiring from the oil pressure switch

15.4 Disconnect the turbocharger oil supply union bolt (arrowed)

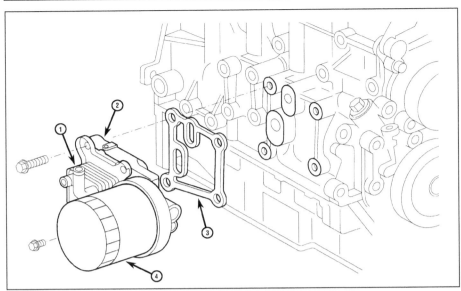

15.5 Oil cooler details

1 *Oil cooler*   2 *Adapter plate*   3 *Metal gasket*   4 *Oil filter*

15.6 Fit new gasket for oil cooler

the union – new ones must be used on reassembly.

5 Unscrew the bolts securing the oil cooler, noting their positions, as they are of different lengths. Remove the oil cooler from the engine, and recover the gasket (a new gasket must be used on refitting) **(see illustration)**.

Refitting

6 Refitting is a reversal of removal, bearing in mind the following points:

a) *Use a new gasket* **(see illustration)**.
b) *Fit the oil cooler mounting bolts to the*

positions noted on removal, and tighten them securely. Refit the oil filter if removed – apply a little oil to the filter sealing ring, and tighten the filter securely by hand (do not use any tools).
c) *Use new copper washers when reconnecting the oil supply union at the top of the cooler, and tighten the union bolt securely.*
d) *On completion, lower the car to the ground. Check and if necessary top up the oil and coolant levels, then start the engine and check for signs of oil or coolant leakage.*

16 Crankshaft oil seals – renewal

Timing belt end seal

1 Remove the crankshaft pulley (see Section 6).

2 Note the fitted depth of the oil seal as a guide for fitting the new one.

3 Using a screwdriver or similar tool, carefully prise the oil seal from its location. Take care not to damage the oil seal contact surfaces or the oil seal seating. An alternative method of removing the seals is to drill a small hole in the seal (taking care not to drill any deeper than necessary), then insert a self-tapping screw and use pliers to pull out the seal.

4 Wipe clean the oil seal contact surfaces and seating, and clean up any sharp edges or burrs which might damage the new seal as it is fitted, or which might cause the seal to leak once in place.

5 The new oil seal may be supplied fitted with a locating sleeve, which must **not** be removed prior to fitting **(see illustration)**. No oil should be applied to the oil seal, which is made of PTFE.

6 Ford technicians use a special seal-fitting tool (303-652), but an adequate substitute can be achieved using a large socket or piece of tubing of sufficient size to bear on the outer edge of the new seal.

7 Locate the new seal (lips facing inwards) over the end of the crankshaft, using the tool **(see illustration)**, socket, or tubing to press

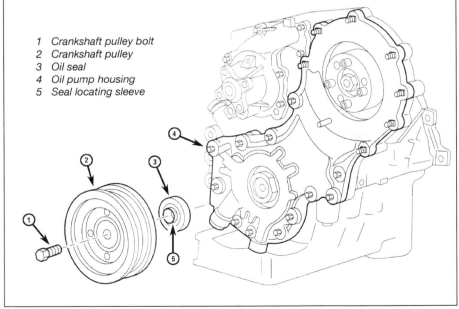

1 *Crankshaft pulley bolt*
2 *Crankshaft pulley*
3 *Oil seal*
4 *Oil pump housing*
5 *Seal locating sleeve*

16.5 Crankshaft oil seal details

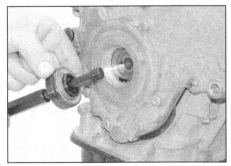

16.7 Using locating tool to press the seal in squarely (locating sleeve not required when using tool)

16.11 The new oil seal is renewed complete with carrier

the seal squarely and fully into position, to the previously-noted depth. Once the seal is fully fitted, remove the locating sleeve, if necessary.

8 The remainder of reassembly is the reverse of the removal procedure, referring to the relevant text for details where required. Check for signs of oil leakage when the engine is restarted.

Flywheel end seal

9 Remove the transmission as described in Chapter 7A, and the clutch assembly as described in Chapter 6.

10 Unbolt the flywheel (see Section 17).

11 Unbolt and remove the oil seal carrier; the seal is renewed complete with the carrier, and is not available separately. A complete set of new carrier retaining bolts should also be obtained for reassembly **(see illustration)**.

12 Clean the end of the crankshaft, polishing off any burrs or raised edges, which may have caused the seal to fail in the first place. Clean also the seal carrier mating face on the engine block, using a suitable solvent for degreasing if necessary.

13 The new oil seal is supplied fitted with a locating sleeve, which must **not** be removed prior to fitting (it will drop out on its own when the carrier is bolted into position) **(see illustration)**. No oil should be applied to the oil seal, which is made of PTFE.

14 Offer up the carrier into position, feeding the locating sleeve over the end of the crankshaft. Insert the new seal carrier

16.14a Fit new seal assembly, complete with locating sleeve over the end of the crankshaft . . .

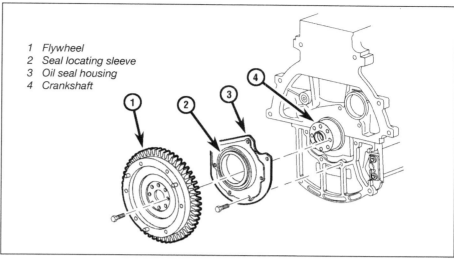

1 Flywheel
2 Seal locating sleeve
3 Oil seal housing
4 Crankshaft

16.13 Crankshaft oil seal details

retaining bolts, and tighten them all by hand **(see illustrations)**.

15 Ford technicians use a special tool (308-204) to centre the oil seal carrier around the end of the crankshaft. In the absence of the tool, this alignment could be confirmed visually, or a large socket/piece of tubing (perhaps wrapped with tape) could be used instead.

16 Ensuring that the correct alignment of the carrier is maintained, tighten the retaining bolts to the specified torque. If the seal locating sleeve is still in position, remove it now.

17 The remainder of the reassembly procedure is the reverse of dismantling, referring to the relevant text for details where required. Check for signs of oil leakage when the engine is restarted.

17 Flywheel – removal, inspection and refitting

Removal

1 Remove the transmission as described in Chapter 7A. Now is a good time to check

16.14b . . . then remove locating sleeve

components such as oil seals and renew them if necessary.

2 Remove the clutch as described in Chapter 6. Now is a good time to check or renew the clutch components and release bearing.

3 Use a centre-punch or paint to make alignment marks on the flywheel and crankshaft, to ensure correct alignment during refitting.

4 Prevent the flywheel from turning by locking the ring gear teeth, or by bolting a strap between the flywheel and the cylinder block/crankcase. Slacken the bolts evenly until all are free.

5 Remove each bolt in turn and ensure that new replacements are obtained for reassembly; these bolts are subjected to severe stresses and so must be renewed, regardless of their apparent condition, whenever they are disturbed.

6 Withdraw the flywheel, remembering that it is very heavy – do not drop it.

Inspection

7 Clean the flywheel to remove grease and oil. Inspect the surface for cracks, rivet grooves, burned areas and score marks. Light scoring can be removed with emery cloth. Check for cracked and broken ring gear teeth. Lay the flywheel on a flat surface and use a straight-edge to check for warpage.

8 Clean and inspect the mating surfaces of the flywheel and the crankshaft. If the crankshaft seal is leaking, renew it (see Section 16) before refitting the flywheel. If the engine has covered a high mileage, it may be worth fitting a new seal as a matter if course, given the amount of work needed to access it.

9 While the flywheel is removed, clean carefully its inboard (right-hand) face, particularly the recesses which serve as the reference points for the crankshaft speed/position sensor. Clean the sensor's tip and check that the sensor is securely fastened.

17.11 Align the bolt holes in the crankshaft – they will only line up one way

17.12 Tool made to lock the flywheel (arrowed) for slackening and tightening the bolts

17.13 Using an angle gauge to carry out the final tightening stages

10 Thoroughly clean the threaded bolt holes in the crankshaft, removing all traces of locking compound.

Refitting

11 Fit the flywheel to the crankshaft so that all bolt holes align – it will fit only one way – check this using the marks made on removal **(see illustration)**. Apply suitable locking compound to the threads of the new bolts, then insert them.

12 Lock the flywheel by the method used on dismantling **(see illustration)**. Working in a diagonal sequence, tighten the bolts to the specified Stage 1 torque wrench setting.

13 Stages 2 and 3 involve tightening the bolts though an angle, rather than to a torque. Each bolt must be rotated through the specified angle – special angle gauges are available from tool outlets. As a guide, a 90° angle is equivalent to a quarter-turn, and this is easily judged by assessing the start and end positions of the socket handle or torque wrench **(see illustration)**.

14 Go around all the bolts, again working in a diagonal sequence, and tighten the bolts through the Stage 2 angle. Once all the bolts have been tightened to Stage 2, go around again, and tighten them all to Stage 3.

15 The remainder of reassembly is the reverse of the removal procedure, referring to the relevant text for details where required.

18 Engine/transmission mountings – inspection and renewal

Inspection

1 The engine/transmission mountings seldom require attention, but broken or deteriorated mountings should be renewed immediately, or the added strain placed on the driveline components may cause damage or wear.

2 During the check, the engine/transmission must be raised slightly, to remove its weight from the mountings.

3 Apply the handbrake, then jack up the front of the vehicle and support it on axle stands (see *Jacking and vehicle support*). Remove the engine undershield where fitted. Position a jack under the sump, with a large block of wood between the jack head and the sump, then carefully raise the engine/transmission just enough to take the weight off the mountings.

4 Check the mountings to see if the rubber is cracked, hardened or separated from the metal components. Sometimes, the rubber will split right down the centre.

5 Check for relative movement between each mounting's brackets and the engine/transmission or body (use a large screwdriver or lever to attempt to move the mountings). If movement is noted, lower the engine and check the mounting nuts and bolts for tightness.

Renewal

6 The engine mountings can be removed if the weight of the engine/transmission is supported by one of the following alternative methods.

7 Either support the weight of the assembly from underneath using a jack and a suitable piece of wood between the jack and the sump (to prevent damage), or from above by attaching a hoist to the engine. A third method is to use a suitable support bar with end pieces which will engage in the water channel each side of the bonnet lid aperture. Using an adjustable hook and chain connected to the engine, the weight of the engine and transmission can then be taken from the mountings.

8 Once the weight of the engine and transmission is suitably supported, any of the mountings can be unbolted and removed.

9 To remove the right-hand engine mounting bracket, undo the bolts securing the bracket to the engine and the nut securing the bracket to the insulator. Remove the bracket from the engine. Unbolt the insulator from the right-hand side of the engine compartment.

10 To remove the left-hand mounting first remove the battery and battery tray as described in Chapter 5A, and the air cleaner assembly as described in Chapter 4C. Unscrew the mounting nuts from the left-hand engine mounting, then unscrew the bolts and remove the upper bracket. Unscrew the bolts and remove the insulator from the left-hand side of the engine compartment.

11 To remove the rear engine mounting/link, apply the handbrake, then jack up the front of the vehicle and support it on axle stands (see *Jacking and vehicle support*). Unscrew the through-bolts and remove the rear engine mounting link from the bracket on the transmission and from the bracket on the underbody. Hold the engine stationary while the bolts are being removed since the link will be under tension.

12 Refitting of all mountings is a reversal of the removal procedure. Do not fully tighten the mounting nuts/bolts until all of the mountings are in position. Check that the mounting rubbers do not twist or distort as the mounting bolts and nuts are tightened to their specified torques.

Chapter 2 Part E:
Engine removal and overhaul procedures

Contents

Auxiliary shaft (Endura-DE engine) – removal, inspection
  and refitting 11
Camshaft and tappets (Endura-E engine) – removal,
  inspection and refitting 13
Crankshaft (except Zetec-SE engine) – inspection 18
Crankshaft (except Zetec-SE engine) – main bearing
  clearance check and refitting 21
Crankshaft (except Zetec-SE engine) – removal 15
Cylinder block/crankcase and bores – cleaning and inspection 16
Cylinder head – dismantling 8
Cylinder head – reassembly 10
Cylinder head and valves – cleaning, inspection and renovation . . . 9
Diesel engine and transmission – removal, separation and refitting . 6
Engine – initial start-up after overhaul 23
Engine overhaul – dismantling sequence 7

Engine overhaul – general information 2
Engine overhaul – reassembly sequence 20
Engine removal – methods and precautions 3
Fuel injection pump drive chain (Endura-DI engine) – removal,
  inspection and refitting 12
General information 1
Main and big-end bearings – inspection 19
Petrol engine and automatic transmission – removal,
  separation and refitting 5
Petrol engine and manual transmission – removal,
  separation and refitting 4
Piston/connecting rod assemblies – big-end bearing
  clearance check and refitting 22
Piston/connecting rod assemblies – inspection and reassembly . . . 17
Piston/connecting rod assemblies – removal 14

Degrees of difficulty

Easy, suitable for novice with little experience	Fairly easy, suitable for beginner with some experience	Fairly difficult, suitable for competent DIY mechanic	Difficult, suitable for experienced DIY mechanic	Very difficult, suitable for expert DIY or professional

Specifications

Engine overhaul data and torque wrench settings
Refer to Specifications in Chapter 2A, 2B, 2C or 2D.

1 General information

How to use this Chapter

Included in this part of Chapter 2 are the general overhaul procedures for the cylinder head, cylinder block/crankcase and internal engine components.

The information ranges from advice concerning preparation for an overhaul and the purchase of replacement parts, to detailed step-by-step procedures covering removal, inspection, renovation and refitting of internal engine parts.

The following Sections have been compiled based on the assumption that the engine has been removed from the car. For information concerning in-car engine repair, as well as the removal and refitting of the external

components necessary for the overhaul, refer to Part A (Endura-E petrol engine), Part B (Zetec-SE petrol engine), Part C (Endura-DE diesel engine), or Part D (Endura-DI diesel engine) of this Chapter, and to Section 7 of this Part.

2 Engine overhaul – general information

It is not always easy to determine when, or if, an engine should be completely overhauled, as a number of factors must be considered.

High mileage is not necessarily an indication that an overhaul is needed, while low mileage does not preclude the need for an overhaul. Frequency of servicing is probably the most important consideration. An engine which has had regular and frequent oil and filter changes, as well as other required

maintenance, will most likely give many thousands of miles of reliable service. Conversely, a neglected engine may require an overhaul very early in its life.

Excessive oil consumption is an indication that piston rings, valve stem oil seals and/or valves and valve guides are in need of attention. Make sure that oil leaks are not responsible before deciding that the rings and/or guides are bad. Perform a cylinder compression check to determine the extent of the work required.

Check the oil pressure with a gauge fitted in place of the oil pressure sender, and compare it with the value given in the Specifications. If it is extremely low, the main and big-end bearings and/or the oil pump are probably worn out.

Loss of power, rough running, knocking or metallic engine noises, excessive valve gear noise and high fuel consumption may also point to the need for an overhaul, especially if they are all present at the same time. If a complete tune-up does not remedy the situation, major mechanical work is the only solution.

An engine overhaul involves restoring the internal parts to the specifications of a new engine. During an overhaul, the pistons and rings are renewed, and the cylinder bores are reconditioned. New main bearings, connecting rod bearings and camshaft bearings are generally fitted, and if necessary, the crankshaft may be reground to restore the journals (note however that some of this work is not possible on the Zetec-SE engine due to the manufacturing processes used). The valves are also serviced as well, since they are usually in less-than-perfect condition at this point. While the engine is being overhauled, other components, such as the starter and alternator, can be overhauled as well. The end result should be a like-new engine that will give many trouble-free miles. **Note:** *Critical cooling system components such as the hoses, drivebelts, thermostat and water pump MUST be renewed when an engine is overhauled. The radiator should be checked carefully, to ensure that it is not clogged or leaking. Also, it is a good idea to renew the oil pump whenever the engine is overhauled.*

Before beginning the engine overhaul, read through the entire procedure to familiarise yourself with the scope and requirements of the job. Overhauling an engine is not difficult if you follow all of the instructions carefully, have the necessary tools and equipment, and pay close attention to all specifications; however, it can be time-consuming. Plan on the vehicle being tied up for a minimum of two weeks, especially if parts must be taken to an engineering works for repair or reconditioning. Check on the availability of parts, and make sure that any necessary special tools and equipment are obtained in advance. Most work can be done with typical hand tools, although a number of precision measuring tools are required for inspecting parts to determine if they must be renewed. Often the engineering works will handle the inspection of parts, and offer advice concerning reconditioning and renewal. **Note:** *Always wait until the engine has been completely dismantled, and all components, especially the engine block, have been inspected before deciding what service and repair operations must be performed by an engineering works. Since the condition of the block will be the major factor to consider when determining whether to overhaul the original engine or buy a reconditioned unit, do not purchase parts or have overhaul work done on other components until the block has been thoroughly inspected.* As a general rule, time is the primary cost of an overhaul, so it does not pay to fit worn or substandard parts.

As a final note, to ensure maximum life and minimum trouble from a reconditioned engine, everything must be assembled with care, and in a spotlessly-clean environment.

3 Engine removal – methods and precautions

If you have decided that an engine must be removed for overhaul or major repair work, several preliminary steps should be taken.

Locating a suitable place to work is extremely important. Adequate work space, along with storage space for the vehicle, will be needed. If a garage is not available, at the very least a flat, level, clean work surface is required.

Cleaning the engine compartment and engine before beginning the removal procedure will help keep tools clean and organised.

The engine can only be withdrawn by removing it complete with the transmission; the vehicle's body must be raised and supported securely, sufficiently high that the engine/transmission can be unbolted as a single unit and lowered to the ground; the engine/transmission unit can then be withdrawn from under the vehicle and separated. An engine hoist or A-frame will therefore be necessary. Make sure the equipment is rated in excess of the combined weight of the engine and transmission. Safety is of primary importance, considering the potential hazards involved in lifting the engine out of the vehicle.

If the engine is being removed by a novice, an assistant should be available. Advice and aid from someone more experienced would also be helpful. There are many instances when one person cannot simultaneously perform all of the operations required when removing the engine from the vehicle.

Plan the operation ahead of time. Arrange for, or obtain, all of the tools and equipment you will need, prior to beginning the job. Some of the equipment necessary to perform engine removal and installation safely and with relative ease are (in addition to an engine hoist) a heavy-duty floor jack, complete sets of spanners and sockets as described at the end of this manual, wooden blocks, and plenty of rags and cleaning solvent for mopping-up spilled oil, coolant and fuel. If the hoist must be hired, make sure that you arrange for it in advance, and perform all of the operations possible without it beforehand. This will save you money and time.

Plan for the vehicle to be out of use for quite a while. An engineering works will be required to perform some of the work which the do-it-yourselfer cannot accomplish without special equipment. These places often have a busy schedule, so it would be a good idea to consult them before removing the engine, in order to accurately estimate the amount of time required to rebuild or repair components that may need work.

Always be extremely careful when removing and refitting the engine. Serious injury can result from careless actions. Plan ahead, take your time, and you will find that a job of this nature, although major, can be accomplished successfully.

4 Petrol engine and manual transmission – removal, separation and refitting

Note: *The engine and manual transmission is lowered from the engine compartment, then separated on the bench.*

Removal

1 Apply the handbrake, then jack up the front of the vehicle and support it on axle stands (see *Jacking and vehicle support*).

2 Where applicable, undo the retaining screws and remove the engine undershield.

3 Depressurise the fuel system with reference to Chapter 4A.

4 Disconnect the battery negative (earth) lead (see Chapter 5A).

5 Drain the cooling system as described in Chapter 1A.

6 If necessary, drain the engine oil with reference to Chapter 1A.

7 Disconnect the wiring for the electric cooling fan on the rear of the radiator.

8 Remove the air cleaner and inlet ducting as described in Chapter 4A.

9 Remove the battery and battery box as described in Chapter 5A.

10 Trace the wiring back from the oxygen sensor on the top of the exhaust manifold to the connector, then disconnect the wiring.

11 Disconnect the accelerator cable from the throttle body housing and release it from the supports. Position it to one side.

12 Loosen the clip and disconnect the top hose from the thermostat housing. Release the engine wiring loom from the clips on the top hose.

13 Unclip the HT leads and position them to one side.

14 Disconnect the wiring from the alternator.

15 Disconnect the heater hose on the bulkhead by releasing the quick release fitting.

16 Disconnect the hose from the top right-hand side of the radiator.

17 Disconnect the engine wiring loom at the two connectors on the bulkhead, and unclip the wiring support bracket.

18 Disconnect the brake servo vacuum line at the inlet manifold.

19 Disconnect the evaporative canister purge vacuum line from the solenoid valve on the bulkhead.

20 Disconnect the wiring from the engine coolant temperature sensor on the right-hand rear of the engine.

21 Remove the oil filler cap and disconnect the crankcase ventilation hose from it, then refit the cap.

22 At the left-hand rear of the engine, disconnect the starter motor wiring and release the main cable from the support clip.

4.23a Disconnect the wiring from the transmission . . .

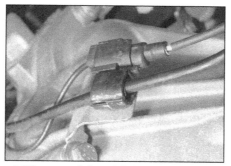

4.23b . . . and detach it from the support

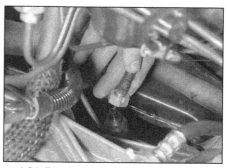

4.24 Disconnecting the speedometer cable from the rear of the transmission

Unscrew the nut and disconnect the main cable from the starter motor.

23 Unbolt the earth lead from the transmission. Also disconnect the wiring and detach it from the support on the transmission **(see illustrations)**.

24 Where applicable, disconnect the speedometer cable from the rear of the transmission **(see illustration)**.

25 Disconnect the vehicle speed sensor wiring at the bulkhead.

26 Remove the cover from the auxiliary drivebelt by unscrewing the bolts at the front right-hand side of the engine.

27 Using a spanner, turn the tensioner pulley clockwise to release the tension, then slip the auxiliary drivebelt from the pulleys and remove it from the engine compartment. If necessary, the tensioner may be unbolted from the cylinder block **(see illustration)**.

28 Unbolt the power steering pump using the information in Chapter 10, and tie it up without disturbing the pipe connections.

29 Working beneath the vehicle, unbolt the lower cover from the crankshaft pulley.

30 Loosen the clip and disconnect the bottom hose from the coolant pump.

31 Unbolt the radiator shroud.

32 Where applicable, unbolt the air conditioning condenser from the top of the radiator. Do not remove the condenser.

33 Loosen the clips and disconnect the two hoses from the bottom right of the radiator.

34 Support the radiator, then unbolt the

lower crossmember and remove it together with the radiator and fan. Where applicable, tie the air conditioning condenser to one side.

35 Where applicable, disconnect the air conditioning compressor wiring plug then unbolt the compressor and tie it to one side.

36 Under the vehicle, remove the exhaust downpipe and catalytic converter with reference to Chapter 4A.

37 Mark the position of the gearchange clamp on the transmission selector rod, then unscrew the clamp bolt and remove the gearchange rod. Tie the rod to one side **(see illustration)**.

38 Unbolt the stabiliser bar from the transmission and tie it to one side **(see illustration)**.

39 Unscrew the though-bolts and remove the rear engine mounting link. Note the link will be under tension, so support the engine until the link is removed.

40 Remove the left- and right-hand driveshafts from the transmission with reference to Chapter 8. Carefully swivel the driveshafts forward and tie them to the subframe leaving sufficient room to lower the engine and transmission assembly.

41 Place cloth rags beneath the fuel feed and return lines on the fuel rail, then squeeze the quick release tags and disconnect the fittings.

42 Fit a hose clamp to the clutch hydraulic hose leading to the slave cylinder. Alternatively tighten the fluid reservoir cap

onto a piece of polythene – this will prevent excessive loss of hydraulic fluid.

43 Pull out the clip and disconnect the hydraulic hose quick release connector from the clutch slave cylinder. Plug the hose and slave cylinder to prevent dust and dirt entering the system. Release the hydraulic hose from the support bracket.

44 Attach a suitable hoist to the engine and transmission and take the weight of the assembly **(see illustration)**. Make sure there is sufficient height beneath the front of the vehicle to withdraw the assembly.

45 Unscrew the nuts from the left-hand engine/transmission mounting.

46 Unscrew the nuts and remove the right-hand engine mounting upper bracket.

47 With the help of an assistant, carefully

4.27 Removing the auxiliary drivebelt tensioner from the cylinder block

4.37 Gearchange rod and clamp on the rear of the transmission

4.38 Unbolting the stabiliser bar from the transmission. Note the location of the washer

4.44 Attaching a hoist to the engine and transmission assembly

4.47 Lowering the engine/transmission assembly to the ground

4.53 Separating the transmission from the rear of the engine

5.12 Disconnecting the wiring from the engine coolant temperature sensor on the left-hand side of the cylinder head

lower the assembly from the engine compartment making sure that it clears the surrounding components and bodywork **(see illustration)**.

48 If the engine is to be overhauled, remove the wiring loom from the engine noting its location and routing.

Separation

49 To separate the transmission from the engine, first remove the starter motor with reference to Chapter 5A.

50 Unscrew and remove the bolts securing the right-hand rear of the transmission to the engine.

51 Move the cable guide to one side, then unscrew the bolts securing the top of the transmission to the engine and withdraw the adapter plate.

52 At the front of the transmission, unscrew and remove the bolts securing the transmission to the engine. Note the location of the TDC sensor cover retained by two of the bolts.

53 With the help of an assistant withdraw the transmission directly from the engine making sure that its weight is not allowed to bear on the clutch friction disc **(see illustration)**.

Refitting

54 Refitting is a reversal of removal, noting the following additional points.

a) Make sure that all mating faces are clean.

b) Apply a smear of high-melting-point grease to the splines of the transmission input shaft. Do not apply too much, otherwise there is the possibility of the grease contaminating the clutch friction disc.

c) Make sure that the clutch release bearing is correctly located in the slave cylinder inside the transmission bellhousing.

d) On the Endura-E engine, ensure that the engine adapter plate is correctly seated on the locating dowels on the engine.

e) Fit new circlips to the grooves in the inner end of each driveshaft CV joint, and ensure that they fully engage as they are fitted into the transmission.

f) Refit and adjust the engine mountings as described in Chapter 2A or 2B.

g) Check and if necessary adjust the gearchange linkage as described in Chapter 7A.

h) Top-up the transmission oil as described in Chapter 1A.

i) Top up and bleed the clutch hydraulic system as described in Chapter 6.

j) Refill the cooling system as described in Chapter 1A.

k) Tighten all nuts and bolts to the specified torque setting, where given.

5 Petrol engine and automatic transmission – removal, separation and refitting

Note: *The engine and automatic transmission is lowered from the engine compartment, then separated on the bench.*

Removal

1 Apply the handbrake, then jack up the front of the vehicle and support it on axle stands (see *Jacking and vehicle support*). Where applicable, remove the engine undershield.

2 Depressurise the fuel system with reference to Chapter 4A.

3 Disconnect the battery negative (earth) lead (see Chapter 5A).

4 Drain the cooling system as described in Chapter 1A.

5 Drain the automatic transmission fluid with reference to Chapter 1A.

6 If necessary, drain the engine oil with reference to Chapter 1A.

7 Remove the battery and battery box as described in Chapter 5A.

8 Remove the air cleaner and inlet ducting as described in Chapter 4A.

9 Lift the flap from the front of the cylinder head cover then disconnect the crankcase ventilation hose.

10 Disconnect the accelerator cable from the throttle body housing and release it from the supports. Position it to one side.

11 Remove the oil filler cap, then unscrew the retaining screws and remove the plastic cover from the top of the cylinder head cover. Refit the oil filler cap.

12 Disconnect the wiring from the following:

a) Throttle position switch.

b) DIS ignition coil.

c) Engine coolant temperature sensor **(see illustration)**.

d) Engine wiring loom plug at the left-hand side of the cylinder head.

e) Vehicle speed sensor on the rear of the transmission.

f) Camshaft position sensor.

g) Oxygen sensor.

h) Injectors.

i) Idle air control valve.

j) Alternator.

13 Disconnect the hoses from the exhaust gas recirculation valve.

14 Disconnect the vacuum hoses from the throttle body housing, inlet manifold and cylinder block.

15 Loosen the clips and disconnect the heater hose, expansion tank hose and thermostat housing hose at the left-hand side of the cylinder head. Also disconnect the expansion tank hose from the top of the radiator.

16 Disconnect the cooling fan wiring from the radiator.

17 Unbolt the radiator shroud.

18 Position a suitable container beneath the transmission, then unscrew the union nuts and disconnect the cooler pipes.

19 Loosen the clips and disconnect the bottom hose and heater hoses from the radiator and coolant pump.

20 Support the radiator, then unbolt the lower crossmember and remove it together with the radiator and fan.

21 Disconnect the solenoid and battery cables from the starter motor.

22 Remove the cover from the auxiliary drivebelt by unscrewing the bolts at the front right-hand side of the engine.

23 Using a spanner, turn the tensioner pulley clockwise to release the tension, then slip the auxiliary drivebelt from the pulleys and remove it from the engine compartment.

24 Unbolt the power steering pump and bracket from the cylinder block and tie it to one side. Note that one of the mounting bolts secures the pipe support.

25 Release the clip and disconnect the

selector cable end fitting from the lever on the transmission, then withdraw the cable from the bracket.

26 Where applicable, disconnect the speedometer cable from the rear of the transmission. Also disconnect the wiring from the reversing light switch.

27 Remove the left- and right-hand driveshafts from the transmission with reference to Chapter 8. Carefully swivel the driveshafts forward and tie them to the subframe leaving sufficient room to lower the engine and transmission assembly.

28 Unscrew the flange nuts and separate the exhaust downpipe from the intermediate section.

29 Unscrew the though-bolts and remove the rear engine mounting link. Note the link will be under tension, so support the engine until the link is removed.

30 Place cloth rags beneath the fuel feed and return lines on the fuel rail, then squeeze the quick release tags and disconnect the fittings. Unclip the lines from the supports.

31 Attach a suitable hoist to the engine and transmission and take the weight of the assembly. Make sure there is sufficient height beneath the front of the vehicle to withdraw the assembly.

32 Unscrew the nuts from the left-hand engine/transmission mounting.

33 Unscrew the nuts and remove the right-hand engine mounting upper bracket.

34 With the help of an assistant, carefully lower the assembly from the engine compartment making sure that it clears the surrounding components and bodywork.

35 If the engine is to be overhauled, remove the wiring loom from the engine noting its location and routing.

Separation

36 To separate the transmission from the engine, first remove the starter motor with reference to Chapter 5A.

37 Unscrew the upper mounting bolts securing the transmission to the engine, noting the location of the wiring support brackets and earth lead.

38 Unclip the vehicle speed sensor and disconnect the wiring plug.

39 Disconnect the wiring from the lock switch on the lower rear of the transmission.

40 Undo the remaining transmission flange bolts and carefully withdraw the transmission from the engine noting the location of the wiring support brackets. Do not allow the weight of the transmission to bear on the input shaft and vibration damper.

41 If necessary, mark the torsional vibration damper in relation to the flywheel then unscrew the mounting bolts and withdraw the damper. Use a wide-bladed screwdriver engaged with the starter ring gear to hold the flywheel stationary. Examine the damper for wear and damage and renew it if necessary.

Refitting

42 Refitting is a reversal of removal, noting the following additional points.

 a) *Fit new circlips to the grooves in the inner end of each driveshaft CV joint, and ensure that they fully engage as they are fitted into the transmission.*

 b) *Refit and adjust the engine mountings as described in Chapter 2A or 2B.*

 c) *Replenish the transmission fluid, and check the level with reference to Chapter 1A.*

 d) *Tighten all nuts and bolts to the specified torque settings, where given.*

 e) *Check and if necessary adjust the selector cable (Chapter 7B) and accelerator cable (Chapter 4A).*

 f) *Refill the cooling system as described in Chapter 1A.*

6 Diesel engine and transmission – removal, separation and refitting

Note: *The engine and manual transmission is lowered from the engine compartment, then separated on the bench.*

Removal

1 Apply the handbrake, then jack up the front of the vehicle and support it on axle stands (see *Jacking and vehicle support*).

2 Where applicable, undo the retaining screws and remove the engine undershield.

3 Disconnect the battery negative (earth) lead (see Chapter 5A).

4 Drain the cooling system as described in Chapter 1B.

5 If necessary, drain the engine oil with reference to Chapter 1B.

6 Remove the auxiliary drivebelt as described in Chapter 1B.

7 Remove the air cleaner and inlet ducting as described in Chapter 4B or 4C.

8 Loosen the clip and disconnect the top hose from the thermostat housing.

9 Loosen the clip and disconnect the vent hose from the expansion tank.

10 Identify the heater hoses on the bulkhead, then loosen the clips and disconnect them.

11 Loosen the clip and disconnect the vent hose from the top of the radiator.

12 Disconnect the following wiring:

 a) *Injection pump wiring loom.*

 b) *Glow plug wiring.*

 c) *Temperature gauge sender unit.*

 d) *Engine coolant temperature sensor.*

 e) *Oil pressure switch on the left-hand side of the cylinder head.*

 f) *Diesel fuel heater on the left-hand side of the cylinder head.*

 g) *Exhaust gas recirculation valve.*

13 On Endura-DE engines, pull out the clip and disconnect the outer accelerator cable from the bracket on the injection pump. Disconnect the inner cable from the lever.

14 Taking precautions against fuel spillage, disconnect the fuel lines at the connections into the engine compartment or the connections to the injector pump. Note the fitted positions of the pipes for use when refitting.

15 Unbolt and remove the earth lead from the transmission.

16 Fit a hose clamp to the clutch hydraulic hose leading to the slave cylinder. Alternatively tighten the fluid reservoir cap onto a piece of polythene – this will prevent excessive loss of hydraulic fluid.

17 Pull out the clip and disconnect the hydraulic hose quick release connector from the clutch slave cylinder. Plug the hose and slave cylinder to prevent dust and dirt entering the system. Release the hydraulic hose from the support bracket.

18 Where applicable, unbolt the power steering pump using the information in Chapter 10, and tie it up without disturbing the pipe connections.

19 Unscrew the bolt from the power steering fluid hose support bracket.

20 Unbolt the auxiliary drivebelt tensioner.

21 Unscrew the bolts and remove the reinforcement bracket from the top of the right-hand engine mounting.

22 Remove the battery and battery box as described in Chapter 5A.

23 Loosen the clips and disconnect the bottom hoses from the radiator.

24 Where applicable, disconnect the air conditioning compressor wiring at the connector and release the wiring from the cable tie.

25 Disconnect the wiring plugs at the bottom left-hand side of the radiator.

26 Unscrew the air conditioning condenser lower mounting bolts and tie the condenser to one side. **Do not** disconnect the refrigerant lines.

27 Support the radiator, then unbolt the lower crossmember and remove it downwards together with the radiator and fan.

28 Where applicable, unbolt the air conditioning compressor and tie it to one side.

29 Disconnect the wiring from the starter motor.

30 Disconnect the wiring from the multi-function switch on the front of the transmission.

31 Mark the position of the gearchange clamp on the transmission selector rod, then unscrew the clamp bolt and remove the gearchange rod. Tie the rod to one side.

32 Unbolt the stabiliser bar from the transmission and tie it to one side.

33 Unscrew the flange nuts and separate the exhaust downpipe from the intermediate section.

34 Disconnect the wiring from the alternator.

35 Disconnect the wiring from the crankshaft position sensor.

36 Where applicable, disconnect the

speedometer cable from the rear of the transmission.

37 On Endura-DI engines, disconnect the coolant hose from the oil cooler at the rear of the engine.

38 Remove the left-hand driveshaft from the transmission with reference to Chapter 8, then carefully swivel the driveshaft forward and tie it to the subframe.

39 Remove the right-hand driveshaft completely as described in Chapter 8.

40 Unscrew the though-bolts and remove the rear engine mounting link. Note the link will be under tension, so support the engine until the link is removed.

41 Attach a suitable hoist to the engine and transmission and take the weight of the assembly. Make sure there is sufficient height beneath the front of the vehicle to withdraw the assembly.

42 Unscrew the nuts from the left-hand engine/transmission mounting.

43 Unscrew the nuts and remove the right-hand engine mounting upper bracket.

44 With the help of an assistant, carefully lower the assembly from the engine compartment making sure that it clears the surrounding components and bodywork.

45 If the engine is to be overhauled, remove the wiring loom from the engine noting its location and routing.

Separation

46 To separate the transmission from the engine, first remove the starter motor with reference to Chapter 5A.

47 Unbolt the air inlet resonator from the transmission.

48 At the front of the transmission, unscrew and remove the bolts securing the transmission to the engine.

49 Unscrew and remove the remaining bolts securing the transmission to the engine.

50 With the help of an assistant withdraw the transmission directly from the engine making sure that its weight is not allowed to bear on the clutch friction disc. Remove the adapter plate from the dowels on the cylinder block.

Refitting

51 Refitting is a reversal of removal, noting the following additional points.
  a) Make sure that all mating faces are clean.
  b) Apply a smear of high-melting-point grease to the splines of the transmission input shaft. Do not apply too much, otherwise there is the possibility of the grease contaminating the clutch friction disc.
  c) Make sure that the clutch release bearing is correctly located in the slave cylinder inside the transmission bellhousing.
  d) Ensure that the engine adapter plate is correctly seated on the locating dowels on the engine.
  e) Fit new circlips to the grooves in the inner end of each driveshaft CV joint, and ensure that they fully engage as they are fitted into the transmission.

  f) Refit and adjust the engine mountings as described in Chapter 2C or 2D.
  g) Check and if necessary adjust the gearchange linkage as described in Chapter 7A.
  h) Top-up the transmission oil as described in Chapter 1B.
  i) Top up and bleed the clutch hydraulic system as described in Chapter 6.
  j) Refill the cooling system as described in Chapter 1B.
  k) Tighten all nuts and bolts to the specified torque setting.

7 Engine overhaul – dismantling sequence

1 It is much easier to disassemble and work on the engine if it is mounted on a portable engine stand. These stands can often be hired from a tool hire shop. Before the engine is mounted on a stand, the flywheel/driveplate should be removed from the engine, so that the engine stand bolts can be tightened into the end of the cylinder block.

2 If a stand is not available, it is possible to disassemble the engine with it blocked up on a sturdy workbench or on the floor. Be extra-careful not to tip or drop the engine when working without a stand.

3 If you are going to obtain a reconditioned engine, all external components must be removed first, to be transferred to the replacement engine (just as they will if you are doing a complete engine overhaul yourself). **Note:** *When removing the external components from the engine, pay close attention to details that may be helpful or important during refitting. Note the fitted position of gaskets, seals, spacers, pins, washers, bolts and other small items. These external components include the following:*

Petrol engine models
  a) Alternator and brackets.
  b) DIS ignition coil, HT leads and spark plugs.
  c) Thermostat and cover.
  d) Fuel injection equipment.
  e) Inlet and exhaust manifolds.
  f) Oil filter.
  g) Engine mountings and lifting brackets.
  h) Ancillary (power steering pump, air conditioning compressor) brackets.
  i) Oil filler tube and dipstick.
  j) Coolant pipes and hoses.
  k) Flywheel/driveplate.

Diesel engine models
  a) Alternator mounting bracket.
  b) Fuel injection pump and mounting bracket, and fuel injectors and glow plugs.
  c) Thermostat and cover.
  d) Inlet and exhaust manifolds.
  e) Oil cooler.

  f) Engine lifting brackets, hose brackets and wiring brackets.
  g) Ancillary (power steering pump, air conditioning compressor) brackets.
  h) Oil pressure warning light switch and oil level sensor (where applicable).
  i) Coolant temperature sensors.
  j) Wiring harnesses and brackets.
  k) Coolant pipes and hoses.
  l) Oil filler tube and dipstick.
  m) Clutch.
  n) Flywheel.

4 If you are obtaining a 'short' motor (which, when available, consists of the engine cylinder block, crankshaft, pistons and connecting rods all assembled), then the cylinder head, sump, oil pump, and timing belt (where applicable) will have to be removed also.

5 If you are planning a complete overhaul, the engine can be disassembled and the internal components removed in the following order:
  a) Engine external components (including inlet and exhaust manifolds).
  b) Timing sprockets and chain/belt.
  c) Cylinder head.
  d) Flywheel/driveplate.
  e) Sump.
  f) Oil pump.
  g) Pistons and connecting rods.
  h) Crankshaft and main bearings.
  i) Tappets and camshaft (Endura-E engine).

Caution: DO NOT attempt to remove the crankshaft or main bearing cap/ladder on the Zetec-SE engines, as it is not possible to refit it accurately using conventional tooling. The manufacturers do not supply torque settings for the main bearing cap/ladder retaining bolts. If the crankshaft is worn excessively, it will be necessary to obtain a new short motor comprising the cylinder block together with the pistons and crankshaft.

6 Before beginning the disassembly and overhaul procedures, make sure that you have all of the correct tools necessary. Refer to the reference section at the end of this manual for further information.

8 Cylinder head – dismantling

Note: *New and reconditioned cylinder heads are available from the manufacturers and from engine overhaul specialists. Due to the fact that some specialist tools are required for the dismantling and inspection procedures, and new components may not be readily available, it may be more practical and economical for the home mechanic to purchase a reconditioned head rather than dismantle, inspect and recondition the original head.*

1 Remove the cylinder head as described in Part A, B, C or D of this Chapter (as applicable).

2 If not already done, remove the inlet and

8.2 Unbolting the engine lifting eyes from the cylinder head

8.6 Compress the valve spring to remove the collets

8.7a Remove the valve spring retainer and spring . . .

exhaust manifolds with reference to the relevant Part of Chapter 4. Also remove all external brackets and elbows **(see illustration)**.

3 Proceed as follows according to engine type.

Endura-E engine

4 Valve removal should commence with No 1 valve (nearest the timing chain end).

5 To remove the valve springs and valves from the cylinder head, a standard valve spring compressor will be required. Fit the spring compressor to the first valve and spring to be removed. Assuming that all of the valves and springs are to be removed, start by compressing the No 1 valve (nearest the timing cover end) spring. Take care not to damage the valve stem with the compressor, and do not over-compress the spring, or the valve stem may bend. When tightening the compressor, it may be found that the spring retainer does not release and the collets are then difficult to remove. In this instance, remove the compressor, then press a piece of tube (or a socket of suitable diameter) so that it does not interfere with the removal of the collets, against the retainer's outer rim. Tap the tube (or socket) with a hammer to unsettle the components.

6 Refit the compressor, and wind it in to enable the collets to be extracted **(see illustration)**.

7 Loosen off the compressor, and remove the retainer and spring. Withdraw the valve from the cylinder head **(see illustrations)**.

8 Pull the valve stem seals from the valve guides using a pair of pliers **(see illustration)**.

9 Repeat the removal procedure with each of the remaining seven valve assemblies in turn. As they are removed, keep the individual valves and their components together, and in their respective order of fitting, by placing them in a separate labelled bag **(see illustration)**.

Zetec-SE and diesel engines

10 Remove the camshafts and tappets as described in Part B, C or D of this Chapter, being careful to store the components as described.

11 Using a valve spring compressor, compress each valve spring in turn until the split collets can be removed. A special valve spring compressor will be required, to reach into the deep wells in the cylinder head without risk of damaging the tappet bores; such compressors are now widely available from most good motor accessory shops. Release the compressor, and lift off the spring upper seat and spring **(see illustration)**.

12 If, when the valve spring compressor is screwed down, the spring upper seat refuses to free and expose the split collets, gently tap the top of the tool, directly over the upper seat, with a light hammer. This will free the seat.

13 Withdraw the valve through the combustion chamber. If it binds in the guide (won't pull through), push it back in, and de-burr the area around the collet groove with a

8.7b . . . followed by the valve

fine file; take care not to mark the tappet bores.

14 Pull the valve stem seals from the valve guides using a pair of pliers. As the seals are removed, note whether they are of different colours for the inlet and exhaust valves – compare with the new parts, and note this for refitting. As a guide, the inlet valve seals are green, and the exhaust seals are red.

15 It is essential that the valves are kept together with their collets, spring seats and springs, and in their correct sequence (unless they are so badly worn that they are to be renewed). If they are going to be kept and used again, place them in a labelled polythene bag or similar small container **(see illustration 8.9)**. Note that No 1 valve is nearest to the timing belt end of the engine.

8.8 Using pliers to pull the valve stem seals from the valve guides

8.9 Use a labelled plastic bag to store and identify valve components

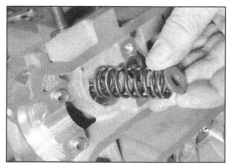

8.11 Removing the valve spring and upper seat

9 Cylinder head and valves – cleaning, inspection and renovation

1 Thorough cleaning of the cylinder head and valve components, followed by a detailed inspection, will enable you to decide how much valve service work must be carried out during the engine overhaul.

Cleaning

2 Scrape away all traces of old gasket material and sealing compound from the cylinder head. Take care not to damage the cylinder head surfaces.
3 Scrape away the carbon from the combustion chambers and ports, then wash the cylinder head thoroughly with paraffin or a suitable solvent.
4 Scrape off any heavy carbon deposits that may have formed on the valves, then use a power-operated wire brush to remove deposits from the valve heads and stems.
5 On the Endura-DE engine, the swirl chambers may be removed from their locations using a soft metal drift inserted through the injector holes (if this is done, mark the swirl chambers so that they can be refitted in their original locations). Before removing the swirl chambers use feeler blades and a straight-edge to measure their projection, and compare with the information given in the Specifications (see Chapter 2C). Alternatively, use a dial test indicator to make the check. Zero the dial test indicator on the gasket surface of the cylinder head, then measure the protrusion of the swirl chamber.
6 If the head is extremely dirty, it should be steam cleaned. On completion, make sure that all oil holes and oil galleries are cleaned.

Inspection and renovation

Note: *Be sure to perform all the following inspection procedures before concluding that the services of an engine overhaul specialist are required. Make a list of all items that require attention.*

Cylinder head

7 Inspect the head very carefully for cracks, evidence of coolant leakage and other damage. If cracks are found, a new cylinder head should be obtained.

8 Use a straight-edge and feeler blade to check that the cylinder head surface is not distorted. On the Endura-DE engine, do not position the straight-edge over the swirl chambers, as these may be proud of the cylinder head face. If the specified distortion limit is exceeded, machining of the gasket face is not recommended by the manufacturers, so the only course of action is to renew the cylinder head.
9 Examine the valve seats in each of the combustion chambers. If they are severely pitted, cracked or burned, then they will need to be renewed or recut by an engine overhaul specialist. If they are only slightly pitted, this can be removed by grinding the valve heads and seats together with coarse, then fine, grinding paste as described below.
10 If the valve guides are worn, indicated by a side-to-side motion of the valve in the guide, new guides must be fitted. If necessary, insert a new valve in the guides to determine if the wear is on the guide or valve. If new guides are to be fitted, the valves must be renewed as a matter of course. Valve guides may be renewed using a press and a suitable mandrel, however, the work is best carried out by an engine overhaul specialist, since if it is not done skillfully, there is a risk of damaging the cylinder head.
11 On the Endura-DE engine, inspect the swirl chambers for burning or cracks and renew the chambers if necessary.
12 On the Zetec-SE and diesel engines, check the tappet bores in the cylinder head for wear. If excessive wear is evident, the cylinder head must be renewed.
13 Except on the Endura-E engine, examine the camshaft bearing surfaces in the cylinder head as described in Chapter 2B, 2C or 2D.

Valves

14 Examine the head of each valve for pitting, burning, cracks and general wear, and check the valve stem for scoring and wear ridges. Rotate the valve, and check for any obvious indication that it is bent. Look for pits and excessive wear on the end of each valve stem. If the valve appears satisfactory at this stage, measure the valve stem diameter at several points using a micrometer **(see illustration)**. Any significant difference in the readings obtained indicates wear of the valve

stem. Should any of these conditions be apparent, the valve(s) must be renewed. If the valves are in satisfactory condition, or if new valves are being fitted, they should be ground (lapped) into their respective seats to ensure a smooth gas-tight seal.
15 Valve grinding is carried out as follows. Place the cylinder head upside-down on a bench, with a block of wood at each end to give clearance for the valve stems.
16 Smear a trace of coarse carborundum paste on the seat face, and press a suction grinding tool onto the valve head. With a semi-rotary action, grind the valve head to its seat, lifting the valve occasionally to redistribute the grinding paste **(see illustration)**. When a dull-matt even surface is produced on both the valve seat and the valve, wipe off the paste and repeat the process with fine carborundum paste. A light spring placed under the valve head will greatly ease this operation. When a smooth unbroken ring of light grey matt finish is produced on both the valve and seat, the grinding operation is complete. Be sure to remove all traces of grinding paste, using paraffin or a suitable solvent, before reassembly of the cylinder head.

Valve components

17 Examine the valve springs for signs of damage and discoloration, and also measure their free length using vernier calipers or a steel rule **(see illustration)** or by comparing the existing spring with a new component.
18 Stand each spring on a flat surface, and check it for squareness. If any of the springs are damaged, distorted or have lost their tension, obtain a complete new set of springs. It is normal to renew the springs as a matter of course during a major overhaul.
19 On Zetec-SE and diesel engines, inspect the tappet buckets and their shims for scoring, pitting (especially on the shims), and wear ridges. Renew any components as necessary. Note that some scuffing is to be expected, and is acceptable provided that the tappets are not scored.

Rocker arm components (Endura-E engine)

20 Check the rocker arm contact surfaces for pits, wear, score marks or any indication that

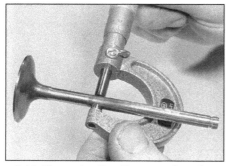

9.14 Measuring the diameter of a valve stem

9.16 Grinding-in a valve seat

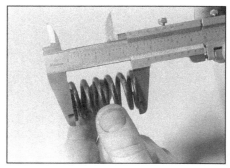

9.17 Checking the valve spring free length

10.2a Fitting a valve stem oil seal (Endura-E engine)

10.2b Using a special tool to fit the valve stem oil seals

the surface-hardening has worn through. Dismantle the rocker shaft and check the components as described in Chapter 2A.

Valve stem oil seals

21 The valve stem oil seals should be renewed as a matter of course.

10 Cylinder head – reassembly

1 On the Endura-DE engine, if the swirl chambers have been removed, refit them to their original locations. Check the protrusion of the swirl chambers as described in Section 9.
2 Lubricate the valve stem oil seals with clean engine oil, then fit them by pushing into position in the cylinder head using a suitable socket or special tool **(see illustrations)**. Ensure that the seals are fully engaged with the valve guide. Note that the inlet and exhaust seals are usually different colours – green for the inlet valves, red for the exhaust valves.
3 Lubricate the valve stems then insert the valves into their original locations. If new valves are being fitted, insert them into the locations to which they have been ground.

Take care not to damage the valve stem oil seal as each valve is fitted **(see illustrations)**.
4 Locate the spring seat over the guide where applicable (on the Zetec-SE engine the seat is incorporated in the valve stem seal). Fit the spring and cap.
5 Compress the valve spring and locate the split collets in the recess in the valve stem **(see illustrations)**. Release the compressor, then repeat the procedure on the remaining valves.
6 With all the valves installed, place the cylinder head flat on the bench and, using a hammer and interposed block of wood, tap

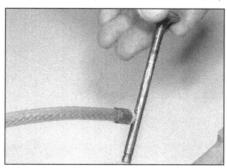

10.3a Oil the valve stems . . .

the end of each valve stem to settle the components.
7 The previously removed components can now be refitted with reference to Section 8 **(see illustration)**.

11 Auxiliary shaft (Endura-DE engine) – removal, inspection and refitting

Note: *A new auxiliary shaft oil seal, housing gasket (or suitable sealant, as applicable), and oil pump drivegear cover plate O-ring will be required on refitting.*

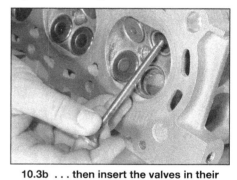

10.3b . . . then insert the valves in their guides

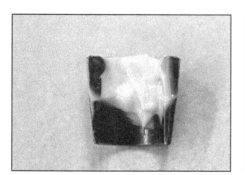

10.5a Apply a small dab of grease to each collet before installation – it will hold them in place on the valve stem

10.5b A dab of grease on a screwdriver will help to fit the collets

10.7 Fit a new gasket when refitting the outlet elbow to the left-hand end of the cylinder head

11.5a Withdraw the auxiliary shaft a little, then remove the thrust plate

11.5b Removing the auxiliary shaft

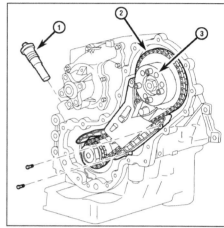

12.3 Unscrew the chain tensioner from the housing

Removal

1 With the engine removed from the vehicle, proceed as follows.
2 Remove the auxiliary shaft sprocket and the oil pump as described in Chapter 2C, Sections 8 and 14.
3 Unbolt and remove the timing belt side cover.
4 Unscrew the bolts and remove the oil seal housing from the cylinder block. The oil seal is integral with the housing.
5 Unscrew the bolts securing the thrust plate to the cylinder block, then carefully withdraw the auxiliary shaft taking care not to allow the oil pump gear to snag on the shaft bearing. Remove the thrust plate from the shaft noting that the oilways are facing outwards (see illustrations).

Inspection

6 Examine the auxiliary shaft and oil pump drivegear for pitting, scoring or wear ridges on the bearing journals, and for chipping or wear of the sprocket teeth. Renew as necessary. Check the auxiliary shaft bearings in the cylinder block for wear and, if worn, have these renewed by your Ford dealer or suitably-equipped engineering works. Wipe them clean if they are still serviceable.
7 Temporarily fit the thrustplate to its position on the auxiliary shaft, and check for excessive wear. If possible, compare the shaft and thrustplate with new components to indicate the amount of wear, and renew them if necessary.

Refitting

8 Lubricate the bearing journals of the auxiliary shaft and the bearings in the cylinder block with fresh engine oil.
9 Lubricate the thrust plate then locate it on the

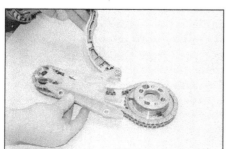

12.6 Examine the chain guides for wear

shaft with the oilways facing outwards (ie, towards the sprocket position). Insert the shaft and thrust plate into the cylinder block, then refit the bolts and tighten to the specified torque.
10 Clean the cylinder block and end of the auxiliary shaft.
11 Smear fresh engine oil on the auxiliary shaft and on the sealing lips of the new oil seal. Before fitting the new seal, locate the special fitting ring inside the sealing lips.
12 Locate the new oil seal housing over the end of the auxiliary shaft, then insert the bolts and tighten to the specified torque.
13 Carefully remove the special ring and make sure that the seal lips are located on the shaft correctly.
14 Refit the timing belt side cover and tighten the bolts.
15 Refit the auxiliary shaft sprocket as described in Chapter 2C.

12 Fuel injection pump drive chain (Endura-DI engine) – removal, inspection and refitting

Removal

1 With the engine removed from the vehicle, proceed as follows.
2 Remove the oil pump as described in Chapter 2D.
3 At the rear of the engine block, locate the drive chain hydraulic tensioner (below and behind the coolant pump). Using the hex in the top of the tensioner body, unscrew and extract the tensioner from the block (see illustration). Be prepared for a small amount of oil spillage as this is done.

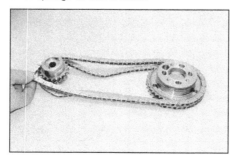

12.9 Two chains ('gemini') which run next to one another, offset by half a link

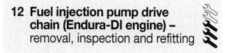

12.5 Fuel injection pump drive chain assembly

1 Hydraulic chain tensioner
2 Chain assembly
3 Injection pump timing hole

4 Temporarily refit the crankshaft pulley if necessary, and turn the engine so that the timing hole in the injection pump sprocket is at the top and aligned – this can be checked by inserting a 6 mm twist drill into the hole in the sprocket and into the injection pump.
5 Unscrew the two bolts securing the chain guides, then carefully slide the two sprockets simultaneously from their locations, and remove the complete chain, guide and sprocket assembly from the engine (see illustration).

Inspection

6 Examine the guides for scoring or wear ridges, and for chipping or wear of the sprocket teeth (see illustration).
7 Check the chains for wear, which will be evident in the form of excess play between the links. If the chains can be lifted at either 'end' of their run so that the sprocket teeth are visible, they have stretched excessively.
8 Check the chain tensioner for signs of wear, and renew if required.
9 At the time of writing, only the chain tensioner is available separately; if the chains or sprockets are worn, the complete assembly, comprising, sprockets, guides and chains must be purchased (see illustration).

12.10 Tightening the chain guide retaining bolts

If possible, compare the old items with new components, or seek the advice of an engineering works, before concluding that renewal is necessary.

Refitting

10 Refitting is a reversal of removal, noting the following points:
 a) *Align the timing holes in the injection pump sprockets when offering the chain and sprocket assembly into position.*
 b) *Tighten the timing chain guide retaining bolts securely to the specified torque (see illustration).*
 c) *Especially if a new chain and sprocket assembly has been fitted, lubricate it thoroughly with fresh engine oil.*
 d) *Refit the chain tensioner, and tighten it to the specified torque.*
 e) *Refit the oil pump as described in Chapter 2D.*

13 Camshaft and tappets (Endura-E engine) – removal, inspection and refitting

Removal

1 Refer to the relevant Sections in Chapter 2A and remove the cylinder head, timing chain and camshaft sprocket, and the sump.
2 Invert the engine so that it is supported on its cylinder head face (on a clean work area). This is necessary to make all of the tappets slide to the top of their stroke, thus allowing the camshaft to be withdrawn. Rotate the camshaft through a full turn, to ensure that all of the tappets slide up their bores, clear of the camshaft.
3 Before removing the camshaft, check its endfloat using a dial gauge mounted on the front face of the engine or feeler blades. Pull the camshaft fully towards the front (timing chain) end of the engine, then insert feeler blades between the camshaft sprocket flange and the camshaft thrust plate to assess the

endfloat clearance **(see illustration)**. The camshaft endfloat must be as specified (see Chapter 2A Specifications).
4 Undo the two retaining bolts, and remove the camshaft thrust plate **(see illustration)**.
5 Carefully withdraw the camshaft from the front end of the engine **(see illustration)**.
6 Extract each tappet in turn. Keep them in order of fitting by inserting them in a card with eight holes in it, numbered 1 to 8 (from the timing chain end of the engine). A valve grinding suction tool will be found to be useful for the removal of tappets **(see illustration)**.

Inspection

7 Examine the camshaft bearing journals and lobes for damage or excessive wear. If evident, the camshaft must be renewed.
8 Examine the camshaft bearing internal surfaces for signs of damage or excessive wear. If evident, the bearings must be renewed by a Ford dealer.
9 If not carried out on removal, check the camshaft endfloat as described in paragraph 3. If the endfloat exceeds the specified tolerance, renew the thrust plate.
10 It is seldom that the tappets wear excessively in their bores, but it is likely that after a high mileage, the cam lobe contact surfaces will show signs of depression or grooving.
11 Where this condition is evident, renew

the tappets. Grinding out the grooves and wear marks will reduce the thickness of the surface hardening, and will accelerate further wear.

Refitting

12 To refit the tappets and the camshaft, it is essential that the crankcase is inverted.
13 Lubricate the tappets and their bores. Insert each tappet fully into its original bore in the cylinder block.
14 Lubricate the camshaft bearings, camshaft and thrust plate, then insert the camshaft into the crankcase from the timing case end.
15 Fit the thrust plate and tighten the retaining bolts to the specified torque setting. Check that the camshaft is able to rotate freely, and that the endfloat is as specified (see Chapter 2A Specifications).

14 Piston/connecting rod assemblies – removal

1 Remove the cylinder head, sump, oil pump pick-up tube and baffle plate (Endura-E, Zetec-SE and Endura-DE engines) with reference to Chapter 2A, 2B or 2C. On Endura-DI engines, unbolt and remove the

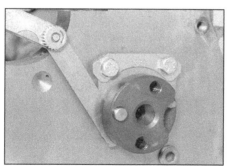

13.3 Checking the camshaft endfloat

13.4 Removing the camshaft thrust plate

13.5 Removing the camshaft from the front end of the engine

13.6 Removing the tappets, using a valve grinding tool suction cup

14.1a Unbolt the oil pick-up pipe/filter and return pipe . . .

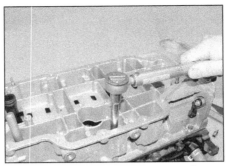

14.1b . . . then unbolt the lower crankcase and remove – Endura-DI engine

14.2 The big-end caps and connecting rods are normally marked with their relevant cylinder number

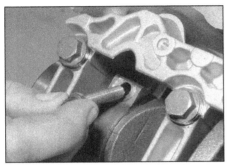

14.3a Removing the bolts . . .

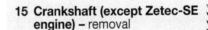

14.3b . . . and big-end bearing caps – Zetec-SE engine

lower crankcase; recover the rubber gasket – a new one must be used when reassembling **(see illustrations)**.

2 Rotate the crankshaft so that No 1 big-end cap (timing end of the engine) is at the lowest point of its travel. If the big-end cap and rod are not already numbered, mark them with a marker pen **(see illustration)**. Mark both cap and rod to identify the cylinder they operate in.

3 Unscrew and remove the big-end bearing cap bolts, and withdraw the cap complete with shell bearing from the connecting rod. Make sure that the shell remains in the cap and if necessary identify it for position **(see illustrations)**.

4 If only the bearing shells are being attended to, push the connecting rod up and off the crankpin, and remove the upper bearing shell. Keep the bearing shells and cap together in their correct sequence if they are to be refitted.

5 If the piston is being removed, push the connecting rod up and remove the piston and rod from the top of the bore. Note that if there is a pronounced wear ridge at the top of the bore, there is a risk of damaging the piston as the rings foul the ridge. However, it is reasonable to assume that a rebore and new pistons will be required in any case if the ridge is so pronounced.

6 Repeat the procedure for the remaining piston/connecting rod assemblies. Ensure that the caps and rods are marked before removal, as described previously, and keep all components in order.

15 Crankshaft (except Zetec-SE engine) – removal

Caution: Do not attempt to remove the crankshaft or main bearing cap/ladder on the Zetec-SE engine, as it is not possible to refit it accurately using conventional tooling. The manufacturers do not supply torque settings for the main bearing cap/ladder retaining bolts. If the crankshaft is worn excessively on the Zetec-SE engine, it will be necessary to obtain a new short motor comprising the cylinder block together with the pistons and crankshaft.

1 Remove the timing belt or chain (as applicable), crankshaft sprocket, engine front plate (Endura-DE engine), sump, oil pick-up

15.2 Checking the crankshaft endfloat with a dial gauge

tube, flywheel/driveplate and left-hand/flywheel end oil seal housing. The pistons/connecting rods must be free of the crankshaft journals, however it is not essential to remove them completely from the cylinder block.

2 Before the crankshaft is removed, check the endfloat. Mount a dial gauge with the probe in line with the crankshaft and just touching the crankshaft **(see illustration)**.

3 Push the crankshaft fully away from the gauge, and zero it. Next, lever the crankshaft towards the gauge as far as possible, and check the reading obtained. The distance that the crankshaft moved is its endfloat; if it is greater than specified, new thrust washers will be required (see Chapter 2A, 2C or 2D Specifications).

4 If no dial gauge is available, feeler blades can be used. Gently lever or push the crankshaft in one direction, then insert feeler blades between the crankshaft web and the main bearing incorporating the thrustwashers to determine the clearance.

5 Check that the main bearing caps have marks to indicate their respective fitted positions in the block. They also have arrow marks pointing towards the timing end of the engine to indicate correct orientation **(see illustration)**.

6 Unscrew the retaining bolts, and remove the main bearing caps. If the caps are reluctant to separate from the block face, lightly tap them free using a plastic- or copper-faced hammer. If the bearing shells are likely to be used again, keep them with

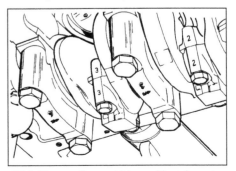

15.5 Connecting rod big-end bearing cap and main bearing cap markings

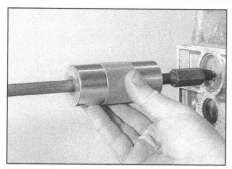

16.1a The core plugs should be removed with a puller – if they are driven into the block, they may be impossible to remove

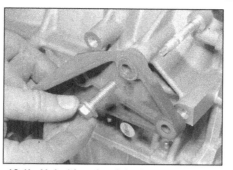
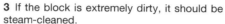

16.1b Unbolting the right-hand driveshaft centre bearing bracket from the rear of the cylinder block

16.1c Unscrew the bolts . . .

their bearing caps for safekeeping. However, unless the engine is known to be of low mileage, it is recommended that they be renewed.

7 Lift the crankshaft out from the crankcase, then extract the upper bearing shells and side thrustwashers. Keep them with their respective caps for correct repositioning if they are to be used again.

16 Cylinder block/crankcase and bores – cleaning and inspection

Cleaning

Caution: If cleaning the cylinder block (with fitted crankshaft) on the Zetec-SE engine, it is recommended that only the external surfaces are cleaned, as otherwise the internal oilways and channels may become contaminated leading to premature wear of the crankshaft and main bearings.

1 For complete cleaning, the core plugs should be removed. Drill a small hole in them, then insert a self-tapping screw and pull out the plugs using a pair of grips or a slide-hammer. Also remove all external components and senders (if not already done), noting their locations **(see illustrations)**. Where applicable, remove the oil sprayers from the bottom of each bore.

2 Scrape all traces of gasket or sealant from the cylinder block, taking care not to damage the head and sump mating faces.

3 If the block is extremely dirty, it should be steam-cleaned.

4 After the block has been steam-cleaned, clean all oil holes and oil galleries one more time. Flush all internal passages with warm water until the water runs clear, dry the block thoroughly and wipe all machined surfaces with a light rust-preventative oil. If you have access to compressed air, use it to speed up the drying process and to blow out all the oil holes and galleries.

> ⚠ **Warning: Wear eye protection when using compressed air.**

5 If the block is not very dirty, you can do an adequate cleaning job with hot soapy water and a stiff brush. Take plenty of time, and do a thorough job. Regardless of the cleaning method used, be sure to clean all oil holes and galleries very thoroughly, dry the block completely and coat all machined surfaces with light oil.

6 The threaded holes in the block must be clean to ensure accurate torque wrench readings during reassembly. Run the proper-size tap into each of the holes to remove rust, corrosion, thread sealant or sludge, and to restore damaged threads **(see illustration)**. If possible, use compressed air to clear the holes of debris produced by this operation. Now is a good time to clean the threads on the head bolts and the main bearing cap bolts as well.

7 Where applicable, refit the main bearing caps, and tighten the bolts finger-tight.

8 After coating the mating surfaces of the new core plugs with suitable sealant, refit them in the cylinder block. Make sure that they are driven in straight and seated properly, or leakage could result. Special tools are available for this purpose, but a large socket, with an outside diameter that will just slip into the core plug, will work just as well.

9 On the diesel engines, remove the oil jets from their locations in the crankcase and clean them. After cleaning the cylinder block, refit the jets.

10 If the engine is not going to be reassembled right away, cover it with a large plastic bag to keep it clean and prevent it rusting.

Inspection

11 Visually check the block for cracks, rust and corrosion. Look for stripped threads in the threaded holes. If there has been any history of internal water leakage, it may be worthwhile having an engine overhaul specialist check the block with special equipment. If defects are found, have the block repaired, if possible, or renewed.

12 Check the cylinder bores for scuffing and scoring. Normally, bore wear will be evident in the form of a wear ridge at the top of the bore. This ridge marks the limit of piston travel.

13 Measure the diameter of each cylinder at the top (just under the ridge area), centre and bottom of the cylinder bore, parallel to the crankshaft axis **(see illustration)**.

14 Next measure each cylinder's diameter at

16.1d . . . and remove the oil trap and gasket from the front of the cylinder block – Zetec-SE engine

16.6 All bolt holes in the block should be cleaned and restored with a tap

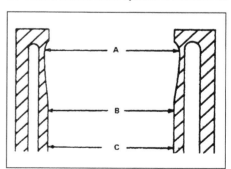

16.13 Measure the diameter of each cylinder just under the wear ridge (A), at the centre (B) and at the bottom (C)

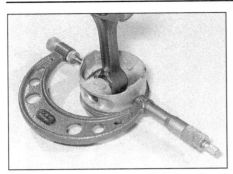

16.15 Measure the piston skirt diameter at right-angles to the gudgeon pin axis, just above the base of the skirt

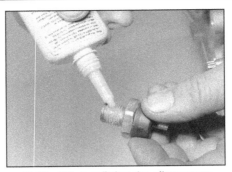

16.19a When refitting the oil pressure switch, apply suitable sealant to the threads . . .

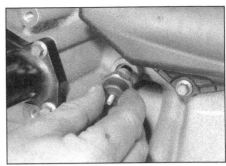

16.19b . . . then insert it in the cylinder block and tighten to the specified torque

the same three locations across the crankshaft axis. If the difference between any of the measurements is greater than 0.20 mm, indicating that the cylinder is excessively out-of-round or tapered, then remedial action must be considered.

15 Repeat this procedure for the remaining cylinders, then measure the diameter of each piston at right-angles to the gudgeon pin axis, and compare the result with the information given in the Specifications **(see illustration)**. By comparing the piston diameters with the bore diameters, an idea can be obtained of the clearances.

16 If the cylinder walls are badly scuffed or scored, or if they are excessively out-of-round or tapered, have the cylinder block rebored (where possible) by an engine overhaul specialist. New pistons (oversize in the case of a rebore) will also be required.

17 If the cylinders are in reasonably good condition, then it may only be necessary to renew the piston rings.

18 If this is the case, the bores should be honed in order to allow the new rings to bed in correctly and provide the best possible seal. The conventional type of hone has spring-loaded stones, and is used with a power drill. You will also need some paraffin or honing oil and rags. The hone should be moved up and down the cylinder to produce a crosshatch pattern, and plenty of honing oil should be used. Ideally, the crosshatch lines should intersect at approximately a 60° angle. Do not take off more material than is necessary to produce the required finish. If new pistons are being fitted, the piston manufacturers may specify a finish with a different angle, so their instructions should be followed. Do not withdraw the hone from the cylinder while it is still being turned, but stop it first (keep the hone moving up-and-down the bore while it slows down). After honing a cylinder, wipe out all traces of the honing oil. If equipment of this type is not available, or if you are not sure whether you are competent to undertake the task yourself, an engine overhaul specialist will carry out the work at a moderate cost.

19 Refit all external components and senders in their correct locations, as noted before removal **(see illustrations)**.

17 Piston/connecting rod assemblies – inspection and reassembly

Inspection

1 Before the inspection process can begin, the piston/connecting rod assemblies must be cleaned, and the original piston rings removed from the pistons.

2 Carefully expand the old rings over the top of the pistons. The use of two or three old feeler blades will be helpful in preventing the rings dropping into empty grooves **(see illustration)**. Note that the oil control scraper ring is in two sections.

3 Scrape away all traces of carbon from the top of the piston. A hand-held wire brush or a piece of fine emery cloth can be used once the majority of the deposits have been scraped away.

4 Remove the carbon from the ring grooves in the piston by cleaning them using an old ring. Break the ring in half to do this. Be very careful to remove only the carbon deposits; do not remove any metal, or scratch the sides of the ring grooves. Protect your fingers – piston rings are sharp.

5 Once the deposits have been removed, clean the piston/connecting rod assembly with paraffin or a suitable solvent, and dry thoroughly. Make sure the oil return holes in the ring grooves are clear.

6 If the pistons and cylinder bores are not

17.2 Using feeler blades to remove piston rings

damaged or worn excessively, and if the cylinder block does not need to be rebored, the original pistons can be re-used. Normal piston wear appears as even vertical wear on the piston thrust surfaces, and slight looseness of the top ring in its groove. New piston rings, however, should always be used when the engine is reassembled.

7 Carefully inspect each piston for cracks around the skirt, at the gudgeon pin bosses, and at the piston ring lands (between the piston ring grooves).

8 Look for scoring and scuffing on the sides of the skirt, holes in the piston crown, and burned areas at the edge of the crown. If the skirt is scored or scuffed, the engine may have been suffering from overheating and/or abnormal combustion, which caused excessively-high operating temperatures. The cooling and lubricating systems should be checked thoroughly. Scorch marks on the sides of the pistons show that blow-by has occurred and the rings are not sealing correctly. A hole in the piston crown is an indication that abnormal combustion (pre-ignition, knocking or detonation) has been occurring. If any of the above problems exist, the causes must be corrected, or the damage will occur again. On petrol engines, the causes may include inlet air leaks, incorrect fuel/air mixture or incorrect ignition timing. On diesel engines, incorrect injection pump timing or a faulty injector may be the cause.

9 Corrosion of the piston, in the form of small pits, indicates that coolant is leaking into the combustion chamber and/or the crankcase. Again, the cause must be corrected, or the problem may persist in the rebuilt engine.

10 If new rings are being fitted to old pistons, measure the piston ring-to-groove clearance by placing a new piston ring in each ring groove and measuring the clearance with a feeler blade. Check the clearance at three or four places around each groove. Where no values are specified, if the measured clearance is excessive – say greater than 0.10 mm – new pistons will be required. If the new ring is excessively tight, the most likely cause is dirt remaining in the groove.

11 Check the piston-to-bore clearance by measuring the cylinder bore (see Section 16)

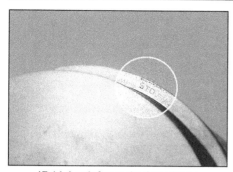

17.14 Look for etched markings identifying the piston ring top surface

and the piston diameter. Measure the piston across the skirt, at a 90° angle to the gudgeon pin, approximately half-way down the skirt. Subtract the piston diameter from the bore diameter to obtain the clearance. If this is greater than the figures given in the Specifications, the block will have to be rebored and new pistons and rings fitted.

12 Check the fit of the gudgeon pin by twisting the piston and connecting rod in opposite directions. Any noticeable play indicates excessive wear, which must be corrected. If the pistons or connecting rods are to be renewed on petrol engines, the work should be carried out by a Ford garage or engine overhaul specialist. Note in the case of the diesel engines, the gudgeon pins are secured by circlips, so the pistons and connecting rods can be separated without difficulty. Note the position of the piston relative to the rod before dismantling, and use new circlips on reassembly.

13 Before refitting the rings to the pistons, check their end gaps by inserting each of them in their cylinder bores. Use the piston to make sure that they are square. Using feeler blades, check that the gaps are within the tolerances given in the Specifications. Genuine rings are supplied pre-gapped; no attempt should be made to adjust the gaps by filing.

Reassembly

14 Install the new rings by fitting them over the top of the piston, starting with the oil control scraper ring sections. Use feeler

18.4 Measure the diameter of each crankshaft journal at several points, to detect taper and out-of round conditions

blades in the same way as when removing the old rings. New rings generally have their top surfaces identified, and must be fitted the correct way round **(see illustration)**. Note that the first and second compression rings have different sections. Be careful when handling the compression rings; they will break if they are handled roughly or expanded too far. With all the rings in position, space the ring gaps at 120° to each other. The oil control scraper ring expander must also be positioned opposite to the actual ring.

18 Crankshaft (except Zetec-SE engine) – inspection

1 Clean the crankshaft and dry it with compressed air if available. Be sure to clean the oil holes with a pipe cleaner or similar probe.

⚠️ *Warning: Wear eye protection when using compressed air.*

2 Check the main and big-end bearing journals for uneven wear, scoring, pitting and cracking.

3 If the crankshaft has been reground, check for burrs around the crankshaft oil holes (the holes are usually chamfered, so burrs should not be a problem unless regrinding has been carried out carelessly). Remove any burrs with a fine file or scraper, and thoroughly clean the oil holes as described previously.

4 Using a micrometer, measure the diameter of the main bearing and connecting rod journals, and compare the results with the Specifications **(see illustration)**. By measuring the diameter at a number of points around each journal's circumference, you will be able to determine whether or not the journal is out-of-round. Take the

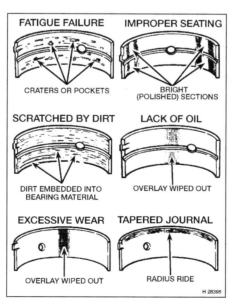

19.2 Typical bearing failures

measurement at each end of the journal, near the webs, to determine if the journal is tapered. If any of the measurements vary by more than 0.025 mm, the crankshaft will have to be reground, and undersize bearings fitted.

5 Check the oil seal contact surfaces at each end of the crankshaft for wear and damage. If an excessive groove is evident in the surface of the crankshaft, consult an engine overhaul specialist who will be able to advise whether a repair is possible or if a new crankshaft is necessary.

19 Main and big-end bearings – inspection

1 Even though the main and big-end bearings should be renewed during the engine overhaul, the old bearings should be retained for close examination, as they may reveal valuable information about the condition of the engine. The size of the bearing shells is stamped on the back metal, and this information should be given to the supplier of the new shells.

2 Bearing failure occurs because of lack of lubrication, the presence of dirt or other foreign particles, overloading the engine, and corrosion. Regardless of the cause of bearing failure, it must be corrected before the engine is reassembled, to prevent it from happening again **(see illustration)**.

3 When examining the bearings, remove them from the engine block, the main bearing caps, the connecting rods and the rod caps, and lay them out on a clean surface in the same general position as their location in the engine. This will enable you to match any bearing problems with the corresponding crankshaft journal.

4 Dirt and other foreign particles get into the engine in a variety of ways. Dirt may be left in the engine during assembly, or it may pass through filters or the crankcase ventilation system. It may get into the oil, and from there into the bearings. Metal chips from machining operations and normal engine wear are often present. Abrasives are sometimes left in engine components after reconditioning, especially when parts are not thoroughly cleaned using the proper cleaning methods. Whatever the source, these foreign objects often end up embedded in the soft bearing material, and are easily recognised. Large particles will not embed in the bearing, and will score or gouge the bearing and journal. The best prevention for this cause of bearing failure is to clean all parts thoroughly, and keep everything spotlessly-clean during engine assembly. Frequent and regular engine oil and filter changes are also recommended.

5 Lack of lubrication (or lubrication breakdown) has a number of interrelated causes. Excessive heat (which thins the oil), overloading (which squeezes the oil from the bearing face) and oil leakage (from excessive bearing clearances, worn oil pump or high engine speeds) all contribute to lubrication breakdown. Blocked oil passages, which usually are the result of misaligned oil holes in a bearing shell, will also oil-starve a bearing and destroy it. When lack of lubrication is the cause of bearing failure, the bearing material is wiped or extruded from the steel backing of the bearing. Temperatures may increase to the point where the steel backing turns blue from overheating.

6 Driving habits can have a definite effect on bearing life. Full-throttle, low-speed operation (labouring the engine) puts very high loads on bearings, which tends to squeeze out the oil film. These loads cause the bearings to flex, which produces fine cracks in the bearing face (fatigue failure). Eventually, the bearing material will loosen in pieces and tear away from the steel backing. Short-trip driving leads to corrosion of bearings, because insufficient engine heat is produced to drive off the condensed water and corrosive gases. These products collect in the engine oil, forming acid and sludge. As the oil is carried to the engine bearings, the acid attacks and corrodes the bearing material.

7 Incorrect bearing installation during engine assembly will lead to bearing failure as well. Tight-fitting bearings leave insufficient bearing oil clearance, and will result in oil starvation. Dirt or foreign particles trapped behind a bearing shell result in high spots on the bearing which lead to failure.

8 If new bearings are to be fitted, the bearing running clearances should be measured before the engine is finally reassembled, to ensure that the correct bearing shells have been obtained (see Sections 21 and 22). If the crankshaft has been reground, the engineering works which carried out the work will advise on the correct size bearing shells to suit the work carried out.

20 Engine overhaul – reassembly sequence

1 Before reassembly begins, ensure that all new parts have been obtained and that all necessary tools are available. Read through the entire procedure to familiarise yourself with the work involved, and to ensure that all items necessary for reassembly of the engine are at hand. In addition to all normal tools and materials, jointing and thread locking compound will be needed during engine reassembly. Do not use any kind of silicone-based sealant on any part of the fuel system or inlet manifold, and never use exhaust sealants upstream (on the engine side) of the catalytic converter.

2 In order to save time and avoid problems, engine reassembly can be carried out in the following order.

  a) *Tappets and camshaft (Endura-E engine).*
  b) *Crankshaft and main bearings.*
  c) *Pistons and connecting rods.*
  d) *Oil pump.*
  e) *Sump.*
  f) *Flywheel/driveplate.*
  g) *Cylinder head.*
  h) *Timing sprockets and chain/belt.*
  i) *Engine external components (including inlet and exhaust manifolds).*

3 Ensure that everything is clean prior to reassembly. As mentioned previously, dirt and metal particles can quickly destroy bearings and result in major engine damage. Use clean engine oil to lubricate during reassembly.

21 Crankshaft (except Zetec-SE engine) – main bearing clearance check and refitting

1 It is assumed at this point that the cylinder block/crankcase and crankshaft have been cleaned and repaired or reconditioned as necessary. Position the engine upside-down.

2 Remove the main bearing cap bolts, and lift out the caps. Lay the caps out in the proper order, to ensure correct installation.

3 If they're still in place, remove the old bearing shells from the block and the main bearing caps. Wipe the bearing recesses of the block and caps with a clean, lint-free cloth. They must be kept spotlessly-clean.

Main bearing clearance check

4 Wipe clean the main bearing shell seats in the crankcase, and clean the backs of the bearing shells. Insert the respective upper shells (dry) into position in the crankcase. Note that the upper shells have grooves in them (the lower shells are plain, and have a wider location lug). Note also that the No 1 lower shell on the diesel engines has a groove. Where the old main bearings are being refitted, ensure that they are located in their original positions. Make sure that the tab on each bearing shell fits into the notch in the block or cap **(see illustrations)**. No lubrication should be used at this time.

Caution: Don't hammer the shells into place, and don't damage the bearing faces.

5 Before the crankshaft can be permanently installed, the main bearing running clearance should be checked; this can be done in either of two ways. One method is to fit the main bearing caps to the cylinder block, with the bearing shells in place. With the cap retaining bolts tightened to the specified torque, measure the internal diameter of each assembled pair of bearing shells using a vernier dial indicator or internal micrometer. If the diameter of each corresponding crankshaft journal is measured and then subtracted from the bearing internal diameter, the result will be the main bearing running clearance. The second (and more accurate) method is to use a product known as Plastigauge. This consists of a fine thread of perfectly-round plastic which is compressed between the bearing cap and the journal. When the cap is removed, the deformation of the plastic thread is measured with a special card gauge supplied with the kit. The running clearance is determined from this gauge. The procedure for using Plastigauge is as follows.

6 Place the crankshaft thrustwashers into position in the crankcase, so that their oil grooves are facing outwards (away from the central web) **(see illustration)**. Hold them in position with a little grease. Clean the bearing surfaces of the shells in the block, and the crankshaft main bearing journals with a clean, lint-free cloth.

21.4a Fit the bearing shells to their locations in the crankcase

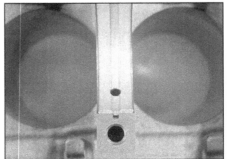

21.4b The tab on each bearing shell must engage with the notch in the cylinder block or cap, and the oil holes in the upper shells must align with the block oilways

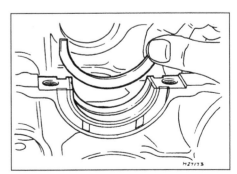

21.6 Place the crankshaft thrustwashers into position in the crankcase so that their oil grooves are facing outwards

21.7 Lowering the crankshaft in the main bearings

21.8 Lay the Plastigauge strips on the main bearing journals, parallel to the crankshaft centre-line

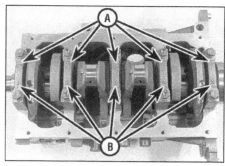

21.9 The crankshaft main bearing cap arrows point to the timing belt end of the engine (A), and the bearing numbers (B) are consecutive from the timing belt end

7 With the crankshaft clean, carefully lay it in position in the main bearings **(see illustration)**. Do not use any lubricant; the crankshaft journals and bearing shells must be perfectly clean and dry.

8 Cut several pieces of the appropriate-size Plastigauge (they should be slightly shorter than the width of the main bearings), and place one piece on each crankshaft journal axis **(see illustration)**.

9 With the bearing shells in position in the caps, fit the caps to their numbered or previously-noted locations **(see illustration)**. Take care not to disturb the Plastigauge.

10 Starting with the centre main bearing and working outward, tighten the main bearing cap bolts progressively to their specified torque setting. Don't rotate the crankshaft at any time during this operation.

11 Remove the bolts and carefully lift off the main bearing caps, keeping them in order. Don't disturb the Plastigauge or rotate the crankshaft. If any of the bearing caps are difficult to remove, tap them from side-to-side with a soft-faced mallet.

12 Compare the width of the crushed Plastigauge on each journal to the scale printed on the gauge to obtain the main bearing running clearance **(see illustration)**.

13 If the clearance is not as specified, the bearing shells may be the wrong size (or excessively-worn if the original shells are being re-used). Before deciding that different

size shells are needed, make sure that no dirt or oil was trapped between the bearing shells and the caps or block when the clearance was measured. If the Plastigauge was wider at one end than at the other, the journal may be tapered.

14 Carefully scrape away all traces of the Plastigauge material from the crankshaft and bearing shells, using a fingernail or something similar which is unlikely to score the shells.

Final crankshaft refitting

15 Carefully lift the crankshaft out of the engine. Clean the bearing surfaces of the shells in the block, then apply a thin layer of clean engine oil to each shell. Coat the thrustwasher bearing surfaces as well.

16 Make sure the crankshaft journals are clean, then lay the crankshaft back in place in the block. Clean the bearing surfaces of the shells in the caps, then lubricate them with oil. Install the caps in their respective positions, with the arrows pointing to the timing belt/chain end of the engine.

17 Working on one cap at a time, from the centre main bearing outwards (and ensuring that each cap is tightened down squarely and evenly onto the block), tighten the main bearing cap bolts to the specified torque wrench setting. On the diesel engines, angle-tighten the bolts in the same sequence using an angle-tightening adapter on a socket.

18 Rotate the crankshaft a number of times by hand, to check for any obvious binding.

19 Check the crankshaft endfloat (refer to Section 15).

20 Refit the crankshaft left-hand/flywheel end oil seal housing and a new seal, as described in Chapters 2A, 2C or 2D (as applicable).

21 Refit the components removed in Section 15.

22 Piston/connecting rod assemblies – big-end bearing clearance check and refitting

1 Clean the backs of the big-end bearing shells and the recesses in the connecting rods and big-end caps. If new shells are being fitted, ensure that all traces of the protective grease are cleaned off using paraffin. Wipe the shells and connecting rods dry with a lint-free cloth.

2 Press the big-end bearing shells into the connecting rods and caps in their correct positions. On the Endura-E engine and the diesel engines, make sure that the location tabs are engaged with the cut-outs in the connecting rods **(see illustration)**. On the Zetec-SE engine, make sure that the shells are located centrally and aligned with the split faces of the connecting rod and cap – the shells are finally held in position when the big-end cap bolts are tightened to the specified torque (see later in this Section) **(see illustration)**.

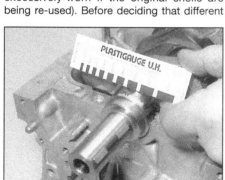

21.12 Compare the width of the crushed Plastigauge to the scale on the envelope to determine the main bearing running clearance

22.2a The location tab on each big-end bearing shell must engage with the notch in the connecting rod or cap

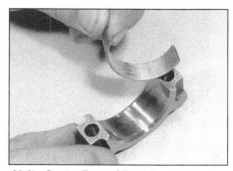

22.2b On the Zetec-SE engine, make sure that the shells are located centrally and aligned with the split faces of the connecting rod and cap

22.4a With the compressor fitted, use the handle of a hammer to gently drive the piston into the cylinder

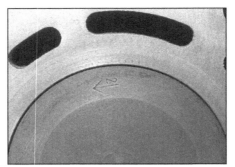

22.4b Make sure that the arrow on the piston crown is facing the timing end of the engine

22.8a Angle-tightening the big-end bearing cap bolts

Big-end bearing clearance check

3 Lubricate No 1 piston and piston rings, and check that the ring gaps are spaced at 120° intervals to each other.

4 Fit a ring compressor to No 1 piston, then insert the piston and connecting rod into No 1 cylinder. Make sure that the arrow on the piston crown is facing the timing end of the engine. With No 1 crankpin at its lowest point, drive the piston carefully into the cylinder with the wooden handle of a hammer, at the same time guiding the connecting rod onto the crankpin (see illustrations).

5 To measure the big-end bearing running clearance, refer to the information contained in Section 21; the same general procedures apply, however note that there are no specifications for the Zetec-SE engine. If the

Plastigauge method is being used, ensure that the crankpin journal and the big-end bearing shells are clean and dry, then engage the connecting rod with the crankpin. Place the Plastigauge strip on the crankpin, fit the bearing cap in its previously-noted position, then tighten the bolts to the specified torque. Do not rotate the crankshaft during this operation. Remove the cap and check the running clearance by measuring the Plastigauge as previously described.

6 Repeat the above procedures on the remaining piston/connecting rod assemblies.

Final refitting

7 Having checked the running clearance of all the crankpin journals and taken any corrective action necessary, clean off all traces of Plastigauge from the bearing shells and crankpin.

8 Liberally lubricate the crankpin journals and big-end bearing shells. Refit the bearing caps once more, ensuring correct positioning as previously described. Tighten the bearing cap bolts to the specified torque and angles, and turn the crankshaft each time to make sure that it is free before moving on to the next assembly (see illustrations).

Diesel engines

9 Use a little grease to stick the new gasket in place, then offer the lower crankcase into position and loosely secure with the bolts (see illustrations). The bolts are of two different lengths, with the longer bolts fitted to the 'inside' of the lower crankcase.

10 The lower crankcase must now be aligned with the cylinder block before the bolts are tightened. Using a straight-edge and feeler blades, check the protrusion or gap all round (see illustration). Spacer shims are available in various thicknesses to correct the alignment – unless new components have been fitted, use the same spacers found on removal.

11 Tighten the lower crankcase bolts to the specified torque (where given), ensuring that the alignment with the cylinder block is not lost (see illustration).

All engines

12 On completion, refit the oil pump pick-up tube and baffle plate (Zetec-SE engine), sump and cylinder head as described in Chapter 2A, 2B, 2C or 2D.

22.8b Torx big-end bolts – Zetec-SE engine

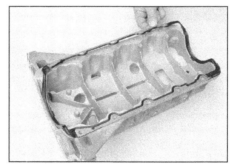

22.9a Lay the gasket into position . . .

22.9b . . . then refit the lower crankcase

22.10 Check the alignment of the lower crankcase

22.11 Tighten the lower crankcase bolts to the specified torque

23 Engine –
initial start-up after overhaul

1 With the engine refitted in the vehicle, double-check the engine oil and coolant levels (see *Weekly checks*). Make a final check that everything has been reconnected, and that there are no tools or rags left in the engine compartment.

Petrol engine models

2 With the spark plugs removed and the ignition and fuel injection systems disabled by disconnecting the low tension wires from the coil (Chapter 5B) and depressurising the fuel system by removing the fuel pump fuse (Chapter 4A), crank the engine on the starter motor until the oil pressure light goes out.
3 Refit the spark plugs and connect the low tension wires. Refit the fuel pump fuse.
4 Start the engine, noting that this may take a little longer than usual, due to the fuel pump being empty.
5 While the engine is idling, check for fuel, water and oil leaks. Where applicable, check the power steering pipe/hose unions for leakage. Do not be alarmed if there are some odd smells and smoke from parts getting hot and burning off oil deposits.
6 Keep the engine idling until hot water is felt circulating through the top hose, then switch it off.
7 After a few minutes, recheck the oil and coolant levels, and top-up as necessary (see *Weekly checks*).
8 There is no requirement to retighten the cylinder head bolts.
9 If new pistons, rings or crankshaft bearings have been fitted, the engine must be run-in for the first 500 miles (800 km). Do not operate the engine at full-throttle, nor allow it to labour in any gear during this period. It is recommended that the oil and filter be changed at the end of this period.

Diesel engine models

10 Prime the fuel system as described in Chapter 4B or 4C.
11 Turn the ignition key and wait for the pre-heating warning light to go out.
12 Start the engine. Additional cranking may be necessary to completely bleed the fuel system before the engine starts.
13 Once started, keep the engine running at fast tickover. Check that the oil pressure light goes out, then check that there are no leaks of oil, fuel and coolant. Where applicable, check the power steering pipe/hose unions for leakage. Do not be alarmed if there are some odd smells and smoke from parts getting hot and burning off oil deposits.
14 Keep the engine idling until hot coolant is felt circulating through the radiator top hose, indicating that the engine is at normal operating temperature, then stop the engine and allow it to cool.
15 Recheck the oil and coolant levels and top up if necessary (see *Weekly checks*).
16 On Endura-DE engines, check the idle speed (Chapter 4B).
17 If new pistons, rings or bearings have been fitted, the engine must be run-in at reduced speeds and loads for the first 500 miles (800 km) or so. Do not operate the engine at full throttle, or allow it to labour in any gear during this period. It is recommended that the engine oil and filter be changed at the end of this period.

Notes

Chapter 3
Cooling, heating and air conditioning systems

Contents

Air conditioning system – general information and precautions 10
Air conditioning system components – removal and refitting 11
Auxiliary drivebelt check and renewal . . . . .See Chapter 1A or 1B
Coolant level check . . . . .See *Weekly checks*
Coolant pump – removal and refitting 7
Coolant renewal and pressure cap check . . . . . .See Chapter 1A or 1B
Cooling system electrical switches and sensors –
  testing, removal and refitting 6
Cooling system hoses – disconnection and renewal 2

Electric cooling fan – testing, removal and refitting 5
General information and precautions 1
Heater/ventilation system components – removal and refitting 9
Heating and ventilation system – general information 8
Hose and fluid leak check . . . . .See Chapter 1A or 1B
Pollen filter renewal . . . . .See Chapter 1A or 1B
Radiator – removal, inspection and refitting 3
Thermostat – removal, testing and refitting 4

Degrees of difficulty

Easy, suitable for novice with little experience		Fairly easy, suitable for beginner with some experience		Fairly difficult, suitable for competent DIY mechanic	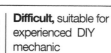	Difficult, suitable for experienced DIY mechanic		Very difficult, suitable for expert DIY or professional	

Specifications

Torque wrench settings	Nm	lbf ft
Coolant pump pulley securing bolts:		
Petrol engines	11	8
Diesel engines:		
Endura-DE	11	8
Endura-DI	24	18
Coolant pump securing bolts:		
Petrol engines	10	7
Diesel engines:		
Endura-DE	33	24
Endura-DI	10	7
Thermostat housing securing bolts:		
Petrol engines	18	13
Diesel engines:		
Endura-DE	18	13
Endura-DI	23	17

1 General information and precautions

General information

The cooling system is of pressurised type, comprising a pump driven by the auxiliary drivebelt (all petrol engines and Endura-DI diesel engine) or the timing belt (Endura-DE diesel engine), an aluminium crossflow radiator, electric cooling fan, and a thermostat. The system functions as follows. Cold coolant from the radiator passes through the hose to the coolant pump, where it is pumped around the cylinder block and head passages. After cooling the cylinder bores, combustion surfaces and valve seats, the coolant reaches the underside of the thermostat, which is initially closed. The coolant passes through the heater, and is returned via the cylinder block to the coolant pump.

When the engine is cold, the coolant circulates only through the cylinder block, cylinder head and heater. When the coolant reaches a predetermined temperature, the thermostat opens and the coolant passes through to the radiator. As the coolant circulates through the radiator, it is cooled by the inrush of air when the car is in forward motion. Airflow is supplemented by the action of the electric cooling fan when necessary. Once the coolant has passed through the radiator, and has cooled, the cycle is repeated.

The electric cooling fan, mounted on the rear of the radiator, is controlled by a thermostatic switch. At a predetermined coolant temperature, the switch actuates the fan.

An expansion tank is fitted to allow for the expansion of the coolant when hot. The expansion tank is connected to the top of the radiator.

Refer to Section 10 for information on the air conditioning system.

Precautions

 Warning: Do not attempt to remove the radiator filler cap, or disturb any part of the cooling system, while the engine is hot; there is a high risk of scalding. If the radiator filler cap must be removed before the engine and radiator have fully cooled (even though this is not recommended) the pressure in the cooling system must first be relieved. Cover the cap with a thick layer of cloth, to avoid scalding, and slowly unscrew the filler cap until a hissing sound can be heard. When the hissing has stopped, indicating that the pressure has reduced, slowly unscrew the filler cap until it can be removed; if more hissing sounds are heard, wait until they have stopped before unscrewing the cap completely. At all times, keep well away from the filler cap opening.

 Warning: Do not allow antifreeze to come into contact with skin, or with the painted surfaces of the vehicle. Rinse off spills immediately, with plenty of water. Never leave antifreeze lying around in an open container, or in a puddle on the driveway or garage floor. Children and pets are attracted by its sweet smell, but antifreeze can be fatal if ingested.

 Warning: If the engine is hot, the electric cooling fan may start rotating even if the engine is not running; be careful to keep hands, hair and loose clothing well clear when working in the engine compartment.

Warning: Refer to Section 10 for precautions to be observed when working on models equipped with air conditioning.

2 Cooling system hoses – disconnection and renewal

Note: *Refer to the warnings given in Section 1 of this Chapter before proceeding. Do not attempt to disconnect any hose while the system is still hot.*

1 If the checks described in the relevant part of Chapter 1 reveal a faulty hose, it must be renewed as follows.

2 First drain the cooling system (see Chapter 1A or 1B). If the coolant is not due for renewal, it may be re-used if it is collected in a clean container.

3 Before disconnecting a hose, first note its routing in the engine compartment, and whether it is secured by any clips or ties. Use a pair of pliers to release the spring clamps (or a screwdriver to slacken screw-type clamps) then move them along the hose, clear of the relevant inlet/outlet union. Carefully work the hose free **(see illustration)**.

4 Note that the radiator inlet and outlet unions are fragile; do not use excessive force when attempting to remove the hoses. If a hose proves to be difficult to remove, try to release it by rotating the hose ends before attempting to free it.

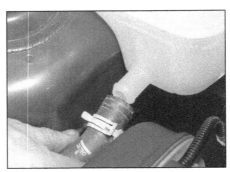

2.3 Disconnecting a coolant hose from the coolant reservoir

If all else fails, cut the coolant hose with a sharp knife, then slit it so that it can be peeled off in two pieces. Although this may prove expensive if the hose is otherwise undamaged, it is preferable to buying a new radiator.

5 When fitting a hose, first slide the clamps onto the hose, then work the hose into position. If spring-type clamps were originally fitted, it is a good idea to replace them with screw-type clamps when refitting the hose. If the hose is stiff, use a little soapy water (washing-up liquid is ideal) as a lubricant, or soften the hose by soaking it in hot water.

6 Work the hose into position, checking that it is correctly routed and secured. Slide each clamp along the hose until it passes over the flared end of the relevant inlet/outlet union, before tightening the clamps securely.

7 Refill the cooling system with reference to Chapter 1A or 1B.

8 Check thoroughly for leaks as soon as possible after disturbing any part of the cooling system.

3 Radiator – removal, inspection and refitting

Removal

1 Disconnect the battery negative lead with reference to Chapter 5A.

2 Drain the cooling system as described in Chapter 1A or 1B.

3 Loosen the hose clip, and disconnect the top hose from the radiator. Similarly, where applicable, disconnect the expansion tank hose from the top of the radiator.

4 Apply the handbrake, then jack up the front of the vehicle and support securely on axle stands (see *Jacking and vehicle support*).

5 Where applicable, remove the securing screws and withdraw the shield from under the radiator.

6 Disconnect the cooling fan wiring plug from the fan motor, and unclip the wiring harness from the cooling fan shroud **(see illustration)**.

7 Where applicable, release the wiring connectors from the lower left-hand side of

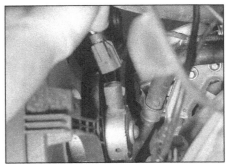

3.6 Disconnect the wiring plug from the cooling fan motor

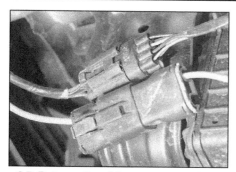

3.7 Release the wiring connectors from the radiator support member

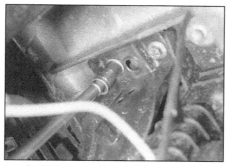

3.10 Unscrew the radiator support member bolts

3.11 Lower the radiator/cooling fan assembly from under the front of the vehicle

the radiator support member **(see illustration)**.

8 Disconnect the hose(s) from the lower right-hand side of the radiator.

9 On models with automatic transmission, place a suitable container beneath the automatic transmission fluid cooler pipes at the transmission, then unscrew the union nuts, and disconnect the pipes from the transmission. Allow the fluid to drain into the container, then plug or cover the open ends of the transmission and the pipes to prevent dirt entry and further fluid spillage.

10 Support the radiator assembly, then unscrew the four bolts securing the radiator support member to the front of the vehicle **(see illustration)**. On vehicles with air conditioning, support the condenser from the front top crossmember to keep it in position.

11 Carefully lower the radiator/fan assembly (complete with the automatic transmission

fluid cooler pipes, where applicable), and withdraw the assembly from under the front of the vehicle **(see illustration)**.

12 If a new radiator is to be fitted, remove the fan assembly and, where applicable, the automatic transmission fluid cooler pipes, and transfer them to the new radiator.

Inspection

13 If the radiator has been removed due to suspected blockage, reverse-flush it as described in Chapter 1A or 1B. Clean dirt and debris from the radiator fins, using an air line (in which case, wear eye protection) or a soft brush. Be careful, as the fins are easily damaged, and are sharp.

14 If necessary, a radiator specialist can perform a 'flow test' on the radiator, to establish whether an internal blockage exists.

15 A leaking radiator must be referred to a specialist for permanent repair. Do not

attempt to weld or solder a leaking radiator, as damage may result.

16 In an emergency, minor leaks from the radiator can be cured by using a suitable radiator sealant (in accordance with its manufacturer's instructions) with the radiator *in situ*.

17 Inspect the radiator mounting rubbers, and renew them if necessary **(see illustration)**.

Refitting

18 Refitting is a reversal of removal, bearing in mind the following points.

  a) *Ensure that the mounting rubbers are correctly located between the radiator and the support member.*

  b) *Ensure that all hoses are correctly reconnected, and their retaining clips securely tightened.*

  c) *On completion, refill the cooling system as described in Chapter 1A or 1B and, on models with automatic transmission, check and if necessary top up the automatic transmission fluid level as described in Chapter 1A.*

3.17 Inspect the radiator mounting rubbers (arrowed) and renew if necessary

4.5a Unscrew the securing bolts . . .

---

4 Thermostat –
removal, testing and refitting

Zetec-SE engines

Note: *A new thermostat housing gasket and a new thermostat sealing ring will be required on refitting.*

Removal

1 Disconnect the battery negative lead with reference to Chapter 5A.

2 Drain the cooling system as described in Chapter 1A or 1B (as applicable).

3 Loosen the clamps, and disconnect the two coolant hoses from the thermostat housing.

4 Remove the alternator as described in Chapter 5A.

5 Unscrew the four securing bolts, and remove the thermostat housing from the cylinder head. Recover the gasket **(see illustrations)**.

6 Lift out the thermostat, and recover the sealing ring **(see illustration)**.

4.5b . . . then remove the thermostat housing (gasket arrowed) – Zetec-SE engine

4.6 Removing the thermostat – Zetec-SE engine

4.8 Testing the thermostat

Testing

7 A rough test of the thermostat's operation may be made by suspending it with a piece of string in a container full of water. Heat the water to bring it to the boil – the thermostat must open by the time the water boils. If not, renew it.

8 The opening temperature is usually marked on the thermostat. If a thermometer is available, the precise opening temperature of the thermostat may be determined, and compared with the value marked on the thermostat **(see illustration)**.

9 A thermostat which fails to close as the water cools must also be renewed.

Refitting

10 Thoroughly clean the mating faces of the thermostat housing and the cylinder head.

11 Refit the thermostat, using a new sealing ring. Ensure that the thermostat air bleed valve is uppermost.

12 Refit the thermostat housing, using a new gasket, and tighten the securing bolts to the specified torque.

13 Refit the alternator as described in Chapter 5A.

14 Reconnect the coolant hoses, then fill the cooling system as described in Chapter 1A.

15 On completion, reconnect the battery negative lead.

Endura-E engines

Note: *A new thermostat cover gasket and a new thermostat sealing ring will be required on refitting.*

Removal

16 Proceed as described in paragraphs 1 and 2.

17 Where applicable, disconnect the wiring from the cooling fan switch mounted in the thermostat housing.

18 Unscrew the securing bolts, and lift off the thermostat housing. Recover the gasket. If necessary, disconnect the coolant hoses from the thermostat housing to enable the housing to be withdrawn.

19 Using pliers, compress the thermostat retaining clip, and remove it from the housing.

20 Lift out the thermostat and recover the sealing ring.

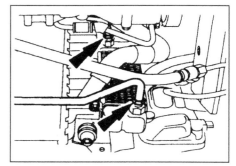

4.24 Thermostat cover location (arrowed) – Endura-DE engine

Testing

21 Proceed as described in paragraphs 7 to 9.

Refitting

22 Refitting is a reversal of removal, bearing in mind the following points.

  a) Thoroughly clean the mating faces of the thermostat cover and the cylinder head.

  b) Refit the thermostat using a new sealing ring.

  c) Refit the thermostat housing, using a new gasket.

  d) Refill the cooling system as described in Chapter 1A.

Diesel engines

Note: *A new thermostat sealing ring will be required on refitting.*

Removal

23 Proceed as described in paragraphs 1 and 2.

24 Unscrew the securing bolts, and lift off the thermostat cover **(see illustration)**.

25 Lift out the thermostat and recover the sealing ring.

Testing

26 Proceed as described in paragraphs 7 to 9.

Refitting

27 Refitting is a reversal of removal, bearing in mind the following points.

  a) Thoroughly clean the mating faces of the thermostat housing and cover.

  b) Refit the thermostat using a new sealing ring.

  c) Refill the cooling system as described in Chapter 1B.

5 Electric cooling fan – testing, removal and refitting

Testing

1 On all models, the cooling fan is controlled by the Powertrain Control Module (PCM – see the relevant part of Chapter 4), using signals provided by the engine coolant temperature

sensor (or cylinder head temperature sensor on Endura-DI diesel engines).

2 The fan operation can be checked by connecting the fan motor directly to a 12-volt power supply. Disconnect the motor wiring plug, and apply 12-volts across the motor terminals (the black wire is the earth) – take great care not to short out the power supply wires.

3 If the fan fails to operate, the fan motor is almost certainly at fault.

4 Testing of the fan motor control circuit must be entrusted to a Ford dealer, who will have the necessary specialist diagnostic equipment to test the powertrain control system – do not attempt to test the system using conventional test equipment, as the Powertrain Control Module may be damaged.

Removal

5 Using suitable lengths of wire or string, support the radiator by tying it to the engine compartment front panel.

6 Disconnect the battery negative lead with reference to Chapter 5A.

7 Apply the handbrake, then jack up the front of the vehicle and support securely on axle stands (see *Jacking and vehicle support*).

8 Where applicable, remove the securing screws and withdraw the shield from under the radiator.

9 Disconnect the cooling fan wiring plug from the fan motor, and unclip the wiring harness from the cooling fan shroud.

10 Where applicable, release the wiring plugs from the left-hand side of the radiator support member.

11 Ensure that the radiator assembly is securely suspended from the front panel, then unscrew the four bolts securing the radiator support member to the front of the vehicle.

12 On models with automatic transmission, proceed as follows.

  *a) Slacken the union nuts securing the transmission fluid cooler pipes to the fluid cooler – **do not** disconnect the pipes **(see illustration)**.*

  b) Unclip the fluid cooler pipes from the fan shroud.

  c) Working at the bottom of the fluid cooler,

5.12a Slacken the transmission fluid cooler pipe unions (arrowed)

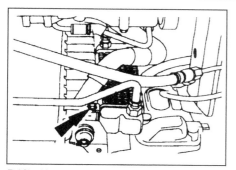

5.12b Unscrew the bolt (arrowed) securing the fluid cooler to the radiator

unscrew the bolt securing the fluid cooler to the radiator (see illustration).

d) Pull the bottom of the fluid cooler away from the radiator, then lower the fluid cooler from the side of the radiator, and support it, taking care not to strain the fluid pipes.

13 Lower the fan shroud assembly from the radiator.

14 If desired, the fan motor can be removed from the shroud after unscrewing the three securing nuts (see illustration).

Refitting

15 Refitting is a reversal of removal, bearing in mind the following points.

a) Ensure that the fan shroud locating lugs are correctly positioned.

b) On automatic transmission models, take care not to strain the fluid cooler pipes, and if any fluid leakage has occurred, check and top up the fluid level as described in Chapter 1A.

c) Ensure that the mounting rubbers are correctly located between the radiator and the support member.

6 Cooling system electrical switches and sensors – testing, removal and refitting

Coolant temperature sensor

1 Testing of the coolant temperature sensor circuit must be entrusted to a Ford dealer, who will have the necessary specialist diagnostic equipment to test the powertrain control system – do not attempt to test the system using conventional test equipment, as the Powertrain Control Module may be damaged.

Zetec-SE engines

2 The sensor is located in a housing, beneath the ignition coil, at the left-hand end of the cylinder head.

3 Disconnect the battery negative lead with reference to Chapter 5A.

4 Drain the cooling system as described in Chapter 1A.

5 Unscrew the securing bolts, and remove the HT lead cover from the camshaft cover,

5.14 Fan motor securing nuts (arrowed)

then disconnect the HT leads from the ignition coil (see illustration).

6 Disconnect the ignition coil wiring plug.

7 Unscrew the four securing bolts, and remove the ignition coil (see illustration).

8 Disconnect the wiring plug from the coolant temperature sensor (see illustration).

9 Unscrew the coolant temperature sensor from its housing.

10 Refitting is a reversal of removal, but refit the camshaft cover with reference to Chapter 2B and on completion, refill the cooling system as described in Chapter 1A.

Endura-E engines

11 The sensor is located at the left-hand bottom corner of the inlet manifold.

12 Disconnect the battery negative lead with reference to Chapter 5A.

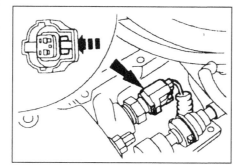

6.8 Disconnect the coolant temperature sensor wiring plug (arrowed) – Zetec-SE engines

13 Drain the cooling system as described in Chapter 1A.

14 Disconnect the wiring plug from the coolant temperature sensor.

15 Unscrew the sensor from the manifold.

16 Refitting is a reversal of removal. Refill the cooling system as described in Chapter 1A.

Diesel engines

17 The sensor is located in the thermostat housing at the front of the engine (see illustration).

18 Disconnect the battery negative lead with reference to Chapter 5A.

19 Drain the cooling system as described in Chapter 1B.

20 Disconnect the wiring plug from the coolant temperature sensor.

21 Unscrew the sensor from the thermostat housing.

22 Refitting is a reversal of removal. Refill the cooling system as described in Chapter 1B.

Temperature gauge sender

23 The coolant temperature gauge is fed with a stabilised voltage supply from the instrument panel feed (via the ignition switch and a fuse), and its earth is controlled by the sender. The sender contains a thermistor (thermal resistor), an electronic component whose electrical resistance decreases at a predetermined rate as its temperature rises. When the coolant is cold, the sender resistance is high, current flow through the

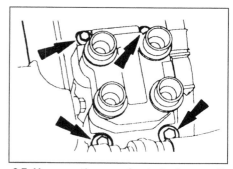

6.5 Unscrew the securing bolts (arrowed) and remove the HT lead cover – Zetec-SE engines

6.7 Unscrew the securing bolts (arrowed) and remove the ignition coil – Zetec-SE engines

6.17 Coolant sensor location (arrowed) – Endura-DE engine

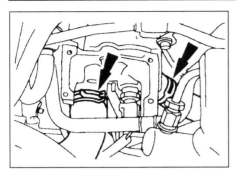

6.29 Disconnect the two coolant hoses (arrowed) from the sensor/sender housing – Zetec-SE engines

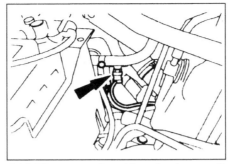

6.30 Disconnect the wiring plug (arrowed) from the temperature sender – Zetec-SE engines

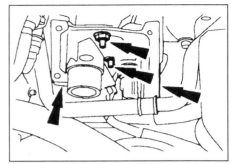

6.31 Unscrew the sensor/sender housing securing nuts (arrowed) – Zetec-SE engines

gauge is reduced, and the gauge needle points towards the 'cold' end of the scale. If the sender is faulty, it must be renewed.

24 If the gauge develops a fault, first check the other instruments; if they do not work at all, check the instrument panel electrical feed. If the readings are erratic, there may be a fault in the voltage stabiliser, which will necessitate renewal of the stabiliser. If the fault lies in the temperature gauge alone, check it as follows.

25 If the gauge needle remains at the 'cold' end of the scale, disconnect the sender wire, and earth it to the cylinder head. If the needle then deflects when the ignition is switched on, the sender unit is proved faulty, and should be renewed. If the needle still does not move, remove the instrument panel (Chapter 12) and check the continuity of the wiring between the sender unit and the gauge, and the feed to the gauge unit. If continuity is shown, and the fault still exists, then the gauge is faulty, and the gauge unit should be renewed.

26 If the gauge needle remains at the 'hot' end of the scale, disconnect the sender wire. If the needle then returns to the 'cold' end of the scale when the ignition is switched on, the sender unit is proved faulty, and should be renewed. If the needle still does not move, check the remainder of the circuit as described previously.

Zetec-SE engines

27 The sensor is located in a housing,

beneath the ignition coil, at the left-hand end of the cylinder head.

28 Proceed as described in paragraphs 2 to 8.

29 Release the clamps, and disconnect the two coolant hoses from the sensor/sender housing **(see illustration)**.

30 Disconnect the wiring plug from the temperature sender, then unscrew the bolt securing the exhaust gas recirculation pipe bracket, and release the wiring connector from the bracket **(see illustration)**.

31 Unscrew the four securing nuts, and withdraw the sensor/sender housing from the engine **(see illustration)**.

32 Unscrew the sender from the housing.

33 Refitting is a reversal of removal, bearing in mind the following points.

a) Tighten all fixings to the specified torque, where given.

b) Thoroughly clean the mating faces of the sensor/sender housing and the cylinder head, and use a new housing gasket.

c) On completion, refill the cooling system as described in Chapter 1A.

Endura-E engines

34 The sender is located at the rear of the engine, in one of the heater hoses **(see illustration)**.

35 Disconnect the battery negative lead with reference to Chapter 5A.

36 Drain the cooling system as described in Chapter 1A, or be prepared for some leakage when the heater hose is disconnected.

37 Release the wiring looms from the clips on the bulkhead, then disconnect the wiring plug from the coolant temperature sensor.

38 Trace the heater hose along to its connection at the cylinder head, then release the hose clip and disconnect the hose.

39 Release the heater hose from any cable-ties, then lift it up from the rear of the engine for better access.

40 Unscrew the sensor from the hose, using a spanner or slip-joint pliers on the raised flats below the sensor location, to prevent the hose from twisting.

41 Refitting is a reversal of removal. Tighten the sensor securely, to prevent leaks, and replace any cable-ties destroyed during removal. Refill the cooling system as described in Chapter 1A.

Diesel engines

42 The sender is located in the thermostat housing, and the removal and refitting procedure is as described for the coolant temperature sensor in paragraphs 17 to 22.

Cooling fan switch

43 The electric cooling fan is controlled by the Powertrain Control Module, using signals provided by the engine coolant temperature sensor.

7 Coolant pump – removal and refitting

Zetec-SE engines

Removal

1 Disconnect the battery negative lead with reference to Chapter 5A.

2 Drain the cooling system as described in Chapter 1A.

3 Slacken the four bolts securing the coolant pump pulley **(see illustration)**.

4 Remove the alternator as described in Chapter 5A.

5 Unscrew the securing bolts, and remove the coolant pump pulley.

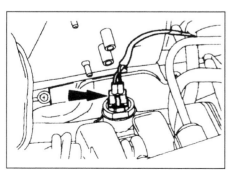

6.34 Coolant temperature gauge sender location (arrowed) – Endura-E engines

7.3 Slacken the coolant pump pulley securing bolts (arrowed) – Zetec-SE engines

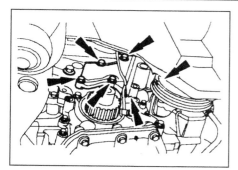

7.8 Coolant pump securing bolts (arrowed) – Zetec-SE engines

6 Unscrew the securing bolt, and remove the auxiliary drivebelt idler pulley.

7 Remove the timing belt covers as described in Chapter 2B.

8 Unscrew the six securing bolts, then withdraw the coolant pump **(see illustration)**.

Refitting

9 Commence refitting by thoroughly cleaning the mating faces of the coolant pump and the cylinder block.

10 Refit the coolant pump, using a new gasket, and tighten the securing bolts to the specified torque.

11 Further refitting is a reversal of removal, bearing in mind the following points.

a) Refit the timing belt covers as described in Chapter 2B.
b) Tighten all fixings to the specified torque (where given).
c) Refit and tension the auxiliary drivebelt as described in Chapter 1A.
d) On completion, refill the cooling system as described in Chapter 1A.

Endura-E engines

Removal

12 Disconnect the battery negative lead with reference to Chapter 5A.

13 Drain the cooling system as described in Chapter 1A.

14 Slacken the coolant pump pulley securing bolts, then remove the auxiliary drivebelt as described in Chapter 1A.

15 Unscrew the securing bolts, and remove the coolant pump pulley.

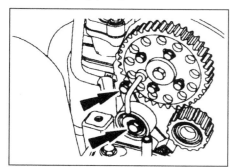

7.24 Remove the two securing bolts (arrowed) and remove the timing belt tensioner pulley – Endura-DE engine

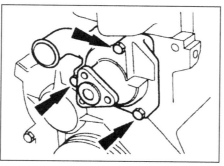

7.17 Coolant pump securing bolts (arrowed) – Endura-E engine

16 Slacken the clip, and disconnect the coolant hose from the coolant pump.

17 Unscrew the three securing bolts, and withdraw the coolant pump **(see illustration)**. Recover the gasket.

Refitting

18 Commence refitting by thoroughly cleaning the mating faces of the coolant pump and the cylinder block.

19 Refit the coolant pump, using a new gasket, and tighten the securing bolts to the specified torque.

20 Further refitting is a reversal of removal, bearing in mind the following points.

a) Tighten all fixings to the specified torque (where given).
b) Refit and tension the auxiliary drivebelt as described in Chapter 1A.
c) On completion, refill the cooling system as described in Chapter 1A.

Endura-DE engines

Removal

21 Disconnect the battery negative lead with reference to Chapter 5A.

22 Drain the cooling system as described in Chapter 1B.

23 Remove the timing belt and the fuel injection pump drivebelt as described in Chapter 2C.

24 Unscrew the two securing bolts, and remove the timing belt tensioner pulley/automatic tensioner assembly **(see illustration)**. Where applicable, recover the tensioner spring.

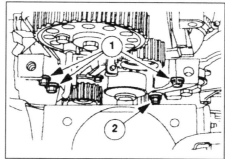

7.26 Engine mounting bracket securing bolts. Loosen bolts (1) and slacken bolt (2) – Endura-DE engine

25 Accurately mark the position of the engine mounting on the body, then unscrew the four securing bolts, and remove the mounting from the vehicle body.

26 Unscrew the four bolts securing the right-hand engine mounting bracket to the engine. Note that the bracket is slotted around the lower front bolt location, so this bolt need only be loosened to remove the bracket **(see illustration)**. If necessary, raise the engine to give sufficient clearance to remove the mounting bracket bolts (the lower front bolt can be left in place), and withdraw the bracket.

27 Unscrew the securing bolt, and remove the timing belt idler sprocket (engines with a standard timing belt tensioner) or adjusting eccentric (engines with an automatic timing belt tensioner).

28 Loosen the clamp, and disconnect the coolant hose from the elbow on the coolant pump.

29 Unscrew the remaining coolant pump securing bolts, then raise the engine until the coolant pump can be manipulated out from the engine compartment **(see illustration)**. Recover the gasket.

Refitting

30 Refitting is a reversal of removal, bearing in mind the following points.

a) Thoroughly clean the mating faces of the coolant pump and the cylinder block.
b) Tighten all fixings to the specified torque (where given).
c) Ensure that the engine mounting is aligned with the marks made before removal.
d) Fit a new fuel injection pump drivebelt and timing belt as described in Chapter 2C.
e) On completion, refill the cooling system as described in Chapter 1B.

Endura-DI engines

Removal

31 Remove the battery and battery box as described in Chapter 5A.

32 Drain the cooling system as described in Chapter 1B.

33 Undo the retaining bolt then unclip the

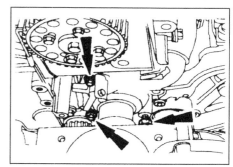

7.29 Unscrew the remaining coolant pump securing bolts (arrowed) – Endura-DE engine

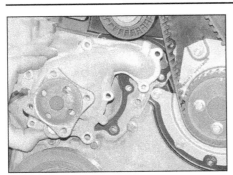

7.41 Unscrew the seven coolant pump securing bolts and withdraw the pump and gasket – Endura-DI engine

coolant expansion tank and position it to one side.

34 Slacken the coolant pump pulley bolts, then remove the auxiliary drivebelt as described in Chapter 1B.

35 Unbolt and remove the coolant pump pulley.

36 Remove the rear engine mounting/link as described in Chapter 2D.

37 Release the coolant hoses likely to restrict access to the engine right-hand mounting and move them to one side. Similarly move aside the wiring and clutch hydraulic fluid pipe for access to the engine/transmission left-hand mounting.

38 Attach a suitable hoist to the engine/transmission and take the weight of the assembly.

39 Undo the mounting nuts/bolts and release the engine/transmission left-hand mounting insulator.

40 Remove the timing belt covers and the engine right-hand mounting and mounting bracket as described in Chapter 2D.

41 Unscrew the seven coolant pump securing bolts and withdraw the pump and gasket **(see illustration)**. It may be necessary to raise or lower the engine slightly to increase the working clearance.

Refitting

42 Clean the pump mating surfaces carefully; the gasket must be renewed whenever it is disturbed. Refit the pump and tighten the bolts to the specified torque wrench setting.

9.3 Unscrew the heater/ventilation control unit securing screws

43 The remainder of the refitting procedure is the reverse of dismantling, noting the following points:

a) *Tighten all fixings to the specified torque wrench settings (where given).*

b) *Where applicable, check the timing belt for contamination and renew if required, as described in Chapter 2D.*

c) *On completion, refill the cooling system as described in Chapter 1B.*

8 Heating and ventilation system – general information

The heater/ventilation system consists of a four-speed blower motor (housed behind the facia), face-level vents in the centre and at each end of the facia, and air ducts to the front footwells.

The control unit is located in the facia, and the controls operate flap valves and a coolant valve, to deflect and mix the air flowing through the various parts of the heater/ventilation system. The flap valves are contained in the air distribution housing, which acts as a central distribution unit, passing air to the various ducts and vents.

Cold air enters the system through the grille at the rear of the engine compartment.

The air (boosted by the blower fan if required) then flows through the various ducts, according to the settings of the controls. Stale air is expelled through ducts at

the rear of the vehicle. If warm air is required, the cold air is passed through the heater matrix, which is heated by the engine coolant.

A recirculation switch enables the outside air supply to be closed off, while the air inside the vehicle is recirculated. This can be useful to prevent unpleasant odours entering from outside the vehicle, but should only be used briefly, as the recirculated air inside the vehicle will soon deteriorate.

9 Heater/ventilation system components – removal and refitting

Heater/ventilation control unit
Removal

1 Disconnect the battery negative lead with reference to Chapter 5A.

2 Remove the radio/cassette player as described in Chapter 12.

3 Working at the top of the heater/ventilation control unit, unscrew the two securing screws **(see illustration)**.

4 Release the two securing clips at the sides of the panel, then pull the control panel forwards from the facia.

5 Disconnect the wiring plugs from the rear of the unit.

6 Disconnect the air distribution control cable end fitting from the rear of the control unit, then withdraw the unit **(see illustration)**.

Refitting

7 Refitting is a reversal of removal, but ensure that the air distribution control cable end fitting engages correctly with the gear at the rear of the control unit (turn the control knob as necessary), and check the operation of the heater/ventilation controls before finally refitting the unit to the facia.

Heater blower motor switch
Removal

8 Remove the heater/ventilation control unit as described previously in this Section.

9 Working at the rear of the control unit, remove the blower motor switch securing screw, then turn the switch clockwise, and release if from the control unit **(see illustrations)**.

9.6 Disconnecting the air distribution control cable from the heater/ventilation control unit

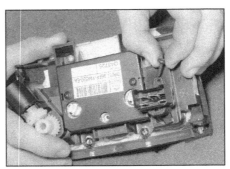

9.9a Remove the securing screw . . .

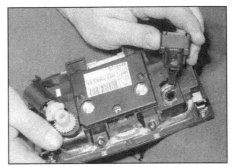

9.9b . . . and release the heater blower motor switch

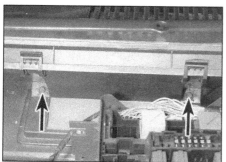

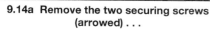

9.14a Remove the two securing screws (arrowed) . . .

9.14b . . . and withdraw the pollen filter housing

9.15a Remove the securing screws . . .

Refitting

10 Refer to paragraph 7.

Heater blower motor

Warning: On left-hand-drive models with air conditioning, read the precautions given in Section 10, and have the system discharged by a Ford dealer or an air conditioning specialist. Do not carry out the following work unless the system had been discharged.

Removal

11 Disconnect the battery negative lead with reference to Chapter 5A.
12 Drain the cooling system as described in Chapter 1A or 1B (as applicable).
13 Remove the scuttle cover panel as described in Chapter 11, Section 26.
14 Remove the two securing screws and

withdraw the pollen filter housing **(see illustrations)**. Lift the housing over the mounting brackets as it is withdrawn.
15 Remove the two securing screws, and withdraw the blower motor cover **(see illustrations)**.
16 Working in the scuttle, unscrew the two screws securing the blower motor to the heater housing **(see illustration)**.
17 Working in the passenger's footwell, disconnect the blower motor wiring plug **(see illustration)**.
18 Pull the wiring grommet from the motor housing, then withdraw the blower motor from the scuttle, pulling the wiring and plug through the bulkhead **(see illustrations)**.

Refitting

19 Refitting is a reversal of removal, bearing in mind the following points.

a) Make sure that the motor wiring grommet

is securely located in the bulkhead.
b) Refill the cooling system as described in Chapter 1A or 1B (as applicable).
c) Where applicable, have the air conditioning system recharged by a Ford dealer or an air conditioning specialist, then check the operation of the air conditioning system.

Heater blower motor resistor

Removal

20 The resistor is located in the passenger's side footwell.
21 Disconnect the battery negative lead with reference to Chapter 5A.
22 Disconnect the resistor wiring plug.
23 Unscrew the securing screw, and withdraw the resistor **(see illustration)**.

Refitting

24 Refitting is a reversal of removal.

9.15b . . . and withdraw the blower motor cover

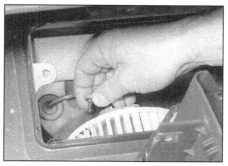

9.16 Remove the blower motor securing screws

9.17 Disconnect the blower motor wiring plug (arrowed)

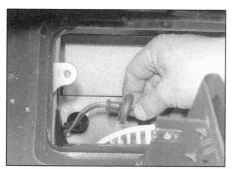

9.18a Pull out the wiring grommet . . .

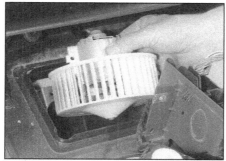

9.18b . . . then withdraw the blower motor

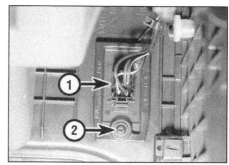

9.23 Heater blower motor resistor (1) and securing screw (2)

Air recirculation control motor

Removal

25 Remove the complete facia assembly as described in Chapter 11.

26 Disconnect the control motor wiring plug.

27 Unscrew the three securing screws, and withdraw the motor from the heater assembly **(see illustration)**.

Refitting

28 Refitting is a reversal of removal.

Heater matrix

Warning: On models with air conditioning, read the precautions given in Section 10, and have the system discharged by a Ford dealer or an air conditioning specialist. Do not carry out the following work unless the system had been discharged.

Note: *On models with air conditioning, Ford special tool No 34-001 will be required to release the refrigerant line connectors from the evaporator.*

Removal

29 Disconnect the battery negative lead with reference to Chapter 5A.

30 Drain the cooling system as described in Chapter 1A or 1B (as applicable).

31 Remove the scuttle cover panel as described in Chapter 11, Section 26.

32 On models with air conditioning, disconnect the refrigerant lines from the evaporator, accessible in the scuttle – **do not** do this unless the air conditioning system has

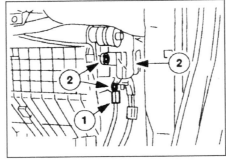

9.27 Air recirculation control valve motor mounting details

1 Wiring plug   2 Securing screws

been discharged. Plug or cover the open ends of the refrigerant lines and the evaporator.

33 Disconnect the wiring plug from the heater coolant valve, and the windscreen wiper motor, then unclip the wiring harness, and move it clear of the heater matrix housing **(see illustration)**.

34 Slacken the hose clips, and disconnect the heater coolant hoses from the top of the heater matrix pipes **(see illustration)**.

35 Slide the coolant valve from the top of the heater matrix housing **(see illustration)**.

36 Remove the four securing screws, and withdraw the heater matrix housing cover from the scuttle **(see illustrations)**.

37 On models with air conditioning, pull the evaporator from the heater housing.

38 Carefully pull the heater matrix from the heater housing, taking care not to damage the

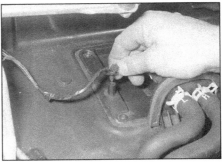

9.33 Unclip the wiring harness and move it clear of the matrix housing

matrix fins on the plastic lugs in front of the matrix **(see illustration)**.

Refitting

39 Refitting is a reversal of removal, bearing in mind the following points.

a) *Refill the cooling system as described in Chapter 1A or 1B (as applicable).*

b) *Where applicable, have the air conditioning system recharged by a Ford dealer or an air conditioning specialist, then check the operation of the air conditioning system.*

Coolant valve

Removal

40 Disconnect the battery negative lead with reference to Chapter 5A.

41 Remove the scuttle cover panel as described in Chapter 11, Section 26.

42 Disconnect the wiring plug from the now-exposed coolant valve **(see illustration)**.

9.34 Disconnect the coolant hoses from the heater matrix pipes

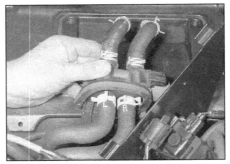

9.35 Slide the coolant valve from the heater matrix housing

9.36a Remove the four securing screws . . .

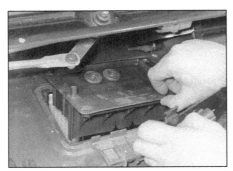

9.36b . . . and withdraw the heater matrix housing cover

9.38 Pull out the heater matrix

9.42 Disconnecting the coolant valve wiring plug

43 Slacken the hose clips, and disconnect the four coolant hoses from the coolant valve (be prepared for some coolant spillage), then slide the valve from the heater matrix housing. Note the locations of the hoses, to ensure correct refitting. Clamp or plug the open ends of the hoses to prevent further coolant spillage.

Refitting

44 Refitting is a reversal of removal, bearing in mind the following points.
  a) *Ensure that the coolant hoses are correctly reconnected to the valve as noted before removal.*
  b) *On completion check the coolant level and top-up if necessary, then check the operation of the heater.*

Heater assembly

 Warning: On models with air conditioning, read the precautions given in Section 10, and have the system discharged by a Ford dealer or an air conditioning specialist. Do not carry out the following work unless the system had been discharged.

Removal

45 Disconnect the battery negative lead with reference to Chapter 5A.
46 Drain the cooling system as described in Chapter 1A or 1B (as applicable).
47 Remove the complete facia assembly as described in Chapter 11.
48 Remove the scuttle cover panel as described in Chapter 11, Section 26.
49 On models with air conditioning, disconnect the refrigerant lines from the evaporator, accessible in the scuttle – **do not** do this unless the air conditioning system has been discharged. Plug or cover the open ends of the refrigerant lines and the evaporator.
50 Disconnect the wiring plug from the heater coolant valve.
51 Slacken the hose clips, and disconnect the coolant hoses from the top of the heater matrix pipes **(see illustration 9.34)**.
52 Working inside the vehicle, disconnect the wiring plugs from the following components **(see illustration)**.

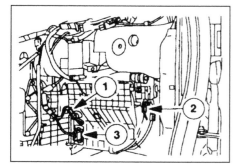

9.52 Disconnect the heater wiring plugs

1 *Blower motor wiring plug*
2 *Air recirculation control valve wiring plug*
3 *Blower motor resistor wiring plug*

  a) *Heater blower motor.*
  b) *Air recirculation valve control motor.*
  c) *Blower motor resistor.*
53 On models with air conditioning, disconnect the drain hose from the condenser.
54 Unscrew the three nuts securing the heater assembly to the bulkhead, then lift the assembly from the bulkhead, and withdraw it from the vehicle **(see illustration)**.

Refitting

55 Refitting is a reversal of removal, bearing in mind the following points.
  a) *Refit the facia as described in Chapter 11.*
  b) *Refill the cooling system as described in Chapter 1A or 1B (as applicable).*
  c) *Where applicable, have the air conditioning system recharged by a Ford dealer or an air conditioning specialist, then check the operation of the air conditioning system.*

10 Air conditioning system – general information and precautions

General information

1 Air conditioning is available on certain models. It enables the temperature of incoming air to be lowered, and also dehumidifies the air, which makes for rapid demisting and increased comfort.
2 The cooling side of the system works in the same way as a domestic refrigerator. Refrigerant gas is drawn into a belt-driven compressor, and passes into a condenser mounted in front of the radiator, where it loses heat and becomes liquid. The liquid passes through an expansion valve to an evaporator, where it changes from liquid under high pressure to gas under low pressure. This change is accompanied by a drop in temperature, which cools the evaporator. The refrigerant returns to the compressor, and the cycle begins again.
3 Air blown through the evaporator passes to the heater assembly, where it is mixed with hot air blown through the heater matrix, to achieve the desired temperature in the passenger compartment.

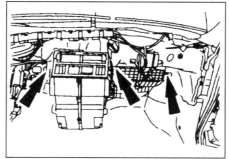

9.54 Heater assembly securing nuts (arrowed)

4 The heating side of the system works in the same way as on models without air conditioning (see Section 8).
5 The operation of the system is controlled electronically. Any problems with the system should be referred to a Ford dealer or an air conditioning specialist.

Many car accessory shops sell one-shot air conditioning recharge aerosols. These generally contain refrigerant, compressor oil, leak sealer and system conditioner. Some also have a dye to help pinpoint leaks.

 Warning: These products must only be used as directed by the manufacturer, and do not remove the need for regular maintenance.

Precautions

 Warning: The air conditioning system is under high pressure. Do not loosen any fittings or remove any components until after the system has been discharged. Air conditioning refrigerant should be properly discharged at a dealer service department or an automotive air conditioning repair facility capable of handling R134a refrigerant. Always wear eye protection when disconnecting air conditioning system fittings.

6 When an air conditioning system is fitted, it is necessary to observe the following special precautions whenever dealing with any part of the system, its associated components, and any items which necessitate disconnection of the system:
  a) *While the refrigerant used – R134a – is less damaging to the environment than the previously-used R12, it is still a very dangerous substance. It must not be allowed into contact with the skin or eyes, or there is a risk of frostbite. It must also not be discharged in an enclosed space – while it is not toxic, there is a risk of suffocation. The refrigerant is heavier than air, and so must never be discharged over a pit.*
  b) *The refrigerant must not be allowed to come in contact with a naked flame, otherwise a poisonous gas will be created*

– under certain circumstances, this can form an explosive mixture with air. For similar reasons, smoking in the presence of refrigerant is highly dangerous, particularly if the vapour is inhaled through a lighted cigarette.

c) *Never discharge the system to the atmosphere – R134a is not an ozone-depleting ChloroFluoroCarbon (CFC) like R12, but is instead a hydrofluorocarbon, which causes environmental damage by contributing to the 'greenhouse effect' if released into the atmosphere.*

d) *R134a refrigerant must not be mixed with R12; the system uses different seals (now green-coloured, previously black) and has different fittings requiring different tools, so that there is no chance of the two types of refrigerant becoming mixed accidentally.*

e) *If for any reason the system must be disconnected, entrust this task to your Ford dealer or a refrigeration engineer.*

f) *It is essential that the system be professionally discharged prior to using any form of heat – welding, soldering, brazing, etc – in the vicinity of the system, before having the vehicle oven-dried at a temperature exceeding 70°C after repainting, and before disconnecting any part of the system.*

11 Air conditioning system components – removal and refitting

⚠️ **Warning: Read the precautions given in Section 10, and have the system discharged by a Ford dealer or an air conditioning specialist. Do not carry out the following work unless the system had been discharged.**

Compressor

Removal

1 Disconnect the battery negative lead with reference to Chapter 5A.

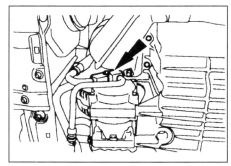

11.4 Slacken the union bolt (arrowed) securing the connector block to the compressor

2 Apply the handbrake, then jack up the front of the vehicle and support securely on axle stands (see *Jacking and vehicle support*).

3 Remove the auxiliary drivebelt as described in Chapter 1A or 1B (as applicable).

4 Slacken the union bolt which secures the refrigerant line connector block to the compressor. Do not slacken the bolt unless the air conditioning system has been discharged **(see illustration)**.

5 Disconnect the compressor wiring plug.

6 Support the compressor, then unscrew the four compressor mounting bolts **(see illustration)**.

7 Remove the union bolt, and disconnect the refrigerant line connector block from the compressor, then lower the compressor and withdraw it from under the vehicle. Plug the openings in the connector block and the compressor to prevent dirt entry.

Refitting

8 Refitting is a reversal of removal, but refit and tension the auxiliary drivebelt as described in Chapter 1A or 1B (as applicable). On completion, have the air conditioning system recharged by a Ford dealer or an air conditioning specialist, then check the operation of the air conditioning system.

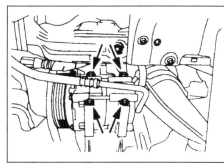

11.6 Air conditioning compressor securing bolts (arrowed)

Evaporator

9 Removal and refitting of the evaporator is described as part of the heater matrix removal and refitting procedure in Section 9.

Condenser

Note: *Ford special tool No 34-001 will be required to release the refrigerant line connectors.*

Removal

10 The condenser is located in front of the radiator.

11 Disconnect the battery negative lead with reference to Chapter 5A.

12 Remove the right-hand headlight as described in Chapter 12, Section 7.

13 Using the special tool, disconnect the refrigerant line connecting the evaporator to the condenser, at the condenser **(see illustration)**. Plug the open ends of the pipes to prevent dirt entry. **Do not** disconnect the line unless the air conditioning system has been discharged.

14 Apply the handbrake, then jack up the front of the vehicle and support securely on axle stands (see *Jacking and vehicle support*).

15 Working under the front of the vehicle, again using the special tool, disconnect the refrigerant line connecting the dehydrator to the condenser, at the condenser. Plug the

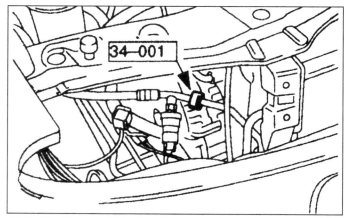

11.13 Use the special tool to disconnect the refrigerant line at the condenser

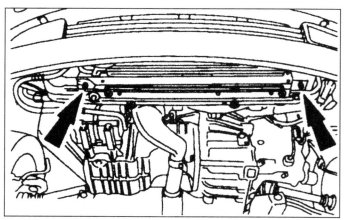

11.17 Unscrew the two bolts (arrowed) securing the condenser to the radiator support member

open ends of the pipes to prevent dirt entry. Again, **do not** disconnect the line unless the air conditioning system has been discharged.

16 Remove the securing screws, and withdraw the undershield from under the radiator/condenser assembly.

17 Unscrew the two bolts securing the condenser to the radiator support member **(see illustration)**.

18 Using suitable lengths of wire or string, support the radiator by tying it to the engine compartment front panel.

19 Where applicable, unclip the wiring plug from the lower left-hand side of the radiator support member.

20 Ensure that the radiator assembly is securely suspended from the front panel, then unscrew the four bolts securing the radiator support member to the front of the vehicle, and withdraw the support member.

21 Unhook the top end of the condenser from its supports, then withdraw the condenser from under the front of the vehicle.

Refitting

22 Refitting is a reversal of removal, bearing in mind the following points.

a) *Use new O-rings when reconnecting the refrigerant lines.*

b) *Refit the headlight with reference to Chapter 12 if necessary.*

c) *On completion, have the air conditioning system recharged by a Ford dealer or an air conditioning specialist, then check*

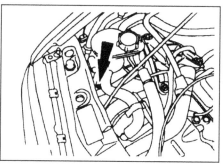

11.26 Dehydrator upper securing bolt (arrowed)

the operation of the air conditioning system.

Dehydrator

Note: *Ford special tool No 34-003 will be required to release the refrigerant line connectors.*

Removal

23 The dehydrator is located at the right-hand front corner of the engine compartment.

24 Disconnect the battery negative lead with reference to Chapter 5A.

25 Using the special tool, disconnect the refrigerant lines from the dehydrator. **Do not** disconnect the lines unless the air conditioning system has been discharged.

26 Unscrew the dehydrator upper securing bolt **(see illustration)**.

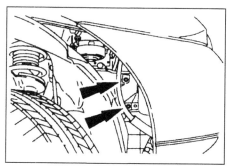

11.29 Dehydrator lower securing bolts (arrowed)

27 Apply the handbrake, then jack up the front of the vehicle and support securely on axle stands (see *Jacking and vehicle support*).

28 Working under the wheelarch, unscrew the four securing screws, and carefully pull the wheelarch liner back to expose the two dehydrator lower securing bolts.

29 Unscrew the two lower securing bolts, and withdraw the dehydrator downwards from under the front of the vehicle **(see illustration)**.

Refitting

30 Refitting is a reversal of removal, but use new O-rings when reconnecting the refrigerant lines. On completion, have the air conditioning system recharged by a Ford dealer or an air conditioning specialist, then check the operation of the air conditioning system.

Chapter 4 Part A:
Fuel and exhaust systems – petrol engine models

Contents

Accelerator cable – removal, refitting and adjustment 6
Accelerator pedal – removal and refitting 7
Air cleaner assembly and air inlet components –
   removal and refitting 5
Air filter element renewal ....See Chapter 1A
Exhaust system – general information, removal and refitting 17
Fuel cut-off switch – removal and refitting 13
Fuel filter renewal ....See Chapter 1A
Fuel injection system – checking 14
Fuel injection system components – removal and refitting 15
Fuel lines and fittings – general information 4

Fuel pump/fuel gauge sender unit – removal and refitting 10
Fuel pump/fuel pressure – checking 8
Fuel system – depressurisation 2
Fuel tank – removal, inspection and refitting 9
Fuel tank filler pipe – removal and refitting 12
Fuel tank roll-over valve – removal and refitting 11
General information and precautions 1
Hose and leak check ....See Chapter 1A
Manifolds – removal and refitting 16
Unleaded petrol – general information and usage 3

Degrees of difficulty

Easy, suitable for novice with little experience	Fairly easy, suitable for beginner with some experience	Fairly difficult, suitable for competent DIY mechanic 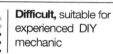	Difficult, suitable for experienced DIY mechanic	Very difficult, suitable for expert DIY or professional

Specifications

General

System type	Sequential Electronic Fuel injection (SEFi)
Fuel octane requirement	95 RON unleaded
Regulated fuel pressure:	
Pressure regulator vacuum hose disconnected	2.7 ± 0.2 bar
Engine running and pressure regulator vacuum hose connected ...	2.1 ± 0.2 bar
Hold pressure – engine stopped after five minutes	1.8 bars minimum

Torque wrench settings

	Nm	lbf ft
Camshaft position sensor	10	7
Crankshaft position sensor	7	5
Cylinder head temperature sensor	10	7
Engine coolant temperature sensor	12	9
Exhaust downpipe-to-manifold nuts:		
Stage 1	30	22
Stage 2	38	28
Exhaust flange bolts/nuts	47	35
Exhaust manifold	53	39
Fuel injector bolts	6	4
Fuel pressure regulator screws:		
Endura-E engine	10	7
Zetec-SE engine	6	4
Fuel rail to cylinder head (Zetec-SE engine)	23	17
Fuel rail-to-inlet manifold bolts (Endura-E engine)	18	13
Fuel supply pipe retaining plate bolts	10	7
Idle air control valve:		
Endura-E engine	8	6
Zetec-SE engine	10	7
Inlet manifold	18	13
Shrader valve retaining bolts	10	7

1 General information and precautions

General information

The fuel system consists of a fuel tank (mounted under the body, beneath the rear seats), fuel hoses, an electric fuel pump mounted in the fuel tank, and a sequential electronic fuel injection system controlled by a EEC V engine management electronic control unit (Powertrain Control Module).

The electric fuel pump supplies fuel under pressure to the fuel rail, which distributes fuel to the injectors. A pressure regulator controls the system pressure in relation to inlet tract depression. From the fuel rail, fuel is injected into the inlet ports, just above the inlet valves, by four fuel injectors. On the Endura-E engine a plastic moulded fuel rail is fitted, whereas on the Zetec-SE engine the fuel rail is of aluminium alloy. The Endura-E fuel rail is mounted on the inlet manifold, and the Zetec-SE fuel rail is mounted in the cylinder head.

The amount of fuel supplied by the injectors is precisely controlled by the Powertrain Control Module (PCM). The module uses the signals from the crankshaft position sensor and the camshaft position sensor, to trigger each injector separately in cylinder firing order (sequential injection), with benefits in terms of better fuel economy and leaner exhaust emissions.

The Powertrain Control Module is the heart of the entire engine management system, controlling the fuel injection, ignition and emissions control systems. The module receives information from various sensors which is then computed and compared with pre-set values stored in its memory, to determine the required period of injection.

Information on crankshaft position and engine speed is generated by a crankshaft position sensor. The inductive head of the sensor runs just above the engine flywheel and scans a series of 36 protrusions on the flywheel periphery. As the crankshaft rotates, the sensor transmits a pulse to the system's ignition module every time a protrusion passes it. There is one missing protrusion in the flywheel periphery at a point corresponding to 90° BTDC. The ignition module recognises the absence of a pulse from the crankshaft position sensor at this point to establish a reference mark for crankshaft position. Similarly, the time interval between absent pulses is used to determine engine speed. This information is then fed to the Powertrain Control Module for further processing.

On the Zetec-SE engine, the camshaft position sensor is located in the cylinder head so that it registers with a lobe on the camshaft. On the Endura-E engine, it is located on the timing cover and registers with a plate located beneath the camshaft

sprocket retaining bolts. The camshaft position sensor functions in the same way as the crankshaft position sensor, producing a series of pulses; this gives the Powertrain Control Module a reference point, to enable it to determine the firing order, and operate the injectors in the appropriate sequence.

The mass air flow sensor is based on a 'hot-wire' system, sending the Powertrain Control Module a constantly-varying (analogue) voltage signal corresponding to the mass of air passing into the engine. Since air mass varies with temperature (cold air being denser than warm), measuring air mass provides the module with a very accurate means of determining the correct amount of fuel required to achieve the ideal air/fuel mixture ratio.

Engine temperature information is supplied by the coolant temperature sensor or, on certain later Zetec-SE engines, by a cylinder head temperature sensor. Both components are NTC (Negative Temperature Coefficient) thermistors – that is, a semi-conductor whose electrical resistance decreases as its temperature increases. The sensors provide the Powertrain Control Module with a constantly-varying (analogue) voltage signal, corresponding to the temperature of the engine coolant or cylinder head, as applicable. This is used to refine the calculations made by the module, when determining the correct amount of fuel required to achieve the ideal air/fuel mixture ratio. While the coolant temperature sensor measures the temperature of the engine coolant, the cylinder head temperature sensor is seated in a blind hole in the cylinder head, and measures the temperature of the metal directly.

Inlet air temperature information is supplied by the inlet air temperature sensor. This component is also an NTC thermistor – see the previous paragraph – providing the module with a signal corresponding to the temperature of air passing into the engine. This is used to refine the calculations made by the module, when determining the correct amount of fuel required to achieve the ideal air/fuel mixture ratio.

On later Endura-E, and 1.25 litre Zetec-SE engines, inlet air temperature and density information for air/fuel mixture ratio calculations is provided by a temperature and manifold absolute pressure (TMAP) sensor. The TMAP sensor is located in the inlet manifold and consists of a pressure transducer and a temperature sensor which directly replaces the mass air flow and inlet air temperature sensors. The TMAP sensor provides information to the Powertrain Control Module relating to inlet manifold vacuum and barometric pressure, and the temperature of the air in the inlet manifold. When the ignition is switched on with the engine stopped, the sensor calculates barometric pressure and, when the engine is running, the sensor calculates inlet manifold vacuum.

A throttle position sensor is mounted on the end of the throttle valve spindle, to provide the Powertrain Control Module with a constantly-varying (analogue) voltage signal corresponding to the throttle opening. This allows the module to register the driver's input when determining the amount of fuel required by the engine.

Road speed is monitored by the vehicle speed sensor. This component is a Hall-effect generator, mounted on the transmission's speedometer drive. It supplies the module with a series of pulses corresponding to the vehicle's road speed, enabling the module to control features such as the fuel shut-off on overrun.

The clutch pedal position is monitored by a switch fitted to the pedal bracket. This sends a signal to the Powertrain Control Module.

Where power steering is fitted, a pressure-operated switch is screwed into the power steering system's high-pressure pipe. The switch sends a signal to the Powertrain Control Module to increase engine speed to maintain idle speed during power steering assistance.

The oxygen sensor in the exhaust system provides the module with constant feedback – 'closed-loop' control – which enables it to adjust the mixture to provide the best possible operating conditions for the catalytic converter.

The air inlet side of the system consists of an air cleaner housing, the mass air flow sensor, an inlet hose and duct, and a throttle housing.

The throttle valve inside the throttle housing is controlled by the driver, through the accelerator pedal. As the valve opens, the amount of air that can pass through the system increases. As the throttle valve opens further, the mass air flow sensor signal alters, and the Powertrain Control Module opens each injector for a longer duration, to increase the amount of fuel delivered to the inlet ports.

Both the idle speed and mixture are under the control of the Powertrain Control Module, and cannot be adjusted.

Precautions

Warning: Many of the procedures in this Chapter require the removal of fuel lines and connections, which may result in some fuel spillage. Before carrying out any operation on the fuel system, refer to the precautions given in 'Safety first!' at the beginning of this manual, and follow them implicitly. Petrol is a highly-dangerous and volatile liquid, and the precautions necessary when handling it cannot be overstressed.

Note: *Residual pressure will remain in the fuel lines long after the vehicle was last used. When disconnecting any fuel line, first depressurise the fuel system as described in Section 2.*

2 Fuel system – depressurisation

Note: *Refer to the warning note in Section 1 before proceeding.*

Warning: The following procedure will merely relieve the pressure in the fuel system – remember that fuel will still be present in the system components, and take precautions accordingly before disconnecting any of them.

1 The fuel system referred to in this Chapter is defined as the fuel tank and tank-mounted fuel pump/fuel gauge sender unit, the fuel filter, the fuel injector, fuel pressure regulator, and the metal pipes and flexible hoses of the fuel lines between these components. All these contain fuel, which will be under pressure while the engine is running and/or while the ignition is switched on.

2 The pressure will remain for some time after the ignition has been switched off, and must be relieved before any of these components is disturbed for servicing work.

3 The simplest depressurisation method is to disconnect the fuel pump electrical supply by removing the fuel pump fuse (refer to the wiring diagrams or the label on the relevant fusebox for exact location) and starting the engine; allow the engine to idle until it stops through lack of fuel. Turn the engine over once or twice on the starter to ensure that all pressure is released, then switch off the ignition; do not forget to refit the fuse when work is complete.

4 If an adapter is available to fit the Schrader-type valve on the fuel rail pressure test/release fitting (identifiable by its blue plastic cap, and located on the union of the fuel feed line and the fuel rail), this may be used to release the fuel pressure. The Ford adapter (tool number 23-033) operates similar to a drain tap – turning the tap clockwise releases the pressure. If the adapter is not available, place cloth rags around the valve, then remove the cap and allow the fuel pressure to dissipate. Refit the cap on completion.

5 Note that, once the fuel system has been depressurised and drained (even partially), it will take significantly longer to restart the engine – perhaps several seconds of cranking – before the system is refilled and pressure restored.

3 Unleaded petrol – general information and usage

All petrol models are designed to run on fuel with a minimum octane rating of 95 (RON). All models have a catalytic converter, and so must be run on unleaded fuel **only**. Under no circumstances should leaded fuel (UK '4-star' or LRP) be used, as this will damage the converter.

Super unleaded petrol (98 octane) can also be used in all models if wished, though there is no advantage in doing so.

4 Fuel lines and fittings – general information

Note: *Refer to the warning note in Section 1 before proceeding.*

Quick-release couplings

1 Quick-release couplings are employed at many of the unions in the fuel feed and return lines.

2 Before disconnecting any fuel system component, relieve the residual pressure in the system (see Section 2), and equalise tank pressure by removing the fuel filler cap.

Warning: This procedure will merely relieve the increased pressure necessary for the engine to run – remember that fuel will still be present in the system components, and take precautions accordingly before disconnecting any of them.

3 Release the protruding locking lugs on each union, by squeezing them together and carefully pulling the coupling apart. Use rag to soak up any spilt fuel. Where the unions are colour-coded, the pipes cannot be confused. Where both unions are the same colour, note carefully which pipe is connected to which, and ensure that they are correctly reconnected on refitting.

4 To reconnect one of these couplings, press them together until the locking lugs snap into their groove. Switch the ignition on and off five times to pressurise the system, and check for any sign of fuel leakage around the disturbed coupling before attempting to start the engine.

Checking fuel lines

5 Checking procedures for the fuel lines are included in Chapter 1A, Section 7.

Component renewal

6 If any damaged sections are to be renewed, use original-equipment replacement hoses or pipes, constructed from exactly the same material as the section being replaced. Do not install substitutes constructed from inferior or inappropriate material; this could cause a fuel leak or a fire.

7 Before detaching or disconnecting any part of the fuel system, note the routing of all hoses and pipes, and the orientation of all clamps and clips. Replacement sections must be installed in exactly the same manner.

8 Before disconnecting any part of the fuel system, be sure to relieve the fuel system pressure (see Section 2), and equalise tank pressure by removing the fuel filler cap. Also disconnect the battery negative (earth) lead –

see Chapter 5A, Section 1. Cover the fitting being disconnected with a rag, to absorb any fuel that may spray out.

5 Air cleaner assembly and air inlet components – removal and refitting

Air cleaner assembly

All engines except 1.25 litre Zetec-SE from February 2000

1 Loosen the clip and disconnect the air inlet duct from the mass air flow sensor on the air cleaner.

2 Disconnect the wiring from the air flow sensor and air intake temperature sensor.

3 Unscrew the screws securing the cover to the air cleaner housing.

4 Withdraw the cover and remove the filter element.

5 Release the retaining strap from the rear of the air cleaner base, then lift the front of the base from the rubber grommets.

6 Disconnect the remaining hose and detach the air cleaner base from the air inlet duct. Withdraw the assembly from the engine compartment.

7 Check the rubber grommets for deterioration and renew them if necessary.

8 Refitting is the reverse of the removal procedure. Ensure that the base pegs seat fully in their rubber grommets, and that the mass air flow sensor is correctly located.

1.25 litre Zetec-SE engines from February 2000

9 Loosen the clip and disconnect the air duct from the throttle body housing.

10 Detach the crankcase ventilation hose from the rear of the air cleaner cover.

11 Unscrew the six screws securing the cover to the air cleaner housing.

12 Withdraw the cover and remove the filter element.

13 Undo the six air cleaner housing securing screws and lift the housing off the inlet manifold.

14 Refitting is the reverse of the removal procedure.

Air inlet components

All engines except 1.25 litre Zetec-SE from February 2000

15 To remove the air inlet duct between the mass air flow sensor and throttle housing, loosen the retaining clips and carefully ease off the duct.

16 To remove the air inlet duct attached to the air cleaner base, first remove the air cleaner assembly as described in paragraphs 1 to 6. Unbolt the resonator then disconnect it from the duct. If necessary, the silencers may be detached from the duct.

17 Refitting is the reverse of the removal procedure.

1.25 litre Zetec-SE engines from February 2000

18 Firmly apply the handbrake then jack up the front of the vehicle and support it on axle stands (see *Jacking and vehicle support*).
19 Remove the left-hand front road wheel, then remove the wheelarch liner.
20 Remove the locking pin from the air inlet duct collar, rotate the duct clockwise and withdraw it from under the wheelarch.
21 Refitting is the reverse of the removal procedure.

6 Accelerator cable – removal, refitting and adjustment

Note: *The following procedure is only applicable to models without traction control. On models with traction control, a two-piece accelerator cable is used so that the effective length of the cable can be altered during traction control intervention, thus enabling the engine speed to be electronically regulated. Removal, refitting and adjustment of this cable type entails the use of Ford diagnostic equipment and the work should be entrusted to a Ford dealer.*

Removal

1 Fold back the carpet and insulation in the driver's footwell to gain access to the accelerator pedal.
2 Disconnect the inner cable from the top of the pedal.
3 From within the engine compartment, detach the outer cable from the adjuster/support bracket by removing the metal retaining clip **(see illustration)**. On later engines with the air cleaner assembly mounted on the engine, remove the air cleaner cover as described in Section 5 if additional working clearance is required.
4 Disconnect the inner cable from the quadrant on the throttle housing by pivoting the quadrant then extracting the retaining clip (manual transmission models) or releasing the end fitting (automatic transmission models).
5 Release the cable from the supports in the engine compartment, and withdraw it from the bulkhead.

6.3 Metal retaining clip on the accelerator cable adjuster/support bracket

Refitting

6 Refitting is a reversal of removal. When the cable is reconnected at each end, adjust the cable as follows.

Adjustment

7 Remove the outer cable metal retaining clip at the adjuster/support bracket and lubricate the cable adjuster grommet with soapy water.
8 Remove any slack by pulling the cable as far as possible out of the adjuster. Have an assistant depress the accelerator pedal fully – the cable outer will move back into the adjuster – and hold it there while the clip is refitted.
9 Check that the throttle quadrant moves smoothly and easily from the fully-closed to the fully-open position and back again as the assistant depresses and releases the accelerator pedal. Re-adjust the cable if required.

7 Accelerator pedal – removal and refitting

Removal

1 Peel back the carpet and insulation from the driver's footwell to allow access to the accelerator pedal.
2 Detach the accelerator cable from the pedal (see Section 6), then release the circlip from the pivot shaft and remove the accelerator pedal.

Refitting

3 Refit in the reverse order of removal. On completion, check the action of the pedal and the cable to ensure that the throttle has full unrestricted movement, and fully returns when released.
4 Check and if necessary adjust the accelerator cable as described in Section 6.

8 Fuel pump/fuel pressure – checking

Note: *Refer to the warning note in Section 1 before proceeding.*

Fuel pump

1 Switch on the ignition, and listen for the fuel pump (the sound of an electric motor running, audible from beneath the rear seats). Assuming there is sufficient fuel in the tank, the pump should start and run for approximately one or two seconds, then stop, each time the ignition is switched on. **Note:** *If the pump runs continuously all the time the ignition is switched on, the electronic control system is running in the backup (or 'limp-home') mode referred to by Ford as 'Limited Operation Strategy' (LOS). This almost certainly indicates a fault in the EEC V module*

itself, and the vehicle should therefore be taken to a Ford dealer for a full test of the complete system, using the correct diagnostic equipment; do not waste time or risk damaging the components by trying to test the system without such facilities.
2 Listen for fuel return noises from the fuel pressure regulator. It should be possible to feel the fuel pulsing in the regulator and in the feed hose from the fuel filter.
3 If the pump does not run at all, check the fuse, relay and wiring (see Chapter 12). Check also that the fuel cut-off switch has not been activated and if so, reset it (Section 13).

Fuel pressure

4 A fuel pressure gauge will be required for this check and should be connected in the fuel line between the fuel filter and the fuel rail, in accordance with the gauge maker's instructions. On Zetec-SE engines, a pressure gauge equipped with an adapter to suit the Schrader-type valve on the fuel rail pressure test/release fitting (identifiable by its blue plastic cap, and located on the union of the fuel feed line and the fuel rail) will be required. If the Ford special tool 29-033 is available, the tool can be attached to the valve, and a conventional-type pressure gauge attached to the tool.
5 If using the service tool, ensure that its tap is turned fully anti-clockwise, then attach it to the valve. Connect the pressure gauge to the service tool. If using a fuel pressure gauge with its own adapter, connect it in accordance with its maker's instructions.
6 Start the engine and allow it to idle. Note the gauge reading as soon as the pressure stabilises, and compare it with the regulated fuel pressure figures listed in the Specifications.
  a) If the pressure is high, check for a restricted fuel return line. If the line is clear, renew the fuel pressure regulator.
  b) If the pressure is low, pinch the fuel return line. If the pressure now goes up, renew the fuel pressure regulator. If the pressure does not increase, check the fuel feed line, the fuel pump and the fuel filter.
7 Detach the vacuum hose from the fuel pressure regulator; the pressure shown on the gauge should increase. Note the increase in pressure, and compare it with that listed in the *Specifications*. If the pressure increase is not as specified, check the vacuum hose and pressure regulator.
8 Reconnect the regulator vacuum hose, and switch off the engine. Verify that the hold pressure stays at the specified level for five minutes after the engine is turned off.
9 Carefully disconnect the fuel pressure gauge, depressurising the system first as described in Section 2. Be sure to cover the fitting with a rag before slackening it. Mop up any spilt petrol.
10 Run the engine, and check that there are no fuel leaks.

9 Fuel tank – removal, inspection and refitting

Note: *Refer to the warning note in Section 1 before proceeding.*

Removal

1 Run the fuel level as low as possible prior to removing the tank.
2 Relieve the residual pressure in the fuel system (see Section 2), and equalise tank pressure by removing the fuel filler cap.
3 Disconnect the battery negative (earth) lead (see Chapter 5A).
4 Where possible, syphon or pump out the remaining fuel from the fuel tank (there is no drain plug). The fuel must be emptied into a suitable container for storage.
5 Chock the front wheels then jack up the rear of the car and support it on axle stands (see *Jacking and vehicle support*). Remove the rear roadwheels.
6 Unhook the exhaust system mounting rubbers at the front and rear and allow the exhaust system to rest on the rear suspension crossmember. There is no need to disconnect the exhaust from the exhaust manifold.
7 Unscrew the nuts and remove the exhaust heat shields from the underbody.
8 Loosen the clip and disconnect the filler pipe lower vent hose from the rear of the fuel tank.
9 Position a container beneath the fuel filter at the front of the tank, then disconnect the fuel supply hose from the filter inlet by squeezing the locking lugs on the quick-release fitting **(see illustration)**. Be prepared for some loss of fuel. The supply hose remains attached to the fuel pump until the tank is lowered.
10 At the rear of the tank, disconnect the hose leading to the evaporative emission canister from the fuel tank vent valve, then release the valve from the bracket.
11 Support the fuel tank using a jack and block of wood.

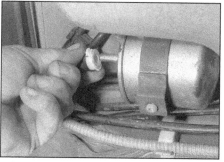

9.9 Disconnecting the fuel supply hose quick-release fitting from the fuel filter

12 Unscrew and remove the tank mounting bolts **(see illustration)**.
13 Partially lower the fuel tank and at the same time loosen the clip and disconnect the lower filler pipe from the tank **(see illustration)**.
14 Squeeze the locking lugs on the quick-release fitting and disconnect the fuel return pipe. Note the return pipe is identified by a red colour band.
15 Disconnect the wiring from the fuel pump/fuel gauge sender on top of the tank.
16 Lower the fuel tank and withdraw it from under the vehicle. If necessary, disconnect the supply hose from the fuel pump. The filter may also be removed at this time **(see illustration)**.
17 Check the condition of the filler pipe seal and renew it if necessary.

Inspection

18 Whilst removed, the fuel tank can be inspected for damage or deterioration. Removal of the fuel pump/fuel gauge sender unit (see Section 10) will allow a partial inspection of the interior. If the tank is contaminated with sediment or water, swill it out with clean fuel. Do not under any circumstances undertake any repairs on a leaking or damaged fuel tank; this work must be carried out by a professional who has

9.12 Fuel tank mounting bolt

experience in this critical and potentially-dangerous work.
19 Whilst the fuel tank is removed from the vehicle, it should be placed in a safe area where sparks or open flames cannot ignite the fumes coming out of the tank. Be especially careful inside garages where a natural-gas type appliance is located, because the pilot light could cause an explosion.
20 Check the condition of the lower filler pipe and renew it if necessary.

Refitting

21 Refitting is a reversal of the removal procedure. Ensure that all connections are securely fitted. When refitting the quick-release couplings, press them together until the locking lugs snap into their groove. If evidence of contamination was found, do not return any previously-drained fuel to the tank unless it is carefully filtered first.

10 Fuel pump/fuel gauge sender unit – removal and refitting

Note: *Refer to the warning note in Section 1 before proceeding. Ford specify the use of their service tool 23-026 (a large ring spanner with projecting teeth to engage the fuel pump/sender unit retaining ring's slots) for this*

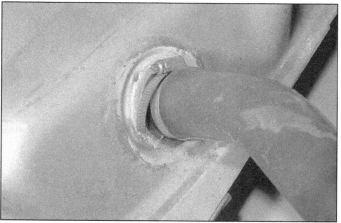

9.13 Lower filler pipe connection to the fuel tank

9.16 Filter location on the fuel tank

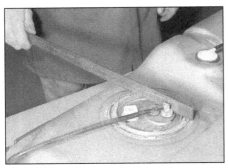

10.3a Using a long metal bar to loosen the special retaining ring from the fuel pump/fuel gauge sender unit

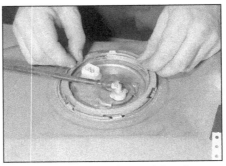

10.3b Removing the retaining ring

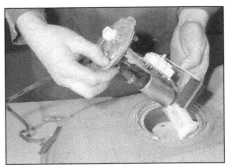

10.4 Withdrawing the fuel pump/sender unit from the tank

task. In practice it was found that a long metal bar could be used with success (see text).

Removal

1 A combined fuel pump and fuel gauge sender unit is located in the top face of the fuel tank. The combined unit can only be detached and withdrawn from the tank after the tank is released and lowered from under the vehicle. Refer to Section 9 and remove the fuel tank, then proceed as follows.

2 With the fuel tank removed, disconnect the fuel supply pipe (if still attached to the tank) from the inlet stub by squeezing the quick-release lugs. Note that the fuel supply pipe connector is identified by a white band.

3 Unscrew and remove the special retaining ring then remove the insert **(see illustrations)**.

4 Carefully withdraw the fuel pump/sender unit from the fuel tank taking care not to damage the strainer and pump components **(see illustration)**.

5 Remove the rubber seal from the periphery of the pump. The seal must be renewed whenever the pump/sender unit is removed from the tank.

Refitting

6 Refitting is a reversal of removal, but fit a new rubber seal and tighten the retaining ring securely. Refit the fuel tank as described in Section 9.

11 Fuel tank roll-over valve – removal and refitting

Note: *Refer to the warning note in Section 1 before proceeding.*

Removal

1 The roll-over valve is located in a rubber grommet in the top of the fuel tank, in the hose leading rearwards to the carbon canister. Its purpose is to prevent fuel loss if the vehicle becomes inverted in a crash.

2 Remove the fuel tank as described in Section 9.

3 Release the vent hose from the clip on the top of the tank **(see illustration)**.

4 Carefully prise the roll-over valve from the rubber grommet and remove it together with the hose.

5 Check the condition of the rubber grommet and renew it if necessary.

Refitting

6 Refitting is a reversal of removal, but apply a light smear of clean engine oil to the rubber grommet, to ease fitting.

12 Fuel tank filler pipe – removal and refitting

Note: *Refer to the warning note in Section 1 before proceeding.*

Removal

1 Remove the fuel tank as described in Section 9.

2 With the vehicle still raised, unscrew and remove the filler pipe lower mounting bolt.

3 Open the filler flap, then lift the plastic cover and unscrew the filler pipe upper mounting bolt.

4 Withdraw the filler pipe from under the vehicle.

5 If necessary, loosen the clips and disconnect the lower filler pipe and vent hose from the bottom of the filler pipe.

6 Check the condition of the filler pipe and hose and renew if necessary.

Refitting

7 Refitting is a reversal of removal.

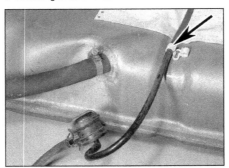

11.3 Vent hose clip on the top of the fuel tank

13 Fuel cut-off switch – removal and refitting

Note: *To reset the switch after an accident, use a coin to remove the plug in the passenger footwell trim, then depress the button on top of the switch.* **Do not** *reset the switch if fuel has escaped from the fuel system.*

Removal

1 The fuel cut-off switch is located behind the front passenger footwell side trim. First disconnect the battery negative (earth) lead (see Chapter 5A).

2 Pull up the weatherstrips from the door apertures and release them from the side trim. Using a sharp instrument, remove the trim clips, then on 5-door models only prise out the cover and remove the rear securing screw. Prise out the front clips and remove the trim.

3 Unscrew and remove the switch securing screws, then disconnect the wiring plug and remove the switch.

Refitting

4 Refitting is a reversal of removal, but make sure that the switch is reset. Start the engine to prove this.

14 Fuel injection system – checking

Note: *Refer to the warning note in Section 1 before proceeding.*

1 If a fault appears in the fuel injection system, first ensure that all the system wiring connectors are securely connected and free of corrosion – also refer to paragraphs 6 to 9 below. Then ensure that the fault is not due to poor maintenance; ie, check that the air cleaner filter element is clean, the spark plugs are in good condition and correctly gapped, the valve clearances are correct, the cylinder compression pressures are correct, the ignition system wiring is in good condition and securely connected, and the engine breather hoses are clear and undamaged, referring to Chapter 1A, Chapter 2A or 2B and Chapter 5B.

2 If these checks fail to reveal the cause of the problem, the vehicle should be taken to a suitably-equipped Ford dealer for testing. A diagnostic connector is incorporated in the engine management system wiring harness, into which dedicated electronic test equipment can be plugged. The test equipment is capable of 'interrogating' the engine management system ECU (Powertrain Control Module) electronically and accessing its internal fault log (reading fault codes).

3 Fault codes can only be extracted from the ECU using a dedicated fault code reader. A Ford dealer will obviously have such a reader, but they are also available from other suppliers, including Haynes. It is unlikely to be cost-effective for the private owner to purchase a fault code reader, but a well-equipped local garage or auto-electrical specialist will have one.

4 Using this equipment, faults can be pinpointed quickly and simply, even if their occurrence is intermittent. Testing all the system components individually in an attempt to locate the fault by elimination is a time-consuming operation that is unlikely to be fruitful (particularly if the fault occurs dynamically), and carries a high risk of damage to the ECU's internal components.

5 Experienced home mechanics equipped with an accurate tachometer and a carefully-calibrated exhaust gas analyser may be able to check the exhaust gas CO content and the engine idle speed; if these are found to be out

of specification, then the vehicle must be taken to a suitably-equipped Ford dealer for assessment. Neither the air/fuel mixture (exhaust gas CO content) nor the engine idle speed are manually adjustable; incorrect test results indicate the need for maintenance (possibly, injector cleaning) or a fault within the fuel injection system.

Limited Operation Strategy

6 Certain faults, such as failure of one of the engine management system sensors, will cause the system will revert to a backup (or 'limp-home') mode, referred to by Ford as 'Limited Operation Strategy' (LOS). This is intended to be a 'get-you-home' facility only – the engine management warning light will come on when this mode is in operation.

7 In this mode, the signal from the defective sensor is substituted with a fixed value (it would normally vary), which may lead to loss of power, poor idling, and generally-poor running, especially when the engine is cold.

8 However, the engine may in fact run quite well in this situation, and the only clue (other than the warning light) would be that the exhaust CO emissions (for example) will be higher than they should be.

9 Bear in mind that, even if the defective sensor is correctly identified and renewed, the engine will not return to normal running until the fault code is erased, taking the system out of LOS. This also applies even if the cause of the fault was a loose connection or damaged piece of wire – until the fault code is erased, the system will continue in LOS.

15 Fuel injection system components – removal and refitting

Note: *Refer to the warning note in Section 1 before proceeding.*

Throttle body housing

1 The housing is located on the left-hand side of the inlet manifold. First disconnect the battery negative (earth) lead (see Chapter 5A).

2 Remove the air inlet duct or air cleaner assembly, as necessary, as described in Section 5.

3 Disconnect the accelerator cable from the lever on the throttle body housing.

4 Disconnect the throttle position sensor multiplug **(see illustration)**.

5 Unscrew and remove the mounting bolts and withdraw the throttle housing from the inlet manifold. On the Zetec-SE engine also unbolt and remove the support bracket. Discard the gasket and obtain a new one **(see illustrations)**.

6 Refitting is a reversal of removal, but clean the mating faces and fit a new gasket, and tighten the mounting bolts securely. Check and if necessary adjust the accelerator cable as described in Section 6.

Fuel rail and injectors

7 Relieve the residual pressure in the fuel system (see Section 2), and equalise tank pressure by removing the fuel filler cap.

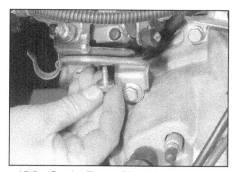

15.4 Disconnecting the throttle position sensor multiplug

15.5a On the Zetec-SE engine, unscrew the lower support bracket bolt . . .

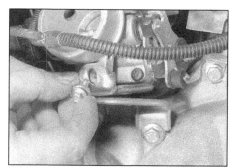

15.5b . . . and upper bolt . . .

15.5c . . . then unscrew the mounting bolts . . .

15.5d . . . remove the throttle body housing . . .

15.5e . . . and remove the gasket from the groove in the inlet manifold

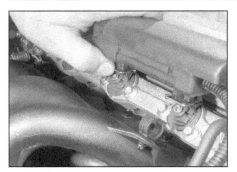

15.26a Depress the wire clips on the injectors . . .

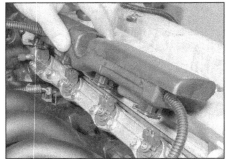

15.26b . . . and disconnect the wiring loom adapter

15.28 Disconnecting the quick-release fuel feed and return hoses from the fuel rail

Warning: This procedure will merely relieve the increased pressure necessary for the engine to run – remember that fuel will still be present in the system components, and take precautions accordingly before disconnecting any of them.

8 Disconnect the battery negative (earth) lead (see Chapter 5A).

Endura-E engine

9 Disconnect the wiring from the idle air control valve. Unscrew the two bolts and remove the idle air control valve.

10 Pull out the accelerator cable adjustment clip, then release the outer cable from the support bracket and disconnect the inner cable from the throttle lever on the throttle housing.

11 Remove the air inlet resonator, then loosen the clips and disconnect the air inlet duct from the air cleaner and throttle housing. Remove the duct from the engine compartment.

12 Disconnect the crankcase ventilation hoses from the inlet manifold.

13 Unscrew the bolt and remove the accelerator cable retaining bracket.

14 Disconnect the HT leads from the spark plugs, then unclip the lead supports and position the leads to one side. When disconnecting the leads, pull on the end fittings and not the leads.

15 Disconnect the wiring from the throttle position sensor. To do this, depress the locking wire and pull off the plug.

16 Disconnect the wiring from the fuel injectors, then undo the injector wiring loom retaining screws, disconnect the loom multiplug, and position the loom to one side.

17 Pull the vacuum hose from the fuel pressure regulator on the end of the fuel rail.

18 Unscrew and remove the fuel rail mounting bolts.

19 Undo the single screw and remove the fuel supply and return pipe retaining bracket.

20 Disconnect the fuel supply and return pipes from the fuel rail by squeezing the lugs on the special quick-release fittings.

21 Carefully pull the injectors from the inlet manifold and withdraw them together with the fuel rail.

22 Remove the clips and carefully pull the injectors from the fuel rail.

23 Using a screwdriver prise the O-rings from the grooves at each end of the injectors. Discard the O-rings and obtain new ones.

24 Refitting is the reverse of the removal procedure, noting the following points:

a) *Lubricate the new O-rings with clean engine oil to aid refitting.*

b) *Ensure that the hoses and wiring are routed correctly, and secured on reconnection by any clips or ties provided.*

c) *Adjust the accelerator cable as described in Section 6.*

d) *On completion, switch the ignition on to activate the fuel pump and pressurise the system, without cranking the engine. Check for signs of fuel leaks around all disturbed unions and joints before attempting to start the engine.*

Zetec-SE engine

25 On later engines with the air cleaner assembly mounted on the engine, remove the air cleaner as described in Section 5. On all engines, lift the cover from the centre of the fuel injector wiring loom holder, and disconnect the vent hose.

26 The wiring loom adapter must now be disconnected from the injectors. To do this, depress two of the injector clips and lift the adapter up a little until it releases from the injectors. Now depress the remaining two clips and lift the complete adapter from the injectors **(see illustrations)**. Position the adapter to one side.

27 If it is only required to remove the injectors, proceed to paragraph 32.

28 To remove the fuel rail, disconnect the feed and return hoses from the left-hand end of the rail by squeezing together the lugs of the quick-release fittings **(see illustration)**.

29 Unscrew the mounting bolts and lift the fuel rail from the cylinder head **(see illustrations)**.

30 Recover the bolt hole adapters from the cylinder head **(see illustration)**.

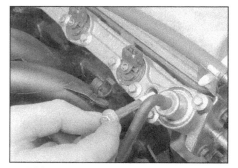

15.29a Unscrew the mounting bolts . . .

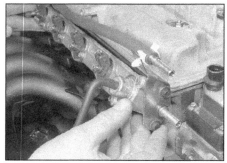

15.29b . . . and lift the fuel rail from the cylinder head

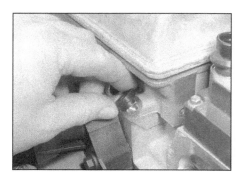

15.30 Remove the bolt hole adapters . . .

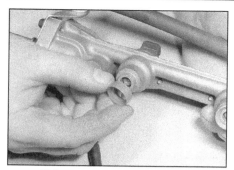

15.31 . . . and the fuel rail seals

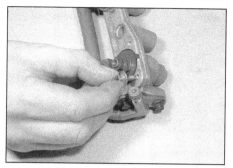

15.32a Unscrew the bolts . . .

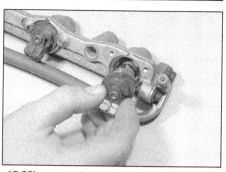

15.32b . . . and remove the injectors from the fuel rail

31 Recover the seals from the inner ends of the fuel rail **(see illustration)**.

32 To remove the injectors, unscrew the two retaining bolts from each injector and carefully prise the injectors from the fuel rail **(see illustrations)**. If they are tight, use a soft-faced tool inserted from the holes on the inner end of the fuel rail.

33 Remove the O-ring seals from the grooves in the injectors. Discard them and obtain new ones.

34 Refitting is a reversal of removal, but fit new O-ring seals and lubricate them with a little fresh engine oil before inserting the injectors in the fuel rail **(see illustration)**. Tighten the bolts to the specified torque.

Fuel pressure regulator

35 Relieve the residual pressure in the fuel system (see Section 2), and equalise tank pressure by removing the fuel filler cap.

 Warning: This procedure will merely relieve the increased pressure necessary for the engine to run – remember that fuel will still be present in the system components, and take precautions accordingly before disconnecting any of them.

36 Disconnect the battery negative (earth) lead (see Chapter 5A).

Endura-E engine

37 Loosen the clips and disconnect the air inlet duct from the air cleaner and throttle housing.

38 Disconnect the vacuum pipe from the fuel pressure regulator.

39 On early models, undo the single screw and remove the fuel supply and return pipe retaining bracket. Disconnect the fuel return pipe from the fuel rail by squeezing the lugs on the special quick-release fittings.

40 Where the regulator is secured by screws, undo the two screws and remove the fuel pressure regulator from the fuel rail.

41 Where the regulator is secured by a spring clip, extract the clip and remove the fuel pressure regulator from the fuel rail.

42 Using a screwdriver, prise the O-ring from the groove in the fuel pressure regulator. Discard the O-ring and obtain a new one.

43 Refitting is a reversal of removal, but lubricate the new O-ring with clean engine oil to aid installation. Where applicable, tighten the mounting screws to the specified torque.

Zetec-SE engine

44 On later engines with the air cleaner assembly mounted on the engine, remove the air cleaner as described in Section 5.

45 Disconnect the vacuum pipe from the fuel pressure regulator, then undo the two screws and remove the fuel pressure regulator from the fuel rail.

46 Using a screwdriver, prise the O-rings from the grooves in the fuel pressure regulator. Discard the O-rings and obtain new ones.

47 Refitting is a reversal of removal, but lubricate the new O-rings with clean engine oil to aid installation. Tighten the mounting screws to the specified torque.

Idle air control valve

48 The valve is located on the inlet manifold. On later engines with the air cleaner assembly mounted on the engine, remove the air cleaner as described in Section 5 for improved access.

49 Depress the wire clip and disconnect the wiring from the valve **(see illustration)**.

50 Unscrew the mounting bolts and remove the valve from the inlet manifold **(see illustration)**.

51 Recover the O-ring seals from the inlet manifold and discard them **(see illustration)**. Obtain new seals.

52 Refitting is a reversal of removal, but note the following points.

 a) *Clean the mating surfaces, and fit new O-ring seals.*

 b) *Once the wiring and battery are reconnected, start the engine and allow it*

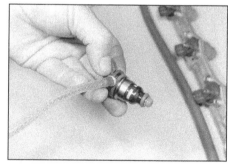

15.34 Oil the O-ring seals before refitting the injectors

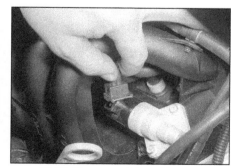

15.49 Disconnect the wiring . . .

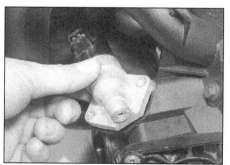

15.50 . . . then unbolt and remove the idle air control valve . . .

15.51 . . . and recover the O-ring seals from the inlet manifold

15.54 Disconnecting the wiring from the mass air flow sensor

15.55 One of the mass air flow sensor mounting screws

15.69a Camshaft position sensor located on the right-hand rear of the cylinder head – Zetec-SE engine

to idle. When it has reached normal operating temperature, check that the idle speed is stable, and that no induction (air) leaks are evident. Switch on all electrical loads (headlights, heated rear window, etc), and check that the idle speed is still satisfactory.

Mass air flow sensor

53 Loosen the clip and disconnect the air inlet duct from the mass air flow sensor on the air cleaner cover. If necessary, remove the air cleaner cover for improved access.
54 Disconnect the wiring from the sensor **(see illustration)**.
55 Unscrew the crosshead mounting screws and remove the sensor from the air cleaner cover **(see illustration)**.
56 Refitting is a reversal of removal.

15.69b Disconnect the wiring . . .

Powertrain Control Module

Note: *The module is fragile. Take care not to drop it, or subject it to any other kind of impact. Do not subject it to extremes of temperature, or allow it to get wet.*
57 The Module (engine management module) is located behind the passenger footwell side trim. First disconnect the battery negative (earth) lead (see Chapter 5A).
58 Remove the fuel cut-off switch as described in Section 13.
59 Drill out or cut off the two rivets and remove the security shield from over the module.
60 Release the module from its bracket and withdraw it downwards.
61 Undo the screw and swivel the wiring multiplug away from the module. **Do not** pull on the wiring, only on the multiplug itself.
62 Withdraw the module from inside the vehicle.
63 Refitting is a reversal of removal. Take care when refitting the multiplug, and tighten the retaining bolt by hand first. Use new pop rivets when refitting the security shield.

Crankshaft position sensor

64 The sensor is located on the front left-hand side of the engine. For improved access, apply the handbrake then jack up the front of the vehicle and support it on axle stands (see *Jacking and vehicle support*).
65 Unbolt (Endura-E) or unclip (Zetec-SE) the cover from the crankshaft position sensor on the front of the engine, then disconnect the wiring.

66 Unscrew the mounting bolt and withdraw the sensor.
67 Refitting is a reversal of removal.

Camshaft position sensor

68 On the Endura-E engine the sensor is located on the timing chain cover. On the Zetec-SE engine it is located on the right-hand rear of the cylinder head.
69 Depress the wire clip and disconnect the wiring from the camshaft position sensor **(see illustrations)**. Where applicable on the Endura-E engine, release the fuel feed and return hoses from their clip.
70 Unscrew the mounting bolt and withdraw the sensor from the cylinder head or timing chain cover (as applicable) **(see illustrations)**.
71 Remove the O-ring from the groove in the sensor **(see illustration)**.
72 Refitting is a reversal of removal but fit a new O-ring. Smear a little engine oil on the seal before fitting the sensor.

Coolant temperature sensor

73 Drain the cooling system (see Chapter 1A).
74 Unbolt the plastic cover from the top of the cylinder head cover.
75 Disconnect the HT leads from the ignition coil, then disconnect the low tension wiring from the coil.
76 Unbolt and remove the ignition coil.
77 Disconnect the wiring from the coolant temperature sensor.
78 Unscrew and remove the sensor.
79 Refitting is a reversal of removal. Clean

15.70a . . . then unscrew the mounting bolt . . .

15.70b . . . and withdraw the camshaft position sensor from the cylinder head

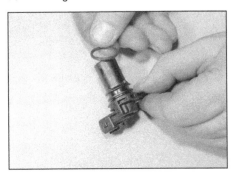

15.71 Removing the O-ring from the camshaft position sensor

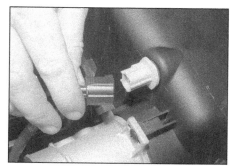

15.81a Disconnect the wiring . . .

the threads of the sensor and mounting hole, then refit the sensor and tighten it to the specified torque.

Inlet air temperature sensor

80 The sensor is located in the air cleaner cover. If necessary, remove the air cleaner cover for improved access.
81 Disconnect the wiring from the sensor, then twist the sensor through 90° and remove it **(see illustrations)**.
82 Refitting is a reversal of removal.

Throttle position sensor

83 The sensor is located on the throttle body housing on the left-hand side of the inlet manifold. On later engines with the air cleaner assembly mounted on the engine, remove the air cleaner as described in Section 5 for improved access.
84 Disconnect the wiring by depressing the retaining clip. Remove the retaining screws, and withdraw the unit from the throttle housing. *Do not* force the sensor's centre to rotate past its normal operating sweep; the unit will be seriously damaged.
85 Refitting is a reversal of removal, but ensure that the sensor is correctly orientated, by locating its centre on the D-shaped throttle shaft (throttle closed), and aligning the sensor body so that the bolts pass easily into the throttle housing.

Vehicle speed sensor

86 The sensor is mounted on the rear of the transmission at the base of the speedometer drive cable.
87 Where applicable, undo the retaining nut, and withdraw the speedometer cable from the vehicle speed sensor. Use two spanners to loosen the nut – one to counterhold the sensor, and the other to unscrew the cable nut.
88 Disconnect the wiring from the vehicle speed sensor, then unscrew the sensor from the top of the drive pinion.
89 Refitting is a reversal of removal.

Temperature and manifold absolute pressure sensor

90 The sensor is mounted in the inlet manifold.
91 Remove the air cleaner as described in Section 5 for improved access.

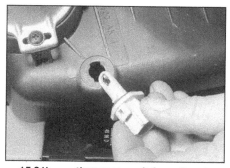

15.81b . . . then remove it from the air cleaner cover

92 Disconnect the sensor wiring connector.
93 Undo the sensor mounting screws, lift off the sensor and recover the gasket.
94 Refitting is a reversal of removal, using a new gasket.

Cylinder head temperature sensor

95 The sensor is located in the centre of the head, between Nos 2 and 3 spark plugs.
96 Disconnect the HT leads from the spark plugs as necessary for access – make sure that the leads are numbered for position (with No 1 at the timing belt end). Prise out the rubber bung used to secure the sensor wiring.
97 Disconnect the wiring from the temperature sensor.
98 Unscrew and remove the sensor. **Note:** *The sensor cannot be re-used – a new one must be fitted, since the mating face of the sensor is deformed when fully tightened, to ensure a good contact with the cylinder head. If the old sensor were re-used, it would result in inaccurate readings.*
99 Refitting is a reversal of removal. Clean the sensor mounting hole, then fit the sensor and tighten it to the specified torque.

Manual transmission multi-function switch

100 Refer to Chapter 7A.

Clutch pedal position switch

101 Inside the vehicle, reach up under the clutch pedal and disconnect the return spring from the bracket.
102 Disconnect the wiring from the clutch switch, then twist the switch and remove it from the pedal bracket.
103 Refitting is a reversal of removal.

Power steering pressure switch

104 Refer to Chapter 10.

Oxygen sensor

105 Refer to Chapter 4D, Section 2.

16 Manifolds – removal and refitting

Note: *Refer to the warning note in Section 1 before proceeding.*

Inlet manifold

1 Apply the handbrake, then jack up the front of the vehicle and support it on axle stands (see *Jacking and vehicle support*).
2 On the Endura-E engine, depressurise the fuel system as described in Section 2.
3 Disconnect the battery negative (earth) lead (see Chapter 5A).
4 Disconnect the wiring from the DIS ignition coil and throttle position sensor.
5 Loosen the clips and disconnect the air intake duct from the air cleaner and throttle body housing. Remove the duct from the engine compartment. On later engines with the air cleaner assembly mounted on the engine, remove the complete air cleaner as described in Section 5.
6 On the Endura-E engine, release the spark plug HT lead supports from the inlet manifold and move the leads to one side.
7 Disconnect the accelerator cable from the throttle body housing, then pull out the adjustment clip and detach the cable from the bracket. Release the cable from the further support on the inlet manifold.
8 On the Endura-E engine, remove the oil filler cap from the valve cover, and disconnect the crankcase ventilation hose from the T-piece.
9 On the Zetec-SE engine disconnect the crankcase ventilation hose from the PCV valve.
10 On the Endura-E engine, disconnect the engine wiring loom connectors at the rear of the engine and unclip the wiring bracket.
11 Disconnect the brake servo vacuum hose from the inlet manifold.
12 Disconnect the carbon canister purge valve vacuum line from the inlet manifold **(see illustration)**.
13 On the Endura-E engine, disconnect the wiring from the camshaft position (CMP) sensor.
14 Disconnect the wiring from the engine coolant temperature sensor (Endura-E) and oil pressure switch (Endura-E and Zetec-SE).
15 On the Endura-E engine, release the heater hose from the rear of the inlet manifold.
16 Unbolt and remove the engine oil level dipstick tube.

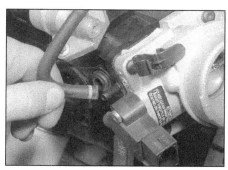

16.12 Disconnecting the carbon canister purge valve vacuum line from the inlet manifold

16.22a Unscrew the mounting bolts . . .

16.22b . . . and withdraw the inlet manifold from the cylinder head

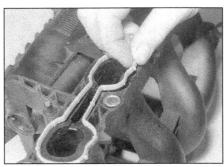

16.22c Removing the gasket from the groove in the inlet manifold

Endura-E engine

17 Identify the positions of the fuel supply and return hoses on the fuel rail, then disconnect them by squeezing the lugs on the quick-release fittings. Be prepared for some fuel loss.

18 Unbolt the cover from the crankshaft position sensor on the front of the engine, then disconnect the wiring from the sensor.

19 Unbolt the cable guide from the inlet manifold.

20 Unscrew the three nuts and remove the inlet manifold protection cover.

21 Progressively unscrew the self-locking nuts and remove the inlet manifold from the cylinder head. Recover the gasket.

Zetec-SE engine

22 Progressively unscrew the inlet manifold mounting bolts and withdraw the manifold from the cylinder head. Recover the gasket from the groove in the inlet manifold **(see illustrations)**.

All engines

23 Tape over the inlet ports on the cylinder head to prevent entry of dustand dirt. Alternatively place cloth rags in the ports.

24 Refitting is a reversal of removal, but note the following additional points.

a) Clean the mating faces of the inlet manifold and cylinder head and use a new gasket.

b) Tighten the nuts/bolts to the specified torque.

Exhaust manifold

25 On the Endura-E engine, the exhaust manifold is located on the front of the engine, while on the Zetec-SE engine it is on the rear.

26 Disconnect the wiring from the oxygen sensor located on top of the exhaust manifold. If preferred, remove the sensor completely as described in Chapter 4D, Section 2.

27 Unbolt and remove the shroud components from the exhaust manifold **(see illustration)**.

28 Unscrew the bolts/nuts securing the exhaust downpipe/catalytic converter to the exhaust manifold.

29 Unscrew the mounting bolts and nuts and withdraw the exhaust manifold from the cylinder head **(see illustrations)**.

30 Remove the gasket from the studs on the cylinder head **(see illustration)**.

31 Check the sealing ring located in the groove in the top of the catalytic converter, and renew it if necessary.

32 Refitting is a reversal of removal, but fit a new gasket and tighten the bolts and nuts to the specified torque.

16.27 Removing the shroud from the exhaust manifold

16.29a Unscrew the mounting bolts . . .

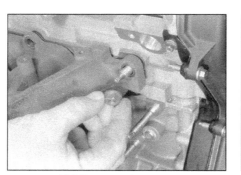

16.29b . . . and nuts . . .

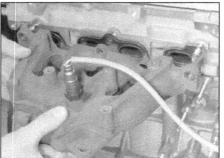

16.29c . . . and withdraw the exhaust manifold from the cylinder head

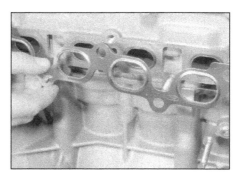

16.30 Recover the gasket from the studs on the cylinder head

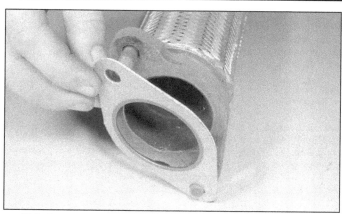

17.9 Removing the gasket fitted between the front pipe and intermediate pipe

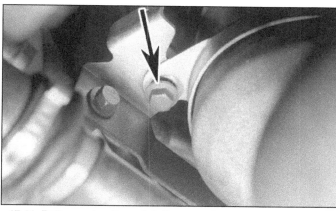

17.11 Bolt securing the catalytic converter strap to the support bracket

17 Exhaust system – general information, removal and refitting

General information

1 On new vehicles the exhaust system consists of two sections; the front downpipe and catalytic converter, and the remaining system consisting of a resonator, tailpipe and silencer. The front section is attached to the rear section by a flanged joint with a gasket.

2 For service replacements, it is possible to obtain the catalytic converter and front down-pipe each separately, however the original pipe must be cut with a hacksaw to accommodate either new item. Similarly, it is possible to obtain the rear silencer separately from the resonator and intermediate pipe. It is not possible to obtain a Ford manufactured intermediate pipe and resonator separately from the tailpipe.

3 The rear section of the exhaust is located above the rear axle, making it necessary to lower the rear axle where the complete rear section is to be renewed.

4 The system is suspended throughout its entire length by rubber mountings.

Removal and refitting

5 To remove a part of the system, first jack up the front or rear of the car, and support it on axle stands (see *Jacking and vehicle support*). Alternatively, position the car over an inspection pit, or on car ramps.

Front downpipe and catalytic converter

6 Disconnect the battery negative (earth) lead (see Chapter 5A).

7 Unbolt and remove the heatshields from the exhaust manifold.

8 Unscrew the nuts securing the downpipe to the exhaust manifold.

9 Unscrew the flange nuts and separate the front pipe from the intermediate section. Recover the gasket **(see illustration)**.

10 Where necessary, unscrew the bolts and move the heatshield away from the catalytic converter.

11 Unscrew the bolts securing the catalytic converter strap to the support bracket **(see illustration)**.

12 Undo the bolt and lower the gearchange stabiliser bar from the transmission.

13 Unscrew the bolt securing the rear engine mounting link to the transmission.

14 Carefully withdraw the front pipe and catalytic converter; it may be necessary to rock the engine slightly in order to provide enough room to remove the catalytic converter. Remove the sealing ring from the top of the catalytic converter **(see illustrations)**.

15 Unscrew the bolt and remove the strap from the catalytic converter. If necessary, unbolt the support bracket from the rear of the cylinder block **(see illustration)**.

16 If a new catalytic converter is to be fitted, cut the original pipe at a point 350 mm (Zetec-SE) or 604 mm (Endura-E) forward of the flange joint face. Ensure the cut is made at 90° to the pipe.

17 Refitting is a reversal of removal, but note the following points.

a) Fit a new gasket to the front pipe rear flange.

b) Fit a new sealing ring between the downpipe/catalytic converter and exhaust manifold and fit new nuts.

c) Tighten all nuts/bolts to the specified torque.

d) Delay tightening the clamp bolt until the remaining joints have been tightened.

Intermediate pipe, resonator and original tailpipe

18 If the complete original rear section is to be renewed, the rear axle must be lowered with reference to Chapter 10 to allow room to withdraw the exhaust. If the rear silencer alone is to be renewed, refer to paragraph 23 onwards.

19 Unscrew the flange nuts and separate the front pipe from the intermediate section. Recover the gasket.

20 With the help of an assistant, disconnect the rubber mountings from the stubs and

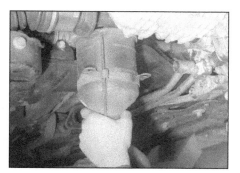

17.14a Removing the front pipe and catalytic converter

17.14b Removing the sealing ring from the top of the catalytic converter

17.15 Catalytic converter support bracket on the rear of the cylinder block

withdraw the exhaust forwards over the rear axle.

21 Check the condition of the rubber mountings and renew as necessary.

22 Refitting is a reversal of removal, but note the following points.

   a) *Fit a new gasket to the front pipe rear flange.*

   b) *Tighten the nuts to the specified torque.*

Tailpipe and silencer

23 If the original rear section is fitted, cut it just forward of the rear silencer at a point 1850 mm (Zetec-SE) or 1830 mm (Endura-E) rearward of the flange joint face. Ensure the cut is made at 90° to the pipe.

24 If a service tailpipe and silencer is fitted, unscrew the nuts and remove the clamp, then separate the tailpipe from the intermediate section.

25 Disconnect the rubber mountings and remove the tailpipe and silencer from under the vehicle.

26 Fit the new tailpipe and silencer using a reversal of the removal procedure. Make sure the intermediate and tailpipe sections are correctly aligned before tightening the clamp nuts.

Heat shield(s)

27 The heat shields are secured to the underside of the body by special nuts. Each shield can be removed separately but note that they overlap making it necessary to loosen another section first. If a shield is being removed to gain access to a component located behind it, it may prove sufficient in some cases to remove the retaining nuts and/or bolts, and simply lower the shield, without disturbing the exhaust system. Otherwise remove the exhaust section as described earlier.

Chapter 4 Part B:
Fuel and exhaust systems – Endura-DE diesel engine models

Contents

Accelerator cable – removal, refitting and adjustment 5
Accelerator pedal – removal and refitting 6
Air cleaner assembly and air inlet components –
   removal and refitting 4
Air filter element renewal . . . . .See Chapter 1B
Cold start cable – adjustment, removal and refitting 12
Exhaust system – general information and component renewal 22
Fuel filter renewal . . . . .See Chapter 1B
Fuel filter water draining . . . . .See Chapter 1B
Fuel gauge sender unit – removal and refitting 8
Fuel heater – removal and refitting 20
Fuel injection pump timing – checking and adjustment 15
Fuel injection pump – removal and refitting 16
Fuel injectors – removal, testing and refitting 18
Fuel shut-off solenoid – removal and refitting 19
Fuel system – priming and bleeding 2
Fuel system – contamination problems 3
Fuel tank – removal, inspection and refitting 7
Fuel tank filler pipe – removal and refitting 10
Fuel tank roll-over valve – removal and refitting 9
General information and precautions 1
Idle speed – checking and adjustment 11
Idle speed control system – adjustment, removal and refitting 13
Injection pipes – removal and refitting 17
Manifolds – removal and refitting 21
Maximum speed – checking and adjustment 14

Degrees of difficulty

Easy, suitable for novice with little experience	**Fairly easy,** suitable for beginner with some experience	**Fairly difficult,** suitable for competent DIY mechanic	**Difficult,** suitable for experienced DIY mechanic	**Very difficult,** suitable for expert DIY or professional

Specifications

General

System type . . . . Rear mounted fuel tank, combined lift and injection pump, indirect injection

Application . . . . 1.8 litre Endura-DE engine

Firing order . . . . 1-3-4-2 (No 1 at timing belt end)

Fuel

Fuel type . . . . Commercial diesel fuel for road vehicles (DERV)

Injection pump

Make and type . . . . Bosch VE

Rotation (viewed from crankshaft pulley end) . . . . Clockwise

Drive . . . . By toothed belt from crankshaft

Injectors

Type . . . . Pintle

Needle seat leakage/injector dribble . . . . Holds 125 bar for 10 seconds

Adjustment data

Idle speed:
  Models without air conditioning . . . . 920 ± 50 rpm
  Models with air conditioning . . . . 950 ± 50 rpm
Injection pump timing . . . . By timing pins, at TDC
Maximum no-load speed:
  Continuous . . . . 4800 rpm
  Intermittent . . . . 5350 ± 50 rpm
Deceleration time (no load at idle) . . . . 5 seconds maximum

Torque wrench settings

	Nm	lbf ft
Crankshaft pulley/vibration damper	35	26
Engine mounting bracket bolts	50	37
Engine mounting bracket nut (centre)	69	51
Engine mounting bracket nuts (outer)	120	89
Exhaust manifold	24	18
Fuel injector delivery pipe unions	20	15
Fuel injectors	75	55
Glow plugs	28	21
Injection pump drivebelt tensioner	50	37
Injection pump mounting bolts	20	15
Injection pump rear support bracket	20	15
Injection pump sprocket	20	15
Inlet manifold lower section to cylinder head	23	17
Inlet manifold upper section to lower section	23	17
TDC timing pin blanking plug	24	18

1 General information and precautions

General information

The fuel system consists of a fuel tank (mounted under the body, beneath the rear seats), fuel filter, fuel injection pump, injectors, fuel lines and hoses, fuel gauge sender unit mounted in the fuel tank, and EEC V engine management electronic control (Powertrain Control Module).

Fuel is drawn from the tank by the transfer pump incorporated in the injection pump. It then passes through the fuel filter, located in the engine bay, where foreign matter and water are removed. The injection pump is belt-driven from the crankshaft and supplies fuel under very high pressure to each injector in turn as it is needed. The engine has two drivebelts, one to drive the injection pump and the other to drive the camshaft, oil pump, auxiliary shaft and water pump. The amount of fuel delivered is determined by the pump governor, which reacts to throttle position and to engine speed. Injection timing is varied automatically to suit the prevailing speed and load.

Rigid pipes connect the pump to the four injectors. Each injector sprays fuel into a pre-combustion or 'swirl' chamber as its piston approaches TDC on the compression stroke. This system is known as indirect injection. The injectors only open under very high pressure. Lubrication is provided by allowing a small quantity of fuel to leak back past the injector internal components. The leaked-back fuel is returned to the pump and then to the fuel tank.

Two systems, both automatically controlled by the powertrain control module, assist cold starting. A cold start advance solenoid on the injection pump advances the injection timing during cold starts. The amount of time the solenoid remains energised decreases as the engine temperature increases. The pre-heater or 'glow' plugs fitted to each swirl chamber are electrically heated before, during and immediately after starting and are particularly effective during a cold start. A warning light illuminates when the ignition is switched on, showing that the glow plugs are in operation. When the light goes out, pre-heating is complete and the engine can be started. The glow plugs are controlled by the powertrain control module, and the amount of time they remain on is dependent on engine temperature.

Except on models with air conditioning, cold start idle speed is controlled by a waxstat system comprising a wax element and cable connected to the idle lever on the injection pump. Models with air conditioning are fitted with an idle speed control motor located beneath the battery tray with a cable connected to the idle lever on the injection pump. The idle speed motor is controlled by the powertrain control module and it is operative with the engine cold or warm.

A light load retard device is fitted, and is controlled by the powertrain control module. Under normal light load conditions, the injection timing is retarded by 3°. During full load conditions with the engine temperature below 50°C and engine speed above 3500 rpm, the device is energised thus effectively advancing the injection timing by 3°.

To stop the engine, a solenoid valve is fitted to the rear of the fuel pump. The valve is of the 'fail safe' type, so it must be energised to allow the engine to run. When power is removed from the valve, its plunger moves under spring pressure and interrupts fuel delivery.

The fuel system on diesel engines is normally very reliable. Provided that clean fuel is used and the specified maintenance is conscientiously carried out, no problems should be experienced. The injection pump and injectors may require overhaul after a high mileage has been covered, but this cannot be done on a DIY basis.

Precautions

Warning: It is necessary to take certain precautions when working on the fuel system components, particularly the *fuel injectors. Before carrying out any operations on the fuel system, refer to the precautions given in 'Safety first!' at the beginning of this manual, and to any additional warning notes at the start of the relevant Sections.*

2 Fuel system – priming and bleeding

Note: *The valve fitted between the filter and the pump on later engines is used at the factory only to fill and bleed the system on production. Check regularly that it is tightly closed.*

1 As this system is intended to be 'self-bleeding', no hand-priming pump or separate bleed screws/nipples are fitted.

2 When any part of the system has been disturbed therefore, air must be purged from the system by cranking the engine on the starter motor until it starts. When it has started, keep the engine running for approximately 5 minutes to ensure that all air has been removed from the system. To minimise the strain on the battery and starter motor when trying to start the engine, crank it in 10-second bursts, pausing for 30 seconds each time, until the engine starts.

3 Depending on the work that has been carried out, it may be possible to partially prime the system so as to spare the battery by reducing the amount of cranking time required to start the engine. To spare the battery, fill the filter with clean fuel via its vent screw opening, but it is essential that no dirt is introduced into the system and that no diesel fuel is poured over vulnerable components when doing this.

4 If a hand-operated vacuum pump is available, this can be connected to the pump's fuel return union and used to suck fuel through the supply lines and filter. This will obviously save the battery a good deal of work. If a long length of clear plastic tubing is used to connect the vacuum pump to the injection pump union, it will be easier to see when fuel emerges free from air bubbles. Do not forget to energise the fuel shut-off solenoid by switching on the ignition to position II so that fuel can pass through the pump.

5 If air has entered the injector pipes, slacken each union at the injectors and crank the engine until fuel emerges, then tighten securely all unions and mop up the spilt fuel. Start the engine and keep it running for a few minutes to ensure that all air has been expelled.

3 Fuel system – contamination problems

1 If, at any time, sudden fuel filter blockage, poor starting or otherwise unsatisfactory engine performance should be traced to the appearance of black sludge or slime within the fuel system, this may be due to corrosion caused by the presence of various micro-organisms in the fuel. These can live in the fuel tank if water is allowed to remain there in significant quantities, their waste products causing corrosion of steel and other metallic components of the fuel system.

2 If the fuel system is thought to be contaminated in this way, immediately seek the advice of a Ford dealer or diesel specialist. Thorough treatment is required to cure the problem and to prevent it from occurring again.

3 If you are considering treating the vehicle on a DIY basis proceed as follows. Do not re-use contaminated fuel.

4 First drain and remove the fuel tank, flush it thoroughly with clean diesel fuel and use an electric torch to examine as much as possible of its interior. If the contamination is severe, the tank must be steam-cleaned internally and then flushed again with clean diesel fuel.

5 Disconnect the fuel feed and return hoses from the injection pump, remove the fuel filter element and flush through the system's feed and return lines with clean diesel fuel.

6 Renew the filter element, refit the fuel tank and reconnect the fuel lines, then fill the tank with clean diesel fuel and bleed the system as described above. Watch carefully for signs of the problem occurring again.

7 While it is unlikely that such contamination will be found beyond the fuel filter, if it is thought to have reached the injection pump,

the pump may require cleaning. This is a task only for a diesel specialist. Do not attempt to disturb any part of the pump (other than the few adjustments detailed in this Manual) or to clean it yourself.

8 The most common cause of excessive quantities of water being in the fuel is condensation from the water vapour in the air. Diesel fuel tanks (whether underground storage tanks or that in the vehicle) are more susceptible to this problem than petrol tanks because of petrol's higher vapour pressure. Water formation in the vehicle's tank can be minimised by keeping the tank as full as possible at all times and by using the vehicle regularly.

9 Note that proprietary additives are available to inhibit the growth of micro-organisms in vehicle fuel tanks or storage tanks.

10 If you buy all your fuel from the same source and suspect that to be the source of the contamination, the owner or operator should be advised. Otherwise, the risk of taking on contaminated fuel can be minimised by using only reputable filling stations which have a good turnover.

4 Air cleaner assembly and air inlet components – removal and refitting

Air cleaner assembly

1 Loosen the clip and disconnect the air inlet tube from the rear of the air cleaner cover.

2 Unscrew the screws securing the cover to the air cleaner housing. Withdraw the cover and remove the filter element.

3 Release the retaining strap from the rear of the air cleaner base, then lift the base from the rubber grommets.

4 Disconnect the inlet duct and withdraw the base from the engine compartment.

5 Check the rubber grommets for deterioration and renew them if necessary.

6 Refitting is the reverse of the removal procedure. Ensure that the base pegs seat fully in their rubber grommets.

Air inlet components

7 To remove the air inlet components between the air cleaner and inlet manifold,

first pull the tube from the air cleaner cover. Loosen the clip and disconnect the tube from the flexible tube, then release it from the mounting and withdraw it from the engine compartment. Loosen the clips and disconnect the resonator and connector.

8 To remove the flexible tube, loosen the clips and disconnect the tube from the inlet manifold and rigid tube.

9 To remove the primary inlet ducts first remove the air cleaner base, then unscrew the mounting bolt and lift out the ducts. Separate the resonator and silencer.

10 Refitting is a reversal of removal.

5 Accelerator cable – removal, refitting and adjustment

Removal

1 On the front of the injection pump, pull out the adjustment clip from the ferrule on the outer cable, and pull the outer cable from the support bracket **(see illustration)**.

2 Disconnect the inner cable end fitting from the speed control (throttle) lever on the pump **(see illustration)**.

3 Inside the vehicle, fold back the carpet and insulation in the driver's footwell to gain access to the accelerator pedal.

4 Disconnect the inner cable from the top of the pedal.

5 Release the cable from the supports in the engine compartment, and withdraw it from the bulkhead.

Refitting

6 Refitting is a reversal of removal. When the cable is reconnected at each end, adjust the cable as follows.

Adjustment

7 Remove the adjustment clip from the outer cable ferrule, and lubricate the cable adjuster grommet with soapy water.

8 Remove any slack by pulling the cable as far as possible out of the adjuster. Have an assistant depress the accelerator pedal fully – the cable outer will move back into the adjuster – and hold it there while the clip is refitted.

9 Check that the speed control (throttle) lever moves smoothly and easily from the fully-closed to the fully-open position and back again as the assistant depresses and releases the accelerator pedal. Re-adjust the cable if required.

6 Accelerator pedal – removal and refitting

Removal

1 Peel back the carpet and insulation from the driver's footwell to allow access to the accelerator pedal.

5.1 Accelerator cable adjustment clip and ferrule

5.2 Inner accelerator cable fitting to speed control lever on the injection pump

2 Detach the accelerator cable from the pedal (see Section 5), then release the circlip from the pivot shaft and remove the accelerator pedal.

Refitting

3 Refit in the reverse order of removal. On completion, check the action of the pedal and the cable to ensure that the throttle has full unrestricted movement, and fully returns when released.
4 Check and if necessary adjust the accelerator cable as described in Section 5.

7 Fuel tank – removal, inspection and refitting

Note: *Refer to the warning note in Section 1 before proceeding.*

Removal

1 Run the fuel level as low as possible prior to removing the tank. Remove the fuel filler cap.
2 Disconnect the battery negative (earth) lead (see Chapter 5A).
3 Where possible, syphon or pump out the remaining fuel from the fuel tank (there is no drain plug). The fuel must be emptied into a suitable container for storage.
4 Chock the front wheels then jack up the rear of the vehicle and support it on axle stands (see *Jacking and vehicle support*). Remove the rear roadwheels.
5 Unhook the exhaust system mounting rubbers at the front, centre and rear and allow the exhaust system to rest on the rear suspension crossmember. There is no need to disconnect the exhaust from the exhaust manifold.
6 Unscrew the nuts and remove the exhaust heat shields from the underbody.
7 Loosen the clip and disconnect the filler pipe lower vent hose from the rear of the fuel tank.
8 Position a container beneath the vent valve at the rear of the fuel tank, then disconnect the hose and remove the valve from its mounting bracket.
9 Support the fuel tank using a trolley jack and block of wood.
10 Unscrew and remove the tank mounting bolts.
11 Partially lower the fuel tank and at the same time disconnect the bottom of the filler pipe from the rubber seal in the tank.
12 Disconnect the wiring from the fuel gauge sender unit on top of the tank.
13 Squeeze the locking lugs on the quick-release fitting and disconnect the fuel return pipe. Note the return pipe is identified by a red colour band.
14 Similarly squeeze the locking lugs and disconnect the fuel supply pipe from the fuel gauge sender unit. Note the supply pipe is identified by a white colour band.
15 Lower the fuel tank and withdraw it from under the vehicle.

16 Check the condition of the filler pipe seal and renew it if necessary.

Inspection

17 Whilst removed, the fuel tank can be inspected for damage or deterioration. Removal of the fuel gauge sender unit (see Section 8) will allow a partial inspection of the interior. If the tank is contaminated with sediment or water, swill it out with clean fuel. Do not under any circumstances undertake any repairs on a leaking or damaged fuel tank; this work must be carried out by a professional who has experience in this critical and potentially-dangerous work.
18 Whilst the fuel tank is removed from the vehicle, it should be placed in a safe area where sparks or open flames cannot ignite the fumes coming out of the tank. Be especially careful inside garages where a natural-gas type appliance is located, because the pilot light could cause an explosion.
19 Check the condition of the filler pipe seal in the fuel tank, and renew it if necessary.

Refitting

20 Refitting is a reversal of the removal procedure. Apply a light smear of clean engine oil to the filler pipe seal, to ease fitting. Ensure that all connections are securely fitted. When refitting the quick-release couplings, press them together until the locking lugs snap into their groove. If evidence of contamination was found, do not return any previously-drained fuel to the tank unless it is carefully filtered first.

8 Fuel gauge sender unit – removal and refitting

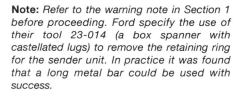

Note: *Refer to the warning note in Section 1 before proceeding. Ford specify the use of their tool 23-014 (a box spanner with castellated lugs) to remove the retaining ring for the sender unit. In practice it was found that a long metal bar could be used with success.*

Removal

1 The fuel gauge sender unit is located in the top face of the fuel tank. The unit can only be detached and withdrawn from the tank after the tank is released and lowered from under the vehicle. Refer to Section 7 and remove the fuel tank, then proceed as follows.
2 With the fuel tank removed, disconnect the fuel supply pipe (still attached to the tank) from the inlet stub by squeezing the quick-release lugs. Note that the fuel supply pipe connector is identified by a white band.
3 Unscrew and remove the special retaining ring.
4 Carefully withdraw the fuel gauge sender unit from the fuel tank.
5 Remove the inlet from the bottom of the sender unit.

Refitting

6 Refitting is a reversal of removal, but tighten the retaining ring securely. Refit the fuel tank as described in Section 7.

9 Fuel tank roll-over valve – removal and refitting

Note: *Refer to the warning note in Section 1 before proceeding.*

Removal

1 The roll-over valve is located in a rubber grommet in the top of the fuel tank, in the hose leading rearwards to the vent valve. Its purpose is to prevent fuel loss if the vehicle becomes inverted in a crash.
2 Remove the fuel tank as described in Section 7.
3 Release the vent hose from the clip on the top of the tank.
4 Carefully prise the roll-over valve from the rubber grommet and remove it together with the hose.
5 Check the condition of the rubber grommet and renew it if necessary.

Refitting

6 Refitting is a reversal of removal, but apply a light smear of clean engine oil to the rubber grommet, to ease fitting.

10 Fuel tank filler pipe – removal and refitting

Note: *Refer to the warning note in Section 1 before proceeding.*

Removal

1 Remove the fuel tank (see Section 7).
2 With the vehicle still raised, unscrew and remove the filler pipe lower mounting bolt.
3 Open the filler flap, then lift the plastic cover and unscrew the filler pipe upper mounting bolt.
4 Withdraw the filler pipe from under the vehicle.
5 If necessary, loosen the clips and disconnect the lower vent hose from the filler pipe.
6 Check the condition of the filler pipe seal and renew it if necessary.

Refitting

7 Refitting is a reversal of removal, but apply a light smear of clean engine oil to the seal, to ease fitting.

11 Idle speed – checking and adjustment

1 The usual type of tachometer (rev counter), which works from ignition system pulses, cannot be used on diesel engines. If it is not felt that adjusting the idle speed 'by ear' is satisfactory, one of the following alternatives must be used:

a) *Purchase or hire of an appropriate tachometer.*

b) *Delegation of the job to a Ford dealer or other specialist.*

2 The adjustment must be carried out with the engine at normal operating temperature. If necessary, take the vehicle on a short run.

3 On models with air conditioning, mark the position of the idle speed control cable in relation to the clip located on the injection pump, then release it from the clip.

4 Start the engine and allow it to idle, then check that the idle speed is as given in the Specifications. If adjustment is necessary, proceed as follows.

5 Loosen the idle speed adjustment screw locknut then turn the screw as necessary until the engine is idling at the specified speed. Tighten the locknut on completion **(see illustration)**.

6 Increase the engine speed by temporarily moving the idle lever on the injection pump. With the lever released, check that the engine returns to the specified idling speed.

7 On models with air conditioning, refit the idle speed control cable and adjust it as described in Section 13.

8 Disconnect the tachometer (if applicable).

12 Cold start cable – adjustment, removal and refitting

Adjustment

1 The cold start cable is fitted to models without air conditioning only. It is located on the cylinder head side of the injection pump **(see illustration)**. The adjustment must be carried out with the engine cold.

2 Release the clip securing the cold start cable to the support bracket.

3 Hold the idle lever fully against its stop, then position the outer cable so that there is between 1.0 and 2.0 mm play in the inner cable. With the cable held in this position, refit the clip to the support bracket.

Removal

4 Drain the cooling system (see Chapter 1B).

5 Release the clip securing the cold start cable to the support bracket.

6 Disconnect the inner cable from the idle lever on the injection pump.

7 Unscrew the cold start cable wax element from the thermostat housing and withdraw the cable from the engine compartment. Be prepared for some loss of coolant – place cloth rags beneath the thermostat housing.

Refitting

8 Refitting is a reversal of removal, but adjust the cable as described in paragraphs 1 to 3. Refill the cooling system as described in Chapter 1B.

13 Idle speed control system – adjustment, removal and refitting

Note: *This work requires the use of a tachometer and the FDS 2000 Ford Diagnostic Tester – this Section is included for the benefit of those who have access to these instruments. If necessary, have the work carried out by a Ford dealer.*

Adjustment

1 The idle speed control system is fitted to models with air conditioning only. The system consists of a control motor located beneath the battery tray with a cable connected to the idle lever on the injection pump.

2 Connect the tester to the diagnostic socket in accordance with the manufacturer's instructions. The adjustment is carried out with the ignition switched off.

3 Release the idle speed control cable from the clip on the injection pump.

4 Using the tester, extend the idle speed control motor plunger.

5 Move the outer cable away from the idle lever until the lever is touching the high idle adjustment screw, then secure the outer cable in this position by refitting the clip. **Note:** *Push the outer cable rather than pull it, as a precaution against stretching it.*

6 Disconnect the tester then connect a tachometer to the engine.

7 Start the engine and allow it to idle.

8 Move the main speed control (throttle) lever to increase the engine speed above 1400 rpm. Check that the idle speed control cable moves the idle lever against the high idle adjustment screw, then backs it off slightly. If this is not the case, carry out the idle speed control cable adjustment again.

9 Switch off the engine and disconnect the tachometer.

Removal

10 Release the idle speed control cable from the clip on the injection pump.

11 Disconnect the inner cable from the idle lever.

12 Remove the battery and tray as described in Chapter 5A.

13 Disconnect the inner cable from the control motor, and the outer cable from the support.

Refitting

14 Refitting is a reversal of removal, but adjust the cable as described in paragraphs 1 to 9.

14 Maximum speed – checking and adjustment

Caution: The maximum speed adjustment screw is sealed by the manufacturers at the factory, using paint or a locking wire and a lead seal. There is no reason why it should require adjustment. Do not disturb the screw if the vehicle is still within the warranty period, otherwise the warranty will be invalidated.

1 The maximum no load speed may be checked if wished, using one of the methods described in Section 11. Running the engine with the wheels free is not recommended, because of the risk of damage or injury if anything goes wrong.

2 When checking the maximum speed, do not hold the engine at this speed for more than five seconds. Keep well clear of the water pump/alternator drivebelt and pulleys.

3 The engine speed should drop from maximum to idle within the specified time when the throttle is released. If not, check that the throttle linkage is not binding or obstructed. If this is in order, seek specialist advice.

15 Fuel injection pump timing – checking and adjustment

Injection pump timing is carried using the TDC setting method described in Chapter 2C. At the time of writing, no information was available in connection with the internal setting of the injection pump plunger using a dial test indicator. Where necessary, the

11.5 Idle speed adjustment screw and locknut

12.1 The cold start cable is located on the rear of the injection pump

injection pump should be checked and adjusted by a Ford dealer or diesel engine specialist.

16 Fuel injection pump – removal and refitting

Caution: Be careful not to allow dirt into the injection pump or injector pipes during this procedure. New sealing rings should be used on the fuel pipe banjo unions when refitting.

Removal

1 Disconnect the battery negative (earth) lead (see Chapter 5A).
2 Apply the handbrake, then jack up the front of the vehicle and support it on axle stands (see *Jacking and vehicle support*). Remove the right-hand front roadwheel.
3 Using a hoist, support the weight of the engine. Alternatively, use a purpose-made support bar across the engine compartment, located in the front wing drain channels.
4 Unscrew and remove the bolts from the right-hand engine mounting bracket and lift off the upper bracket **(see illustration)**. Unscrew the nuts and remove the lower mounting bracket. Make sure the engine is supported adequately.
5 Remove the alternator as described in Chapter 5A.
6 Unscrew and remove the bolts securing the crankshaft pulley/vibration damper to the sprocket flange. To do this, have an assistant temporarily engage 4th gear and depress the footbrake pedal in order to hold the crankshaft stationary. Remove the pulley.
7 Unscrew and remove the three lower bolts from the lower timing cover.
8 On models with air conditioning, loosen the power-assisted steering pump drive pulley bolts. Using an Allen key, loosen the PAS pump drivebelt tensioner central screw, then back off the tensioner adjustment bolt until the drivebelt can be removed. Fully remove the bolts and remove the pulley from the PAS pump.
9 Unscrew the remaining bolts and release the clip, then remove the upper, intermediate and lower timing covers from the engine.

16.4 Right-hand engine mounting upper bracket (1) and lower bracket (2)

10 Using a socket on the crankshaft pulley bolt, turn the engine clockwise until the slot in the injection pump drive gear is at the 11 o'clock position. To make this task easier, remove the glow plugs as described in Chapter 5C.
11 Working under the vehicle, unbolt and remove the alternator bracket.
12 Unscrew the timing pin blank plug from the cylinder block, then screw in the timing pin (refer to Chapter 2C).
13 Slowly turn the crankshaft in its normal direction of rotation, until the crankshaft web just contacts the TDC pin.
Caution: Take care when turning the crankshaft to avoid bending the TDC pin.
14 On engines with a standard timing belt tensioner, insert the camshaft timing pin (refer to Chapter 2C).
15 Insert the injection pump timing pin (refer to Chapter 2C).
16 Remove the timing belt as described in Chapter 2C. Ford recommend that the belt is renewed every time it is removed.
17 Pull out the adjustment clip securing the accelerator cable ferrule to the support on the injection pump, then release the outer cable and disconnect the inner cable from the speed control (throttle) lever.
18 On models without air conditioning release the clip securing the cold start cable to the support bracket, then disconnect the inner cable from the idle lever on the injection pump.
19 On models with air conditioning release the idle speed control cable from the clip on the injection pump, then disconnect the inner cable from the idle lever.
20 Release the wiring loom from the clip, then disconnect the multiplug.
21 Note the location of the fuel leak-off pipe then disconnect it at the fuel return union.
22 Identify the fuel inlet and return pipes then disconnect the quick-release fittings by squeezing the lugs together. Be prepared for some loss of fuel by placing cloth rags beneath the pipes.
23 Disconnect the fuel injector leak-off pipes from the injectors.
24 Release the fuel supply pipe from the support clips, then unscrew the union nuts at the injector pump and injectors and remove the delivery pipes as an assembly.
25 Loosen the injection pump drivebelt tensioner bolt then lever the tensioner away from the drivebelt and secure it by retightening the bolt. Take care not to damage the drivebelt.
26 With the timing pin inserted, loosen the injection pump sprocket bolts. Take care not to bend the timing pin.
27 Slip the drivebelt from the sprocket. Ford recommend that the drivebelt is renewed after removal.
28 Remove the timing pin, then unscrew the bolts and remove the sprocket from the injection pump.

29 Unscrew the bolts from the injection pump rear support bracket.
30 Support the weight of the injection pump. Unscrew and remove the front mounting bolts from within the timing gear housing and withdraw the injection pump from the engine.
31 Unbolt the rear support bracket from the injection pump.

Refitting

32 Before fitting a new pump, remove the blanking plugs and prime it with clean fuel, poured in through the return port.
33 Commence refitting by fitting the rear support bracket to the injection pump. Do not fully tighten the bolts at this stage.
34 Locate the injection pump on the timing gear housing, insert the bolts and tighten them progressively to the specified torque.
35 Insert the rear bracket-to-cylinder block bolts and tighten to the specified torque.
36 Fully tighten the rear support bracket-to-injection pump bolts.
37 Refit the sprocket and hand-tighten the retaining bolts at this stage. Refit the timing pin.
38 With the timing pins in position, locate a new drivebelt on the crankshaft and injection sprockets.
39 Loosen the tensioner bolt and allow the spring to tension the drivebelt. Tighten the bolt to the specified torque.
40 Tighten the sprocket retaining bolts to the specified torque, making sure that the elongated holes are centralised as the bolts are tightened.
41 Fit a new timing belt with reference to Chapter 2C.
42 Refit the delivery pipes and tighten the union nuts to the specified torque. Locate the fuel supply pipe in the support clips.
43 Reconnect the fuel injector leak-off pipes to the injectors.
44 Reconnect the fuel inlet and return pipes making sure that the quick-release fittings are correctly engaged.
45 Reconnect the fuel leak-off pipe at the fuel return union.
46 Reconnect the multiplug and refit the wiring loom to the clip.
47 On models with air conditioning refit the idle speed control cable. If necessary, adjust it with reference to Section 13.
48 On models without air conditioning refit the cold start cable. If necessary, adjust it with reference to Section 12.
49 Refit the accelerator cable and adjust it with reference to Section 5.
50 Refit the alternator bracket and tighten the retaining bolts.
51 Refit the lower, intermediate and upper timing covers and tighten the bolts.
52 On models with air conditioning refit the power-assisted steering pump pulley and hand-tighten the bolts, then locate the drivebelt on the pulleys and tension it with reference to Chapter 1B. Tighten the pulley bolts securely, then check and if necessary retension the drivebelt.

53 Refit the crankshaft pulley/vibration damper to the sprocket flange and tighten the bolts to the specified torque while holding the crankshaft stationary as described for removal.
54 Refit the alternator as described in Chapter 5A.
55 Refit the right-hand engine mounting lower bracket and tighten the nuts to the specified torque. Refit the upper bracket and tighten the bolts to the specified torque.
56 Disconnect the hoist or support bar from the engine.
57 Refit the right-hand front roadwheel and lower the vehicle to the ground.
58 Reconnect the battery negative (earth) lead (see Chapter 5A).
59 Prime and bleed the fuel system as described in Section 2.
60 Start the engine, and bring it to operating temperature. Check and if necessary adjust the idle speed as described in Section 11.

17 Injection pipes – removal and refitting

Caution: Be careful not to allow dirt into the injection system during this procedure.

Removal
1 The injection pipes should be removed as a set. Individual pipes may then be renewed if necessary after releasing the anti-rattle clips.
2 Disconnect the battery negative (earth) lead (see Chapter 5A). Clean around the pipe unions at the injectors and at the pump.
3 Protect the alternator against fuel spillage, then disconnect the fuel leak-off pipes from the injectors.
4 Release the fuel supply pipe from the clips on numbers 2 and 4 injectors.
5 Counterhold the pump adapters and unscrew the pipe union nuts.
6 Similarly unscrew the injector union nuts, counterholding the injector bodies as the nuts are slackened.
7 Remove the pipe assembly. Plug or cap open unions to keep fuel in and dirt out.

Refitting
8 When refitting, make sure that all the anti-rattle clips are in place. Do not bend or strain the pipes. Blow through the pipes with compressed air (from an air line or a foot pump) to expel any debris.
9 Refit the pipe assembly to both the injectors and injection pump, initially hand-tightening the union nuts. With the assembly in place, fully tighten the nuts to the specified torque.
10 Refit the fuel supply pipe to the clips and reconnect the fuel leak-off pipes to the injectors.
11 Reconnect the battery negative (earth) lead (see Chapter 5A).
12 Prime and bleed the fuel system as described in Section 2.
13 Run the engine and check the disturbed unions for leaks.

18 Fuel injectors – removal, testing and refitting
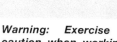

 Warning: Exercise extreme caution when working on the fuel injectors. Never expose the hands or any part of the body to injector spray, as the high working pressure can cause the fuel to penetrate the skin, with possibly fatal results. You are strongly advised to have any work which involves testing the injectors under pressure carried out by a dealer or fuel injection specialist.
Caution: Be careful not to allow dirt into the injection system during this procedure.

Removal
1 Disconnect the battery negative (earth) lead (see Chapter 5A). Clean around the injectors and the injection pipe unions.
2 Disconnect the fuel return hoses from the injectors **(see illustration)**.
3 Remove the injection pipes as described in Section 17.
4 Unscrew and remove the injectors. A 27 mm box spanner or deep socket will be required **(see illustrations)**.
5 Retrieve the heat protection washers from the injector bores. Obtain new washers for reassembly **(see illustration)**.

18.2 Disconnecting a fuel return hose from an injector

6 Take care not to drop the injectors, nor allow the needles at their tips to become damaged.

Testing
7 Testing of injectors is quite simple, but requires a special high pressure pump and gauge. Should such equipment be available, use it in accordance with its maker's instructions, referring to the Specifications for the desired values. Do not expose the skin to spray from the injectors – the pressure is high enough to penetrate the skin.
8 Defective injectors should be renewed or professionally repaired. DIY repair is not a practical proposition.

Refitting
9 Commence refitting by inserting new heat protection washers, domed faces downwards, to the injector bores.
10 Insert the injectors and screw them in by hand, then tighten them to the specified torque. No outer sealing washer is used and the injectors are a taper fit in the head.
11 Refit the injection pipes with reference to Section 17.

19 Fuel shut-off solenoid – removal and refitting

Caution: Be careful not to allow dirt into the injection system during this procedure.
1 If the fuel shut-off solenoid is disconnected, the engine will not run. The same applies if the

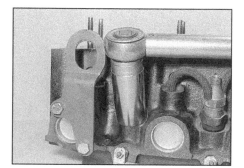

18.4a Removing an injector using a deep socket

18.4b Removing an injector . . .

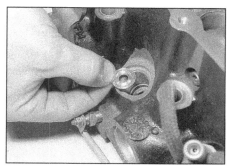

18.5 . . . followed by the heat protection washer

solenoid is defective. If the plunger jams in the raised position, the engine will not stop. A defective solenoid should be removed for inspection or renewal as follows:

2 Disconnect the battery negative (earth) lead (see Chapter 5A).

3 Disconnect the electrical lead from the solenoid **(see illustration)**.

4 Wipe clean the area around the solenoid, then unscrew it from the fuel injection pump using a deep socket or box spanner. **Caution: If the solenoid has recently been energised, it may be hot.**

5 A defective solenoid must be renewed.

6 Refit the solenoid and tighten moderately.

7 Reconnect the solenoid lead and the battery earth lead. Run the engine to check for correct operation.

20 Fuel heater – removal and refitting

Removal

1 Obtain a container in which to catch any fuel spillage.

2 Disconnect the battery negative (earth) lead (see Chapter 5A).

3 Disconnect the multiplug from the base of the fuel heater located on the left-hand end of the cylinder head **(see illustration)**.

4 Disconnect the fuel inlet pipe from the inlet pipe by squeezing the lugs on the quick-release fitting.

5 Release the fuel outlet pipe from the clip, then disconnect it from the filter by squeezing the lugs on the quick-release fitting.

6 Remove the single retaining screw and detach the heater and bracket assembly from the engine.

7 Release the two clips and separate the heater from the bracket.

Refitting

8 Refitting is the reverse of the removal procedure. On completion, prime and bleed the fuel system as described in Section 2.

21 Manifolds – removal and refitting

Inlet

Removal

1 Loosen the clip and disconnect the air inlet duct from the inlet manifold.

2 Undo the retaining bolts, lift the plastic upper section clear of the inlet manifold and collect the four O-ring seals from the grooves in the mating face **(see illustration)**. If required, the connector can be detached from the upper section by unscrewing the four retaining bolts.

3 Detach the crankcase breather hose and unbolt the EGR valve from the manifold end face. Recover the gasket.

4 Unscrew the retaining bolts and nuts, and withdraw the manifold lower section from the cylinder head. Collect the gasket.

Refitting

5 Refitting is a reversal of the removal procedure. Ensure that the mating faces are clean. Ensure that a new gasket is fitted between the manifold and the cylinder head and tighten the retaining bolts/nuts to the specified torque, working from the centre outwards to avoid warping the manifold. Locate new ring seals into the grooves in plastic upper section prior to fitting it into position and tightening the bolts. Fit a new gasket to the EGR valve before tightening the bolts.

Exhaust

Removal

6 Apply the handbrake, then jack up the front of the vehicle and support it on axle stands (see *Jacking and vehicle support*).

7 Unbolt and remove the shroud components from the exhaust manifold and catalytic converter.

8 Unscrew the bolts/nuts securing the exhaust downpipe/catalytic converter to the exhaust manifold.

9 Unbolt the EGR valve tube and recover the gasket.

10 Unscrew the mounting bolts and nuts and withdraw the exhaust manifold from the cylinder head.

11 Remove the gasket from the studs on the cylinder head.

12 Check the sealing ring located in the groove in the top of the catalytic converter, and renew it if necessary.

Refitting

13 Refitting is a reversal of removal, but fit new gaskets and tighten the bolts and nuts to the specified torque.

22 Exhaust system – general information and component renewal

General information

1 On new vehicles the exhaust system consists of two sections; the front downpipe and catalytic converter, and the remaining system consisting of a resonator, tailpipe and silencer. The front section is attached to the rear section by a flanged joint with a gasket.

2 For service replacements, it is possible to obtain the catalytic converter and front downpipe each separately, however the original pipe must be cut with a hacksaw to accommodate either new item. Similarly, it is possible to obtain the rear silencer separately from the resonator and intermediate pipe. It is not possible to obtain a Ford manufactured intermediate pipe and resonator separately from the tailpipe.

3 The rear section of the exhaust is located above the rear axle, making it necessary to lower the rear axle where the complete rear section is to be renewed.

4 The system is suspended throughout its entire length by rubber mountings.

Removal and refitting

5 To remove a part of the system, first jack up the front or rear of the car, and support it on axle stands (see *Jacking and vehicle support*). Alternatively, position the car over an inspection pit, or on car ramps.

19.3 Fuel shut-off solenoid electrical connector

20.3 The fuel heater is located on the left-hand end of the cylinder head

21.2 Inlet manifold and mounting bolts

Front downpipe and catalytic converter

6 Disconnect the battery negative (earth) lead (see Chapter 5A).

7 Unbolt and remove the heatshields from the exhaust manifold.

8 Unscrew the nuts securing the downpipe to the exhaust manifold.

9 Unscrew the flange nuts and separate the front pipe from the intermediate section. Recover the gasket.

10 Where necessary, unscrew the bolts and move the heatshield away from the catalytic converter.

11 Unscrew the bolts securing the catalytic converter strap to the support bracket.

12 Undo the bolt and lower the gearchange stabiliser bar from the transmission.

13 Unscrew the bolt securing the rear engine mounting link to the transmission.

14 Carefully withdraw the front pipe and catalytic converter; it may be necessary to rock the engine slightly in order to provide enough room to remove the catalytic converter. Remove the sealing ring from the top of the catalytic converter.

15 Unscrew the bolt and remove the strap from the catalytic converter. If necessary, unbolt the support bracket from the rear of the cylinder block.

16 If a new catalytic converter is to be fitted, cut the original pipe at a point 350 mm forward of the flange joint face. Ensure the cut is made at 90° to the pipe.

17 Refitting is a reversal of removal, but note the following points.
   a) *Fit a new gasket to the front pipe rear flange.*
   b) *Fit a new sealing ring between the downpipe/catalytic converter and exhaust manifold and fit new nuts.*
   c) *Delay tightening the clamp bolt until the remaining joints have been tightened.*

Intermediate pipe, resonator and original tailpipe

18 If the complete original rear section is to be renewed, the rear axle must be lowered with reference to Chapter 10 to allow room to withdraw the exhaust. If the rear silencer alone is to be renewed, refer to paragraph 23 onwards.

19 Unscrew the flange nuts and separate the front pipe from the intermediate section. Recover the gasket.

20 With the help of an assistant, disconnect the rubber mountings from the stubs and withdraw the exhaust forwards over the rear axle.

21 Check the condition of the rubber mountings and renew as necessary.

22 Refitting is a reversal of removal, using a new gasket on the front pipe rear flange.

Tailpipe and silencer

23 If the original rear section is fitted, cut it just forward of the rear silencer at a point 1850 mm rearward of the flange joint face. Ensure the cut is made at 90° to the pipe.

24 If the service tailpipe and silencer is fitted, unscrew the nuts and remove the clamp, then separate the tailpipe from the intermediate section.

25 Disconnect the rubber mountings and remove the tailpipe and silencer from under the vehicle.

26 Fit the new tailpipe and silencer using a reversal of the removal procedure. Make sure the intermediate and tailpipe sections are correctly aligned before tightening the clamp nuts.

Heat shield(s)

27 The heat shields are secured to the underside of the body by special nuts. Each shield can be removed separately but note that they overlap making it necessary to loosen another section first. If a shield is being removed to gain access to a component located behind it, it may prove sufficient in some cases to remove the retaining nuts and/or bolts, and simply lower the shield, without disturbing the exhaust system. Otherwise remove the exhaust section as described earlier.

Notes

Chapter 4 Part C:
Fuel and exhaust systems –
Endura-DI diesel engine models

Contents

Accelerator pedal – removal and refitting 5
Air cleaner assembly and air inlet components –
  removal and refitting 4
Air filter element renewal . . . . .See Chapter 1B
Diesel injection system – checking 10
Diesel injection system electronic components –
  removal and refitting 11
Exhaust system – general information and component renewal 18
Fuel filter renewal . . . . .See Chapter 1B
Fuel filter water draining . . . . .See Chapter 1B
Fuel gauge sender unit – removal and refitting 7
Fuel injection pump – removal and refitting 13

Fuel injection pump timing – checking and adjustment 12
Fuel injectors – removal, testing and refitting 15
Fuel system – contamination problems 3
Fuel system – priming and bleeding 2
Fuel tank – removal, inspection and refitting 6
Fuel tank filler pipe – removal and refitting 9
Fuel tank roll-over valves – removal and refitting 8
General information and precautions 1
Injection pipes – removal and refitting 14
Manifolds – removal and refitting 17
Turbocharger – general information, removal and refitting 16

Degrees of difficulty

Easy, suitable for novice with little experience	Fairly easy, suitable for beginner with some experience	Fairly difficult, suitable for competent DIY mechanic	Difficult, suitable for experienced DIY mechanic	Very difficult, suitable for expert DIY or professional
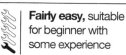				

Specifications

General

System type	Bosch VP-30 combined lift and injection pump, chain-driven from crankshaft. Direct injection via five-hole, pencil-type injectors, electronic pump control unit (PCU) linked to revised EEC-V engine management Powertrain Control Module (PCM)
Application	1.8 litre Endura-DI engine
Firing order	1-3-4-2 (No 1 at timing belt end)
Idle speed	800 ± 50 rpm (regulated by EEC V engine management system – no adjustment possible)

Fuel

Fuel type	Commercial diesel fuel for road vehicles (DERV)

Injection pump

Make and type	Bosch VP-30 electronic, distributor-type
Rotation (viewed from crankshaft pulley end)	Clockwise
Drive	By twin 'gemini' chains from crankshaft
Injection pump timing	By timing pin, at TDC

Injectors

Type	Pencil-type, five-hole

Turbocharger

Type	Garrett GT15, integral with exhaust manifold.

Torque wrench settings

	Nm	lbf ft
Catalytic converter-to-turbocharger nuts	47	35
Crankshaft position sensor bolt	10	7
Cylinder head temperature sensor	20	15
Exhaust manifold	25	18
Injection pump bracket bolts	22	16
Injection pump locking screw	12	9
Injection pump oil seal housing nuts	10	7
Injection pump rear mounting bolts	20	15
Injection pump timing belt sprocket bolts (use locking fluid)	42	31
Injection pump-to-drive pulley bolts	33	24
Injector clamp bolt	23	17
Injector pipe unions	28	21
Inlet manifold	23	17
Turbocharger oil feed/return flange bolts	10	7

1 General information and precautions

General information

The fuel system consists of a fuel tank (mounted under the body, beneath the rear seats), fuel filter, electronic fuel injection pump with pump control unit, injectors, fuel lines and hoses, fuel gauge sender unit mounted in the fuel tank, and EEC V engine management electronic control unit (Powertrain Control Module).

Fuel is drawn from the tank by the transfer pump incorporated in the injection pump. It then passes through the fuel filter, located in the engine bay, where foreign matter and water are removed. The injection pump is driven from the crankshaft via a twin-row ('gemini') chain and supplies fuel under very high pressure to each injector in turn as it is needed. The camshaft is driven from the injection pump via a toothed timing belt.

The Endura-DI engine is very much a 'state-of-the-art' unit, in that it features a full electronic engine management system, very similar to that fitted to the Fiesta petrol models. An extensive array of sensors is fitted, which supply information on many different parameters to the Powertrain Control Module (PCM).

Information on crankshaft position and engine speed is generated by a crankshaft position sensor. The inductive head of the sensor runs just above the engine flywheel, and scans a series of 36 protrusions on the flywheel periphery. As the crankshaft rotates, the sensor transmits a pulse every time a protrusion passes it. There is one missing protrusion in the flywheel periphery at a point corresponding to 90° BTDC. The PCM recognises the absence of a pulse from the crankshaft position sensor at this point to establish a reference mark for crankshaft position. Similarly, the time interval between absent pulses is used to determine engine speed.

Information on the quantity and temperature of the inlet air is derived from the MAP sensor and the inlet air temperature sensor. The manifold absolute pressure (or MAP) sensor is connected to the inlet manifold by a vacuum hose, and measures the pressure in the inlet system. The inlet air temperature sensor measures the temperature of the inlet air before it enters the turbocharger. The temperature and quantity of air has a direct bearing on the quantity of fuel to be injected for optimum efficiency.

The traditional coolant temperature sensor has been replaced by a cylinder head temperature sensor. The new sensor is seated in a blind hole in the cylinder head, and measures the temperature of the metal directly. Information on engine temperature is critical for accurate fuelling calculations, and is also used to control the pre-heating system for cold starts.

The clutch pedal sensor informs the PCM whether the clutch is engaged or disengaged. When the clutch pedal is depressed, the quantity of fuel injected is momentarily reduced, to make gearchanging smoother.

The amount of fuel delivered is determined by the pump's internal quantity and timing solenoid valves, which are controlled by the pump control unit (PCU), mounted on top of the pump. The pump is internally equipped with a pulse ring fitted to the main rotor, and an angle sensor determines the pump rotor's position and speed, in much the same way as the crankshaft position sensor and engine flywheel, except that there are four gaps in the pump rotor 'teeth' – one for each cylinder. The pump control unit is supplied with information from the 'main' engine management module (PCM), and from this, is able to calculate the most appropriate values for injection timing and quantity (injection duration). The electronically-controlled pump internals enable these calculated values to be delivered with great accuracy, for improved efficiency and reduced emissions.

No accelerator cable is fitted on the Endura-DI engine – instead, a sensor located next to the accelerator pedal informs the PCM of the accelerator position, and this information is used to determine the most appropriate fuelling requirements from the injection pump. The engine idle speed is also controlled by the PCM, and cannot be adjusted. From the signals it receives from the various sensors, the PCM can control the idle speed very accurately, compensating automatically for additional engine loads or unfavourable ambient/engine temperatures.

Rigid pipes connect the pump to the four injectors. Each injector has five holes, to disperse the fuel evenly, and sprays fuel directly into the combustion chamber as its piston approaches TDC on the compression stroke. This system is known as direct injection. The pistons have an off-centre recess machined into their crowns, the shape of which has been calculated to improve 'swirl' (fuel/air mixing). The injectors open in two stages, to promote smoother combustion – the rate of opening is fixed by two internal springs. Lubrication is provided by allowing a small quantity of fuel to leak back past the injector internal components. The leaked-back fuel is returned to the pump and then to the fuel tank.

Cold-starting performance is automatically controlled by the PCM and pump control unit. Under cold start conditions, the injection pump timing is advanced by the pump control unit, while the PCM operates the glow plug system. The pre-heater or 'glow' plugs fitted to each cylinder are electrically heated before, during and immediately after starting, and are particularly effective during a cold start. A warning light illuminates when the ignition is switched on, showing that the glow plugs are in operation. When the light goes out, pre-heating is complete and the engine can be started. In very cold conditions, the glow plugs remain on after the engine has started (post-heating) – this helps the engine to run more smoothly during warm-up, and reduces exhaust emissions.

Older diesel engines, including the previous Endura-DE, had injection pumps which were equipped with a solenoid valve to cut the fuel supply when the ignition switch is turned off, to stop the engine (the valve was usually known as a 'stop' solenoid). The Endura-DI injection pump does not have a stop solenoid – instead, the PCM is able to 'switch off' the injection pump via the pump control unit, and this forms part of the vehicle immobiliser system.

The fuel system on diesel engines is normally very reliable. Provided that clean fuel is used and the specified maintenance is conscientiously carried out, no problems should be experienced. The injection pump and injectors may require overhaul after a high mileage has been covered, but this cannot be done on a DIY basis.

Precautions

 Warning: It is necessary to take certain precautions when working on the fuel system components, particularly the fuel injectors. Before carrying out any operations on the fuel system, refer to the precautions given in 'Safety first!' at the beginning of this manual, and to any additional warning notes at the start of the relevant Sections. In particular, note that the injectors on direct injection diesel engines operate at extremely high pressures (approximately 1100 bar), making the injector spray extremely hazardous.

2 Fuel system –
priming and bleeding

1 As this system is intended to be 'self-bleeding', no hand-priming pump or separate bleed screws/nipples are fitted.

2 When any part of the system has been disturbed therefore, air must be purged from the system by cranking the engine on the starter motor until it starts. When it has started, keep the engine running for approximately 5 minutes to ensure that all air has been removed from the system. To minimise the strain on the battery and starter motor when trying to start the engine, crank it in 10-second bursts, pausing for 30 seconds each time, until the engine starts.

3 Depending on the work that has been carried out, it may be possible to partially prime the system so as to spare the battery by reducing the amount of cranking time required to start the engine. To spare the battery, fill the filter with clean fuel via its vent screw opening, but it is essential that no dirt is introduced into the system and that no diesel fuel is poured over vulnerable components when doing this.

4 If a hand-operated vacuum pump is available, this can be connected to the pump's fuel return union and used to suck fuel through the supply lines and filter. This will obviously save the battery a good deal of work. If a long length of clear plastic tubing is used to connect the vacuum pump to the injection pump union, it will be easier to see when fuel emerges free from air bubbles. Turn the ignition switch to position II so that fuel can pass through the pump.

5 If air has entered the injector pipes, slacken each union at the injectors and crank the engine until fuel emerges, then tighten securely all unions and mop up the spilt fuel. Start the engine and keep it running for a few minutes to ensure that all air has been expelled.

3 Fuel system –
contamination problems

1 If, at any time, sudden fuel filter blockage, poor starting or otherwise unsatisfactory engine performance should be traced to the appearance of black sludge or slime within the fuel system, this may be due to corrosion caused by the presence of various micro-organisms in the fuel. These can live in the fuel tank if water is allowed to remain there in significant quantities, their waste products causing corrosion of steel and other metallic components of the fuel system.

2 If the fuel system is thought to be contaminated in this way, immediately seek the advice of a Ford dealer or diesel specialist. Thorough treatment is required to cure the problem and to prevent it from occurring again.

3 If you are considering treating the vehicle on a DIY basis, proceed as follows. Do not re-use the contaminated fuel.

4 First drain and remove the fuel tank, flush it thoroughly with clean diesel fuel, and use an electric torch to examine as much as possible of its interior. If the contamination is severe, the tank must be steam-cleaned internally and then flushed again with clean diesel fuel.

5 Disconnect the fuel feed and return hoses from the injection pump, remove the fuel filter element and flush through the system's feed and return lines with clean diesel fuel.

6 Renew the filter element, refit the fuel tank and reconnect the fuel lines, then fill the tank with clean diesel fuel and bleed the system as described above. Watch carefully for signs of the problem occurring again.

7 While it is unlikely that such contamination will be found beyond the fuel filter, if it is thought to have reached the injection pump, the pump may require cleaning. This is a task only for a diesel specialist. Do not attempt to disturb any part of the pump or to clean it yourself.

8 The most common cause of excessive quantities of water being in the fuel is condensation from the water vapour in the air. Diesel fuel tanks (whether underground storage tanks or that in the vehicle) are more susceptible to this problem than petrol tanks because of petrol's higher vapour pressure. Water formation in the vehicle's tank can be minimised by keeping the tank as full as possible at all times, and by using the vehicle regularly.

9 Note that proprietary additives are available to inhibit the growth of micro-organisms in vehicle fuel tanks or storage tanks. Modern

diesel fuels should by now contain these additives in any case.

10 If you buy all your fuel from the same source and suspect that to be the source of the contamination, the owner or operator should be advised. Otherwise, the risk of taking on contaminated fuel can be minimised by using only reputable filling stations which have a good turnover.

4 Air cleaner assembly and air
inlet components – removal and refitting

Air cleaner assembly

1 Disconnect the wiring from the inlet air temperature sensor.

2 Release the hose clip and disconnect the air inlet duct from the air cleaner cover. Note that the hose clip may not be of the screw type, and will have to be separated by prising the crimped section with a small screwdriver. The clip can be re-used if care is taken, but it may be preferable to fit a screw-drive clip when refitting.

3 Disconnect the breather hose leading to the cylinder head cover.

4 Lift the air cleaner to release it from the rubber grommets, and disconnect the hose from the port underneath.

5 Check the rubber grommets for deterioration and renew them if necessary.

6 Refitting is the reverse of the removal procedure. Ensure that the air cleaner pegs seat fully in their rubber grommets.

Air inlet components

7 If removing the inlet duct between the air cleaner and turbocharger, first ensure that the engine is cool. Release the hose clip and carefully ease the duct off the turbocharger. Note that the hose clip may not be of the screw type, and will have to be separated by prising the crimped section with a small screwdriver. The clip can be re-used if care is taken, but it may be preferable to fit a screw-drive clip when refitting.

8 To remove the air inlet duct attached to the air cleaner base, first remove the air cleaner assembly as described in paragraphs 1 to 4.

9 Prise up the two clips securing the duct to the engine compartment front panel, then separate the two halves of the duct at the sleeve joint next to the battery.

10 Refitting is a reversal of removal.

5 Accelerator pedal –
removal and refitting

Removal

1 Peel back the carpet and insulation from the driver's footwell to allow access to the accelerator pedal.

2 Disconnect the wiring plug from the accelerator position sensor, then unscrew the bolts and remove the accelerator pedal assembly.

Refitting

3 Refit in the reverse order of removal. On completion, check the action of the pedal with the engine running.

6 Fuel tank – removal, inspection and refitting

Refer to Chapter 4B, Section 7.

7 Fuel gauge sender unit – removal and refitting

Refer to Chapter 4B, Section 8.

8 Fuel tank roll-over valves – removal and refitting

Refer to Chapter 4B, Section 9.

9 Fuel tank filler pipe – removal and refitting

Refer to Chapter 4B, Section 10.

10 Diesel injection system – checking

Note: *Refer to the warning note in Section 1 before proceeding.*

1 If a fault appears in the diesel injection system, first ensure that all the system wiring connectors are securely connected and free of corrosion. Then ensure that the fault is not due to poor maintenance; ie, check that the air cleaner filter element is clean, the valve clearances are correct, the cylinder compression pressures are correct, the fuel filter has been changed and the engine breather hoses are clear and undamaged, referring to Chapter 1B and Chapter 2D.

2 If these checks fail to reveal the cause of the problem, the vehicle should be taken to a suitably-equipped Ford dealer for testing. A diagnostic connector is incorporated in the engine management system wiring harness, into which dedicated electronic test equipment can be plugged. The test equipment is capable of 'interrogating' the engine management system PCM electronically and accessing its internal fault log (reading fault codes).

3 Fault codes can only be extracted from the PCM using a dedicated fault code reader. A Ford dealer will obviously have such a reader, but they are also available from other suppliers, including Haynes. It is unlikely to be cost-effective for the private owner to purchase a fault code reader, but a well-equipped local garage or auto-electrical specialist will have one.

4 Using this equipment, faults can be pinpointed quickly and simply, even if their occurrence is intermittent. Testing all the system components individually in an attempt to locate the fault by elimination is a time-consuming operation that is unlikely to be fruitful (particularly if the fault occurs dynamically), and carries a high risk of damage to the ECU's internal components.

5 Experienced home mechanics equipped with a diesel tachometer or other diagnostic equipment may be able to check the engine idle speed; if found to be out of specification, the vehicle must be taken to a suitably-equipped Ford dealer for assessment. The engine idle speed is not manually adjustable; incorrect test results indicate the need for maintenance (possibly, injector cleaning or recalibration) or a fault within the injection system.

6 If excessive smoking or knocking is evident, it may be due to a problem with the fuel injectors. Proprietary treatments are available which can be added to the fuel, in order to clean the injectors. Injectors do deteriorate with prolonged use, however, and it is reasonable to expect them to need reconditioning or renewal after 60 000 miles or so. Accurate testing, overhaul and calibration of the injectors must be left to a specialist.

11 Diesel injection system electronic components – removal and refitting

Crankshaft position sensor

1 The sensor is located at the flywheel end of the engine, low down at the rear (**see illustration**). For improved access, apply the handbrake then jack up the front of the vehicle and support it on axle stands (see *Jacking and vehicle support*).

2 Where fitted, unclip the cover from the crankshaft position sensor, then disconnect the wiring plug.

3 Unscrew the mounting bolt and withdraw the sensor. If a spacer is fitted between the sensor and engine, it is vital that this is refitted when refitting the sensor, or the sensor head will hit the rotor teeth.

4 Refitting is a reversal of removal.

Cylinder head temperature sensor

5 The switch is screwed into the left-hand (flywheel) end of the cylinder head, behind the vacuum pump and below the oil pressure warning light switch (**see illustration**).

6 Disconnect the battery negative (earth) lead (see Chapter 5A).

7 To improve access to the switch, it will be necessary to remove (or partially remove) the air cleaner inlet duct, referring to Section 4 if necessary.

8 It will also be helpful to release the hoses and remove the crankcase ventilation system oil separator from the left-hand end of the cylinder head.

9 Trace the wiring from the sensor, and disconnect it at the plug, which is clipped to the brake vacuum pump at the front of the engine (**see illustration**).

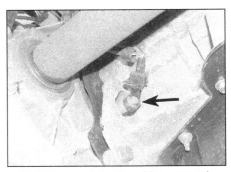

11.1 The crankshaft position sensor is located at the rear of the engine (arrowed)

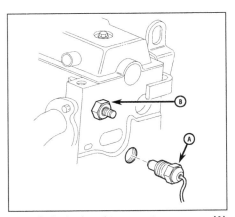

11.5 Cylinder head temperature sensor (A) is fitted below oil pressure switch (B)

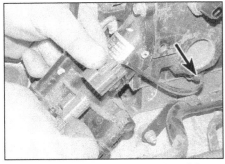

11.9 Unclip and disconnect the wiring plug, then remove the sensor (arrowed)

11.10 Cylinder head temperature sensor (arrowed)

10 The sensor can now be unscrewed and removed **(see illustration)**. However, access to the sensor is such that great difficulty may be experienced in getting a tool to fit onto it. Ultimately, it may be necessary to cut the sensor wiring, unscrew the sensor using a thin-wall socket or box spanner, then re-make the wiring after fitting, using a suitable connector.

11 Refitting is a reversal of removal. Clean the threads of the sensor and mounting hole, then refit the sensor and tighten it to the specified torque.

Inlet air temperature sensor

12 The sensor is located in the air cleaner inlet duct.

13 Disconnect the wiring from the sensor, then twist the sensor anti-clockwise and remove it **(see illustration)**.

14 Refitting is a reversal of removal.

Vehicle speed sensor

15 Refer to Chapter 7A, Section 7.

Manifold absolute pressure sensor

16 The MAP sensor is located in the centre of the engine compartment bulkhead.

17 Disconnect the vacuum hose from the port at the base of the sensor, then disconnect the wiring plug behind it.

18 Unscrew and remove the two mounting bolts, and withdraw the sensor from the bulkhead.

19 Prior to refitting, remove the vacuum hose from the inlet manifold connection, and check it for signs of perishing or splitting, especially at the pipe ends.

20 Refitting is a reversal of removal, ensuring that the wiring plug and vacuum hose are securely reconnected.

Fuel control valve

21 The control valve is fitted to the top of the fuel filter (at the right-hand rear corner of the engine compartment), and contains a bi-metal strip. Its function is to close the fuel return to the fuel tank at low fuel temperatures, allowing fuel which has been warmed by passing through the injection pump to flow back into the filter, thus warming the fuel being drawn from the tank.

11.13 Disconnecting the air temperature sensor at the air cleaner

22 Noting their positions for refitting, disconnect the fuel supply and outlet pipes from the connections at the fuel filter.

23 Extract the wire clip securing the control valve and return pipe, and release it from the top of the filter. Once again noting the fitted positions of the fuel pipes, disconnect them from each end of the valve (note that the return pipe may in this case be black, and smaller in diameter than the supply pipe).

24 Refitting is a reversal of removal. Ensure that the pipe connections are correctly and securely remade, then run the engine and check for signs of fuel leakage.

EGR valve

25 Refer to Chapter 4D, Section 3.

Clutch pedal position switch

26 Remove the trim panel above the driver's footwell to gain access to the clutch pedal.

27 Reach up and disconnect the wiring from the clutch switch at the top of the pedal, then twist the switch anti-clockwise and remove it from the pedal bracket.

28 Refitting is a reversal of removal.

Accelerator pedal sensor

29 The accelerator pedal sensor is integral with the pedal assembly, which is removed as described in Section 5.

Injection pump control unit

30 The pump control unit is integral with the injection pump, and cannot be separated from it. If a new injection pump is fitted, the PCM must be electronically 'matched' to the engine management module (ECU), otherwise the pump will not function correctly (or even at all, if the immobiliser function is not correctly set up) – this is a task for a Ford dealer, as specialised electronic equipment is required.

Powertrain Control Module

Note: *The module is fragile. Take care not to drop it, or subject it to any other kind of impact. Do not subject it to extremes of temperature, or allow it to get wet. The module wiring plug must never be disconnected while the ignition switch is on.*

31 The Powertrain Control Module is located behind the passenger footwell side trim. First

disconnect the battery negative (earth) lead (see Chapter 5A).

32 Drill out or cut off the two rivets and remove the security shield from over the module.

33 Release the module from its bracket and withdraw it downwards.

34 Undo the screw and swivel the wiring multiplug away from the module. **Do not** pull on the wiring, only on the multiplug itself.

35 Withdraw the module from inside the vehicle.

36 Refitting is a reversal of removal. Take care when refitting the multiplug, and tighten the retaining bolt by hand first. Use new pop rivets when refitting the security shield.

12 Fuel injection pump timing – checking and adjustment

Injection pump timing is carried using the TDC setting method described in Section 13. It would appear that no further checking or setting of the pump timing is possible – at least, not without dedicated test equipment. Where necessary, the injection pump should be checked and adjusted by a Ford dealer or diesel engine specialist.

13 Fuel injection pump – removal and refitting

Caution: Be careful not to allow dirt into the injection pump or injector pipes during this procedure.
Note: *If a new injection pump is fitted, there is a possibility that the engine may not run properly (or even at all) until both the Powertrain Control Module (PCM) and the new pump control unit have been electronically 'configured' using Ford diagnostic equipment. In particular, the immobiliser may not function correctly, leading to the engine not starting.*

Removal

1 Disconnect the battery negative (earth) lead (see Chapter 5A).

2 Remove the timing belt as described in Chapter 2D.

3 Remove the injection pipes as described in Section 14.

4 Remove the alternator as described in Chapter 5A, then unbolt and remove the alternator mounting bracket.

5 On models with air conditioning, remove the four bolts securing the air conditioning compressor, using the information in Chapter 3 if necessary. The refrigerant lines **must not** be disconnected – unbolt the compressor, and tie it up to one side.

6 If the car was raised to remove the alternator, refit the front wheel (if removed) and lower the car to the ground.

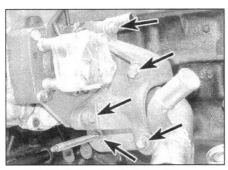

13.7 Undo the four bolts and the one retaining nut (arrowed)

13.9 Remove the seal housing retaining nuts

13.13 Undo the three pump retaining bolts (arrowed)

7 Unbolt and remove the injection pump rear mounting bracket, which is secured by four bolts and one nut **(see illustration)**.

8 Slacken the three bolts securing the injection pump sprocket, and remove the sprocket from the pump. The sprocket may need to be prevented from turning as this is done – it should prove sufficient to select a gear and apply the handbrake, but it may be necessary to suitably lock the flywheel ring gear as described in Chapter 2D, Section 7. The sprocket is sealed to the inner pulley using RTV sealant, and may need to be prised free; recover the metal gasket.

9 Remove the seven nuts which secure the injection pump oil seal housing, and withdraw the seal housing from around the pump inner pulley **(see illustration)**. Withdraw the timing belt backplate from the oil pump housing studs, noting which way round it fits.

10 Noting their positions for refitting, prise out the plastic retaining clips and disconnect the fuel supply and return pipes from the connections at the pump. The supply pipe is marked with a white band, and the return pipe has a red band.

11 Disconnect the wiring connector from the pump control unit, on top of the injection pump. The connector is secured by a clip, which slides forwards to release.

Caution: As with any ECU, take care while the wiring connector is unplugged that the pump control unit is not damaged by static discharge across the exposed wiring pins – it may be advisable to cover the pins with a strip of paper, taped in place (do not use tape directly, as this may contaminate the pins).

12 Unscrew and remove the four bolts securing the injection pump to the drive pulley. As with removal of its timing belt sprocket, it may be necessary to prevent the pulley from turning as the bolts are loosened.

13 The three pump mounting bolts can now be slackened, and the pump removed **(see illustration)**. The bolts are accessible through the elongated holes in the drive pulley – support the pump as the bolts are unscrewed, noting that the bolts cannot be removed completely. When the bolts have been fully slackened, carefully withdraw the pump from the engine. Recover the metal gasket from the pump mounting face.

Refitting

14 Ensure that the engine is still set at TDC, using the information in Chapter 2D, if necessary.

15 Offer the pump into position, with a new gasket, and fit the three mounting bolts, tightening them to the specified torque. Using a 6 mm drill bit, align the hole in the pump drive pulley with the hole in the pump rotor mounting face **(see illustration)**.

16 Keeping the drill bit in position, refit the four pump drive pulley bolts, and tighten them to the specified torque.

17 If a new pump is being fitted, note that a new pump is supplied locked in the TDC position. The locking is achieved by a small screw near the pump control unit – remove the screw, fit the small horseshoe spacer provided with the new pump, and tighten the screw to the specified torque **(see illustration)**.

18 Refit the timing belt backplate over the oil pump housing studs.

19 Before fitting the new injection pump oil seal housing, fit the plastic protector sleeve (which should be included with the oil seal housing) over the shoulder of the injection pump drive pulley.

20 Fit the new oil seal housing over the protector sleeve, and secure with the seven nuts. Note that the PTFE oil seal should not be oiled in any way prior to fitting. Tighten the seven nuts in a diagonal sequence to the

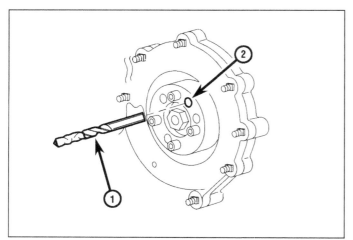

13.15 Injection pump timing hole (2) and 6 mm drill bit (1)

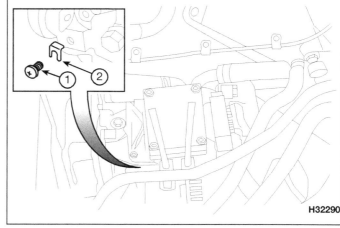

13.17 Injection pump locking screw (1) and horseshoe spacer (2)

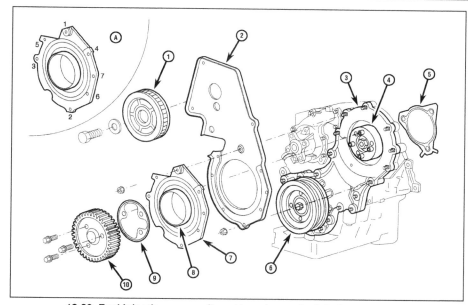

13.20 Fuel injection pump oil seal housing and related components

1 Camshaft pulley
2 Timing belt backplate
3 Oil pump housing
4 Fuel injection pump rotor
5 Metal gasket

6 Crankshaft pulley
7 Fuel injection pump oil
   seal housing
8 Protector sleeve
9 Metal gasket

10 Fuel injection pump
   sprocket
A Oil seal housing bolt
   tightening sequence

specified torque, then remove the protector sleeve **(see illustration)**.

21 Fit a new metal gasket to the pump drive pulley. Apply a coating of Loctite RTV 5910 sealant to the pulley (avoiding the three sprocket bolt holes). The three bolts should be cleaned, then lightly coated with Loctite 518 locking fluid. Offer up the timing belt sprocket, aligning the bolt holes carefully, then fit the three bolts and tighten to the specified torque.

22 Refit the injection pump rear mounting bracket, and tighten the four bolts and nut to the specified torque.

23 Refit the alternator, and (where applicable) the air conditioning compressor, using the information in Chapter 5A and Chapter 3 respectively.

24 Remove the covers from the injection pump unions, and from the injectors. Install the injector pipe assembly (Ford state that a new pipe assembly must be fitted whenever it

is disturbed), and tighten the unions at the pump to the specified torque. Fit the unions to the injectors, screwing them all the way on, but tightening them by hand only at this stage.

25 Reconnect the wiring plug to the pump control unit, and secure it in position with the locking catch.

26 Refit the fuel supply pipe (colour-coded white) to the injection pump, and secure by pressing the plastic retaining clip fully home.

27 Before reconnecting the return pipe, the injection pump should be primed with fuel, to reduce the length of time spent cranking the engine at start-up. If a new pump has been fitted (or the old pump has been off the engine for some time), priming with fuel is essential, as the fuel lubricates the pump internals, which may otherwise be dry. Follow the procedures in Section 2. If a vacuum pump is not available, a new pump can be partially primed by pouring in clean fuel via the fuel supply and return connections – take

precautions against fuel spillage on delicate components by covering the surrounding area with clean rags, and be very careful not to introduce dirt into the pump.

28 Refit the fuel return pipe (colour-coded red) to the injection pump, and secure by pressing the plastic retaining clip fully home.

29 Refit the timing belt as described in Chapter 2D.

30 Making sure that the fuel pipe unions at the injectors are fully screwed on but only hand-tight, place some clean rags around each union, to reduce the fuel spray. Keeping well clear of the injectors, crank the engine on the starter until fuel (probably preceded by air) emerges from all four pipe unions. If the engine starts, or tries to start, switch off immediately.

31 Clean up any spilt fuel, then tighten the injector pipe unions to the specified torque.

32 Start the engine, and let it idle, noting that it may take a while before a stable idle speed is achieved, as the PCM may have to re-learn some of the 'adaptive' values. As the engine warms-up, check for signs of leakage from the fuel unions. If no leakage is evident, take the car for a short journey (of at least 5 miles) to allow the PCM to complete its 'learning' process.

33 If a new injection pump has been fitted, refer to the Note at the start of this Section. Otherwise, if fuel is present at the injector unions (see paragraph 30), and the pump control unit wiring has been reconnected, the engine should start. If the engine shows signs of firing, but will not run, a push-start or tow-start may coax it to life, but this should only be attempted by the experienced DIY mechanic. If the battery has been weakened by repeated attempts to start, charge it using a battery charger before continuing.

14 Injection pipes – removal and refitting

Caution: Be careful not to allow dirt into the injection system during this procedure.

Removal

1 The injection pipes should be removed as a set. At the time of writing, it is not clear whether individual pipes are available – if so, the pipes can be separated after releasing the anti-rattle clips.

2 Disconnect the battery negative (earth) lead (see Chapter 5A).

3 Where fitted, cut the cable-ties securing the insulation cover fitted over the pump, and remove the cover.

4 Clean around the pipe unions at the injectors and at the pump. Counter-hold the pump adapters with one spanner, and unscrew the pipe union nuts with another **(see illustration)**.

5 Unscrew the injector union nuts, then remove each pair of pipes from the engine **(see illustration)**.

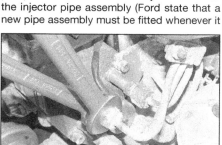

14.4 Unscrewing the pipe unions at the injector pump

14.5 Unscrew the injector union nuts

14.6a Cover the injection pump unions with a plastic bag . . .

6 Plug or cap all open unions to keep fuel in and dirt out – we used a plastic bag taped over the pump, and fingers cut from old rubber gloves over the injectors **(see illustrations)**.

7 Ford state that new pipes must be used when refitting – consult a Ford dealer or diesel specialist for advice on this point, but it would seem prudent to fit new pipes if a new pump is being installed.

Refitting

8 When refitting, make sure that all the anti-rattle clips are in place. Do not bend or strain the pipes. Blow through the pipes with compressed air (from an air line or a foot pump) to expel any debris.

9 Refit the pipe assemblies to both the injectors and injection pump, initially hand-tightening the union nuts. With the assembly in place, fully tighten the nuts to the specified torque.

10 Reconnect the battery negative (earth) lead.

11 If only the pipes have been removed, there should be no need to bleed the system (Section 2).

12 Run the engine and check the disturbed unions for leaks.

---

15 Fuel injectors – removal, testing and refitting

![warning triangle] **Warning: Exercise extreme caution when working on the fuel injectors. Never expose the hands or any part of the body to injector spray, as the high working pressure can cause the fuel to penetrate the skin, with possibly fatal results. You are strongly advised to have any work which involves testing the injectors under pressure carried out by a dealer or fuel injection specialist.**
Caution: Be careful not to allow dirt into the injection system during this procedure.

Removal

1 Disconnect the battery negative (earth) lead (see Chapter 5A). Clean around the injectors and the injection pipe unions.

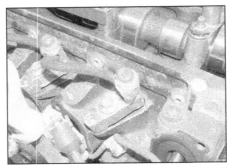

14.6b . . . and the injectors with fingers cut from a rubber glove

2 Remove the injection pipes as described in Section 14.

3 Unscrew the retaining bolts and remove the injector clamp plates, noting how they are fitted over the flat section of the injectors **(see illustration)**. New clamp bolts must be obtained for refitting.

4 The injectors are released by turning them 90° clockwise, then pulling them upwards and out. Recover the copper heat shield washers from each injector **(see illustration)**, and discard them – new washers must be used on reassembly.

5 Take care not to drop the injectors, nor allow the needles at their tips to become damaged.

Testing

6 Testing of injectors requires a special high-pressure test rig, and is best left to a professional. If the skin is exposed to spray

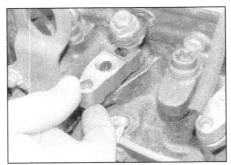

15.3 Undo the retaining bolt and remove the injector clamp plate

15.10 Tighten the injector clamp bolts to the specified torque

---

from the injectors, the pressure is high enough for diesel fuel to penetrate the skin, with potentially fatal results.

7 Defective injectors should be renewed or professionally repaired. DIY repair is not a practical proposition.

Refitting

8 Commence refitting by inserting new heat shield washers, domed faces downwards, to the injector bores.

9 Insert the injectors and turn them anti-clockwise to secure.

10 Refit the injector clamps, tightening the new retaining bolts to the specified torque **(see illustration)**.

11 Refit the injection pipes with reference to Section 14 **(see illustration)**.

---

16 Turbocharger – general information, removal and refitting

General information

1 The turbocharger increases engine efficiency by raising the pressure in the inlet manifold above atmospheric pressure. Instead of the air simply being sucked into the cylinders, it is forced in. Additional fuel is supplied by the injection pump, in proportion to the increased amount of air.

2 Energy for the operation of the turbocharger comes from the exhaust gas. The gas flows through a specially-shaped housing (the turbine housing) and in so doing,

15.4 Recover the copper washer from the injector recess in the cylinder head

15.11 Refit the injection pipes, tightening the unions up evenly

spins the turbine wheel. The turbine wheel is attached to a shaft, at the end of which is another vaned wheel, known as the compressor wheel. The compressor wheel spins in its own housing, and compresses the inducted air on the way to the inlet manifold.

3 Boost pressure (the pressure in the inlet manifold) is limited by a wastegate, which diverts the exhaust gas away from the turbine wheel in response to a pressure-sensitive actuator.

4 The turbo shaft is pressure-lubricated by its own dedicated oil feed pipe. The shaft 'floats' on a cushion of oil. Oil is returned to the sump via a return pipe that connects to the sump.

5 The turbocharger on the Endura-DI engine is integral with the exhaust manifold, and is not available separately.

Precautions

6 The turbocharger operates at extremely high speeds and temperatures. Certain precautions must be observed to avoid premature failure of the turbo, or injury to the operator.

Do not operate the turbo with any parts exposed. Foreign objects falling onto the rotating vanes could cause excessive damage and (if ejected) personal injury.

Cover the turbocharger air inlet ducts to prevent debris entering, and clean using lint-free cloths only.

Do not race the engine immediately after start-up, especially if it is cold. Give the oil a few seconds to circulate.

Always allow the engine to return to idle speed before switching it off – do not blip the throttle and switch off, as this will leave the turbo spinning without lubrication.

Allow the engine to idle for several minutes before switching off after a high-speed run.

Observe the recommended intervals for oil and filter changing, and use a reputable oil of the specified quality. Neglect of oil changing, or use of inferior oil, can cause carbon formation on the turbo shaft and subsequent failure. Thoroughly clean the area around all oil pipe unions before disconnecting them, to prevent the ingress of dirt. Store dismantled components in a sealed container to prevent contamination.

Removal

7 The turbocharger should only be removed with the engine completely cool. Disconnect the battery negative (earth) lead (see Chapter 5A).

8 Remove the air cleaner and inlet duct as described in Section 4.

9 Undo the four nuts securing the catalytic converter to the turbocharger.

10 Remove the EGR valve as described in Chapter 4D, Section 3.

11 Anticipating some oil spillage, undo the two bolts and disconnect the oil feed and

return pipe flange from the turbocharger. Recover the O-ring seal from the flange.

12 Remove the exhaust manifold nuts which can be accessed from above.

13 Apply the handbrake, then jack up the front of the vehicle and support it on axle stands (see *Jacking and vehicle support*).

14 Undo the nuts and bolts securing the catalytic converter to the intermediate pipe. Separate the joint and recover the gasket.

15 Refer to Chapter 7A and disconnect the gearchange linkage and stabiliser bar from the transmission. Move the linkage to one side and retain it using a cable tie.

16 Unscrew the bolt securing the rear engine mounting link to the transmission.

17 Undo the remaining bolts accessible from below and remove the catalytic converter and gasket.

18 Disconnect the air outlet duct from the turbocharger.

19 Support the manifold from below, then remove the remaining manifold bolts. Lower the manifold and turbocharger and remove the assembly from under the car. Recover the manifold gasket.

20 It is not advisable to separate the wastegate assembly from the turbocharger without first consulting a Ford dealer or turbocharger specialist, as the setting may be lost. Interfering with the wastegate setting may lead to a reduction in performance, or could result in engine damage.

21 If on inspection, there are any signs of internal oil contamination on the turbine or compressor wheels, this indicates failure of the turbocharger oil seals. Renewing these seals is a job best left to a turbocharger specialist. In the event of any problem with the turbocharger, one of these specialists will usually be able to rebuild a defective unit, or offer a rebuilt unit on an exchange basis, either of which will prove cheaper than a new unit.

Refitting

22 Refitting is a reversal of removal, noting the following points:

a) *Clean the mating surfaces, and use new gaskets and O-rings on all disturbed joints.*

b) *Tighten all nuts and bolts to the specified torque (where given).*

c) *Reconnect and adjust the gearchange linkage as described in Chapter 7A.*

d) *Refit the EGR valve as described in Chapter 4D, Section 3.*

17 Manifolds – removal and refitting

Inlet manifold

Removal

1 Remove the turbocharger and exhaust manifold as described in Section 16.

2 Disconnect the MAP sensor vacuum hose from the inlet manifold.

3 Unscrew and remove the two nuts and six bolts securing the inlet manifold, then unscrew the stud nearest the power steering pump bracket – the stud has a Torx end fitting, to make unscrewing it easier. Withdraw the manifold from the cylinder head. Recover the manifold gasket, and discard it – a new one should be obtained for refitting.

Refitting

4 Refitting is a reversal of the removal procedure, noting the following points:

a) *Ensure that the mating faces are clean.*

b) *Ensure that a new gasket is fitted between the manifold and the cylinder head.*

c) *With the manifold in place, refit and tighten the stud next to the power steering pump.*

d) *Tighten the retaining nuts and bolts to the specified torque, working from the centre outwards to avoid warping the manifold.*

e) *Refit the turbocharger and exhaust manifold as described in Section 16.*

Exhaust manifold

5 The exhaust manifold is removed with the turbocharger, as described in Section 16. The turbocharger housing is integral with the exhaust manifold.

18 Exhaust system – general information and component renewal

General information

1 The catalytic converter is mounted at an angle, directly below the exhaust manifold. Immediately below the converter is a short flexible section of pipe, connecting to the factory-fitted one-piece rear section, which contains the centre and rear silencers. To renew either silencer, the original rear section must be cut through mid-way between the centre and rear silencers.

2 Before making any cut, offer up the replacement exhaust section for comparison, and if necessary, adjust the cutting points as required. Bear in mind that there must be some 'overlap' allowance, as the original and replacement sections are sleeved together.

3 The system is suspended throughout its entire length by rubber mountings, with a rigid support bracket fitted below the catalytic converter.

4 To remove a part of the system, first jack up the front or rear of the car, and support it on axle stands (see *Jacking and vehicle support*). Alternatively, position the car over an inspection pit, or on car ramps.

5 Ford recommend that all nuts (such as flange joint nuts, clamp joint nuts, or converter-to-manifold nuts) are renewed on reassembly – given that they may be in less-than-perfect condition as a result of corrosion, this seems a good idea, especially as it will make subsequent removal easier.

6 Make sure that the mating faces of the exhaust system joints are cleaned thoroughly before assembling, and use new gaskets where applicable.

Catalytic converter

Removal

7 To prevent possible damage to the flexible section of pipe behind the flange joint, Ford technicians cable-tie two strips of thick metal on either side, down the length of the flexible section.

8 Remove the four nuts securing the converter to the turbocharger.

9 Loosen and remove the nuts at the flange joint just in front of the first exhaust mounting rubbers.

10 Refer to Chapter 7A and disconnect the gearchange linkage and stabiliser bar from the transmission. Move the linkage to one side and retain it using a cable tie.

11 Unscrew the bolt securing the rear engine mounting link to the transmission.

12 Support the converter, then remove the bolts securing the converter to the support bracket.

13 With the converter supported, separate the flange joint, and feed the converter rearwards and out from under the car, taking great care not to drop it or knock it, as the internals are fragile. The converter is a bulky component, and it may be necessary to rotate it as it is withdrawn – try not to bend the flexible section if possible.

Refitting

14 Refitting is a reversal of removal. Use new nuts, bolts and gaskets as necessary, and tighten all fasteners to the specified torque (where given). **Note:** *Exhaust sealant paste should not be used on any part of the exhaust system upstream of the catalytic converter (between the engine and the converter) – even if the sealant does not contain additives harmful to the converter, pieces of it may break off and foul the element, causing local overheating.*

Centre silencer

Removal

15 If the original rear section is still intact, it must be cut at a point between the centre and rear silencers. Before making the cut, offer up the replacement exhaust section for comparison, and suitably mark the cutting point on the existing system. Bear in mind that there must be some 'overlap' allowance, as the original and replacement sections are sleeved together. Take care to cut the pipe at right-angles to the pipe (and to **only** cut the pipe); clean up any rough edges.

16 If a new rear silencer has been fitted, there will be a clamped sleeve joint at the rear of the centre silencer. Loosen the clamp nuts, but do not try to separate the sleeve joint at this stage.

17 Loosen and remove the nuts, and separate the exhaust at the flange joint in front of the centre silencer (use new nuts when refitting).

18 Unhook the centre silencer from its rubber mountings. If a sleeve joint is used at the rear, twist and pull the pipes to separate the joint. Remove the centre silencer from under the car.

Refitting

19 Refitting is a reversal of removal. Clean up any sleeve joints before mating them together. Use new nuts, and tighten all fasteners securely.

Rear silencer

Removal

20 If the original rear section is still intact, it must be cut at a point between the centre and rear silencers. Before making the cut, offer up the replacement exhaust section for comparison, and suitably mark the cutting point on the existing system. Bear in mind that there must be some 'overlap' allowance, as the original and replacement sections are sleeved together. Take care to cut the pipe at right-angles to the pipe (and to **only** cut the pipe); clean up any rough edges.

21 Unhook the rear silencer from its mounting rubber(s).

22 If the rear silencer has been renewed previously, loosen the clamp nuts until the joint is free, then twist and pull the pipes relative to each other, to free and separate the sleeve joint.

23 Remove the rear silencer from under the car.

Refitting

24 Refitting is a reversal of removal. Clean up any sleeve joints before mating them together. Use new nuts (or a new clamp), and tighten the nuts securely.

Heat shield(s)

25 The heat shields are secured to the underside of the body by special nuts, or by bolts. The shields are fitted above the exhaust, to reduce radiated heat affecting the cabin or fuel tank.

26 Each shield can be removed separately, but note that some overlap each other, making it necessary to loosen another section first. If a shield is being removed to gain access to a component located behind it, it may prove sufficient in some cases to remove the retaining nuts and/or bolts, and simply lower the shield, without disturbing the exhaust system. Otherwise, remove the exhaust section as described earlier.

Chapter 4 Part D:
Emission control systems

Contents

Catalytic converter – general information and precautions 4
Diesel engine emission control systems –
   testing and component renewal 3
General information and precautions 1
Petrol engine emission control systems –
   testing and component renewal 2

Degrees of difficulty

Easy, suitable for novice with little experience	Fairly easy, suitable for beginner with some experience	Fairly difficult, suitable for competent DIY mechanic 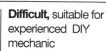	Difficult, suitable for experienced DIY mechanic 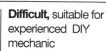	Very difficult, suitable for expert DIY or professional

Specifications

Torque wrench settings	Nm	lbf ft
Petrol engines		
EGR valve mounting bolts	31	23
EGR valve pipe to EGR valve union	55	41
EGR valve pipe to exhaust manifold union	73	54
Oxygen (lambda) sensor	42	31
Diesel engines		
EGR valve mounting bolts (Endura-DE engines)	20	15
EGR valve and tube clamp rings (Endura-DI engines)	19	14

1 General information and precautions

1 All petrol engines have the ability to use unleaded petrol and also have various other features built into the fuel system to help minimise harmful emissions. In addition, all models are equipped with the crankcase emission-control system described below. All models are also equipped with a closed-loop catalytic converter and an evaporative emission control system. In certain territories, some petrol models are equipped with an exhaust gas recirculation system.
2 All diesel engine models are also designed to meet strict emission requirements and are also equipped with a crankcase emission control system. In addition to this, all models are fitted with a two-way catalytic converter to reduce harmful exhaust emissions. To further reduce emissions, an exhaust gas recirculation (EGR) system is fitted.
3 The emission control systems function as follows.

Petrol models

Crankcase emission control

4 To reduce the emission of unburned hydrocarbons from the crankcase into the atmosphere, the engine is sealed and the blow-by gases and oil vapour are drawn from inside the crankcase, through an oil separator and regulating (PCV – positive crankcase ventilation) valve, into the inlet manifold to be burned by the engine during normal combustion **(see illustration)**.
5 Under all conditions the gases are forced out of the crankcase by the (relatively) higher crankcase pressure.

Exhaust emission control

6 To minimise the amount of pollutants which reduce emissions, an exhaust gas recirculation (EGR) system is fitted.

escape into the atmosphere, all models are fitted with a catalytic converter in the exhaust system. The system is of the closed-loop type, in which an oxygen (lambda) sensor in

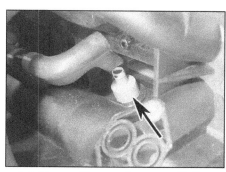

1.4 The positive crankcase ventilation (PCV) valve is located on the oil separator housing fitted to the front of the cylinder block – Zetec-SE engine

the exhaust manifold provides the fuel-injection/ignition system Powertrain Control Module (PCM) with constant feedback, enabling the PCM to adjust the mixture to provide the best possible conditions for the converter to operate.

7 The oxygen sensor has a heating element built-in that is controlled by the PCM through a relay to quickly bring the sensor's tip to an efficient operating temperature. The sensor's tip is sensitive to oxygen and sends the PCM a varying voltage depending on the amount of oxygen in the exhaust gases; if the intake air/fuel mixture is too rich, the exhaust gases are low in oxygen so the sensor sends a low-voltage signal, the voltage rising as the mixture weakens and the amount of oxygen rises in the exhaust gases. Peak conversion efficiency of all major pollutants occurs if the intake air/fuel mixture is maintained at the chemically-correct ratio for the complete combustion of petrol of 14.7 parts (by weight) of air to 1 part of fuel (the 'stoichiometric' ratio). The sensor output voltage alters in a large step at this point, the PCM using the signal change as a reference point and correcting the intake air/fuel mixture accordingly by altering the fuel injector pulse width.

Evaporative emission control

8 To minimise the escape into the atmosphere of unburned hydrocarbons, an evaporative emissions control system is also fitted to all models. The fuel tank filler cap is sealed and a charcoal canister is mounted behind the fuel tank on the underbody. The canister collects the petrol vapours generated in the tank when the car is parked and stores them until they can be cleared from the canister (under the control of the fuel-injection/ignition system PCM) via the purge valve into the inlet tract to be burned by the engine during normal combustion. The purge valve is located on the bulkhead in the engine compartment.

9 To ensure that the engine runs correctly when it is cold and/or idling and to protect the catalytic converter from the effects of an over-rich mixture, the purge control valve is not opened by the PCM until the engine has warmed-up, and the engine is under load; the valve solenoid is then modulated on and off to allow the stored vapour to pass into the inlet tract.

Diesel models

Crankcase emission control

10 To reduce the emission of unburned hydrocarbons from the crankcase into the atmosphere, the engine is sealed and the blow-by gases and oil vapour are drawn from inside the crankcase, through a hose located on the rear of the engine, into the inlet manifold to be burned by the engine during normal combustion. A further hose from the cylinder head cover to the crankcase ensures the blow-by gases are circulated freely. Since

the inlet manifold depression does not vary on a diesel engine, there is no regulating valve as fitted to petrol engines.

Exhaust emission control

11 To minimise the level of exhaust pollutants released into the atmosphere, a catalytic converter is fitted in the exhaust system of all models.

12 The catalytic converter consists of a canister containing a fine mesh impregnated with a catalyst material, over which the hot exhaust gases pass. The catalyst speeds up the oxidation of harmful carbon monoxide, unburnt hydrocarbons and soot, effectively reducing the quantity of harmful products released into the atmosphere via the exhaust gases.

Exhaust gas recirculation system

13 This system is designed to recirculate small quantities of exhaust gas into the inlet manifold, and therefore into the combustion process. This process reduces the level of oxides of nitrogen present in the final exhaust gas which is released into the atmosphere.

14 The volume of exhaust gas recirculated is controlled by a regulator supplied with vacuum from the brake servo vacuum pump. The regulator is controlled by the Powertrain Control Module.

Catalytic converter precautions

15 For long life and satisfactory operation of the catalytic converter, certain precautions must be observed. These are as follows.

16 For petrol engines, only use unleaded fuel. Leaded fuel will damage the catalyst and the oxygen sensor.

17 Do not run the engine for long periods if it is misfiring. Unburnt fuel entering the catalytic converter can cause it to overheat, resulting in permanent damage. For the same reason, do not try to start the engine by pushing or towing the car, nor crank it on the starter motor for long periods.

18 Do not strike or drop the catalytic converter. The ceramic honeycomb which forms part of its internal structure may be damaged.

19 Always renew seals and gaskets upstream of the catalytic converter (between

the engine and converter) whenever they are disturbed.

2 Petrol engine emission control systems – testing and component renewal

Crankcase emission control

1 The components of this system require no attention other than to check that the hose and PCV valve are clear and undamaged at regular intervals. If the hoses are blocked the oil separator housing should be removed from the front of the cylinder block and cleaned; when refitting the housing, fit a new gasket **(see illustration)**.

Evaporative emission control system

Testing

2 If the system is thought to be faulty, disconnect the hoses from the charcoal canister and purge control valve and check that they are clear by blowing through them. If the purge control valve or charcoal canister are thought to be faulty, they must be renewed.

Charcoal canister renewal

3 The charcoal canister is located under the rear of the vehicle, behind the fuel tank. First chock the front wheels then jack up the rear of the vehicle and support it on axle stands (see *Jacking and vehicle support*).

4 Unscrew the mounting bolts and lower the canister cover from the underbody.

5 Disconnect the hoses and remove the canister from under the vehicle.

6 Fit the new canister using a reversal of the removal procedure.

Purge valve renewal

7 The purge valve is mounted on the left-hand end of the engine compartment bulkhead **(see illustration)**.

8 To renew the purge valve, first disconnect the wiring plug.

9 Disconnect the hoses from the valve noting their locations, then detach the valve from its mounting bracket.

2.1 Always fit a new gasket if the oil separator housing is removed – Zetec-SE engine

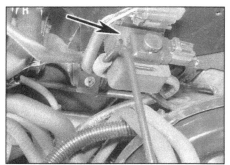

2.7 Evaporative emission control system purge valve location on the bulkhead in the engine compartment – Zetec-SE engine

10 Fit the new purge valve using a reversal of the removal procedure.

Exhaust emission control

Testing

11 The performance of the catalytic converter can be checked only by measuring the exhaust gases using a good-quality, carefully-calibrated exhaust gas analyser.
12 If the CO level at the tailpipe is too high, the vehicle should be taken to a Ford dealer so that the complete fuel injection and ignition systems, including the oxygen sensor, can be thoroughly checked using the special diagnostic equipment. Once these have been checked and are known to be free from faults, the fault must be in the catalytic converter, which must be renewed.

Catalytic converter renewal

13 Refer to Chapter 4A.

Oxygen (lambda) sensor renewal

Note: *The oxygen sensor is delicate and will not work if it is dropped or knocked, if its power supply is disrupted, or if any cleaning materials are used on it.*

14 Trace the wiring back from the oxygen sensor to the connector and disconnect the wiring.
15 Unscrew the sensor and remove it from the exhaust manifold.
16 Clean the threads of the sensor and the threads in the exhaust manifold. If necessary for improved access to the manifold, remove the manifold shroud components.
17 Insert the sensor in the manifold and tighten to the specified torque.
18 Refit the manifold shrouds where removed.
19 Reconnect the wiring making sure that it is in no danger of contacting the exhaust manifold.

Exhaust gas recirculation system

Testing

20 Testing of the system should be entrusted to a Ford dealer.

Valve renewal

21 Unbolt and remove the shroud components from the exhaust manifold.
22 Disconnect the EGR vacuum hose and the two pressure transducer pipes.
23 Remove the oxygen (lambda) sensor as described previously.
24 Unscrew the EGR valve pipe union nut from the exhaust manifold.
25 With the assembly on the bench, unscrew the pipe union nut and remove the EGR pipe and pressure transducer pipes from the valve. To obtain a gas tight seal, a new EGR pipe assembly must be used when refitting.
26 Refitting is a reversal of removal, noting the following points:
a) *Fit the new EGR pipe assembly to the EGR valve but do not tighten the pipe union nut until the valve has been refitted.*

b) *Offer the valve into position, and fit the mounting bolts and EGR valve pipe-to-manifold union hand-tight.*
c) *Tighten the valve mounting bolts to the specified torque then tighten the pipe unions.*
d) *Refit the remainder of the disturbed components.*

---

3 Diesel engine emission control systems – testing and component renewal

Crankcase emission control

1 The components of this system require no attention other than to check that the hoses are clear and undamaged at regular intervals.

Exhaust emission control

Testing

2 The performance of the catalytic converter can be checked only by measuring the exhaust gases using a good-quality, carefully-calibrated exhaust gas analyser.
3 Before assuming that the catalytic converter is faulty, it is worth checking the problem is not due to a faulty injector. Refer to your Ford dealer for further information.

Catalytic converter renewal

4 Refer to Chapter 4B.

Exhaust gas recirculation system

Testing

5 Testing of the system should be entrusted to a Ford dealer.

Valve renewal (Endura-DE engine)

6 Loosen the clips and disconnect the air inlet duct from the inlet manifold and air cleaner.
7 Depress the clip and disconnect the wiring from the exhaust gas recirculation valve at the left-hand end of the cylinder head **(see illustration)**.
8 Disconnect the vacuum pipe.
9 Unscrew the mounting bolts and remove the valve from the inlet manifold and transfer tube flange. Recover the gaskets.

3.7 Exhaust gas recirculation valve – Endura-DE engine

10 Tape over or cover with cloth rag the openings in the inlet manifold and EGR transfer tube.
11 Clean the mating faces of the valve and inlet manifold.
12 Using new gaskets fit the new valve to the inlet manifold and transfer tube. Tighten the bolts to the specified torque.
13 Reconnect the vacuum pipe and wiring, then refit the air inlet duct.

Valve renewal (Endura-DI engine)

14 Disconnect the EGR valve vacuum pipe and wiring connector.
15 Disconnect the inlet air temperature sensor wiring connector.
16 Slacken the clip and disconnect the air inlet duct.
17 Disconnect the EGR valve tube from the exhaust manifold.
18 Release the clamp ring securing the EGR valve to the inlet manifold.
19 Withdraw the EGR valve and recover the gaskets.
20 Tape over or cover with cloth rag the openings in the inlet and exhaust manifolds.
21 Clean the mating faces of the valve and manifolds.
22 Using new gaskets refit the valve using a reverse of the removal procedure

---

4 Catalytic converter – general information and precautions

The catalytic converter is a reliable and simple device which needs no maintenance in itself, but there are some facts of which an owner should be aware if the converter is to function properly for its full service life.

Petrol models

a) *DO NOT use leaded petrol ('4-star' or LRP) in a car equipped with a catalytic converter – the lead will coat the precious metals, reducing their converting efficiency and will eventually destroy the converter.*
b) *Always keep the ignition and fuel systems well-maintained in accordance with the manufacturer's schedule.*
c) *If the engine develops a misfire, do not drive the car at all (or at least as little as possible) until the fault is cured.*
d) *DO NOT push- or tow-start the car – this will soak the catalytic converter in unburned fuel, causing it to overheat when the engine does start.*
e) *DO NOT switch off the ignition at high engine speeds.*
f) *DO NOT use fuel or engine oil additives – these may contain substances harmful to the catalytic converter.*
g) *DO NOT continue to use the car if the engine burns oil to the extent of leaving a visible trail of blue smoke.*
h) *Remember that the catalytic converter*

operates at very high temperatures. DO NOT, therefore, park the car in dry undergrowth, over long grass or piles of dead leaves after a long run.

i) Remember that the catalytic converter is FRAGILE – do not strike it with tools during servicing work.

j) In some cases a sulphurous smell (like that of rotten eggs) may be noticed from the exhaust. This is common to many catalytic converter-equipped cars and once the car has covered a few thousand miles the problem should disappear.

k) The catalytic converter, used on a well-maintained and well-driven car, should last for between 50 000 and 100 000 miles – if the converter is no longer effective it must be renewed.

Diesel models

Refer to the information given in parts f, g, h and i of the petrol models information given above.

Chapter 5 Part A:
Starting and charging systems

Contents

Alternator – removal and refitting 7
Alternator – testing and overhaul 8
Alternator drivebelt – removal, refitting and tensioning 6
Battery – removal and refitting 4
Battery – testing and charging 3
Battery check . . . . .See *Weekly checks*
Charging system – testing 5
Electrical fault finding – general information 2

Electrical system check . . . . .See *Weekly checks*
General information, precautions and battery disconnection 1
Ignition switch – removal and refitting . . . . .See Chapter 12
Oil pressure warning light switch – removal and refitting 12
Starter motor – removal and refitting 10
Starter motor – testing and overhaul 11
Starting system – testing 9

Degrees of difficulty

Easy, suitable for novice with little experience	**Fairly easy,** suitable for beginner with some experience	**Fairly difficult,** suitable for competent DIY mechanic	**Difficult,** suitable for experienced DIY mechanic	**Very difficult,** suitable for expert DIY or professional

Specifications

System type . . . . 12-volt, negative earth

Battery

Type . . . . Lead-acid, low-maintenance or 'maintenance-free'
Charge condition:
   Poor . . . . 12.5 volts
   Normal . . . . 12.6 volts
   Good . . . . 12.7 volts

Alternator

Type . . . . Bosch, Magnetti Marelli or Mitsubishi
Output . . . . 70 amps
Regulated voltage . . . . 13.5 to 14.8 volts

Starter motor

Type . . . . Bosch or Magnetti Marelli

Torque wrench settings

	Nm	lbf ft
Alternator drive coupling bolts (Endura-DI engines)	12	9
Alternator drive pulley bracket bolts (Endura-DI engines)	25	18
Alternator mountings:		
1.25 and 1.4 litre Zetec-SE engines:		
Upper and lower bolts	50	37
Rear support bolt	25	18
1.6 litre Zetec-SE engines	45	33
1.3 litre Endura-E engines	25	18
Diesel engines	25	18
Starter motor mounting bolts	35	26
Starter motor mounting bracket:		
Bolt	25	18
Nut	6	4

1 General information, precautions and battery disconnection

General information

The engine electrical system consists mainly of the charging and starting systems. Because of their engine-related functions, these components are covered separately from the body electrical devices such as the lights, instruments, etc (which are covered in Chapter 12). Information on the ignition system is covered in Part B of this Chapter.

The electrical system is of 12-volt negative earth type.

The battery is of the low-maintenance or 'maintenance-free' (sealed for life) type and is charged by the alternator, which is belt-driven from the crankshaft pulley.

The starter motor is of the pre-engaged type incorporating an integral solenoid. On starting, the solenoid moves the drive pinion into engagement with the flywheel ring gear before the starter motor is energised. Once the engine has started, a one-way clutch prevents the motor armature being driven by the engine until the pinion disengages from the flywheel.

Precautions

Further details of the various systems are given in the relevant Sections of this Chapter. While some repair procedures are given, the usual course of action is to renew the component concerned. The owner whose interest extends beyond mere component renewal should obtain a copy of the *Automobile Electrical & Electronic Systems Manual*, available from the publishers of this manual.

It is necessary to take extra care when working on the electrical system to avoid damage to semi-conductor devices (diodes and transistors), and to avoid the risk of personal injury. In addition to the precautions given in *Safety First!* at the beginning of this manual, observe the following when working on the system:

Always remove rings, watches, etc before

working on the electrical system. Even with the battery disconnected, capacitive discharge could occur if a component's live terminal is earthed through a metal object. This could cause a shock or nasty burn.

Do not reverse the battery connections. Components such as the alternator, electronic control units, or any other components having semi-conductor circuitry could be irreparably damaged.

If the engine is being started using jump leads and a slave battery, connect the batteries *positive-to-positive* and *negative-to-negative* (see *Jump starting*). This also applies when connecting a battery charger.

Never disconnect the battery terminals, the alternator, any electrical wiring or any test instruments when the engine is running.

Do not allow the engine to turn the alternator when the alternator is not connected.

Never 'test' for alternator output by 'flashing' the output lead to earth.

Never use an ohmmeter of the type incorporating a hand-cranked generator for circuit or continuity testing.

Always ensure that the battery negative lead is disconnected when working on the electrical system.

Before using electric-arc welding equipment on the car, disconnect the battery, alternator and components such as the fuel injection/ignition electronic control unit to protect them from the risk of damage.

Battery disconnection

Several systems fitted to the vehicle require battery power to be available at all times, either to ensure their continued operation (such as the clock) or to maintain control unit memories (such as that in the engine management system's ECU) which would be wiped if the battery were to be disconnected. Whenever the battery is to be disconnected, first note the following, to ensure that there are no unforeseen consequences of this action:

a) *First, on any vehicle with central locking, it is a wise precaution to remove the key from the ignition, and to keep it with you, so that it does not get locked in if the central locking should engage accidentally*

when the battery is reconnected.

b) *On cars equipped with an engine management system, the system's ECU will lose the information stored in its memory – referred to by Ford as the 'KAM' (Keep-Alive Memory) – when the battery is disconnected. This includes idling and operating values, and any fault codes detected; in the case of the fault codes, if it is thought likely that the system has developed a fault for which the corresponding code has been logged, the vehicle must be taken to a Ford dealer for the codes to be read, using the special diagnostic equipment necessary for this. Whenever the battery is disconnected, the information relating to idle speed control and other operating values will have to be re-programmed into the unit's memory. The ECU does this by itself, but until then, there may be surging, hesitation, erratic idle and a generally inferior level of performance. To allow the ECU to relearn these values, start the engine and run it as close to idle speed as possible until it reaches its normal operating temperature, then run it for approximately two minutes at 1200 rpm. Next, drive the vehicle as far as necessary – approximately 5 miles of varied driving conditions is usually sufficient – to complete the relearning process.*

c) *If the battery is disconnected while the alarm system is armed or activated, the alarm will remain in the same state when the battery is reconnected. The same applies to the engine immobiliser system (where fitted).*

d) *If a Ford 'Keycode' audio unit is fitted, and the unit and/or the battery is disconnected, the unit will not function again on reconnection until the correct security code is entered. Details of this procedure, which varies according to the unit and model year, are given in the 'Ford Audio Systems Operating Guide' supplied with the vehicle when new, with the unit itself being given in a 'Radio Passport' and/or a 'Keycode Label' at the same time. Ensure you have the correct code before you disconnect the battery. For obvious security reasons, the procedure* is not given in this manual. If you do not have the code or details of the correct procedure, but can supply proof of ownership and a legitimate reason for wanting this information, the vehicle's selling dealer may be able to help.

Devices known as 'memory-savers' (or 'code-savers') can be used to avoid some of the above problems. Precise details vary according to the device used. Typically, it is plugged into the cigarette lighter, and is connected by its own wires to a spare battery; the vehicle's own battery is then disconnected from the electrical system, leaving the 'memory-saver' to pass sufficient current to maintain audio unit security codes and ECU memory values, and also to run permanently-live circuits such as the clock, all the while isolating the battery in the event of a short-circuit occurring while work is carried out.

 Warning: Some of these devices allow a considerable amount of current to pass, which can mean that many of the vehicle's systems are still operational when the main battery is disconnected. If a 'memory-saver' is used, ensure that the circuit concerned is actually 'dead' before carrying out any work on it.

2 Electrical fault finding – general information

Refer to Chapter 12.

3 Battery – testing and charging

Testing

Standard and low-maintenance battery

1 If the vehicle covers a small annual mileage it is worthwhile checking the specific gravity of the electrolyte every three months to determine the state of charge of the battery. Use a hydrometer to make the check and compare the results with the following table. Note that the specific gravity readings assume an electrolyte temperature of 15°C (60°F); for every 10°C (18°F) below 15°C (60°F) subtract 0.007. For every 10°C (18°F) above 15°C (60°F) add 0.007.

	Ambient temperature	
	Above 25°C	**Below 25°C**
Fully-charged	1.210 to 1.230	1.270 to 1.290
70% charged	1.170 to 1.190	1.230 to 1.250
Discharged	1.050 to 1.070	1.110 to 1.130

2 If the battery condition is suspect, first check the specific gravity of electrolyte in each cell. A variation of 0.040 or more between any cells indicates loss of electrolyte or deterioration of the internal plates.

3 If the specific gravity variation is 0.040 or more, the battery should be renewed. If the cell variation is satisfactory but the battery is discharged, it should be charged as described later in this Section.

Maintenance-free battery

4 In cases where a 'sealed for life' maintenance-free battery is fitted, topping-up and testing of the electrolyte in each cell is not possible. The condition of the battery can therefore only be tested using a battery condition indicator or a voltmeter.

5 Certain models may be fitted with a 'Delco' type maintenance-free battery, with a built-in charge condition indicator. The indicator is located in the top of the battery casing, and indicates the condition of the battery from its colour. If the indicator shows green, then the battery is in a good state of charge. If the indicator turns darker, eventually to black, then the battery requires charging, as described later in this Section. If the indicator shows clear/yellow, then the electrolyte level in the battery is too low to allow further use, and the battery should be renewed. **Do not** attempt to charge, load or jump start a battery when the indicator shows clear/yellow.

All battery types

6 If testing the battery using a voltmeter, connect the voltmeter across the battery and compare the result with those given in the Specifications under 'charge condition'. The test is only accurate if the battery has not been subjected to any kind of charge for the previous six hours. If this is not the case, switch on the headlights for 30 seconds, then wait four to five minutes before testing the battery after switching off the headlights. All other electrical circuits must be switched off, so check that the doors and tailgate/bootlid are fully shut when making the test.

7 If the voltage reading is less than 12.2 volts, then the battery is discharged, whilst a reading of 12.2 to 12.4 volts indicates a partially-discharged condition.

8 If the battery is to be charged, remove it from the vehicle (Section 4) and charge it as described later in this Section.

Charging

Standard and low-maintenance battery

Note: *The following is intended as a guide only. Always refer to the manufacturer's recommendations (often printed on a label attached to the battery), and always disconnect both terminal leads before charging a battery.*

9 Charge the battery at a rate of 3.5 to 4 amps and continue to charge the battery at this rate until no further rise in specific gravity is noted over a four hour period.

10 Alternatively, a trickle charger charging at the rate of 1.5 amps can safely be used overnight.

11 Specially rapid 'boost' charges which are

claimed to restore the power of the battery in 1 to 2 hours are not recommended, as they can cause serious damage to the battery plates through overheating.

12 While charging the battery, note that the temperature of the electrolyte should never exceed 37.8°C (100°F).

Maintenance-free battery

Note: *The following is intended as a guide only. Always refer to the manufacturer's recommendations (often printed on a label attached to the battery), and always disconnect both terminal leads before charging a battery.*

13 This battery type takes considerably longer to fully recharge than the standard type, the time taken being dependent on the extent of discharge, but it can take anything up to three days.

14 A constant voltage type charger is required, to be set, when connected, to 13.9 to 14.9 volts with a charger current below 25 amps. Using this method, the battery should be usable within three hours, giving a voltage reading of 12.5 volts, but this is for a partially-discharged battery and, as mentioned, full charging can take considerably longer.

15 If the battery is to be charged from a fully-discharged state (condition reading less than 12.2 volts), have it recharged by your Ford dealer or local automotive electrician, as the charge rate is higher and constant supervision during charging is necessary.

4 Battery – removal and refitting

Note: *Refer to the warnings given in 'Safety First!' and in Section 1 of this Chapter before starting work.*

Removal

1 The battery is located on the left-hand side of the engine compartment, on a platform on the vehicle structure above the transmission **(see illustration)**.

2 Loosen the clamp nut, then detach the earth lead from the battery negative (earth)

4.1 The battery location in the Endura-DE engine compartment

4.4 Removing the clamp bar from the top of the battery

terminal post. This is the terminal to disconnect before working on, or disconnecting, any electrical component on the vehicle. Position the lead away from the battery.

3 Pivot up the plastic cover from the positive terminal, then loosen the positive lead clamp nut. Detach the positive lead from the terminal and position it away from the battery.

4 Unscrew the nuts and remove the clamp bar from the top of the battery **(see illustration)**. Lift the battery from its location, keeping it in an upright position to avoid the possibility of corrosive electrolyte spilling onto the paintwork.

5 If necessary, unbolt the battery box from the platform and detach the wiring supports.

6 Clean the battery terminal posts, clamps and the battery casing. If the platform is rusted as a result of battery acid spilling onto it, clean it thoroughly and re-paint.

7.2 Disengaging the auxiliary drivebelt from the alternator pulley

7 If you are renewing the battery, make sure that you get the correct one. Dispose of the old battery in a responsible fashion. Most local authorities have facilities for the collection and disposal of such items.

Refitting

8 Refitting is a reversal of removal. Smear the battery terminals with a petroleum-based jelly after reconnecting to protect against corrosion. Always connect the positive terminal clamp first and the negative terminal clamp last.

5 Charging system – testing

Note: *Refer to the warnings given in 'Safety First!' and in Section 1 of this Chapter before starting work.*

1 If the ignition warning light fails to illuminate when the ignition is switched on, first check the alternator wiring connections for security. If satisfactory, check that the warning light bulb has not blown, and that the bulbholder is secure in its location in the instrument panel. If the light still fails to illuminate, check the continuity of the warning light feed wire from the alternator to the bulbholder. If all is satisfactory, the alternator is at fault and should be renewed or taken to an auto-electrician for testing and repair.

2 If the ignition warning light illuminates when the engine is running, stop the engine and check that the drivebelt is intact and correctly tensioned (see Chapter 1A or 1B) and that the alternator connections are secure. If all is so far satisfactory, have the alternator checked by an auto-electrician for testing and repair.

3 If the alternator output is suspect even though the warning light functions correctly, the regulated voltage may be checked as follows.

4 Connect a voltmeter across the battery terminals and start the engine.

5 Increase the engine speed until the voltmeter reading remains steady; the reading should be approximately 12 to 13 volts, and no more than 14 volts.

6 Switch on as many electrical accessories

(eg, the headlights, heated rear window and heater blower) as possible, and check that the alternator maintains the regulated voltage at around 13 to 14 volts.

7 If the regulated voltage is not as stated, the fault may be due to worn brushes, weak brush springs, a faulty voltage regulator, a faulty diode, a severed phase winding or worn or damaged slip rings. The alternator should be renewed or taken to an auto-electrician for testing and repair.

6 Alternator drivebelt – removal, refitting and tensioning

Refer to the procedure given for the auxiliary drivebelt in Chapter 1A or 1B.

7 Alternator – removal and refitting

Note: *Refer to the warnings given in 'Safety First!' and in Section 1 of this Chapter before starting work.*

Removal

1 Loosen the clamp nut, then detach the earth lead from the battery negative (earth) terminal post. Position the lead well away from the battery.

1.25 and 1.4 litre Zetec-SE engine models

2 Fit a ring spanner on the auxiliary drivebelt tensioner, and rotate it clockwise to release the tension. Note the routing of the drivebelt, then disengage it from the pulleys and remove it **(see illustration)**.

3 Unscrew the nut and disconnect the battery positive cable from the terminal on top of the alternator **(see illustration)**. A socket will be required as the plastic terminal cover is brittle and easily broken with a ring spanner.

4 Depress the wire clip and disconnect the field winding wiring from the top of the alternator **(see illustration)**.

5 Unscrew and remove the lower mounting bolt **(see illustration)**.

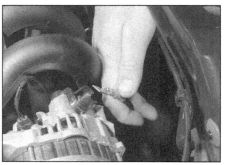

7.3 Disconnecting the battery positive cable from the alternator terminal

7.4 Disconnecting the field winding wiring

7.5 Alternator lower mounting bolt

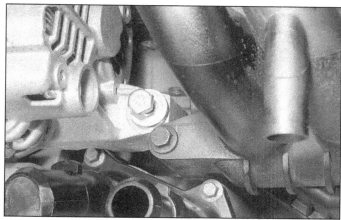

7.6 Bolt securing the rear of the alternator to the cylinder block

7.7 Unscrew and remove the upper mounting bolt, then remove the alternator from the engine

6 Unscrew and remove the bolt securing the rear of the alternator to the cylinder block **(see illustration)**.

7 Support the alternator then unscrew and remove the upper mounting bolt and remove the alternator **(see illustration)**.

1.6 litre Zetec-SE engine models

8 Fit a ring spanner on the auxiliary drivebelt tensioner, and rotate it clockwise to release the tension. Note the routing of the drivebelt, then disengage it from the pulleys and remove it.

9 Unscrew the nut and disconnect the battery positive cable from the terminal on top of the alternator. A socket will be required as the plastic terminal cover is brittle and easily broken with a ring spanner.

10 Disconnect the field winding wiring from the top of the alternator.

11 Unscrew and remove the alternator front mounting bolts.

12 Unscrew the nut from the alternator upper mounting stud, then unscrew the stud from the cylinder head. The stud can be removed using a suitable stud extractor or, alternatively, screw two nuts onto the stud, lock them together and unscrew the inner nut.

13 Withdraw the alternator from the engine.

Endura-E engine models with automatic tensioner

14 Apply the handbrake, then jack up the front of the vehicle and support on axle stands (see *Jacking and vehicle support*). Remove the right-hand front roadwheel.

15 Remove the catalytic converter as described in Chapter 4A.

16 Unscrew the bolts from the crankshaft pulley lower cover then unclip it from the coolant hose.

17 Fit a ring spanner on the auxiliary drivebelt tensioner, and rotate it clockwise to release the tension. Note the routing of the drivebelt, then disengage it from the pulleys and remove it.

18 On models with air conditioning, unbolt the compressor and support it to one side with wire or string (refer to Chapter 3).

19 Disconnect the wiring from the rear of the alternator.

20 Unscrew and remove the rear mounting bolts.

21 Support the alternator, then unscrew and remove the front mounting bolts. Withdraw the alternator from the engine compartment.

Endura-E engine models without automatic tensioner

22 Apply the handbrake, then jack up the front of the vehicle and support on axle stands (see *Jacking and vehicle support*). Remove the right-hand front roadwheel.

23 Slacken the alternator upper mounting/adjustment bolt and the two lower mounting nuts and bolts and move the alternator toward the engine to release the drivebelt tension. Note how the drivebelt is routed, then remove the belt from the pulleys.

24 Disconnect the wiring from the rear of the alternator.

25 Unscrew and remove the alternator upper mounting/adjuster bolt.

26 Support the alternator and unscrew and remove the lower mounting nuts and bolts. Withdraw the alternator from the engine compartment.

Endura-DE engine models

27 Apply the handbrake, then jack up the front of the vehicle and support on axle stands (see *Jacking and vehicle support*). Remove the right-hand front roadwheel.

28 Loosen the adjustment clamp bolts, then release the drivebelt tension by backing off the adjustment bolt. Note the routing of the drivebelt, then withdraw it downwards from the pulleys.

29 On models with air conditioning, unbolt the compressor and support it to one side with wire or string (refer to Chapter 3).

30 Unbolt and remove the drivebelt tensioner.

31 Disconnect the wiring from the alternator.

32 Support the alternator, then unscrew and remove the mounting bolts and withdraw the alternator downwards from the engine compartment.

Endura-DI engine models

33 Apply the handbrake, then jack up the front of the vehicle and support on axle stands (see *Jacking and vehicle support*). Remove the right-hand front roadwheel.

34 Remove the auxiliary drivebelt as described in Chapter 1B.

35 Disconnect the wiring from the alternator.

36 Undo the two bolts securing the alternator drive pulley bracket to the front of the engine.

37 Undo the three alternator drive coupling bolts and remove the drive coupling and pulley assembly.

38 Remove the electric cooling fan assembly from the radiator as described in Chapter 3.

39 Support the alternator, then unscrew and remove the mounting bolts and withdraw the alternator downwards from the engine compartment.

Refitting

40 Refitting is a reversal of removal, but refer to Chapter 3 for details of refitting cooling system components and Chapter 1A or 1B for details of refitting the auxiliary drivebelt.

**8 Alternator –
testing and overhaul**

If the alternator is thought to be suspect, it should be removed from the vehicle and taken to an auto-electrician for testing. Most auto-electricians will be able to supply and fit brushes at a reasonable cost. However, check on the cost of repairs before proceeding as it may prove more economical to obtain a new or exchange alternator.

9 Starting system – testing

Note: *Refer to the precautions given in 'Safety First!' and in Section 1 of this Chapter before starting work.*

1 If the starter motor fails to operate when the ignition key is turned to the appropriate position, the following possible causes may be to blame.
  a) *The battery is faulty.*
  b) *The electrical connections between the switch, solenoid, battery and starter motor are somewhere failing to pass the necessary current from the battery through the starter to earth.*
  c) *The solenoid is faulty.*
  d) *The starter motor is mechanically or electrically defective.*

2 To check the battery, switch on the headlights. If they dim after a few seconds, this indicates that the battery is discharged – recharge (see Section 3) or renew the battery. If the headlights glow brightly, operate the ignition switch and observe the lights. If they dim, then this indicates that current is reaching the starter motor, therefore the fault must lie in the starter motor. If the lights continue to glow brightly (and no clicking sound can be heard from the starter motor

solenoid), this indicates that there is a fault in the circuit or solenoid – see following paragraphs. If the starter motor turns slowly when operated, but the battery is in good condition, then this indicates that either the starter motor is faulty, or there is considerable resistance somewhere in the circuit.

3 If a fault in the circuit is suspected, disconnect the battery leads (including the earth connection to the body), the starter/solenoid wiring and the engine/transmission earth strap. Thoroughly clean the connections, and reconnect the leads and wiring, then use a voltmeter or test lamp to check that full battery voltage is available at the battery positive lead connection to the solenoid, and that the earth is sound. Smear petroleum jelly around the battery terminals to prevent corrosion – corroded connections are amongst the most frequent causes of electrical system faults.

4 If the battery and all connections are in good condition, check the circuit by disconnecting the wire from the solenoid terminal. Connect a voltmeter or test lamp between the wire end and a good earth (such as the battery negative terminal), and check that the wire is live when the ignition switch is turned to the 'start' position. If it is, then the circuit is sound – if not, the circuit wiring can be checked as described in Chapter 12.

5 The solenoid contacts can be checked by connecting a voltmeter or test lamp between

the battery positive feed connection on the starter side of the solenoid, and earth. When the ignition switch is turned to the 'start' position, there should be a reading or lighted bulb, as applicable. If there is no reading or lighted bulb, the solenoid is faulty and should be renewed.

6 If the circuit and solenoid are proved sound, the fault must lie in the starter motor. In this event, it may be possible to have the starter motor overhauled by a specialist, but check on the cost of spares before proceeding, as it may prove more economical to obtain a new or exchange motor.

10 Starter motor – removal and refitting

Note: *Refer to the warnings given in 'Safety First!' and in Section 1 of this Chapter before starting work.*

Removal

1 Loosen the clamp nut, then detach the earth lead from the battery negative (earth) terminal. Position the lead away from the battery.

Zetec-SE engine models

2 Apply the handbrake, then jack up the front of the vehicle and support on axle stands (see *Jacking and vehicle support*).

3 Working beneath the front of the engine, unscrew the two nuts and disconnect the wiring from the starter motor.

4 Unscrew and remove the lower then upper starter mounting bolts from the transmission bellhousing, noting that the upper bolts secure the throttle body housing support bracket **(see illustrations)**.

5 Support the starter motor, then unscrew and remove the rear support bolt and withdraw the unit to the right from the transmission bellhousing and downwards from the engine compartment. As there is limited working room, take care not to damage the wiring or terminals, or the surrounding pipes and dipstick tube **(see illustrations)**.

10.4a Removing the starter motor lower mounting bolt

10.4b The starter motor upper mounting bolts also secure the throttle body housing support bracket

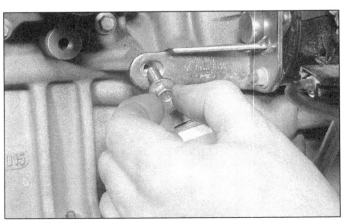

10.5a Unscrew and remove the rear support bolt . . .

10.5b . . . then withdraw the starter motor

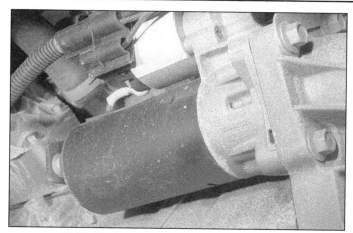

10.14 Starter motor on the Endura-DE engine

12.1 Oil pressure switch location on the Endura-DE engine

Endura-E engine models

6 Apply the handbrake, then jack up the front of the vehicle and support on axle stands (see *Jacking and vehicle support*).

7 Unclip and remove the air duct leading from the air cleaner to the throttle housing.

8 Working beneath the vehicle, disconnect the wiring at the connector above the starter motor.

9 Unscrew and remove the starter motor upper mounting bolts.

10 Unscrew and remove the lower mounting bolt, then withdraw the starter motor and lower it for access to the wiring. Unscrew the nuts and disconnect the wiring, then withdraw the starter motor from the engine compartment.

Endura-DE engine models

11 Apply the handbrake, then jack up the front of the vehicle and support on axle stands (see *Jacking and vehicle support*).

12 Working beneath the vehicle, unscrew the nuts and disconnect the wiring from the starter motor.

13 Unscrew the nuts and bolt, and remove the starter motor rear support bracket.

14 Unscrew the mounting bolts and withdraw the starter motor from the transmission **(see illustration)**.

Endura-DI engine models

15 Apply the handbrake, then jack up the front of the vehicle and support on axle stands (see *Jacking and vehicle support*).

16 Remove the electric cooling fan assembly from the radiator as described in Chapter 3.

17 Working beneath the vehicle, unscrew the nuts and disconnect the wiring from the starter motor.

18 Unscrew the mounting bolts and withdraw the starter motor from the transmission.

Refitting

19 Refitting is a reversal of removal, but tighten the mounting bolts to the specified torque.

11 Starter motor – testing and overhaul

If the starter motor is thought to be suspect, it should be removed from the vehicle and taken to an auto-electrician for testing. Most auto-electricians will be able to supply and fit brushes at a reasonable cost. However, check on the cost of repairs before proceeding as it may prove more economical to obtain a new or exchange motor.

12 Oil pressure warning light switch – removal and refitting

Removal

1 On petrol engines, the oil pressure switch is located on the front of the cylinder block. On diesel engines, it is located on the left-hand end of the cylinder head **(see illustration)**.

2 On petrol engine models, apply the handbrake then jack up the front of the vehicle and support on axle stands (see *Jacking and vehicle support*).

3 Disconnect the wiring from the oil pressure warning light switch.

4 Unscrew the switch and remove it from the cylinder block/head. Be prepared for some loss of oil.

Refitting

5 Clean the threads of the switch and the threads in the cylinder block/head. Also wipe away any oil which may have escaped from the switch hole.

6 Apply suitable sealant to the threads, then insert the switch and tighten securely.

7 Reconnect the wiring and where necessary lower the vehicle to the ground.

8 Check and if necessary top-up the engine oil as described in *Weekly checks*.

Notes

Chapter 5 Part B:
Ignition system – petrol engine models

Contents

Crankshaft position sensor – removal and refitting 4
Electronic ignition HT coil – removal, testing and refitting 3
Ignition system – general information and precautions 1
Ignition system – testing 2

Ignition system check . . . . See Chapter 1A
Ignition timing – checking and adjustment 5
Spark plug renewal . . . . See Chapter 1A

Degrees of difficulty

Easy, suitable for novice with little experience		**Fairly easy,** suitable for beginner with some experience		**Fairly difficult,** suitable for competent DIY mechanic		**Difficult,** suitable for experienced DIY mechanic		**Very difficult,** suitable for expert DIY or professional

Specifications

General

System type . . . . Electronic distributorless ignition system (DIS) with ignition module controlled by EEC V engine management module (Powertrain control module)

Firing order:
   1.25, 1.4 and 1.6 litre Zetec-SE engines 1-3-4-2
   1.3 litre Endura-E engine 1-2-4-3
Location of No 1 cylinder . . . . Timing belt end

Ignition system data

Ignition timing . . . . Controlled by the Powertrain Control Module (PCM)
Electronic Ignition (EI) coil resistances:
   Primary windings . . . . 0.4 to 0.6 ohms
   Secondary windings . . . . 10 500 to 16 500 ohms

Torque wrench setting	**Nm**	**lbf ft**
Ignition coil	6	4

1 Ignition system – general information and precautions

General information

The ignition system is integrated with the fuel injection system to form a combined engine management system under the control of the Powertrain control module (PCM) (see Chapter 4A for further information). The main ignition system components include the ignition switch, the battery, the crankshaft speed/position sensor, the ignition coil, and the spark plugs.

A Distributorless Ignition System (DIS) is fitted where the main functions of the conventional distributor are replaced by a computerised module within the Powertrain Control Module. The remote ignition coil unit combines a double-ended pair of coils – each time a coil receives an ignition signal, two sparks are produced, one at each end of the secondary windings. One spark goes to a cylinder on its compression stroke and the other goes to the corresponding cylinder on its exhaust stroke. The first will give the correct power stroke, but the second spark will have no effect (a 'wasted spark'), occurring as it does during exhaust conditions.

The information contained in this Chapter concentrates on the ignition-related components of the engine management system. Information covering the fuel, exhaust and emission control components can be found in the applicable Parts of Chapter 4.

Precautions

The following precautions must be observed, to prevent damage to the ignition system components and to reduce risk of personal injury.

a) *Do not keep the ignition on for more than 10 seconds if the engine will not start.*
b) *Ensure that the ignition is switched off before disconnecting any of the ignition wiring.*

c) *Ensure that the ignition is switched off before connecting or disconnecting any ignition test equipment, such as a timing light.*
d) *Do not earth the coil primary or secondary circuits.*

⚠️ *Warning: Voltages produced by an electronic ignition system are considerably higher than those produced by conventional ignition systems. Extreme care must be taken when working on the system with the ignition switched on. Persons with surgically-implanted cardiac pacemaker devices should keep well clear of the ignition circuits, components and test equipment.*

2 Ignition system – testing

1 If the engine either will not turn over at all, or only turns very slowly, check the battery and starter motor as described in Chapter 5A.
2 If the engine turns over at normal speed but will not start, check the HT circuit by connecting a timing light (following the manufacturer's instructions) and turning the engine over on the starter motor; if the light flashes, voltage is reaching the spark plugs, so these should be checked first. If the light does not flash, check the HT leads themselves using the information given in Chapter 1A.
3 If there is still no spark, check the coil's primary and secondary winding resistance as described in Section 3; renew the coil if faulty, but be careful to check carefully the wiring connections themselves before doing so, to ensure that the fault is not due to dirty or poorly-fastened connectors.
4 If these checks fail to reveal the cause of the problem the vehicle should be taken to a suitably-equipped Ford dealer for testing. A wiring block connector is incorporated in the engine management circuit into which a special electronic diagnostic tester can be plugged. The tester will locate the fault quickly and simply, alleviating the need to test all the system components individually which is a time consuming operation that carries a high risk of damaging the PCM. If necessary, the

system wiring and wiring connectors can be checked as described in Chapter 12.
5 If the engine runs but has an irregular misfire, check the low tension wiring on the ignition coil ensuring that all connections are clean and securely fastened.
6 Check that the coil HT leads are clean and dry. Check the leads themselves and the spark plugs (by substitution, if necessary).
7 Regular misfiring is probably due to a fault in the HT leads or spark plugs. Use a timing light (as described above) to check whether HT voltage is present at all leads.
8 If HT voltage is not present on any particular lead, the fault will be in that lead or in the ignition coil. If HT is present on all leads, the fault will be in the spark plugs; check and renew them if there is any doubt about their condition.
9 If no HT is present, check the coil; its secondary windings may be breaking down under load.

3 Electronic ignition HT coil – removal, testing and refitting

Removal

1 On the Endura-E engine the ignition coil is bolted to the right-hand rear of the engine. On the Zetec-SE engine the ignition coil is bolted to the coolant outlet elbow on the left-hand end of the cylinder head.
2 Make sure the ignition is switched off, then disconnect the low tension wiring from the coil.
3 Identify the HT leads for position then carefully pull them from the terminals on the coil.
4 Unscrew the mounting bolts and remove the ignition coil from the engine compartment (see illustration).

Testing

5 Using an ohmmeter, measure the resistances of the ignition coil's primary and secondary windings and compare with the information given in the Specifications. Renew the coil if necessary.

Refitting

6 Refitting is a reversal of removal.

4 Crankshaft position sensor – removal and refitting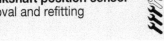

Removal

1 The crankshaft position sensor is located on the front left-hand end of the cylinder block. For improved access apply the handbrake, then jack up the front of the vehicle and support it on axle stands (see *Jacking and vehicle support*).
2 Unhook the metal cover from the sensor (see illustration).

3.4 Ignition coil bolted to the top of the coolant outlet elbow on the left-hand end of the cylinder head (showing removal together with the elbow during engine overhaul)

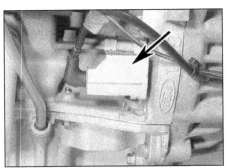

4.2 Unhook the metal cover . . .

4.3 . . . then disconnect the wiring

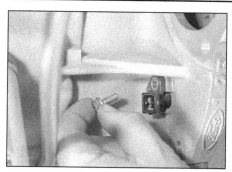

4.4a Unscrew the bolt . . .

4.4b . . . and withdraw the crankshaft position sensor

3 Depress the wire clip and disconnect the wiring from the sensor **(see illustration)**.

4 Unscrew the bolt and withdraw the sensor from the engine rear flange **(see illustrations)**.

Refitting

5 Refitting is a reversal of removal.

5 Ignition timing – checking and adjustment

Due to the nature of the ignition system, the ignition timing is constantly being monitored and adjusted by the engine management PCM, and nominal values cannot be given. Therefore, it is not possible for the home mechanic to check the ignition timing.

The only way in which the ignition timing can be checked is using special electronic test equipment, connected to the engine management system diagnostic connector (refer to Chapter 4A). No adjustment of the ignition timing is possible. Should the ignition timing be incorrect, then a fault must be present in the engine management system.

Notes

Chapter 5 Part C:
Pre-heating system – diesel engine models

Contents

Fuel heater – general information, removal and refitting 3
Glow plugs – removal, inspection and refitting 2
Pre-heating system – description and testing 1

Degrees of difficulty

Easy, suitable for novice with little experience	**Fairly easy,** suitable for beginner with some experience	**Fairly difficult,** suitable for competent DIY mechanic	**Difficult,** suitable for experienced DIY mechanic	**Very difficult,** suitable for expert DIY or professional

Specifications

Glow plugs
Type . . . .   Bosch 0 250 201 049

Torque wrench setting

	Nm	lbf ft
Glow plugs	28	21

1 Pre-heating system – description and testing

Description

1 Each swirl chamber has a heater plug (commonly called a glow plug) screwed into it. The plugs are electrically operated before, during, and a short time after start-up when the engine is cold. Electrical feed to the glow plugs and glow plug indicator lamp are controlled by the Powertrain Control Module (PCM).

2 The glow plugs are energised when the ignition is switched on, and they remain on together with the indicator lamp for a period varying between 1 and 10 seconds, depending on the temperature of the engine coolant. After the indicator lamp is extinguished, the glow plugs remain energised for a period up to 3 seconds, however if the engine is started in this period the glow plugs will remain on for a period up to 40 seconds depending on the engine coolant temperature. With the coolant at 80°C the period is 0 seconds and with the coolant at –40°C the period is 40 seconds.

3 A warning light in the instrument panel tells the driver that pre-heating is taking place. When the light goes out, the engine is ready to be started. If no attempt is made to start, the timer then cuts off the supply in order to avoid draining the battery and overheating the glow plugs.

Testing

4 If the system malfunctions, testing is ultimately by substitution of known good units, but some preliminary checks may be made as follows.

5 Connect a voltmeter or 12-volt test lamp between the glow plug supply cable and earth (engine or vehicle metal). Make sure that the live connection is kept clear of the engine and bodywork.

6 Have an assistant switch on the ignition and check that voltage is applied to the glow plugs. Note the time for which the warning light is lit and the total time for which voltage is applied before the system cuts out. Switch off the ignition.

7 If the results of the check do not come within the periods indicated in paragraph 2, refer to Chapters 4B and 12 and check the relevant temperature sensor and power supply.

8 If an ammeter of suitable range (0 to 50 amp approx) is available, connect it between the glow plug feed wire and the bus bar. During the pre-heating period the ammeter should show a current draw of approximately 8 amps per working plug, ie, 32 amps if all four plugs are working. If one or more plugs appear not to be drawing current, remove the bus bar and check each plug separately with a continuity tester or self-powered test lamp.

9 If there is no supply at all to the glow plugs, the associated wiring is at fault.

10 To locate a defective glow plug, disconnect the main supply cable and the interconnecting wire or strap from the top of the glow plugs. Be careful not to drop the nuts and washers.

11 Use a continuity tester, or a 12-volt test lamp connected to the battery positive terminal, to check for continuity between each glow plug terminal and earth. The resistance of a glow plug in good condition is very low (less than 1 ohm), so if the test lamp does not light or the continuity tester shows a high resistance the glow plug is certainly defective.

12 If an ammeter is available, the current draw of each glow plug can be checked. After an initial surge of around 15 to 20 amps, each plug should draw around 10 amps. Any plug which draws much more or less than this is probably defective.

13 As a final check the glow plugs can be removed and inspected as described in Section 2.

2 Glow plugs – removal, inspection and refitting

Removal

Caution: If the pre-heating system has just been energised, or if the engine has been running, the glow plugs may be very hot.

1 Disconnect the battery negative (earth) lead (see Chapter 5A).

2.2 Glow plug feed wire connection

2.3 Unscrewing a glow plug terminal nut

2 Disconnect the feed wire from the bus bar **(see illustration)**.

3 Unscrew the terminal nut from each plug to be removed. Remove the nuts, washers and bus bar **(see illustration)**.

4 Clean around the glow plug seats then unscrew and remove them **(see illustration)**.

Inspection

5 Inspect the glow plugs for damage. Burnt or eroded glow plug tips can be caused by a bad injector spray pattern. Have the injectors checked if this sort of damage is found.

6 If the glow plugs are in good physical condition, check them electrically using a 12-volt test lamp or continuity tester as described in the previous Section.

7 The glow plugs can be energised by applying 12 volts to them to verify that they heat up evenly and in the required time. Observe the following precautions:

2.4 Glow plug removed from cylinder head

a) Support the glow plug by clamping it carefully in a vice or self-locking pliers. Remember it will become red-hot.

b) Make sure that the power supply or test lead incorporates a fuse or overload trip to protect against damage from a short-circuit.

c) After testing, allow the glow plug to cool for several minutes before attempting to handle it.

8 A glow plug in good condition will start to glow red at the tip after drawing current for 5 seconds or so. Any plug which takes much longer to start glowing, or which starts glowing in the middle instead of at the tip, is defective.

Refitting

9 When refitting, apply a little anti-seize compound to the glow plug threads. Screw

3.1 The fuel heater is located on the left-hand end of the cylinder head

the glow plugs into place and tighten them to the specified torque.

10 Refit the bus bar and washers and secure with the nuts. Make sure that the clamping areas are clean.

11 Reconnect the feed wire and the battery earth lead.

3 Fuel heater – general information, removal and refitting

General information

1 An electrically-operated fuel heater is fitted in the fuel line leading to the fuel filter housing, to prevent the fuel 'waxing' at low temperatures **(see illustration)**. The heater is controlled by an internal thermostat. When the fuel is below a predetermined temperature, current to the heater warms the fuel.

Removal

Caution: Be careful not to allow dirt into the fuel system during the following procedure.

2 Obtain a container to catch spilt fuel.

3 Disconnect the battery negative (earth) lead (see Chapter 5A).

4 Disconnect the multiplug from the base of the fuel heater.

5 Depress the tabs on the quick release connector and disconnect the fuel supply pipe from the heater inlet pipe.

6 Release the fuel filter inlet pipe from the support clip.

7 Depress the tabs on the quick release connector and disconnect the inlet pipe from the fuel filter.

8 Unscrew the bolt and remove the fuel heater and bracket from the engine compartment.

9 Release the two clips and remove the heater from the bracket.

Refitting

10 Refitting is the reverse of the removal procedure. On completion, prime the fuel system with reference to Chapter 4B, then carry out leak checks directly after the engine is first started.

Chapter 6
Clutch

Contents

Clutch – general check .See Chapter 1A or 1B
Clutch assembly – removal, inspection and refitting 7
Clutch hydraulic hoses – removal and refitting 4
Clutch hydraulic system – bleeding 5
Clutch master cylinder – removal and refitting 2

Clutch pedal – removal, inspection, refitting and adjustment 6
Clutch release bearing – removal, inspection and refitting 8
Clutch slave cylinder – removal and refitting 3
General information 1

Degrees of difficulty

Easy, suitable for novice with little experience		Fairly easy, suitable for beginner with some experience		Fairly difficult, suitable for competent DIY mechanic		Difficult, suitable for experienced DIY mechanic		Very difficult, suitable for expert DIY or professional	

Specifications

General

Clutch type . . . . Single dry plate, diaphragm spring, hydraulically-operated release mechanism

Clutch disc

Diameter:
    Petrol engine models . . . . 180.0 mm
    Diesel engine models:
        Endura-DE engine . . . . 210.0 mm
        Endura-DI engine . . . . 220.0 mm
Friction material thickness (new) . . . . 8.3 mm (approximate)

Clutch pedal

Pedal travel* . . . . 125.0 ± 3.0 mm
*Not applicable to later models – see text, Section 6

Torque wrench settings

	Nm	lbf ft
Clutch slave cylinder	10	7
Clutch slave cylinder pre-loading valve	10	7
Pressure plate-to-flywheel bolts	30	22
Slave cylinder bleed valve	14	10

1 General information

The clutch consists of a friction disc, a pressure plate assembly, a release bearing and hydraulic slave cylinder; all of these components are contained in the large cast-aluminium alloy bellhousing, sandwiched between the engine and the transmission.

The hydraulic master cylinder is located in the pedal bracket on the bulkhead, and the clutch fluid reservoir is shared with the brake fluid reservoir on the top of the brake master cylinder. Inside the reservoir each circuit has its own compartment, so that in the event of fluid loss in the clutch circuit the brake circuit remains fully operational.

The clutch disc (friction disc) is fitted between the engine flywheel and the clutch pressure plate, and is allowed to slide on the transmission input shaft splines.

The pressure plate assembly is bolted to the engine flywheel. When the engine is running, drive is transmitted from the crankshaft, via the flywheel, to the friction disc (these components being clamped securely together by the pressure plate assembly) and from the friction disc to the transmission input shaft.

To interrupt the drive, the spring pressure must be relaxed by the hydraulically-operated release mechanism. Depressing the clutch pedal operates the master cylinder which in turn operates the slave cylinder and presses the release bearing against the pressure plate spring fingers. This causes the springs to deform and releases the clamping force on the pressure plate.

When the pedal is released, the diaphragm spring forces the pressure plate into contact with the friction linings on the friction disc. The disc is now firmly sandwiched between the pressure plate and the flywheel, thus transmitting engine power to the transmission.

On pre-August 1999 models, a pre-loading valve is fitted on the fluid inlet to the slave cylinder. This valve maintains a pressure of approximately 1.0 bar between the valve and the slave cylinder in order to keep the release bearing constantly pressed against the pressure plate. Upstream of the valve there is no pressure, in order to prevent vibrations being transmitted to the clutch pedal. On later models, the pre-loading valve is not fitted and the pre-load is produced by a spring.

Wear of the friction material on the friction disc is automatically compensated for by the operation of the hydraulic system. As the friction material on the disc wears, the pressure plate moves towards the flywheel causing the clutch diaphragm spring inner fingers to move outwards. When the clutch pedal is released, excess fluid is expelled through the master cylinder into the fluid reservoir.

2 Clutch master cylinder – removal and refitting

Removal

1 Remove the filler cap from the brake master cylinder reservoir on top of the brake master cylinder, and syphon the hydraulic fluid from the reservoir until it is below the outlet to the clutch master cylinder. Alternatively, open the slave cylinder bleed screw, and gently pump the clutch pedal to expel the fluid through a plastic tube connected to the screw; tighten the screw when all the fluid has been removed.

⚠ **Warning: Do not syphon the fluid by mouth, as it is poisonous; use a syringe or an old poultry baster.**

2 Wipe clean the area around the master cylinder fluid outlets on the engine compartment bulkhead. Remove the clip and disconnect the hydraulic fluid supply hose from the master cylinder inlet stub. Plug the hose to prevent further loss of fluid.

3 Extract the clip from the quick release connection on the master cylinder, then remove the pressure hose and tie it to one side. Plug the end of the hose or tape over the end.

4 Inside the vehicle, reach up under the clutch pedal and disconnect the return spring from the bracket.

5 Extract the retaining clip and withdraw the pin attaching the master cylinder pushrod to the clutch pedal. Use a punch to drive it out.

6 Pull up the clutch pedal to release it from the master cylinder pushrod.

7 Unscrew and remove the bolts securing the master cylinder to the bracket. Note that it will be necessary to depress the brake pedal in order to reach all of the bolts.

8 Withdraw the master cylinder from the bracket together with the sponge rubber padding.

9 If the master cylinder is faulty it must be renewed, as the manufacturers do not supply a repair kit.

Refitting

10 Locate the master cylinder in the bracket together with the sponge padding then insert the mounting bolts. Tighten the bolts securely.

11 Apply a smear of grease to the pushrod pin, then align the pushrod eye with the pedal, insert the pin from the left-hand side of the bracket and fit the retaining clip.

12 Reconnect the return spring to the bracket.

13 In the engine compartment, clean the end of the pressure hose then insert it in the quick release connection on the master cylinder and refit the clip.

14 Fit the supply hose to the top of the master cylinder and retain with the clip.

15 Check and if necessary adjust the pedal travel as described in Section 6.

16 Refill the master cylinder reservoir with fresh fluid, then bleed the hydraulic system as described in Section 5.

3 Clutch slave cylinder – removal and refitting

Removal

1 Remove the transmission as described in Chapter 7A. Note that this procedure includes locating a hose clamp on the hydraulic pressure hose, releasing the pressure line from the support, then disconnecting the line from the pre-loading valve (where fitted) by extracting the clip from the quick release connection **(see illustrations)**.

3.1a Hose clamp fitted to the clutch hydraulic pressure hose

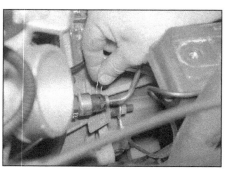

3.1b Extract the clip . . .

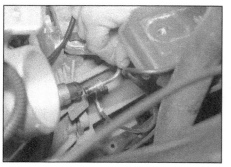

3.1c . . . and disconnect the line from the pre-loading valve

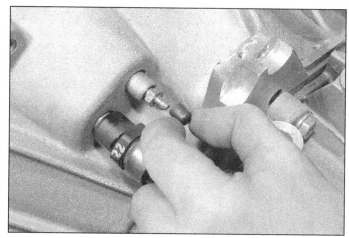

3.2a Remove the protective cap . . .

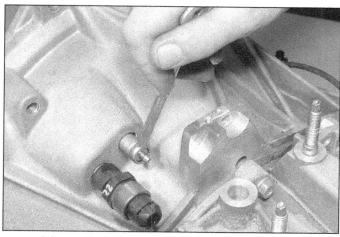

3.2b . . . then unscrew and remove the bleed screw

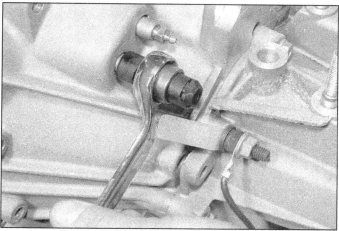

3.3a Unscrew the pre-loading valve . . .

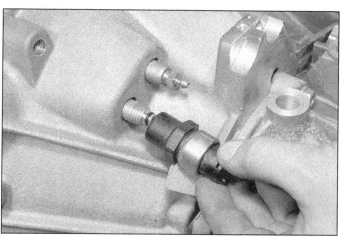

3.3b . . . and remove it from the slave cylinder inlet

2 Remove the protective cap from the slave cylinder bleed screw, then unscrew and remove the bleed screw **(see illustrations)**. Be prepared for some loss of fluid by placing a cloth rag around the screw.

3 Unscrew and remove the pre-loading valve (where fitted) from the slave cylinder inlet on the outside of the bellhousing **(see illustrations)**.

4 Inside the bellhousing, unscrew and remove the mounting bolts, then withdraw the slave cylinder over the transmission input shaft **(see illustrations)**.

5 With the slave cylinder removed, it is recommended that the transmission input shaft oil seal is renewed. Use a suitable tool to hook it out of the transmission casing and over the input shaft. Refer to Chapter 7A if necessary.

6 Remove the release bearing from the slave cylinder by tapping the cylinder on the workbench or against a block of wood.

7 If the slave cylinder is faulty it must be renewed, as the manufacturers do not supply repair kits.

Refitting

8 Locate the release bearing on the slave

3.4a Unscrew the mounting bolts . . .

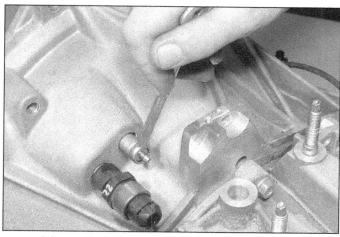

3.4b . . . and withdraw the slave cylinder over the transmission input shaft

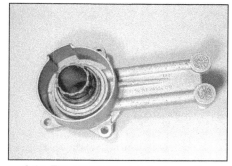

3.4c The clutch slave cylinder on the bench, with the release bearing removed

cylinder making sure it is correctly seated.

9 Locate a new oil seal over the input shaft and into the transmission housing (refer to Chapter 7A), then slide the slave cylinder onto the shaft.

10 Insert the mounting bolts and tighten them progressively to the specified torque. As the bolts are tightened make sure that the oil seal enters the transmission housing correctly.

Caution: Do not exceed the torque wrench setting, otherwise the pre-loading valve may not function correctly.

11 Refit the pre-loading valve (where applicable) to the slave cylinder and tighten to the specified torque.

12 Refit and tighten the bleed screw and fit the protective cap.

13 Refit the transmission as described in Chapter 7A and reconnect the pre-loading valve. Refill the master cylinder reservoir with fresh fluid, then bleed the hydraulic system as described in Section 5.

4 Clutch hydraulic hoses – removal and refitting

Caution: Hydraulic fluid can damage vehicle paintwork. Take the necessary precautions to prevent spillage of fluid.

Removal

1 Remove the filler cap from the brake master cylinder reservoir on top of the brake master cylinder, and syphon the hydraulic fluid from the reservoir until it is below the outlet to the clutch master cylinder. Alternatively, open the slave cylinder bleed screw, and gently pump the clutch pedal to expel the fluid through a plastic tube connected to the screw; tighten the screw when all the fluid has been removed.

2 To remove the supply hose, remove the clips then disconnect the hose from the reservoir and master cylinder.

3 To remove the pressure hose, first wipe all traces of dirt from the master cylinder and slave cylinder. Extract the clip from the quick release connections on the master cylinder and slave cylinder, then remove the hose.

Refitting

4 Refitting is a reversal of removal, but on completion bleed the hydraulic system as described in Section 5.

5 Clutch hydraulic system – bleeding

Warning: Hydraulic fluid is poisonous; wash off immediately and thoroughly in the case of skin contact, and seek immediate medical advice if any fluid is swallowed or gets into the eyes. Certain types of hydraulic fluid are flammable, and

may ignite when allowed into contact with hot components; when servicing any hydraulic system, it is safest to assume that the fluid is flammable, and to take precautions against the risk of fire as though it is petrol that is being handled. Hydraulic fluid is also an effective paint stripper, and will attack plastics; if any is spilt, it should be washed off immediately, using copious quantities of fresh water. Finally, it is hygroscopic (it absorbs moisture from the air) – old fluid may be contaminated and unfit for further use. When topping-up or renewing the fluid, always use the recommended type, and ensure that it comes from a freshly-opened sealed container.

1 The correct operation of any hydraulic system is only possible after removing all air from the components and circuit; this is achieved by bleeding the system.

2 During the bleeding procedure, add only clean, unused hydraulic fluid of the recommended type; never re-use fluid that has already been bled from the system. Ensure that sufficient fluid is available before starting work.

3 If there is any possibility of incorrect fluid being already in the system, the hydraulic circuit must be flushed completely with uncontaminated, correct fluid.

4 If hydraulic fluid has been lost from the system, or air has entered because of a leak, ensure that the fault is cured before continuing further.

5 The bleed screw is screwed into the slave cylinder extension which is positioned on the top of the transmission bellhousing.

6 First check that all the hydraulic hoses are securely fitted to the master and slave cylinders. Clean any dirt from around the bleed screw.

7 Unscrew the brake master cylinder fluid reservoir cap, and top up the fluid level to the upper (MAX) level line; refit the cap loosely, and remember to maintain the fluid level at least above the lower (MIN) level line throughout the procedure, or there is a risk of further air entering the system.

8 There are a number of one-man, do-it-yourself bleeding kits currently available from motor accessory shops. It is recommended that one of these kits is used whenever possible, as they greatly simplify the bleeding operation, and reduce the risk of expelled air and fluid being drawn back into the system. If such a kit is not available, the basic (two-man) method must be used, which is described in detail below.

9 If a kit is to be used, prepare the vehicle as described previously, and follow the kit manufacturer's instructions, as the procedure may vary slightly according to the type being used; generally, they are as outlined below in the relevant sub-section.

Bleeding

Basic (two-man) method

10 Collect a clean glass jar, a suitable length of plastic or rubber tubing which is a tight fit

over the bleed screw, and a ring spanner to fit the screw. The help of an assistant will also be required.

11 Remove the protective cap from the slave cylinder bleed screw. Fit the spanner and tube to the screw, place the other end of the tube in the jar, and pour in sufficient fluid to cover the end of the tube.

12 Ensure that the fluid level is maintained at least above the lower level line in the reservoir throughout the procedure.

13 Loosen the bleed screw half a turn, then have the assistant slowly depress and release the clutch pedal several times until fluid free of air bubbles emerges (see illustration). On the final stroke have the assistant hold the pedal fully depressed. Note that the pedal must be fully depressed and fully released each time.

14 With the pedal held down, tighten the bleed screw and have the assistant fully release the pedal slowly. Check the reservoir fluid level and top-up if necessary, then check the operation of the pedal. After the initial free movement, increased pressure should be felt as the clutch pressure plate diaphragm spring is operated.

15 If the pedal feels spongy, air still remains in the hydraulic system and the bleeding operation must be repeated as described in the previous paragraphs.

16 With the hydraulic system bled, tighten the bleed screw securely then remove the tube and spanner and refit the dust cap. Do not overtighten the bleed screw.

Using a one-way valve kit

17 As the name implies, these kits consist of a length of tubing with a one-way valve fitted, to prevent expelled air and fluid being drawn back into the system; some kits include a translucent container, which can be positioned so that the air bubbles can be more easily seen flowing from the end of the tube.

18 The kit is connected to the bleed screw, which is then opened. The user returns to the driver's seat, depresses the clutch pedal with a smooth, steady stroke, and slowly releases it; this is repeated until the expelled fluid is clear of air bubbles.

19 Note that these kits simplify work so much that it is easy to forget the clutch fluid reservoir level; ensure that this is maintained at least above the lower level line at all times.

5.13 Bleeding the clutch hydraulic circuit

Using a pressure-bleeding kit

20 These kits are usually operated by the reservoir of pressurised air contained in the spare tyre. However, note that it will probably be necessary to reduce the pressure to a lower level than normal; refer to the instructions supplied with the kit.

21 By connecting a pressurised, fluid-filled container to the clutch fluid reservoir, bleeding can be carried out simply by opening the bleed screw and allowing the fluid to flow out until no more air bubbles can be seen in the expelled fluid.

22 This method has the advantage that the large reservoir of fluid provides an additional safeguard against air being drawn into the system during bleeding.

All methods

23 When bleeding is complete, and correct pedal feel is restored, check that the bleed screw is securely tightened and wash off any spilt fluid. Refit the dust cap to the bleed screw.

24 Check the hydraulic fluid level in the master cylinder reservoir, and top-up if necessary.

25 Discard any hydraulic fluid that has been bled from the system; it will not be fit for re-use.

26 If the clutch is not operating correctly after carrying out the bleeding procedure, the master cylinder or slave cylinder may be faulty.

6 Clutch pedal – removal, inspection, refitting and adjustment

Removal

1 Disconnect the battery negative (earth) lead (see Chapter 5A).

2 Inside the vehicle, reach up under the clutch pedal and disconnect the return spring from the bracket.

3 Disconnect the wiring from the clutch switch, then twist the switch and remove it from the pedal bracket.

4 Extract the retaining clip and withdraw the pin attaching the master cylinder pushrod to the clutch pedal. If necessary, use a punch to drive it out. Pull up the clutch pedal to release it from the master cylinder pushrod.

5 Extract the retaining clip from the left-hand end of the pedal pivot shaft, then push the pivot shaft to the right until it clears the clutch pedal.

6 Withdraw the clutch pedal from the pedal bracket.

7 If necessary, prise out the bushes on each side of the pedal.

Inspection

8 Clean the bushes and pedal and inspect them for wear and damage. The bushes may be renewed separately, however if they are worn excessively, the pivot shaft must be checked and if necessary renewed as well. Refer to Chapter 9 for details of removing the brake pedal.

9 Check the return spring and renew it if necessary.

Refitting

10 Refitting is a reversal of removal, but apply multi-purpose grease to the pedal pivot shafts and bushes and make sure that the retaining clips are fully engaged with their grooves.

Adjustment

Note: *Adjustment is only necessary on pre-1999 models. On later models the pedal stop screw is not fitted and adjustment is not required.*

11 Check that the clutch pedal operates freely and that there is no obstruction or excess matting on the floor. If the pedal is spongy, the hydraulic system must be bled to remove any air as described in Section 5.

12 With the pedal fully released, measure the distance from the floor to the pedal rubber (second groove from bottom) and record.

13 Now fully depress the pedal and measure the distance again. The difference between the two measurements is the pedal travel. If this is not as given in the Specifications,

adjust the position of the pedal stop screw by loosening the locknut, repositioning the adjustment screw then tightening the locknut. Note that if the pedal travel is excessive, the master cylinder will be damaged.

7 Clutch assembly – removal, inspection and refitting

 Warning: Dust created by clutch wear and deposited on the clutch components may contain asbestos, which is a health hazard. DO NOT blow it out with compressed air, or inhale any of it. DO NOT use petrol or petroleum-based solvents to clean off the dust. Brake system cleaner or methylated spirit should be used to flush the dust into a suitable receptacle. After the clutch components are wiped clean with rags, dispose of the contaminated rags and cleaner in a sealed, marked container.

Note: *Although some friction materials may no longer contain asbestos, it is safest to assume that they do, and to take precautions accordingly.*

Removal

1 Unless the complete engine/transmission unit is to be removed from the car and separated for major overhaul (see Chapter 2E), the clutch can be reached by removing the transmission as described in Chapter 7A.

2 Before disturbing the clutch, use chalk or a marker pen to mark the relationship of the pressure plate assembly to the flywheel.

3 Working in a diagonal sequence, slacken the pressure plate bolts by half a turn at a time, until spring pressure is released and the bolts can be unscrewed by hand. Hold the flywheel stationary using a suitable tool engaged with the starter ring gear teeth – a piece of metal can be tightened to one of the bolt holes, or alternatively an assistant can use a wide-bladed screwdriver engaged with the teeth **(see illustrations)**.

4 Prise the pressure plate assembly off its

7.3a Home-made tool for holding the flywheel stationary while loosening the clutch pressure plate bolts

7.3b Unscrewing the bolts retaining the clutch pressure plate

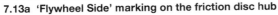

7.13a 'Flywheel Side' marking on the friction disc hub

7.13b Using the centralising tool to hold the friction disc on the flywheel

locating dowels, and collect the friction disc, noting which way round the disc is fitted.

Inspection

Note: *Due to the amount of work necessary to remove and refit clutch components, it is usually considered good practice to renew the clutch friction disc, pressure plate assembly and release bearing as a matched set, even if only one of these is actually worn enough to require renewal. It is also worth considering the renewal of the clutch components on a preventive basis if the engine and/or transmission have been removed for some other reason.*

5 When cleaning clutch components, read first the warning at the beginning of this Section; remove dust using a clean, dry cloth, and working in a well-ventilated atmosphere.

6 Check the friction disc linings for signs of wear, damage or oil contamination. If the friction material is cracked, burnt, scored or damaged, or if it is contaminated with oil or grease (shown by shiny black patches), the friction disc must be renewed. Check the depth of the rivets below the friction material surface. If any are at or near the surface of the friction material, then the friction disc must be renewed.

7 If the friction material is still serviceable, check that the centre boss splines are unworn, that the torsion springs are in good condition and securely fastened, and that all the rivets are tight. If any wear or damage is found, the friction disc must be renewed.

8 If the friction material is fouled with oil, this must be due to an oil leak from the crankshaft oil seal, from the sump-to-cylinder block joint, or from the transmission input shaft. Renew the seal or repair the joint, as appropriate, as described in the appropriate part of Chapter 2 or 7A, before installing the new friction disc.

9 Check the pressure plate assembly for obvious signs of wear or damage; shake it to check for loose rivets or worn or damaged fulcrum rings, and check that the drive straps securing the pressure plate to the cover do not show signs of overheating (such as a deep yellow or blue discoloration). If the diaphragm spring is worn or damaged, or if its pressure is

in any way suspect, the pressure plate assembly should be renewed.

10 Examine the machined bearing surfaces of the pressure plate and of the flywheel; they should be clean, completely flat, and free from scratches or scoring. If either is discoloured from excessive heat, or shows signs of cracks, it should be renewed – although minor damage of this nature can sometimes be polished away using emery paper.

11 Check that the release bearing contact surface rotates smoothly and easily, with no sign of noise or roughness. Also check that the surface itself is smooth and unworn, with no signs of cracks, pitting or scoring. If there is any doubt about its condition, the bearing must be renewed.

Refitting

12 On reassembly, ensure that the disc contact surfaces of the flywheel and pressure plate are completely clean, smooth, and free from oil or grease. Use solvent to remove any protective grease from new components.

13 Fit the friction disc so that its spring hub assembly faces away from the flywheel; there may also be a marking showing which way round the plate is to be refitted. Depending on the type of centralising tool being used, the friction disc may be held in position at this stage **(see illustrations)**.

14 Refit the pressure plate assembly,

aligning the marks made on dismantling (if the original pressure plate is re-used), and locating the pressure plate on its locating dowels **(see illustration)**. Fit the pressure plate bolts, but tighten them only finger-tight, so that the friction disc can still be moved.

15 The friction disc must now be centralised, so that when the transmission is refitted, its input shaft will pass through the splines at the centre of the friction disc.

16 Centralisation can be achieved by passing a screwdriver or other long bar through the friction disc and into the hole in the crankshaft; the friction disc can then be moved around until it is centred on the crankshaft hole. Alternatively, a clutch-aligning-tool can be used to eliminate the guesswork; these can be obtained from most accessory shops. The normal type consists of a spigot bar with several different adapters, but a more recent type consists of a tool which clamps the friction disc to the pressure plate before locating the two items on the flywheel. A home-made aligning tool can be fabricated from a length of metal rod or wooden dowel which fits closely inside the crankshaft hole, and has insulating tape wound around it to match the diameter of the friction disc splined hole.

17 When the friction disc is centralised, tighten the pressure plate bolts evenly and in a diagonal sequence to the specified torque setting **(see illustration)**.

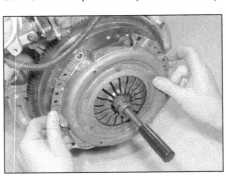

7.14 Refitting the pressure plate assembly onto the friction disc

7.17 Tightening the clutch pressure plate bolts

18 Apply a thin smear of molybdenum disulphide grease to the splines of the friction disc and the transmission input shaft.
Caution: Do not apply too much grease as there is a risk that it will contaminate the friction disc material.
19 Refit the transmission as described in Chapter 7A.

8 Clutch release bearing – removal, inspection and refitting

Removal

1 For access to the clutch release bearing, the transmission must be removed as described in Chapter 7A.
2 Withdraw the release bearing from the slave

8.2 **Removing the release bearing from the clutch slave cylinder**

cylinder inside the transmission bellhousing. If necessary, use a screwdriver to carefully prise out the bearing **(see illustration)**.

Inspection

3 Note that it is often considered worthwhile to renew the release bearing as a matter of course regardless of its condition, considering the amount of work necessary to access it. Check that the contact surface rotates smoothly and easily, with no sign of noise or roughness, and that the surface itself is smooth and unworn, with no signs of cracks, pitting or scoring. If there is any doubt about its condition, the bearing must be renewed.

Refitting

4 Align the tag with the cut-out in the slave cylinder, then slide the release bearing fully into position.
5 Refit the transmission with reference to Chapter 7A.

Chapter 7 Part A:
Manual transmission

Contents

Gearchange linkage – adjustment 3
Gearchange linkage and lever – removal, overhaul and refitting 4
General information 1
Manual transmission – removal and refitting 8
Manual transmission oil – general information 2
Manual transmission oil level check . . . . .See Chapter 1A or 1B

Manual transmission overhaul – general information 9
Oil seals – renewal 5
Reversing light switch and multi-function switch – testing, removal
  and refitting 6
Speedometer drive pinion – removal and refitting 7

Degrees of difficulty

Easy, suitable for novice with little experience 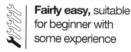	Fairly easy, suitable for beginner with some experience	Fairly difficult, suitable for competent DIY mechanic	Difficult, suitable for experienced DIY mechanic	Very difficult, suitable for expert DIY or professional

Specifications

General

Type	Manual, five forward speeds and reverse. Synchromesh on all forward speeds
Designation	iB5

Gear ratios

Petrol engine models:

1st	3.58 to 1
2nd	2.04 to 1
3rd	1.32 to 1
4th	0.95 to 1
5th	0.76 to 1
Reverse	3.62 to 1

Diesel engine models:

1st	3.58 to 1
2nd	1.93 to 1
3rd	1.28 to 1
4th	0.95 to 1
5th	0.76 to 1
Reverse	3.62 to 1

Final drive ratio

1.3 litre Endura-E petrol engine models:

Hatchback/Van	3.84 to 1
Courier/Combi	4.06 to 1
1.25 litre Zetec-SE petrol engine models	4.27 to 1
1.4 litre Zetec-SE petrol engine models	4.27 to 1
1.6 litre Zetec-SE petrol engine models	3.82 to 1
Diesel engine models	3.82 to 1

Torque wrench settings

	Nm	lbf ft
Anti-roll bar link to suspension strut	50	37
Driveshaft nut	270	199
Gearchange clamp bolt	23	17
Left-hand engine mounting nuts	70	52
Lower suspension arm to hub carrier	52	38
Multi-function switch	7	5
Rear engine mounting:		
To engine	50	37
To subframe	70	52
Right-hand driveshaft centre bearing bolts	24	18
Right-hand engine mounting	69	51
Steering track rod ends	36	27
Transmission earth lead	44	32
Transmission filler/level plug	35	26
Transmission-to-engine bolts	44	32

1 General information

The transmission is contained in a cast-aluminium alloy casing bolted to the engine's left-hand end, and consists of the gearbox and final drive differential – often called a transaxle. The transmission unit type is stamped on a plate attached to the transmission.

Drive is transmitted from the crankshaft via the clutch to the input shaft, which has a splined extension to accept the clutch friction disc, and rotates in sealed ball-bearings. From the input shaft, drive is transmitted to the output shaft, which rotates in a roller bearing at its left-hand end, and a taper roller bearing at its right-hand end. From the output shaft, the drive is transmitted to the differential crownwheel, which rotates with the differential and planetary gears, thus driving the sun gears and driveshafts. The rotation of the planetary gears on their shaft allows the inner roadwheel to rotate at a slower speed than the outer roadwheel when the car is cornering.

The input and output shafts are arranged side-by-side, parallel to the crankshaft and driveshafts, so that their gear pinion teeth are in constant mesh. In the neutral position, the output shaft gear pinions rotate freely, so that drive cannot be transmitted to the crownwheel.

Gear selection is via a floor-mounted lever and selector rod mechanism.

The transmission selector rod causes the appropriate selector fork to move its respective synchro-sleeve along the output shaft, to lock the gear pinion to the synchro-hub. Since the synchro-hubs are splined to the output shaft, this locks the pinion to the shaft, so that drive can be transmitted. To ensure that gearchanging can be made quickly and quietly, a synchromesh system is fitted to all forward gears, consisting of baulk rings and spring-loaded fingers, as well as gear pinions and synchro-hubs. The synchromesh cones are formed on the mating faces of the baulk rings and gear pinions.

2 Manual transmission oil – general information

1 Since transmission oil renewal is not part of the manufacturer's maintenance schedule, no drain plug is fitted to the transmission and the unit can be considered to be 'sealed for life'.

2 If, for any reason, it is felt necessary to renew the transmission oil, this can only be achieved by removing the transmission from the car and partially dismantling the casings.

3 Procedures for oil level checking and topping-up are contained in Chapters 1A and 1B.

3 Gearchange linkage – adjustment

1 Firmly apply the handbrake, then jack up the front of the vehicle and support it securely on axle stands (see *Jacking and vehicle support*).

2 On petrol engine models, unbolt the heatshield(s) from the underbody for access to the bottom of the gear lever. It is not necessary to completely remove the heatshields, only pull down one side of them **(see illustration)**.

3 Loosen the clamp bolt and disconnect the gearchange rod from the transmission selector shaft.

4 Slide the selector shaft back and forth to find its central position, then turn the selector shaft to the right and left to find the central position in the transverse plane. Hold the selector shaft in the centralised position, then insert a suitable rod (or punch) into the hole in the selector shaft in the transmission, and move it as far forwards as possible.

5 Locate the gearchange rod on the selector shaft, then have an assistant position the gear lever approximately in the 4th position.

6 Using a 9 mm drill bit inserted through the special hole in the bottom of the gear lever housing, lock the gear lever in 4th position. It will be necessary for the assistant to move the gear lever slightly until the drill locates correctly **(see illustration)**.

7 With the gearchange rod and gear lever in 4th, tighten the clamp bolt to the specified torque.

8 Check the adjustment, by moving the gear lever in all positions.

9 Refit the heatshields, then lower the car to the ground.

4 Gearchange linkage and lever – removal, overhaul and refitting

Removal

1 Working inside the vehicle carefully unscrew the knob from the top of the gear lever, then lift the gaiter and frame from the centre console **(see illustration)**.

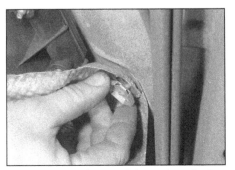

3.2 Unscrew the special nuts in order to bend down the underbody heatshields

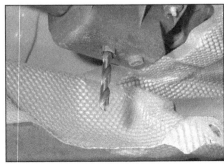

3.6 Insert a 9 mm drill bit through the special hole

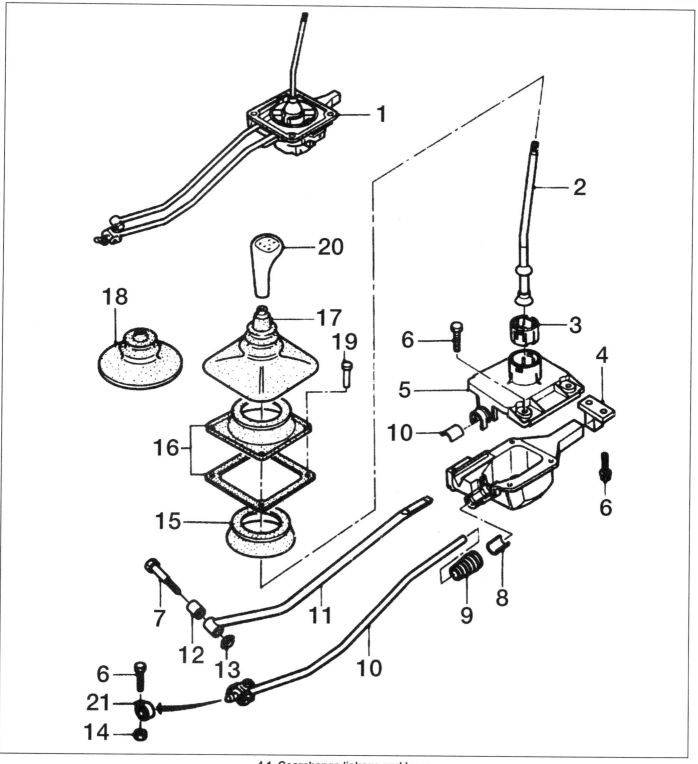

4.1 Gearchange linkage and lever

1 Assembly
2 Gear lever
3 Bearing
4 Support bracket
5 Housing
6 Bolt

7 Stabiliser bar pivot
   bolt
8 Bush
9 Boot
10 Rod and clevis

11 Stabiliser bar
12 Bush
13 Washer
14 Nut
15 Insert

16 Boot retainer
17 Gaiter
18 Boot
19 Rivet
20 Knob
21 Collar

4.5 Unscrewing the bolt securing the gearchange stabiliser rod to the transmission

2 Remove the inner gaiter over the gear lever.

3 Apply the handbrake, then jack up the front of the vehicle and support it on axle stands (see *Jacking and vehicle support*).

4 Unbolt the heatshield(s) from the underbody for access to the bottom of the gear lever.

5 Unscrew the bolt securing the gearchange stabiliser rod to the transmission and tie the rod to one side **(see illustration)**. Note that the washer is located next to the transmission.

6 Mark the position of the gearchange rod clamp on the transmission selector shaft, then unscrew and remove the clamp bolt and disconnect the gearchange rod.

7 Unscrew the gear lever support bracket mounting bolts on the underbody, and withdraw the gearchange linkage from under the car.

Overhaul

8 Unbolt the stabiliser rod from the gear lever housing.

9 Withdraw the noise damping pad over the gear lever, and remove the support bracket from the rear of the housing.

10 Using a screwdriver carefully press out the locking lugs, then withdraw the gear lever from the top of the housing.

11 Mount the inverted gear lever in a vice, then lever off the mounting sleeve using two screwdrivers.

12 Remove the rubber boot from the gearchange rod, then lever off the housing cover and remove the rod.

13 Clean all components and examine them for wear and damage. Obtain new items as necessary.

14 If necessary the bush in the stabiliser rod can be removed by pressing it out using suitable diameter metal tubes and a vice. Press in the new bush using the same method.

15 Reassemble the linkage using a reversal of dismantling, but apply a little grease to the bearing surfaces.

Refitting

16 Refitting is a reversal of removal, but adjust the linkage as described in Section 3.

5 Oil seals – renewal

1 Oil leaks frequently occur due to wear or deterioration of the differential side gear seals and/or the transmission selector shaft oil seal and speedometer drive pinion O-ring. Renewal of these seals is relatively easy, since the repairs can be performed without removing the transmission from the vehicle, however if the input shaft oil seal requires renewal the transmission must be removed.

Differential side gear seals

2 The differential side gear oil seals are located at the sides of the transmission, where the driveshafts enter the transmission. If leakage at the seal is suspected, raise the vehicle and support it securely on axle stands (see *Jacking and vehicle support*). If the seal is leaking, oil will be found on the side of the transmission below the driveshaft.

3 Referring to Chapter 8, disconnect the driveshaft from the transmission. Note that it is not necessary to remove the driveshaft completely, the shaft can be left attached to the hub carrier and slid off from the differential gear splines as the hub assembly is pulled outwards. On the right-hand driveshaft, if the stub has not been removed from the transmission, it will be necessary to remove the left-hand driveshaft then use a screwdriver or similar tool to drive the stub from the right-hand side of the transmission.

Note: *With the driveshaft removed from the transmission, do not allow it to hang down under its own weight as this could damage the constant velocity joints/gaiters.*

4 Wipe clean the old oil seal and note its fitted depth below the casing edge. This is necessary to determine the correct fitted position of the new oil seal. The fitted depth will be approximately 5 mm.

5 Using a large screwdriver or lever, carefully prise the oil seal out of the transmission casing, taking care not to damage the casing **(see illustration)**. If the oil seal is reluctant to move, it is sometimes helpful to carefully drive it into the transmission a little way, applying the force at one point only. This will have the effect of swivelling the seal out of the casing, and it can then be pulled out. If the oil seal is particularly difficult to remove, an oil seal removal tool may be obtained from a garage or accessory shop.

6 Wipe clean the oil seal seating in the transmission casing.

7 Dip the new oil seal in clean oil, then press it a little way into the casing by hand, making sure that it is square to its seating with its closed end facing outwards **(see illustration)**.

8 Using suitable tubing or a large socket, carefully drive the oil seal fully into the casing up to its previously-noted fitted depth **(see illustration)**.

 HAYNES HiNT *Wrap adhesive tape around the socket to indicate the depth to fit the oil seal*

9 Refit the driveshaft with reference to Chapter 8. On the right-hand driveshaft fit the stub first and make sure the circlip is fully engaged with the groove in the differential gears.

Transmission selector shaft seal

10 Apply the handbrake, then jack up the front of the vehicle and support it on axle stands (see *Jacking and vehicle support*).

11 Mark the position of the gearchange rod clamp on the transmission selector shaft.

12 Unscrew and remove the clamp bolt and disconnect the gearchange rod.

13 Remove the rubber boot for access to the oil seal.

5.5 Prising the oil seal from the transmission

5.7 Locating a new oil seal on the transmission aperture

5.8 Driving the new oil seal into the transmission casing

14 Using a suitable tool or grips, pull the oil seal out of the transmission casing. Ford technicians use a slide hammer, with an end fitting which locates over the oil seal extension. In the absence of this tool, if the oil seal is particularly tight, drill one or two small holes in the oil seal, and screw in self-tapping screws. The oil seal can then be removed from the casing by pulling on the screws.

15 Wipe clean the oil seal seating in the transmission.

16 Dip the new oil seal in clean oil, then press it a little way into the casing by hand, making sure that it is square to its seating and with its closed end facing outwards.

17 Using suitable tubing or a large socket, carefully drive the oil seal fully into the casing.

18 Locate the rubber boot over the selector shaft.

19 The gearchange linkage rod can now be reconnected and adjusted using the procedure described in Section 3.

Speedometer drive pinion seal

20 The procedure is covered in Section 7.

Input shaft seal

21 Remove the clutch slave cylinder from the transmission as described in Chapter 6.

22 Hook out the oil seal using a suitable tool, taking care not to damage the input shaft. If it is tight, drill one or two small holes in the oil seal, and screw in self-tapping screws. The oil seal can then be removed from the casing by pulling on the screws.

23 Wipe clean the oil seal seating in the transmission.

24 Dip the new oil seal in clean oil, then locate it over the input shaft and press it a little way into the casing by hand, making sure that it is square to its seating and with its closed end facing outwards.

25 Locate the clutch slave cylinder over the input shaft and refit it with reference to Chapter 6. The action of tightening the mounting bolts evenly presses the oil seal into the transmission casing.

6 Reversing light switch and multi-function switch – testing, removal and refitting

Reversing light switch

Testing

1 The reversing light circuit is controlled by a plunger-type switch that is screwed into the front of the transmission casing, near the bellhousing. If a fault develops in the circuit, first ensure that the circuit fuse has not blown.

2 To test the switch, disconnect the wiring connector, and use a multimeter (set to the resistance function) or a battery-and-bulb test circuit to check that there is continuity between the switch terminals only when reverse gear is selected. If this is not the case, and there are no obvious breaks or other damage to the wires, the switch is faulty, and must be renewed.

Removal

3 Apply the handbrake, then jack up the front of the vehicle and support it on axle stands (see *Jacking and vehicle support*).

4 Disconnect the wiring from the reversing light switch.

5 Unscrew the switch from the front of the transmission.

Refitting

6 Clean the location in the transmission, and the threads of the switch.

7 Insert the switch and tighten securely.

8 Reconnect the wiring.

9 Check and top-up the transmission oil level if necessary, with reference to Chapter 1A or 1B.

10 Lower the vehicle to the ground.

Multi-function switch

Testing

11 The multi-function switch is incorporated in the engine management system. Testing should be referred to a Ford dealer.

Removal

12 Apply the handbrake, then jack up the

front of the vehicle and support it on axle stands (see *Jacking and vehicle support*).

13 Disconnect the wiring from the multi-function switch.

14 Unbolt the retaining bracket and remove the switch from the transmission.

Refitting

15 Refitting is a reversal of removal.

7 Speedometer drive pinion – removal and refitting

Removal

1 Disconnect the battery negative (earth) lead (see Chapter 5A).

2 Where applicable, undo the retaining nut, and withdraw the speedometer cable from the vehicle speed sensor in the top face of the transmission. Use two spanners to loosen the nut – one to counterhold the sensor, and the other to unscrew the cable nut.

3 Disconnect the wiring from the vehicle speed sensor, then unscrew the sensor from the top of the drive pinion (see illustration).

4 Grip the drive pinion retaining pin with self-locking grips or pliers, and withdraw it from the drive pinion housing.

5 Pull the drive pinion and bearing out of the housing, but take care not to tilt it, because the pinion and bearing are not secured and can easily be separated if the pinion is snagged (see illustration).

6 Using a small screwdriver, prise the O-ring from the groove in the bearing; obtain a new one for reassembly.

7 Wipe clean the drive pinion and bearing, also the seating bore in the transmission casing.

Refitting

8 Refitting is a reversal of the removal procedure, but lightly oil the new O-ring before inserting the assembly in the transmission casing. Drive in the retaining roll pin using a hammer (see illustration).

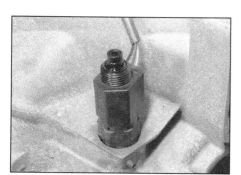

7.3 Vehicle speed sensor on the rear of the transmission

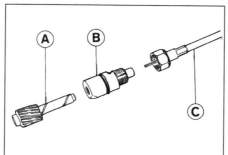

7.5 Speedometer drive pinion (A) pinion bearing (B) and drive cable (C)

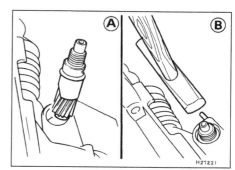

7.8 Insert the speedometer drive pinion/bearing (A) and secure with a new retaining pin (B)

8.9 Support bar across the engine compartment supporting the engine

8.12a Removing the left-hand suspension strut and driveshaft complete

8.12b Tie the brake caliper to the inner wing panel using wire

8 Manual transmission – removal and refitting

Zetec-SE engine models

Removal

1 The manual transmission is removed downwards from the engine compartment, after disconnecting it from the engine. Due to the weight of the unit, it will be necessary to have a suitable method of supporting the transmission as it is lowered during removal and subsequently raised during its refitting. A trolley jack fitted with a suitable saddle to support the transmission as it is removed will be ideal, but failing this, an engine lift hoist and sling will suffice. The weight of the engine will also need to be supported whilst the transmission is detached from it – an engine support bar fitted in the front wing drain channel each side is ideal for this purpose, but care must be taken not to damage the wings or their paintwork. If this type of tool is not available (or cannot be fabricated), the engine can be supported by blocks or a second jack from underneath.
2 Disconnect and remove the battery as described in Chapter 5A.
3 Unscrew the bolts securing the battery tray to the body. Cut the plastic cable tie and remove the tray.
4 Loosen the clips and remove the air inlet

duct from between the air mass air flow sensor on the air cleaner and the throttle housing.
5 Apply the handbrake, then jack up the front of the vehicle and support it on axle stands (see *Jacking and vehicle support*). Remove both front roadwheels. Where fitted, undo the screws and remove the engine undershield or, alternatively, unbolt the plastic cover from under the crankshaft pulley.
6 Unbolt the exhaust front downpipe from the intermediate pipe with reference to Chapter 4A.
7 Unscrew the bolt securing the gearchange stabiliser rod to the transmission and tie the rod to one side.
8 Mark the position of the gearchange rod clamp on the transmission shaft, then unscrew and remove the clamp bolt and disconnect the gearchange rod.
9 Using a hoist, support the weight of the engine. Alternatively, use a purpose-made support bar across the engine compartment, located in the front wing drain channels **(see illustration)**.
10 Unbolt and remove the rear engine mounting link (see Chapter 2B, Section 17). Hold the engine stationary while the bolts are being removed since the link will be under tension.
11 Unscrew and remove the clamp bolts and disconnect the lower suspension arms from the hub carriers on each side as described in Chapter 10.
12 Using a lever, remove the left-hand driveshaft from the transmission while pulling

out the suspension strut (refer to Chapter 8). Tie the driveshaft to one side making sure that the joints are not bent more that 18° otherwise they may be damaged. If preferred to give additional working room, remove the left-hand strut complete with driveshaft with reference to Chapter 8. If this course of action is taken, tie up the brake caliper with a piece of wire **(see illustrations)**.
13 Unscrew and remove the two bolts securing the right-hand driveshaft centre bearing to the rear of the engine and temporarily support it.
14 Using a drift entered from the left-hand side of the transmission, carefully drive the inner end of the right-hand driveshaft from the transmission taking care to prevent it from dropping. Tie the driveshaft to one side making sure that the joints are not bent more that 18° otherwise they may be damaged.
15 Disconnect the wiring from the multi-function switch on the front of the transmission **(see illustration)**.
16 Where fitted, unscrew and remove the pivot bolt from the front of the left-hand lower suspension arm, and remove the small bracket from the front of the subframe **(see illustration)**.
17 Unbolt the reinforcement bar, then pull out the transmission breather and unscrew the mounting nuts from the left-hand engine mounting. Note that the arrow on the breather points to the front of the car **(see illustrations)**.
18 Disconnect the vacuum hose from the EGR valve (see Chapter 4D, Section 2).

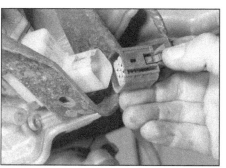

8.15 Disconnecting the wiring from the multi-function switch on the front of the transmission

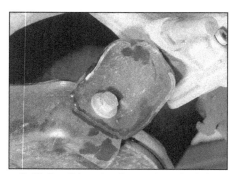

8.16 Small bracket located on the left-hand front lower suspension arm front pivot bolt

8.17a Unbolt the reinforcement bar . . .

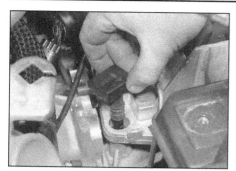

8.17b . . . then pull out the transmission breather . . .

8.17c . . . and unscrew the nuts from the left-hand mounting

8.22 Releasing the clutch hydraulic line from the support

19 Lower the engine and transmission until the left-hand engine mounting is clear of the mounting studs.

20 Unbolt the bracket from the throttle housing.

21 Fit a hose clamp to the clutch hydraulic hose leading to the slave cylinder. Alternatively tighten the fluid reservoir cap onto a piece of polythene – this will prevent excessive loss of hydraulic fluid.

22 Pull out the clip and disconnect the hydraulic hose quick release connector from the clutch slave cylinder. Plug the hose and slave cylinder to prevent dust and dirt entering the system. Release the hydraulic line from the support **(see illustration)**.

23 Unscrew the retaining nut and disconnect the speedometer drive cable from the vehicle speed sensor on the transmission **(see illustration)**.

24 Support the transmission on a trolley jack, then unscrew and remove the bolts securing the right-hand rear of the transmission to the engine.

25 Unscrew and remove the remaining bolts securing the transmission to the engine. Note the lower bolts are on the engine sump side, and also note that the uppermost bolt secures the transmission earth lead.

26 With the help of an assistant withdraw the transmission directly from the engine until the input shaft is clear of the clutch pressure plate assembly, then lower it to the ground and remove from under the car **(see illustration)**.

Refitting

27 Refitting is a reversal of removal, but note the following additional points:

a) *Make sure that all mating faces are clean.*

b) *Apply a smear of high-melting-point grease to the splines of the transmission input shaft. Do not apply too much, otherwise there is the possibility of the grease contaminating the clutch friction disc.*

c) *Ensure that the engine adapter plate is correctly seated on the locating dowels on the engine.*

d) *Fit new circlips to the grooves in the inner end of each driveshaft CV joint, and ensure that they fully engage as they are fitted into the transmission.*

e) *Refit and adjust the engine mountings as described in Chapter 2B.*

f) *Check and if necessary adjust the gearchange linkage as described in Section 3.*

g) *Top-up the transmission oil as described in Chapter 1A.*

h) *Top-up and bleed the clutch hydraulic system as described in Chapter 6.*

i) *Tighten all nuts and bolts to the specified torque settings.*

Endura-E engine models

Removal

28 The manual transmission is removed downwards from the engine compartment, after disconnecting it from the engine. Due to the weight of the unit, it will be necessary to have a suitable method of supporting the transmission as it is lowered during removal and subsequently raised during its refitting. A trolley jack fitted with a suitable saddle to support the transmission as it is removed will be ideal, but failing this, an engine lift hoist and sling will suffice. The weight of the engine will also need to be supported whilst the transmission is detached from it – an engine support bar fitted in the front wing drain channel each side is ideal for this purpose, but care must be taken not to damage the wings or their paintwork. If this type of tool is not available (or cannot be fabricated), the engine can be supported by blocks or a second jack from underneath.

8.23 Disconnecting the speedometer drive cable from the vehicle speed sensor on the rear of the transmission

29 Loosen the clips and remove the air inlet duct.

30 Disconnect and remove the battery as described in Chapter 5A.

31 Unscrew the bolts securing the battery tray to the body. Cut the plastic cable tie and remove the tray.

32 Apply the handbrake, then jack up the front of the vehicle and support it on axle stands (see *Jacking and vehicle support*). Remove both front roadwheels.

33 Where fitted, undo the retaining screws and remove the engine undershield.

34 Disconnect the oxygen sensor wiring at the plug.

35 If necessary, disconnect the wiring from the starter motor and release the wiring from the bracket. This is not essential as the starter motor may be left in position while the transmission is being removed.

36 Unbolt the transmission earth lead from the top of the transmission.

37 Unscrew the retaining nut and disconnect the speedometer drive cable from the speed sensor on the transmission.

38 Disconnect the wiring plug leading to the vehicle speed sensor.

39 Place cloth rags beneath the fuel supply and return hoses at the fuel rail, then depress the quick-release fittings and disconnect the hoses. Identify each hose for position to aid reassembly.

40 Remove the clutch hydraulic pipe with reference to Chapter 6.

41 Using a hoist, support the weight of the

8.26 Withdrawing the transmission from the engine

engine. Alternatively, use a purpose-made support bar across the engine compartment, located in the front wing drain channels.

42 Pull out the transmission breather then unscrew the nuts retaining the left-hand engine mounting to the transmission. Note that the arrow on the breather points to the front of the car.

43 Unbolt the auxiliary drivebelt lower cover from the underbody.

44 Disconnect the wiring from the multi-function switch on the front of the transmission.

45 Unbolt the exhaust front downpipe from the intermediate pipe with reference to Chapter 4A.

46 Unscrew the bolt securing the gearchange stabiliser rod to the transmission and tie the rod to one side.

47 Mark the position of the gearchange rod clamp on the transmission shaft, then unscrew and remove the clamp bolt and disconnect the gearchange rod.

48 Unbolt and remove the rear engine mounting link (see Chapter 2A). Hold the engine stationary while the bolts are being removed since the link will be under tension.

49 Unbolt the exhaust pipe mounting bracket from the cylinder block.

50 Disconnect the steering track rod end from the left-hand hub carrier as described in Chapter 10.

51 Unscrew and remove the clamp bolts and disconnect the lower suspension arms from the hub carriers on each side as described in Chapter 10.

52 Unscrew the nuts and disconnect the anti-roll bar link from the left-hand front suspension strut (refer to Chapter 10).

53 Using a lever, remove the left-hand driveshaft from the transmission while pulling out the suspension strut (refer to Chapter 8). Tie the driveshaft to one side making sure that the joints are not bent more that 18° otherwise they may be damaged.

54 Unscrew and remove the two bolts securing the right-hand driveshaft centre bearing to the rear of the engine and temporarily support it.

55 Using a drift entered from the left-hand side of the transmission, carefully drive the inner end of the right-hand driveshaft from the transmission taking care to prevent it from dropping. Tie the driveshaft to one side making sure that the joints are not bent more that 18° otherwise they may be damaged.

56 Lower the transmission and engine until there is free access to the transmission from the left-hand side of the car.

57 Unscrew and remove the bolts securing the right-hand rear of the transmission to the engine.

58 Move the cable guide to one side, then unscrew the bolts securing the top of the transmission to the engine and withdraw the adapter plate.

59 At the front of the transmission, unscrew and remove the bolts securing the

transmission to the engine. Note the location of the TDC sensor cover retained by two of the bolts.

60 With the help of an assistant withdraw the transmission directly from the engine until the input shaft is clear of the clutch pressure plate assembly, then lower it to the ground and remove from under the car.

Refitting

61 Refitting is a reversal of removal, but note the following additional points:
  a) *Make sure that all mating faces are clean.*
  b) *Apply a smear of high-melting-point grease to the splines of the transmission input shaft. Do not apply too much, otherwise there is the possibility of the grease contaminating the clutch friction disc.*
  c) *Ensure that the engine adapter plate is correctly seated on the locating dowels on the engine.*
  d) *Fit new circlips to the grooves in the inner end of each driveshaft CV joint, and ensure that they fully engage as they are fitted into the transmission.*
  e) *Refit and adjust the engine mountings as described in Chapter 2A.*
  f) *Check and if necessary adjust the gearchange linkage as described in Section 3.*
  g) *Top-up the transmission oil as described in Chapter 1A.*
  h) *Top up and bleed the clutch hydraulic system as described in Chapter 6.*
  i) *Tighten all nuts and bolts to the specified torque setting.*

Diesel engine models

Removal

62 The manual transmission is removed downwards from the engine compartment, after disconnecting it from the engine. Due to the weight of the unit, it will be necessary to have a suitable method of supporting the transmission as it is lowered during removal and subsequently raised during its refitting. A trolley jack fitted with a suitable saddle to support the transmission as it is removed will be ideal, but failing this, an engine lift hoist and sling will suffice. The weight of the engine will also need to be supported whilst the transmission is detached from it – an engine support bar fitted in the front wing drain channel each side is ideal for this purpose, but care must be taken not to damage the wings or their paintwork. If this type of tool is not available (or cannot be fabricated), the engine can be supported by blocks or a second jack from underneath.

63 Disconnect and remove the battery as described in Chapter 5A.

64 Unscrew the bolts securing the battery tray to the body.

65 Loosen the clips securing the air inlet duct to the inlet manifold and resonator. Release the duct from the support clip then withdraw it from the air cleaner.

66 Unscrew the mounting bolts and remove the air inlet resonator.

67 Fit a hose clamp to the clutch hydraulic hose leading to the slave cylinder. Alternatively tighten the fluid reservoir cap onto a piece of polythene – this will prevent excessive loss of hydraulic fluid.

68 Pull out the clip and disconnect the hydraulic hose quick release connector from the clutch slave cylinder. Plug the hose and slave cylinder to prevent dust and dirt entering the system.

69 Unscrew and remove the two upper bolts securing the transmission to the engine, noting the location of the bracket.

70 Using a hoist, support the weight of the engine. Alternatively, use a purpose-made support bar across the engine compartment, located in the front wing drain channels.

71 Pull out the transmission breather, then unscrew the nuts securing the left-hand engine mounting to the transmission. Note that the arrow on the breather points to the front of the car.

72 Unscrew the nuts and remove the right-hand engine mounting bracket.

73 Remove the wheel trim from the right-hand front wheel, then loosen the driveshaft nut using a 32 mm socket and extension bar.

74 Apply the handbrake, then jack up the front of the vehicle and support it on axle stands (see *Jacking and vehicle support*). Remove both front roadwheels.

75 Where fitted, undo the retaining screws and remove the engine undershield.

76 Unscrew the bolt securing the gearchange stabiliser rod to the transmission and tie the rod to one side.

77 Mark the position of the gearchange linkage clamp on the transmission shaft, then unscrew and remove the clamp bolt and disconnect the gearchange linkage.

78 Unbolt and remove the rear engine mounting link (see Chapter 2C or 2D). Hold the engine stationary while the bolts are being removed since the link will be under tension.

79 Disconnect the wiring from the multi-function switch on the front of the trans-mission.

80 Unscrew the retaining nut and disconnect the speedometer drive cable from the speed sensor on the transmission.

81 Unscrew and remove the clamp bolts and disconnect the lower suspension arms from the hub carriers on each side as described in Chapter 10.

82 Using a lever, remove the left-hand driveshaft from the transmission while pulling out the suspension strut (refer to Chapter 8). Tie the driveshaft to one side making sure that the joints are not bent more that 18° otherwise they may be damaged.

83 Unscrew and remove the two bolts securing the right-hand driveshaft centre bearing to the rear of the engine and temporarily support it.

84 Push the right-hand driveshaft from the hub carrier while pulling the carrier outwards. If the driveshaft is tight, use a suitable puller mounted on the wheel studs to force it out. Support the driveshaft on an axle stand.

85 Using a drift entered from the left-hand side of the transmission, carefully drive the inner end of the right-hand driveshaft from the transmission taking care to prevent it from dropping. Remove the driveshaft from under the car.

86 Lower the engine and transmission until the rear engine mounting is clear of the mounting studs.

87 Support the weight of the transmission on a trolley jack, then unscrew and remove the bolt securing the exhaust resonator bracket.

88 Unscrew and remove the bolts securing the transmission to the engine.

89 With the help of an assistant withdraw the transmission directly from the engine until the input shaft is clear of the clutch pressure plate assembly, then lower it to the ground and remove from under the car.

Refitting

90 Refitting is a reversal of removal, but note the following additional points:
a) *Make sure that all mating faces are clean.*
b) *Apply a smear of high-melting-point grease to the splines of the transmission input shaft. Do not apply too much, otherwise there is the possibility of the grease contaminating the clutch friction disc.*
c) *Ensure that the engine adapter plate is correctly seated on the locating dowels on the engine.*
d) *Fit new circlips to the grooves in the inner end of each driveshaft CV joint, and ensure that they fully engage as they are fitted into the transmission.*
e) *Refer to Chapter 8 when refitting the right-hand driveshaft, and if necessary use a suitable puller to draw it into the hub carrier. Fit a new driveshaft nut and tighten it to the specified torque.*
f) *Refit and adjust the engine mountings as described in Chapter 2C or 2D.*
g) *Check and if necessary adjust the gearchange linkage as described in Section 3.*
h) *Top-up the transmission oil as described in Chapter 1B.*
i) *Top up and bleed the clutch hydraulic system as described in Chapter 6.*
j) *Tighten all nuts and bolts to the specified torque settings.*

9 Manual transmission overhaul – general information

1 Overhauling a manual transmission unit is a difficult and involved job for the DIY home mechanic. In addition to dismantling and reassembling many small parts, clearances must be precisely measured and, if necessary, changed by selecting shims and spacers. Internal transmission components are also often difficult to obtain, and in many instances, extremely expensive. Because of this, if the transmission develops a fault or becomes noisy, the best course of action is to have the unit overhauled by a specialist repairer, or to obtain an exchange reconditioned unit.

2 Nevertheless, it is not impossible for the more experienced mechanic to overhaul the transmission, provided the special tools are available, and the job is done in a deliberate step-by-step manner, so that nothing is overlooked.

3 The tools necessary for an overhaul include internal and external circlip pliers, bearing pullers, a slide hammer, a set of pin punches, a dial test indicator, and possibly a hydraulic press. In addition, a large, sturdy workbench and a vice will be required.

4 During dismantling of the transmission, make careful notes of how each component is fitted, to make reassembly easier and more accurate.

5 Before dismantling the transmission, it will help if you have some idea what area is malfunctioning. Certain problems can be closely related to specific areas in the transmission, which can make component examination and replacement easier. Refer to the *Fault finding* Section at the rear of this manual for more information.

Notes

Notes

Chapter 7 Part B:
Automatic transmission

Contents

Automatic transmission – removal and refitting 7
Automatic transmission fluid renewal . . . . .See Chapter 1A
Automatic transmission fluid level check . . . . .See Chapter 1A
Automatic transmission overhaul – general 8
Fluid seals – renewal 6
Gear selector mechanism – removal and refitting 3
General information and precautions 1
Reversing light/inhibitor switch – removal and refitting 5
Selector cable – removal, refitting and adjustment 2
Speedometer drive pinion – removal and refitting 4

Degrees of difficulty

Easy, suitable for novice with little experience | **Fairly easy,** suitable for beginner with some experience | **Fairly difficult,** suitable for competent DIY mechanic | **Difficult,** suitable for experienced DIY mechanic | **Very difficult,** suitable for expert DIY or professional

Specifications

General
Type . . . . Hydraulically-controlled continuously-variable automatic transmission
Designation . . . . CTX

Torque wrench settings

	Nm	lbf ft
Drain plug	33	24
Oil filler pipe to transmission	20	15
Oil pipe to connector	20	15
Oil pipe to radiator cooler	20	15
Oil strainer	8	6
Radiator support crossmember	25	18
Rear engine mounting to body	56	41
Selector cable bracket to transmission	40	30
Sump	8	6
Torsional vibration damper	30	22
Transmission to engine	44	32

1 General information and precautions

The CTX transmission is an automatic transmission providing continuously-variable drive over the entire speed range. Torque from the engine is transmitted to the transmission via an input shaft and a multi-plate wet clutch (rather than a conventional torque converter employed on most automatic transmissions).

A steel thrust-link drivebelt made of disc-shaped steel elements transmits the torque from the primary cone pulley (driven by the engine) to the secondary cone pulley. The secondary cone pulley is linked by a series of gears to the final drive gear which drives the differential unit and the driveshafts.

The continuous variation in ratio is produced by altering the diameter of the path followed by the drivebelt around the two cone pulleys. This alteration of the drivebelt path is produced by a hydraulic control system which moves one half of each cone pulley in an axial direction. The secondary pulley cone is also spring-loaded, to keep the drivebelt at the required tension needed to transmit the torque. The hydraulic control system is governed by the position of the transmission selector lever, the accelerator pedal and the load resistance encountered (such as up or down gradients), as well as road speed.

The selector lever is connected to the transmission selector shaft by a cable.

A gear-type pump delivers fluid (according to the input speed) to the hydraulic control system. A transmission fluid cooler is attached to the right-hand side of the radiator.

As with conventional automatic transmission systems, the CTX type has a parking mechanism. The parking pawl engages with the teeth on the outside of the secondary pulley. A starter inhibitor switch prevents the engine from being started in selector positions R, D or L.

When accelerating, the engine speed may sound higher than would normally be expected, similar to a slipping clutch on a manual transmission vehicle. The reverse is true when decelerating, with the engine speed dropping faster than the comparable drop in road speed. These are normal characteristics of the CTX transmission.

Precautions

When the vehicle is parked and left with the engine running, or when any checks and/or adjustments are being carried out, the handbrake must be applied and the selector lever moved to the P position.

Do not allow the engine speed to rise above the normal idle speed when the vehicle is stationary with the selector lever in the R, D or L position.

The engine must not run at more than 3000 rpm with the selector lever in the R, D or L position when the driving (front) roadwheels are clear of the ground.

It is not permissible to tow a vehicle fitted with the CTX automatic transmission otherwise internal damage will occur to the transmission. The vehicle may be towed with the front wheels lifted clear of the ground, or it may be loaded onto a trailer or breakdown truck.

2 Selector cable – removal, refitting and adjustment

Removal

1 Disconnect the battery negative (earth) lead (see Chapter 5A).
2 Refer to Chapter 11 and remove the centre console.
3 Move the selector lever to position P (the lever on the transmission selector shaft should also be in position P – the most forward position). This is important for correct subsequent adjustment of the selector cable.
4 Detach the selector gate from the selector lever housing by undoing its two securing screws. Slide it off over the selector lever, having unscrewed the selector lever knob.
5 Using a suitable screwdriver as a lever, prise free the plastic connecting eye of the selector lever from the cable, then prise free the cable retaining clip, and withdraw the cable from the selector housing. If necessary, cut the carpet at the front to allow extra access **(see illustration)**.
6 Chock the rear wheels then jack up the front of the car and support it on axle stands (see *Jacking and vehicle support*).
7 Working beneath the vehicle, disconnect the cable from the transmission lever by pulling out the special clip and turning it through 90°.
8 Pull out the outer cable support clip, and withdraw the cable to the rear.
9 Pull free the rubber gaiter from the floor, and then withdraw the selector cable from the vehicle.

Refitting

10 Feed the selector cable up through the floor, refit the rubber gaiter, then lower the vehicle to the ground.
11 Reconnect the selector cable to the lever and housing, ensuring that the annular bead of the cable eye faces the end of the pin. Use a suitable pair of pliers to press the pin in until it is heard to clip into engagement **(see illustration)**.
12 The selector lever must now be moved to the P position, and the vehicle then raised and supported at the front end again.
13 Reconnect the cable to the transmission, then adjust the cable as follows before refitting the centre console and selector gate assembly.

Adjustment

14 The vehicle must be raised and supported on axle stands at the front end to make the cable adjustment check (see *Jacking and vehicle support*).
15 With the selector lever set in the P position, the parking pawl engaged and the gears immobilised, check that the lever/selector shaft drilling and the cable yoke are in alignment, and that the connecting pin is an easy fit. If required, draw the gaiter back from the yoke, and screw the yoke in the appropriate direction to reposition it on the cable so that the pin fits freely. Fit the pin and retaining clip, then relocate the bellows.
16 The vehicle can now be lowered to the ground.

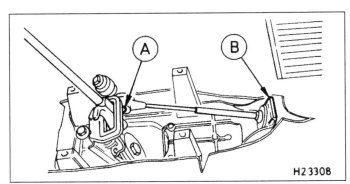

2.5 Selector cable fitting to selector lever (A) and selector cable abutment retaining clip arrangement (B)

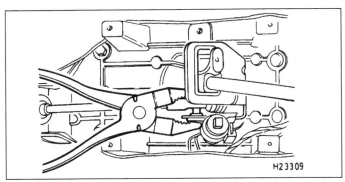

2.11 Securing the selector cable to the selector lever

3   Gear selector mechanism – removal and refitting

Removal

1 Refer to Section 2, paragraphs 1 to 5 inclusive, to disconnect the cable from the selector housing unit.
2 Pull free the quadrant illumination light bulbholder, then undo the four retaining bolts and remove the selector housing unit **(see illustration)**.
3 To remove the selector lever from the housing, release the clip and extract the lever pivot pin.

Refitting

4 Reassemble and refit in the reverse order of removal.

4   Speedometer drive pinion – removal and refitting

Removal

1 Disconnect the battery negative (earth) lead (see Chapter 5A).
2 Undo the retaining nut, and withdraw the speedometer cable from the transmission.
3 Grip the drive pinion retaining roll pin with self-locking grips or pliers, and withdraw it from the drive pinion housing.
4 Pull the drive pinion and bearing out of the housing, but take care not to tilt it, because the pinion and bearing are not secured and can easily be separated if the pinion is snagged.
5 Using a small screwdriver, prise the O-ring from the groove in the bearing; obtain a new one for reassembly.
6 Wipe clean the drive pinion and bearing, also the seating bore in the transmission casing.

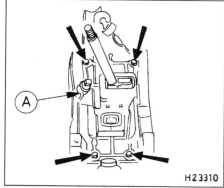

H23310

3.2 Selector lever housing retaining bolts (arrowed), and selector cover illumination bulbholder (A)

Refitting

7 Refitting is a reversal of the removal procedure, but lightly oil the new O-ring before inserting the assembly in the transmission. Drive in the retaining roll pin as far as the stop. When fitted, it should protrude by approximately 5.0 mm.

5   Reversing light/inhibitor switch – removal and refitting

1 Disconnect the battery negative (earth) lead (see Chapter 5A).
2 The switch is located on the rear of the transmission, and prevents the engine from being started with the selector lever in any position except P or N. Access to the switch is gained after raising and supporting the vehicle at the front end on axle stands (see *Jacking and vehicle support*).
3 Detach the switch multiplug, then unscrew and remove the switch from the transmission, together with its O-ring. As the switch is removed, catch any fluid spillage in a suitable container, and plug the switch aperture in the transmission to prevent any further loss.
4 Refitting is a reversal of the removal procedure. Use a new O-ring, and tighten the switch securely. Ensure that the wiring connection is securely made. On completion, check and if necessary top-up the automatic transmission fluid (see Chapter 1A) then check that the engine only starts when the selector is in the P or N position.

6   Fluid seals – renewal

Differential side gear seals

1 The procedure is the same as described for the oil seals on the manual transmission (refer to Chapter 7A).

Speedometer drive pinion seal

2 The procedure is covered in Section 4 of this Chapter.

7   Automatic transmission – removal and refitting

Removal

1 The automatic transmission is removed downwards from the engine compartment, after disconnecting it from the engine. Due to the weight of the unit, it will be necessary to have a suitable method of supporting the transmission as it is lowered during removal, and subsequently raised during its refitting. A trolley jack fitted with a suitable saddle to support the transmission as it is removed will

be ideal, but failing this, an engine lift hoist and sling will suffice. The weight of the engine will also need to be supported whilst the transmission is detached from it. An engine support bar fitted in the front wing drain channel on each side is ideal for this purpose. If this type of tool is not available (or cannot be fabricated), the engine can be supported by blocks or a second jack from underneath.
2 Remove the battery as described in Chapter 5A.
3 Cut the plastic cable ties, then unbolt and remove the battery tray.
4 Loosen the clips and remove the air inlet duct from between the air cleaner and throttle housing.
5 Disconnect the accelerator cable from the throttle housing with reference to Chapter 4A.
6 Disconnect the hoses from the exhaust gas recirculation (EGR) valve at the left-hand end of the cylinder head.
7 Unscrew the front suspension strut upper mounting nut on each side five turns. The nuts are on top of the front suspension strut turrets.
8 Remove the radiator grille as described in Chapter 11.
9 Unscrew the upper mounting bolts securing the transmission to the engine, noting the location of the wiring support brackets and earth lead.
10 Unclip the vehicle speed sensor and disconnect the wiring plug.
11 Apply the handbrake, then jack up the front of the vehicle and support it on axle stands (see *Jacking and vehicle support*). Remove both front roadwheels.
12 Position a container beneath the transmission, then unscrew the drain plug and drain the fluid. On completion, wipe the drain plug clean and refit it, tightening it to the specified torque.
Caution: Make sure the fluid has had time to cool before loosening the drain plug.
13 Undo the screws and remove the radiator lower cover.
14 Disconnect the fluid cooler hoses from the transmission by unscrewing the outer union nut while holding the inner adapter with a further spanner. Be prepared for some fluid loss.
15 Disconnect the electric cooling fan wiring at the connector and unclip it from the radiator.
16 Using plastic cable ties or string, tie the radiator to the bonnet lock plate on the front crossmember. Make sure the radiator is secure.
17 Support the radiator lower support crossmember, then unscrew the mounting bolts and lower it from the underbody and radiator together with the electric cooling fan. Leave the radiator suspended by the cable ties.
18 On models with power-assisted steering remove the auxiliary drivebelt as described in Chapter 1A, then unbolt the pump together with its mounting bracket from the cylinder

block and tie it to one side. Refer to Chapter 10 for more information if necessary.

19 Unclip the selector cable from the lever on the transmission, then withdraw the cable from the bracket and tie it to one side.

20 Unscrew the retaining nut and pull the speedometer drive cable from the speed sensor on the rear of the transmission.

21 Remove the brake pipe bracket from the left-hand front suspension strut (refer to Chapter 9).

22 Unscrew the nuts and disconnect the anti-roll bar links from the front suspension struts on each side (refer to Chapter 10).

23 Unclip the ABS sensors on each side (refer to Chapter 9).

24 Disconnect the steering track rod ends from the hub carriers on each side of the car (refer to Chapter 10).

25 Unscrew and remove the clamp bolts and disconnect the lower suspension arms from the hub carriers on each side as described in Chapter 10.

26 Disconnect the wiring from the lock switch on the lower rear of the transmission.

27 Using a lever, remove the left-hand driveshaft from the transmission while pulling out the suspension strut (refer to Chapter 8). Tie the driveshaft to one side making sure that the joints are not bent more that 18° otherwise they may be damaged.

28 Unscrew and remove the two bolts securing the right-hand driveshaft centre bearing to the rear of the engine and temporarily support it.

29 Using a drift entered from the left-hand side of the transmission, carefully drive the inner end of the right-hand driveshaft from the transmission taking care to prevent it from dropping. Tie the driveshaft to one side making sure that the joints are not bent more that 18° otherwise they may be damaged.

30 Remove the starter motor as described in Chapter 5A.

31 Unbolt the exhaust front downpipe from the intermediate pipe with reference to Chapter 4A.

32 Unbolt and remove the rear engine mounting/link (see Chapter 2A or 2B). Hold the engine stationary while the bolts are being removed, since the mounting will be under tension.

33 Using a hoist, support the weight of the engine and transmission. Alternatively, use a purpose-made support bar across the engine compartment, located in the front wing drain channels.

34 Undo the nuts and bolts and remove the left-hand engine mounting bracket from the transmission and insulator.

35 Unscrew the nuts and remove the right-hand engine mounting upper bracket.

36 Lower the engine and transmission until the left-hand engine mounting is clear of the mounting studs and the top of the transmission is level with the crossmember.

37 Support the transmission on a trolley jack, then unscrew and remove the upper rear and lower front bolts (with heads facing the right-hand side) securing the transmission to the engine.

38 At this stage it is advisable to have an assistant at the ready. Undo the remaining transmission bolts and carefully withdraw the transmission from the engine noting the location of the wiring support brackets. Do not allow the weight of the transmission to bear on the input shaft and vibration damper.

39 Lower the jack and remove the transmission from under the car.

40 If necessary, mark the torsional vibration damper in relation to the flywheel then unscrew the mounting bolts and withdraw the damper. Use a wide-bladed screwdriver engaged with the starter ring gear to hold the flywheel stationary. Examine the damper for wear and damage and renew it if necessary.

Refitting

41 If removed, refit the torsional vibration damper to the flywheel and tighten the mounting bolts to the specified torque while holding the flywheel stationary using the method previously described.

42 Do not lubricate the transmission input shaft, as this may contaminate and adversely affect the operation of the torsional vibration damper.

43 Raise the transmission on the jack and align the input shaft with the centre of the torsional vibration damper. Check that the engine adapter plate is correctly fitted, then engage the transmission input shaft with the vibration damper and push the transmission onto the engine.

44 Insert all mounting bolts then progressively tighten them to the specified torque.

45 The remaining refitting procedure is a reversal of removal, but note the following additional points:

a) *Fit new circlips to the grooves in the inner end of each driveshaft CV joint, and ensure that they fully engage as they are fitted into the transmission.*

b) *Refit and adjust the engine mountings as described in Chapter 2A or 2B.*

c) *Replenish the transmission fluid, and check the level with reference to Chapter 1A.*

d) *Tighten all nuts and bolts to the specified torque settings.*

e) *Check and if necessary adjust the selector cable (Section 2) and accelerator cable (Chapter 4A).*

8 Automatic transmission overhaul – general

In the event of a fault occurring on the transmission, it is first necessary to determine whether it is of an electrical, mechanical or hydraulic nature, and to do this, special test equipment is required. It is therefore essential to have the work carried out by a Ford dealer if a transmission fault is suspected.

Do not remove the transmission from the car for possible repair before professional fault diagnosis has been carried out, since most tests require the transmission to be in the vehicle.

Chapter 8
Driveshafts

Contents

Driveshaft gaiter check .See Chapter 1A or 1B
Driveshaft inner joint gaiter – renewal 3
Driveshaft outer joint gaiter – renewal 4
Driveshaft overhaul – general information 6

Driveshafts – removal and refitting 2
General information 1
Right-hand driveshaft intermediate bearing – inspection
   and renewal 5

Degrees of difficulty

| **Easy,** suitable for novice with little experience | | **Fairly easy,** suitable for beginner with some experience | | **Fairly difficult,** suitable for competent DIY mechanic | | **Difficult,** suitable for experienced DIY mechanic | | **Very difficult,** suitable for expert DIY or professional | 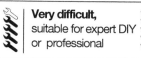 |

Specifications

General

Driveshaft type . . . .   Solid steel shafts with inner and outer constant velocity (CV) joints, both outer joints are of the ball-and-cage type and the inner joints of the tripod (spider-and-yoke) type. Right-hand driveshaft is fitted with a support bearing.

Lubricant:
  Type/specification . . . .   Special grease (Ford specification WSD-M1C230-A) supplied in sachets with gaiter kits – joints are otherwise pre-packed with grease and sealed
  Quantity (per joint):
    Inner joint . . . .   125 g
    Outer joint:
      Petrol engine models . . . .   30 g
      Diesel engine models . . . .   40 g

Torque wrench settings

	Nm	lbf ft
Hub nut*	270	199
Right-hand driveshaft support bearing plate nuts	24	18

* Use new nuts

2.2 Relieve the staking on the front hub nut

2.3 Slackening the suspension strut top mounting nut

2.6 Slacken the track rod end balljoint nut . . .

1 General information

Drive is transmitted from the differential to the front wheels by means of two, unequal-length driveshafts.

Each driveshaft is fitted with an inner and outer constant velocity (CV) joint. The inner constant velocity joint is of the spider-and-yoke type and the outer joint is of the ball-and-cage type. Each outer joint is splined to engage with the wheel hub, and is threaded so that it can be fastened to the hub by a large nut. The inner joint is also splined to engage with the differential sunwheel (left-hand side) or the intermediate shaft (right-hand side).

On the right-hand driveshaft, the inner constant velocity (CV) joint is located approximately halfway along the shaft length, and the joint outer member is supported by the rear of the cylinder block via a support bearing and bracket.

2 Driveshafts – removal and refitting

Removal

Note 1: *A new front hub nut will be required on refitting. If work is being carried out on the left-hand driveshaft, a new circlip will be*

required on refitting, and on the right-hand driveshaft new dust cover retaining clips will be required. Where applicable, Nyloc-type self-locking nuts must be renewed on refitting.
Note 2: *The driveshaft outer joint splines may be a tight fit in the hub and it is possible that a puller/extractor will be required to draw the hub assembly off of the driveshaft during removal.*

1 Remove the relevant wheel trim, or the wheel centre plate (alloy wheels) for access to the front hub nut.
2 Ensure that the handbrake is applied, then relieve the staking on the front hub nut, using a suitable punch. Slacken the hub nut using a suitable socket and extension bar. Do not remove the hub nut at this stage **(see illustration)**.
Caution: Take care, as the hub nut is tightened to a very high torque.
3 Working in the engine compartment, remove the plastic cover, and slacken the relevant suspension strut top mounting nut, using a ring spanner. Counterhold the strut piston rod using a suitable Allen key or hexagon bit **(see illustration)**. **Do not** remove the nut.
4 Slacken the relevant front wheel nuts, then jack up the front of the vehicle, and support securely on axle stands (see *Jacking and vehicle support*). Remove the roadwheel.
5 Where applicable, unscrew the retaining screws and remove the undershield from beneath the engine/transmission unit.
6 Slacken the track rod end balljoint nut, and

unscrew it as far as the ends of the threads. Counterhold the balljoint pin using a suitable Allen key or hexagon bit **(see illustration)**.
7 Disconnect the track rod end balljoint from the hub carrier using a balljoint separator tool (leave the nut fitted to protect the threads), taking care not to damage the balljoint rubber seal **(see illustration)**. Once the balljoint has been released, remove the balljoint nut.
8 Unscrew the pinch-nut and bolt securing the hub carrier to the lower arm balljoint **(see illustration)**. Push the end of the lower arm down to free the balljoint from the hub carrier. If the balljoint is very tight, it may be necessary to lever down using a large screwdriver, or similar tool, but take care not to damage the balljoint rubber seal.
9 Unscrew the nut securing the anti-roll bar drop link to the suspension strut. If necessary, counterhold the drop link pin using a spanner on the flats provided **(see illustration)**.
10 Proceed as follows, according to which driveshaft is being removed.

Left-hand driveshaft

11 On automatic transmission models, drain the transmission fluid as described in Chapter 1A.
12 The hub must now be freed from the end of the driveshaft. It should be possible to pull the hub off the driveshaft, but if the end of the driveshaft is tight in the hub, temporarily refit the hub nut to protect the driveshaft threads, then tap the end of the driveshaft with a soft-faced hammer, or use a suitable puller to free it. Support the driveshaft using wire or string –

2.7 . . . then disconnect the track rod end balljoint from the hub carrier using a balljoint separator tool

2.8 Unscrew the pinch-nut and bolt securing the hub carrier to the lower arm balljoint

2.9 Unscrew the nuts securing the anti-roll bar drop link to the suspension strut

do not allow the driveshaft to hang down under its own weight, as this may result in damage to the constant velocity joints.
Caution: When freeing the driveshaft from the hub, make sure that the driveshaft does not disengage from the inner constant velocity joint.

13 Insert a lever between the inner driveshaft joint and the transmission housing, positioning a thin piece of wood between the lever and housing to protect it. Carefully lever the driveshaft inner joint out of the differential, taking great care not to damage the transmission housing **(see illustration)**. Manoeuvre the driveshaft out of position, ensuring that the constant velocity joints are not placed under excessive strain, and remove the driveshaft from underneath the vehicle. Whilst the driveshaft is removed, plug the differential aperture with a clean, lint-free cloth to prevent dirt entry.
Caution: The manufacturers recommend that the inner driveshaft joints are not bent at an angle of more than 18°.

Right-hand driveshaft

14 Release the larger retaining clip securing the dust cover in position on the driveshaft intermediate shaft in the transmission, and slide the cover along the driveshaft **(see illustration)**.
15 Slacken and remove the nuts securing the intermediate support bearing plate to its mounting bracket **(see illustration)**.
16 Free the outer constant velocity joint from the hub as described in paragraph 12. Release the inner end of the driveshaft from the intermediate shaft, and remove the driveshaft assembly from underneath the vehicle, taking care not to place any strain on the constant velocity joints **(see illustration)**.
Caution: The manufacturers recommend that the inner driveshaft joints are not bent at an angle of more than 18°.

Refitting

Left-hand driveshaft

17 Before installing the driveshaft, examine the driveshaft oil seal in the transmission for signs of damage or deterioration and, if necessary, renew it, referring to Chapter 7A

2.13 Levering the driveshaft inner joint out of the differential

for further information. (Having got this far it is worth renewing the seal as a matter of course.)
18 Remove the circlip from the end of the driveshaft inner joint splines and discard it. Fit a new circlip, making sure it is correctly located in the groove **(see illustration)**.
19 Thoroughly clean the driveshaft splines, and the apertures in the transmission and hub assembly. Apply a thin film of grease to the oil seal lips, and to the driveshaft splines and shoulders. Check that all gaiter clips are securely fastened.
20 Offer up the driveshaft, and locate the joint splines with those of the differential sun gear, taking great care not to damage the oil seal. Push the joint fully into position, then check that the circlip is correctly located and securely holds the joint in position.
21 Align the outer constant velocity joint splines with those of the hub, and slide the joint back into position in the hub.
22 Fit a new hub nut, and use it to draw the outer joint fully into position in the hub.
23 Locate the lower arm balljoint in the hub carrier and refit the pinch-bolt and nut, tightening to the specified torque (see Chapter 10 Specifications).
24 Reconnect the track rod end balljoint to the hub carrier, and tighten a new retaining nut to the specified torque (see Chapter 10 specifications). Counterhold the balljoint pin as during removal.
25 Reconnect the anti-roll bar drop link to the strut and tighten its retaining nut to the specified torque (see Chapter 10 specifi-

2.14 Release the retaining clip securing the dust cover to the intermediate shaft

cations). Again, if necessary, counterhold the drop link pin.
26 The remainder of the refitting procedure is a reversal of removal, bearing in mind the following points.
  a) Renew any Nyloc-type self-locking nuts on refitting.
  b) Do not fully tighten the hub nut until the vehicle is resting on its wheels.
  c) Do not forget to tighten the suspension strut top mounting nut.
  d) Tighten all fixings to the specified torque.
  e) On manual transmission models check, and if necessary top-up the transmission oil as described in Chapter 1A or 1B.
  f) On automatic transmission models refill the transmission with fresh fluid as described in Chapter 1A.

Right-hand driveshaft

27 Prior to refitting, check the driveshaft support bearing for signs of freeplay or roughness. If necessary, renew the bearing as described in Section 5.
28 Ensure the driveshaft splines are clean and dry, then slide the inner dust cover onto the shaft.
29 Manoeuvre the driveshaft into position, aligning its splines with those of the intermediate shaft and engaging the support bearing plate with its mounting bracket on the rear of the cylinder block. Refit the support bearing plate nuts, tightening them lightly only at this stage.
30 Thoroughly clean the driveshaft splines, and the apertures in the hub assembly, then locate the outer constant velocity joint splines

2.15 Remove the nuts (arrowed) securing the intermediate support bearing plate to its mounting bracket

2.16 Release the inner end of the driveshaft from the intermediate shaft

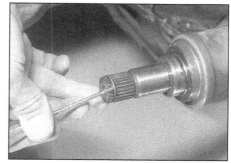

2.18 Removing the circlip from the left-hand driveshaft inner joint

with those of the hub, and slide the joint back into position in the hub.

31 Slide the inner dust cover into position over the driveshaft/intermediate shaft, and secure it in position with new retaining clips.

32 Carry out the operations described in paragraphs 22 to 26, but ignore the reference to topping-up/refilling the transmission with oil/fluid and, on completion, tighten the intermediate support bearing plate mounting nuts to the specified torque before refitting the undershield (where applicable).

3 Driveshaft inner joint gaiter – renewal

1 The inner joint gaiter can be renewed either with the driveshaft removed from the vehicle, or with it *in situ*. If it is wished to fully remove the driveshaft, refer to Section 2 first. Note that if both the inner and outer gaiters are being renewed at the same time, the outer gaiter can be removed from the inner end of the driveshaft.

Driveshaft fitted

2 Remove the relevant wheel trim or the wheel centre plate (alloy wheels), then slacken the relevant front wheel nuts. Apply the handbrake, then jack up the front of the vehicle, and support securely on axle stands (see *Jacking and vehicle support*). Remove the roadwheel.

3 Where applicable, undo the retaining screws and remove the undershield from beneath the engine/transmission unit.

4 Slacken the track rod end balljoint nut, and unscrew it as far as the ends of the threads. Counterhold the balljoint pin using a suitable Allen key or hexagon bit.

5 Disconnect the track rod end balljoint from the hub carrier using a balljoint separator tool (leave the nut fitted to protect the threads), taking care not to damage the balljoint rubber seal. Once the balljoint has been released, remove the balljoint nut.

6 Unscrew the nut securing the anti-roll bar drop link to the suspension strut. If necessary, counterhold the drop link pin using a spanner on the flats provided.

7 Unscrew the pinch-nut and bolt securing the hub carrier to the lower arm balljoint.

8 Mark the driveshaft in relation to the joint outer member to ensure correct refitting.

9 Note the fitted location of both of the inner joint gaiter retaining clips. Release the clips from the gaiter, and slide the gaiter back along the driveshaft to expose the inner joint.

10 Push the end of the lower arm down to free the balljoint from the hub carrier. If the balljoint is very tight, it may be necessary to lever down using a large screwdriver, or similar tool, but take care not to damage the balljoint rubber seal.

11 Pull the front suspension strut/hub carrier assembly outwards, while guiding the tripod joint out of the outer member. As the joint tripod is being withdrawn from the outer member, take precautions to prevent the bearing rollers falling off. Wipe away all excess grease and, if necessary, wrap tape around the tripod joint to secure the rollers in position.

12 Using a punch, paint or a suitable marker pen, make alignment marks between the tripod joint and driveshaft. Prise the circlip from the end of the driveshaft, then remove the tripod joint assembly **(see illustrations)**. If the joint is a tight fit, it maybe necessary to use a puller to draw it off the shaft – if a puller is used, take great care not to damage the rollers.

13 Slide the gaiter off the end of the driveshaft. If necessary, the outer gaiter can now be renewed with reference to Section 4.

14 Where applicable, remove the tape from the joint, and thoroughly clean the constant velocity joint components using paraffin, or a suitable solvent, and dry the components thoroughly. Carry out a visual inspection of all the components.

15 Check the spider, rollers and outer member for signs of wear, pitting or scuffing on their bearing surfaces. Also check that the spider rollers rotate smoothly and easily, with no traces of roughness.

16 If on inspection, the spider, rollers or outer member reveals signs of wear or damage, it will be necessary to renew the complete driveshaft as an assembly, since no components are available separately. If the joint components are in satisfactory condition,

obtain a repair kit from your Ford dealer, consisting of a new gaiter, retaining clips, tripod circlip and the correct type and quantity of grease.

17 Clean the driveshaft, and tape over the splines on its inner end to protect the new gaiter as it is fitted.

18 Slide the new gaiter onto the driveshaft then remove the tape from the driveshaft end.

19 If necessary, again wind tape around the tripod to retain the rollers, then push the tripod onto the driveshaft splines, if necessary using a soft-faced mallet to drive it fully onto the splines. Note that the tripod assembly must be fitted with the chamfered edge leading (towards the driveshaft), and with the previously-made marks on the tripod and driveshaft aligned. Secure the tripod in position using the new circlip, making sure that the circlip locates correctly in the driveshaft groove.

20 Where applicable, remove the tape from around the tripod, then work the grease supplied with the repair kit fully into the roller bearings. Fill the joint outer member with any excess grease.

21 Guide the tripod joint back into the outer member, making sure that the previously-made marks are aligned.

22 Slide the gaiter along the driveshaft, and locate it in the recesses on the driveshaft and joint outer member.

23 Ensure that the gaiter is not twisted or distorted, then carefully lift the lip of the gaiter at the outer member end to equalise air pressure in the gaiter.

24 Fit the large metal retaining clip to the gaiter. Remove any slack in the gaiter retaining clip by carefully compressing the raised section of the clip. In the absence of the special tool, a pair of side cutters may be used. Secure the small retaining clip using the same procedure.

25 Locate the lower arm balljoint in the hub carrier, then refit the pinch-bolt and nut and tighten to the specified torque setting (see Chapter 10 Specifications).

26 Reconnect the track rod balljoint to the hub carrier, and tighten a new retaining nut to the specified torque (see Chapter 10 Specifications). Counterhold the balljoint pin as during removal.

27 Reconnect the anti-roll bar drop link to the strut and tighten its retaining nut to the specified torque (see Chapter 10 Specifications). Again, if necessary, counterhold the drop link pin.

28 Where applicable, refit the engine undershield and the roadwheel, then lower the vehicle to the ground and tighten the wheel nuts to the specified torque (see Chapter 10 Specifications).

Driveshaft removed

29 Mount the driveshaft in a vice and remove all traces of dirt from the outside of the inner joint.

30 Mark the driveshaft in relation to the joint outer member, to ensure correct refitting.

3.12a Make alignment marks between the tripod joint and the driveshaft

3.12b . . . then prise the circlip from the end of the driveshaft

31 Note the fitted location of both of the inner joint gaiter retaining clips, then release both the large and small retaining clips from the gaiter.

32 Slide the gaiter along the driveshaft and lift off the outer member. As the outer member is being removed, take precautions to prevent the bearing rollers falling off the tripod. Wipe away all excess grease and wrap tape around the tripod joint to secure the rollers in position.

33 Carry out the operations described in paragraphs 12 to 24.

34 Check that the constant velocity joint moves freely in all directions, then refit the driveshaft to the car as described in Section 2.

4 Driveshaft outer joint gaiter – renewal

1 The outer joint gaiter can be renewed either with the driveshaft removed from the vehicle, or with it *in situ*. If it is wished to fully remove the driveshaft, refer to Section 2 first. Note that if both the outer and inner gaiters are being renewed at the same time, the inner gaiter can also be removed from the outer end of the driveshaft or alternatively both gaiters can be removed from the inner end of the driveshaft (see Section 3).

Driveshaft fitted

2 Carry out the operations described in paragraphs 2 to 7 of Section 3.

3 Note the fitted location of both of the outer joint gaiter retaining clips. Release both clips and slide the gaiter back along the driveshaft to expose the inner joint.

4 Scoop away all excess grease from the joint assembly to reveal the outer joint circlip.

5 Push the end of the lower arm down to free the balljoint from the hub carrier. If the balljoint is very tight, it may be necessary to lever down using a large screwdriver, or similar tool, but take care not to damage the balljoint rubber seal.

6 With the aid of an assistant expand the driveshaft outer joint circlip while at the same time pulling the hub assembly outwards **(see illustration)**. Free the hub and joint assembly from the end of the driveshaft, taking care not to place any excess strain on the inner joint, then slide off the gaiter.

7 Thoroughly clean the constant velocity joint components using paraffin, or a suitable solvent, and dry them thoroughly. Carry out a visual inspection of the joint components.

8 Move the inner splined driving member from side-to-side, to expose each ball in turn at the top of its track. Examine the balls for cracks, flat spots, or signs of surface pitting.

9 Inspect the ball tracks on the inner and outer members. If the tracks have widened, the balls will no longer be a tight fit. At the

same time, check the ball cage windows for wear or cracking between the windows.

10 If on inspection, any of the constant velocity joint components are found to be worn or damaged, it will be necessary to renew the complete joint assembly (where available), or even the complete driveshaft. Refer to your Ford dealer for further information on parts availability. If the joint is in satisfactory condition, obtain a repair kit consisting of a new gaiter, circlip, retaining clips, and the correct type and quantity of grease.

11 Where necessary, renew the inner gaiter using the information described in Section 3.

12 Clean the driveshaft and tape over the splines on its outer end to prevent damage to the new gaiter as it is fitted.

13 Slide the new gaiter onto the driveshaft, then remove the tape from the driveshaft end.

14 Remove the circlip from the joint inner member and install the new one supplied with the repair kit, making sure it is correctly located in the groove **(see illustration)**.

15 Work the grease supplied with the repair kit fully into the joint assembly and fill the gaiter with any excess grease **(see illustration)**.

16 Align the driveshaft splines with those of the outer joint inner member. Slide the joint onto the driveshaft until its circlip clicks into the driveshaft groove **(see illustration)**.

17 Slide the gaiter along the driveshaft, and locate it in the recesses on the driveshaft and joint outer member.

18 Ensure that the gaiter is not twisted or distorted, then carefully lift the lip of the gaiter at the outer member end to equalise air pressure in the gaiter.

19 Fit the large metal retaining clip to the gaiter and remove any slack in the clip by carefully compressing its raised section. In the absence of the special tool, a pair of side cutters may be used. Secure the small retaining clip using the same procedure.

20 Locate the lower arm balljoint in the hub carrier, then refit the pinch-bolt and nut and tighten to the specified torque setting (see Chapter 10 Specifications).

21 Reconnect the track rod end balljoint to the hub carrier, and tighten its retaining nut to the specified torque (see Chapter 10 Specifications). Counterhold the balljoint pin as during removal.

22 Reconnect the anti-roll bar drop link to the strut and tighten its retaining nut to specified torque (see Chapter 10 Specifications). Again, if necessary, counterhold the drop link pin.

23 Where applicable, refit the engine undershield and the roadwheel, then lower the vehicle to the ground and tighten the wheel nuts to the specified torque (see Chapter 10 Specifications).

Driveshaft removed

24 Mount the driveshaft in a vice and remove all traces of dirt from the outside of the inner joint.

25 Note the fitted location of both of the

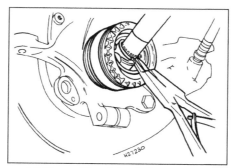

4.6 Expand the driveshaft outer joint circlip whilst pulling the hub assembly outwards

4.15 Work the grease into the joint assembly

4.14 Fit a new circlip (arrowed) to the joint outer member

4.16 Slide the joint into the driveshaft until the circlip (A) engages with the driveshaft groove (B)

retaining clips, then release both the large and small retaining clips from the gaiter.

26 Slide the gaiter along the driveshaft and wipe away all excess grease from the outer joint.

27 Using circlip pliers, expand the circlip, then remove the outer joint from the end of the driveshaft. The gaiter can then be slid off the driveshaft end.

28 Carry out the operations described in paragraphs 7 to 19.

29 Check that the constant velocity joint moves freely in all directions, then refit the driveshaft to the vehicle as described in Section 2.

5 Right-hand driveshaft intermediate bearing – inspection and renewal

Note: *A suitable bearing puller will be required to draw the bearing off the driveshaft.*

1 With the driveshaft removed as described in Section 2, proceed as follows.

2 If not already done, slide the dust cover from the inner end of the driveshaft.

3 Check that the bearing outer race rotates smoothly and easily, without any signs of roughness or undue free play between the inner and outer races. If necessary, renew the bearing as follows.

4 Using a long-reach universal bearing puller, carefully draw the bearing off the driveshaft inner end.

5 Apply a smear of grease to the inner race of the new bearing, then fit the bearing over the end of the driveshaft. Using a soft-faced hammer, and a suitable piece of tubing which bears only on the bearing inner race, tap the new bearing into position on the driveshaft, until it abuts the constant velocity joint outer member.

6 Check that the bearing rotates freely, then refit the driveshaft as described in Section 2.

6 Driveshaft overhaul – general information

1 If any of the checks described in Chapter 1A or 1B reveal wear in any driveshaft joint, first remove the wheel trim or centre cap (alloy wheels).

2 If the hub nut staking is still effective, the driveshaft nut should be correctly tightened – if in doubt, relieve the staking using a suitable punch, then tighten the nut to the specified torque and re-stake the nut (ideally, a new nut should be fitted). Refit the wheel trim or centre cap (as applicable), and repeat the check on the remaining front hub nut.

3 Road test the vehicle, and listen for a metallic clicking from the front as the vehicle is driven slowly in a circle on full-lock. If a clicking noise is heard, this indicates wear in the outer constant velocity joint. This means that the joint must be renewed; reconditioning is not possible.

4 If vibration, consistent with road speed, is felt through the car when accelerating, there is a possibility of wear in the inner constant velocity joints.

5 To check the joints for wear, remove the driveshafts, then dismantle them as described in Section 3 and 4 – if any wear or free play is found, the affected joint must be renewed. In the case of the inner joints (and on some models, the outer joints), this means that the complete driveshaft assembly must be renewed, as the joints are not available separately. Refer to your Ford dealer for information on the availability of driveshaft components.

Chapter 9
Braking system

Contents

Anti-lock braking system (ABS) – general information 20
Anti-lock braking system components – removal and refitting 21
Brake caliper – removal, overhaul and refitting 8
Brake disc – inspection, removal and refitting 6
Brake drum – removal, inspection and refitting 7
Brake fluid renewal . . . . .See Chapter 1A or 1B
Brake pad and disc wear check . . . . .See Chapter 1A or 1B
Brake pads – renewal 4
Brake pedal – removal and refitting 11
Brake pressure-regulating valve (models without ABS) – testing,
   removal and refitting 17
Brake shoe and drum wear check . . . . .See Chapter 1A or 1B
Brake shoes – renewal 5
General information 1
Handbrake – adjustment 14
Handbrake cables – removal and refitting 16
Handbrake lever – removal and refitting 15
Handbrake 'on' warning light switch – removal and refitting 19
Hydraulic fluid level check .See Weekly checks
Hydraulic fluid renewal . . . . .See Chapter 1A or 1B
Hydraulic pipes and hoses – renewal 3
Hydraulic system – bleeding 2
Master cylinder – removal, overhaul and refitting 10
Stop-light switch – removal, refitting and adjustment 18
Vacuum pump (diesel engine models) – removal and refitting 22
Vacuum pump (diesel engine models) – testing and overhaul 23
Vacuum servo unit – testing, removal and refitting 12
Vacuum servo unit check valve – removal, testing and refitting 13
Wheel cylinder – removal, overhaul and refitting 9

Degrees of difficulty

| **Easy,** suitable for novice with little experience | | **Fairly easy,** suitable for beginner with some experience | | **Fairly difficult,** suitable for competent DIY mechanic | | **Difficult,** suitable for experienced DIY mechanic | | **Very difficult,** suitable for expert DIY or professional |  |

Specifications

Front brakes

Disc diameter . . . . 240.0 mm
Disc thickness:
  Models with solid discs:
    New . . . . 12.0 mm
    Minimum . . . . 8.0 mm
  Models with ventilated discs:
    New . . . . 20.0 mm
    Minimum . . . . 18.0 mm
Maximum disc run-out . . . . 0.1 mm
Brake pad friction material minimum thickness . . . . 1.5 mm

Rear brakes

Drum internal diameter:
  Hatchback and Van models not fitted with ABS:
    New . . . . 180.0 mm
    Maximum diameter after machining . . . . 181.0 mm
  Courier/Combi models, and Hatchback and Van models with ABS:
    New . . . . 203.0 mm
    Maximum diameter after machining . . . . 204.0 mm
Brake shoe friction material minimum thickness . . . . 1.0 mm

Torque wrench settings

	Nm	lbf ft
ABS wheel sensor retaining bolt	10	7
Brake caliper:		
Guide pin bolts	25	18
Mounting bracket bolts	58	43
Handbrake cable adjusting nut	4	3
Handbrake lever retaining nuts	24	18
Hydraulic hose union	13	10
Hydraulic pipe union nut	13	10
Master cylinder retaining nuts	24	18
Rear hub nut	235	173
Vacuum pump mounting bolts – diesel engine	20	15
Vacuum servo unit mounting nuts	25	18

1 General information

The braking system is of the servo-assisted, dual-circuit hydraulic type. The arrangement of the hydraulic system is such that each circuit operates one front and one rear brake from a tandem master cylinder. Under normal circumstances, both circuits operate in unison. However, in the event of hydraulic failure in one circuit, full braking force will still be available at two wheels.

All models are fitted with front disc brakes and rear drum brakes. The front disc brakes are actuated by single-piston sliding type calipers, which ensure that equal pressure is applied to each disc pad. The rear drum brakes incorporate leading and trailing shoes, which are actuated by twin-piston wheel cylinders. A self-adjust mechanism is incorporated, to automatically compensate for brake shoe wear. As the brake shoe linings wear, the footbrake operation automatically operates the adjuster mechanism, which effectively lengthens the shoe strut and repositions the brake shoes, to remove the lining-to-drum clearance.

On models not fitted with an anti-lock braking system (ABS) a pressure-regulating valve is situated in the hydraulic circuit to each rear brake. The valves regulate the hydraulic pressure applied to the rear brakes and so help to prevent rear wheel lock-up during emergency braking. Refer to Section 20 for further information on the ABS system.

The handbrake provides an independent mechanical means of rear brake application.

On diesel engine models, since there is no throttling of the inlet manifold, the manifold is not a suitable source of vacuum to operate the vacuum servo unit. The servo unit is therefore connected to a separate vacuum pump which is bolted onto the front of the cylinder head and operated by an eccentric on the camshaft.

 Warning: When servicing any part of the system, work carefully and methodically; also observe scrupulous cleanliness

when overhauling any part of the hydraulic system. Always renew components (in axle sets, where applicable) if in doubt about their condition, and use only genuine Ford replacement parts, or at least those of known good quality. Note the warnings given in 'Safety first!' and at relevant points in this Chapter concerning the dangers of asbestos dust and hydraulic fluid.

2 Hydraulic system – bleeding

 Warning: Hydraulic fluid is poisonous; wash off immediately and thoroughly in the case of skin contact, and seek immediate medical advice if any fluid is swallowed or gets into the eyes. Certain types of hydraulic fluid are inflammable, and may ignite when allowed into contact with hot components; when servicing any hydraulic system, it is safest to assume that the fluid is inflammable, and to take precautions against the risk of fire as though it is petrol that is being handled. Hydraulic fluid is also an effective paint stripper, and will attack plastics; if any is spilt, it should be washed off immediately, using copious quantities of fresh water. Finally, it is hygroscopic (it absorbs moisture from the air) – old fluid may be contaminated and unfit for further use. When topping-up or renewing the fluid, always use the recommended type, and ensure that it comes from a freshly-opened sealed container.

General

1 The correct operation of any hydraulic system is only possible after removing all air from the components and circuit; this is achieved by bleeding the system.

2 During the bleeding procedure, add only clean, unused hydraulic fluid of the recommended type; never re-use fluid that has already been bled from the system. Ensure that sufficient fluid is available before starting work.

3 If there is any possibility of incorrect fluid being already in the system, the brake components and circuit must be flushed completely with uncontaminated, correct fluid, and new seals should be fitted to the various components.

4 If hydraulic fluid has been lost from the system, or air has entered because of a leak, ensure that the fault is cured before proceeding further.

5 Park the vehicle on level ground, switch off the engine and select first or reverse gear then chock the wheels and release the handbrake. On models equipped with ABS, disconnect the battery negative lead with reference to Chapter 5A.

6 Check that all pipes and hoses are secure, unions tight and bleed screws closed. Clean any dirt from around the bleed screws.

7 Unscrew the master cylinder reservoir cap, and top the master cylinder reservoir up to the MAX level line; refit the cap loosely, and remember to maintain the fluid level at least above the MIN level line throughout the procedure, or there is a risk of further air entering the system.

8 There are a number of one-man, do-it-yourself brake bleeding kits currently available from motor accessory shops. It is recommended that one of these kits is used whenever possible, as they greatly simplify the bleeding operation, and also reduce the risk of expelled air and fluid being drawn back into the system. If such a kit is not available, the basic (two-man) method must be used, which is described in detail below.

9 If a kit is to be used, prepare the vehicle as described previously, and follow the kit manufacturer's instructions, as the procedure may vary slightly according to the type being used; generally, they are as outlined below in the relevant sub-section.

10 Whichever method is used, the same sequence must be followed (paragraphs 11 and 12) to ensure that the removal of all air from the system.

Bleeding sequence

11 If the system has been only partially disconnected, and suitable precautions were taken to minimise fluid loss, it should be necessary only to bleed that part of the system (ie, the primary or secondary circuit).

12 If the complete system is to be bled, then it should be done working in the following sequence:
a) *Left-hand rear brake.*
b) *Right-hand front brake.*
c) *Right-hand rear brake.*
d) *Left-hand front brake.*

Bleeding

Basic (two-man) method

13 Collect together a clean glass jar, a suitable length of plastic or rubber tubing which is a tight fit over the bleed screw, and a ring spanner to fit the screw. The help of an assistant will also be required.

14 Remove the dust cap from the first bleed screw in the sequence **(see illustration)**. Fit the spanner and tube to the screw, place the other end of the tube in the jar, and pour in sufficient fluid to cover the end of the tube.

15 Ensure that the master cylinder reservoir fluid level is maintained at least above the MIN level line throughout the procedure.

16 Have the assistant fully depress the brake pedal several times to build up pressure, then maintain it on the final downstroke.

17 While pedal pressure is maintained, unscrew the bleed screw (approximately one turn) and allow the compressed fluid and air to flow into the jar. The assistant should maintain pedal pressure, following it down to the floor if necessary, and should not release it until instructed to do so. When the flow stops, tighten the bleed screw again, have the assistant release the pedal slowly, and recheck the reservoir fluid level.

18 Repeat the steps given in paragraphs 16 and 17 until the fluid emerging from the bleed screw is free from air bubbles. If the master cylinder has been drained and refilled, and air is being bled from the first screw in the sequence, allow approximately five seconds between cycles for the master cylinder passages to refill.

19 When no more air bubbles appear, securely tighten the bleed screw, remove the tube and spanner, and refit the dust cap. Do not overtighten the bleed screw.

20 Repeat the procedure on the remaining screws in the sequence, until all air is removed from the system and the brake pedal feels firm again.

Using a one-way valve kit

21 As their name implies, these kits consist of a length of tubing with a one-way valve fitted, to prevent expelled air and fluid being drawn back into the system; some kits include a translucent container, which can be positioned so that the air bubbles can be more easily seen flowing from the end of the tube.

22 The kit is connected to the bleed screw, which is then opened **(see illustration)**. The user returns to the driver's seat, depresses the brake pedal with a smooth, steady stroke, and slowly releases it; this is repeated until the expelled fluid is clear of air bubbles.

23 Note that these kits simplify work so much that it is easy to forget the master cylinder reservoir fluid level; ensure that this is maintained at least above the MIN level line at all times.

Using a pressure-bleeding kit

24 These kits are usually operated by the reservoir of pressurised air contained in the spare tyre. However, note that it will probably be necessary to reduce the pressure to a lower level than normal; refer to the instructions supplied with the kit.

25 By connecting a pressurised, fluid-filled container to the master cylinder reservoir, bleeding can be carried out simply by opening each screw in turn (in the specified sequence), and allowing the fluid to flow out until no more air bubbles can be seen in the expelled fluid.

26 This method has the advantage that the large reservoir of fluid provides an additional safeguard against air being drawn into the system during bleeding.

27 Pressure-bleeding is particularly effective when bleeding 'difficult' systems, or when bleeding the complete system at the time of routine fluid renewal.

All methods

28 When bleeding is complete, and firm pedal feel is restored, wash off any spilt fluid, securely tighten the bleed screws, and refit their dust caps.

29 Check the hydraulic fluid level in the master cylinder reservoir, and top-up if necessary (see *Weekly checks*).

30 Discard any hydraulic fluid that has been bled from the system; it will not be fit for re-use.

31 Check the feel of the brake pedal. If it feels at all spongy, air must still be present in the system, and further bleeding is required. Failure to bleed satisfactorily after a reasonable repetition of the bleeding procedure may be due to worn master cylinder seals. **Note:** *If difficulty is experienced in bleeding the braking circuit on models with ABS, this maybe due to air being trapped in the ABS hydraulic unit. If this is the case then the vehicle should be taken to a Ford dealer so that the system can be bled using special electronic test equipment.*

32 Finally, check the operation of the clutch. Since the clutch shares the same fluid reservoir as the braking system, it may also be necessary to bleed the clutch as described in Chapter 6.

3 Hydraulic pipes and hoses – renewal

Caution: On models equipped with ABS, disconnect the battery before disconnecting any braking system hydraulic union and do not reconnect the battery until after the hydraulic system has been bled. Failure to do this could lead to air entering the ABS hydraulic unit requiring the unit to be bled using special Ford test equipment (see Section 21).

Note: *Before starting work, refer to the note at the beginning of Section 2 concerning the dangers of hydraulic fluid.*

1 If any pipe or hose is to be renewed, minimise fluid loss by first removing the master cylinder reservoir cap, then tightening it down onto a piece of polythene to obtain an airtight seal. Alternatively, flexible hoses can be sealed, if required, using a proprietary brake hose clamp; metal brake pipe unions can be plugged (if care is taken not to allow dirt into the system) or capped immediately they are disconnected. Place a wad of rag under any union that is to be disconnected, to catch any spilt fluid.

2 If a flexible hose is to be disconnected, unscrew the brake pipe union nut before removing the spring clip which secures the hose to its mounting bracket **(see illustration)**.

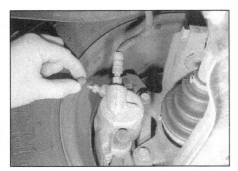

2.14 Removing a brake caliper bleed screw dust cap (right-hand brake shown)

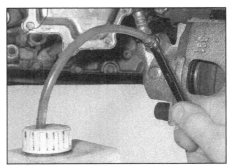

2.22 Bleeding the hydraulic system using a one-way valve kit

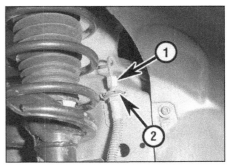

3.2 Unscrew the brake pipe union nut (1) before removing the spring clip (2)

3 To unscrew the union nuts, it is preferable to obtain a brake pipe spanner of the correct size; these are available from most large motor accessory shops. Failing this, a close-fitting open-ended spanner will be required, though if the nuts are tight or corroded, their flats may be rounded-off if the spanner slips. In such a case, a self-locking wrench is often the only way to unscrew a stubborn union, but it follows that the pipe and the damaged nuts must be renewed on reassembly. Always clean a union and surrounding area before disconnecting it. If disconnecting a component with more than one union, make a careful note of the connections before disturbing any of them.

4 If a brake pipe is to be renewed, it can be obtained, cut to length and with the union nuts and end flares in place, from Ford dealers. All that is then necessary is to bend it to shape, following the line of the original, before fitting it to the car. Alternatively, most motor accessory shops can make up brake pipes from kits, but this requires very careful measurement of the original, to ensure that the replacement is of the correct length. The safest answer is usually to take the original to the shop as a pattern.

5 On refitting, do not overtighten the union nuts. It is not necessary to exercise brute force to obtain a sound joint.

6 Ensure that the pipes and hoses are correctly routed, with no kinks, and that they are secured in the clips or brackets provided. After fitting, remove the polythene from the reservoir, and bleed the hydraulic system as described in Section 2. Wash off any spilt fluid, and check carefully for fluid leaks.

4.2 Prising the pad spring from the caliper

4 Brake pads – renewal

⚠️ **Warning: Renew both sets of front brake pads at the same time – never renew the pads on only one wheel, as uneven braking may result. Note that the dust created by wear of the pads may contain asbestos, which is a health hazard. Never blow it out with compressed air, and don't inhale any of it. An approved filtering mask should be worn when working on the brakes. DO NOT use petrol or petroleum-based solvents to clean brake parts; use brake cleaner or methylated spirit only.**

1 Chock the rear wheels, apply the handbrake, then jack up the front of the vehicle and support it on axle stands (see *Jacking and vehicle support*). Remove the front roadwheels.

2 Using a flat-bladed screwdriver, carefully

4.3 Prise out the plastic covers . . .

prise the pad spring out from the caliper noting its correct fitted position **(see illustration)**.

3 Remove the plastic covers from the ends of the guide bushes to gain access to the caliper guide pin bolts **(see illustration)**.

4 Slacken and remove the guide pin bolts, then lift the caliper assembly away from the disc **(see illustrations)**. Suspend the caliper from suspension strut coil spring using a suitable piece of wire or string; do not allow the caliper to hang down by the hose.

5 Remove the outer pad from the caliper mounting bracket, then unclip the inner pad from the caliper piston **(see illustrations)**.

6 Measure the thickness of the friction material on each brake pad **(see illustration)**. If either pad is worn at any point to the specified minimum thickness or less, all four pads must be renewed. Also, the pads should be renewed if any are fouled with oil or grease; there is no satisfactory way of degreasing friction material, once contaminated. If any of the brake pads are worn unevenly, or are

4.4a . . . then slacken . . .

4.4b . . . and remove the guide pin bolts . . .

4.4c . . . and lift the caliper from the disc

4.5a Remove the outer pad from the caliper mounting bracket . . .

4.5b . . . then unclip the inner pad from the caliper piston

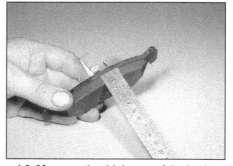

4.6 Measure the thickness of the brake pad friction material

fouled with oil or grease, trace and rectify the cause before reassembly.

7 If the brake pads are still serviceable, carefully clean them using a clean, fine wire brush or similar, paying particular attention to the sides and back of the metal backing plate. Clean out the grooves in the friction material, and pick out any large embedded particles of dirt or debris. Carefully clean the pad locations in the caliper and piston.

8 Brush the dust and dirt from the caliper and piston, but **do not** inhale it, as it is injurious to health. Inspect the dust seal around the piston for damage, and the piston for evidence of fluid leaks, corrosion or damage. If attention is necessary, refer to Section 8.

9 Prior to fitting the pads, check that the guide pin bolts are a reasonably tight-fit in the caliper bushes. If there is any sign of freeplay between either bush and bolt, both the bushes and bolts should be renewed – the bushes are a push-fit in the caliper body.

10 If new brake pads are to be fitted, the caliper piston must be pushed back into the cylinder to make room for them. Either use a G-clamp or similar tool, or use suitable pieces of wood as levers. Provided that the master cylinder reservoir has not been overfilled with hydraulic fluid, there should be no spillage, but keep a careful watch on the fluid level while retracting the piston. If the fluid level rises above the MAX level line at any time, the surplus should be syphoned off, or ejected via a plastic tube connected to one of the bleed screws (see Section 2). **Note:** *Do not syphon the fluid by mouth, as it is poisonous; use a syringe or an old poultry baster.*

11 Fit the outer pad to the caliper mounting bracket, ensuring that the pad friction material is against the brake disc, then clip the inner pad into position in the caliper piston.

12 Slide the caliper into position over the brake disc, and install the guide pin bolts. Tighten both guide pin bolts to the specified torque setting, then refit the plastic caps to the ends of the guide bushes.

13 Engage the pad spring with the outer pad, then engage the spring ends correctly in the caliper body holes, as noted before removal.

14 Depress the brake pedal repeatedly until the pads are pressed into firm contact with the brake disc, and normal (non-assisted) pedal pressure is restored.

15 Repeat the procedure to inspect or remove the pads on the remaining brake caliper.

16 Refit the roadwheels, then lower the vehicle to the ground and tighten the roadwheel nuts to the specified torque setting (see Chapter 10 Specifications).

17 Check the hydraulic fluid level as described in *Weekly checks*.

> **HAYNES HiNT** *New pads will not give full braking efficiency until they have bedded-in. Be prepared for this, and avoid hard braking as far as possible for the first hundred miles or so after pad renewal.*

5 Brake shoes – renewal

> ⚠ *Warning: Brake shoes must be renewed on both rear wheels at the same time – never renew the shoes on only one wheel, as uneven braking may result. Also, the dust created by wear of the shoes may contain asbestos, which is a health hazard. Never blow it out with compressed air, and don't inhale any of it. An approved filtering mask should be worn when working on the brakes. DO NOT use petrol or petroleum-based solvents to clean brake parts; use brake cleaner or methylated spirit only.*

1 Remove the brake drum as described in Section 7.

2 Working carefully, and taking the necessary precautions to avoid inhalation of dust, remove all traces of brake dust from the brake drum, backplate and shoes.

3 Measure the thickness of the friction material of each brake shoe at several points; if either shoe is worn at any point to the specified minimum thickness or less, all four shoes must be renewed as a set. The shoes should also be renewed if any are fouled with oil or grease; there is no satisfactory way of degreasing friction material, once contaminated.

4 If either of the brake shoes are worn unevenly, or fouled with oil or grease, trace and rectify the cause before reassembly.

5 To renew the brake shoes, proceed as follows. If all the components are in good condition, refit the brake drum as described in Section 7.

6 If desired, to improve access to the brake components, proceed as follows.

a) Where applicable, unscrew the securing bolt, and move the ABS wheel sensor clear of the working area to avoid possible damage.

b) Unscrew the four securing bolts, and remove the rear stub axle (or stub axle/hub assembly on Courier and Combi models) from the trailing arm.

7 Note the position of each shoe, and the location of each of the springs. Also make a note of the self-adjuster component locations, to aid refitting later.

8 Using a pair of pliers, remove the shoe retainer springs by depressing and sliding them downwards, then withdraw the retainer pins from the brake backplate **(see illustration)**.

9 Ease the shoes out one at a time from the lower anchor point, to release the tension of the return spring, then disconnect the lower return spring from both shoes, using pliers if necessary **(see illustration)**.

10 Ease the upper end of both shoes out from the wheel cylinder pistons, taking care not to damage the wheel cylinder seals, and disconnect the handbrake cable from the lever on the trailing shoe. The brake shoe and adjuster strut assembly can then be manoeuvred out of position and away from the backplate. Do not depress the brake pedal until the brakes are reassembled; wrap a strong elastic band around the wheel cylinder pistons to retain them **(see illustrations)**.

5.8 Remove the shoe retaining springs and the pins

5.9 Disconnect the lower return spring from both shoes

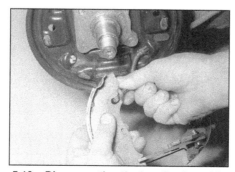

5.10a Disconnecting the handbrake cable from the lever on the trailing shoe

5.10b Wrap a strong elastic band around the wheel cylinder pistons to retain them

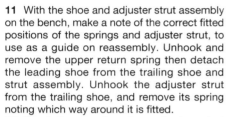

5.14a Adjuster strut components correctly assembled for refitting

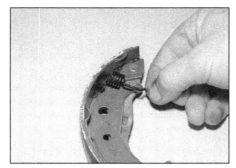

5.14b Fit the adjuster strut retaining spring

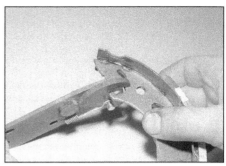

5.15 Engage the adjuster strut with the leading shoe

11 With the shoe and adjuster strut assembly on the bench, make a note of the correct fitted positions of the springs and adjuster strut, to use as a guide on reassembly. Unhook and remove the upper return spring then detach the leading shoe from the trailing shoe and strut assembly. Unhook the adjuster strut from the trailing shoe, and remove its spring noting which way around it is fitted.

12 Carefully examine the adjuster strut assembly for signs of wear or damage, paying particular attention to the self-adjust ratchet mechanism, and renew if necessary.

13 Depending on the type of brake shoes being installed, it may be necessary to remove the handbrake lever from the original trailing shoe, and install it on the new shoe. Secure the lever in position with a new retaining clip. All return springs should be renewed, regardless of their apparent condition; spring kits are available from Ford dealers.

14 Fit the adjuster strut retaining spring to the trailing shoe, ensuring that the shorter hook of the spring is engaged with the shoe **(see illustrations)**.

15 Fully extend the adjuster strut ratchet, then engage the adjuster strut with the leading shoe, and fully release the ratchet **(see illustration)**.

16 Attach the adjuster strut to the retaining spring on the trailing shoe, then ease the strut into position in its slot in the trailing shoe **(see illustration)**.

17 Hook the leading shoe onto the return spring, then manipulate the shoes until the return spring can be connected to the trailing shoe **(see illustration)**.

18 Remove the elastic band fitted to the wheel cylinder. Peel back the rubber protective caps, and check the wheel cylinder for fluid leaks or other damage. Also check that both cylinder pistons are free to move easily. Refer to Section 9, if necessary, for information on wheel cylinder renewal.

19 Prior to installation, clean the backplate and apply a thin smear of high-temperature brake grease or anti-seize compound to all those surfaces of the backplate which bear on the shoes, particularly the wheel cylinder pistons and lower anchor point. Do not use too much lubricant, and don't allow the lubricant to foul the friction material.

20 Ensure that the adjuster strut self-adjust mechanism is fully released then manoeuvre the shoe and strut assembly into position and attach the handbrake cable to the lever on the trailing shoe. Engage the upper ends of both shoes with the wheel cylinder pistons, then fit the lower return spring to both shoes and ease the shoes into position on the lower anchor point **(see illustration)**.

21 Centralise the shoes relative to the backplate by tapping them. Refit the shoe retainer pins and secure them in position with the springs.

22 Where applicable, refit the rear stub axle (or stub axle/hub assembly on Courier and Combi models), and tighten the securing bolts to the specified torque (see Chapter 10 Specifications).

23 Where applicable, refit the ABS wheel sensor, and tighten the securing bolt to the specified torque.

24 Refit the brake drum as described in Section 7.

25 Repeat the procedure to inspect or renew the shoes on the remaining rear brake.

26 Once the brake drums have been refitted, adjust the lining-to-drum clearance by repeatedly depressing the brake pedal. Whilst doing this, have an assistant listen to the rear drums, to check that the adjuster strut is functioning correctly – a clicking sound should be emitted by the strut as the pedal is operated.

27 Adjust the handbrake as described in Section 14 then check the brake fluid level as described in *Weekly checks*.

> **HAYNES HiNT** *New shoes will not give full braking efficiency until they have bedded-in. Be prepared for this, and avoid hard braking as far as possible for the first hundred miles or so after shoe renewal.*

6 Brake disc – inspection, removal and refitting

Note: *Before starting work, refer to the note at the beginning of Section 4 concerning the dangers of asbestos dust.*

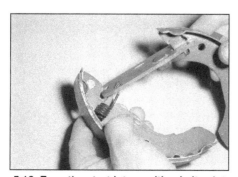

5.16 Ease the strut into position in its slot in the trailing shoe

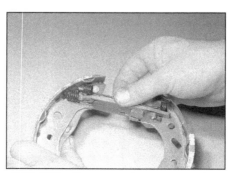

5.17 Fitting the upper shoe return spring

5.20 Fit the lower return spring and ease the shoes into position over the lower anchor point

6.4 Checking brake disc run-out using a dial gauge

7.4 Unscrew the rear hub nut . . .

7.5 . . . and withdraw the hub/brake drum – Hatchback and Van models

Inspection

Note: *If either disc requires renewal, BOTH should be renewed at the same time, to ensure even and consistent braking. New brake pads should also be fitted.*

1 Apply the handbrake, then jack up the front of the car and support it on axle stands (see *Jacking and vehicle support*). Remove the appropriate front roadwheel.

2 Slowly rotate the disc so that the full area of both sides can be checked. Remove the brake pads if better access is required to the inboard surface. Light scoring is normal in the area swept by the brake pads, but if heavy scoring or cracks are found, the disc must be renewed.

3 It is normal to find a lip of rust and brake dust around the disc's perimeter – this can be scraped off if required. If, however, a lip has formed due to excessive wear of the brake pad swept area, then the disc's thickness must be measured using a micrometer. Take measurements at several places around the disc, at the inside and outside of the pad swept area. If the disc has worn at any point to the specified minimum thickness or less, the disc must be renewed.

4 If the disc is thought to be warped, it can be checked for run-out. Using spacers, refit at least two wheel nuts and tighten them securely to seat the disc in position. Either use a dial gauge mounted on any convenient fixed point, while the disc is slowly rotated, or use feeler blades to measure (several points around the disc) the clearance between the disc and a fixed point, such as the caliper mounting bracket **(see illustration)**. If the measurements obtained are at the specified maximum or beyond, the disc is excessively warped, and must be renewed, however, it is worth checking first that the hub bearing is in good condition (see Chapter 1A or 1B and/or 10). Remove the nuts and spacers.

5 Check the disc for cracks, especially around the wheel stud holes, and any other wear or damage, and renew if necessary.

Removal

6 With the front of the vehicle raised and the wheel removed, slacken and remove the two bolts securing the brake caliper mounting bracket to the hub carrier. Slide the caliper

assembly (complete with the brake pads) off of the disc, and suspend the assembly from the suspension strut coil spring, using a piece of wire or string, to avoid placing any strain on the hydraulic brake hose.

7 Use chalk or paint to mark the relationship of the disc to the hub then, where applicable, remove the retaining clip(s) from wheel studs, and remove the disc. If the disc is tight, lightly tap its rear face with a hide or plastic mallet.

Refitting

8 Refitting is the reverse of the removal procedure, noting the following points:
   a) *Ensure that the mating surfaces of the disc and hub are clean and flat.*
   b) *If a new disc has been fitted, use a suitable solvent to wipe any preservative coating from the disc, before refitting the caliper.*
   c) *Slide the caliper into position, making sure the pads pass either side of the disc, and tighten the caliper bracket bolts to the specified torque setting.*
   d) *Refit the roadwheel then lower the vehicle to the ground and tighten the wheel nuts to the specified torque. Apply the footbrake several times to force the pads back into contact with the disc before driving the vehicle.*

7   Brake drum – removal, inspection and refitting

Note: *Before starting work, refer to the note at the beginning of Section 5 concerning the dangers of asbestos dust.*

Note: *The manufacturer's procedure for removal of the brake drum is to undo the four bolts that hold the hub/brake drum assembly to the rear axle flange. However, in our experience, as the vehicle gets older so the bolts become covered in road dirt which results in them being increasingly difficult to remove due to corrosion. It is for this reason that we offer the following alternative method.*

Hatchback and Van models

Removal

1 An integral hub/brake drum assembly is used, incorporating the rear wheel bearings.

2 Working at the handbrake lever inside the car, back off the handbrake cable adjustment, as described in Section 14.

3 Remove the relevant wheel trim or the wheel centre plate (alloy wheels), then slacken the relevant wheel nuts. Chock the front wheels, and select 1st gear (manual transmission) or P (automatic transmission), then jack up the rear of the vehicle, and support securely on axle stands (see *Jacking and vehicle support*). Remove the rear roadwheel.

4 Using a screwdriver, prise the dust cap from the centre of the hub/brake drum, then unscrew the hub nut **(see illustration)**.

5 Withdraw the hub/brake drum from the stub axle **(see illustration)**. If the drum is tight (this should not be the case if the handbrake cable has been backed off), this may be due to the tightness of the hub bearing on the stub axle, or due to the brake shoes binding on the inner circumference of the drum. If the bearing is tight, tap the periphery of the hub/brake drum using a hide or plastic mallet, or use a universal puller, secured to the hub/brake drum with the wheel nuts, to pull it off. If the brake shoes are binding, proceed as follows.

6 Referring to Section 14, fully slacken the handbrake cable adjuster nut to obtain maximum freeplay in the cable. If this still fails to release the drum, remove the small rubber grommet from the rear of the backplate. Insert a screwdriver through the hole and release the handbrake operating lever by pushing the lever until the stop lug can pass over the surface of the shoe, allowing the brake shoes to retract fully **(see illustration)**. The

7.6 Insert a screwdriver through the hole (arrowed) to release the handbrake operating lever – Hatchback and Van models

7.19 Brake backplate rubber grommet location (arrowed) – Courier and Combi models

hub/brake drum should then be free to be removed.

Inspection

7 Working carefully, remove all traces of brake dust from the drum, but *avoid inhaling the dust, as it is injurious to health.*

8 Scrub clean the outside of the drum, and check it for obvious signs of wear or damage such as cracks around the roadwheel bolt holes; renew the drum if necessary.

9 Examine carefully the inside of the drum. Light scoring of the friction surface is normal, but if heavy scoring is found, the drum must be renewed. It is usual to find a lip on the drum's inboard edge which consists of a mixture of rust and brake dust; this should be scraped away to leave a smooth surface which can be polished with fine (120 to 150 grade) emery paper. If the lip is due to the friction surface being recessed by wear, then the drum must be refinished (within the specified limits) or renewed.

10 If the drum is thought to be excessively worn or oval, its internal diameter must be measured at several points using an internal micrometer. Take measurements in pairs, the second at right-angles to the first, and compare the two to check for signs of ovality. Minor ovality can be corrected by machining; otherwise, renew the hub/brake drum.

Refitting

11 If a new hub/brake drum is to be installed, use a suitable solvent to remove any preservative coating that may have been applied to its interior.

12 Apply a smear of gear oil to the stub axle, and slide on the hub/brake drum, being careful not to get oil onto the brake shoes or the friction surface of the drum.

13 Fit the rear hub nut, tightening it to the specified torque setting, and tap the dust cap securely into position in the centre of the hub/brake drum.

14 Depress the footbrake several times to operate the self-adjusting mechanism until normal, non-assisted pedal action returns. Refit the roadwheel then lower the vehicle to the ground and tighten the wheel nuts to the specified torque.

15 On completion, adjust the handbrake as described in Section 14.

Courier and Combi models

Removal

16 Working at the handbrake lever inside the car, back off the handbrake cable adjustment, as described in Section 14.

17 Remove the relevant wheel trim or the wheel centre plate (alloy wheels), then slacken the relevant wheel nuts. Chock the front wheels, and select 1st gear (manual transmission) or P (automatic transmission), then jack up the rear of the vehicle, and support securely on axle stands (see *Jacking and vehicle support*). Remove the rear roadwheel.

18 Prise off the retaining clip, located on one of the wheel studs, and withdraw the drum from the hub. If the drum is tight (this should not be the case if the handbrake cable has been backed off), this may be due to the brake shoes binding on the inner circumference of the drum. If the brake shoes are binding, proceed as follows.

19 Referring to Section 14, fully slacken the handbrake cable adjuster nut to obtain maximum freeplay in the cable. If this still fails to release the drum, remove the small rubber grommet from the rear of the backplate. Insert a screwdriver through the hole and release the adjuster strut self-adjust mechanism by moving the strut quadrant, allowing the brake shoes to retract fully **(see illustration)**. The drum should then be free to be removed.

Inspection

20 Proceed as described in paragraphs 7 to 10 inclusive.

Refitting

21 If a new drum is to be installed, use a suitable solvent to remove any preservative coating that may have been applied to its interior.

22 Ensure that the mating faces of the hub and drum are clean, then slide the drum into position on the hub, and refit the retaining clip to the wheel stud.

23 Depress the footbrake several times to operate the self-adjusting mechanism until normal, non-assisted pedal action returns. Refit the roadwheel then lower the vehicle to the ground and tighten the wheel nuts to the specified torque.

24 On completion, adjust the handbrake as described in Section 14.

8.5 Unscrewing a caliper guide pin bolt

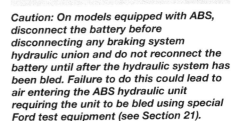

8 Brake caliper – removal, overhaul and refitting

Caution: On models equipped with ABS, disconnect the battery before disconnecting any braking system hydraulic union and do not reconnect the battery until after the hydraulic system has been bled. Failure to do this could lead to air entering the ABS hydraulic unit requiring the unit to be bled using special Ford test equipment (see Section 21).

Note: *Before starting work, refer to the note at the beginning of Section 2 concerning the dangers of hydraulic fluid, and to the warning at the beginning of Section 4 concerning the dangers of asbestos dust.*

Removal

1 Apply the handbrake, then jack up the front of the vehicle and support it on axle stands (see *Jacking and vehicle support*). Remove the appropriate roadwheel.

2 Minimise fluid loss by first removing the master cylinder reservoir cap, and then tightening it down onto a piece of polythene, to obtain an airtight seal. Alternatively, use a brake hose clamp, a G-clamp or a similar tool to clamp the flexible hose running to the caliper.

3 Clean the area around the caliper hose union, then loosen the union nut.

4 Using a flat-bladed screwdriver, carefully prise the pad spring out from the caliper noting its correct fitted position.

5 Remove the plastic covers from the ends of the guide bushes to gain access to the caliper guide pin bolts, then slacken and remove the guide pin bolts **(see illustration)**.

6 Lift the caliper assembly away from the disc and unclip the inner pad from the caliper piston **(see illustration)**. Unscrew the caliper from the end of the brake hose and remove it from the vehicle. Plug or cover the end of the hose to minimise fluid loss and to prevent dirt entry.

Overhaul

7 With the caliper on the bench, wipe away all traces of dust and dirt, but *avoid inhaling the dust, as it is injurious to health.*

8.6 Lift the caliper away from the disc

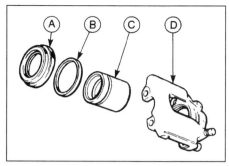

8.8 Brake caliper components

A *Dust cover* C *Piston*
B *Piston seal* D *Caliper body*

8 Withdraw the partially ejected piston from the caliper body **(see illustration)**.

 HAYNES HINT *If the piston cannot be withdrawn by hand, it can be pushed out by applying compressed air to the brake hose union hole. Only low pressure should be required, such as is generated by a foot pump. As the piston is expelled take great care not to trap your fingers between the piston and caliper.*

9 Using a small screwdriver, prise the dust seal from the piston, then extract the piston hydraulic seal from the caliper bore, taking great care not to damage the bore.
10 Thoroughly clean all components, using only methylated spirit, isopropyl alcohol or clean hydraulic fluid as a cleaning medium. Never use mineral-based solvents such as petrol or paraffin, as they will attack the hydraulic system rubber components. Dry the components immediately, using compressed air or a clean, lint-free cloth. Use compressed air to blow clear the fluid passages.
11 Check all components, and renew any that are worn or damaged. Check particularly the cylinder bore and piston – these should be renewed (note that this means the renewal of the complete caliper body assembly) if they are scratched, worn or corroded in any way. Similarly, check the condition of the guide pin bolts and their bushes – both bolts should be undamaged and (when cleaned) a reasonably tight sliding fit in their bushes. If there is any doubt about the condition of any component, renew it.
12 If the assembly is fit for further use, obtain the appropriate repair kit; the components are available from Ford dealers in various combinations. All rubber seals should be renewed as a matter of course; these should never be re-used.
13 Before commencing reassembly, ensure that all components are clean and dry.
14 Soak the piston and the new piston (fluid) seal in clean hydraulic fluid. Smear clean fluid on the cylinder bore surface.

15 Fit the new piston (fluid) seal, using only your fingers (no tools) to manipulate it into the cylinder bore groove.
16 Fit the new dust seal to the piston groove, then carefully ease the piston squarely into the cylinder bore using a twisting motion. Press the piston fully into position then seat the outer lip of the dust seal on the caliper body.

Refitting

17 Screw the caliper body fully onto the flexible hose union.
18 Ensure that the outer brake pad is still correctly fitted in the caliper mounting bracket, and clip the inner pad into position in the caliper piston.
19 Slide the caliper over the disc, making sure that the pads remain correctly positioned, and fit the guide pin bolts. Tighten both guide pin bolts to the specified torque, then refit the plastic covers to the bushes.
20 Engage the pad spring with the outer pad and engage the spring ends correctly in the caliper body holes, as noted before removal.
21 Tighten the brake hose union, then remove the brake hose clamp or polythene (where fitted).
22 Bleed the hydraulic system as described in Section 2. Note that, provided precautions were taken to minimise brake fluid loss, it should only be necessary to bleed the relevant front brake.
23 Refit the roadwheel, then lower the vehicle to the ground and tighten the roadwheel nuts to the specified torque.

9 Wheel cylinder – removal, overhaul and refitting

Caution: On models equipped with ABS, disconnect the battery before disconnecting any braking system hydraulic union and do not reconnect the battery until after the hydraulic system has been bled. Failure to do this could lead to air entering the ABS hydraulic unit requiring the unit to be bled using special Ford test equipment (see Section 21).
Note: *Before starting work, refer to the note at the beginning of Section 2 concerning the*

9.3 Unhook the brake shoe upper return spring (arrowed) – Hatchback model

dangers of hydraulic fluid, and to the warning at the beginning of Section 5 concerning the dangers of asbestos dust.

Removal

1 Remove the brake drum as described in Section 7.
2 Minimise fluid loss by first removing the master cylinder reservoir cap, and then tightening it down onto a piece of polythene, to obtain an airtight seal. Alternatively, use a brake hose clamp, a G-clamp or a similar tool to clamp the flexible hose at the nearest convenient point to the wheel cylinder.
3 Carefully unhook the brake shoe upper return spring, and remove it from both brake shoes **(see illustration)**. Pull the upper ends of the shoes away from the wheel cylinder to disengage them from the pistons.
4 Wipe away all traces of dirt around the brake pipe union at the rear of the wheel cylinder, and unscrew the union nut. Carefully ease the pipe out of the wheel cylinder, and plug or tape over its end to prevent dirt entry. Wipe off any spilt fluid immediately.
5 Unscrew the two wheel cylinder retaining bolts from the rear of the backplate, and remove the cylinder, taking great care not to allow surplus hydraulic fluid to contaminate the brake shoe linings **(see illustration)**.

Overhaul

6 It is not possible to overhaul the cylinder, since no components are available separately. If faulty, the complete wheel cylinder assembly must be renewed.

Refitting

7 Ensure that the backplate and wheel cylinder mating surfaces are clean and dry then spread the brake shoes and manoeuvre the wheel cylinder into position. Engage the brake pipe, and screw in the union nut two or three turns to ensure that the thread has started.
8 Insert the two wheel cylinder retaining bolts, tightening them securely, then tighten the brake pipe union nut to the specified torque.
9 Remove the clamp from the flexible brake hose, or the polythene from the master cylinder reservoir (as applicable).
10 Ensure that the brake shoes are correctly

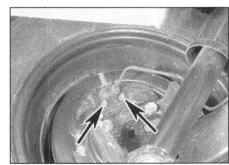

9.5 Rear wheel cylinder securing bolts (arrowed) – Courier model

located in the cylinder pistons, then carefully refit the brake shoe return spring, ensuring it is correctly located in both shoes. Also check that the adjuster strut components are correctly located on the shoes.

11 Refit the brake drum as described in Section 7.

12 Bleed the brake hydraulic system as described in Section 2. Providing suitable precautions were taken to minimise loss of fluid, it should only be necessary to bleed the relevant rear brake.

10 Master cylinder – removal, overhaul and refitting

Caution: On models equipped with ABS, disconnect the battery before disconnecting any braking system hydraulic union and do not reconnect the battery until after the hydraulic system has been bled. Failure to do this could lead to air entering the ABS hydraulic unit requiring the unit to be bled using special Ford test equipment (see Section 21).

Note: *Before starting work, refer to the warning at the beginning of Section 2 concerning the dangers of hydraulic fluid.*

Removal

1 Exhaust the vacuum present in the brake servo unit by repeatedly depressing the brake pedal.

2 Remove the master cylinder reservoir cap and syphon the hydraulic fluid from the reservoir. **Note:** *Do not syphon the fluid by mouth, as it is poisonous; use a syringe or an old poultry baster.* Alternatively, open any convenient bleed screw in the system, and gently pump the brake pedal to expel the fluid through a plastic tube connected to the bleed screw (see Section 2). Disconnect the wiring connector from the brake fluid level sender unit in the reservoir cap.

3 On diesel engine models, if desired, to improve access, slacken the retaining clamps and remove the air intake ducting from behind the reservoir.

4 On manual transmission models, release

the retaining clip and disconnect the clutch master cylinder fluid supply hose from the side of the reservoir **(see illustration)**. Be prepared for fluid spillage.

5 On models not fitted with ABS, wipe clean the area around the brake pipe unions on the side of the master cylinder, and place absorbent rags beneath the pipe unions to catch any surplus fluid. Make a note of the correct fitted positions of the unions, then unscrew the union nuts and carefully withdraw the pipes **(see illustration)**. Plug or tape over the pipe ends and master cylinder orifices, to minimise the loss of brake fluid, and to prevent the entry of dirt into the system. Wash off any spilt fluid immediately with cold water.

6 On models with ABS, wipe clean the area around the brake pipe unions on both the master cylinder and ABS hydraulic unit, and place absorbent rags beneath the pipe unions to catch any surplus fluid. Unscrew the union nuts securing each pipe to both the master cylinder and hydraulic unit and remove the pipes from the engine compartment. Plug or tape over the master cylinder and hydraulic unit orifices, to minimise the loss of brake fluid, and to prevent the entry of dirt into the system. Wash off any spilt fluid immediately with cold water.

7 Slacken and remove the nuts securing the master cylinder to the vacuum servo unit **(see illustration)**. Note the locations of any brackets secured by the nuts. Remove the master cylinder from the engine compartment along with its sealing ring – discard the sealing ring a new one must be used on refitting.

Overhaul

8 The master cylinder can be overhauled after obtaining the relevant repair kit from a Ford dealer. Ensure that the correct repair kit is obtained for the master cylinder being worked on. Note the locations of all components to ensure correct refitting, and lubricate the new seals using clean brake fluid. Follow assembly instructions supplied with the repair kit.

Refitting

9 Ensure the mating surfaces are clean and

dry then fit the new sealing ring to the rear of the master cylinder.

10 Carefully fit the master cylinder to the servo unit, ensuring that the servo unit pushrod enters the master cylinder bore centrally. Fit the retaining nuts and tighten them to the specified torque setting. Where applicable, make sure that any brackets secured by the master cylinder retaining nuts are in position as noted before removal.

11 Reconnect the brake pipes to the master cylinder and, on models with ABS, the hydraulic unit and tighten the union nuts securely. Make sure that the pipes are correctly reconnected as noted before removal.

12 On manual transmission models securely reconnect the clutch fluid hose to the side of the reservoir, and secure with the clip.

13 On diesel engine models, refit the air intake ducting, and tighten the retaining clamps.

14 Refill the master cylinder reservoir with new fluid, then bleed the complete hydraulic system as described in Section 2. Thoroughly check the operation of the braking system before using the vehicle on the road.

11 Brake pedal – removal and refitting

Removal

1 Remove the stop-light switch as described in Section 18.

2 On manual transmission models, using pliers, carefully unhook the return spring from the clutch pedal.

3 Remove the retaining clip from the left-hand end of the pedal pivot shaft and push the shaft slightly towards the brake pedal.

4 Remove the retaining clip from the right-hand end of the pivot shaft then slide the shaft sufficiently to the left until the pedal can be lowered from its mounting bracket.

5 Insert a screwdriver into the groove in the plastic retaining clip, then use the screwdriver to spread the clip, and release it from the

10.4 Disconnect the clutch master cylinder hose (arrowed) from the brake fluid reservoir – manual transmission models

10.5 Unscrewing a master cylinder brake pipe union nut

10.7 Master cylinder securing nut (arrowed)

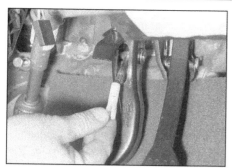

11.5 Removing the pushrod-to-brake pedal retaining clip

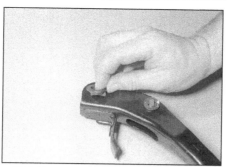

11.6 Remove the pivot bushes from the brake pedal

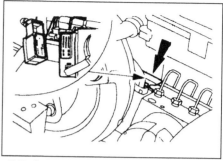

12.7 On models with ABS, disconnect the ABS hydraulic unit wiring connector (arrowed)

groove in the pushrod **(see illustration)**. Disconnect the servo unit/linkage pushrod from the pedal.

6 Remove the pivot bushes from either side of the pedal **(see illustration)**.

7 Inspect the pedal for signs of wear or damage, paying particular attention to the pivot bushes, and renew worn components as necessary.

Refitting

8 Apply some multi-purpose grease to the bearing surfaces of the pedal, pivot shaft and bushes. Fit the bushes to the pedal.

9 Manoeuvre the pedal assembly into position under the facia, ensuring that the servo/linkage unit pushrod engages correctly with the pedal, then slide the pivot shaft fully into position.

10 Refit the right-hand retaining clip to the pivot shaft groove, then secure the shaft in position by refitting the left-hand clip to the groove.

11 Secure the servo/linkage pushrod in position with the retaining clip (make sure that the clip engages with the groove in the pushrod end fitting), then refit the stop-light switch as described in Section 18.

12 On manual transmission models, hook the return spring back onto the clutch pedal.

13 Check the operation of the brake pedal before using the vehicle on the road.

12 Vacuum servo unit – testing, removal and refitting

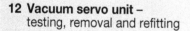

Testing

1 To test the operation of the servo unit, depress the footbrake several times to exhaust the vacuum, then start the engine whilst keeping the pedal firmly depressed. As the engine starts, there should be a noticeable 'give' in the brake pedal as the vacuum builds up. Allow the engine to run for at least two minutes, then switch it off. If the brake pedal is now depressed it should feel normal, but further applications should result in the pedal feeling firmer, with the pedal stroke decreasing with each application.

2 If the servo does not operate as described, first inspect the servo unit check valve as described in Section 13.

3 If the servo unit still fails to operate satisfactorily, the fault lies within the unit itself. Repairs to the unit are not possible – if faulty, the servo unit must be renewed.

Removal

4 Remove the master cylinder as described in Section 10.

5 Carefully ease the vacuum hose end fitting out from the servo unit, taking great care not to displace the rubber grommet.

6 Where applicable, disconnect the wiring connectors from the emission control system components mounted on the bracket, situated directly above the servo unit. Slacken and remove the retaining screw then unclip the bracket assembly and remove it from the engine compartment.

7 On models equipped with ABS, disconnect the wiring connector from the ABS hydraulic unit **(see illustration)**.

8 On left-hand-drive models, reach up behind the facia, then prise off the retaining clip securing the servo unit pushrod to the brake pedal (see Section 11). Slacken and remove the four nuts securing the servo unit to its mounting bracket, then manoeuvre the unit forwards and out of the engine compartment.

9 On right-hand-drive models, slacken and remove the four nuts securing the servo unit to its mounting brackets. Pull the servo unit gently forwards until access to the pushrod clevis pin can be gained. Slide out the

retaining clip, then withdraw the clevis pin and manoeuvre the servo unit out from the engine compartment **(see illustrations)**.

10 If the servo unit is faulty it must be renewed – overhaul of the unit is not possible.

Refitting

11 On left-hand-drive models, carefully manoeuvre the servo unit into position, making sure that the pushrod engages correctly with the brake pedal locating piece. Ensure that the pushrod is correctly located, then refit the servo unit securing nuts and tighten them to the specified torque. Secure the pushrod to the pedal with the retaining clip.

12 On right-hand-drive models, apply a smear of multi-purpose grease to the servo unit clevis and clevis pin. Manoeuvre the unit into position, aligning it with the cross-linkage, then refit the clevis pin and secure it in position with the retaining clip. Seat the unit on the bracket and tighten its mounting nuts to the specified torque.

13 Where applicable, refit the emission control system component bracket and securely tighten its retaining screw, then reconnect the wiring connectors to the emission control system components. Where necessary, also reconnect the ABS hydraulic unit wiring connector.

14 Ensure that the rubber grommet is correctly located in the servo unit, then ease the vacuum hose end fitting back into position.

15 Refit the master cylinder as described in Section 10 and bleed the complete hydraulic system as described in Section 2.

12.9a Unscrew the four servo securing nuts (arrowed) . . .

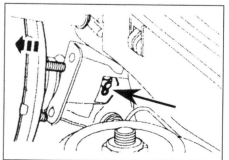

12.9b . . . then remove the clevis pin and retaining clip (arrowed)

13.1 Vacuum servo unit check valve location (arrowed)

13 Vacuum servo unit check valve – removal, testing and refitting

Removal

1 The valve is integral with the servo vacuum hose **(see illustration)**.
2 Carefully ease the vacuum hose end fitting out from its rubber grommet on the front of the servo unit **(see illustration)**.
3 Work back along the vacuum hose, freeing it from any relevant retaining clips, then unscrew the union nut securing the hose to the manifold/pump (as applicable) and remove the hose assembly from the vehicle. The check valve and hose cannot be separated.

Testing

4 Examine the check valve and hose for signs of damage, and renew if necessary. The valve may be tested by blowing through the hose in both directions. Air should flow through the valve in one direction only – when blown through from the servo unit end of the hose. Renew the valve and hose assembly if this is not the case.
5 Examine the servo unit rubber sealing grommet for signs of damage or deterioration, and renew as necessary.

Refitting

6 Manoeuvre the hose assembly into position and connect the engine end of the hose to the

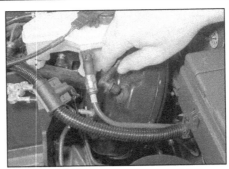

13.2 Ease the vacuum hose end fitting from the servo unit

manifold/pump (as applicable), tightening its union nut securely.
7 Ensure the hose is correctly routed and fit the sealing grommet into position in the servo unit. Ease the hose end fitting into position in the servo, taking care not to displace or damage the grommet.
8 On completion, start the engine and check that there are no air leaks.

14 Handbrake – adjustment

Caution: If the handbrake is incorrectly adjusted, the rear brake automatic adjustment mechanism will not be able to function correctly. This will lead to the brake shoe-to-drum clearance becoming excessive as the shoe linings wear, resulting in excessive brake pedal travel.
1 Fully release the handbrake then apply the footbrake firmly several times to ensure that the self-adjust mechanism is fully adjusted.
2 Unclip the handbrake lever gaiter to gain access to the adjuster nut on the side of the lever.
3 From the fully-released position, pull the handbrake lever up noting the number of clicks emitted from the handbrake ratchet mechanism. Position the handbrake lever on the sixth notch of mechanism then slacken the adjusting nut until it rotates freely. Adjust the handbrake by tightening the adjuster nut to the specified torque then clip the gaiter back into position **(see illustration)**.

15 Handbrake lever – removal and refitting

Removal

1 Disconnect the battery negative lead (see Chapter 5A).
2 Chock the wheels to prevent the vehicle rolling whilst the handbrake is released.
3 From inside the vehicle, unclip the handbrake lever gaiter and remove it from the lever.
4 Slacken and remove the cable adjusting nut from the side of the lever, then unscrew the two lever retaining nuts **(see illustration)**. Manoeuvre the lever assembly out of position, disconnecting the warning light switch wiring connector as it becomes accessible.

Refitting

5 Refitting is a reversal of removal, tightening the lever retaining nuts to the specified torque. Prior to refitting the gaiter, adjust the handbrake cable as described in Section 14.

16 Handbrake cables – removal and refitting

Removal

1 The handbrake cable consists of three sections, a short front section which connects the lever to the equalizer plate and the left- and right-hand rear sections which link the equalizer plate to the rear brakes. Each section can be removed individually as follows.

Front cable

2 Remove the handbrake lever as described in Section 15.
3 Firmly chock the front wheels, then jack the rear of the vehicle and support it on axle stands (see *Jacking and vehicle support*).
4 To gain access to the equalizer plate mechanism which links the handbrake cables, undo the retaining nuts and remove the exhaust system centre heat shield **(see illustration)**. **Note:** *On some models it may*

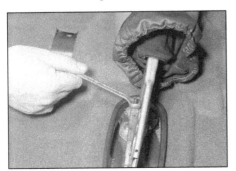

14.3 Slackening the handbrake adjuster nut

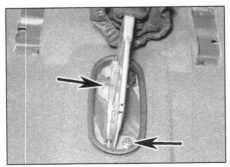

15.4 Handbrake lever securing nuts (arrowed)

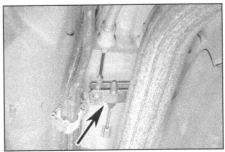

16.4 Remove the exhaust heat shield for access to the handbrake equalizer plate mechanism (arrowed)

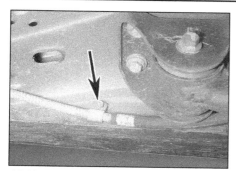

16.10 Unbolt the handbrake cable bracket (arrowed) from the vehicle floor

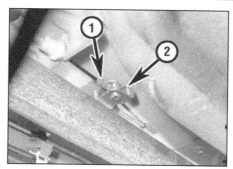

16.11 Detach the front end of the inner cable (1) from the equalizer plate (2)

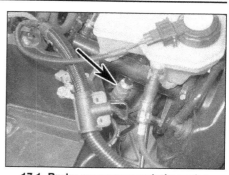

17.1 Brake pressure regulating valve (arrowed) screwed into master cylinder – Hatchback model

prove necessary to free the rear of the exhaust system from its mounting rubbers and lower the system slightly to gain the necessary clearance required to remove the heat shield (see the relevant part of Chapter 4).

5 Detach the front cable from the equalizer plate, then free the cable grommet from the body and remove the cable from the vehicle.

Rear cable

6 Carry out the operations described in paragraphs 3 and 4.

7 Undo the retaining nuts and remove the exhaust system centre heat shield from the vehicle.

8 Remove the relevant set of brake shoes as described in Section 5.

9 Release the securing clip, then free the handbrake outer cable from the brake backplate.

10 Work back along the cable, noting its correct routing whilst freeing it from any clips or ties. Where necessary, unbolt the handbrake cable brackets from the vehicle floor **(see illustration)**.

11 Detach the front end of the inner cable from the handbrake lever equalizer plate, then remove the outer cable retaining clip from the bracket on the floor, and remove the cable from the vehicle **(see illustration)**.

Refitting

12 Refitting is a reversal of the removal procedure, bearing in mind the following points.
  a) Ensure that the cable is correctly routed and retained by all the relevant clips and ties.
  b) Refit the brake shoes with reference to Section 5.
  c) Prior to refitting the gaiter, adjust the handbrake as described in Section 14.

17 Brake pressure-regulating valve – testing, removal and refitting

1 On models not equipped with ABS, a pressure regulating valve is fitted into the hydraulic circuit to each rear brake. The valves are screwed into the rear brake outlet ports of the master cylinder **(see illustration)**. The valves regulate the hydraulic pressure being applied to the rear brakes to help prevent rear wheels locking up under hard braking.

Hatchback and Van models

Testing

2 Specialist equipment is required to check the performance of the valves, therefore if the valves are thought to be faulty the car should be taken to a suitably-equipped Ford dealer for testing. Repairs are not possible and, if faulty, the valves must be renewed.

Removal

Note: Before starting work, refer to the warning at the beginning of Section 2 concerning the dangers of hydraulic fluid.

3 Exhaust the vacuum present in the servo unit by repeatedly depressing the brake pedal.

4 Remove the master cylinder reservoir cap and syphon the hydraulic fluid from the reservoir. **Note:** Do not syphon the fluid by mouth, as it is poisonous; use a syringe or an old poultry baster. Alternatively, open any convenient bleed screw in the system, and gently pump the brake pedal to expel the fluid through a plastic tube connected to the screw (see Section 2).

5 Wipe clean the area around the relevant valve and place absorbent rags beneath the pipe unions to catch any surplus fluid.

6 Slacken the union nut and disconnect the brake pipe from the valve, then unscrew the valve and remove it from the master cylinder. Plug or tape over the pipe end and master cylinder orifice, to minimise the loss of brake fluid, and to prevent the entry of dirt into the system. Wash off any spilt fluid immediately with cold water.

Refitting

7 Ensure that the threads of the valve and master cylinder are clean and dry and fit the valve, tightening it securely. Reconnect the brake pipe and tighten its union nut securely.

8 Refill the master cylinder reservoir, and bleed the complete hydraulic system as described in Section 2.

Courier and Combi models

Testing

9 Specialist equipment is required to check the performance of the valves, therefore if the valves are thought to be faulty the car should be taken to a suitably-equipped Ford dealer for testing. Repairs are not possible and, if faulty, the valves must be renewed.

Removal

Note: Before starting work, refer to the warning at the beginning of Section 2 concerning the dangers of hydraulic fluid.

10 For this operation, the vehicle must be raised for access underneath at the rear, but must still be resting on its wheels. Suitable ramps (or an inspection pit) will therefore be required. If positioning the vehicle on a pair of ramps, chock the front roadwheels.

11 Minimise fluid loss by first removing the master cylinder reservoir cap, and then tightening it down onto a piece of polythene, to obtain an airtight seal.

12 Disconnect the four brake pipes from the valve, and drain any escaping fluid into a suitable container for disposal **(see illustration)**. Due to its location, care will be needed not to spill the fluid onto the hands – wear suitable protective gloves. Plug or cap the disconnected pipes and valve openings, to prevent dirt entry and further fluid loss.

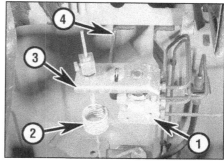

17.12 Rear brake pressure regulating valve components – Courier and Combi models

1 Valve   *3 Operating lever*
2 Operating spring *4 Mounting bracket*

13 Unbolt the valve from its mounting bracket, unhook the linkage from the rear axle, then withdraw the valve. The intermediate bracket may be unbolted if required.

Refitting

14 Refitting is the reverse of the removal procedure, but have the valve adjusted at the earliest opportunity, and bleed the complete hydraulic system as described in Section 2. Check the operation of the brakes before taking the vehicle out on the road.

18 Stop-light switch – removal, refitting and adjustment

Removal

1 The stop-light switch is located on the pedal bracket behind the facia **(see illustration)**.
2 Disconnect the battery negative lead (see Chapter 5A).
3 To remove the switch, reach up behind the facia, disconnect the wiring connector, then rotate the switch slightly anti-clockwise and remove it from the bracket.

Refitting and adjustment

4 On left-hand-drive models, insert the switch into position aligning its locating tabs with the bracket cut-out. Pull the brake pedal fully upwards then push the switch fully downwards, to ensure the plunger is fully depressed, and secure the switch in position by rotating it clockwise. This procedure will automatically set the switch adjustment.
5 On right-hand-drive models, insert the switch into position aligning its locating tabs with the bracket cut-out. Hold the brake pedal in the at-rest position then push the switch fully downwards, to ensure the plunger is fully depressed, and secure the switch in position by rotating it clockwise. This procedure will automatically set the switch adjustment.
6 Reconnect the wiring connector, then reconnect the battery negative lead, and check the stop-light operation before using the vehicle on the road.

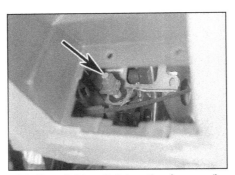

18.1 Stop-light switch location (arrowed) – viewed through fusebox aperture in facia with fuse/relay box removed

19 Handbrake 'on' warning light switch – removal and refitting

Removal

1 Remove the handbrake lever assembly as described in Section 15 **(see illustration)**.
2 Remove the securing screw, and withdraw the switch.

Refitting

3 Refitting is a reversal of removal, but on completion, adjust the handbrake cable as described in Section 14.

20 Anti-lock braking system (ABS) – general information

Note: *On models equipped with traction control, the ABS hydraulic unit is a dual-function unit and controls both the anti-lock braking system and the traction control system.*

1 ABS is available as an option on most models. The system comprises the hydraulic unit and the four roadwheel sensors. The hydraulic unit contains the electronic control unit (ECU), the hydraulic solenoid valves (one set for each brake) and the electrically-driven pump. The purpose of the system is to prevent the wheel(s) locking during heavy braking. This is achieved by automatic release of the brake on the relevant wheel, followed by re-application of the brake.
2 The solenoid valves are controlled by the ECU, which itself receives signals from the four wheel sensors (which are fitted to the wheel hubs), which monitor the speed of rotation of each wheel. By comparing these signals, the ECU can determine the speed at which the vehicle is travelling. It can then use this speed to determine when a wheel is decelerating at an abnormal rate, compared to the speed of the vehicle, and therefore predicts when a wheel is about to lock. During normal operation, the system functions in the same way as a non-ABS braking system.

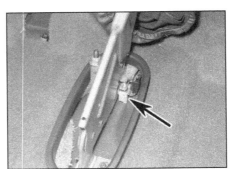

19.1 Handbrake 'on' warning light switch location (arrowed)

3 If the ECU senses that a wheel is about to lock, it operates the relevant solenoid valve(s) in the hydraulic unit, which then isolates from the master cylinder the relevant brake(s) on the wheel(s) which is/are about to lock, effectively sealing-in the hydraulic pressure.
4 If the speed of rotation of the wheel continues to decrease at an abnormal rate, the ECU operates the electrically-driven pump which pumps the hydraulic fluid back into the master cylinder, releasing the brake. Once the speed of rotation of the wheel returns to an acceptable rate, the pump stops, and the solenoid valves switch again, allowing the hydraulic master cylinder pressure to return to the caliper/wheel cylinder (as applicable), which then re-applies the brake. This cycle can be carried out many times a second.
5 The action of the solenoid valves and return pump creates pulses in the hydraulic circuit. When the ABS system is functioning, these pulses can be felt through the brake pedal.
6 The ABS also incorporates a low-speed traction control system. The hydraulic unit incorporates an additional set of solenoid valves which operate the traction control system. The system operates at speeds up to approximately 30 mph (60 km/h) using the signals supplied by the wheel sensors (see paragraph 2). If the ECU senses that a driving wheel is about to lose traction, it prevents this by momentarily applying the relevant front brake.
7 The operation of the ABS and the traction control system is entirely dependent on electrical signals. To prevent the system responding to any inaccurate signals, a built-in safety circuit monitors all signals received by the ECU. If an inaccurate signal or low battery voltage is detected, the system is automatically shut down, and the warning light(s) on the instrument panel is/are illuminated, to inform the driver that the system is not operational. Normal braking should still be available, however.
8 If a fault does develop in the ABS/traction control system, the vehicle must be taken to a Ford dealer for fault diagnosis and repair.

21 Anti-lock braking system components – removal and refitting

Hydraulic unit

1 Removal and refitting of the hydraulic unit should be entrusted to a Ford dealer since special electronic test equipment will be required to bleed the hydraulic system on refitting. The electronic test equipment allows the hydraulic unit to be switched into a special mode which purges the unit of all trapped air – it is not possible to remove trapped air from the unit by bleeding the system conventionally.

Wheel sensor

Removal

2 Disconnect the battery negative lead (see Chapter 5A).

3 Apply the handbrake or chock the front wheels, as applicable, then jack up the relevant end of the vehicle and support securely on axle stands (see *Jacking and vehicle support*). To improve access, remove the roadwheel.

4 Trace the wiring back from the sensor, releasing it from all the relevant clips and ties whilst noting its correct routing, and disconnect the wiring connector.

5 Slacken and remove the retaining bolt and withdraw the sensor from its housing.

Refitting

6 Ensure that the mating faces of the sensor and the housing are clean, and apply a little multi-purpose grease to the housing bore before refitting.

7 Make sure the sensor tip is clean, then ease the sensor into position in the housing. Refit the retaining bolt and tighten it to the specified torque.

8 Work along the sensor wiring, making sure it is correctly routed, securing it in position with all the relevant clips and ties.

9 Reconnect the sensor wiring connector, then refit the roadwheel, lower the vehicle, and tighten the wheel nuts to the specified torque.

22 Vacuum pump (diesel engine models) – removal and refitting

Removal

1 Disconnect the battery negative lead (see Chapter 5A).

2 Remove the cylinder head cover.

3 Using a suitable socket or spanner on the crankshaft pulley bolt, turn the crankshaft until the vacuum pump pushrod (operated by the lobe on the end of the camshaft) is fully retracted into the cylinder head **(see illustration)**.

4 Unscrew the union nut and disconnect the vacuum hose from the top of the pump **(see illustration)**.

5 Release the retaining clip and disconnect the oil return hose from the base of the pump **(see illustration)**. Be prepared for some oil spillage as the hose is disconnected and mop up any spilt oil.

6 Unscrew the bolt securing the fuel heater bracket to the side of the cylinder head **(see illustration)**. Move the fuel heater to one side for access to the lower vacuum pump securing bolt.

7 Evenly and progressively slacken the bolts securing the pump to the front of the cylinder head. Note that there is no need to completely remove the lower bolt, as the

22.3 The vacuum pump pushrod (1) must be fully retracted into the cylinder head (the pushrod must be resting on the lowest point of the cam lobe 2)

lower end of the pump is slotted **(see illustrations)**.

8 Remove the pump from the engine compartment, along with its sealing ring. Discard the sealing ring, a new one should be used on refitting **(see illustration)**.

Refitting

9 Ensure the pump and cylinder head mating surfaces are clean and dry and fit the new sealing ring to the pump recess.

10 Manoeuvre the pump into position, ensuring the sealing ring remains correctly seated, and tighten the pump mounting bolts securely.

22.4 Disconnecting the vacuum hose from the vacuum pump

22.5 Disconnecting the oil return hose from the vacuum pump

22.6 Unscrew the bolt (arrowed) securing the fuel heater bracket

22.7a Vacuum pump lower securing bolt location (arrowed)

22.7b Unscrewing the vacuum pump upper securing bolt

22.8 Use a new sealing ring (arrowed) when refitting the vacuum pump

11 Reconnect the oil return hose to the base of the pump and secure it in position with the retaining clip.
12 Reconnect the vacuum hose to the pump, tightening its union nut securely.
13 Refit the fuel heater bracket and tighten the securing bolt.
14 Refit the cylinder head cover.

23 Vacuum pump (diesel engine models) – testing and overhaul

Note: *A vacuum gauge will be required for this check.*

1 The operation of the braking system vacuum pump can be checked using a vacuum gauge.
2 Disconnect the vacuum pipe from the pump, and connect the gauge to the pump union using a suitable length of hose.
3 Start the engine and allow it to idle, then measure the vacuum created by the pump. As a guide, after one minute, a minimum of approximately 500 mm Hg should be recorded. If the vacuum registered is significantly less than this, it is likely that the pump is faulty. However, seek the advice of a Ford dealer before condemning the pump.
4 Overhaul of the vacuum pump is not possible, since no components are available separately for it. If faulty, the complete pump assembly must be renewed.

Chapter 10
Suspension and steering

Contents

Auxiliary drivebelt check and renewal . . . . .See Chapter 1A or 1B
Front hub bearings – renewal 3
Front hub carrier – removal and refitting 2
Front suspension anti-roll bar – removal and refitting 5
Front suspension crossmember – removal and refitting 7
Front suspension lower arm – removal and refitting 6
Front suspension strut – removal, overhaul and refitting 4
General information 1
Power steering fluid cooler – removal and refitting 22
Power steering fluid pressure switch – removal and refitting 24
Power steering hydraulic system – bleeding 23
Power steering pump – removal and refitting 21
Rear axle assembly (Hatchback and Van models) – removal and
   refitting 11
Rear axle assembly pivot bushes (Hatchback and Van models) –
   renewal 12
Rear hub – removal and refitting 8
Rear hub bearings – renewal 9
Rear shock absorber (Courier and Combi models) – removal,
   inspection and refitting 14
Rear strut (Hatchback and Van models) – removal, overhaul
   and refitting 10
Rear suspension assembly (Courier and Combi models) –
   removal and refitting 15
Rear suspension components (Courier and Combi models) –
   general 13
Rear suspension ride height (Courier and Combi models) –
   adjustment 16
Roadwheel nut tightness check . . . . .See Chapter 1A or 1B
Steering and suspension check . . . . .See Chapter 1A or 1B
Steering column – removal and refitting 18
Steering gear – removal and refitting 20
Steering gear rubber gaiters – renewal 19
Steering wheel – removal and refitting 17
Track rod end – removal and refitting 25
Wheel alignment and steering angles – general information 26

Degrees of difficulty

Easy, suitable for novice with little experience	Fairly easy, suitable for beginner with some experience	Fairly difficult, suitable for competent DIY mechanic	Difficult, suitable for experienced DIY mechanic 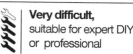	Very difficult, suitable for expert DIY or professional

Specifications

Wheel alignment and steering angles

Front wheel castor:
  Hatchback models:
    Manual steering . . . . 2°35' to 0°05'
    Power steering . . . . 3°29' to 0°59'
  Van models:
    Manual steering . . . . 2°33' to 0°03'
    Power steering . . . . 3°28' to 0°58'
  Courier models:
    Manual steering . . . . 1°35' to –0°55'
    Power steering . . . . 2°13' to –0°17'
  Combi models:
    Manual steering . . . . 1°57' to –0°33'
    Power steering . . . . 2°34' to 0°04'
Front wheel camber:
  Hatchback and Van models:
    Manual steering . . . . 0°44' to –2°04'
    Power steering . . . . 0°47' to –2°01'
  Courier models . . . . 0°49' to –1°59'
  Combi models
    Manual steering . . . . 0°43' to –2°00'
    Power steering . . . . 0°47' to –2°01'

Wheel alignment and steering angles (continued)

Front wheel toe-setting (all models):
Allowable tolerance . . . .   0°25' (2.5 mm) toe-in to 0°25' (2.5 mm) toe-out
Setting value after adjustment . . . .   0°00' (0 mm) ± 0°10' (1.0 mm)
Rear wheel camber:
Hatchback and Van models . . . .   -0°30' to –2°00'
Courier and Combi models . . . .   0°06' to –1°24'
Rear wheel toe-setting:
Hatchback and Van models . . . .   0°43' (4.3 mm) to 0°03' (0.3 mm) toe-in
Courier and Combi models . . . .   0°45' (4.5 mm) to 0°05' (0.5 mm) toe-in

Torque wrench settings

	Nm	lbf ft
Front suspension		
Anti-roll bar clamp bolts	23	17
Anti-roll bar drop link nuts	50	37
Front crossmember securing bolts	103	76
Front hub nut	270	199
Hub carrier-to-suspension strut pinch-bolt	85	63
Lower arm securing nuts and bolts	80	59
Lower arm-to-hub carrier pinch-bolt and nut	51	38
Suspension strut piston rod nut	59	44
Suspension strut top mounting nut	48	35
Rear suspension – Hatchback and Van models		
Rear axle assembly mounting bracket-to-floor bolts	50	37
Rear axle assembly mounting bracket-to-trailing arm bolts	120	89
Rear hub nut	235	173
Stub axle-to-trailing arm bolts	66	49
Suspension strut lower securing bolt	120	89
Suspension strut top mounting nut	34	25
Steering		
Flexible coupling-to-steering column shaft pinch-bolt	28	21
Flexible coupling-to-steering gear pinion pinch-bolt	26	19
Power steering fluid pressure switch	11	8
Power steering gear fluid pipe unions	31	23
Power steering pump bracket securing bolts	25	18
Power steering pump high-pressure fluid pipe union nut:		
All except 2000 onward diesel engine models	65	48
2000 onward diesel engine models	22	16
Power steering pump securing bolts:		
All except 2000 onward diesel engine models	25	18
2000 onward diesel engine models	18	13
Steering column securing nuts	12	9
Steering gear securing nuts and bolts	48	35
Steering wheel securing bolt	45	33
Track rod end locknuts	63	46
Track rod end-to-hub carrier nuts	37	27
Roadwheels		
Wheel nuts	85	63

1 General information

The front suspension is of independent type, with a subframe, MacPherson struts, lower arms, and an anti-roll bar. The struts, which incorporate coil springs and integral shock absorbers, are attached at their upper ends to the reinforced strut mountings on the body shell. The lower end of each strut is bolted to the top of a cast hub carrier, which carries the hub, and the brake disc and caliper. The hubs run within non-adjustable bearings in the hub carriers. The lower end of each hub carrier is attached, via a balljoint, to a pressed-steel lower arm assembly. The balljoints are integral with the lower arms. Each lower arm is attached at its inboard end to the subframe, via flexible rubber bushes, and controls both lateral and fore and aft movement of the front wheels. An anti-roll bar is fitted to all models. The anti-roll bar is mounted on the subframe, and is connected to the suspension struts via vertical drop links.

On Hatchback and Van models, the rear suspension is semi-independent, with an inverted V-section beam welded between tubular trailing arms. This inverted V-section beam allows a limited torsional flexibility, giving each rear wheel a certain degree of independent movement, whilst maintaining optimum track and wheel camber control. This type of arrangement is called a 'twist beam' rear axle. The axle is attached to the body via rubber bushes. The rear suspension struts, which are similar to the MacPherson struts used at the front, are attached at their upper ends to the reinforced strut mountings in the luggage compartment. At their lower ends, the struts are attached to the rear of the trailing arms. The rear hubs are integral with the brake drums, and the hub/drums run on stub axles which are bolted to the rear of the trailing arms.

Courier and Combi models are fitted with a modified version of the twist beam rear axle,

2.2 Relieve the staking on the front hub nut

2.3 Lift the plastic cover from the suspension strut top mounting

using four linked torsion bars in place of springs and an anti-roll bar. The ends of the torsion bars are splined to allow adjustment within their mounting brackets.

The steering is of conventional rack-and-pinion type, incorporating a collapsible safety column. The column is joined to the steering gear via a flexible coupling. The steering gear is mounted on the front suspension subframe. The steering gear track rods are attached via the track rod ends to the steering arms on the hub carriers.

Certain models are available with power steering. The power steering pump is belt-driven from the crankshaft pulley.

2 Front hub carrier – removal and refitting

Removal

Note: *A balljoint separator tool will be required for this operation. Where applicable, Nyloc-type self-locking nuts must be renewed on refitting. A new hub nut will be required on refitting.*

1 Remove the relevant wheel trim, or the wheel centre plate (alloy wheels) for access to the front hub nut.

2 Ensure that the handbrake is applied, then relieve the staking on the front hub nut, using a suitable punch **(see illustration)**. Slacken the hub nut using a suitable socket and extension bar. Do not remove the hub nut at this stage.
Caution: Take care, as the hub nut is tightened to a very high torque.

3 Working in the engine compartment, lift off the plastic cover, then slacken the relevant suspension strut top mounting nut, using a ring spanner **(see illustration)**. Counterhold the strut piston rod using a suitable Allen key or hexagon bit. **Do not** remove the nut.

4 Slacken the relevant front wheel nuts, then jack up the front of the vehicle, and support

securely on axle stands (see *Jacking and vehicle support*). Remove the roadwheel.

5 Working under the wheeelarch, unbolt the brake hose bracket from the suspension strut **(see illustration)**.

6 Unscrew the bolts securing the brake caliper mounting bracket to the hub carrier, then slide the caliper/bracket assembly from the hub carrier and brake disc (there is no need to remove the brake pads) **(see illustration)**. Suspend the caliper/bracket assembly from the strut coil spring using wire or string – do not allow the caliper to hang on the brake hose.

7 Slacken the track rod end balljoint nut, and unscrew it as far as the ends of the threads.

Counterhold the balljoint pin using a suitable Allen key or hexagon bit **(see illustration)**.

8 Disconnect the track rod end balljoint from the hub carrier using a balljoint separator tool (leave the nut fitted to protect the threads), taking care not to damage the balljoint rubber seal. Once the balljoint has been released, remove the balljoint nut.

9 Where applicable, unbolt the ABS wheel sensor from the hub carrier, and suspend it clear of the working area to prevent any possibility of damage during the following procedure.

10 Unscrew the hub nut from the end of the driveshaft, and lift off the washer **(see illustration)**.

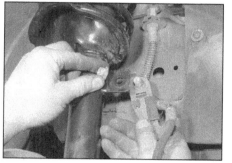

2.5 Unbolt the brake hose bracket from the suspension strut

2.6 Unscrew the bolts securing the brake caliper mounting bracket to the hub carrier

2.7 Slackening the track rod end balljoint nut

2.10 Unscrew the hub nut and lift off the washer

2.12a Unscrew the pinch-bolt and nut securing the hub carrier to the lower arm balljoint . . .

11 Where applicable, prise the locating clip from the wheel stud, then lift off the brake disc.

12 Unscrew the pinch-nut and bolt securing the hub carrier to the lower arm balljoint. Push the end of the lower arm down to free the balljoint from the hub carrier **(see illustrations)**. If the balljoint is very tight, it may be necessary to lever down using a large screwdriver, or similar tool, but take care not to damage the balljoint rubber seal.

13 The hub must now be freed from the end of the driveshaft. It should be possible to pull the hub carrier off the driveshaft, but if the end of the driveshaft is tight in the hub, temporarily refit the hub nut to protect the driveshaft threads, then tap the end of the driveshaft with a soft-faced hammer, or use a suitable puller to free it. Support the driveshaft using wire or string – **do not** allow the driveshaft to hang down under its own weight, as this may result in damage to the constant velocity joints.

Caution: When freeing the driveshaft from the hub, make sure that the driveshaft does not disengage from the inner constant velocity joint.

14 Unscrew the pinch-bolt securing the hub carrier to the lower end of the suspension strut. Using a suitable lever, or a large screwdriver, spread the slot in the top of the hub carrier, until the hub carrier can be pulled from the end of the strut. If necessary, tap the hub carrier down to free it from the strut, using a soft-faced mallet.

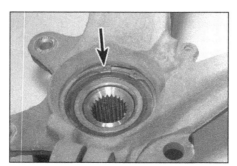

2.12b . . . then push the end of the lower arm down to free the balljoint from the hub carrier

Refitting

15 Refitting is a reversal of removal, bearing in mind the following points.
a) *Renew any Nyloc-type self-locking nuts on refitting.*
b) *Use a new hub nut.*
c) *Make sure that the slot for the pinch-bolt in the strut aligns with the corresponding holes in the hub carrier.*
d) *Do not fully tighten the hub nut until the vehicle is resting on its wheels.*
e) *Do not forget to tighten the suspension strut top mounting nut.*
f) *Tighten all fixings to the specified torque.*

3 Front hub bearings – renewal

Note: *A press, a suitable puller, or similar improvised tools will be required for this operation. Obtain a bearing overhaul kit before proceeding. A new bearing retaining circlip should be used on refitting.*

1 With the hub carrier removed as described in Section 2, proceed as follows.

2 The hub must now be removed from the bearing/hub carrier assembly. It is preferable to use a press to do this, but it is possible to drive out the hub using a metal tube of suitable diameter. Alternatively a suitable puller can be used.

3 Securely support the hub carrier, on two metal bars for instance, with the inner face uppermost then, using a metal bar or tube of

suitable diameter, press or drive the hub from the hub bearing **(see illustration)**. Alternatively, use the puller to separate the hub from the bearing. Note that the part of the bearing inner race will remain on the hub.

4 Using a suitable puller, pull the half inner bearing race from the hub. Alternatively, support the bearing race on suitably thin metal bars, and press or drive the hub from the bearing race.

5 Remove the bearing retaining circlip from the inner face of the hub carrier – discard the circlip, a new one must be used on refitting **(see illustration)**.

6 Temporarily refit the half inner bearing race to the bearing, making sure that the bearing cage and the seal are in position then, using a puller, pull the bearing from the hub carrier, applying pressure to the inner race. Alternatively, support the hub carrier, and press or drive out the bearing.

7 Before fitting the new bearing, thoroughly clean the bearing location in the hub carrier.

8 Using a press or a suitable puller, fit the new bearing to the hub carrier. The outer face of the bearing should contact the shoulder in the hub carrier. It may be possible to improvise a suitable puller using a socket, nut, washers, and length of threaded bar.

9 Fit a new bearing retaining clip to the inner face of the hub carrier.

10 Press or draw the hub into the bearing. The bearing inner track must be supported during this operation. This can be achieved using a socket, nut washers, and a length of threaded bar.

11 Refit the hub carrier (see Section 2).

4 Front suspension strut – removal, overhaul and refitting

Removal

Note: *Where applicable, Nyloc-type self-locking nuts must be renewed on refitting.*

1 Working in the engine compartment, remove the plastic cover, then slacken the relevant suspension strut top mounting nut, using a ring spanner. Counterhold the strut piston rod using a suitable Allen key or hexagon bit **(see illustration)**. **Do not** remove the nut.

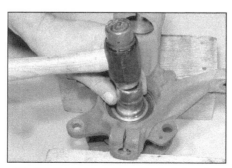

3.3 Driving the hub from the hub bearing

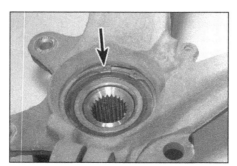

3.5 Remove the bearing circlip from the inner face of the hub carrier

4.1 Slackening the suspension strut top mounting nut

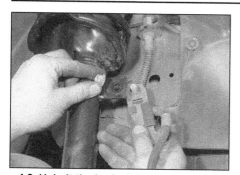

4.3 Unbolt the brake hose bracket from the suspension strut

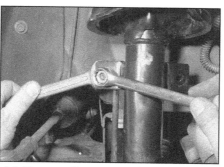

4.4 Unscrew the nut securing the anti-roll bar drop link to the suspension strut

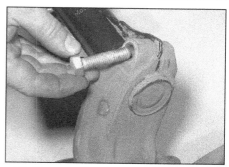

4.5 Unscrew the pinch-bolt securing the hub carrier to the suspension strut

2 Slacken the relevant front wheel nuts. Ensure that the handbrake is fully applied, then jack up the front of the vehicle, and support securely on axle stands (see *Jacking and vehicle support*). Remove the roadwheel.

3 Working under the wheelarch, unbolt the brake hose bracket from the suspension strut **(see illustration)**.

4 Unscrew the nut securing the anti-roll bar drop link to the suspension strut. If necessary, counterhold the drop link pin using a spanner on the flats provided **(see illustration)**.

5 Unscrew the pinch-bolt securing the hub carrier to the lower end of the suspension strut **(see illustration)**. Using a suitable lever, or a large screwdriver, spread the slot in the top of the hub carrier, until the hub carrier can be pulled from the end of the strut. If necessary, tap the hub carrier down to free it from the strut, using a soft-faced mallet.

6 Support the strut from under the wheeelarch then, working in the engine compartment, unscrew the suspension strut top mounting nut, using a ring spanner. Again, counterhold the strut piston rod using a suitable Allen key or hexagon bit.

7 Lower the strut assembly from under the wheeelarch.

8 Where applicable, lift the damper weight from the suspension turret in the engine compartment. Recover the top mounting insulator, which fits under the damper weight (it may be stuck in position under the wheeelarch) **(see illustrations)**.

Overhaul

Note: *A spring compressor tool will be required for this operation.*

9 With the suspension strut resting on a bench, or clamped in a vice, fit a spring compressor tool, and compress the coil spring to relieve the pressure on the spring seats **(see illustration)**. Ensure that the compressor tool is securely located on the spring, in accordance with the tool manufacturer's instructions.

10 Counterhold the strut piston rod with the Allen key or hexagon bit used during removal, and unscrew the piston rod nut **(see illustration)**.

11 Remove the piston rod nut, followed by the thrust bearing, the upper spring seat, the spring (with compressor tool still fitted), the gaiter, the rubber bump stop, and the dust cover – note that the gaiter clips into the dust cover.

12 With the strut assembly now completely dismantled, examine all the components for wear, damage or deformation, and check the thrust bearing for smoothness of operation. Renew any of the components as necessary.

13 Examine the strut for signs of fluid leakage. Check the strut piston for signs of pitting along its entire length, and check the strut body for signs of damage. While holding it in an upright position, test the operation of the strut by moving the piston through a full stroke, and then through short strokes of 50 to 100 mm. In both cases, the resistance felt should be smooth and continuous. If the resistance is jerky or uneven or if there is any visible sign of wear or damage to the strut, renewal is necessary.

14 If any doubt exists as to the condition of the coil spring, carefully remove the spring compressors and check the spring for distortion and signs of cracking. Renew the spring if it is damaged or distorted, or if there is any doubt as to its condition.

15 Inspect all other components for damage or deterioration, and renew any that are suspect.

16 Slide the dust cover, followed by rubber bump stop and the gaiter, onto the strut

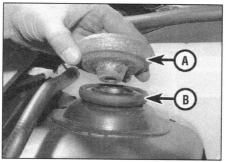

4.8a Lift off the damper weight (A) and recover the top mounting insulator (B)

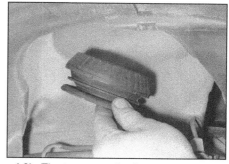

4.8b The top mounting insulator may be stuck in position under the wheeelarch

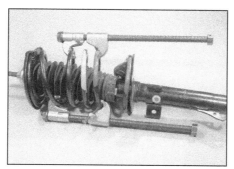

4.9 Spring compressor tools fitted to suspension strut coil spring

4.10 Counterhold the strut piston rod with the Allen key and unscrew the piston rod nut

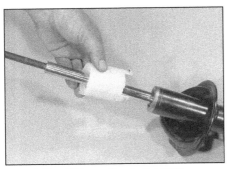

4.16a Slide on the dust cover . . .

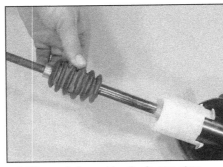

4.16b . . . followed by the bump stop . . .

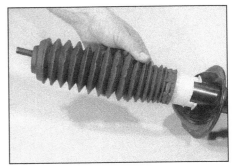

4.16c . . . and the gaiter

piston **(see illustrations)**. Clip the gaiter into position on the dust cover.

17 If the spring compressor tool has been removed from the spring, refit it and compress the spring sufficiently to enable it to be refitted to the strut.

18 Slide the spring over the strut, and position it so that the lower end of the spring is resting against the stop on the lower seat **(see illustrations)**.

19 Refit the upper spring seat, and rotate it as necessary to position the stop against the upper end of the spring **(see illustration)**.

20 Refit the thrust bearing, then refit the piston rod nut, and tighten to the specified torque **(see illustrations)**. Counterhold the piston rod using an Allen key or hexagon bit as during removal.

21 Slowly slacken the spring compressor tool to relieve the tension in the spring. Check that the ends of the spring locate correctly against the stops on the spring seats. If necessary, turn the spring and the upper seat so that the components locate correctly before the compressor tool is removed. Remove the compressor tool when the spring is fully seated.

Refitting

22 Refitting is a reversal of removal, bearing in mind the following points:
  a) Make sure that the slot for the pinch-bolt in the strut aligns with the corresponding holes in the hub carrier **(see illustration)**.
  b) Make sure that the top mounting insulator is correctly seated on the strut mounting in the engine compartment.

  c) Renew any Nyloc-type self-locking nuts on refitting.
  d) Tighten all fixings to the specified torque.
  e) Do not forget to tighten the suspension strut top mounting nut.

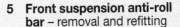

5 Front suspension anti-roll bar – removal and refitting

Removal

Note: Where applicable, Nyloc-type self-locking nuts must be renewed on refitting.

1 Remove the front suspension crossmember as described in Section 7.

4.18a Slide the spring over the strut . . .

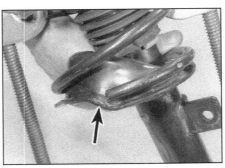

4.18b . . . and position it so that the lower end of the spring is resting against the stop (arrowed)

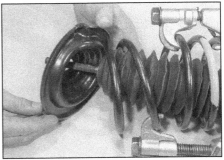

4.19 Refit the upper spring seat . . .

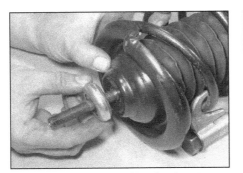

4.20a . . . followed by the thrust bearing . . .

4.20b . . . and the piston rod nut

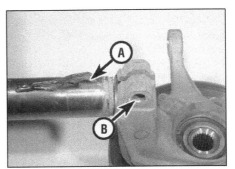

4.22 Make sure that the slot (A) for the pinch-bolt in the strut aligns with the holes (B) in the hub carrier

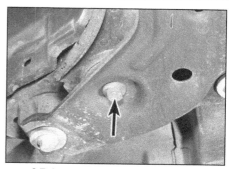

6.2 Push the lower arm down to free the balljoint from the hub carrier

6.6 Lower arm front securing bolt (arrowed)

6.7 Lower arm rear securing bolt (arrowed)

2 Unscrew the bolts securing the anti-roll bar mounting clamps to the subframe, then carefully manipulate the anti-roll bar assembly out from under the vehicle.

3 If desired, the drop links can be removed from the anti-roll bar after unscrewing the securing nuts. If necessary, counterhold the drop link pins using a spanner on the flats provided.

Refitting

4 Refitting is a reversal of removal, bearing in mind the following points.
 a) *Renew any Nyloc-type self-locking nuts on refitting.*
 b) *Tighten all fixings to the specified torque.*
 c) *Refit the front suspension crossmember as described in Section 7.*

6 Front suspension lower arm – removal and refitting

Removal

Note: *Where applicable, Nyloc-type self-locking nuts must be renewed on refitting.*

1 Remove the wheel trims or the wheel centre plates (alloy wheels), then slacken the front wheel nuts. Apply the handbrake, then jack up the front of the vehicle, and support securely on axle stands (see *Jacking and vehicle support*). Remove the roadwheels.

2 Unscrew the pinch-nut and bolt securing the hub carrier to the lower arm balljoint. Push the end of the lower arm down to free the balljoint from the hub carrier **(see illustration)**. If the balljoint is very tight, it may be necessary to lever down using a large screwdriver, or a balljoint separator tool, but take care not to damage the balljoint rubber seal.

3 Working on each side of the vehicle in turn, where applicable, unclip the ABS wheel sensor wiring from the anti-roll bar drop link.

4 Again working on both sides of the vehicle, unscrew the nuts securing the anti-roll bar drop links to the suspension struts. If

necessary, counterhold the drop link pins using a spanner on the flats provided.

5 If necessary, rotate the anti-roll bar towards the rear of the vehicle to allow improved access to the lower arm. The anti-roll bar clamp bolts can be slackened to allow the anti-roll bar to rotate more easily.

6 Unscrew the nut and bolt (counterhold the bolt as the nut is unscrewed) securing the front of the lower arm to the subframe **(see illustration)**.

7 Unscrew the bolt securing the rear of the lower arm, noting that the bolts also secures the subframe, then manipulate the lower arm out from under the vehicle **(see illustration)**.

Refitting

8 Refitting is a reversal of removal, bearing in mind the following points.
 a) *Renew any Nyloc-type self-locking nuts on refitting.*
 b) *Tighten all fixings to the specified torque.*

7 Front suspension crossmember – removal and refitting

Removal

Note: *A balljoint separator tool will be required for this operation. Where applicable, Nyloc-type self-locking nuts must be renewed on refitting. Special tools (Ford Tool No 15-097) will be required to align the crossmember with the body when refitting – do not attempt this procedure without these tools, as incorrect front suspension/steering geometry may result. On models with power steering, new power steering fluid pipe sealing rings should be used on refitting.*

1 Disconnect the battery negative lead, with reference to Chapter 5A.

2 Working in the driver's footwell, unscrew the pinch-bolt securing the lower end of the steering column universal joint to the steering gear pinion.

3 Similarly, slacken the pinch-bolt securing the flexible coupling to the steering column shaft.

4 Disconnect the exhaust downpipe/catalytic converter assembly from the manifold, as described in Chapter 4A, 4B or 4C, as applicable.

5 Remove the wheel trims or the wheel centre plates (alloy wheels), then slacken the front wheel nuts. Apply the handbrake, then jack up the front of the vehicle, and support securely on axle stands (see *Jacking and vehicle support*). Remove the roadwheels.

6 On models with manual transmission, disconnect the gearchange linkage from the transmission, as described in Chapter 7A.

7 On models with automatic transmission, disconnect the selector cable from the transmission as described in Chapter 7B.

8 Working on one side of the vehicle, slacken the track rod end balljoint nut, and unscrew it as far as the ends of the threads. Counterhold the balljoint pin using a suitable Allen key or hexagon bit.

9 Disconnect the track rod end balljoint from the hub carrier using a balljoint separator tool (leave the nut fitted to protect the threads), taking care not to damage the balljoint rubber seal. Once the balljoint has been released, remove the balljoint nut.

10 Repeat the procedure given in paragraphs 8 and 9 to disconnect the remaining track rod end.

11 Remove the exhaust downpipe/catalytic converter assembly as described in Chapter 4A, 4B or 4C, as applicable.

12 Working on each side of the vehicle in turn, unscrew the pinch-nut and bolt securing the hub carrier to the lower arm balljoint. Push the end of the lower arm down to free the balljoint from the hub carrier. If the balljoint is very tight, it may be necessary to lever down using a large screwdriver, or a balljoint separator tool, but take care not to damage the balljoint rubber seal.

13 Again working on each side of the vehicle in turn, unscrew the nut securing the anti-roll bar drop link to the suspension strut. If necessary, counterhold the drop link pin using a spanner on the flats provided.

14 Unscrew and remove the rear

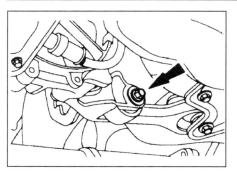

7.14 Remove the rear engine/transmission mounting link through-bolt

engine/transmission mounting link through-bolt **(see illustration)**.

15 Where applicable, unclip the ABS wheel sensor wires from the clips on each side of the crossmember.

16 Support the crossmember using a trolley jack, with a block of wood between the jack and the crossmember to spread the load.

17 Progressively unscrew and remove the seven crossmember securing bolts, so that the crossmember is supported by the jack **(see illustration)**. Do not lower the crossmember at this stage.

18 On models with power steering, proceed as follows.

a) *Lower the crossmember slightly for access to the power steering fluid pipe connections on the steering gear.*

b) *Place a container beneath the steering gear to catch escaping fluid, then unscrew the union nuts, and allow the fluid to drain into the container. Plug or cover the open ends of the pipes and steering gear to prevent dirt entry and further fluid loss.*

c) *Release the power steering fluid pipes from the bracket on the crossmember.*

19 Where applicable, remove the seal which fits between the steering gear pinion and the bulkhead, then lower the crossmember assembly, and withdraw it from under the vehicle.

20 If desired, the steering gear, anti-roll bar and lower arms can be removed from the crossmember with reference to the relevant Sections of this Chapter.

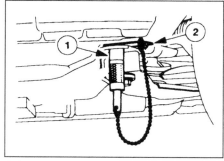

7.25 Using special tool 15-097 to align the crossmember with the body

1 *Guide pin*   2 *Locking plate*

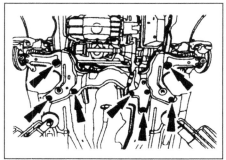

7.17 Crossmember securing bolts (arrowed)

Refitting

21 Where applicable, commence refitting by refitting the lower arms, anti-roll bar and/or steering gear to the crossmember, with reference to the relevant Sections of this Chapter.

22 Position the crossmember on the jack with the wooden block between the crossmember and the jack, then raise the jack to lift the crossmember into position under the vehicle. Ensure that the crossmember is securely supported, and make sure that the steering gear pinion-to-bulkhead seal is fitted.

23 On models with power steering, reconnect the power steering fluid pipes to the steering gear using new sealing rings, and tighten the union nuts, then refit the seal which fits between the steering gear pinion and the bulkhead.

24 It is now necessary to obtain two special alignment tools (Ford Tool No 15-097) to align the crossmember with the body before refitting the securing bolts.

25 Fit the tools to the alignment holes at the front of the crossmember, then slide the locking plates into the locking grooves, and tighten the alignment tool sleeves **(see illustration)**.

26 Raise the crossmember into position, making sure that the pins on the alignment tools engage with the alignment holes in the body.

27 Refit the crossmember securing bolts, and tighten them to the specified torque, then remove the alignment tools.

28 Further refitting is a reversal of removal, bearing in mind the following points.

a) *Make sure that the seal between the steering gear pinion and the bulkhead is correctly located.*

b) *Renew any Nyloc-type self-locking nuts on refitting.*

c) *Tighten all fixings to the specified torque.*

d) *Refit the exhaust downpipe/catalytic converter assembly as described in Chapter 4A, 4B or 4C, as applicable.*

e) *On models with automatic transmission, reconnect the selector cable to the transmission as described in Chapter 7B.*

f) *On models with manual transmission, reconnect the gearchange linkage to the transmission as described in Chapter 7A.*

g) *Ensure that the front wheels and the steering wheel are in the straight-ahead position before reconnecting the universal joint to the steering gear pinion and the steering column shaft.*

h) *On completion, where applicable, refill and bleed the power steering hydraulic system as described in Section 23.*

8 Rear hub – removal and refitting

Hatchback and Van models

1 An integral hub/brake drum assembly is used, which incorporates the rear wheel bearings.

2 Removal and refitting of the hub/brake drum assembly is described in Chapter 9, Section 7.

Courier and Combi models

Removal

3 Remove the relevant wheel trim or the wheel centre plate (alloy wheels), then slacken the relevant wheel nuts. Chock the front wheels, and select 1st gear (manual transmission) or P (automatic transmission), then jack up the rear of the vehicle, and support securely on axle stands (see *Jacking and vehicle support*). Remove the rear roadwheel.

4 Remove the brake drum as described in Chapter 9.

5 Using a screwdriver, prise the dust cap from the centre of the hub, then unscrew the hub nut.

6 Withdraw the hub from the stub axle.

Refitting

7 Slide the hub onto the stub axle, then fit the hub nut and tighten to the specified torque.

8 Carefully tap the dust cap into position until it is seated on the shoulder in the hub. If the dust cap was damaged during removal, fit a new one.

9 Refit the brake drum (see Chapter 9).

10 Refit the roadwheel, then lower the vehicle to the ground, tighten the wheel nuts to the specified torque, and refit the wheel trim or centre plate, as applicable.

9 Rear hub bearings – renewal

Hatchback and Van models

Note: *Obtain a bearing overhaul kit before proceeding. The kit should contain the bearing components, a grease seal and suitable grease.*

1 With the hub/brake drum removed as described in Chapter 9, Section 7, proceed as follows.

9.3 Prising the grease seal from the inboard hub bore

9.4 Lifting out the outer bearing cone

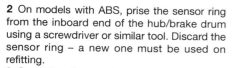

9.5 Driving out a bearing cup

2 On models with ABS, prise the sensor ring from the inboard end of the hub/brake drum using a screwdriver or similar tool. Discard the sensor ring – a new one must be used on refitting.

3 Carefully prise out the grease seal from the inboard hub bore, using a screwdriver **(see illustration)**. Take great care not to damage the bore surface.

4 Lift the inner and outer bearing cones out from the hub bore **(see illustration)**.

5 The bearing cups must now be removed from the hub bore by driving them out with a suitable punch. Drive each cup out from its respective end, by tapping alternately at diagonally opposite points **(see illustration)**. Do not allow the cups to tilt in the bore, or the surfaces may become burred and prevent the new bearings from seating correctly as they are fitted.

6 Clean the hub bore and the stub axle thoroughly before commencing reassembly.

7 Carefully tap the new bearing cups into position in the hub bore, using a piece of tubing of a slightly smaller diameter than the bearing cups. Make sure that the cups are fitted squarely, and that they abut their respective shoulders in the hub.

8 Pack the inner bearing cone with grease (suitable grease should be supplied with the new bearing kit), then fit the bearing cone to the cup in the hub.

9 Lubricate the inner lip of the new grease seal, then lightly tap the seal into position using a block of wood. Note that the seal lips should face in towards the bearings in the hub.

10 On models with ABS, fit the new sensor ring to the inboard end of the hub/brake drum. Press the sensor ring into position using a tube of suitable diameter. Make sure that the ring seats correctly on the hub shoulder. *Caution: The sensor ring teeth are easily damaged – take great care to avoid damage when fitting. It is not advisable to tap the ring into position, as this may cause damage.*

11 Pack the outer bearing cone with grease, then fit it to the bearing cone in the hub.

12 Refit the hub/brake drum as described in Chapter 9.

Courier and Combi models

13 The rear wheel bearings are integral with the hubs, and cannot be renewed independently. If a bearing is worn or damaged, the complete hub must be renewed as described in Section 8.

10 Rear strut (Hatchback and Van models) – removal, overhaul and refitting

Removal

Note: *A new strut top mounting nut should be used on refitting.*

1 Remove the relevant rear wheel trim or the wheel centre plate (alloy wheels), then slacken the relevant rear wheel nuts. Chock the front wheels, and select 1st gear (manual transmission) or P (automatic transmission), then jack up the rear of the vehicle, and support securely on axle stands (see *Jacking and vehicle support*). Remove the rear roadwheel.

2 Support the trailing arm using a trolley jack, then unscrew the nut and bolt securing the lower end of the strut assembly to the trailing arm. Counterhold the bolt using a second spanner as the nut is unscrewed **(see illustration)**.

3 Support the strut then, working in the luggage compartment, unscrew the strut top mounting nut **(see illustration)**. If necessary, lower the jack supporting the trailing arm until

the strut can be manipulated out from under the vehicle.

Overhaul

Note: *A spring compressor tool will be required for this operation.*

4 With the suspension strut resting on a bench, or clamped in a vice, fit a spring compressor tool, and compress the coil spring to relieve the pressure on the spring seats. Ensure that the compressor tool is securely located on the spring, in accordance with the tool manufacturer's instructions.

5 Remove the strut top mounting retaining circlip using circlip pliers.

6 Remove the top mounting, followed by the upper spring seat, the spring (with compressor tool still fitted), the gaiter, the rubber bump stop, and the dust cover.

7 With the strut assembly now completely dismantled, examine all the components for wear, damage or deformation. Renew any of the components as necessary.

8 Examine the strut for signs of fluid leakage. Check the strut piston for signs of pitting along its entire length, and check the strut body for signs of damage. While holding it in an upright position, test the operation of the strut by moving the piston through a full stroke, and then through short strokes of 50 to 100 mm. In both cases, the resistance felt should be smooth and continuous. If the resistance is jerky or uneven or if there is any visible sign of wear or damage to the strut, renewal is necessary.

10.2 Unscrewing the rear strut lower securing nut and bolt

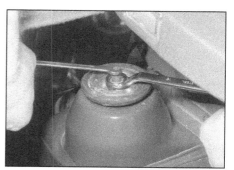

10.3 Unscrewing the rear strut top mounting nut

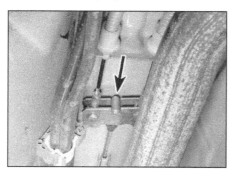

10.11 Rear suspension strut components

1 Circlip	5 Bump stop
2 Top mounting	6 Gaiter
3 Upper spring seat	7 Dust cover
4 Strut body	

9 If any doubt exists as to the condition of the coil spring, carefully remove the spring compressors and check the spring for distortion and signs of cracking. Renew the spring if it is damaged or distorted, or if there is any doubt as to its condition.

10 Inspect all other components for damage or deterioration, and renew any that are suspect.

11 Slide the dust cover, followed by rubber bump stop and the gaiter, onto the strut piston **(see illustration)**.

12 If the spring compressor tool has been removed from the spring, refit it and compress the spring sufficiently to enable it to be refitted to the strut.

13 Slide the spring over the piston rod, and position it so that the lower end of the spring is resting against the stop on the lower seat.

14 Refit the upper spring seat, and rotate it as necessary to position the stop against the upper end of the spring.

15 Refit the top mounting, then fit a new top mounting retaining circlip

16 Slowly slacken the spring compressor tool to relieve the tension in the spring. Check that the ends of the spring locate correctly against the stops on the spring seats. If necessary, turn the spring and the upper seat so that the components locate correctly before the compressor tool is removed. Remove the compressor tool when the spring is fully seated.

Refitting

17 Refitting is a reversal of removal, but use a new strut top mounting nut, and do not fully tighten the strut mountings until the weight of the vehicle is resting on the wheels.

11 Rear axle assembly (Hatchback and Van models) – removal and refitting

Removal

1 Disconnect the battery negative lead, with reference to Chapter 5A.

2 Working at the handbrake lever inside the car, back off the handbrake cable adjustment, as described in Chapter 9.

3 Remove the rear wheel trims or the wheel centre plates (alloy wheels), then slacken the rear wheel nuts. Chock the front wheels, and select 1st gear (manual transmission) or P (automatic transmission), then jack up the rear of the vehicle, and support securely on axle stands (see *Jacking and vehicle support*). Remove the rear roadwheels.

4 Unhook the rear of the exhaust system from its rubber mountings, then lower the rear of the system and support on a jack or axle stand.

5 Unscrew the securing nuts, and remove the centre section and then the rear section of the exhaust heat shielding from the vehicle floor.

6 Working at the now-exposed handbrake equaliser, disconnect the handbrake cables from the equaliser as follows. If necessary, slacken off the handbrake adjuster to enable

the cables to be disconnected (see Chapter 9) **(see illustration)**.

a) *Disconnect the primary (front) cable from the equaliser.*

b) *Prise off the clips securing the secondary (rear) cables to the brackets on the vehicle floor.*

c) *Release the secondary cables from the brackets.*

d) *Disconnect the secondary cables from the equaliser.*

7 Working under the rear of the vehicle, detach the handbrake cables from the clips under the vehicle floor. Where applicable, remove the screws securing the clips to the floor to enable the cables to be released **(see illustration)**.

8 Similarly, where applicable, detach the handbrake cables from the clips on the rear axle assembly.

9 On models with ABS, separate the two halves of the rear wheel sensor wiring connector at the bracket under the vehicle floor, then detach the connector from the bracket.

10 Working on each side of the vehicle in turn, place a container under the brake fluid rigid pipe-to-flexible hose connection at the bracket on the vehicle floor, then unscrew the union nut, and disconnect the brake fluid rigid pipe from the flexible hose **(see illustration)**. Be prepared for fluid spillage, and plug or cover the open ends of the pipe and hose to prevent dirt entry and further fluid loss (the hose can be sealed with a brake hose clamp is desired).

11 Pull out the retaining clips, and detach the brake fluid flexible hoses from the brackets on the floor.

12 Slacken, but do not remove, the bolts securing the lower ends of the suspension struts to the trailing arms. Counterhold the nuts as the bolts are loosened.

13 Support the rear axle assembly using a jack positioned beneath the axle beam. Use a block of wood between the jack and the axle beam to spread the load.

14 Make a final check to ensure that all relevant cables, wires and hoses have been disconnected to allow removal of the axle assembly.

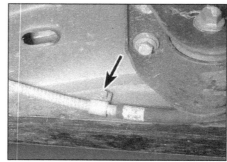

11.6 Heat shield removed to expose handbrake cable equaliser (arrowed)

11.7 Remove the screws (arrowed) securing the handbrake cable clips to the vehicle floor

11.10 Place a container beneath the brake pipe-to-hose connection (arrowed)

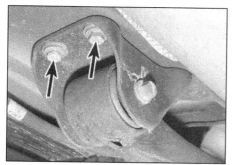

11.15 Two of the rear axle assembly mounting bracket securing bolts (arrowed)

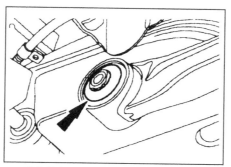

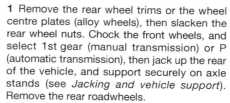

12.6 Prise the pivot bush dust cover (arrowed) from the trailing arm

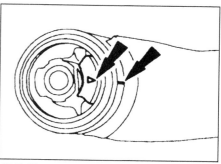

12.7 Make an alignment mark on the bush housing corresponding to the alignment arrow on the bush

15 Unscrew the four bolts on each side of the vehicle securing the axle assembly mounting brackets to the vehicle floor **(see illustration)**.

16 Ensure that the axle assembly is securely supported by the jack, then unscrew and remove the bolts securing the lower ends of the suspension struts to the trailing arms.

17 Lower the axle assembly out from under the rear of the vehicle.

18 If desired, the brake assemblies and mounting brackets can be removed from the axle assembly, bearing in mind the following points.

a) *Each stub axle assembly is secured to the trailing arm by four bolts.*

b) *The brake backplates are secured by rivets (accessible with the hub/brake drum removed) which must be renewed on refitting.*

c) *Mark the hub/brake drum assemblies so that they can be refitted to the correct sides of the axle assembly.*

Refitting

19 If the brake assemblies and/or mounting brackets have been removed from the axle assembly, refit them noting the following points, as applicable.

a) *Ensure that the hub/brake drum assemblies are refitted to the correct sides of the axle assembly as noted before removal.*

b) *Use new rivets to secure the brake backplates to the trailing arms.*

c) *Do not fully tighten the through-bolts and nuts securing the trailing arms to the axle assembly mounting brackets until the weight of the vehicle is resting on its wheels.*

20 Refitting of the axle assembly is a reversal of removal, bearing in mind the following points.

a) *Do not fully tighten the axle assembly mounting bolts until the weight of the vehicle is resting on its wheels.*

b) *Tighten all fixings to the specified torque.*

c) *Bleed the brake hydraulic system as described in Chapter 9.*

d) *Adjust the handbrake as described in Chapter 9.*

12 Rear axle assembly pivot bushes (Hatchback and Van models) – renewal

1 Remove the rear wheel trims or the wheel centre plates (alloy wheels), then slacken the rear wheel nuts. Chock the front wheels, and select 1st gear (manual transmission) or P (automatic transmission), then jack up the rear of the vehicle, and support securely on axle stands (see *Jacking and vehicle support*). Remove the rear roadwheels.

2 Support the rear axle assembly using a jack positioned beneath the axle beam. Use a block of wood between the jack and the axle beam to spread the load.

3 Working on each side of the vehicle in turn, release the handbrake cable from the clips on the axle beam and the trailing arms. Where applicable, remove the screws securing the clips trailing arms to enable the cables to be released.

4 Unscrew the through-bolts and nuts (on both sides of the vehicle) securing the trailing arms to the mounting brackets on the vehicle floor.

5 Using the jack, carefully lower the axle assembly until the pivot bushes (in the trailing arms) are clear of the axle mounting brackets and the body sidemembers. Take care not to place the brake fluid lines under strain.

6 Carefully prise the pivot bush outer dust cover from the relevant trailing arm **(see illustration)**.

7 Make an alignment mark on the bush housing on the trailing arm corresponding to the position of the alignment arrow on the end of the bush **(see illustration)**.

8 Using a metal tube of suitable diameter, flat washers and a long bolt and nut, draw the bush out of its location in the trailing arm.

9 Thoroughly clean the bush housing in the trailing arm.

10 Carefully prise the outer dust cover from the new bush, then mark a line along the side of the bush, corresponding with the alignment arrow on the end of the bush.

11 Lubricate the bush housing, and the new bush, with a soapy solution (eg, washing-up liquid) to aid fitting.

12 Locate the new bush in position against the housing, together with the metal tube, washers, bolt and nut used for removal. Align the line made on the side of the bush with the alignment mark made before removal on the trailing arm, then draw the bush into the housing until it is fully engaged.

13 Fit the outer dust cover to the bush.

14 If desired, repeat the procedure given in paragraphs 6 to 13 for the remaining bush.

15 Further refitting is a reversal of removal, but do not fully tighten the trailing arm-to-mounting bracket through-bolts and nuts to the specified torque until the weight of the vehicle is resting on its wheels.

13 Rear suspension components (Courier and Combi models) – general

Although it is possible to remove the rear suspension torsion bars and anti-roll bars independently of the complete rear axle assembly, it is essential to have certain special tools available to carry out the work successfully.

Due to the complexity of the tasks, and the requirement for special tools to accurately set the suspension geometry and vehicle ride height on refitting, the removal and refitting of individual rear suspension components is considered to be beyond the scope of DIY work, and should be entrusted to a Ford dealer.

Procedures for removal and refitting of the rear shock absorbers, and the complete rear suspension assembly are given in Sections 14 and 15 respectively.

14 Rear shock absorber (Courier and Combi models) – removal, inspection and refitting

Removal

1 Remove the relevant rear wheel trim or the wheel centre plate (alloy wheels), then slacken the relevant rear wheel nuts. Chock the front wheels, and select 1st gear (manual

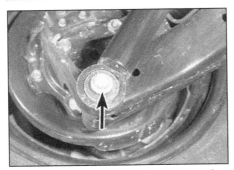

14.3 Rear shock absorber lower mounting bolt (arrowed) – Courier and Combi models

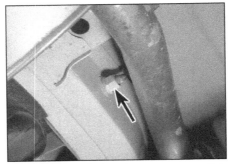

14.4 Rear shock absorber upper mounting nut (arrowed) – Courier and Combi models

15.3 Disconnect the brake fluid hoses from the brackets (arrowed) on the axle beam – Courier and Combi models

transmission) or P (automatic transmission), then jack up the rear of the vehicle, and support securely on axle stands (see *Jacking and vehicle support*). Remove the rear roadwheel.

2 Support the rear axle assembly using a jack positioned beneath the axle beam. Use a block of wood between the jack and the axle beam to spread the load.

3 Unscrew the bolt securing the lower end of the shock absorber to the trailing arm **(see illustration)**.

4 Unscrew the nut and bolt securing the top of the shock absorber to the bracket on the body, then withdraw the shock absorber from under the rear of the vehicle **(see illustration)**.

Inspection

5 The shock absorber can be tested by

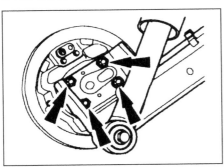

15.6 Hub assembly securing bolts (arrowed) – Courier and Combi models

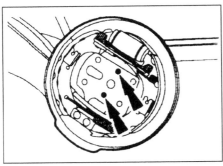

15.8 Drill out the rivets (arrowed) securing the brake backplates – Courier and Combi models

clamping the lower mounting eye in a vice, then fully extending and contracting the shock absorber several times. Any evidence of jerky movement or lack of resistance indicates the need for renewal.

Refitting

6 Refitting is a reversal of removal, but do not finally tighten the shock absorber fixings until the weight of the vehicle is resting on its wheels.

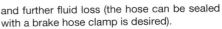

15 Rear suspension assembly (Courier and Combi models) – removal and refitting

Removal

1 Remove the rear wheel trims or the wheel centre plates (alloy wheels), then slacken the rear wheel nuts. Chock the front wheels, and select 1st gear (manual transmission) or P (automatic transmission), then jack up the rear of the vehicle, and support securely on axle stands (see *Jacking and vehicle support*). Remove the rear roadwheels.

2 Working on each side of the vehicle in turn, place a container under the brake fluid rigid pipe-to-flexible hose connection at the bracket on the rear axle beam, then unscrew the union nut, and disconnect the brake fluid rigid pipe from the flexible hose. Be prepared for fluid spillage, and plug or cover the open ends of the pipe and hose to prevent dirt entry

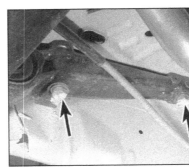

15.12 Unscrew the two bolts (arrowed) on each side securing the axle assembly – Courier and Combi models

and further fluid loss (the hose can be sealed with a brake hose clamp is desired).

3 Unscrew the union locknuts, and detach the brake fluid flexible hoses from the brackets on the axle beam **(see illustration)**.

4 Working on each side of the vehicle in turn, unscrew the union nuts, and disconnect the brake fluid pipes from the rear brake wheel cylinders, then release the brake pipes from the clips on the rear axle assembly, and remove the brake pipes.

5 Remove the brake drums, with reference to Chapter 9 if necessary.

6 Working on each side of the vehicle in turn, unscrew the four securing bolts on each side securing the hub assemblies to the trailing arms, then remove hub assemblies **(see illustration)**.

7 Release the handbrake cables from the clips on the trailing arms.

8 Drill out the two rivets on each side securing the brake backplates to the trailing arms **(see illustration)**. Suspend the backplates using wire or string to avoid straining the handbrake cables.

9 Unhook the brake pressure regulating valve spring from the bracket on the axle beam.

10 Support the rear axle assembly using a jack positioned beneath the axle beam. Use a block of wood between the jack and the axle beam to spread the load.

11 Remove the bolts securing the lower ends of the shock absorbers to the trailing arms.

12 Ensure that the rear axle assembly is adequately supported, then unscrew the two bolts on each side securing the front of the axle assembly to the vehicle floor **(see illustration)**.

13 Lower the axle assembly out from under the rear of the vehicle.

Refitting

14 Refitting is a reversal of removal, bearing in mind the following points.

a) Do not fully tighten the axle assembly securing bolts or the shock absorber-to-trailing arm bolts until the weight of the vehicle is resting on its wheels.

b) Tighten all fixings to the specified torque.

c) Use new rivets to secure the brake backplates to the trailing arms.

d) Refit the brake drums with reference to Chapter 9 if necessary.

e) On completion, bleed the brake hydraulic system as described in Chapter 9.

16 Rear suspension ride height (Courier and Combi models) – adjustment

Checking and adjustment of the ride height requires the use of Ford special tools to accurately compress the suspension to a pre-determined value. Special tools are also required to reposition the torsion bars.

This operation is considered to be beyond the scope of DIY work, and should be entrusted to a Ford dealer.

17 Steering wheel – removal and refitting

Removal

Note: Suitable thread-locking compound will be required to coat the threads of the steering wheel securing bolt on refitting.

1 Disconnect the battery negative lead, with reference to Chapter 5A, then wait at least two minutes before proceeding. If this waiting period is not observed, there is a danger of accidentally activating the airbag(s) and/or seat belt tensioner(s).

2 Remove the steering column shrouds as described in Chapter 11, Section 29.

17.5 Removing the anti-theft immobiliser transceiver unit securing screw. Transceiver unit arrowed

17.7 Removing the steering wheel securing bolt

3 Remove the airbag unit from the steering wheel as described in Chapter 12.

4 Ensure that the front wheels are pointing in the straight-ahead position, and check that the steering lock is engaged.

5 Where applicable, disconnect the wiring plug and remove the securing screw, then withdraw the anti-theft immobiliser transceiver unit from the ignition switch/steering lock assembly **(see illustration)**.

6 Disconnect the airbag module wiring harness connector, which is located on the right-hand side of the steering column **(see illustration)**.

7 Unscrew and remove the steering wheel securing bolt **(see illustration)**.

8 Turn the ignition key to position I and withdraw the steering wheel from the column. Grip the steering wheel on each side, then pull and withdraw it from the splines on the end of the column.

9 Once the steering wheel has been removed, turn the ignition key back to position 0.

10 If a new steering wheel is to be fitted, remove the airbag rotary switch assembly from the old wheel, as described in Chapter 12, Section 27, and fit it to the new steering wheel.

Refitting

11 Where applicable, fit the airbag rotary switch assembly, and make sure that the assembly is centralised, as described in Chapter 12, Section 29.

12 Make sure that the front wheels are

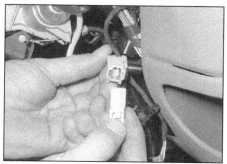

17.6 Disconnecting the airbag module wiring connector

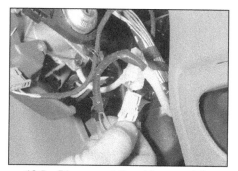

18.5a Disconnect the airbag module wiring harness connector . . .

pointing in the straight-ahead position, and turn the ignition key to position I, then fit the steering wheel to the column, making sure that the airbag rotary switch tabs engage correctly over the steering lock plunger assembly.

13 Thoroughly clean the threads of the steering wheel securing bolt, then coat the threads with suitable locking compound. Refit the steering wheel securing bolt, and tighten to the specified torque, then turn the ignition key back to position 0.

14 The remainder of the refitting procedure is a reversal of removal, but refit the airbag unit as described in Chapter 12.

18 Steering column – removal and refitting

Removal

 Warning: Before proceeding, refer to Chapter 12, and take note of the precautions to be observed when working with an airbag. If the steering wheel is left fitted to the steering column, handle the assembly with care, and note the precautions given for storing an airbag.

Note: New steering column securing nuts should be used on refitting.

1 Removal and refitting of the steering column is described here leaving the steering wheel in place on the column.

2 Disconnect the battery negative lead, with reference to Chapter 5A, then wait at least two minutes before proceeding. If this waiting period is not observed, there is a danger of accidentally activating the airbag(s) and/or seat belt tensioner(s).

3 Remove the steering column shrouds as described in Chapter 11, Section 29.

4 Ensure that the front wheels are pointing in the straight-ahead position, and check that the steering lock is engaged.

5 Working around the steering column, disconnect the following wiring plugs.

a) Airbag module wiring harness connector **(see illustration)**.

b) Anti-theft immobiliser transceiver unit wiring connector **(see illustration)**.

18.5b . . . then the anti-theft immobiliser transceiver unit wiring connector . . .

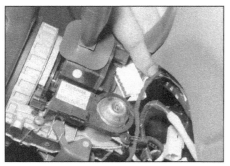

18.5c . . . the steering column stalk switch wiring connectors (wash/wipe switch shown) . . .

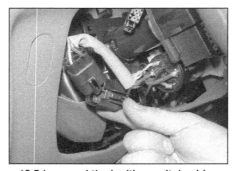

18.5d . . . and the ignition switch wiring connector

18.6 Disconnecting the bonnet release cable

c) *Steering column stalk switch wiring connectors* **(see illustration)**.
d) *Ignition switch wiring connector* **(see illustration)**.

Where applicable, release the cable-tie securing the immobiliser wiring to the receiver unit.

6 Disconnect the end of the bonnet release cable from the release lever under the steering column, then release the cable sheath from the steering column lock housing **(see illustration)**.

7 Working in the footwell, unscrew the pinch-bolt securing the universal joint to the lower end of the steering column shaft, then withdraw the retaining cage, and remove the shaft alignment collar **(see illustration)**.

8 Unscrew the two steering column securing

nuts, and withdraw the column assembly from inside the vehicle **(see illustration)**.

Refitting

9 Refitting is a reversal of removal, bearing in mind the following points.
a) *Use new steering column securing nuts.*
b) *Tighten all fixings to the specified torque.*
c) *Ensure that the steering column universal joint pinch-bolt alignment collar retaining cage is correctly installed.*

19 Steering gear rubber gaiters – renewal

1 Remove the relevant track rod end as described in Section 25.

2 Where applicable, on models with power steering, disconnect the steering gear breather pipe to enable the gaiter to be removed **(see illustration)**.

3 Remove the inboard and outboard securing clips, then slide the gaiter off the end of the track rod.

4 Thoroughly clean the track rod, then slide the new gaiter into position.

5 Fit the gaiter securing clips, using new clips if necessary, making sure that the gaiter is not twisted.

6 On models with power steering, reconnect the steering gear breather pipe.

7 Refit the track rod end as described in Section 25.

20 Steering gear – removal and refitting

Removal

Note: *Any self-locking nuts should be renewed on refitting.*

1 Remove the front suspension crossmember as described in Section 7, noting the following points.
a) *There is no need to disconnect the hub carriers from the lower arm balljoints.*
b) *There is no need to disconnect the anti-roll bar drop links from the suspension struts.*
c) *Lower the crossmember to give sufficient clearance to allow the steering gear to be withdrawn from under the vehicle – there is no need to remove the crossmember completely.*

2 Unscrew the steering gear securing nuts and bolts, then manipulate the steering gear out from under the vehicle **(see illustration)**.

Refitting

3 Refit the steering gear to the crossmember, and tighten the securing nuts and bolts to the specified torque.

4 Raise the crossmember, and refit it to the vehicle as described in Section 7.

18.7 Universal joint-to-steering column shaft pinch-bolt (1) and retaining cage (2)

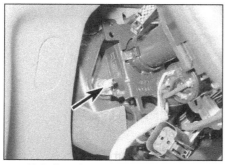

18.8 Steering column securing nut (arrowed)

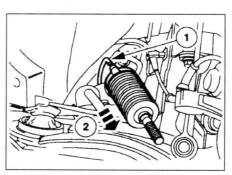

19.2 On models with power steering, disconnect the steering gear breather pipe (1) to enable the gaiter to be removed (2)

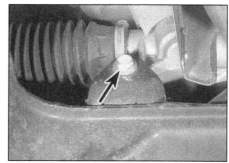

20.2 Steering gear securing bolt (arrowed)

21 Power steering pump – removal and refitting

Zetec-SE engine models

Note: *A new power steering pump high pressure pipe sealing ring will be required on refitting.*

1 Disconnect the battery negative lead, with reference to Chapter 5A.

2 Remove the auxiliary drivebelt as described in Chapter 1A.

3 On models with air conditioning, undo the coolant expansion tank retaining bolt, unclip the tank and move it to one side.

4 Working under the power steering pump, unscrew the bolt securing the high-pressure power steering fluid pipe bracket **(see illustration)**.

5 Place a container beneath the high-pressure pipe union on the pump, then unscrew the union nut, and disconnect the pipe from the pump. Allow the fluid to drain into the container.

6 Slacken the hose clamp, and disconnect the low-pressure fluid hose from the pump.

7 Plug or cover the open ends of the pipe, hose and pump, to prevent dirt entry and further fluid loss.

8 Unscrew the three bolts securing the power steering pump mounting bracket to the engine, then remove the pump/bracket assembly **(see illustration)**.

9 To remove the pump from the mounting bracket, the pump pulley must be removed, using a suitable puller. The puller legs can be engaged with the holes in the face of the pulley.

10 Once the pulley has been removed, the pump can be removed from the bracket after unscrewing the four securing bolts **(see illustration)**.

11 If a new power steering pump is being fitted, remove and discard the fluid pipe unions fitted to the new assembly.

12 Where applicable, refit the pump to the mounting bracket, then refit and tighten the securing bolts. Refit the pulley to the pump using a suitable puller or a press – note that the pulley should be flush with the end of the pump shaft.

13 Further refitting is a reversal of removal, bearing in mind the following points.

a) *Use a new sealing ring when reconnecting the high-pressure fluid pipe to the pump.*

b) *Refit the auxiliary drivebelt as described in Chapter 1A.*

c) *On completion, bleed the power steering hydraulic circuit as described in Section 23.*

Endura-E engine models

Without air conditioning

14 Disconnect the battery negative lead, with reference to Chapter 5A.

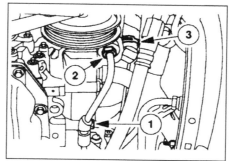

21.4 High pressure fluid pipe bracket securing bolt (1), high pressure pipe union (2) and low pressure fluid hose connection (3) – Zetec-SE engine models

15 Remove the auxiliary drivebelt as described in Chapter 1A.

16 On 1999 models onward, disconnect the alternator wiring multiplug and release the wiring harness from the power steering pump.

17 On pre-1999 models, insert an Allen key into the centre of the pump drive spindle to prevent it from turning, then unscrew and remove the three pump pulley retaining bolts. Withdraw the pulley from the pump. On later models, the pulley is a press-fit on the pump spindle and it is not necessary to remove the pulley to allow removal of the pump. If it is necessary to remove the pulley after removal of the pump, a suitable removal tool (Ford tool 13-022) will be required.

18 Position a suitable container beneath the power steering pump, then unscrew and detach the fluid high pressure pipe and fluid return hose from the pump. As they are detached from the pump, allow the fluid to drain from the pipe and hose (and the pump) into the container. Plug the exposed ends of the pipe, hose and the pump connections, to prevent the ingress of dirt and excessive fluid loss.

19 Unscrew the four retaining bolts (three from the front or top, and one from the rear) and withdraw the pump from the vehicle.

20 Refitting is a reversal of removal, bearing in mind the following points.

a) *If removed, refit the later type press-fit pulley to the pump using Ford tool 21-192, until the pulley is flush with the end of the spindle.*

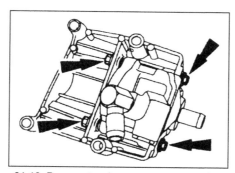

21.10 Power steering pump-to-mounting bracket bolts (arrowed) – Zetec-SE engine models

21.8 Power steering pump mounting bracket bolts (arrowed) – Zetec-SE engine models

b) *Use a new sealing ring when reconnecting the high-pressure fluid pipe to the pump.*

c) *Refit the auxiliary drivebelt as described in Chapter 1A.*

d) *On completion, bleed the power steering hydraulic circuit as described in Section 23.*

With air conditioning

21 Disconnect the battery negative lead, with reference to Chapter 5A.

22 Remove the right-hand headlamp, as described in Chapter 12, Section 7.

23 Unscrew the two securing bolts, and remove the upper auxiliary drivebelt cover.

24 Apply the handbrake, then jack up the front of the vehicle and support securely on axle stands (see *Jacking and vehicle support*).

25 Unscrew the two securing bolts and remove the lower auxiliary drivebelt cover **(see illustration)**.

26 Remove the auxiliary drivebelt as described in Chapter 1A, then lower the vehicle to the ground.

27 Place a container beneath the high-pressure pipe union on the pump, then unscrew the union nut, and disconnect the pipe from the pump. Allow the fluid to drain into the container.

28 Slacken the hose clamp, and disconnect the low-pressure fluid hose from the pump.

29 Plug or cover the open ends of the pipe, hose and pump, to prevent dirt entry and further fluid loss.

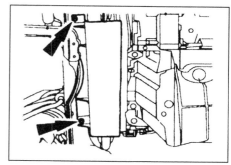

21.25 Lower auxiliary drivebelt cover securing bolts (arrowed) – Endura-E engine models with air conditioning

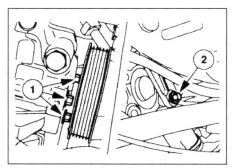

21.30 Power steering pump front securing bolts (1) and rear securing bolt (2) – Endura-E engine models with air conditioning

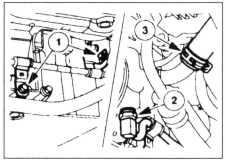

21.34a High-pressure fluid pipe securing bolts (1), high-pressure pipe union (2) and low-pressure hose connection (3) – Endura-DE diesel engine models

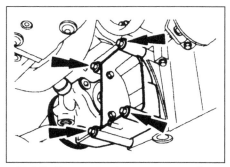

21.34b Power steering pump mounting bracket securing bolts (arrowed) – Endura-DE diesel engine models

30 Unscrew the three front securing bolts, and the single rear securing bolt, and withdraw the pump from the engine **(see illustration)**.

31 If desired, the pulley can be removed from the pump using a suitable puller. The puller legs can be engaged with the holes in the face of the pulley.

32 Where applicable, refit the pulley to the pump using a suitable puller or a press – note that the pulley should be flush with the end of the pump spindle.

33 Refitting is a reversal of removal, bearing in mind the following points.

  a) *Tighten the three front pump securing bolts before tightening the rear securing bolt.*

  b) *Use a new sealing ring when reconnecting the high-pressure fluid pipe to the pump.*

  c) *Refit the auxiliary drivebelt as described in Chapter 1A.*

  d) *On completion, bleed the power steering hydraulic circuit as described in Section 23.*

Diesel engine models

Without air conditioning

34 Proceed as described previously in paragraphs 1 to 13 for Zetec-SE engine models, noting that the high-pressure power steering fluid pipe is secured by two brackets, and the pump bracket is secured by four bolts **(see illustrations)**.

Pre-2000 with air conditioning

35 Disconnect the battery negative lead, with reference to Chapter 5A.

36 Withdraw the power steering fluid reservoir from its location and place it to one side.

37 Remove the right-hand headlamp, as described in Chapter 12, Section 7.

38 Unscrew the two securing bolts, and remove the upper auxiliary drivebelt cover.

39 Apply the handbrake, then jack up the front of the vehicle and support securely on axle stands (see *Jacking and vehicle support*).

40 Unscrew the two securing bolts and remove the lower auxiliary drivebelt cover.

41 Remove the auxiliary drivebelt as

described in Chapter 1B, then lower the vehicle to the ground.

42 Insert an Allen key into the centre of the pump drive spindle to prevent it from turning, then unscrew and remove the three pump pulley retaining bolts. Withdraw the pulley from the pump.

43 Undo the high-pressure pipe support bracket bolt.

44 Place a container beneath the high-pressure pipe union on the pump, then unscrew the union nut, and disconnect the pipe from the pump. Allow the fluid to drain into the container.

45 Slacken the hose clamp, and disconnect the low-pressure fluid hose from the pump.

46 Plug or cover the open ends of the pipe, hose and pump, to prevent dirt entry and further fluid loss.

47 Undo the two bolts and remove the auxiliary drivebelt tensioner bracket.

48 Undo the three bolts and withdraw the pump from the engine.

49 Refitting is a reversal of removal, bearing in mind the following points.

  a) *Use a new sealing ring when reconnecting the high-pressure fluid pipe to the pump.*

  b) *Refit the auxiliary drivebelt as described in Chapter 1B.*

  c) *On completion, bleed the power steering hydraulic circuit as described in Section 23.*

2000 onward with air conditioning

Note: *The power steering pump fitted to 2000 onward diesel engine models with air conditioning is of the electro-hydraulic type.*

50 Disconnect the battery negative lead, with reference to Chapter 5A.

51 Release the securing band and remove the power steering pump cover.

52 Disconnect the pump electrical connector.

53 Place a container beneath the low-pressure hose connection on the pump. Slacken the hose clamp, and disconnect the low-pressure fluid hose. Allow the fluid to drain into the container.

54 Plug or cover the open ends of the hose

and pump, to prevent dirt entry and further fluid loss.

55 Apply the handbrake, then jack up the front of the vehicle and support securely on axle stands (see *Jacking and vehicle support*).

56 Move the container to beneath the high-pressure pipe union on the pump, then unscrew the union nut, and disconnect the pipe from the pump. Allow the fluid to drain into the container.

57 Undo the bolt and release the power steering pump earth cable.

58 Undo the pump mounting bracket retaining bolts and withdraw the pump and mounting bracket. Undo the remaining bolts and separate the pump from the bracket.

59 Refitting is a reversal of removal, bearing in mind the following points.

  a) *Use a new sealing ring when reconnecting the high-pressure fluid pipe to the pump.*

  b) *On completion, bleed the power steering hydraulic circuit as described in Section 23.*

22 Power steering fluid cooler – removal and refitting

Removal

1 The fluid cooler takes the form of a pipe assembly fitted in front of the radiator.

2 Apply the handbrake, then jack up the front of the vehicle and support securely on axle stands.

3 Remove the securing screws, and withdraw the shield from under the radiator.

4 Where applicable, remove the securing screws, and withdraw the engine undershield.

5 Working under the front of the vehicle, place a container under the fluid pipe unions on the right-hand side of the vehicle, the unscrew the union nuts, and disconnect the pipes. Allow the fluid to drain into the container, then plug or cover the open ends of the pipes to prevent dirt entry and further fluid loss.

6 Repeat the procedure for the pipe

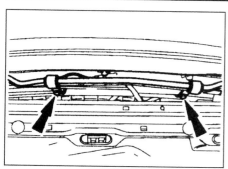

22.8 Power steering fluid cooler securing bolts (arrowed)

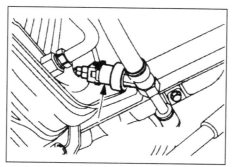

24.2 Power steering fluid pressure switch location (arrowed)

25.2 Unscrewing the track rod end balljoint nut

connections on the left-hand side of the vehicle.

7 Unscrew the bolts securing the high-pressure pipe bracket.

8 Unscrew the two securing bolts, and withdraw the fluid cooler pipes from the front of the vehicle **(see illustration)**.

Refitting

9 Refitting is a reversal of removal, but on completion bleed the power steering hydraulic system as described in Section 23.

23 Power steering hydraulic system – bleeding

Note: *Ford recommend that the power steering system is bled using a hand-operated vacuum pump connected to the reservoir filler neck – this should only be necessary if persistent problems are experienced with air in the hydraulic system.*

Conventional bleeding

1 Check the power steering fluid level as described in *Weekly checks*.

2 Turn the steering wheel quickly from lock-to-lock several times, then recheck the fluid level and top-up if necessary.

3 Start the engine and allow it to idle, then *slowly* turn the steering wheel from lock-to-lock several times – do not hold the steering wheel on full lock for more than 15 seconds at a time. Check for air bubbles in the fluid reservoir – if air bubbles are visible, the system requires further bleeding.

4 Stop the engine, then lower the vehicle to the ground, and recheck the fluid level.

5 If air bubbles appear in the reservoir when the system is operated, or if the pump is noisy in operation (not to be confused with a slipping drivebelt), repeat the bleeding procedure.

Bleeding using a vacuum pump

Note: *During the bleeding procedure, the pressure will drop, so adequate pressure should be maintained using the vacuum pump. If the pressure drops by more than*

0.07 bar in 5 minutes, the system should be checked for leaks.

6 Connect a vacuum pump to the fluid reservoir filler neck using a suitable adapter (Ford Tool No 13-016 is available for this purpose).

7 Start the engine, and slowly turn the steering to the right, just off full-lock.

8 Stop the engine, and apply a vacuum of 0.51 bar, using the vacuum pump, until the air is purged from the system (this will take at least 5 minutes).

9 Depressurise the system using the vacuum pump.

10 Repeat the procedure given in paragraphs 7 to 9 with the steering turned to just off full left lock.

11 Disconnect the vacuum pump from the fluid reservoir, and top up the fluid level if necessary.

12 Start the engine, and turn the steering wheel from lock-to-lock. If the system is excessively noisy in operation, repeat the bleeding procedure.

13 If problems with air in the system persist, leave the vehicle overnight, then repeat the bleeding procedure.

24 Power steering fluid pressure switch – removal and refitting

Removal

1 The power steering fluid pressure switch provides a signal to the engine management electronic control unit, which is used to reduce the engine speed if the power steering fluid pressure becomes too high.

2 The switch is located in the high pressure fluid pipe **(see illustration)**.

3 Disconnect the battery negative lead, with reference to Chapter 5A.

4 Place a container beneath the switch location to catch any escaping fluid.

5 Disconnect the wiring plug from the switch, then unscrew the switch from the fluid pipe.

6 Be prepared for fluid spillage, and plug or cover the orifice in the pipe to prevent dirt entry and further fluid loss.

Refitting

7 Refitting is a reversal of removal, but tighten the switch securely, and on completion bleed the power steering hydraulic circuit as described in Section 23.

25 Track rod end – removal and refitting

Note: *A balljoint separator tool will be required for this operation. Where applicable, Nyloc-type self-locking nuts must be renewed on refitting.*

Removal

1 Remove the relevant front wheel trim or the wheel centre plate (alloy wheels), then slacken the wheel nuts. Apply the handbrake, then jack up the front of the vehicle, and support securely on axle stands (see *Jacking and vehicle support*). Remove the roadwheel.

2 Slacken the track rod end balljoint nut, and unscrew it as far as the ends of the threads. Counterhold the balljoint pin using a suitable Allen key or hexagon bit **(see illustration)**.

3 Disconnect the track rod end balljoint from the hub carrier using a balljoint separator tool (leave the nut fitted to protect the threads), taking care not to damage the balljoint rubber seal. Once the balljoint has been released, remove the balljoint nut.

4 Slacken the track rod end locknut, then unscrew the track rod end from the track rod, counting the number of turns necessary to remove it.

Refitting

5 Screw the track rod end onto the track rod the number of turns noted during removal, then tighten the locknut while holding the balljoint in position.

6 Engage the track rod end balljoint pin with the hub carrier, then fit a new securing nut. Tighten the nut to the specified torque, while counterholding the balljoint pin as during removal.

7 Refit the roadwheel, then lower the vehicle to the ground, and tighten the wheel nuts.

8 Check the front wheel alignment (see Section 26) at the earliest opportunity.

26 Wheel alignment and steering angles – general information

Front wheel alignment

1 Accurate front wheel alignment is essential to good steering and for even tyre wear. Before considering the steering angles, check that the tyres are correctly inflated, that the front wheels are not buckled, the hub bearings are not worn and that the steering linkage is in good order. without slackness or wear at the joints.

2 Wheel alignment consists of four factors:

Camber, is the angle at which the roadwheels are set from the vertical when viewed from the front or rear of the vehicle. Positive camber is the angle (in degrees) that the wheels are tilted outwards at the top from the vertical. The camber angle is given for reference only and cannot be adjusted.

Castor, is the angle between the steering axis and a vertical line when viewed from each side of the vehicle. Positive castor is indicated when the steering axis is inclined towards the rear of the vehicle at its upper end. This angle is not adjustable.

Steering axis inclination (kingpin inclination), is the angle, when viewed from the front or rear of the vehicle, between the vertical and an imaginary line drawn between the upper and lower front suspension strut mountings. This angle is not adjustable.

Toe, is the amount by which the distance between the front inside edges of the roadwheel rim differs from that between the rear inside edges. If the distance between the front edges is less than that at the rear, the wheels are said to toe-in. If the distance between the front inside edges is greater than that at the rear, the wheels toe-out.

3 Owing to the need for precision gauges to measure the small angles of the steering and suspension settings, it is preferable that checking of camber and castor is left to a service station having the necessary equipment. Camber and castor is set during production of the vehicle, and any deviation from the specified angle will be due to accident damage or gross wear in the suspension mountings.

4 To check the front wheel alignment, first make sure that the lengths of both track rods are equal when the steering is in the straight-ahead position. The track rod lengths can be adjusted if necessary by releasing the locknuts from the track rod ends and rotating the track rods. If necessary, self-locking grips can be used to rotate the track rods.

5 Obtain a tracking gauge. These are available in various forms from accessory stores, or one can be fabricated from a length of steel tubing suitably cranked to clear the sump and transmission, and having a setscrew and locknut at one end.

6 With the gauge, measure the distances between the two wheel inner rims (at hub height) at the rear of the wheel. Push the vehicle forward to rotate the wheel through 180° (half a turn) and measure the distance between the wheel inner rims, again at hub height, at the front of the wheel. This last measurement should differ from the first by the appropriate toe-in which is given in the Specifications. The vehicle must be on level ground.

7 If the toe-in is found to be incorrect, release the track rod end locknuts and turn both track rods equally. Only turn them a quarter-of-a-turn at a time before re-checking the alignment. If necessary use self-locking grips to turn the track rods – **do not** grip the threaded part of the track rod during adjustment. It is important not to allow the track rods to become unequal in length during adjustment, otherwise the alignment of the steering wheel will become incorrect and tyre scrubbing will occur on turns.

8 On completion tighten the locknuts without disturbing the setting. Check that the balljoint is at the centre of its arc of travel.

Rear wheel alignment

9 Figures are provided in the Specifications for rear wheel camber and toe-setting for reference only. No adjustment is possible. Refer to paragraph 2 for a description of the settings.

Chapter 11
Bodywork and fittings

Contents

Body exterior fittings – removal and refitting 26
Bonnet – removal, refitting and adjustment 8
Bonnet lock – removal and refitting 10
Bonnet release cable – removal and refitting 9
Bumpers – removal and refitting 6
Central locking system components – general information 21
Centre console – removal and refitting 30
Door handles and lock components – removal and refitting 13
Door inner trim panel – removal and refitting 12
Door window glass and regulator – removal and refitting 14
Door – removal and refitting 11
Electric window components – removal and refitting 22
Exterior mirrors and associated components –
    removal and refitting 23
Facia assembly – removal and refitting 31
General information 1
Hinge and lock lubrication . . . . See Chapter 1A or 1B
Interior trim – removal and refitting 29

Maintenance – bodywork and underframe 2
Maintenance – upholstery and carpets 3
Major body damage – repair 5
Minor body damage – repair 4
Opening rear quarter windows (3-door models) 15
Radiator grille panel – removal and refitting 7
Rear load door components (Courier and Combi models) –
    removal and refitting 20
Rear load doors (Courier and Combi models) –
    removal and refitting 18
Seat belt components – removal and refitting 28
Seats – removal and refitting 27
Sliding side windows (Combi models) – removal and refitting 16
Sunroof – general information, removal and refitting 25
Tailgate and support struts – removal, refitting and adjustment 17
Tailgate lock components – removal and refitting 19
Windscreen, tailgate and fixed window glass –
    general information 24

Degrees of difficulty

Easy, suitable for novice with little experience	**Fairly easy,** suitable for beginner with some experience	**Fairly difficult,** suitable for competent DIY mechanic	**Difficult,** suitable for experienced DIY mechanic	**Very difficult,** suitable for expert DIY or professional

Specifications

Torque wrench settings

	Nm	lbf ft
Front seat belt height adjuster securing bolts	35	26
Front seat belt stalk/tensioner assembly securing bolt	50	37
Front seat mounting bolts	25	18
Seat belt anchor bolts	38	28
Tailgate hinge bolts	10	7

1 General information

The bodyshell is of three- and five-door Hatchback, 3-door Van, and Courier and Combi light commercial configurations, and is made of pressed steel sections. Most components are welded together, but some use is made of structural adhesives. The front wings are bolted on.

The bonnet, doors and some other vulnerable panels are made of zinc-coated metal, and are further protected by being coated with an anti-chip primer prior to being sprayed.

Extensive use is made of plastic materials, mainly in the interior, but also in exterior components. The front and rear bumpers and

the front grille are injection-moulded from a synthetic material which is very strong, and yet light. Plastic components such as wheelarch liners are fitted to the underside of the vehicle, to improve the body's resistance to corrosion.

2 Maintenance – bodywork and underframe

The general condition of a vehicle's bodywork is the one thing that significantly affects its value. Maintenance is easy, but needs to be regular. Neglect, particularly after minor damage, can lead quickly to further deterioration and costly repair bills. It is important also to keep watch on those parts of the vehicle not immediately visible, for

instance the underside, inside all the wheelarches, and the lower part of the engine compartment.

The basic maintenance routine for the bodywork is washing – preferably with a lot of water, from a hose. This will remove all the loose solids which may have stuck to the vehicle. It is important to flush these off in such a way as to prevent grit from scratching the finish. The wheelarches and underframe need washing in the same way, to remove any accumulated mud which will retain moisture and tend to encourage rust. Paradoxically enough, the best time to clean the underframe and wheelarches is in wet weather, when the mud is thoroughly wet and soft. In very wet weather, the underframe is usually cleaned of large accumulations automatically, and this is a good time for inspection.

Periodically, except on vehicles with a wax-based underbody protective coating, it is a good idea to have the whole of the underframe of the vehicle steam-cleaned, engine compartment included, so that a thorough inspection can be carried out to see what minor repairs and renovations are necessary. Steam-cleaning is available at many garages, and is necessary for the removal of the accumulation of oily grime, which sometimes is allowed to become thick in certain areas. If steam-cleaning facilities are not available, there are one or two excellent grease solvents available, which can be brush-applied; the dirt can then be simply hosed off. Note that these methods should not be used on vehicles with wax-based underbody protective coating, or the coating will be removed. Such vehicles should be inspected annually, preferably just prior to Winter, when the underbody should be washed down, and any damage to the wax coating repaired. Ideally, a completely fresh coat should be applied. It would also be worth considering the use of such wax-based protection for injection into door panels, sills, box sections, etc, as an additional safeguard against rust damage, where such protection is not provided by the vehicle manufacturer.

After washing paintwork, wipe off with a chamois leather to give an unspotted clear finish. A coat of clear protective wax polish will give added protection against chemical pollutants in the air. If the paintwork sheen has dulled or oxidised, use a cleaner/polisher combination to restore the brilliance of the shine. This requires a little effort, but such dulling is usually caused because regular washing has been neglected. Care needs to be taken with metallic paintwork, as special non-abrasive cleaner/polisher is required to avoid damage to the finish. Always check that the door and ventilator opening drain holes and pipes are completely clear, so that water can be drained out. Brightwork should be treated in the same way as paintwork. Windscreens and windows can be kept clear of the smeary film which often appears, by the use of proprietary glass cleaner. Never use any form of wax or other body or chromium polish on glass.

3 Maintenance – upholstery and carpets

Mats and carpets should be brushed or vacuum-cleaned regularly, to keep them free of grit. If they are badly stained, remove them from the vehicle for scrubbing or sponging, and make quite sure they are dry before refitting. Seats and interior trim panels can be kept clean by wiping with a damp cloth. If they do become stained (which can be more apparent on light-coloured upholstery), use a little liquid detergent and a soft nail brush to scour the grime out of the grain of the material. Do not forget to keep the headlining clean in the same way as the upholstery. When using liquid cleaners inside the vehicle, do not over-wet the surfaces being cleaned. Excessive damp could get into the seams and padded interior, causing stains, offensive odours or even rot. If the inside of the vehicle gets wet accidentally, it is worthwhile taking some trouble to dry it out properly, particularly where carpets are involved. *Do not leave oil or electric heaters inside the vehicle for this purpose.*

4 Minor body damage – repair

Repairs of minor scratches

If the scratch is very superficial, and does not penetrate to the metal of the bodywork, repair is very simple. Lightly rub the area of the scratch with a paintwork renovator, or a very fine cutting paste, to remove loose paint from the scratch, and to clear the surrounding bodywork of wax polish. Rinse the area with clean water.

Apply touch-up paint to the scratch using a fine paint brush; continue to apply fine layers of paint until the surface of the paint in the scratch is level with the surrounding paintwork. Allow the new paint at least two weeks to harden, then blend it into the surrounding paintwork by rubbing the scratch area with a paintwork renovator or a very fine cutting paste. Finally, apply wax polish.

Where the scratch has penetrated right through to the metal of the bodywork, causing the metal to rust, a different repair technique is required. Remove any loose rust from the bottom of the scratch with a penknife, then apply rust-inhibiting paint, to prevent the formation of rust in the future. Using a rubber or nylon applicator, fill the scratch with bodystopper paste. If required, this paste can be mixed with cellulose thinners, to provide a very thin paste which is ideal for filling narrow scratches. Before the stopper-paste in the scratch hardens, wrap a piece of smooth cotton rag around the top of a finger. Dip the finger in cellulose thinners, and quickly sweep it across the surface of the stopper-paste in the scratch; this will ensure that the surface of the stopper-paste is slightly hollowed. The scratch can now be painted over as described earlier in this Section.

Repairs of dents

When deep denting of the vehicle's bodywork has taken place, the first task is to pull the dent out, until the affected bodywork almost attains its original shape. There is little point in trying to restore the original shape completely, as the metal in the damaged area will have stretched on impact, and cannot be reshaped fully to its original contour. It is better to bring the level of the dent up to a point which is about 3 mm below the level of the surrounding bodywork. In cases where the dent is very shallow anyway, it is not worth trying to pull it out at all. If the underside of the dent is accessible, it can be hammered out gently from behind, using a mallet with a wooden or plastic head. Whilst doing this, hold a suitable block of wood firmly against the outside of the panel, to absorb the impact from the hammer blows and thus prevent a large area of the bodywork from being 'belled-out'.

Should the dent be in a section of the bodywork which has a double skin, or some other factor making it inaccessible from behind, a different technique is called for. Drill several small holes through the metal inside the area – particularly in the deeper section. Then screw long self-tapping screws into the holes, just sufficiently for them to gain a good purchase in the metal. Now the dent can be pulled out by pulling on the protruding heads of the screws with a pair of pliers.

The next stage of the repair is the removal of the paint from the damaged area, and from an inch or so of the surrounding 'sound' bodywork. This is accomplished most easily by using a wire brush or abrasive pad on a power drill, although it can be done just as effectively by hand, using sheets of abrasive paper. To complete the preparation for filling, score the surface of the bare metal with a screwdriver or the tang of a file, or alternatively, drill small holes in the affected area. This will provide a really good 'key' for the filler paste.

To complete the repair, see the Section on filling and respraying.

Repairs of rust holes or gashes

Remove all paint from the affected area, and from an inch or so of the surrounding 'sound' bodywork, using an abrasive pad or a wire brush on a power drill. If these are not available, a few sheets of abrasive paper will do the job most effectively. With the paint removed, you will be able to judge the severity of the corrosion, and therefore decide whether to renew the whole panel (if this is possible) or to repair the affected area. New body panels are not as expensive as most people think, and it is often quicker and more satisfactory to fit a new panel than to attempt to repair large areas of corrosion.

Remove all fittings from the affected area, except those which will act as a guide to the original shape of the damaged bodywork (eg headlamp shells etc). Then, using tin snips or a hacksaw blade, remove all loose metal and any other metal badly affected by corrosion. Hammer the edges of the hole inwards, in order to create a slight depression for the filler paste.

Wire-brush the affected area to remove the powdery rust from the surface of the remaining metal. Paint the affected area with rust-inhibiting paint; if the back of the rusted area is accessible, treat this also.

Before filling can take place, it will be necessary to block the hole in some way. This can be achieved by the use of aluminium or plastic mesh, or aluminium tape.

Aluminium or plastic mesh, or glass-fibre matting is probably the best material to use for a large hole. Cut a piece to the approximate size and shape of the hole to be filled, then position it in the hole so that its edges are below the level of the surrounding bodywork. It can be retained in position by several blobs of filler paste around its periphery.

Aluminium tape should be used for small or very narrow holes. Pull a piece off the roll, trim it to the approximate size and shape required, then pull off the backing paper (if used) and stick the tape over the hole; it can be overlapped if the thickness of one piece is insufficient. Burnish down the edges of the tape with the handle of a screwdriver or similar, to ensure that the tape is securely attached to the metal underneath.

Filling and respraying

Before using this Section, see the Sections on dent, deep scratch, rust holes and gash repairs.

Many types of bodyfiller are available, but generally speaking, those proprietary kits which contain a tin of filler paste and a tube of resin hardener are best for this type of repair. A wide, flexible plastic or nylon applicator will be found invaluable for imparting a smooth and well-contoured finish to the surface of the filler.

Mix up a little filler on a clean piece of card or board – measure the hardener carefully (follow the maker's instructions on the pack), otherwise the filler will set too rapidly or too slowly. Using the applicator, apply the filler paste to the prepared area; draw the applicator across the surface of the filler to achieve the correct contour and to level the surface. As soon as a contour that approximates to the correct one is achieved, stop working the paste – if you carry on too long, the paste will become sticky and begin to 'pick-up' on the applicator. Continue to add thin layers of filler paste at 20-minute intervals, until the level of the filler is just proud of the surrounding bodywork.

Once the filler has hardened, the excess can be removed using a metal plane or file. From then on, progressively-finer grades of abrasive paper should be used, starting with a 40-grade production paper, and finishing with a 400-grade wet-and-dry paper. Always wrap the abrasive paper around a flat rubber, cork, or wooden block – otherwise the surface of the filler will not be completely flat. During the smoothing of the filler surface, the wet-and-dry paper should be periodically rinsed in water. This will ensure that a very smooth finish is imparted to the filler at the final stage.

At this stage, the 'dent' should be surrounded by a ring of bare metal, which in turn should be encircled by the finely 'feathered' edge of the good paintwork. Rinse the repair area with clean water, until all of the dust produced by the rubbing-down operation has gone.

Spray the whole area with a light coat of – this will show up any imperfections in the surface of the filler. Repair these imperfections with fresh filler paste or bodystopper, and once more smooth the surface with abrasive paper. If bodystopper is used, it can be mixed with cellulose thinners, to form a really thin paste which is ideal for filling small holes. Repeat this spray-and-repair procedure until you are satisfied that the surface of the filler, and the feathered edge of the paintwork, are perfect. Clean the repair area with clean water, and allow to dry fully.

The repair area is now ready for final spraying. Paint spraying must be carried out in a warm, dry, windless and dust-free atmosphere. This condition can be created artificially if you have access to a large indoor working area, but if you are forced to work in the open, you will have to pick your day very carefully. If you are working indoors, dousing the floor in the work area with water will help to settle the dust which would otherwise be in the atmosphere. If the repair area is confined to one body panel, mask off the surrounding panels; this will help to minimise the effects of a slight mis-match in paint colours. Bodywork fittings (eg chrome strips, door handles etc) will also need to be masked off. Use genuine masking tape, and several thicknesses of newspaper, for the masking operations.

Before commencing to spray, agitate the aerosol can thoroughly, then spray a test area (an old tin, or similar) until the technique is mastered. Cover the repair area with a thick coat of primer; the thickness should be built up using several thin layers of paint, rather than one thick one. Using 400 grade wet-and-dry paper, rub down the surface of the primer until it is really smooth. While doing this, the work area should be thoroughly doused with water, and the wet-and-dry paper periodically rinsed in water. Allow to dry before spraying on more paint.

Spray on the top coat, again building up the thickness by using several thin layers of paint. Start spraying at the top of the repair area, and then, using a side-to-side motion, work downwards until the whole repair area and about 2 inches of the surrounding original paintwork is covered. Remove all masking material 10 to 15 minutes after spraying on the final coat of paint.

Allow the new paint at least two weeks to harden, then, using a paintwork renovator or a very fine cutting paste, blend the edges of the paint into the existing paintwork. Finally, apply wax polish.

Plastic components

With the use of more and more plastic body components by the vehicle manufacturers (eg bumpers. spoilers, and in some cases major body panels), rectification of more serious damage to such items has become a matter of either entrusting repair work to a specialist in this field, or renewing complete components. Repair of such damage by the DIY owner is not really feasible, owing to the cost of the equipment and materials required for effecting such repairs. The basic technique involves making a groove along the line of the crack in the plastic, using a rotary burr in a power drill. The damaged part is then welded back together, using a hot air gun to heat up and fuse a plastic filler rod into the groove. Any excess plastic is then removed, and the area rubbed down to a smooth finish. It is important that a filler rod of the correct plastic is used, as body components can be made of a variety of different types (eg polycarbonate, ABS, polypropylene).

Damage of a less serious nature (abrasions, minor cracks etc) can be repaired by the DIY owner using a two-part epoxy filler repair. Once mixed in equal, this is used in similar fashion to the bodywork filler used on metal panels. The filler is usually cured in twenty to thirty minutes, ready for sanding and painting.

If the owner is renewing a complete component himself, or if he has repaired it with epoxy filler, he will be left with the problem of finding a suitable paint for finishing which is compatible with the type of plastic used. At one time, the use of a universal paint was not possible, owing to the complex range of plastics encountered in body component applications. Standard paints, generally speaking, will not bond to plastic or rubber satisfactorily, but suitable paints to match any plastic or rubber finish, can be obtained from dealers. However, it is now possible to obtain a plastic body parts finishing kit which consists of a pre-primer treatment, a primer and coloured top coat. Full instructions are normally supplied with a kit, but basically, the method of use is to first apply the pre-primer to the component concerned, and allow it to dry for up to 30 minutes. Then the primer is applied, and left to dry for about an hour before finally applying the special-coloured top coat. The result is a correctly-coloured component, where the paint will flex with the plastic or rubber, a property that standard paint does not normally posses.

5 Major body damage – repair

Where serious damage has occurred, or large areas need renewal due to neglect, it means that complete new panels will need welding-in, and this is best left to professionals. If the damage is due to impact, it will also be necessary to check completely the alignment of the bodyshell, and this can only be carried out accurately by a Ford dealer using special jigs. If the body is left misaligned, it is primarily dangerous, as the car will not

6.5 Air inlet resonator box securing bolt (arrowed) – viewed from under the left-hand side of the vehicle

6.6a Remove the screw securing the wheelarch liner to the bumper . . .

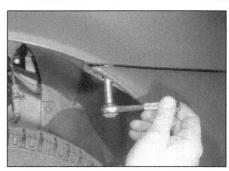

6.6b . . . then unscrew the bumper side securing screw

handle properly, and secondly, uneven stresses will be imposed on the steering, suspension and possibly transmission, causing abnormal wear, or complete failure, particularly to such items as the tyres.

6 Bumpers – removal and refitting

Front bumper

1 Disconnect the battery negative lead, with reference to Chapter 5A.
2 Remove the radiator grille panel as described in Section 7.
3 Remove the headlights as described in Chapter 12, Section.
4 Apply the handbrake, then jack up the front

of the vehicle and support securely on axle stands (see *Jacking and vehicle support*).
5 Where applicable, unscrew the bolt securing the air inlet resonator box to the body panel, to allow access to the left-hand bumper securing bolt **(see illustration)**.
6 Working on each side of the vehicle in turn, remove the screw securing the wheelarch liner to the front bumper assembly. Pull the wheelarch liners away from the bumper for access to the bumper side securing screws, then unscrew the side securing screws **(see illustrations)**.
7 Where applicable, disconnect the wiring plugs from the front bumper-mounted lights.
8 Working through the headlight apertures, unscrew the two bumper securing nuts (one on each side of the vehicle), then pull the bumper forwards, and withdraw it from the vehicle **(see illustration)**.

9 Refitting is a reversal of removal, but refit the headlights with reference to Chapter 12 if necessary.

Rear bumper

Hatchback and Van models

10 Disconnect the battery negative lead, with reference to Chapter 5A.
11 Working at the rear of the rear wheelarches, unscrew the two bumper securing screws on each side of the vehicle **(see illustration)**.
12 Using a screwdriver, carefully prise the number plate light from the rear bumper and unclip the bulbholder from the light.
13 Working in the luggage compartment, unscrew the two bumper securing nuts, then lift the bumper from the rear of the vehicle **(see illustration)**.
14 Refitting is a reversal of removal.

Courier and Combi models

15 To improve access, chock the front wheels, then jack up the rear of the vehicle and support on axle stands (see *Jacking and vehicle support*).
16 Working on each side of the vehicle in turn, unscrew the two bumper lower corner panel securing screws from the rear of the rear wheelarches, then pull the bumper corner panels towards the rear of the vehicle to release them from the main bumper. Withdraw the bumper corner panels **(see illustrations)**.

6.8 Unscrewing a front bumper securing nut

6.11 Rear bumper side securing screws (arrowed) – Hatchback and Van models

6.13 Removing a rear bumper securing nut – Hatchback and Van models

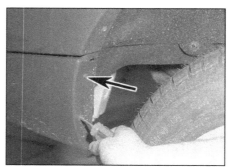

6.16a Remove the securing screws . . .

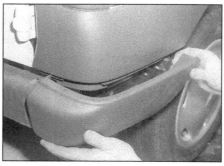

6.16b . . . and remove the rear bumper lower corner panels – Courier and Combi models

6.17 Rear bumper securing nut (arrowed) – Courier and Combi models

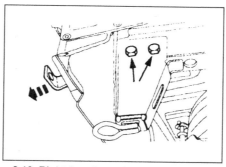

6.18 Right-hand rear bumper mounting bracket bolts (arrowed) – Courier and Combi models

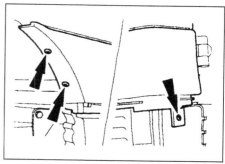

6.19 Rear bumper upper corner panel securing screws (arrowed) – Courier and Combi models

17 Unscrew the now-exposed main bumper securing nuts (one on each side of the vehicle), then withdraw the main bumper from the rear of the vehicle **(see illustration)**.

18 If desired, the bumper mounting brackets can be removed after unscrewing the two bolts securing each bracket to the vehicle body **(see illustration)**. Note that the left-hand bracket bolts also secure the rear exhaust mounting bracket.

19 To remove the bumper upper corner panels, remove the main bumper as described previously, then unscrew the three securing screws in each case, and remove the upper corner panels **(see illustration)**.

20 Refitting is a reversal of removal.

7 Radiator grille panel – removal and refitting

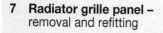

Removal

1 Open the bonnet, then pull the grille panel upwards to release it from the four securing clips **(see illustration)**. **Note:** *On later models the grille is secured with two clips.*

Refitting

2 Refitting is a reversal of removal.

8 Bonnet – removal, refitting and adjustment

Removal

1 Open the bonnet, and support it on its stay.

2 Using a marker pen or paint, mark around the hinge positions on the bonnet.

3 Disconnect the windscreen washer fluid hose from the connector in the scuttle at the left-hand side of the engine compartment. Where applicable, release the hose from the bonnet hinge.

4 With the aid of an assistant, support the bonnet, and unscrew the four bolts securing the bonnet to the hinges **(see illustration)**.

5 Lift off the bonnet.

Refitting

6 Align the marks made on the bonnet before removal, with the hinges, then refit and tighten the bonnet securing bolts.

7 Reconnect the windscreen washer fluid hose, and where applicable clip the hose to the bonnet hinge.

8 Check the bonnet adjustment as follows.

Adjustment

9 Close the bonnet, and check that there is an equal gap at each side, between the bonnet and the wing panels. Check also that the bonnet sits flush in relation to the surrounding body panels.

10 The bonnet should close smoothly and positively without excessive pressure. If this is not the case, adjustment will be required.

11 To adjust the bonnet alignment, slacken the bonnet securing bolts, and move the bonnet on the bolts as required (the bolt holes in the hinges are elongated). To adjust the bonnet closure, adjustable bump stops are fitted to the body front panel. These may be raised or lowered by screwing in or out as necessary. If desired, the bonnet lock can be adjusted as described in Section 10.

9 Bonnet release cable – removal and refitting

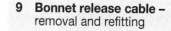

Removal

1 Working inside the vehicle, remove the steering column shrouds, as described in Section 29.

2 Unclip the inner cable from the bonnet release lever **(see illustration)**.

3 Slide the cable sheath grommet from the steering column lock housing.

4 Working in the engine compartment, remove the front grille panel as described in Section 7.

5 Unclip the end of the cable from the lock operating lever, then release the cable sheath

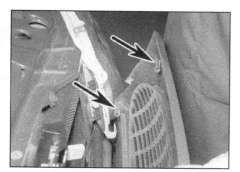

7.1 Pull the grille panel forwards to release the securing clips (arrowed)

8.4 Unscrewing a bonnet securing bolt

9.2 Unclipping the inner cable from the bonnet release lever

9.5 Unclip the bonnet release cable from the lock operating lever (1), and release the cable sheath (2) from the lock body

10.3 Bonnet lock securing bolts (arrowed)

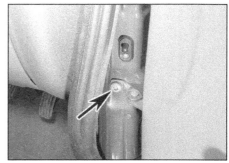

11.2 Unbolt the door check strap from the door pillar

grommet from the lock body **(see illustration)**.

6 Release the cable from the clips and brackets in the engine compartment, noting its routing.

7 Tie a length of string to the end of the cable at the release lever inside the vehicle, then carefully pull the cable through the bulkhead grommet into the engine compartment.

8 Untie the string from the end of the cable and leave it in position to aid refitting.

Refitting

9 Refitting is a reversal of removal, but tie the string to the release lever end of the cable, and use the string to pull the cable into position. Ensure that the cable is routed as noted before removal, and make sure that the bulkhead grommet is correctly seated.

10 Bonnet lock –
removal and refitting

Removal

1 Remove the front grille panel as described in Section 7.

2 Unclip the bonnet release cable inner sleeve from the lock operating lever, then release the cable sheath grommet from the lock body.

3 Unscrew the securing bolts, and remove the lock assembly **(see illustration)**.

Refitting

4 Refitting is a reversal of removal. If necessary, the position of the lock can be altered to adjust the lock operation, by moving the lock within the elongated holes.

11 Door –
removal and refitting

Removal

1 On models with electrical components mounted in the door, remove the door inner trim panel as described in Section 12, and disconnect the wiring from the components inside the door, noting the routing of the wiring. Pull the wiring grommet from the front edge of the door, and feed the wiring through the hole in the door.

2 Unbolt the door check strap from the door pillar **(see illustration)**.

3 Ensure that the door is adequately supported, with the aid of an assistant, or using wooden blocks or similar under the bottom edge of the door (take care not to damage the paintwork).

4 Prise off the retaining clips, then drive out the door hinge pins using a suitable drift, and lift the door from the vehicle **(see illustration)**.

The lower hinge pin should be driven out upwards, and the upper hinge pin downwards.

Refitting

5 Refitting is a reversal of removal, but check the condition of the hinge pins, and renew if necessary.

12 Door inner trim panel –
removal and refitting

Front door

Removal

1 On models with electrical components inside the door, disconnect the battery negative lead, with reference to Chapter 5A.

2 Prise the cover plug from the centre of the door interior handle surround to expose the securing screw **(see illustration)**.

3 Unscrew the securing screw, then withdraw the interior handle surround from the door. Where applicable, disconnect the wiring plug from the loudspeaker mounted in the surround **(see illustration)**.

4 On models with manually-operated windows, use a hooked piece of wire or a similar tool to release the window regulator handle securing clip from the shaft. Pull off the regulator handle, and recover the round

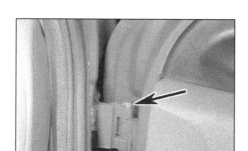

11.4 Prise the retaining clip (arrowed) from the hinge pin

12.2 Prising the cover plug from the door interior handle surround

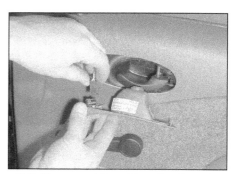

12.3 Disconnect the wiring plug from the loudspeaker in the handle surround

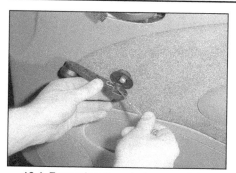

12.4 Removing the window regulator handle

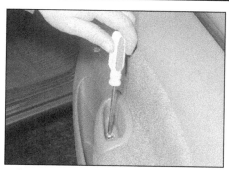

12.5 Unscrewing the trim panel securing screw from the armrest

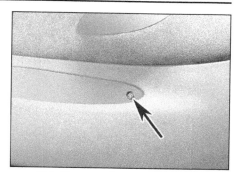

12.6 Unscrew the securing screw (arrowed) from above the door bin

trim plate **(see illustration)**. On models with electric windows, carefully prise out the switch from the door trim panel and disconnect the wiring connector.

5 Prise out the cover plug, then unscrew the door trim panel securing screw from the armrest **(see illustration)**.

6 Prise out the cover plug, and unscrew the door trim panel securing screw from above the door bin **(see illustration)**.

7 On early models, working at the rear edge of the trim panel, prise off the cover plate, and unscrew the trim panel securing screw **(see illustration)**.

8 Prise out the cover plate, and remove the screw securing the mirror trim plate to the door **(see illustration)**.

9 On models with manually-operated door mirrors, working at the front corner of the door, pull the rubber cover from the mirror adjustment lever, then unscrew the plastic collar securing the adjuster lever to the mirror trim plate. Unclip the mirror trim plate, then unclip the mirror adjuster lever from the plate, and remove the plate **(see illustrations)**.

10 On early models with electric door mirrors, unclip the mirror trim plate, then disconnect the wiring from the mirror adjustment switch. On later models the switch is located in the door trim panel – carefully prise out the switch and disconnect the wiring connector.

11 Work around the edge of the trim panel,

and release the securing clips, ideally using a forked tool, then lift up the top edge of the panel, and remove the panel **(see illustration)**.

12 If work is to be carried out on the components inside the door it will be necessary to peel back the protective plastic sheeting from the door. Use a sharp knife to cut the adhesive putty around the edge of the plastic sheeting, then peel the sheeting from the door **(see illustration)**. Do not attempt to peel back the sheeting without cutting the adhesive, as the sheeting will probably tear.

13 If the complete plastic sheeting is to be removed, it will be necessary to drill out the rivets, and remove the trim panel mounting

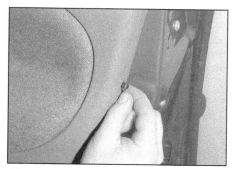

12.7 Prise off the cover plate for access to the rear trim panel securing screw

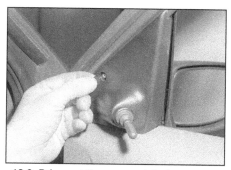

12.8 Prise out the cover plate for access to the mirror trim plate securing screw

12.9a Unscrew the collar securing the adjuster lever to the trim plate . . .

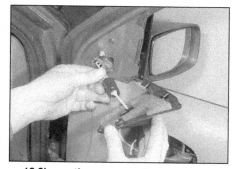

12.9b . . . then remove the mirror trim plate

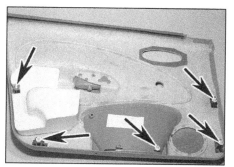

12.11 Front door trim panel removed to show securing clips (arrowed)

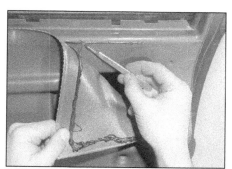

12.12 Removing the protective plastic sheeting from the door

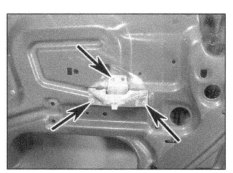

12.13 Removing the door trim panel mounting bracket

12.16 Unscrewing the interior handle surround securing screw – rear door trim panel

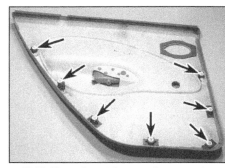

12.19 Rear door trim panel removed to show securing clips (arrowed)

12.21 Drill out the rivets (arrowed) to remove the rear door trim panel mounting bracket

bracket from the door to allow the sheeting to be removed **(see illustration)**. On models with manually-operated windows, recover the insulator from the window winder spindle. It will also be necessary to remove the door-mounted loudspeaker.

Refitting

14 Refitting is a reversal of removal. Where applicable, make sure that the protective plastic sheeting is pushed securely back into position on the door – there should be no need to renew the adhesive, and use new rivets to secure the trim panel mounting bracket.

Rear door

Removal

15 Prise the cover plug from the centre of the door interior handle surround to expose the securing screw.

16 Unscrew the securing screw, then withdraw the interior handle surround from the door **(see illustration)**.

17 Use a hooked piece of wire or a similar tool to release the window regulator handle securing clip from the shaft. Pull off the regulator handle, and recover the round trim plate.

18 Where applicable prise out the cover plate, and unscrew the door trim panel securing screw from the armrest.

19 Using a suitable forked tool, work around the edge of the trim panel, and release the trim panel securing clips, then withdraw the panel from the door **(see illustration)**.

20 If work is to be carried out on the components inside the door it will be necessary to peel back the protective plastic sheeting from the door. Use a sharp knife to cut the adhesive putty around the edge of the plastic sheeting, then peel the sheeting from the door. Do not attempt to peel back the sheeting without cutting the adhesive, as the sheeting will probably tear.

21 If the complete plastic sheeting is to be removed, it will be necessary to drill out the

rivets, and remove the trim panel mounting bracket from the door to allow the sheeting to be removed **(see illustration)**. Recover the insulator from the window winder spindle.

Refitting

22 Refitting is a reversal of removal. Where applicable, make sure that the protective plastic sheeting is pushed securely back into position on the door – there should be no need to renew the adhesive, and use new rivets to secure the trim panel mounting bracket.

13 Door handles and lock components – removal and refitting

Interior handle

Removal

1 Remove the door inner trim panel, and peel back the protective plastic sheeting as described in Section 12.

2 Unclip the handle from the door **(see illustration)**.

3 Move the handle as necessary, and manipulate the nipple on the end of the lock operating cable inner from the handle lever, then release the operating cable from the handle **(see illustration)**. Withdraw the handle.

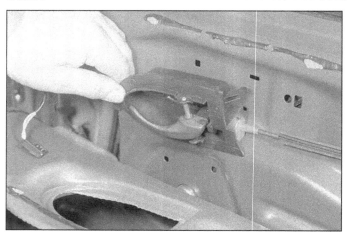

13.2 Unclip the interior handle from the door

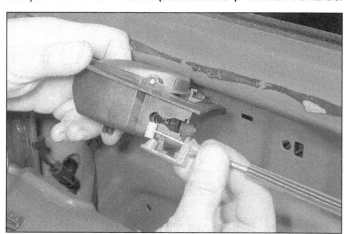

13.3 Disconnect the lock operating cable from the handle

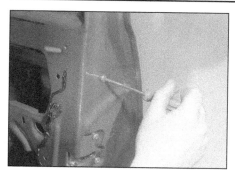

13.6a Unscrew the upper . . .

13.6b . . . and lower securing screws . . .

13.6c . . . and remove the window upper guide rail/lock shield

Refitting

4 Refitting is a reversal of removal, but refit the door trim panel with reference to Section 12.

Front exterior handle

Removal

5 Remove the door inner trim panel, and peel back the protective plastic sheeting as described in Section 12.
6 Working at the rear edge of the door, remove the two screws securing the window upper guide rail/lock shield to the door, then lower the guide rail/lock shield, and manipulate it out through the aperture next to the door lock **(see illustrations)**. Note that the lock shield is secured to the inner door skin with sealant.
7 Working inside the door, remove the two door exterior handle securing screws **(see illustration)**.
8 Disconnect the lock operating rod from the door lock, then manipulate the rod to disconnect it from the exterior handle. Note the fitted position of the lock operating rod to aid refitting **(see illustrations)**.
9 Withdraw the exterior handle from outside the door.

Refitting

10 Refitting is a reversal of removal. When refitting the guide rail/lock shield, ensure that the window rubber is fed into the top of the guide rail before working the shield into

position. Check the operation of the door handle and door window before refitting the door trim panel as described in Section 12.

Rear exterior handle
Removal

11 Remove the door inner trim panel, and peel back the protective plastic sheeting as described in Section 12.
12 Remove the door lock as described later in this Section.
13 Working inside the door, unscrew the two securing screws, then remove the handle from outside the door **(see illustration)**.

Refitting

14 Refitting is a reversal of removal, but refit the door trim panel with reference to Section 12.

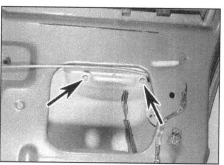

13.7 Remove the two exterior handle securing screws (arrowed)

Front lock cylinder

Removal

15 Proceed as described in paragraphs 5 and 6.
16 Prise off the locking clip, and disconnect the lock cylinder operating rod from the lever on the door lock.
17 Where applicable, disconnect the wiring plug from the central locking microswitch attached to the lock cylinder, then unclip the microswitch from the lock cylinder.
18 Using a suitable pin-punch engaged with one of the holes in the lock cylinder retaining plate, tap the retaining plate collar anti-clockwise to release it from the lock cylinder **(see illustration)**.

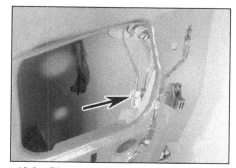

13.8a Disconnect the lock operating rod from the door lock (arrowed) . . .

13.8b . . . then disconnect the rod from the exterior handle

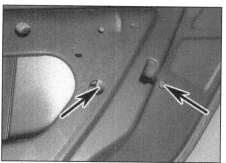

13.13 Rear door exterior handle securing screws (arrowed)

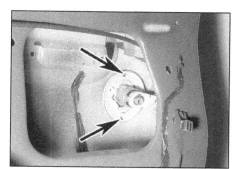

13.18 Engage a pin-punch with one of the holes (arrowed) in the lock cylinder retaining plate

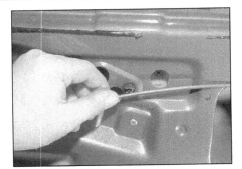

13.19 Removing the front door lock cylinder

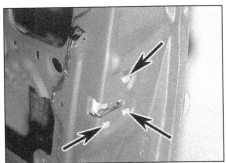

13.22 Release the lock operating cable from the clips on the door

13.26 Unscrew the three lock securing screws (arrowed)

19 Withdraw the retaining plate, then withdraw the lock cylinder from outside the door **(see illustration)**.

Refitting

20 Refitting is a reversal of removal, bearing in mind the following points.
  a) *Tap the retaining plate collar clockwise to secure the lock cylinder – make sure that the retaining plate is correctly fitted.*
  b) *Check the operation of the lock mechanism before refitting the door inner trim panel.*
  c) *Refit the door trim panel with reference to Section 12.*

Front lock

Removal

21 Remove the door interior handle, as described previously in this Section.

22 Release the lock operating cable from the clips on the door **(see illustration)**.

23 On certain models, it may be necessary to remove the foam padding from the side impact protection bar inside the door, to enable clearance for the lock to be removed. If the foam padding is removed, note its exact location so that it can be refitted correctly.

24 Working at the rear edge of the door, remove the two screws securing the window upper guide rail/lock shield to the door, then lower the guide rail/lock shield, and manipulate it out though the aperture next to the door lock (see paragraph 6). Note that the

lock shield is secured to the inner door skin with sealant.

25 Prise off the locking clips, and disconnect the lock operating rods from the lock.

26 Working at the rear edge of the door, unscrew the three lock securing screws **(see illustration)**.

27 Where applicable, disconnect the wiring plug from the microswitch attached to the lock cylinder, then release the door lock wiring harness clip from the door.

28 Manipulate the lock assembly out through the aperture in the door and, on models with central locking, disconnect the wiring plug from the lock motor **(see illustration)**.

29 Where applicable, unclip the door ajar switch from the top of the lock assembly.

30 To remove the lock operating cable from the lock, proceed as follows.
  a) *Remove the two securing screws, or release the securing clips, as applicable, and withdraw the cover from the lock (see illustration).*
  b) *Using a small screwdriver, prise the lock operating cable from the lock body. Note that to release the cable sheath collar from the lock body, the plastic fitting on the cable sheath must be turned to align the small cut-out in the plastic fitting with the hole in the lock body (see illustrations).*

31 If desired, on models with central locking, remove the two securing screws, and separate the lock motor from the lock.

13.28 Manipulate the lock assembly out through the aperture in the door

Refitting

32 Refitting is a reversal of removal, bearing in mind the following points.
  a) *When reconnecting the lock operating cable, align cut-out in plastic fitting on the cable sheath collar with the hole in the lock body.*
  b) *Check the operation of the lock mechanism before refitting the door inner trim panel.*
  c) *Refit the door trim panel with reference to Section 12.*

Rear lock

Removal

33 Remove the door interior handle as described previously in this Section.

34 Working at the rear edge of the door,

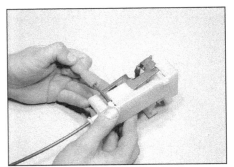

13.30a Removing the cover from the lock

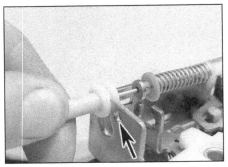

13.30b Align the cut-out in the plastic end fitting with the hole (arrowed) in the lock body

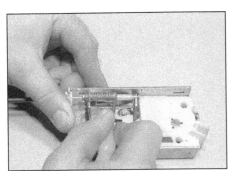

13.30c Release the inner cable from the lock operating lever

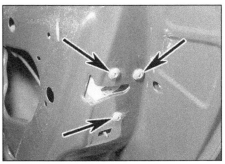

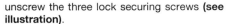

13.34 Rear door lock securing screws (arrowed)

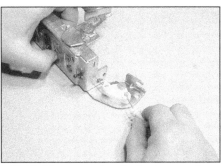

13.38 Disconnecting the lock operating cable from the rear door lock bellcrank

14.4 Front door window glass-to-regulator securing screws (arrowed)

unscrew the three lock securing screws **(see illustration)**.

35 Manipulate the lock out through the aperture in the door and, on models with central locking, disconnect the lock motor wiring plug. Where applicable, unclip the wiring loom from the lock cover.

36 Remove the two securing screws, and withdraw the cover from the lock.

37 Where applicable, unclip the door ajar switch from the top of the lock assembly.

38 To remove the lock operating cable from the lock, proceed as follows.

a) *Remove the two securing screws, or release the securing clips, as applicable, and withdraw the cover from the lock.*

b) *Disconnect the cable from the lock bellcrank. To release the cable sheath collar from the lock body, the plastic fitting on the cable sheath must be turned to align the small cut-out in the plastic fitting with the hole in the lock body **(see illustration)**.*

39 If desired, on models with central locking, the lock motor can be separated from the lock after removing the two securing screws.

Refitting

40 Refitting is a reversal of removal, bearing in mind the following points.

a) *When reconnecting the lock operating*

cable, align cut-out in plastic fitting on the cable sheath with the hole in the lock body.

b) *Check the operation of the lock mechanism before refitting the door inner trim panel.*

c) *Refit the door trim panel with reference to Section 12.*

---

14 Door window glass and regulator – removal and refitting

Front window

Removal

1 Remove the door inner trim panel as described in Section 12.

2 On models with manually-operated windows, temporarily refit the window winder handle. On models with electric windows, temporarily reconnect the battery negative lead, and the door window switch.

3 Make sure that the window is in the fully closed position.

4 Working through the two holes in the door panel, unscrew the two screws securing the lower edge of the window glass to the regulator mechanism **(see illustration)**.

5 Hold the glass in position in the top of the window aperture, then lower the regulator mechanism.

6 Carefully lower the glass to the bottom of the door.

7 Prise the weatherseal from the lower outside edge of the window aperture **(see illustration)**.

8 Carefully tilt the glass, and withdraw it from the outside of the window aperture.

Refitting

9 Refitting is a reversal of removal, but check the operation of the window regulator mechanism before refitting the door trim panel. Check that the rear edge of the window glass engages with the rear guide channel.

Front regulator

Note: *New rivets will be required to secure the regulator mechanism to the door on refitting.*

Removal

10 Remove the door window glass as described previously in this Section.

11 Drill out the rivets securing the regulator mechanism to the door **(see illustration)**.

12 On models with electric windows, working through the lower aperture in the door, disconnect the regulator motor wiring plug.

13 Manipulate the mechanism out through

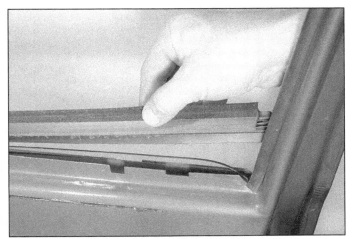

14.7 Prise the weatherseal from the window aperture

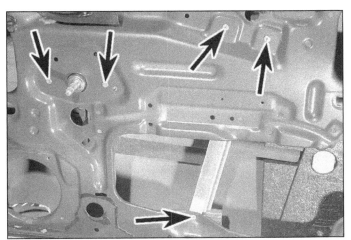

14.11 Window regulator securing rivets (arrowed)

14.13 Removing the window regulator mechanism

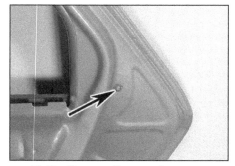

14.18a Remove the securing screw (arrowed) . . .

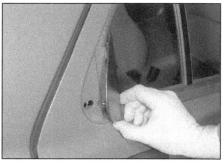

14.18b . . . and remove the trim panel

the lower aperture in the door (see illustration).

Refitting

14 Refitting is a reversal of removal, but check the operation of the window regulator mechanism before refitting the door trim panel, and use new rivets to secure the regulator mechanism, and the motor where applicable, to the door.

Rear window

Removal

15 Remove the door inner trim panel as described in Section 12.
16 Temporarily refit the window winder handle, then fully lower the window glass.
17 Remove the window regulator mechanism as described later in this Section.

18 Working at the rear edge of the door, remove the screw securing the fixed rear quarter window trim panel to the door, then remove the trim panel (see illustrations).
19 Prise the weatherseal from the lower outside edge of the window aperture (see illustration).
20 Unscrew the two upper securing screws, and the centre and lower Torx bolts securing the rear quarter window channel to the door (see illustrations).
21 Withdraw the channel and the rear quarter window from the door as an assembly (see illustration).
22 Carefully tilt the sliding window glass, and withdraw it from the outside of the window aperture.

Refitting

23 Refitting is a reversal of removal, but

ensure that the sliding window glass engages with the channel as the channel is refitted, and check the operation of the window regulator mechanism before refitting the door trim panel.

Rear regulator

Note: *New rivets will be required to secure the regulator mechanism to the door on refitting.*

Removal

24 Remove the door inner trim panel as described in Section 12.
25 Temporarily refit the window winder handle, then fully lower the window glass.
26 Drill out the four rivets securing the regulator mechanism to the door (see illustration).
27 Manipulate the mechanism out through the lower door aperture, sliding the pad on the

14.19 Prise the weatherseal from the outside edge of the door

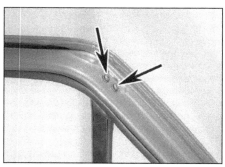

14.20a Unscrew two upper window channel securing screws (arrowed) . . .

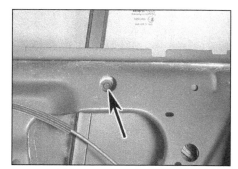

14.20b . . . and the centre . . .

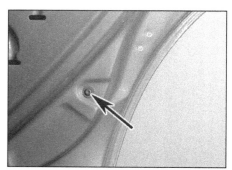

14.20c . . . and lower Torx bolts (arrowed)

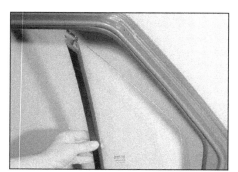

14.21 Withdraw the channel and the rear quarter window as an assembly

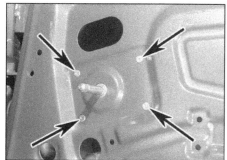

14.26 Drill out the rivets securing the regulator mechanism to the door

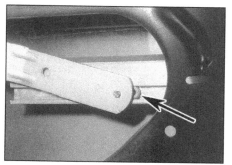

14.27a Slide the pad (arrowed) from the rear of the channel on the glass . . .

14.27b . . . and withdraw the mechanism through the door aperture

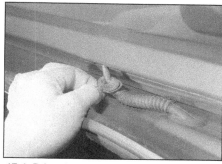

17.4 Prise the washer fluid hose grommet from the tailgate

regulator arm from the rear of the channel on the bottom of the glass **(see illustrations)**.

Refitting

28 Refitting is a reversal of removal, bearing in mind the following points.

 a) *Make sure that the pad on the regulator arm engages correctly with the channel on the bottom of the glass. Fit the pad from the rear of the glass channel.*
 b) *Use new rivets to secure the regulator mechanism to the door.*
 c) *Check the operation of the window regulator mechanism before refitting the door trim panel.*

15 Opening rear quarter windows (3-door models) – removal and refitting

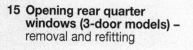

Removal

1 Remove the screws securing the handle assembly at the rear of the window glass to the body.

2 Support the glass panel, then prise off the covers, and remove the screws securing the front edge of the glass to the hinges. Lift the glass panel from the vehicle.

3 If desired, the handle and the hinge fasteners can be removed from the glass after prising off the covers, and removing the fasteners.

Refitting

4 Refitting is a reversal of removal.

16 Sliding side windows (Combi models) – removal and refitting

Removal

1 Working inside the vehicle, remove the two window locks from the glass panels. Each lock assembly is secured by two screws.

2 Slide the front glass panel fully to the rear.

3 Pull the weatherseal as far as possible from the front part of the window aperture, then slide the rear glass panel fully to the front.

4 Pull the remainder of the weatherseal from the rear part of the window aperture, and withdraw the complete weatherseal.

5 Using a small screwdriver, prise the window glass stop from the upper edge of the window aperture – push the stop towards the front of the vehicle, then prise the stop out from the rear of the clip.

6 Remove the window centre channel from the window aperture.

7 Remove the centre channel support rubber from the upper edge of the window aperture by pulling it out from the rear.

8 The glass panels can now be carefully lifted out from the window aperture.

Refitting

9 Refitting is a reversal of removal, but make sure that the window centre channel components and the weatherseal are correctly refitted.

17 Tailgate and support struts – removal, refitting and adjustment

Tailgate

Removal

1 Disconnect the battery negative lead, with reference to Chapter 5A.

2 Using a pencil or marker pen, mark the position of the hinges on the tailgate to aid refitting.

3 Carefully prise the washer nozzle from the tailgate, and disconnect the nozzle from the end of the washer fluid hose.

4 Prise the rubber grommet from the top edge of the tailgate, then pull the washer fluid hose through, and withdraw the hose from the tailgate **(see illustration)**. If desired, to aid

17.6 Tailgate hinge bolts (arrowed)

refitting, tie a length of string to the end of the hose before pulling it through, then pull the hose from the tailgate, and untie the string, leaving the string in position in the tailgate.

5 Support the tailgate, and disconnect the support struts, with reference to paragraphs 8 and 9.

6 Ensure that the tailgate is adequately supported, ideally with the aid of an assistant, then unscrew the bolts securing the hinges to the tailgate, and lift the tailgate from the vehicle **(see illustration)**.

Refitting

7 Refitting is a reversal of removal, bearing in mind the following points.

 a) *Make sure that the hinges are aligned with the marks made before removal.*
 b) *Where applicable, use the string to pull the wiring harness and the washer fluid hose into position in the tailgate.*
 c) *On completion, check the alignment of the tailgate with the surrounding body panels and, if necessary, adjust the position of the tailgate hinges within the elongated holes until satisfactory alignment is achieved.*

Support struts

Removal

8 Open the tailgate, and support it in the open position, using a wooden prop or similar tool. Note that the tailgate is heavy, and will fall closed if either of the support struts are disconnected.

9 Working at the top end of the strut, lever off the retaining clip, and disconnect the end of the strut from the lug on the tailgate **(see illustration)**.

17.9 Lever off the tailgate support strut retaining clip

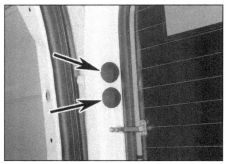

18.3 Prise out the covers (arrowed) for access to the upper door-to-hinge bolts

18.5 Rear load door lower door-to-hinge bolts (arrowed)

19.2a Unscrew the securing screw . . .

10 Repeat the procedure at the bottom end of the strut, and withdraw the strut.

Refitting

11 Refitting is a reversal of removal.

18 Rear load doors (Courier and Combi models) – removal and refitting

Removal

1 Disconnect the battery negative lead, with reference to Chapter 5A.

2 Where applicable, separate the two halves of the heater rear window wiring connector, then pull the wiring through the grommets in the rear edge of the door.

3 Prise out the two covers for access to the upper door-to-hinge bolts **(see illustration)**.

4 Unscrew the bolts securing the door check strap to the bottom of the door.

5 Support the door, ideally with the aid of an assistant, then unscrew the upper and lower bolts securing the door to the hinges, and carefully lift off the door **(see illustration)**.

Refitting

6 Refitting is a reversal of removal.

19 Tailgate lock components – removal and refitting

Lock cylinder

Removal

1 Disconnect the battery negative lead, with reference to Chapter 5A.

2 Unscrew the securing screw, and prise out the clip, then pull the trim panel from the tailgate to release the remaining securing clips **(see illustrations)**.

3 Working inside the tailgate, unscrew the four securing nuts, then withdraw the lock cylinder trim panel/handle from outside the tailgate. Note that two of the nuts also secure the lock operating cable plate **(see illustrations)**.

4 Unclip the lock operating cable from the rear of the lock cylinder.

5 Working inside the tailgate, twist the lock cylinder plastic securing ring anti-clockwise (looking up at the open tailgate) to release it **(see illustration)**.

6 Where applicable, unclip the anti-theft alarm switch from the lock cylinder, by pushing the switch in, and tilting it up, then withdraw the lock cylinder **(see illustration)**.

19.2b . . . then prise out the tailgate trim panel securing clip . . .

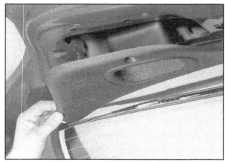

19.2c . . . and withdraw the trim panel

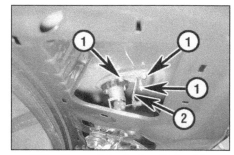

19.3a Three of the lock cylinder trim panel/handle securing nuts (1), and lock operating cable plate (2)

19.3b Removing the lock cylinder trim panel/handle

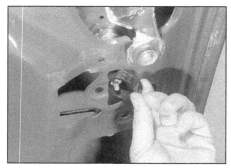

19.5 Removing the lock cylinder plastic securing ring

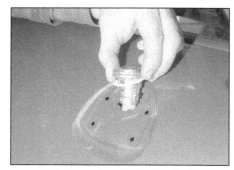

19.6 Removing the lock cylinder

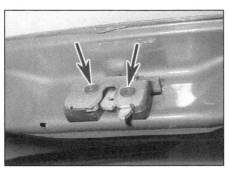

19.9 Lock securing screws (arrowed)

20.1a Prise off the interior handle trim plate . . .

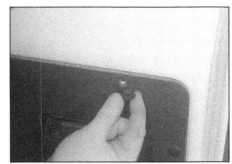

20.1b . . . then prise out the trim panel securing clips

Refitting

7 Refitting is a reversal of removal, bearing in mind the following points.

a) *Check the condition of the seal on the rear of the lock cylinder and renew if necessary.*

b) *Before fully refitting the lock cylinder, fit the plastic securing ring over the rear of the cylinder.*

c) *Make sure that the lock operating cable plate is in position on the lock cylinder trim panel/handle studs.*

d) *Check the operation of the lock mechanism before refitting the tailgate trim panel.*

Lock assembly

Removal

8 Proceed as described in paragraphs 1 and 2.

9 Where applicable, unclip the lock operating rod, then unscrew the two lock securing screws **(see illustration)**. Manipulate the lock out from the tailgate and, where applicable, unclip the anti-theft alarm switch from the lock, by pushing the switch in, and tilting it up.

Refitting

10 Refitting is a reversal of removal, but check the operation of the lock mechanism before refitting the tailgate trim panel.

Lock release motor

Removal

11 Proceed as described in paragraphs 1 and 2.

12 Disconnect the lock operating rod.

13 Separate the two halves of the motor wiring connector, then unscrew the screw securing the earth lead to the tailgate.

14 Remove the two motor securing screws, then withdraw the motor from the tailgate.

Refitting

15 Refitting is a reversal of removal, but make sure that the lock operating rod is correctly positioned in the lock lever. Check the operation of the mechanism before refitting the tailgate trim panel.

20 Rear load door components (Courier and Combi models) – removal and refitting

Interior handle

Removal

1 Open the door, then prise off the interior handle trim plate. Prise out the securing clips and remove the door trim panel **(see illustrations)**.

2 Remove the mounting plate/relay lever assembly securing screws, noting the location of the earth wire on one of the screws, and

20.2 Unscrewing a mounting plate/relay lever assembly securing screw

withdraw the mounting plate/relay lever assembly **(see illustration)**.

3 Disconnect the lock operating cables from the relay lever assembly **(see illustration)**.

4 Disconnect the lock operating rod from relay lever assembly.

5 Remove the securing screw, and remove the interior handle, complete with the operating rod **(see illustrations)**.

Refitting

6 Make sure that lugs on relay lever engage with lock on refitting

Lock cylinder/exterior handle

Removal

7 Remove the interior handle as described previously.

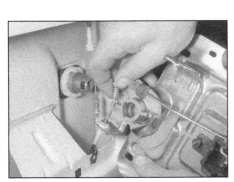

20.3 Disconnecting a lock operating cable from the relay lever assembly

20.5a Remove the securing screw (arrowed) . . .

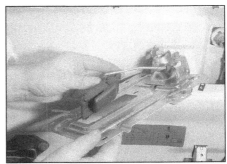

20.5b . . . and remove the interior handle

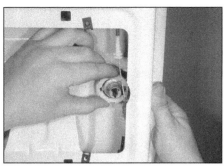

20.8 Removing the lock cylinder retaining clip

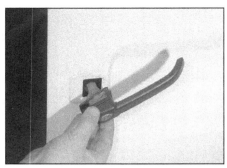

20.9 Removing the lock cylinder/exterior handle assembly

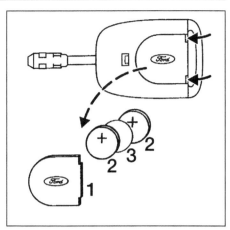

21.4 Central locking remote control transmitter battery renewal

1 Cover   2 Batteries   3 Contact plate

8 Turn the lock cylinder retaining clip anti-clockwise, and remove it from the rear of the lock cylinder **(see illustration)**. Recover spacer plate.
9 Turn the lock cylinder/handle assembly clockwise until it can be withdrawn from the door **(see illustration)**.

Refitting

10 Refitting is a reversal of removal, but make sure that the spacer plate is in position under the retaining clip.

Lock assembly

Removal

11 Working at the top or bottom of the door, as applicable, remove two securing screws, then lift out the lock assembly and disconnect the operating cable.

Refitting

12 Refitting is a reversal of removal.

---

21 Central locking system components – general information

Door lock motor

1 The removal and refitting procedure for the door lock motors is described as part of the door lock removal and refitting procedure in Section 13.

Door lock microswitch

2 Removal and refitting of the microswitches is described as part of the door lock cylinder removal and refitting procedure in Section 13.

Remote control

Batteries renewal

Note: *If it takes longer than 15 seconds to renew the batteries, the remote control system must be reprogrammed as described later in this Section.*
3 Carefully prise off the transmitter cover, using a small screwdriver.
4 Lift out the batteries and the contact plate **(see illustration)**.
5 Fit the new batteries with the '+' side facing

upwards, and the contact plate in between the batteries.
6 Refit the cover.

Reprogramming

7 Insert the ignition key into the ignition switch, and turn the key to position I. Turn the key back to position 0 as soon as the control light in the clock illuminates. The light will illuminate for 30 seconds, during which the transmitter can be reprogrammed as follows.
8 Point the transmitter towards the interior light in the roof console, then press and hold the front button on the transmitter (nearest the key shaft) depressed. Wait until the light on the transmitter begins to flash, then press the rear button on the transmitter three times (continue to hold the front button depressed).
9 Release the front button. If the lights on the transmitter and the clock flash simultaneously, the reprogramming was successful.
10 To end the procedure, turn the ignition key to position II.

---

22 Electric window components – removal and refitting

Window switches

1 Refer to Chapter 12, Section 4.

Window regulator motors

2 The motors are integral with the regulator assemblies, and if faulty, the complete regulator assembly must be renewed. Removal and refitting of the regulator assemblies is described in Section 14.

---

23 Exterior mirrors and associated components – removal and refitting

Mirror glass

Removal

1 On models with electric mirrors, disconnect the battery negative lead, with reference to Chapter 5A.

2 Push the inboard edge of the mirror glass fully into the mirror housing, to leave a gap at the outboard edge of the glass.
3 Carefully pull the outboard edge of the glass outwards, and at the same time, pull the glass towards the outboard edge of the housing, until the glass is released from the mirror **(see illustration)**. Where applicable, disconnect the wiring from the glass.

Refitting

4 Where applicable, reconnect the wiring to the glass.
5 Locate the inboard edge of the glass on the mounting in the mirror housing.
6 With the glass laid in position, press the outboard edge of the glass into the housing until an audible click is heard, and the glass locks in position.

Mirror

Removal

7 Remove the door inner trim panel as described in Section 12 – this is necessary for access to the two lower mirror securing bolts.
8 On models with electric mirrors, trace the wiring harness back from the mirror, and separate the two halves of the wiring connector inside the door. Remove the adhesive tape securing the wiring harness to the door.
9 Unscrew the three securing bolts, and withdraw the mirror, complete with wiring

23.3 Removing the door mirror glass

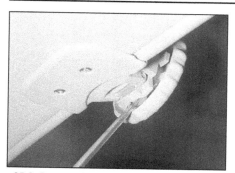

25.3 Depressing the tilting glass sunroof panel locking clip

harness or adjuster cable (as applicable), from the door.

Refitting

10 Refitting is a reversal of removal.

Mirror motor

11 The motor is integral with the mirror, and cannot be renewed separately. If faulty, the complete mirror assembly must be renewed.

Mirror switch

12 On early models the switch is integral with the mirror assembly and is described as part of the mirror removal and refitting procedure earlier in this Section.
13 On later models the switch is located in the front door inner trim panel. Carefully prise the switch from the panel and disconnect the wiring connector.
14 Reconnect the wiring and press the switch back into position to refit.

24 Windscreen, tailgate and fixed window glass – general information

These areas of glass are secured by the tight fit of the weatherseal in the body aperture, and are bonded in position with a special adhesive. Renewal of such fixed glass is a difficult, messy and time-consuming task, which is considered beyond the scope of the home mechanic. It is difficult, unless one has plenty of practice, to obtain a secure, waterproof fit. Furthermore, the task carries a

high risk of breakage; this applies especially to the laminated glass windscreen. In view of this, owners are strongly advised to have this sort of work carried out by one of the many specialist windscreen fitters.

25 Sunroof – general information, removal and refitting

General information

1 Two different types of sunroof may be fitted, depending on model. A manually-operated tilting glass panel may be fitted, or an electric sliding canvas roof may be fitted.

Tilting glass sunroof

Removal

2 Turn the knob to fully open the sunroof panel.
3 Use a small screwdriver to depress the red locking lever underneath the knob, and release the knob assembly from the bracket on the roof **(see illustration)**.
4 Lift the roof panel to the vertical position, and withdraw it from the roof.

Refitting

5 Hold the roof panel vertically, and lower the hinges into the retainers on the roof.
6 Lower the panel, and engage the knob assembly with the bracket on the roof.

Sliding canvas sunroof

> **HAYNES HINT** *If the sunroof mechanism is faulty, and the roof panel is stuck in the open position, the panel can be closed manually as follows.*
> a) *Remove the blanking plug from the roof console panel.*
> b) *Insert the cranked handle supplied with the car in the hole provided in the sunroof motor spindle, then use the handle to turn the motor and close the roof panel.*

Roof assembly

7 Due to the complexity of the sliding canvas sunroof mechanism, considerable expertise is

required to repair, replace or adjust the sunroof components successfully. Removal of the roof first requires the headlining to be removed, which is a tedious operation, and not a task to be undertaken lightly. Therefore, any problems with this type of sunroof should be referred to a Ford dealer.

Roof switch

8 Refer to Chapter 12, Section 4.

26 Body exterior fittings – removal and refitting

Radiator grille panel

1 Refer to Section 7.

Bumpers

2 Refer to Section 6.

Fuel filler flap

Removal

3 The fuel filler flap is a push-fit into the housing, and is easily broken.
4 Open the flap, and carefully prise the integral hinge from the locating holes in the housing – do not use excessive force.

Refitting

5 Refitting is a reversal of removal.

Scuttle cover panel

Removal

6 Working in the engine compartment, unscrew the coolant expansion tank securing screw, then release the expansion tank securing clip, and move the expansion tank clear of the engine compartment bulkhead, taking care not to strain the coolant hoses **(see illustration)**.
7 Pull the rubber weatherseal from the front edge of the engine compartment bulkhead **(see illustration)**.
8 Unclip the cover from the fusebox at the left-hand side of the engine compartment **(see illustration)**.
9 Where applicable, remove the securing screw, and lift the MAP sensor

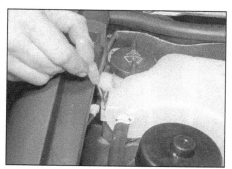

26.6 Releasing the expansion tank securing clip

26.7 Pull the weatherseal from the bulkhead . . .

26.8 . . . then unclip the cover from the fusebox

26.9a Remove the securing screw (arrowed) . . .

26.9b . . . and lift the MAP sensor bracket from the bulkhead

26.10 Pull the oxygen sensor wiring connector from the bulkhead panel

securing bracket from the bulkhead **(see illustrations)**.

10 Where applicable, pull the oxygen sensor wiring connector from the lug on the bulkhead panel **(see illustration)**.

11 Lift screenwash hoses from slot on right-hand side of panel.

12 Remove the screw securing the panel to the fusebox **(see illustration)**.

13 Remove the screws and remove the three clips securing the panel, then withdraw the panel **(see illustrations)**. Release the speedometer cable grommet from the panel as panel is withdrawn.

Refitting

14 Refitting is a reversal of removal.

Rear spoiler

Removal

15 Open the tailgate, and prise out the four spoiler securing nut covers from the top of the tailgate.

16 Unscrew the four securing nuts, and lift off the spoiler.

Refitting

17 Refitting is a reversal of removal.

Wheelarch liners

18 The wheelarch liners are secured by a combination of self-tapping screws and push-fit clips **(see illustration)**. Removal is self-evident, and normally the clips can be

released by pulling the liner away from its mountings.

Engine undershield

19 The engine undershield is secured by a combination of self-tapping screws and push-fit clips. Removal is self-evident, and normally the clips can be released by pulling the undershield away from its mountings.

Body trim strips and badges

20 The various body trim strips and badges are held in position with a special adhesive. Removal requires the trim/badge to be heated, to soften the adhesive, and then cut away from the surface. Due to the high risk of damage to the vehicle paintwork during this operation, it is recommended that this task should be entrusted to a Ford dealer.

---

27 Seats – removal and refitting

Front seat

 Warning: Disconnect the battery negative lead, with reference to Chapter 5A, then wait for two minutes before proceeding. If this waiting period is not observed, there is danger of activating the seat belt tensioner and side airbags.

26.12 Removing the screw securing the scuttle cover panel to the fusebox

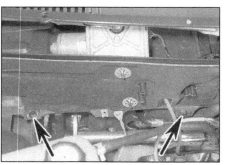

26.13a Remove the two lower screws and clips (arrowed) . . .

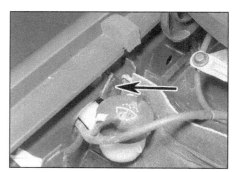

26.13b . . . and the right-hand screw and clip (arrowed) . . .

26.13c . . . and withdraw the scuttle cover panel

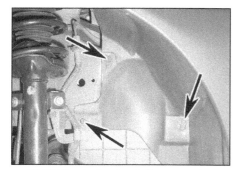

26.18 Front wheelarch liner securing screws (arrowed)

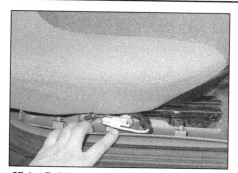

27.1a Pull the trim panel from the seat . . .

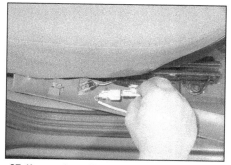

27.1b . . . then disconnect the wiring plug

27.2 Removing a front seat securing bolt

1 Pull the side trim panel from the outside edge of the seat then, where applicable, disconnect the now-exposed wiring plug(s) **(see illustrations)**. Unclip the wiring plug(s) from the trim panel.
2 Slide the seat fully rearwards, then unscrew the two front bolts securing the seat rails to the floor **(see illustration)**.
3 Slide the seat fully forwards, then unclip the trim panel from the inner seat rail, and unscrew the three rear bolts securing the seat rails to the floor (two bolts securing the inner rail, and one bolt securing the outer rail) **(see illustration)**.
4 Lift the seat, complete with the rails, from the vehicle.
5 Refitting is a reversal of removal, but tighten the seat mounting bolts to the specified torque, and in the order: front inner bolt, rear inner bolt, front outer bolt, rear outer bolt.

Rear seat (Hatchback/Van models)

Cushion

6 Working at the front lower edge of the seat cushion, remove the three screws securing the seat cushion to the floor **(see illustration)**.
7 Lift the front of the seat cushion, and push it sharply towards the rear of the vehicle.
8 Lift up the rear of the cushion, and withdraw it from the vehicle.
9 Refitting is a reversal of removal.

Seat back

10 Release the catch, and fold the rear seat back down on top of the cushion.
11 Unscrew the bolts securing the seat back to the hinges, then remove the seat back **(see illustration)**.

12 If desired, the rear seat back catch can now be removed after unscrewing the two securing bolts.
13 Refitting is a reversal of removal.

Rear seats (Combi models)

14 The rear seats can be removed as an assembly, after folding the rear seat back down, and tilting the complete seat assembly forwards.
15 Release the seat assembly from the locking catches, and withdraw it from the vehicle.
16 Refitting is a reversal of removal.

28 Seat belt components – removal and refitting

Front belt

Removal

1 On three-door models, unbolt the lower seat belt anchor rail, and slide the seat belt from the rail. On five-door models, unscrew the lower seat belt anchor bolt.
2 Pull off the plastic cover, then unscrew the upper seat belt anchor bolt **(see illustration)**.
3 Remove the centre pillar trim panel and the sill trim panel with reference to Section 29.
4 Unscrew the inertia reel anchor bolt, and the upper screw, than manipulate the inertia reel out from the door pillar, and withdraw the seat belt assembly **(see illustration)**.

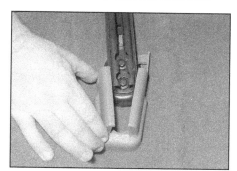

27.3 Unclip the trim panel from the inner seat rail

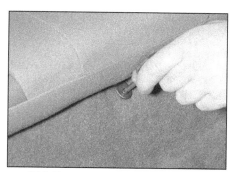

27.6 Removing a rear seat cushion securing screw

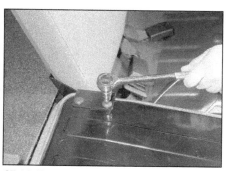

27.11 Removing a rear seat back securing bolt

28.2 Unscrew the upper seat belt anchor bolt

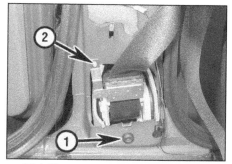

28.4 Unscrew the inertia reel anchor bolt (1) and the upper screw (2)

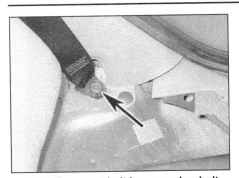

28.16 Rear seat belt lower anchor bolt (arrowed)

Refitting

5 Refitting is a reversal of removal, but tighten the seat belt anchor bolts to the specified torque.

Front belt stalk

Removal

6 Remove the front seat (see Section 27). On models with front seat belt tensioners, release the tensioner wiring harness from the clips under the seat.

7 On January 1999 models onward, prise off the seat back recliner hand wheel trim cap, then remove the hand wheel by extracting the star type retaining clip. Carefully remove the plastic trim panels from both sides of the seat for access to the stalk assembly retaining bolts. Note that the trim panels are secured by a combination of bolts and plastic clips, and the plastic clips are easily broken.

8 Unscrew the bolt securing the stalk assembly to the seat frame. Note that on pre-January 1999 models, the bolt is captive in the stalk assembly (secured by a paper washer) – **do not** attempt to remove the bolt from the stalk assembly.

9 Withdraw the assembly from the seat. On models with seat belt tensioners, handle the assembly by holding the tensioner barrel, or the buckle – **do not** hold the assembly by the stalk.

Refitting

10 Refitting is a reversal of removal, bearing in mind the following points.
  a) *Make sure that the stalk is angled towards the seat.*

29.3 Withdrawing the upper . . .

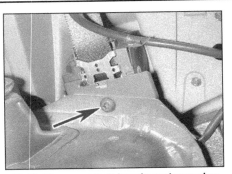

28.19 Rear seat belt inertia reel securing bolt (arrowed)

  b) *Tighten the securing bolt to the specified torque.*
  c) *Refit the seat with reference to Section 27.*

Front belt height adjuster

Removal

11 Pull off the plastic cover, then unscrew the upper seat belt anchor bolt.

12 Remove the centre pillar trim panel with reference to Section 29.

13 Unscrew the two securing bolts, and remove the height adjuster assembly.

Refitting

14 Refitting is a reversal of removal.

Rear inertia reel belt

Removal

15 Remove the rear seat cushion as described in Section 27.

16 Unscrew the seat belt lower anchor bolt **(see illustration)**.

17 Pull off the plastic cover, then unscrew the upper seat belt anchor bolt.

18 Working in the luggage compartment, peel back the trim panel for access to the seat belt inertia reel.

19 Unscrew the inertia reel anchor bolt **(see illustration)**.

20 Manipulate the seat belt upper anchor plate down through the hole in the parcel shelf side trim panel, then feed the remainder of the seat belt through the slot, and withdraw the seat belt from the vehicle.

Refitting

21 Refitting is a reversal of removal, but

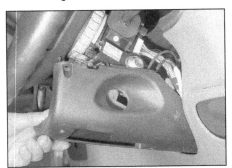

29.4 . . . and lower steering column shrouds

tighten the seat belt anchor bolts to the specified torque.

Rear centre belt and stalks

Removal

22 Remove the rear seat cushion as described in Section 27.

23 Tilt the seat back as necessary for access to the seat belt/stalk anchor bolts.

24 Unscrew the relevant seat belt/stalk anchor bolt(s), and remove the assembly.

Refitting

25 Refitting is a reversal of removal, but tighten the anchor bolt(s) to the specified torque.

29 Interior trim – removal and refitting

General

1 The interior trim panels are secured by a combination of clips and screws. Removal and refitting is generally self-explanatory, noting that it may be necessary to remove or loosen surrounding panels to allow a particular panel to be removed. The following paragraphs describe the removal and refitting of the major panels in more detail.

Door inner trim panels

2 Refer to Section 12.

Steering column shrouds

3 Working under the lower column shroud, unscrew the five securing screws, then withdraw the upper shroud **(see illustration)**.

4 Unclip and lift off the lower shroud **(see illustration)**.

5 Refitting is a reversal of removal.

Sill trim panels

6 Open the door(s), and carefully prise the weather-seal(s) from the edges of the door aperture(s).

7 Using two small screwdrivers, carefully prise out the trim panel lower securing clips, taking care not to damage the trim panel **(see illustration)**. There are three securing clips on three door models, and four clips on five-door models

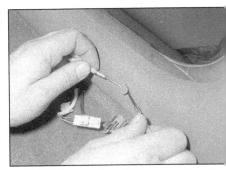

29.7 Prising out a sill trim panel lower securing clip

8 On five-door models, prise out the cover, and remove the securing screw from the rear of the trim panel.

9 Working in the front footwell, tap out the centre pin(s) and prise out the front securing clip(s), or unscrew the securing clip(s), as applicable, then withdraw the trim panel from the sill **(see illustration)**.

10 Refitting is a reversal of removal.

Front pillar trim panel

11 Open the door, and carefully prise the weatherseal from the edge of the door aperture.

12 Carefully prise the trim panel from the pillar to release the three securing clips (one at each end, and one in the centre).

13 Refitting is a reversal of removal.

Centre pillar trim panel

Hatchback and Van models

14 Pull off the plastic cover, then unscrew the upper seat belt anchor bolt.

15 Carefully prise the weatherseal(s) from the edges of the door aperture(s).

16 Carefully prise the trim panel from the pillar to release the three securing clips (one at each end, and one in the centre).

17 Refitting is a reversal of removal, but tighten the seat belt anchor bolt to the specified torque.

Courier and Combi models

18 Carefully prise the rear centre pillar trim panel from the pillar to release the two securing clips.

19 Pull off the plastic cover, then unscrew the upper seat belt anchor bolt.

20 Carefully prise the weatherseal from the edges of the door aperture.

21 Carefully prise the trim panel from the pillar to release the three securing clips (one at each end, and one in the centre).

22 Refitting is a reversal of removal, but tighten the seat belt anchor bolt to the specified torque.

Rear parcel shelf support panel

Hatchback and Van models

23 On models with a loudspeaker and/or a luggage compartment light mounted in the rear parcel shelf support panel, disconnect the battery negative lead, with reference to Chapter 5A.

24 Fold down the rear seat back.

25 Unscrew the seat belt lower anchor bolt.

26 Pull off the plastic cover, then unscrew the upper seat belt anchor bolt

27 Working in the luggage compartment, remove the securing clip, and withdraw the luggage compartment side trim panel.

28 Unscrew the securing bolt, and detach the rear seat belt inertia reel from the side of the luggage compartment.

29 Disconnect the wiring plugs from the rear loudspeaker and, where applicable, the luggage compartment light (both mounted in the parcel shelf support panel).

30 Peel back the weatherseal(s) from the edge of the parcel shelf support panel.

31 Unscrew the four securing screws (three accessible from the luggage compartment, and one from the passenger compartment), then withdraw the parcel shelf support panel **(see illustrations)**. As the panel is withdrawn, feed the seat belt and, where applicable, the wiring, through the holes in the panel.

32 Refitting is a reversal of removal, but tighten the seat belt anchor bolts to the specified torque.

Rear pillar trim panel

Hatchback and Van models

33 Remove the rear parcel shelf support panel, as described previously in this Section.

34 Support the tailgate in the open position, using a wooden prop or similar tool. Note that the tailgate is heavy, and will fall closed if either of the support struts are disconnected.

35 Working at the lower end of the tailgate strut, lever off the retaining clip, and disconnect the end of the strut from the lug on the body.

36 Remove the securing screw from the lower edge of the rear pillar trim panel.

37 Carefully prise the trim panel from the pillar to release the two securing clips (at the top of the panel).

38 Refitting is a reversal of removal, but tighten the seat belt anchor bolts to the specified torque.

Lower rear pillar trim panel

5-door models

39 Remove the rear seat cushion as described in Section 27, then fold the rear seat back down.

40 Carefully peel back the weatherseal from the edge of the trim panel.

41 Remove the securing screw from the top of the panel, then carefully prise the securing clip from the lower end of the panel, and withdraw the panel.

42 Refitting is a reversal of removal.

Luggage compartment trim panel

Courier and Combi models

43 Remove the centre pillar trim panel, as described previously in this Section.

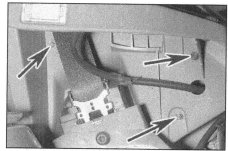

29.31a Three of the rear parcel shelf support panel screws (arrowed) accessible from the luggage compartment . . .

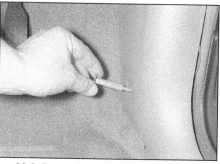

29.9 Removing a sill trim panel front securing clip

44 Remove the securing screw, and withdraw the rear quarter trim panel.

45 Pull off the plastic cover, then unscrew the upper seat belt anchor bolt.

46 Unscrew lower seat belt anchor bolt.

47 Pull the seat belt surround from the trim panel, then manipulate the seat belt through the hole in the panel.

48 Work around the edge of the luggage compartment side trim panel, and release the securing clips (ideally using a forked tool), then withdraw the panel from the vehicle.

49 Refitting is a reversal of removal, but tighten the seat belt anchor bolts to the specified torque.

Carpets

50 The passenger compartment floor carpet is in several pieces, and is secured along the edges by screws or various types of clips.

51 Carpet removal and refitting is reasonably straightforward, but time-consuming, due to the fact that all adjoining trim panels must be released, and the seats and centre console must be removed.

Headlining

52 The headlining is clipped to the roof, and can be withdrawn only once all fittings such as the grab handles, sun visors, sunroof, front, centre and rear pillar trim panels, and associated components have been removed. The door, tailgate and sunroof aperture weatherseals will also have to be prised clear.

53 Note that headlining removal requires considerable skill and experience if it is to be carried out without damage, and is therefore best entrusted to an expert.

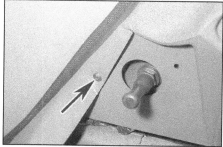

29.31b . . . and one screw (arrowed) accessible from the passenger compartment

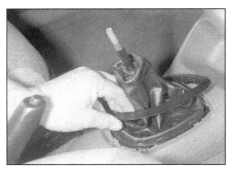

30.3 Prise the surround from the gear lever gaiter . . .

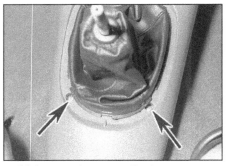

30.4 . . . and unscrew the two screws (arrowed)

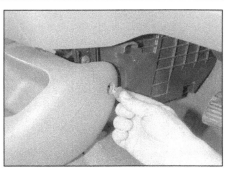

30.5 Prise out the cover plugs for access to the front securing screws

30 Centre console – removal and refitting

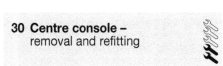

Manual transmission models

Removal

1 On models with a remote tailgate release, disconnect the battery negative lead, with reference to Chapter 5A, then carefully prise the tailgate release switch from the centre console, and disconnect the wiring plug.

2 Unscrew the knob from the end of the gear lever.

3 Carefully prise the surround from the gear lever gaiter **(see illustration)**.

4 Unscrew the two now-exposed centre console rear securing screws **(see illustration)**.

5 Working at the front of the console, prise out the cover plugs (one on each side) to reveal the front securing screws **(see illustration)**. Remove the screws.

6 Withdraw the centre console, and manipulate it over the gear lever.

Refitting

7 Refitting is a reversal of removal, but take care not to damage the gear lever gaiter.

Automatic transmission models

Removal

8 Disconnect the battery negative lead, with reference to Chapter 5A.

9 On models with an electric tailgate release, carefully prise the tailgate release switch from the centre console, and disconnect the wiring plug.

10 Remove the securing screw, and pull off the gear selector lever knob.

11 Carefully prise off the gear selector lever position indicator cover, and disconnect the wiring plug from the illumination light.

12 Proceed as described in paragraphs 4 to 6.

Refitting

13 Refitting is a reversal of removal.

31 Facia assembly – removal and refitting

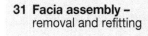

Removal

Note: *This is a difficult procedure, as the wiring harness and heater/ventilation ducting must be released from the rear of the facia (and attached on refitting) with the facia pulled back from the bulkhead, before the assembly can be removed. Access is very difficult, and it is suggested that this Section is read through thoroughly before starting the procedure.*

1 Disconnect the battery negative lead, with reference to Chapter 5A, then wait for two minutes before proceeding. If this waiting period is not observed, there is danger of activating the seat belt tensioner.

2 Remove the centre console as described in Section 30.

3 Remove the steering column assembly as described in Chapter 10.

4 Remove the instrument panel as described in Chapter 12.

5 Remove the radio/cassette player as described in Chapter 12.

6 Remove the heater control unit as described in Chapter 3.

7 Where applicable, remove the passenger's airbag as described in Chapter 12.

8 Carefully prise the weatherseals from the front edges of the door apertures, then prise off the facia side trim panels **(see illustration)**.

9 Remove the sill trim panels and the front pillar trim panels, as described in Section 29.

10 Where applicable, disconnect the wiring plug(s) from the anti-theft alarm control module in the footwell behind the right-hand sill trim panel.

11 Reach in through the glovebox and prise out the cover panel for access to the airbag control unit. Disconnect the airbag control unit wiring plug **(see illustration)**.

12 Pull the fusebox cover from the facia, then remove the two screws securing the fusebox to the facia. Unclip the fusebox from the facia **(see illustration)**.

13 Work around the facia, and remove the ten facia securing bolts. The bolt locations are as follows.

a) Two bolts on either side of the facia

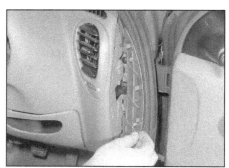

31.8 Prise off the facia side trim panels

31.11 Disconnecting the airbag control unit wiring plug

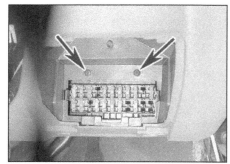

31.12 Remove the two screws (arrowed) securing the fusebox to the facia

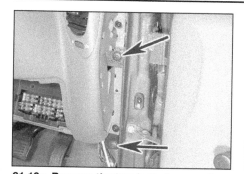

31.13a Remove the two bolts (arrowed) on either side of the facia . . .

31.13b . . . the three bolts at the top of the facia . . .

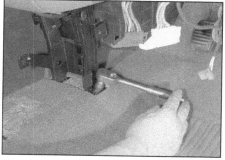

31.13c . . . the lower bolts on either side of the floor tunnel . . .

(revealed by removal of the facia side trim panels) **(see illustration)**.
b) *Three bolts at the top of the facia – prise out the plastic covers for access* **(see illustration)**.
c) *One lower bolt on either side of the floor tunnel (securing the facia mounting brackets to the floor)* **(see illustration)**.
d) *One bolt under the driver's side of the facia (securing the facia to the steering column mounting bracket)* **(see illustration)**.

14 Carefully pull the facia assembly back from the bulkhead, taking care not to strain the wiring harnesses **(see illustration)**. Ensure that the facia is adequately supported to avoid damaging the wiring harnesses.

15 Reach behind the facia, and remove the seven screws securing the heater/ventilation trunking to the facia **(see illustration)**.

16 Working through the radio/cassette player

aperture in the front of the facia, remove the remaining screw securing the heater/ventilation trunking to the facia, then remove the heater/ventilation trunking.

17 Again, reach behind the facia and release the clips securing the wiring harnesses to the facia. Note the routing of the harnesses to aid refitting **(see illustration)**.

18 Release the clips and detach the wiring harnesses from the guide rails. Again, not the routing of the harnesses to aid refitting.

19 With the aid of an assistant, lift out the facia, and withdraw it through one of the door apertures.

Refitting

20 Refitting is a reversal of removal, bearing in mind the following points.
a) *Ensure that the wiring harnesses are routed as noted before removal.*
b) *Where applicable, refit the passenger's airbag as described in Chapter 12.*

c) *Refit the radio/cassette player with reference to Chapter 12.*
d) *Refit the instrument panel with reference to Chapter 12.*
e) *Refit the steering column assembly as described in Chapter 10.*

31.13d . . . and the bolt under the facia . . .

31.14 . . . then pull the facia assembly back from the bulkhead

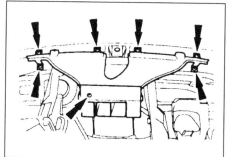

31.15 Heater/ventilation trunking-to-facia securing screws (arrowed)

31.17 Wiring harness-to-facia securing clips (arrowed)

Chapter 12
Body electrical system

Contents

Airbag system – general information, precautions and system de-activation 26
Airbag system components – removal and refitting 27
Anti-theft alarm system and engine immobiliser – general information 25
Auxiliary warning system components – general information, removal and refitting 14
Bulbs (exterior lights) – renewal 5
Bulbs (interior lights) – renewal 6
Cigarette lighter – removal and refitting 12
Clock/temperature display – removal and refitting 13
Electrical fault finding – general information 2
Electrical systems check .... See Weekly checks
Exterior light units – removal and refitting 7
Fuses and relays – general information 3
General information and precautions 1
Headlight beam adjustment components – removal and refitting ... 8
Headlight beam alignment – general information 9
Horn – removal and refitting 16
Instrument panel – removal and refitting 10
Instrument panel components – removal and refitting 11
Lights 'on' warning buzzer – removal and refitting 15
Loudspeakers – removal and refitting 23
Radio aerial – removal and refitting 24
Radio/cassette player – removal and refitting 22
Speedometer cable – removal and refitting 17
Switches – removal and refitting 4
Tailgate wiper motor – removal and refitting 20
Washer fluid level check .... See Weekly checks
Windscreen wiper motor and linkage – removal and refitting 19
Windscreen/tailgate washer system components – removal and refitting 21
Wiper arm – removal and refitting 18
Wiper blades check .... See Weekly checks

Degrees of difficulty

Easy, suitable for novice with little experience 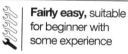	**Fairly easy,** suitable for beginner with some experience 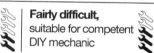	**Fairly difficult,** suitable for competent DIY mechanic	**Difficult,** suitable for experienced DIY mechanic	**Very difficult,** suitable for expert DIY or professional

Specifications

General
System type .... 12-volt negative earth

Fuses
Refer to label on fusebox cover

Bulbs

	Type	Wattage
Headlight (pre-2000 models):		
Main beam	H1	55
Dipped beam	H7	55
Headlight (2000 models onward)	H4	55/60
Front sidelight	Push-fit	5
Front direction indicator light	Bayonet-fit	21
Front direction indicator side repeater light	Push-fit	5
Front foglight	H1	55
Tail/stop-light (Courier and Combi models)	Bayonet-fit	5/21
Tail light	Bayonet-fit	5
Stop-light	Bayonet-fit	21
High-level stop-light	Push-fit	5
Rear direction indicator light	Bayonet-fit	21
Reversing light	Bayonet-fit	21
Rear foglight	Bayonet-fit	21
Number plate light:		
Hatchback and Van models	Push-fit	5
Courier and Combi models	Push-fit	4
Courtesy light	Festoon	10
Map reading lights	Push-fit	5
Luggage compartment light	Push-fit	5
Glovebox light	Push-fit	5

Torque wrench setting

	Nm	lbf ft
Airbag electronic control unit screws	6	4

1 General information and precautions

 Warning: Before carrying out any work on the electrical system, read through the precautions given in 'Safety first!' at the beginning of this manual, and in Chapter 5A.

The electrical system is of 12-volt negative earth type. Power for the lights and all electrical accessories is supplied by a lead-acid type battery, which is charged by the alternator.

This Chapter covers repair and service procedures for the various electrical components not associated with engine. Information on the battery, alternator and starter motor can be found in Chapter 5A.

It should be noted that, prior to working on any component in the electrical system, the battery negative terminal should first be disconnected, to prevent the possibility of electrical short-circuits and/or fires.

Caution: Before disconnecting the battery, refer to the information given in Chapter 5A.

2 Electrical fault finding – general information

Note: *Refer to the precautions given in 'Safety first!' and at the beginning of Chapter 5A before starting work. The following tests relate to testing of the main electrical circuits, and should not be used to test delicate electronic circuits (such as anti-lock braking systems), particularly where an electronic control module is used.*

General

1 A typical electrical circuit consists of an electrical component, any switches, relays, motors, fuses, fusible links or circuit breakers related to that component, and the wiring and connectors which link the component to both the battery and the chassis. To help to pinpoint a problem in an electrical circuit, wiring diagrams are included at the end of this Chapter.

2 Before attempting to diagnose an electrical fault, first study the appropriate wiring diagram, to obtain a more complete understanding of the components included in the particular circuit concerned. The possible sources of a fault can be narrowed down by noting whether other components related to the circuit are operating properly. If several components or circuits fail at one time, the problem is likely to be related to a shared fuse or earth connection.

3 Electrical problems usually stem from simple causes, such as loose or corroded connections, a faulty earth connection, a blown fuse, a melted fusible link, or a faulty relay (refer to Section 3 for details of testing relays). Visually inspect the condition of all fuses, wires and connections in a problem circuit before testing the components. Use the wiring diagrams to determine which terminal connections will need to be checked, in order to pinpoint the trouble-spot.

4 The basic tools required for electrical fault finding include a circuit tester or voltmeter (a 12-volt bulb with a set of test leads can also be used for certain tests); a self-powered test light (sometimes known as a continuity tester); an ohmmeter (to measure resistance); a battery and set of test leads; and a jumper wire, preferably with a circuit breaker or fuse incorporated, which can be used to bypass suspect wires or electrical components. Before attempting to locate a problem with test instruments, use the wiring diagram to determine where to make the connections.

5 To find the source of an intermittent wiring fault (usually due to a poor or dirty connection, or damaged wiring insulation), a 'wiggle' test can be performed on the wiring. This involves wiggling the wiring by hand, to see if the fault occurs as the wiring is moved. It should be possible to narrow down the source of the fault to a particular section of wiring. This method of testing can be used in conjunction with any of the tests described in the following sub-Sections.

6 Apart from problems due to poor connections, two basic types of fault can occur in an electrical circuit – open-circuit, or short-circuit.

7 Open-circuit faults are caused by a break somewhere in the circuit, which prevents current from flowing. An open-circuit fault will prevent a component from working, but will not cause the relevant circuit fuse to blow.

8 Short-circuit faults are caused by a 'short' somewhere in the circuit, which allows the current flowing in the circuit to 'escape' along an alternative route, usually to earth. Short-circuit faults are normally caused by a breakdown in wiring insulation, which allows a feed wire to touch either another wire, or an earthed component such as the bodyshell. A short-circuit fault will normally cause the relevant circuit fuse to blow.

Finding an open-circuit

9 To check for an open-circuit, connect one lead of a circuit tester or voltmeter to either the negative battery terminal or a known good earth.

10 Connect the other lead to a connector in the circuit being tested, preferably nearest to the battery or fuse.

11 Switch on the circuit, bearing in mind that some circuits are live only when the ignition switch is moved to a particular position.

12 If voltage is present (indicated either by the tester bulb lighting or a voltmeter reading, as applicable), this means that the section of the circuit between the relevant connector and the battery is problem-free.

13 Continue to check the remainder of the circuit in the same fashion.

14 When a point is reached at which no voltage is present, the problem must lie between that point and the previous test point with voltage. Most problems can be traced to a broken, corroded or loose connection.

Finding a short-circuit

15 To check for a short-circuit, first disconnect the load(s) from the circuit (loads are the components which draw current from a circuit, such as bulbs, motors, heating elements, etc).

16 Remove the relevant fuse from the circuit, and connect a circuit tester or voltmeter to the fuse connections.

17 Switch on the circuit, bearing in mind that some circuits are live only when the ignition switch is moved to a particular position.

18 If voltage is present (indicated either by the tester bulb lighting or a voltmeter reading, as applicable), this means that there is a short-circuit.

19 If no voltage is present, but the fuse still blows with the load(s) connected, this indicates an internal fault in the load(s).

Finding an earth fault

20 The battery negative terminal is connected to 'earth' – the metal of the engine/transmission unit and the car body – and most systems are wired so that they only receive a positive feed, the current returning via the metal of the car body. This means that the component mounting and the body form part of that circuit. Loose or corroded mountings can therefore cause a range of electrical faults, ranging from total failure of a circuit, to a puzzling partial fault. In particular, lights may shine dimly (especially when another circuit sharing the same earth point is in operation), motors (eg, wiper motors or the radiator cooling fan motor) may run slowly, and the operation of one circuit may have an apparently-unrelated effect on another. Note that on many vehicles, earth straps are used between certain components, such as the engine/transmission and the body, usually where there is no metal-to-metal contact between components, due to flexible rubber mountings, etc.

21 To check whether a component is properly earthed, disconnect the battery, and connect one lead of an ohmmeter to a known good earth point. Connect the other lead to the wire or earth connection being tested. The resistance reading should be zero; if not, check the connection as follows.

22 If an earth connection is thought to be faulty, dismantle the connection, and clean back to bare metal both the bodyshell and the wire terminal or the component earth connection mating surface. Be careful to remove all traces of dirt and corrosion, then use a knife to trim away any paint, so that a clean metal-to-metal joint is made. On reassembly, tighten the joint fasteners

securely; if a wire terminal is being refitted, use serrated washers between the terminal and the bodyshell, to ensure a clean and secure connection. When the connection is remade, prevent the onset of corrosion in the future by applying a coat of petroleum jelly or silicone-based grease, or by spraying on (at regular intervals) a proprietary ignition sealer.

3 Fuses and relays –
general information

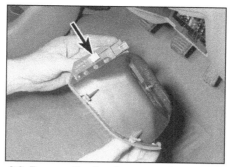

3.3 Remove the fusebox cover for access to the fuses. Note the location of the fuse removal tool (arrowed)

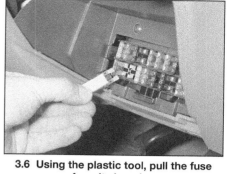

3.6 Using the plastic tool, pull the fuse from its location

Fuses

1 Fuses are designed to break a circuit when a predetermined current is reached, in order to protect the components and wiring which could be damaged by excessive current flow. Any excessive current flow will be due to a fault in the circuit, usually a short-circuit (see Section 2).

2 The main fuses are located in the fusebox, below the driver's side of the facia.

3 For access to the fuses, pull off the fusebox cover **(see illustration)**.

4 A blown fuse can be recognised from its melted or broken wire.

5 To remove a fuse, first ensure that the relevant circuit is switched off.

6 Using the plastic tool provided on the fusebox cover, pull the fuse from its location **(see illustration)**.

7 Before renewing a blown fuse, trace and rectify the cause, and always use a fuse of the correct rating. Never substitute a fuse of a higher rating, or make temporary repairs using wire or metal foil; more serious damage, or even fire, could result.

8 Note that the fuses are colour-coded as follows. Refer to the markings on the fusebox cover for details of the circuits protected.

Colour	Rating
Orange	5A
Red	10A
Blue	15A
Yellow	20A
Clear or white	25A
Green	30A

9 Additional fuses are located in the auxiliary

3.9 Additional fuses are located in the auxiliary fuse/relay box

fuse/relay box, at the rear left-hand corner of the engine compartment **(see illustration)**.

Relays

10 A relay is an electrically-operated switch, which is used for the following reasons:
 a) *A relay can switch a heavy current remotely from the circuit in which the current is flowing, allowing the use of lighter-gauge wiring and switch contacts.*
 b) *A relay can receive more than one control input, unlike a mechanical switch.*
 c) *A relay can have a timer function – for example, the intermittent wiper relay.*

11 Most of the relays are located under the facia, at the rear of the main fusebox. Additional relays are located in the auxiliary fuse/relay box, at the rear left-hand corner of the engine compartment **(see illustration)**.

12 Access to the relays in the fusebox can be

3.11 To gain access to the relays in the auxiliary fuse/relay box, unclip the main cover

obtained by removing the two securing screws, then releasing the securing clips, and lowering the fusebox from the facia **(see illustrations)**.

13 If a circuit or system controlled by a relay develops a fault, and the relay is suspect, operate the system. If the relay is functioning, it should be possible to hear it 'click' as it is energised. If this is the case, the fault lies with the components or wiring of the system. If the relay is not being energised, then either the relay is not receiving a main supply or a switching voltage, or the relay itself is faulty. Testing is by the substitution of a known good unit, but be careful – while some relays are identical in appearance and in operation, others look similar but perform different functions.

14 To remove a relay, first ensure that the relevant circuit is switched off. The relay can

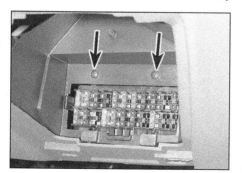

3.12a Remove the two securing screws . . .

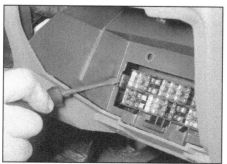

3.12b . . . then release the securing clips . . .

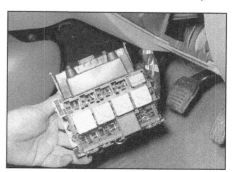

3.12c . . . and lower the fusebox from the facia

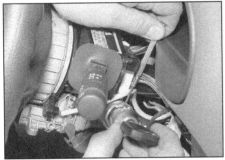

3.15 Removing the direction indicator/hazard flasher relay

then simply be pulled out from the socket, and pushed back into position.

15 The direction indicator/hazard flasher relay is plugged into the bottom of the steering column combination switch assembly, and can be removed after

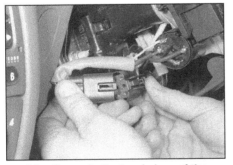

4.4 Removing the steering lock cylinder

4.2 Disconnecting the wiring plug from the anti-theft immobiliser transceiver unit

removing the switch assembly as described in Section 4 (see illustration).

4 Switches – removal and refitting

Note: Disconnect the battery negative lead, with reference to Chapter 5A, before removing any switch, and reconnect the lead after refitting the switch.

Ignition switch/steering lock

Steering column lock cylinder

1 Remove the steering column shrouds as described in Chapter 11, Section 29.
2 Where applicable, disconnect the wiring plug and remove the securing screw, then withdraw the anti-theft immobiliser

transceiver unit from the ignition switch/steering lock assembly (see illustration).
3 Insert the ignition key, and turn it to position I.
4 Using a small screwdriver, depress the locking pin at the top of the lock housing, then pull out the lock cylinder using the key (see illustration).
5 To refit the lock cylinder, push the assembly into the lock housing, until the locking pin engages, then turn the ignition key to position 0 and withdraw the key.

Ignition switch

Caution: Do not remove the ignition switch whilst the steering column lock cylinder is removed.

6 To remove the ignition switch, separate the two halves of the wiring connector, then release the securing clips using a small screwdriver, and withdraw the switch from the end of the lock housing (see illustrations).
7 Refitting is a reversal of removal, but make sure that the plunger on the lock engages correctly with the switch wiper.

Steering column switches

8 Remove the steering column shrouds as described in Chapter 11, Section 29.
9 Disconnect the wiring plugs from the rear of the switches (see illustration).
10 Remove the securing screw from the top of the switch assembly (see illustration).
11 Lift the switch assembly from the steering column (see illustration).

4.6a Separate the two halves of the ignition switch wiring connector . . .

4.6b . . . then release the securing clips . . .

4.6c . . . and withdraw the switch

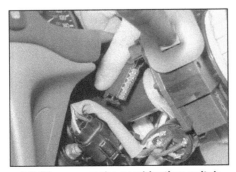

4.9 Disconnect the combination switch wiring plugs . . .

4.10 . . . then remove the securing screw . . .

4.11 . . . and lift the switch assembly from the steering column

4.15 Pushing out a switch from the facia

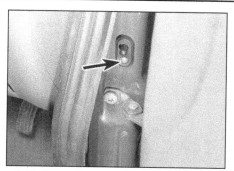

4.28 Door pillar-mounted courtesy light switch securing screw (arrowed)

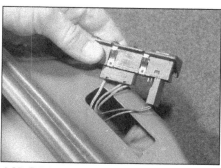

4.35 Prising out the luggage compartment light switch/contact plate assembly

12 If desired, the direction indicator/hazard flasher relay can now be unplugged from the bottom of the switch.
13 Refitting is a reversal of removal.

Facia pushbutton switches

14 Remove the clock/temperature display as described in Section 13.
15 Working through the clock/temperature gauge aperture, push out the relevant switch, then disconnect the wiring plug **(see illustration)**.
16 Refitting is a reversal of removal.

Headlight adjustment switch

17 Carefully prise the switch from the facia using a small screwdriver, and disconnect the wiring plug.
18 Refitting is a reversal of removal.

Heater blower motor switch

19 Refer to Chapter 3.

Stop-light switch

20 Refer to Chapter 9.

Handbrake 'on' warning light switch

21 Refer to Chapter 9.

Electric window switches

22 Carefully prise the switch free from the door inner trim panel using a small screwdriver. Disconnect the wiring plug, then remove the switch.
23 Refitting is a reversal of removal.

Electric mirror switch

24 Refer to Chapter 11, Section 23.

Remote tailgate release switch

25 Carefully prise the switch from the housing, and disconnect the wiring plug.
26 Refitting is a reversal of removal.

Courtesy light switches

Door pillar-mounted switch

27 Where applicable, pull the rubber cover from the switch.
28 Unscrew the switch securing screw, then pull the switch from the door pillar, and disconnect the wiring plug **(see illustration)**.

29 It is advisable to tape or tie the switch wiring in position, to prevent it from dropping down into the door pillar.
30 Refitting is a reversal of removal.

Light-mounted switches

31 The switches are integral with the light units, and cannot be renewed separately.

Glovebox light switch

32 Open the glovebox, and prise out the switch/light unit, then disconnect the wiring plug.
33 Refitting is a reversal of removal.

Luggage compartment light switch

34 The switch is integral with the tailgate electrical contact plate at the rear of the passenger compartment.
35 Open the tailgate, and prise the assembly from the body panel, then disconnect the wiring plugs **(see illustration)**.
36 Refitting is a reversal of removal.

Electric sunroof switch

37 Carefully prise the switch from the housing, and disconnect the wiring plug.
38 Refitting is a reversal of removal.

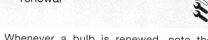

5 Bulbs (exterior lights) – renewal

1 Whenever a bulb is renewed, note the following points.

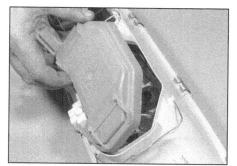

5.3 Removing the headlight bulb cover

a) *Disconnect the battery negative lead before starting work. See Chapter 5A.*
b) *Remember that, if the light has just been in use, the bulb may be extremely hot.*
c) *Always check the bulb contacts and holder, ensuring that there is clean metal-to metal contact between the bulb and its live(s) and earth. Clean off any corrosion or dirt before fitting a new bulb.*
d) *Wherever bayonet-type bulbs are fitted (see Specifications), ensure that the live contact(s) bear firmly against the bulb contact.*
e) *Always ensure that the new bulb is of the correct rating, and that it is completely clean before fitting it; this applies particularly to headlight/foglight bulbs (see below).*

Headlight

2 Remove the headlight (see Section 7).
3 Release the securing clips from each side of the headlight rear cover, or the clip at the bottom of the cover, as applicable, then lift off the cover **(see illustration)**.
4 Pull the wiring plug from the rear of the relevant bulb. On early models, separate main and dipped beam bulbs are fitted, but a combined main/dipped beam bulb is used on later models **(see illustration)**.
5 Release the spring clip by compressing its

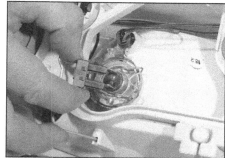

5.4 Disconnect the wiring plug . . .

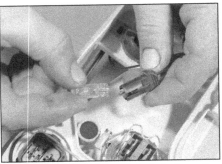

5.5 . . . then release the spring clip and withdraw the bulb

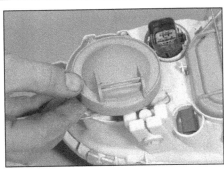

5.11 Removing the sidelight bulb from the bulbholder

5.15 Removing the direction indicator light cover from the headlight assembly

ends, then withdraw the relevant bulb **(see illustration)**.

6 When handling the new bulb, use a tissue or clean cloth, to avoid touching the glass with the fingers; moisture and grease from the skin can cause blackening and rapid failure of this type of bulb. If the glass is accidentally touched, wipe it clean using methylated spirit.

7 Install the new bulb, ensuring that its locating tabs are correctly seated in the light cut-outs. Secure the bulb in position with the spring clip, and reconnect the wiring plug.

8 Refit the cover, and secure with the clips, then refit the headlight as described in Section 7.

Front sidelight

9 Remove the headlight as described in Section 7.

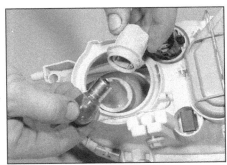

5.16 Removing the front direction indicator light bulb from the bulbholder

10 Release the securing clips from each side of the headlight rear cover, or the clip at the bottom of the cover, as applicable, then lift off the cover.

11 Pull the bulbholder from the rear of the light. The bulb is a push-fit in the bulbholder **(see illustration)**.

12 Fit the new bulb using a reversal of the removal procedure.

13 Refit the headlight as described in Section 7.

Front direction indicator light

14 Remove the headlight as described in Section 7.

15 Release the securing clip, then pull the direction indicator light cover (the round cover) from the rear of the headlight **(see illustration)**.

16 Twist the bulbholder anti-clockwise to remove it from the light unit. The bulb is a bayonet-fit in the bulbholder **(see illustration)**.

17 Fit the new bulb using a reversal of the removal procedure, then refit the headlight as described in Section 7.

Front foglight

18 Remove the foglight as described in Section 7.

19 Pull the rubber cover from the rear of the light unit.

20 Release the securing clip, and pull the bulb from the light.

21 When handling the new bulb, use a tissue

or clean cloth, to avoid touching the glass with the fingers; moisture and grease from the skin can cause blackening and rapid failure of this type of bulb. If the glass is accidentally touched, wipe it clean using methylated spirit.

22 Fit the new bulb using a reversal of the removal procedure. Ensure that the flat on the bulb locates against the shoulder in the light unit.

23 Refit the foglight with reference to Section 7.

Indicator side repeater light

24 Using a screwdriver (rest the screwdriver on a piece of rag to protect the paintwork), push the complete light assembly sideways, and pull it from the wing panel **(see illustration)**.

25 Turn the bulbholder anti-clockwise to remove it from the lens. The bulb is a push-fit in the bulbholder **(see illustration)**.

26 Fit the new bulb using a reversal of the removal procedure.

Rear lights

Hatchback and Van models

27 Open the tailgate, then release the securing clip, and pull the luggage compartment trim panel back from the rear of the light unit.

28 Press the locking tabs at the centre of the bulbholder together, and remove the bulbholder **(see illustration)**.

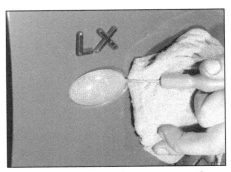

5.24 Use a screwdriver to remove the direction indicator side repeater light

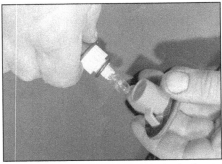

5.25 Turn the bulbholder anti-clockwise to remove it from the lens

5.28 Press the locking tabs to remove the rear light bulbholder – Hatchback and Van models

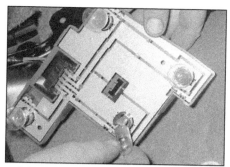

5.29 The bulbs are a bayonet-fit in the bulbholder – Hatchback and Van models

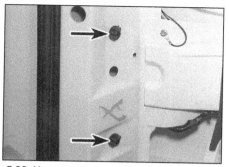

5.32 Unscrew the rear light securing nuts (arrowed) – Courier and Combi models

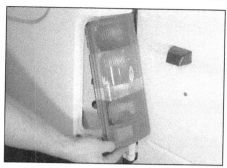

5.33 Remove the light assembly . . .

29 The bulbs are a bayonet-fit in the bulbholder **(see illustration)**.
30 Fit the new bulb using a reversal of the removal procedure.

Courier and Combi models

31 Open the rear doors, and turn the securing clip at the top of the light rear cover anti-clockwise to release it. Withdraw the cover.
32 Unscrew the two now-exposed nuts securing the light unit to the body **(see illustration)**.
33 Working outside the vehicle, pull the lower end of the light unit out slightly, then press

down, and withdraw the complete light assembly **(see illustration)**.
34 Squeeze the upper and lower bulbholder securing clips, and remove the bulbholder from the light unit **(see illustration)**.
35 The bulbs are a bayonet-fit in the bulbholder **(see illustration)**.
36 Fit the new bulb using a reversal of the removal procedure.

Rear number plate light

Hatchback and Van models

37 Carefully prise the light unit from the rear bumper using screwdriver **(see illustration)**.

38 Twist the bulbholder anti-clockwise, and remove it from the light unit **(see illustration)**.
39 The bulb is a push-fit in the bulbholder.
40 Fit the new bulb using a reversal of removal procedure.

Courier and Combi models

41 Carefully prise the light unit from the rear door.
42 Pull the bulbholder from the rear of the light unit **(see illustration)**. The bulb is a bayonet-fit in the bulbholder.
43 Refitting is a reversal of removal.

5.34 . . . then unclip the bulbholder – Courier and Combi models

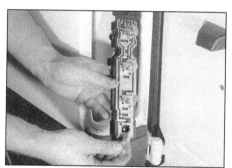

5.35 The bulbs are a bayonet-fit – Courier and Combi models

5.37 Prise the rear number plate light unit from the bumper . . .

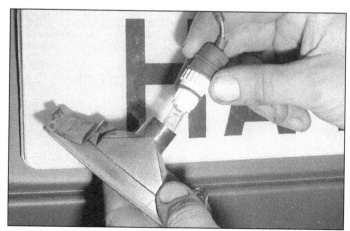

5.38 . . . and twist the bulbholder anti-clockwise to remove it – Hatchback and Van models

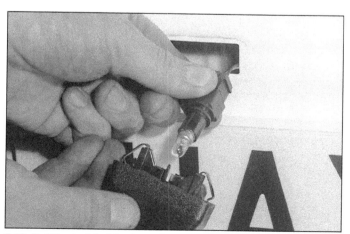

5.42 Pull the bulbholder from the rear number plate light – Courier and Combi models

6.2 Prise off the lens . . .

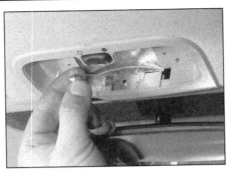

6.3 . . . for access to the courtesy light bulb

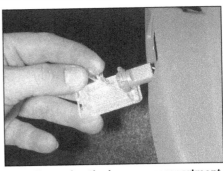

6.11 Removing the luggage compartment light bulb

High-level stop-light

44 Open the tailgate or rear doors as applicable.
45 Undo the two screws and withdraw the light unit from its location.
46 Disconnect the wiring connector and pull the bulbholder from the light unit.
47 Unclip the lens and remove the relevant push-fit bulb from the bulbholder.
48 Refitting is a reversal of removal.

6 Bulbs (interior lights) – renewal

General

1 Refer to Section 5, paragraph 1.

Courtesy lights

2 Carefully prise the lens from the light unit (see illustration).
3 Pull the bulb from the sprung contacts (see illustration).
4 Fit the new bulb using a reversal of the removal procedure.

Map reading lights

5 Carefully prise the light unit from the roof console, and disconnect the wiring plugs.
6 Slide the contact plate back from the bulb, and withdraw the bulb.
7 Fit the new bulb using a reversal of the removal procedure.

Glovebox light

8 Open the glovebox, and pull the bulb from the switch/light assembly.
9 Fit the new bulb using a reversal of the removal procedure.

Luggage compartment light

10 Carefully prise the light unit out from the trim panel.
11 The bulb can now be reached from the back of the light unit. The bulb is a push-fit in the bulbholder (see illustration). If necessary, the bulbholder can be removed by twisting anti-clockwise.
12 Fit the new bulb using a reversal of the removal procedure.

Instrument panel illumination

13 Refer to Section 11.

Warning light bulbs

14 Refer to Section 11.

Clock illumination

15 The bulb is integral with the clock/temperature display unit, and cannot be renewed separately.

Pushbutton switch illumination

16 The bulbs are integral with the switches, and cannot be renewed separately.

Cigarette lighter illumination

17 Open the ashtray.
18 Working at the rear of the ashtray, disconnect the cigarette lighter wiring plugs.
19 Squeeze the rear corners of the ashtray to release the securing lugs, then pull the ashtray from the facia.
20 Working at the rear of the assembly, carefully prise the bulbholder from the cigarette lighter body. The bulb is a push-fit in the bulbholder.
21 Fit the new bulb using a reversal of the removal procedure.

Heater control unit illumination

22 Remove the heater control unit as described in Chapter 3.
23 Twist the relevant bulbholder anti-clockwise and remove it from the rear of the panel. The bulbs are integral with the bulbholders.

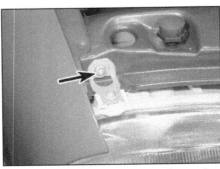

7.2 Remove the screw (arrowed) securing the outboard headlight mounting bracket to the body panel

24 Fit the new bulb using a reversal of the removal procedure.

Heater blower switch illumination

25 Pull the knob from the blower switch for access to the bulb.
26 The bulb is a push-fit in the switch.
27 Fit the new bulb using a reversal of the removal procedure.

7 Exterior light units – removal and refitting

Note: *Disconnect the battery negative lead, with reference to Chapter 5A before removing any light unit, and reconnect the lead after refitting the unit.*

Headlight

Caution: Do not unscrew the Torx screw on the headlight housing.
1 Remove the radiator grille panel as described in Chapter 11.
2 Remove the screw securing the outboard headlight mounting bracket to the body panel (see illustration).
3 Remove the two securing screws from the inner edge of the headlight (see illustration).
4 Withdraw the headlight by moving it towards the centre of the vehicle, and forwards.

7.3 Remove the two screws securing the inner edge of the headlight

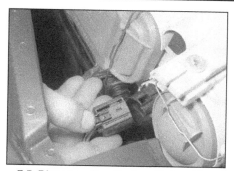

7.5 Disconnecting the headlight wiring plug

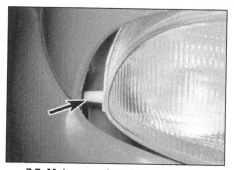

7.7 Make sure that the locating lug (arrowed) engages with the hole in the inner wing panel

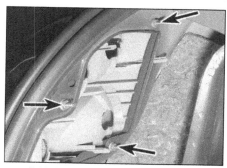

7.15 Rear light unit securing nuts (arrowed) – Hatchback and Van models

5 Disconnect the wiring plug, and withdraw the headlight **(see illustration)**.
6 Note that if desired, the headlight lens can be removed after releasing the metal securing clips around the edge of the lens.
7 Refitting is a reversal of removal, but make sure that the locating lug on the headlight engages with the corresponding hole in the inner wing panel and, on completion, have the headlight beam alignment checked at the earliest opportunity **(see illustration)**.

Front direction indicator light

8 The front direction indicator light is integral with the headlight.

Front foglight

9 Working at the top of the light unit, unscrew the securing screw. Where applicable, also remove the securing screw from the lower, outer corner of the light.
10 Pull the light unit from the bumper.
11 Refitting is a reversal of removal.

Indicator side repeater light

12 The procedure is described as part of the bulb renewal procedure in Section 5.

Rear lights

Hatchback and Van models

Note: *A new rubber seal should be used on refitting.*
13 Open the tailgate, then release the securing clip, and pull the luggage compartment trim panel back from the rear of the light unit.
14 Disconnect the wiring plug from the rear of the bulbholder. If desired, unclip the bulbholder from the light unit.
15 Unscrew the three securing nuts, and withdraw the light unit from the rear of the vehicle **(see illustration)**. Recover the rubber seal.
16 Refitting is a reversal of removal, but use a new rubber seal, and make sure that the seal is seated correctly.

Courier and Combi models

17 The procedure is described as part of the bulb renewal procedure in Section 5.

Rear number plate light

18 The procedure is described as part of the bulb renewal procedure in Section 5.

High-level stop-light

19 The procedure is described as part of the bulb renewal procedure in Section 5.

8 Headlight beam adjustment components – removal and refitting

Adjuster switch

1 Refer to Section 4.

Adjuster motor

Note: *On later models the motor cannot be separated from the headlight.*

Removal

2 If necessary for access, remove the headlight as described in Section 7.
3 Release the securing clips from each side, or from the bottom of the headlight rear cover, then pull off the cover.
4 Disconnect the wiring plug from the rear of the motor.
5 Twist the motor anti-clockwise, and pull it from the headlight.

Refitting

6 Refitting is a reversal of removal but, where applicable, refit the headlight with reference to Section 7.

9 Headlight beam alignment – general information

1 All later vehicles are equipped with a four-position electrical vertical beam adjuster unit – this can be used to adjust the headlight beam, to compensate for the relevant load which the vehicle is carrying. An adjuster switch is provided on the facia. Refer to the vehicle handbook for further information.
2 Accurate adjustment of the headlight beam is only possible using optical beam-setting equipment, and this work should therefore be

carried out by a Ford dealer or suitably-equipped workshop.
3 For reference, the headlights can be finely adjusted by rotating the adjuster screws fitted to the top of each light unit. The screws are accessible through the top of the body front panel. The vertical adjustment screw is mounted at the inner end of the headlight. The horizontal adjustment screw is mounted at the outer end of the headlight **(see illustration)**. Note if the vertical adjustment is altered, this will affect the horizontal adjustment, which will have to be adjusted too.

10 Instrument panel – removal and refitting

Removal

Caution: When the instrument panel has been removed, do not rest it face down on the lens.
Note: *A speedometer cable is not fitted to later models (January 1999 onward) which are equipped with an electronically-controlled instrument panel. In this case ignore all references to disconnection of the speedometer cable and removal of the cable grommets from the bulkhead.*
1 Disconnect the battery negative lead, with reference to Chapter 5A.
2 Remove the steering column shrouds, with reference to Chapter 11, Section 29, if necessary.

9.3 Headlight beam adjustment screws

1 Vertical alignment screw
2 Horizontal alignment screw

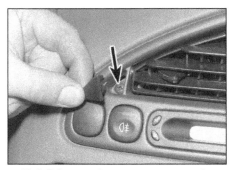

10.4 Prise out the cover to expose the instrument panel/heater/ventilation nozzle/switch trim panel securing screw (arrowed)

3 Remove the steering column combination switch assembly as described in Section 4.

4 Working at the passenger's side edge of the instrument panel/heater/ventilation nozzle/switch trim panel, prise out the cover to expose the trim panel securing screw. Remove the securing screw **(see illustration)**.

5 Working above the instrument panel, unscrew the remaining trim panel securing screws **(see illustration)**.

6 Ease the trim panel forwards to release the retaining clips at the bottom of the panel, then pull the panel forwards and disconnect the wiring plugs from the switches and clock/temperature display (where applicable) mounted in the panel. Withdraw the panel **(see illustration)**.

7 Working in the scuttle at the rear of the

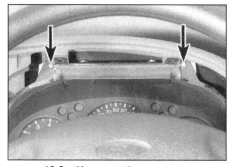

10.9a Unscrew the upper . . .

10.9b . . . and lower instrument panel securing screws (arrowed)

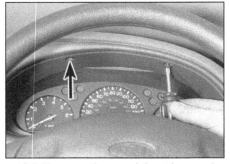

10.5 Unscrew the remaining trim panel securing screws

engine compartment, prise the speedometer cable grommet from the inner bulkhead – if desired, to improve access, remove the windscreen wiper motor and linkage as described in Section 19 **(see illustration)**.

8 Prise the grommet from the outer bulkhead at the rear of the engine compartment. Note the routing of the speedometer cable to ensure correct refitting.

9 Working inside the vehicle, remove the four instrument panel securing screws **(see illustrations)**.

10 The speedometer cable must now be disconnected from the transmission. On most models, access is easiest from under the vehicle. If desired, apply the handbrake, then jack up the front of the vehicle and support securely on axle stands (see *Jacking and vehicle support*).

11 If necessary, counterhold the vehicle speed sensor at the transmission using a suitable spanner, then unscrew the securing nut, and disconnect the end of the speedometer cable from the transmission **(see illustration)**. Again, note the routing of the speedometer cable to aid refitting.

12 Where applicable, lower the vehicle to the ground.

13 Working inside the vehicle, carefully ease the instrument panel forwards from the facia (if necessary, push the speedometer cable through the bulkhead as the instrument panel is withdrawn), then release the securing clip, and disconnect the speedometer cable from the rear of the panel.

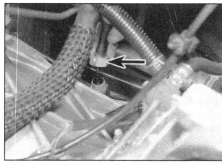

10.11 Disconnecting the speedometer cable (arrowed) from the transmission

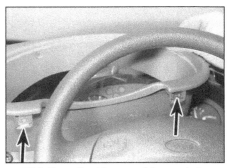

10.6 Ease the trim panel forwards to release the retaining clips (arrowed)

10.7 Speedometer cable grommets (arrowed) at inner and outer bulkhead – viewed with scuttle cover panel and wiper motor removed for clarity

14 Disconnect the wiring plugs from the rear of the instrument panel, then remove the panel **(see illustration)**.

Refitting

15 Refitting is a reversal of removal, bearing in mind the following points.

  a) *Ensure that the speedometer cable is routed as noted before removal.*

  b) *Ensure that the speedometer cable grommets are correctly located in the inner and outer bulkhead panels.*

  c) *Make sure that the speedometer cable securing clip engages correctly with the back of the speedometer.*

  d) *Pull the speedometer cable through into the engine compartment as the instrument panel is refitted.*

10.14 Removing the instrument panel

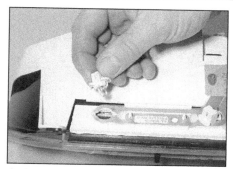

11.2 Remove the bulbholders from the top of the panel

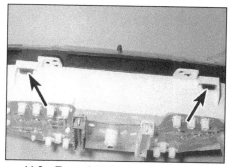

11.3a Two of the lens securing clips (arrowed)

11.3b Removing the lens assembly from the instrument panel

11 Instrument panel components – removal and refitting

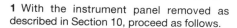

1 With the instrument panel removed as described in Section 10, proceed as follows.

Lens

2 Working at the top of the instrument panel, twist the two bulbholders anti-clockwise, and remove them from the panel **(see illustration)**.
3 Release the four lens retaining lugs, and remove the lens assembly **(see illustrations)**.
4 Refitting is a reversal of removal.

Tachometer

5 Remove the lens assembly as described previously in this Section.
6 Unscrew the two securing screws, and withdraw the tachometer. Note that one of the securing screws also secures the speedometer **(see illustration)**.

Fuel/temperature gauge

7 Remove the lens assembly as described previously in this Section.
8 Remove the two securing screws and withdraw the gauge assembly (one of the screws also secures the speedometer). Note that the fuel gauge and the temperature gauge cannot be separated.
9 Refitting is a reversal of removal.

Speedometer

10 Remove the fuel/temperature gauge assembly and the tachometer as described previously in this Section, then lift out the speedometer.

Illumination/warning light bulbs

11 Twist the bulbholders anti-clockwise to remove them from the panel **(see illustration)**. The bulbs are integral with the bulbholders.
12 Refit by twisting clockwise to lock the bulb in position.

12 Cigarette lighter – removal and refitting

Removal

1 Disconnect the battery negative lead, with reference to Chapter 5A.
2 Open the ashtray, and pull out the ashtray liner.
3 Pull out the cigarette lighter element.
4 Working at the rear of the ashtray, Disconnect the cigarette lighter wiring plugs.
5 Squeeze the rear corners of the ashtray to release the securing lugs, then pull the ashtray from the facia.
6 Working at the rear of the assembly, carefully prise the bulbholder from the cigarette lighter body.

7 Remove the cigarette lighter body as follows.
 a) *Rotate the cigarette lighter body approximately 30° clockwise.*
 b) *Push the rear of the body forwards approximately 10 mm.*
 c) *Rotate the body back to its original position.*
 d) *Push the body forwards, and remove it from the ashtray.*
8 The illumination ring can now be pulled from the ashtray.

Refitting

9 Refitting is a reversal of removal.

13 Clock/temperature display – removal and refitting

Removal

1 Disconnect the battery negative lead, with reference to Chapter 5A.
2 Using a small screwdriver or similar tool, carefully prise the clock/temperature display from the facia – take care not to damage the facia trim.
3 Disconnect the wiring plug(s) and withdraw the unit **(see illustration)**.

Refitting

4 Refitting is a reversal of removal.

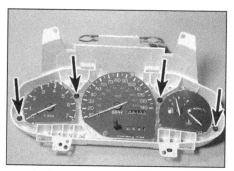

11.6 Instrument securing screws (arrowed)

11.11 Removing an instrument panel warning light bulb

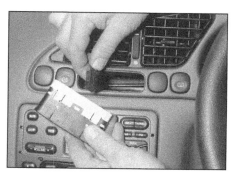

13.3 Removing the clock/temperature display from the facia

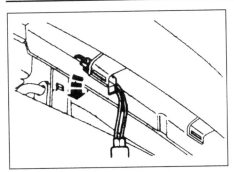

14.9 Unclip the auxiliary warning system air temperature sensor from the front panel

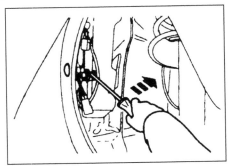

14.15 Using a screwdriver, carefully prise the auxiliary warning system washer fluid level sensor from the reservoir

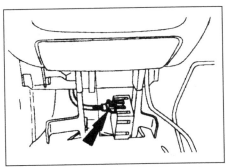

14.20 Disconnect the auxiliary warning system control unit wiring plug (arrowed)

14 Auxiliary warning system components – information, removal and refitting

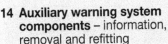

General information

1 Certain models are equipped with an auxiliary warning system.
2 This system comprises a number of sensors, and four warning devices as follows.

 a) *Ice warning – an air temperature sensor provides information which is displayed by the clock/temperature display. Two warning lights in the display (orange and red) will illuminate, depending on the outside temperature. The orange light will illuminate when the air temperature is between 0.5 and 4°C, and the red light will illuminate when the air temperature is below 0.5°C.*
 b) *Low fuel warning – a warning light will illuminate when around 8 litres of fuel remain in the tank. The signal is provided by the fuel gauge sender unit (see the relevant part of Chapter 4).*
 c) *Low washer fluid level – a warning light will illuminate when the washer fluid level requires topping up. The signal is provided by a float and reed switch in the fluid reservoir.*
 d) *Door/tailgate/bonnet ajar warning – a warning light will illuminate if a door, the tailgate or the bonnet is not fully shut. The signals are provided by switches which are shared with the central locking and alarm systems.*

Fuel level sender unit

3 Refer to the relevant part of Chapter 4.

Door/tailgate/bonnet switches

4 The door and tailgate ajar switches are mounted on the locks, and the locks must be removed for access to the switches. The bonnet ajar switch is mounted on the body front panel under the bonnet.

Air temperature sensor

Removal

5 Disconnect the battery negative lead, with reference to Chapter 5A.
6 Apply the handbrake, then jack up the front of the vehicle and support securely on axle stands (see *Jacking and vehicle support*).
7 Remove the two securing screws, and withdraw the lower grille panel from the front bumper.
8 Separate the two halves of the air temperature sensor wiring connector.
9 Unclip the sensor from the front panel (see illustration).

Refitting

10 Refitting is a reversal of removal.

Washer fluid level sensor

Removal

11 Disconnect the battery negative lead, with reference to Chapter 5A.
12 Remove the right-hand front wheel trim or the wheel centre plate (alloy wheels), then slacken the wheel nuts. Apply the handbrake, then jack up the front of the vehicle, and support securely on axle stands (see *Jacking and vehicle support*). Remove the roadwheel.
13 Remove the wheelarch liner, with reference to Chapter 11, Section 26, if necessary.
14 Working at the rear of the wheelarch, locate the sensor wiring connector, then manipulate the connector as necessary to enable the two halves to be separated.
15 Using a screwdriver, carefully prise the sensor from the side of the reservoir (see illustration). Have a suitable container ready to catch escaping fluid. Take care not to damage the rubber grommet.

Refitting

16 Refitting is a reversal of removal.

Control unit

Removal

17 Disconnect the battery negative lead, with reference to Chapter 5A.

18 Remove the centre console as described in Chapter 11.
19 Release the wiring harness from the upper control unit securing clip.
20 Disconnect the control unit wiring plug (see illustration).
21 Release the control unit from the securing clips, and withdraw it from the bracket.

Refitting

22 Refitting is a reversal of removal.

15 Lights 'on' warning buzzer – removal and refitting

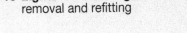

Removal

1 Disconnect the battery negative lead, with reference to Chapter 5A.
2 Working at the driver's side of the facia, pull off the fusebox cover.
3 Remove the two securing screws, and pull the fusebox forward from the facia to expose the relays.
4 The headlight warning buzzer is located at the lower right-hand corner of the relay panel (see illustration). Pull the buzzer from the panel to remove it.

Refitting

5 Refitting is a reversal of removal.

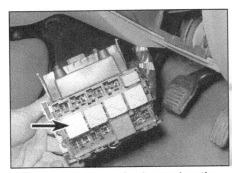

15.4 Headlight warning buzzer location (arrowed) in fuse/relay box

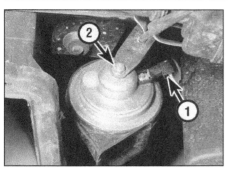

16.4 Horn wiring plug (1) and horn securing nut (2)

18.2 Unscrew the securing nut and washer . . .

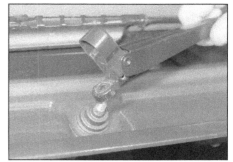

18.3 . . . and withdraw the wiper arm

16 Horn – removal and refitting

Removal

1 The horn is located under the left-hand corner of the front bumper.
2 Disconnect the battery negative lead, with reference to Chapter 5A.
3 Disconnect the wiring plug from the horn.
4 Unscrew the securing nut, and remove the horn from its mounting bracket **(see illustration)**.

Refitting

5 Refitting is a reversal of removal.

17 Speedometer cable – removal and refitting

Removal

1 Remove the instrument panel as described in Section 10, then withdraw the cable through the bulkhead panels into the engine compartment.
2 Release the cable from any brackets or clips, noting its routing, then withdraw the cable from the vehicle.

Refitting

3 Refitting is a reversal of removal, but ensure that the cable is routed as noted before

removal, and refit the instrument panel as described in Section 10.

18 Wiper arm – removal and refitting

Removal

1 Operate the wiper motor, then switch it off so that the wiper arm returns to the at-rest position.

> **HAYNES HiNT**
> *Stick a piece of masking tape along the edge of the wiper blade, to use as an alignment aid on refitting.*

2 Lift up the wiper arm spindle nut cover, then slacken and remove the spindle nut. Recover the washer **(see illustration)**.
3 Lift the blade off the glass, and pull the wiper arm off its spindle. Note that on some models, the wiper arms may be very tight on the spindle splines – it should be possible to lever the arm off the spindle, using a flat-bladed screwdriver (take care not to damage the scuttle cover panel) **(see illustration)**.

Refitting

4 Ensure that the wiper arm and spindle splines are clean and dry, then refit the arm to the spindle. Where applicable, align the wiper blade with the tape fitted on removal.
5 Refit the spindle nut, tightening it securely, and clip the nut cover back into position.

19 Windscreen wiper motor and linkage – removal and refitting

Removal

1 Remove the wiper arms as described in Section 18.
2 Prise off the covers, then unscrew and remove the nuts securing the wiper arm drive spindles to the body panel **(see illustrations)**. Lift off the washers and spacer plates.
3 Remove the scuttle cover panel as described in Chapter 11, Section 26.
4 Disconnect the wiper motor wiring plug **(see illustration)**.
5 Unscrew the two bolts securing the wiper motor mounting plate **(see illustration)**.

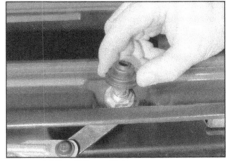

19.2a Prise off the covers . . .

19.2b . . . and unscrew the wiper arm drive spindle securing nuts

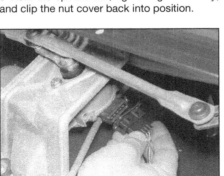

19.4 Disconnect the wiper motor wiring plug

19.5 Unscrew the securing bolts . . .

19.6 ... and withdraw the wiper motor/linkage assembly from the scuttle

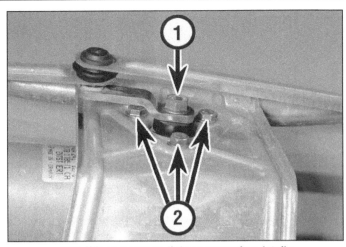

19.7 Wiper motor-to-linkage mounting details

1 Motor-to-drive link spindle nut   2 Motor securing bolts

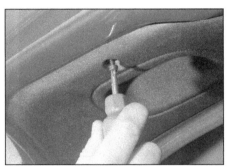

20.2a Unscrewing the tailgate trim panel securing screw

20.2b Removing the tailgate trim panel

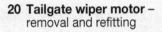

20 Tailgate wiper motor –
removal and refitting

6 Manipulate the wiper motor/linkage assembly out from the scuttle **(see illustration)**.

7 If desired, the motor can be removed from the linkage as follows **(see illustration)**.

a) *Make alignment marks on the linkage drive link and the motor spindle, then unscrew the spindle nut.*

b) *Unscrew the three bolts securing the motor to the mounting plate, then withdraw the motor from the linkage assembly.*

Refitting

8 Refitting is a reversal of removal, bearing in mind the following points.

a) *Ensure that the motor is in the 'parked' position before refitting.*

b) *If the motor has been removed from the linkage, ensure that the marks made on the linkage drive link and motor spindle are aligned on refitting.*

c) *Refit the wiper arms with reference to Section 18.*

Removal

1 Disconnect the battery negative lead, with reference to Chapter 5A.

2 Unscrew the tailgate trim panel securing screw, and prise out the plastic surround, then prise around the edge of the trim panel to release the remaining retaining clips, and withdraw the tailgate trim panel **(see illustrations)**.

3 Remove the wiper arm as described in Section 18.

4 Unscrew the bolt securing the wiper motor earth lead to the tailgate **(see illustration)**.

5 Separate the two halves of the wiper motor wiring connector **(see illustration)**.

6 Unscrew the three securing bolts, and withdraw the motor assembly from the tailgate **(see illustration)**.

Refitting

7 Refitting is a reversal of removal, but refit the wiper arm with reference to Section 18.

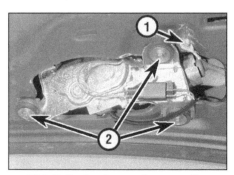

20.4 Tailgate wiper motor mounting details

1 Earth lead securing bolt
2 Wiper motor securing bolts

20.5 Disconnecting the tailgate wiper motor wiring connector

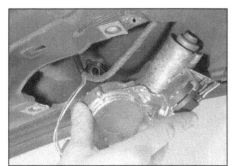

20.6 Withdrawing the tailgate wiper motor

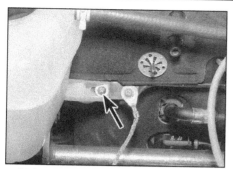

21.2a Remove the screw (arrowed) . . .

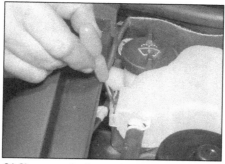

21.2b . . . and release the clip securing the coolant expansion tank

21.3 Pull the washer fluid reservoir filler neck from the reservoir

21 Windscreen/tailgate washer system components – removal and refitting

Washer fluid reservoir

Removal

1 Disconnect the battery negative lead, with reference to Chapter 5A.

2 Working in the engine compartment, remove the screw securing the coolant expansion tank, then release the securing clip using a screwdriver, and move the expansion tank to one side, clear of the washer fluid reservoir filler neck **(see illustrations)**. There is no need to disconnect the coolant hoses from the expansion tank.

3 Pull the washer fluid reservoir filler neck from the reservoir **(see illustration)**.

4 Remove the right-hand front wheel trim or the wheel centre plate (alloy wheels), then slacken the wheel nuts. Apply the handbrake, then jack up the front of the vehicle, and support securely on axle stands (see *Jacking and vehicle support*). Remove the roadwheel.

5 Remove the wheelarch liner, with reference to Chapter 11, Section 26, if necessary.

6 Place a suitable container beneath the reservoir, then drain the fluid from the reservoir into the container, by disconnecting the fluid hose(s) from the pump(s) in the reservoir.

7 Partially open the front door, then unscrew the two reservoir securing nuts, which are accessible at the rear of the door pillar **(see illustration)**.

8 Support the reservoir then, working under the wheelarch, unscrew the reservoir securing bolt **(see illustration)**.

9 Lower the reservoir, and disconnect the fluid pump wiring plug(s), the remaining fluid hose(s) and, where applicable, the fluid level sensor wiring plug. Release the clips securing the hoses and wiring harness(es) to the reservoir, then feed the hoses and harness(es) through the hole in the top of the reservoir, and withdraw the reservoir from under the wheelarch **(see illustrations)**.

Refitting

10 Refitting is a reversal of removal, bearing in mind the following points.
  a) *Check the condition of the filler neck O-ring, and renew if necessary.*
  b) *Make sure that the fluid hose(s) and the filler neck are securely reconnected to the reservoir.*

Washer fluid pump

Removal

11 Disconnect the battery negative lead, with reference to Chapter 5A.

12 Proceed as described in paragraphs 4 to 6. Note that in some cases, it may prove easier to remove the reservoir as described previously in this Section for access to the pump.

13 If not already done, disconnect the fluid hose(s) from the pump, then disconnect the pump wiring plug.

14 Pull the pump from the reservoir, and recover the rubber sealing grommet.

Refitting

15 Examine the rubber sealing grommet, and renew if necessary.

16 Refitting is a reversal of removal, but take care not to push the grommet into the reservoir when refitting the pump. Make sure that the pump is securely fitted in its sealing grommet, and make sure that the fluid hose(s) are securely reconnected.

Windscreen washer nozzle

Removal

17 Open the bonnet and, where applicable, prise out the securing clips, and pull back the underbonnet insulation for access to the washer nozzle.

18 Working under the bonnet, carefully pull

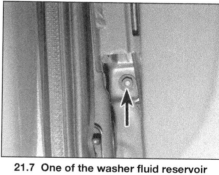

21.7 One of the washer fluid reservoir securing nuts (arrowed)

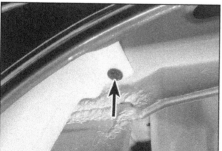

21.8 Washer fluid reservoir securing bolt location (arrowed)

21.9a Disconnect the motor wiring plug . . .

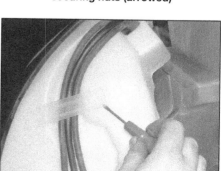

21.9b . . . and release the clips securing the hoses and wiring to the reservoir

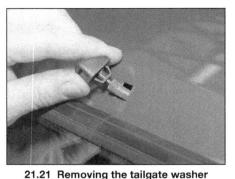

21.19 Removing the windscreen washer nozzle

21.21 Removing the tailgate washer nozzle

22.4 Using DIN removal tools to remove the radio/cassette player

the fluid hose end fitting from the washer nozzle.

19 Carefully prise the washer nozzle from the outside of the bonnet **(see illustration)**.

Refitting

20 Refitting is a reversal of removal, but make sure that the fluid hose end fitting is securely reconnected to the nozzle.

Tailgate washer nozzle

Removal

21 Carefully prise the nozzle from the top of the tailgate, taking care not to damage the paintwork **(see illustration)**.

22 Disconnect the fluid hose, and remove the nozzle. Take care not to allow the hose to drop down into the tailgate.

Refitting

23 Refitting is a reversal of removal, but

22.5 Disconnect the wiring plugs and the aerial lead from the rear of the radio/cassette player unit

make sure that the fluid hose is securely reconnected.

22 Radio/cassette player – removal and refitting

Note: *On models with a security-coded radio/cassette player, once the battery has been disconnected, the unit cannot be re-activated until the appropriate security code has been entered. Do not remove the unit unless the appropriate code is known. The following information applies to radio/cassette players having standard DIN fixings. Two DIN removal tools will be required for this operation.*

Removal

1 Disconnect the battery negative lead, with reference to Chapter 5A.

2 Insert the DIN removal tools into the holes on each side of the radio/cassette player, and push them until they click into place.

3 Pull the tools gently outwards to the left and right to release the locking tangs.

4 Gently pull the radio/cassette player from the facia, using the removal tools **(see illustration)**.

5 Disconnect the wiring plugs and the aerial lead, and withdraw the unit **(see illustration)**.

Refitting

6 Reconnect the wiring plugs and the aerial lead, then push the unit into its housing until the securing clips engage.

7 On completion, reconnect the battery negative lead and, where applicable enter the security code.

23 Loudspeakers – removal and refitting

Door-mounted speakers

Removal

1 Remove the relevant door inner trim panel, as described in Chapter 11.

2 Unscrew the four loudspeaker securing screws, then withdraw the loudspeaker from the door and disconnect the wiring plug **(see illustration)**.

Refitting

3 Refitting is a reversal of removal.

High-frequency (tweeter) speakers

Removal

4 The loudspeaker is integral with the door interior handle surround.

5 Prise off the cover, unscrew the securing screw, then withdraw the interior handle surround from the door. Disconnect the wiring plug from the loudspeaker mounted in the surround, then remove the surround/loudspeaker assembly **(see illustrations)**.

Refitting

6 Refitting is a reversal of removal.

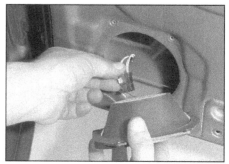

23.2 Removing a main front door-mounted loudspeaker

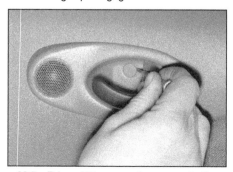

23.5a Prise off the cover for access to the handle surround/loudspeaker securing screw

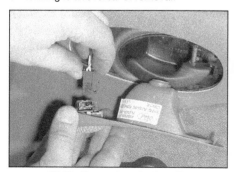

23.5b Removing the handle surround/tweeter loudspeaker

Parcel shelf-mounted speakers

Removal

7 Disconnect the battery negative lead, with reference to Chapter 5A.
8 If removing the right-hand loudspeaker, working in the luggage compartment, remove the luggage compartment light from the rear parcel shelf support panel, by prising the light out and disconnecting the wiring plug.
9 Remove the two securing screws, then withdraw the loudspeaker sideways from the parcel shelf, and disconnect the wiring plug.

Refitting

10 Refitting is a reversal of removal, but make sure that the lugs on the loudspeaker engage correctly with the slots in the trim panel.

24 Radio aerial – removal and refitting

Removal

1 Disconnect the battery negative lead, with reference to Chapter 5A.
2 Carefully prise the courtesy light assembly from the roof console. Disconnect the wiring plugs, and remove the courtesy light assembly (note that the light assembly incorporates the remote control receiver for the central locking system, where applicable).
3 Unscrew the now-exposed securing screw, and disconnect the aerial lead from the base of the aerial **(see illustration)**.
4 Withdraw the aerial from the roof panel. Note that the aerial mast can be unscrewed from the aerial body if desired.

Refitting

5 Refitting is a reversal of removal.

25 Anti-theft alarm system and engine immobiliser – general information

Certain vehicles are equipped with an anti-theft alarm system and/or and engine immobiliser system. Various types of system

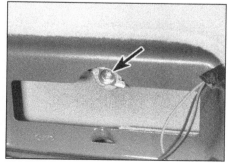

24.3 Radio aerial securing screw (arrowed)

may be fitted depending on vehicle specification, and market.

The anti-theft alarm system, is automatically activated by the central locking system (manually, or via the remote control, where applicable). The engine immobiliser system is operated by a coded unit in the ignition key – the engine can only be started using one of the ignition keys originally supplied with the car when new.

The alarm system has switches on the bonnet, tailgate and each of the doors.

Any faults with the system should be referred to a Ford dealer.

26 Airbag system – general information, precautions and system de-activation

General information

A driver's airbag is fitted as standard equipment on some models, and is available as an option on others. The airbag is fitted to the steering wheel centre pad.

Similarly, a passenger's airbag, located in the facia, is also fitted as standard equipment, or as an option, depending on model.

Later models may also be equipped with side airbags, located in the front seat backs.

The system is armed only when the ignition is switched on, however, a reserve power source maintains a power supply to the system in the event of a break in the main electrical supply. The system is activated by a 'g' sensor (deceleration sensor), incorporated in the electronic control unit. Note that the electronic control unit also controls the front seat belt tensioners.

The airbags are inflated by gas generators, which force the bags out from their locations in the steering wheel, passenger's side facia, and seat backs, where applicable.

Precautions

 Warning: The following precautions must be observed when working on vehicles equipped with an airbag system, to prevent the possibility of personal injury.

General precautions

The following precautions **must** be observed when carrying out work on a vehicle equipped with an airbag.
a) Do not disconnect the battery with the engine running.
b) Before carrying out any work in the vicinity of the airbag, removal of any of the airbag components, or any welding work on the vehicle, de-activate the system as described in the following sub-Section.
c) Do not attempt to test any of the airbag system circuits using test meters or any other test equipment.

d) If the airbag warning light comes on, or any fault in the system is suspected, consult a Ford dealer without delay. Do not attempt to carry out fault diagnosis, or any dismantling of the components.

Precautions to be taken when handling an airbag

a) Transport the airbag by itself, bag upward.
b) Do not put your arms around the airbag.
c) Carry the airbag close to the body, bag outward.
d) Do not drop the airbag or expose it to impacts.
e) Do not attempt to dismantle the airbag unit.
f) Do not connect any form of electrical equipment to any part of the airbag circuit.

Precautions to be taken when storing an airbag unit

a) Store the unit in a cupboard with the airbag upward.
b) Do not expose the airbag to temperatures above 80°C.
c) Do not expose the airbag to flames.
d) Do not attempt to dispose of the airbag – consult a Ford dealer.
e) Never refit an airbag which is known to be faulty or damaged.

De-activation of airbag system

The system must be de-activated as follows, before carrying out any work on the airbag components or surrounding area.
a) Switch off the ignition.
b) Remove the ignition key.
c) Switch off all electrical equipment.
d) Disconnect the battery negative lead, with reference to Chapter 5A.
e) Insulate the battery negative terminal and the end of the battery negative lead to prevent any possibility of contact.
f) Wait for at least two minutes before carrying out any further work.

27 Airbag system components – removal and refitting

Driver's airbag unit

 Warning: Refer to the precautions given in Section 26 before attempting to carry out work on the airbag components.

Removal

1 The airbag unit is an integral part of the steering wheel centre pad.
2 De-activate the airbag system as described in Section 26.
3 Move the steering wheel as necessary for access to the two airbag unit securing screws. The screws are located at the rear of the steering wheel centre pad.

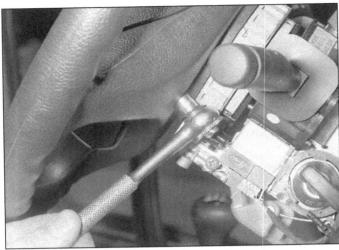

27.4 Unscrewing a driver's airbag unit securing screw

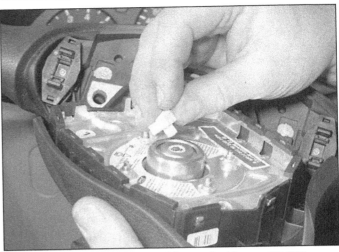

27.6 Disconnecting the airbag unit wiring connector

4 Remove the two airbag unit securing screws **(see illustration)**.

5 Gently ease the airbag unit from the steering wheel.

6 Lift the airbag unit from the steering wheel, then unclip the airbag wiring harness from the rear of the airbag unit (note the harness routing), and disconnect the wiring connector from the rear of the airbag unit **(see illustration)**.

7 Withdraw the airbag unit, and store it in a safe place, with reference to the precautions given in Section 26.

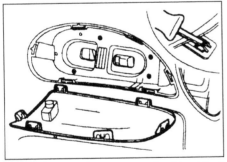

27.11 Release the passenger's side airbag cover securing clips

Refitting

8 Refitting is a reversal of removal, but make sure that the wiring harness is routed as noted before removal, and make sure that the wiring connector is securely reconnected.

Passenger's airbag unit

 Warning: Refer to the precautions given in Section 26 before attempting to carry out work on the airbag components.

Removal

9 De-activate the airbag system as described in Section 26.

10 Carefully prise the passenger's side heating/ventilation nozzle from the facia.

11 Working through the heating/ventilation nozzle housing, release the outer clips securing the airbag cover. If a tool is used to release the clips, ensure that the tool always points towards the centre of the airbag cover, **not** into the facia towards the airbag **(see illustration)**.

12 Work around the edge of the airbag cover, and release the remaining securing clips, then lift the cover from the facia.

13 Unscrew the nut and the Torx screw securing the airbag cover strap to the facia,

then withdraw the cover and strap **(see illustration)**.

14 Unscrew the three Torx bolts securing the airbag, then carefully lift the airbag from the facia **(see illustration)**.

15 Disconnect the two wiring connectors from the rear of the airbag, noting the routing of the wiring, then withdraw the airbag from the facia, and store it in a safe place, with reference to the precautions given in Section 26 **(see illustration)**.

Refitting

16 Refitting is a reversal of removal, bearing in mind the following points.
  a) *Make sure that the wiring harness is routed as noted before removal.*
  b) *Make sure that the wiring connectors are securely reconnected.*
  c) *Make sure that the airbag cover strap is not twisted.*

Electronic control unit

17 In order to remove the airbag electronic control unit, it is necessary to drill an access hole into the facia to reach one of the control unit securing screws. Due to the risk of damage to the control unit during this operation, it is recommended that removal

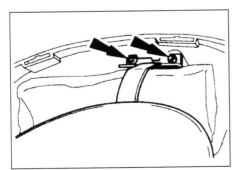

27.13 Unscrew the nut and Torx screw securing the airbag cover strap

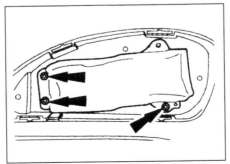

27.14 Unscrew the three airbag securing bolts (arrowed)

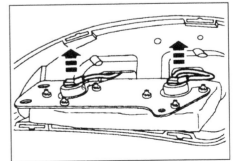

27.15 Disconnect the airbag wiring connectors (arrowed)

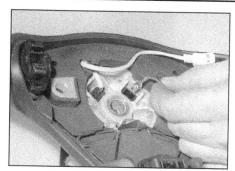

27.22 Disconnect the wiring connectors from the rotary switch assembly

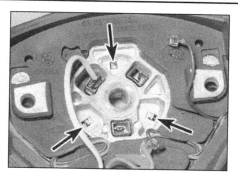

27.23 Release the three rotary switch assembly retaining lugs (arrowed)

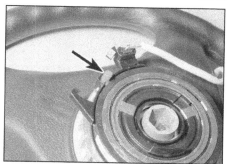

27.24 Depress the locking pin (arrowed) to centralise the rotary switch (viewed with switch fitted to steering wheel)

and refitting of the control unit is entrusted to a Ford dealer.

Airbag rotary switch

Removal

18 Disconnect the battery negative lead, with reference to Chapter 5A.

19 Remove the steering column shrouds, with reference to Chapter 11, Section 29, if necessary.

20 Remove the driver's airbag unit as described previously in this Section.

21 Remove the steering wheel as described in Chapter 10.

22 Disconnect the wiring connectors from the rotary switch assembly **(see illustration)**.

23 Carefully release the three retaining lugs, then withdraw the rotary switch from the steering column **(see illustration)**.

Refitting

Caution: The rotary switch centralising procedure described in the following paragraphs must be carried out before refitting the assembly. If there is any doubt about the centralisation of the switch, repeat the centralising procedure.

24 Depress the locking pin at the lower left-hand corner of the rotary switch **(see illustration)**.

25 Rotate the inner switch rotor fully anti-clockwise against the outer rotor until tight.

26 Rotate the inner switch rotor approximately 3.75 turns clockwise, then release the locking pin. Ensure that the inner rotor is locked in position.

27 Refit the switch using a reversal of the removal procedure, then refit the steering wheel as described in Chapter 10, and refit the driver's airbag as described previously in this Section.

Side airbags

28 The side airbags are located internally within the front seat back and no attempt should be made to remove them. Any suspected problems with the side airbag system should be referred to a Ford dealer.

H32233

Central fusebox (in passenger compartment)

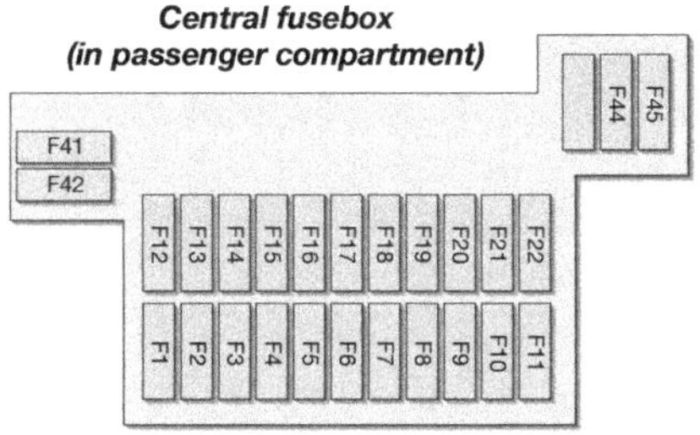

F45
F44

F22	F11
F21	F10
F20	F9
F19	F8
F18	F7
F17	F6
F16	F5
F15	F4
F14	F3
F13	F2
F12	F1

F41 F42

Central fusebox

Fuse	Rating	Circuit protected
F1	15A	Cigar lighter
F2	20A	Interior lights, clock, radio memory
F3	–	Not used
F4	15A	Heated rear screen/exterior mirrors
F5	20A	Horn, alarm
F6	10A	LH sidelight
F7	10A	RH sidelight
F8	15A	Central locking, electric mirrors
F9	15A	Seat height adjustment
F10	15A	Heated front seats
F11	30A	Central locking, electric windows
F12	20A	Wiper motor, screen washer pump
F13	15A	Brake light, instrument panel
F14	10A	Air bag
F15	10A	Heated mirrors
F16	30A	Heater blower motor
F17	15A	Direction indicators
F18	15A	Ignition
F19	10A	Engine management, alarm, radio
F20	30/10A	Headlight washer (Scandinavia only) Dim/dip (RHD only)
F21	–	Not used
F22	10A	Diagnostic plug
F41	10A	Rear fog light (depending on country)
F42	10A	Rear fog light (depending on country)
F43	10A	Daytime running lights (Scandinavia only) High beam locking diode (RHD only)
F44	20A	Door locking module
F45	15A	Luggage compartment release (central locking only)

NOTE: Fuses and wire colour in *italic* refer to post 09/1999

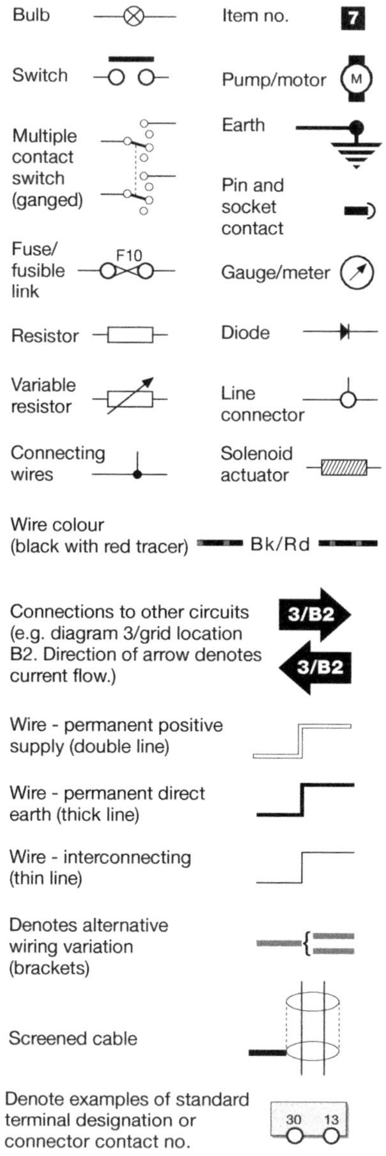

Auxiliary fusebox (in engine bay)

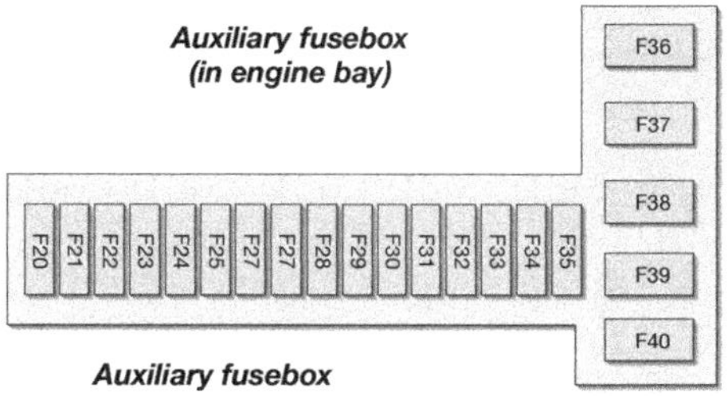

F36	F37	F38	F39	F40

F35
F34
F33
F32
F31
F30
F29
F28
F27
F27
F25
F24
F23
F22
F21
F20

Auxiliary fusebox

Fuse	Rating	Circuit protected
F1	–	Protection diode for EEC V relay
F2	–	Not used
F3	–	Not used
F23	10A	LH main beam
F24	10A	RH main beam
F25	10A	LH low beam
F26	10A	RH low beam
F27	15A	Lambda sensor (petrol) or Fuel heater (diesel)
F28	15A	Engine management
F29	20A	Reversing lights/compressor clutch (a/c)
F30	3A	ABS module
F31	30A	ABS module
F32	3A	EEC V ignition module
F33	30A	ABS module
F34	25A	Transmission
F35	10A	Fuel pump (petrol) or PATS module (diesel engine)
F36	3A 60A	Engine management, blower, fuel pump glow plug (diesel)
F37	40A	Heated windscreen
F38	60A	Central locking, heated rear screen
F39	60A	Headlight washer
F40	60A	Ignition lock

Earth locations

E1	Engine compartment LH side
E2	'A' pillar passenger's side
E3	Vehicle rear end LH side
E4	'A' pillar driver's side
E5	Vehicle rear end RH side
E6	'A' pillar driver's side
E7	On radiator LH side
E8	'A' pillar passenger's side
E9	LH 'A' pillar
E10	Engine compartment front LH side
E11	Engine compartment front RH side
E12	Under centre console
E13	On steering column
E14	Cargo space door LH side (Courier)
E15	Cargo space door RH side (Courier)
E16	In tailgate

Key to symbols

⊗	Bulb
	Switch
	Multiple contact switch (ganged)
F10	Fuse/fusible link
	Resistor
	Variable resistor
	Connecting wires
	Wire colour (black with red tracer) — Bk/Rd
3/B2	Connections to other circuits (e.g. diagram 3/grid location B2. Direction of arrow denotes current flow.)
	Wire - permanent positive supply (double line)
	Wire - permanent direct earth (thick line)
	Wire - interconnecting (thin line)
	Denotes alternative wiring variation (brackets)
	Screened cable
30 13	Denote examples of standard terminal designation or connector contact no.

7	Item no.
Ⓜ	Pump/motor
	Earth
	Pin and socket contact
	Gauge/meter
	Diode
	Line connector
	Solenoid actuator

Diagram 1 : Information for wiring diagrams up to February 2000

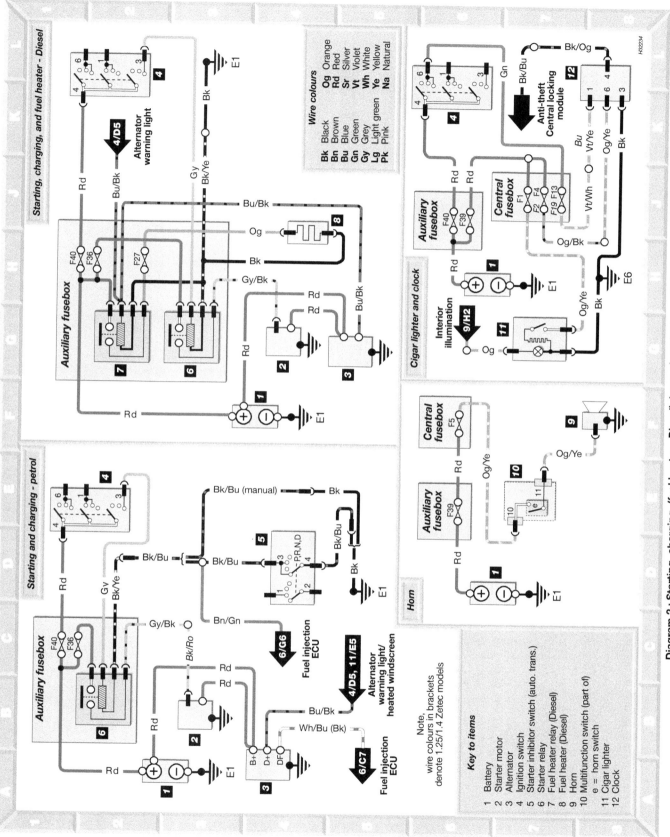

Diagram 2 : Starting, charging, (fuel heater - Diesel), horn, cigar lighter and clock up to Feb 2000

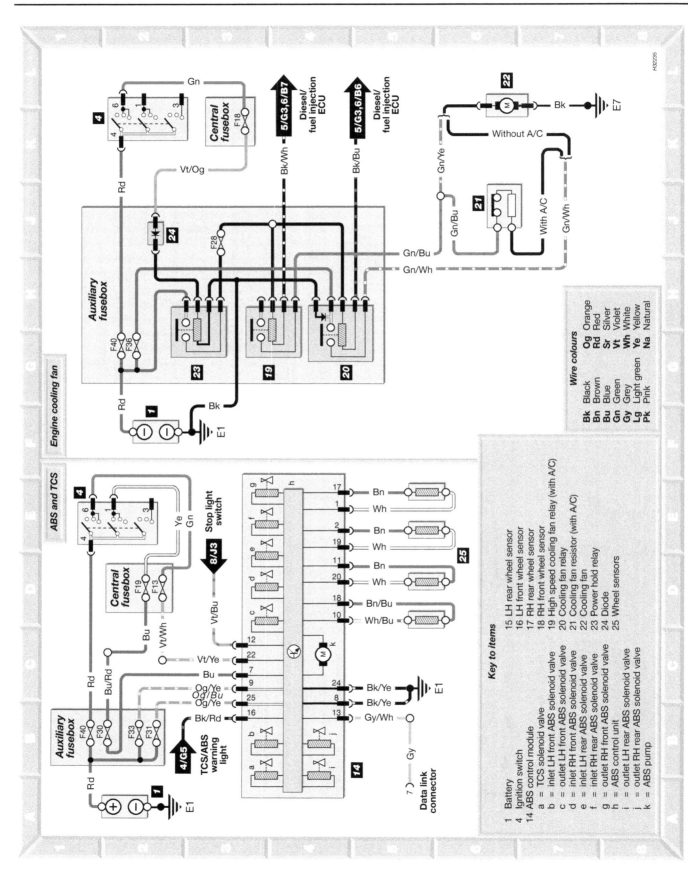

Diagram 3 : ABS/TCS and engine cooling fan up to Feb 2000

Wire colours

Bk	Black	**Og**	Orange
Bn	Brown	**Rd**	Red
Bu	Blue	**Sr**	Silver
Gn	Green	**Vt**	Violet
Gy	Grey	**Wh**	White
Lg	Light green	**Ye**	Yellow
Pk	Pink	**Na**	Natural

Key to items

1 Battery
4 Ignition switch
14 ABS control module

a = TCS solenoid valve
b = inlet LH front ABS solenoid valve
c = outlet LH front ABS solenoid valve
d = inlet RH front ABS solenoid valve
e = inlet LH rear ABS solenoid valve
f = inlet RH rear ABS solenoid valve
g = outlet LH rear ABS solenoid valve
h = ABS control unit
i = outlet LH rear ABS solenoid valve
j = outlet RH rear ABS solenoid valve
k = ABS pump

15 LH rear wheel sensor
16 LH front wheel sensor
17 RH rear wheel sensor
18 RH front wheel sensor
19 High speed cooling fan relay (with A/C)
20 Cooling fan relay
21 Cooling fan resistor (with A/C)
22 Cooling fan
23 Power hold relay
24 Diode
25 Wheel sensors

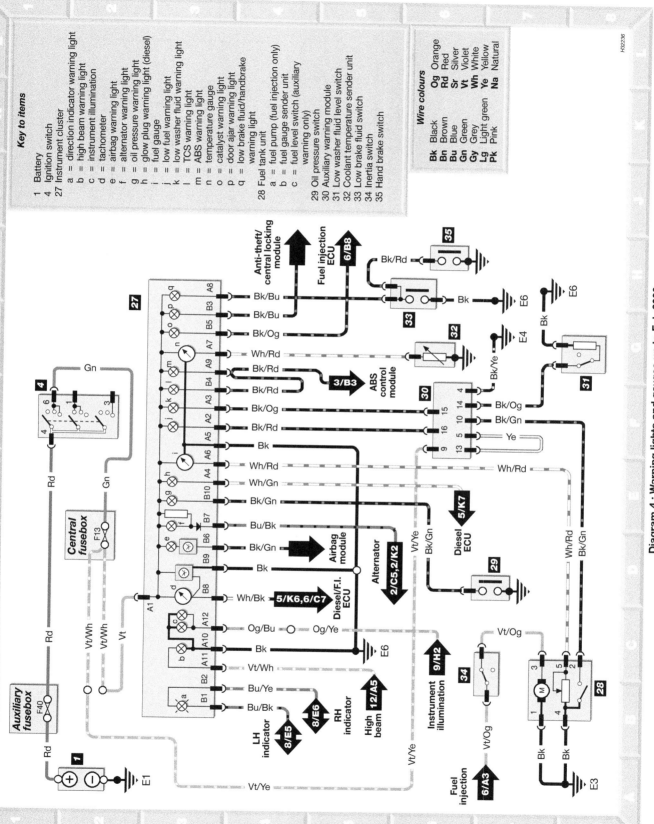

Key to items

1   Battery
4   Ignition switch
27 Instrument cluster
    a = direction indicator warning light
    b = high beam warning light
    c = instrument illumination
    d = tachometer
    e = airbag warning light
    f = alternator warning light
    g = oil pressure warning light
    h = glow plug warning light (diesel)
    i = fuel gauge
    j = low fuel warning light
    k = low washer fluid warning light
    l = TCS warning light
    m = ABS warning light
    n = temperature gauge
    o = catalyst warning light
    p = door ajar warning light
    q = low brake fluid/handbrake
        warning light
28 Fuel tank unit
    a = fuel pump (fuel injection only)
    b = fuel gauge sender unit
    c = fuel level switch (auxiliary
        warning only)
29 Oil pressure switch
30 Auxiliary warning module
31 Low washer fluid level switch
32 Coolant temperature sender unit
33 Low brake fluid switch
34 Inertia switch
35 Hand brake switch

Wire colours

Bk	Black	**Og**	Orange
Bn	Brown	**Rd**	Red
Bu	Blue	**Sr**	Silver
Gn	Green	**Vt**	Violet
Gy	Grey	**Wh**	White
Lg	Light green	**Ye**	Yellow
Pk	Pink	**Na**	Natural

Diagram 4 : Warning lights and gauges up to Feb 2000

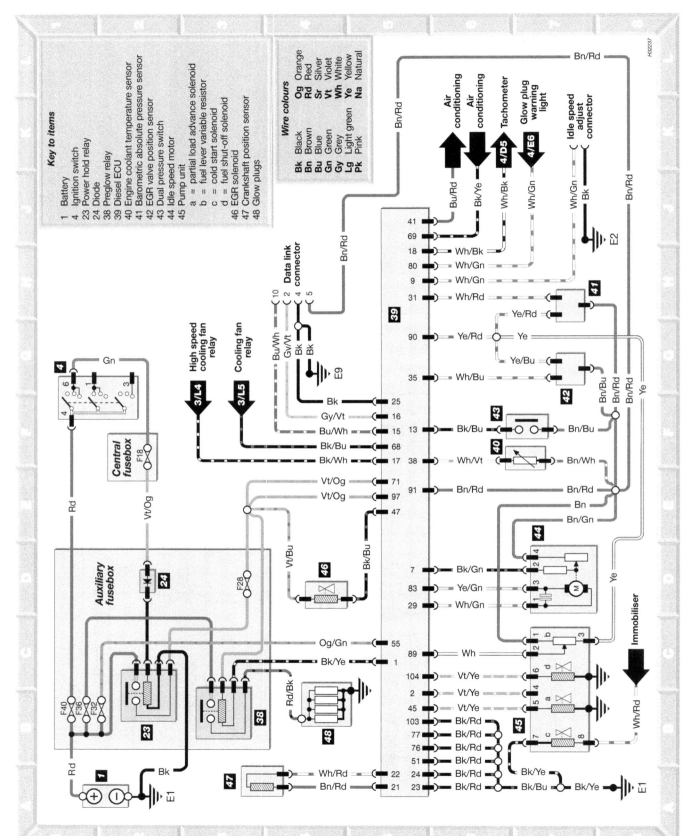

Diagram 5 : Typical diesel engine management up to Feb 2000

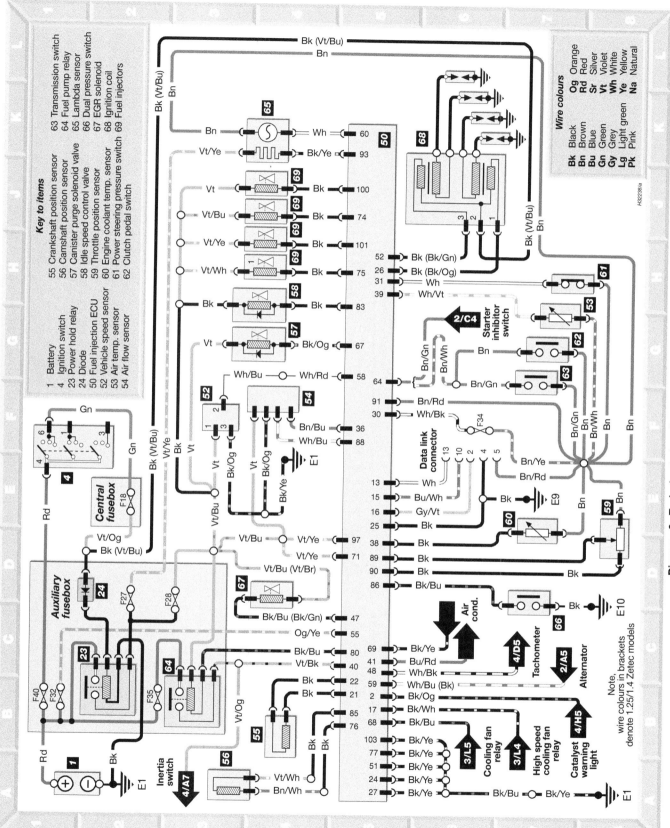

Key to items

1 Battery
4 Ignition switch
23 Power hold relay
24 Diode
50 Fuel injection ECU
52 Vehicle speed sensor
53 Air temp. sensor
54 Air flow sensor
55 Crankshaft position sensor
56 Camshaft position sensor
57 Canister purge solenoid valve
58 Idle speed control valve
59 Throttle position sensor
60 Engine coolant temp. sensor
61 Power steering pressure switch
62 Clutch pedal switch
63 Transmission switch
64 Fuel pump relay
65 Lambda sensor
66 Dual pressure switch
67 EGR solenoid
68 Ignition coil
69 Fuel injectors

Wire colours

Bk Black	Og Orange
Bn Brown	Rd Red
Bu Blue	Sr Silver
Gn Green	Vt Violet
Gy Grey	Wh White
Lg Light green	Ye Yellow
Pk Pink	Na Natural

H32238/a

Diagram 6 : Typical petrol engine management up to Feb 2000

Note,
wire colours in brackets
denote 1.25/1.4 Zetec models

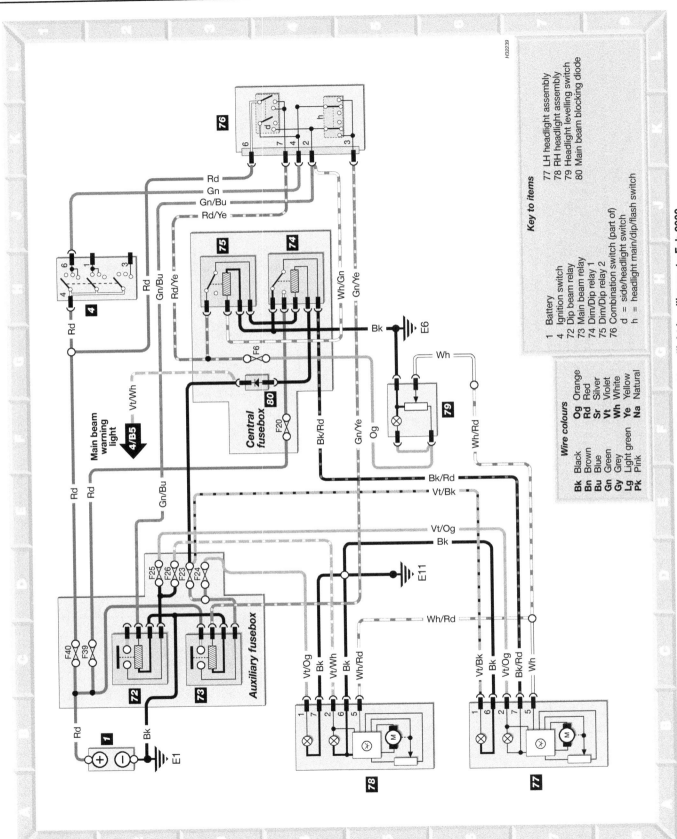

H32239

Key to items

1   Battery
4   Ignition switch
72 Dip beam relay
73 Main beam relay
74 Dim/Dip relay 1
75 Dim/Dip relay 2
76 Combination switch (part of)
    d = side/headlight switch
    h = headlight main/dip/flash switch
77 LH headlight assembly
78 RH headlight assembly
79 Headlight levelling switch
80 Main beam blocking diode

Wire colours

Bk	Black	**Og**	Orange
Bn	Brown	**Rd**	Red
Bu	Blue	**Sr**	Silver
Gn	Green	**Vt**	Violet
Gy	Grey	**Wh**	White
Lg	Light green	**Ye**	Yellow
Pk	Pink	**Na**	Natural

Main beam warning light

4/B5

Central fusebox

Auxiliary fusebox

Diagram 7 : Typical exterior lighting - headlights and headlight levelling up to Feb 2000

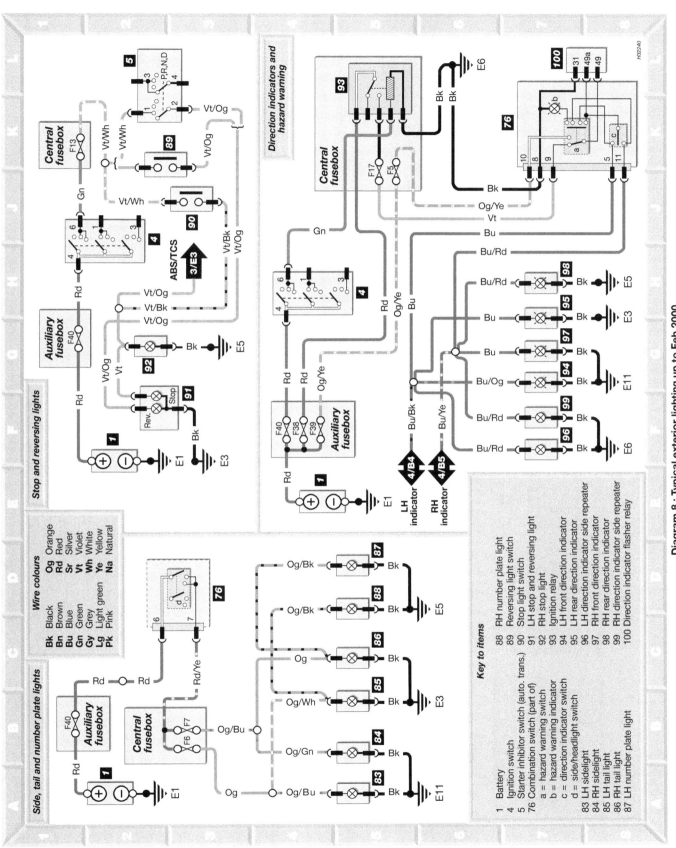

Diagram 8 : Typical exterior lighting up to Feb 2000

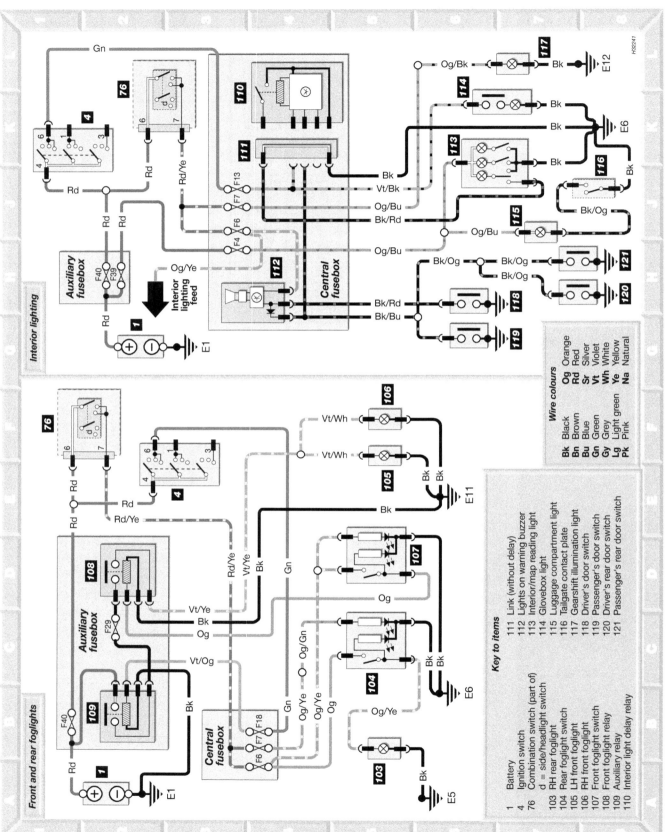

Interior lighting

Front and rear foglights

Wire colours

Bk	Black	**Og**	Orange
Bn	Brown	**Rd**	Red
Bu	Blue	**Sr**	Silver
Gn	Green	**Vt**	Violet
Gy	Grey	**Wh**	White
Lg	Light green	**Ye**	Yellow
Pk	Pink	**Na**	Natural

Key to items

1	Battery	111	Link (without delay)
4	Ignition switch	112	Lights on warning buzzer
76	Combination switch (part of)	113	Interior/map reading light
	d = side/headlight switch	114	Glovebox light
103	RH rear foglight	115	Luggage compartment light
104	Rear foglight switch	116	Tailgate contact plate
105	LH front foglight	117	Gearshift illumination light
106	RH front foglight	118	Driver's door switch
107	Front foglight switch	119	Passenger's door switch
108	Front foglight relay	120	Driver's rear door switch
109	Auxiliary relay	121	Passenger's rear door switch
110	Interior light delay relay		

Diagram 9 : Typical exterior lighting continued and interior lighting up to Feb 2000

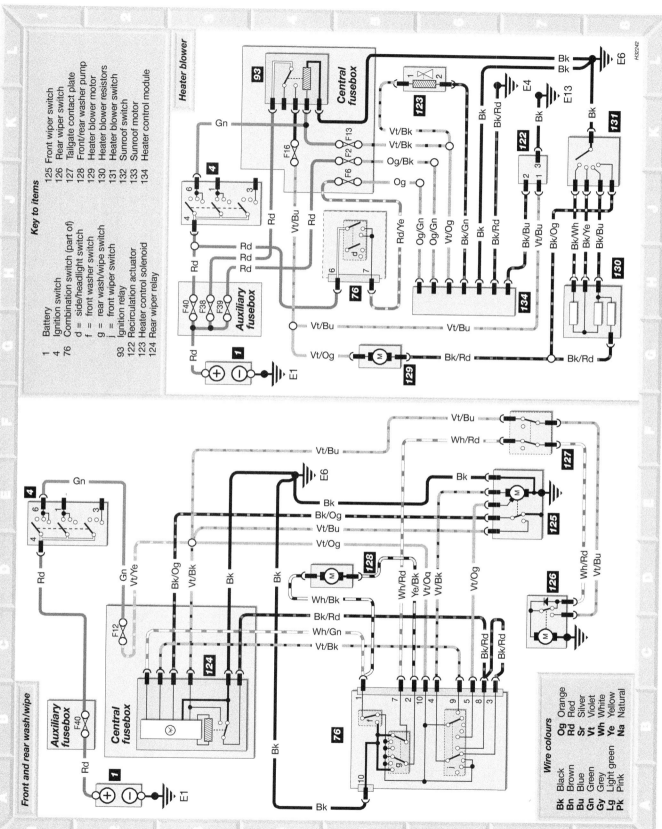

Diagram 10 : Wash/wipe and heater blower up to Feb 2000

Key to items

1 Battery
4 Ignition switch
76 Combination switch (part of)
   d = side/headlight switch
   f = front washer switch
   g = rear wash/wipe switch
   j = front wiper switch
93 Ignition relay
122 Recirculation actuator
123 Heater control solenoid
124 Rear wiper relay
125 Front wiper switch
126 Rear wiper switch
127 Tailgate contact plate
128 Front/rear washer pump
129 Heater blower motor
130 Heater blower resistors
131 Heater blower switch
132 Sunroof switch
133 Sunroof motor
134 Heater control module

Wire colours

Bk Black   Og Orange
Bn Brown   Rd Red
Bu Blue   Sr Silver
Gn Green   Vt Violet
Gy Grey   Wh White
Lg Light green Ye Yellow
Pk Pink   Na Natural

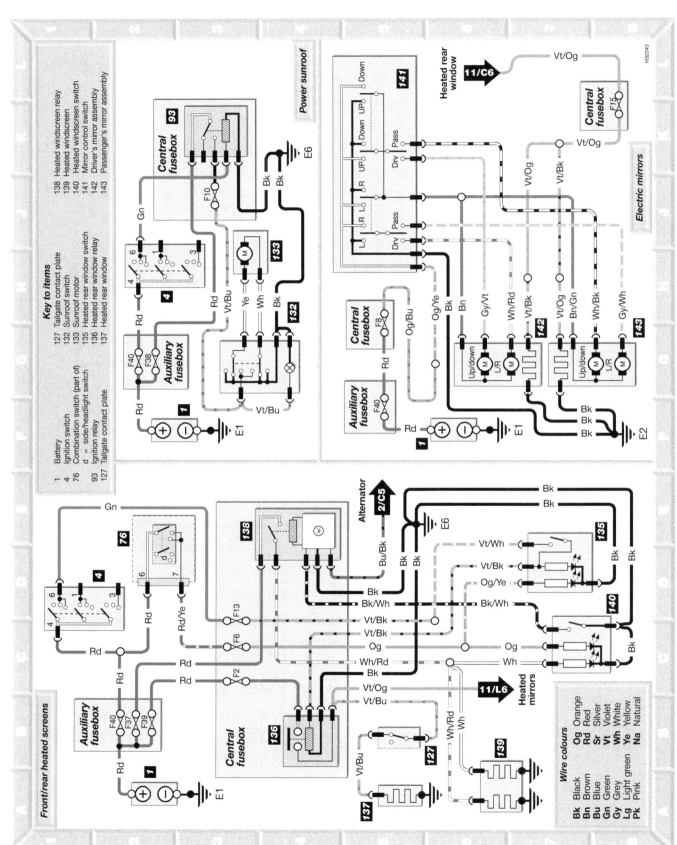

Key to items

127 Tailgate contact plate
132 Sunroof switch
133 Heated motor
135 Heated rear window switch
136 Heated rear window relay
137 Heated rear window

138 Heated windscreen relay
139 Heated windscreen
140 Heated windscreen switch
141 Mirror control switch
142 Driver's mirror assembly
143 Passenger's mirror assembly

1 Battery
4 Ignition switch
76 Combination switch (part of)
   d = side/headlight switch
93 Ignition relay
127 Tailgate contact plate

Power sunroof

Electric mirrors

Front/rear heated screens

Wire colours

Bk	Black	Og	Orange
Bn	Brown	Rd	Red
Bu	Blue	Sr	Silver
Gn	Green	Vt	Violet
Gy	Grey	Wh	White
Lg	Light green	Ye	Yellow
Pk	Pink	Na	Natural

Diagram 11 : Heated front/rear screens, electric mirrors and sunroof up to Feb 2000

H32243

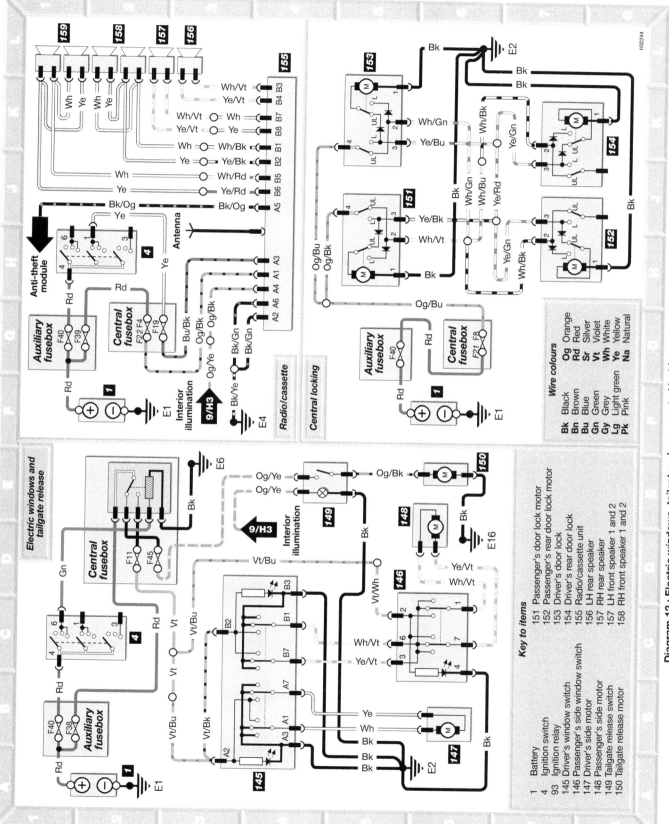

H32244

Wire colours

Bk	Black	**Og**	Orange
Bn	Brown	**Rd**	Red
Bu	Blue	**Sr**	Silver
Gn	Green	**Vt**	Violet
Gy	Grey	**Wh**	White
Lg	Light green	**Ye**	Yellow
Pk	Pink	**Na**	Natural

Key to items

1	Battery
4	Ignition switch
93	Ignition relay
145	Driver's window switch
146	Passenger's side window switch
147	Driver's side motor
148	Passenger's side motor
149	Tailgate release switch
150	Tailgate release motor
151	Passenger's door lock motor
152	Passenger's rear door lock motor
153	Driver's door lock
154	Driver's rear door lock
155	Radio/cassette unit
156	LH rear speaker
157	RH rear speaker
157	LH front speaker 1 and 2
158	RH front speaker 1 and 2

Diagram 12 : Electric windows, tailgate release, central locking and radio/cassette up to Feb 2000

Anti-theft module

Auxiliary fusebox

Central fusebox

Radio/cassette

Central locking

Electric windows and tailgate release

Interior illumination

Fiesta wiring diagrams (from March 2000) **Diagram 1**

Key to symbols

Bulb	—⊗—	Item no.	**2**

Switch —○ ○—

Pump/motor (M)

Multiple contact switch (ganged)

Earth point and location (E22)

Fuse/fusible link and current rating — **F5** 30A

Gauge/meter (↗)

Resistor —▭—

Diode —▶|—

Variable resistor

Wire splice or soldered joint

Connecting wires

Solenoid actuator

Plug and socket contact ■▶

Light emitting diode (LED) ▶|

Wire colour (brown with black tracer) ■■■ Bn/Bk ■■■

Screened cable

Dashed outline denotes part of a larger item, containing in this case an electronic or solid state device.
6 - unspecified connector pin 6.
C2/5 - connector no. 2, pin 9.

Key to circuits

Diagram 1	Information for wiring diagrams
Diagram 2	Starting, charging, horn and power steering
Diagram 3	Engine cooling fan, heating and ventilation
Diagram 4	Heating and ventilation (models with A/C)
Diagram 5	Instrument cluster
Diagram 6	Side, tail, stop, reversing and number plate lights, headlights and headlight levelling
Diagram 7	Direction indicators, hazard warning, fog lights
Diagram 8	Interior lighting, ABS, clock, alarm indicator and cigar lighter
Diagram 9	Sunroof, diagnostic connector, supplementary restraint and audio system
Diagram 10	Electric mirrors, heated front and rear screen
Diagram 11	Front and rear wash/wipe, electric windows and heated seats
Diagram 12	Central locking
Diagram 13	Engine management 1.3L Endura E
Diagram 14	Engine management 1.25L Zetec SE
Diagram 15	Engine management 1.4L Zetec SE
Diagram 16	Engine management 1.6L Zetec SE
Diagram 17	Engine management 1.8L Diesel Endura DE
Diagram 18	Engine management 1.8L Diesel Endura DI

Earth locations

E1	Engine compartment LH side
E3	Vehicle rear end LH side
E4	Driver's 'A' pillar
E5	Vehicle rear end RH side
E6	Driver's 'A' pillar
E7	LH front engine compartment
E9	Passenger's 'A' pillar
E11	RH front engine compartment
E12	Under centre console
E13	On steering column
E14	LH cargo space door (Courier)
E15	RH cargo space door (Courier)
E17	Under centre console
E18	On steering column
E19	Engine compartment LH side

Central fusebox

Fuse	Rating	Circuit protected
F1	15A	Power socket
F2	7.5A	Interior lights, clock
F3	10A	Rear foglight, alarm
F4	20A	Heated rear screen
F5	15A	Horn, hazard flasher
F6	7.5A	LH side light
F7	7.5A	RH side light
F8	15A	Central locking, electric mirrors
F9	-	Spare
F10	15A	Heated front seats, electric sunroof
F11	30A	Central locking, electric windows
F12	20A	Wiper motor, windscreen washer pump
F13	15A	Stop light, instrument cluster
F14	10A	Airbag
F15	7.5A	Heated mirrors
F16	30A	Heater blower motor
F17	15A	Direction indicators
F18	15A	Engine compartment, multifunction electronic module
F19	7.5A	Engine management, radio memory, auxiliary relay
F20	-	Spare
F21	-	Spare
F22	10A	Diagnostic socket

Auxiliary fusebox

Fuse	Rating	Circuit protected
F23	10A	LH main beam
F24	30A	ABS control unit
F25	10A	RH main beam
F26	30A	ABS control unit, cooling fan (models without A/C)
F27	10A	LH dipped beam
F28	3A	ABS control unit
F29	10A	RH dipped beam
F30	15A	Engine management
F31	30A	Diesel pump - 1.8L Diesel Endura DI
	20A	Fuel pump - 1.25L/1.4L Zetec SE
	10A	Fuel pump - 1.3 Endura E/1.6L Zetec SE
F32	20A	A/C clutch, front fog lights
F33	3A	Engine management control unit
F34	30A	Octane adjust
F35	-	Spare
F36	10A	Catalytic converter
	15A	Fuel heater - 1.8L Diesel Endura DE
F37	3A	Engine management - 1.8L Diesel Endura DI
F38	30A	Glow plug heater - 1.8L Diesel Endura DI
F51	60A	Engine management, glow plug heater (Diesel), fuel pump
F52	40A	Heated front screen
F53	60A	Ignition
F54	60A	Glow plug heater - 1.8L Diesel Endura DI
F55	60A	Battery
F56	60A	Ignition

Wire colours

Bk	Black	**Na**	Natural
Bn	Brown	**Og**	Orange
Bu	Blue	**Rd**	Red
DG	Dark green	**Sr**	Silver
Gn	Green	**Vt**	Violet
Gy	Grey	**Wh**	White
LG	Light green	**Ye**	Yellow

Key to items

1 Battery
2 Ignition switch
3 Auxiliary fusebox
   a = starter inhibitor relay
   b = fuel heater relay
   c = power hold relay
4 Central fusebox
5 Alternator
6 Starter motor
7 Horn switch
8 Multi-function switch
9 Horn
10 Power steering pump
11 Power steering pump relay

Diagram 2

H32246

Starting system

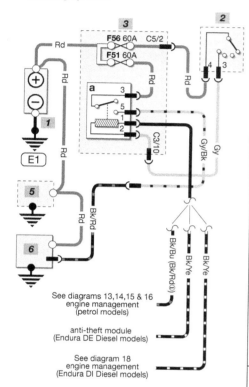

See diagrams 13,14,15 & 16
engine management
(petrol models)

anti-theft module
(Endura DE Diesel models)

See diagram 18
engine management
(Endura DI Diesel models)

① 1.25L Zetec SE only

Horn

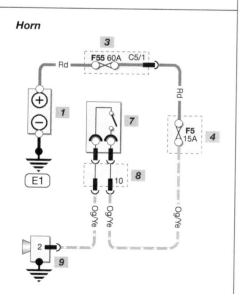

Charging system - all models except
(1.8L Diesel Endura DE)

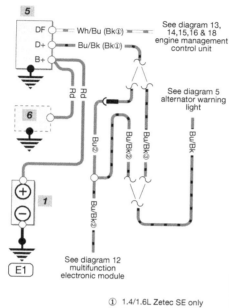

See diagram 13,
14,15,16 & 18
engine management
control unit

See diagram 5
alternator warning
light

See diagram 12
multifunction
electronic module

① 1.4/1.6L Zetec SE only
② With heated windscreen
③ Without heated windscreen

Charging system
(1.8L Diesel Endura DE)

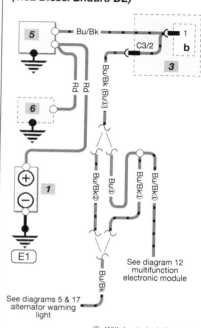

See diagram 12
multifunction
electronic module

See diagrams 5 & 17
alternator warning
light

① With heated windscreen
② Without heated windscreen

Power steering system

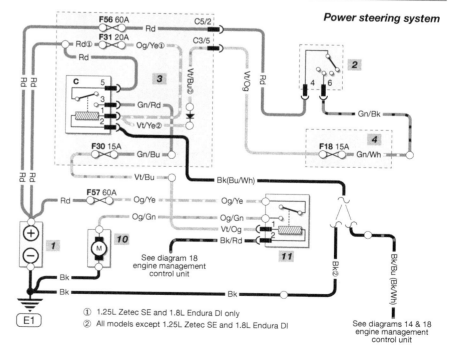

See diagram 18
engine management
control unit

See diagrams 14 & 18
engine management
control unit

① 1.25L Zetec SE and 1.8L Endura DI only
② All models except 1.25L Zetec SE and 1.8L Endura DI

Wire colours

Bk	Black	**Na**	Natural
Bn	Brown	**Og**	Orange
Bu	Blue	**Rd**	Red
DG	Dark green	**Sr**	Silver
Gn	Green	**Vt**	Violet
Gy	Grey	**Wh**	White
LG	Light green	**Ye**	Yellow

Key to items

1 Battery
2 Ignition switch
3 Auxiliary fusebox
  c = power hold relay
  d = cooling fan relay
  e = high speed cooling fan relay
4 Central fusebox
  a = ignition relay

15 Engine cooling fan
16 Engine cooling fan resistor
17 Heater control
  a = off
  b = recirculation on
  c = recirculation switch illumination
  d = illumination
  e = temp. selector switch

18 Heater control solenoid valve
19 Heater blower motor
20 Heater blower switch
21 Heater blower motor
22 Recirculation air actuator

Diagram 3

H32247

Engine cooling fan (models without A/C)

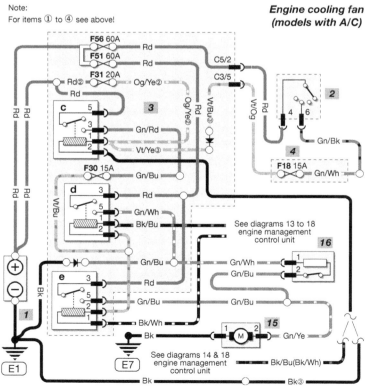

Note:
For items ① to ④ see above!

Engine cooling fan (models with A/C)

① Petrol models only
② 1.25L Zetec SE and 1.8L Endura DI only
③ All models except 1.25L Zetec SE and 1.8L Endura DI
④ Diesel models only

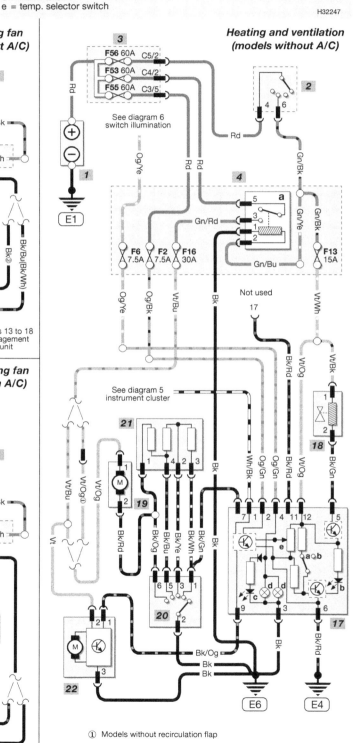

Heating and ventilation (models without A/C)

① Models without recirculation flap

Wire colours

Bk	Black	**Na**	Natural
Bn	Brown	**Og**	Orange
Bu	Blue	**Rd**	Red
DG	Dark green	**Sr**	Silver
Gn	Green	**Vt**	Violet
Gy	Grey	**Wh**	White
LG	Light green	**Ye**	Yellow

Key to items

1 Battery
2 Ignition switch
3 Auxiliary fusebox
  c = power hold relay
  d = cooling fan relay
  e = high speed cooling fan relay
  f = auxiliary relay
  g = A/C switch relay (all models
    except 1.25L Zetec SE)
  h = A/C wide open throttle relay
4 Central fusebox
  a = ignition relay

15 Engine cooling fan
16 Engine cooling fan resistor
17 Heater control
  a = off
  b = recirculation on
  c = recirculation switch illumination
  d = illumination
  e = temp. selector switch
  f = A/C switch illumination
  g = A/C on
18 Heater control solenoid valve
19 Heater blower motor

20 Heater blower switch
21 Heater blower motor
22 Recirculation air actuator
23 A/C compressor cycling switch
24 A/C dual pressure switch
25 A/C compressor clutch
26 A/C compressor clutch diode

Diagram 4

H32248

*Heating and ventilation
(models with A/C)*

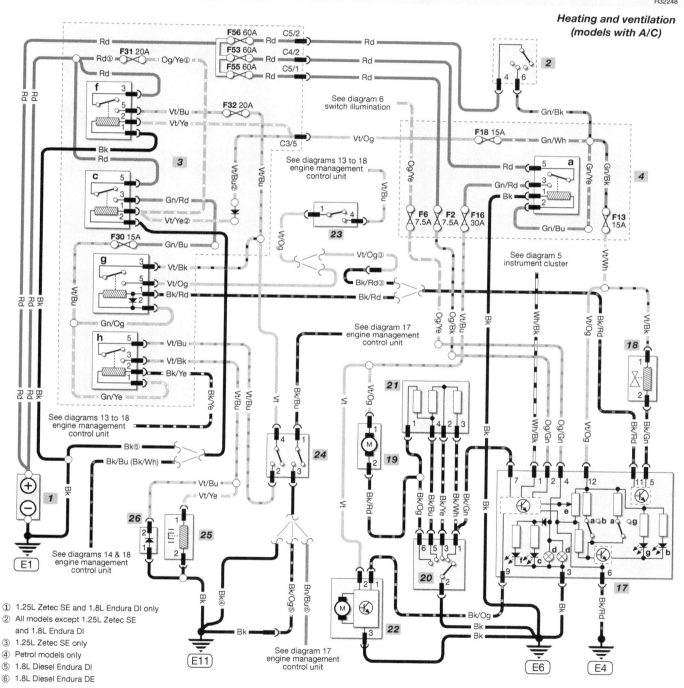

① 1.25L Zetec SE and 1.8L Endura DI only
② All models except 1.25L Zetec SE
  and 1.8L Endura DI
③ 1.25L Zetec SE only
④ Petrol models only
⑤ 1.8L Diesel Endura DI
⑥ 1.8L Diesel Endura DE

Diagram 5

Wire colours

Bk	Black	**Na**	Natural
Bn	Brown	**Og**	Orange
Bu	Blue	**Rd**	Red
DG	Dark green	**Sr**	Silver
Gn	Green	**Vt**	Violet
Gy	Grey	**Wh**	White
LG	Light green	**Ye**	Yellow

Key to items

1 Battery
2 Ignition switch
3 Auxiliary fusebox
  c = power hold relay
4 Central fusebox
30 Brake fluid level switch
31 Handbrake switch
32 Oil pressure switch
33 Fuel gauge sender unit/fuel pump
34 Low washer fluid level switch
35 Coolant temperature sensor
  (1.8L Diesel Endura DE only)

36 Instrument cluster
  a = tachometer
  b = coolant temperature gauge
  c = glow plug warning light
  d = fuel gauge
  e = low fuel warning light
  f = speedometer
  g = control unit
  h = alternator warning light
  i = oil pressure warning light
  j = check engine warning light
  k = bkake system warning light

36 Instrument cluster continued
  l = ABS warning light
  m = TCS warning light
  n = instrument illumination
  o = low washer fluid warning light
  p = door ajar warning light
  q = airbag warning light
  r = main beam warning light
  s = LH indicator warning light
  t = RH indicator warning light
37 Vehicle speed sensor

H32249

Instrument cluster

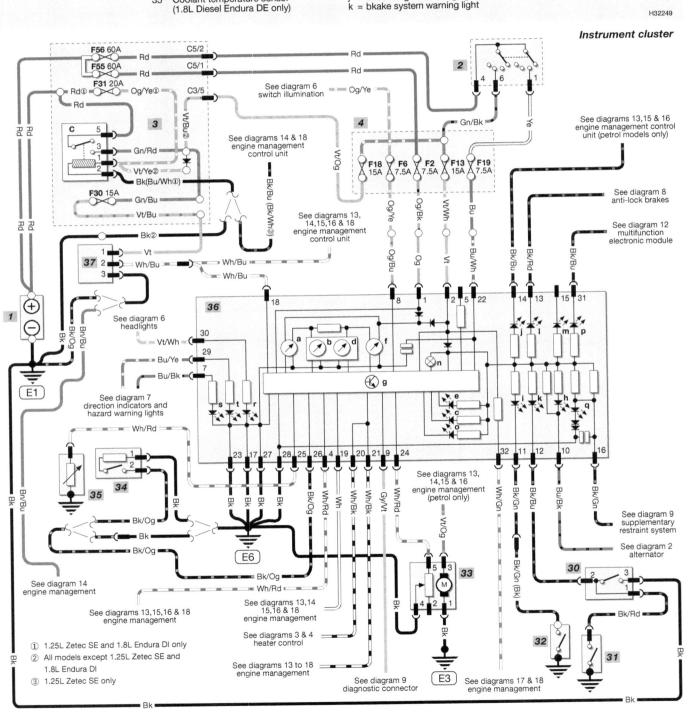

① 1.25L Zetec SE and 1.8L Endura DI only
② All models except 1.25L Zetec SE and 1.8L Endura DI
③ 1.25L Zetec SE only

Wire colours

Bk	Black	**Na**	Natural
Bn	Brown	**Og**	Orange
Bu	Blue	**Rd**	Red
DG	Dark green	**Sr**	Silver
Gn	Green	**Vt**	Violet
Gy	Grey	**Wh**	White
LG	Light green	**Ye**	Yellow

Key to items

1 Battery
2 Ignition switch
3 Auxiliary fusebox
  i = dipped beam relay
  j = main beam relay
4 Central fusebox
8 Multifunction switch
  a = flash/dip/main
  b = side/headlight
40 LH headlight assembly

41 RH headlight assembly
42 LH rear light assembly
  a = tail
  b = stop light
  c = reversing light
43 RH rear light assembly
  a = tail
  b = stop light
  c = reversing light
44 LH number plate light

45 RH number plate light
46 High level brake light
47 Stop light switch
48 Starter inhibitor/reversing light switch
49 Transmission range sensor
50 Headlight levelling rheostat

Diagram 6

H32250

Headlights

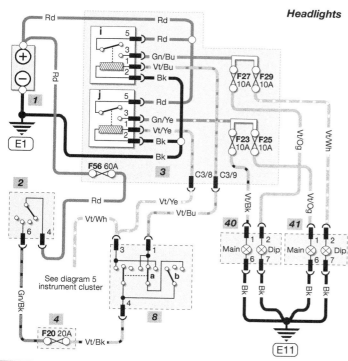

Side, tail, number plate lights and switch illumination feed

See diagrams 3,4,5,7,9 & 10
Switch illumination feed

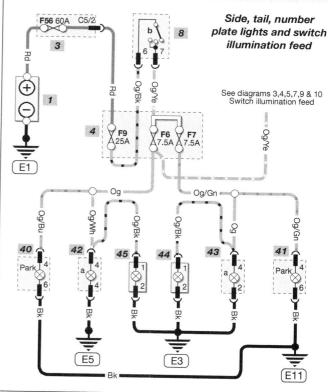

Stop and reversing lights

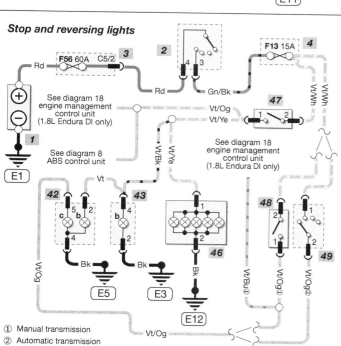

See diagram 18
engine management
control unit
(1.8L Endura DI only)

See diagram 8
ABS control unit

See diagram 18
engine management
control unit
(1.8L Endura DI only)

① Manual transmission
② Automatic transmission

Headlight levelling

See diagram 6
Headlights

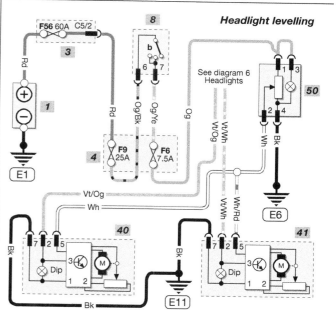

Wire colours

Bk	Black	**Na**	Natural
Bn	Brown	**Og**	Orange
Bu	Blue	**Rd**	Red
DG	Dark green	**Sr**	Silver
Gn	Green	**Vt**	Violet
Gy	Grey	**Wh**	White
LG	Light green	**Ye**	Yellow

Key to items

1 Battery
2 Ignition switch
3 Auxiliary fusebox
  f = auxiliary relay
  k = front foglight relay
4 Central fusebox
  a = ignition relay
8 Multifunction switch
  c = hazard warning light
  d = direction indicator

40 LH headlight assembly
41 RH headlight assembly
42 LH rear light assembly
  d = direction indicator
43 RH rear light assembly
  d = direction indicator
  e = foglight
55 Direction indicator flasher relay
56 LH indicator side repeater
57 RH indicator side repeater

58 Front foglight switch
59 LH front foglight
60 RH front foglight
61 Rear foglight switch
62 Multifunction electronic module
  a = rear foglight relay
  b = microprocessor
  c = voltage regulator (models
    with double locking)

Diagram 7

H32251

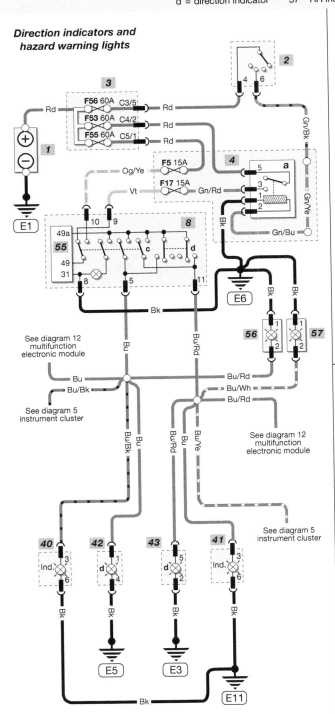

Direction indicators and hazard warning lights

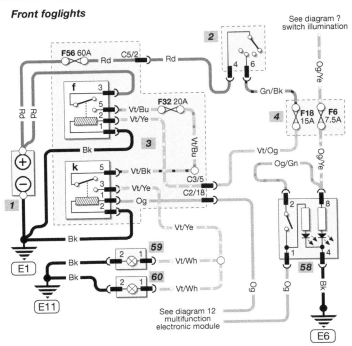

Front foglights

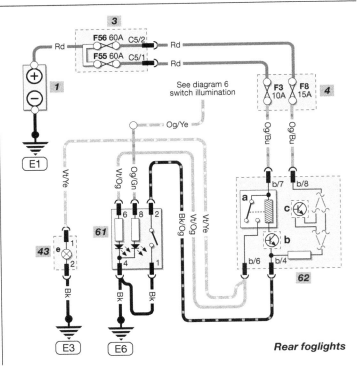

Rear foglights

Wire colours

Bk	Black	**Na**	Natural
Bn	Brown	**Og**	Orange
Bu	Blue	**Rd**	Red
DG	Dark green	**Sr**	Silver
Gn	Green	**Vt**	Violet
Gy	Grey	**Wh**	White
LG	Light green	**Ye**	Yellow

Key to items

1   Battery
2   Ignition switch
3   Auxiliary fusebox
4   Central fusebox
8   Multifunction switch
   b = side/headlight
62   Multifunction electronic module
   b = microprocessor
   c = voltage regulator
   d = buzzer
65   Front interior light
66   LH front door switch

67   RH front door switch
68   Gearshift illumination
69   Luggage compartment light
70   Tailgate contact plate
71   ABS control module
   a = ABS pump motor
   b = TCS solenoid valve
   c = LH front inlet solenoid valve
   d = LH front outlet solenoid valve
   e = RH front inlet solenoid valve
   f = RH front outlet solenoid valve
   g = LH rear inlet solenoid valve
   h = LH rear outlet solenoid valve

71   ABS control module (continued)
   i = RH rear inlet solenoid valve
   j = RH rear outlet solenoid valve
   k = control unit
72   LH front wheel sensor
73   LH rear wheel sensor
74   RH front wheel sensor
75   RH rear wheel sensor
76   Clock and alarm 'on' indicator
77   Cigar lighter

Diagram 8

H32252

Interior lighting

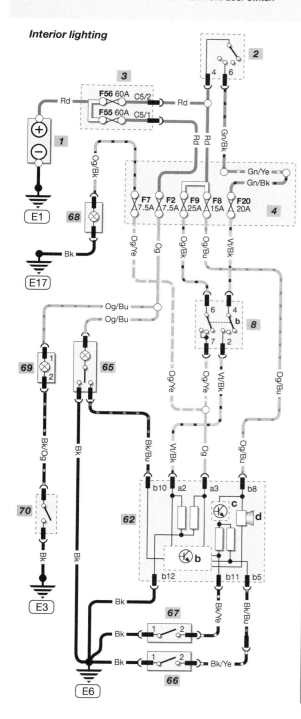

Anti-lock brakes

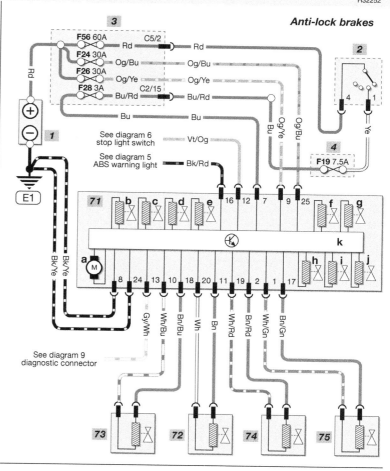

Clock, alarm 'on' indicator and cigar lighter

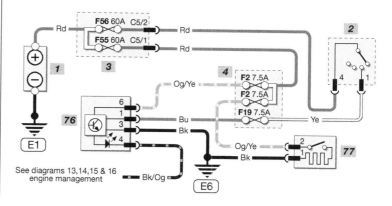

Wire colours

Bk	Black	**Na**	Natural
Bn	Brown	**Og**	Orange
Bu	Blue	**Rd**	Red
DG	Dark green	**Sr**	Silver
Gn	Green	**Vt**	Violet
Gy	Grey	**Wh**	White
LG	Light green	**Ye**	Yellow

Key to items

1 Battery
2 Ignition switch
3 Auxiliary fusebox
4 Central fusebox
 a = ignition relay
80 Sunroof switch
81 Sunroof motor
82 Airbag control unit
83 Driver's side airbag
84 Passenger's side airbag
85 Driver's airbag sensor
86 Passenger's airbag sensor
87 Driver's seat belt tensioner
88 Passenger's seat belt tensioner
89 Driver's airbag
90 Passenger's airbag
91 Steering wheel clock springs
92 Audio unit
93 LH front door speaker
94 LH front tweeter
95 LH rear speaker
96 RH front door speaker
97 RH front tweeter
98 RH rear speaker
99 Diagnostic connector

Diagram 9

H32253

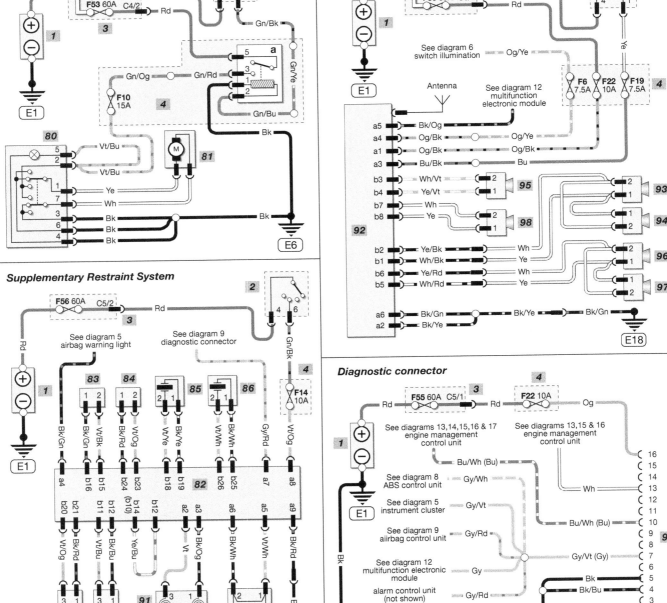

Electric sunroof

Audio system

Supplementary Restraint System

Diagnostic connector

Wire colours

Bk	Black	**Na**	Natural
Bn	Brown	**Og**	Orange
Bu	Blue	**Rd**	Red
DG	Dark green	**Sr**	Silver
Gn	Green	**Vt**	Violet
Gy	Grey	**Wh**	White
LG	Light green	**Ye**	Yellow

Key to items

1 Battery
2 Ignition switch
3 Auxiliary fusebox
4 Central fusebox
b = heated rear window relay
c = heated rear window timer relay
d = heated windscreen relay

70 Tailgate contact plate
103 Mirror control switch
104 Driver's mirror assembly
105 Passenger's mirror assembly
106 Heated rear window element
107 LH heated rear window element
108 RH heated rear window element

109 Heated rear window switch
110 LH heated windscreen element
111 RH heated windscreen element
112 Heated windscreen switch

Diagram 10

H32254

Electric mirrors

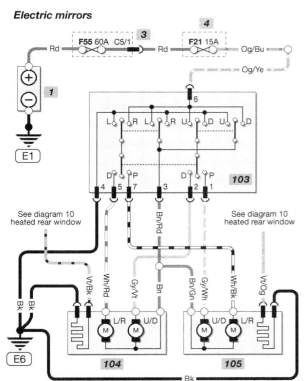

Heated windscreen

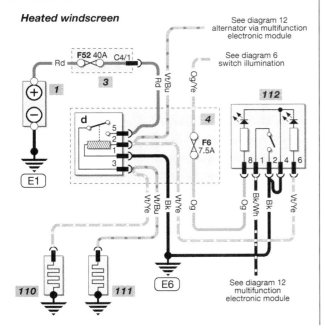

Heated rear window (models without timer)

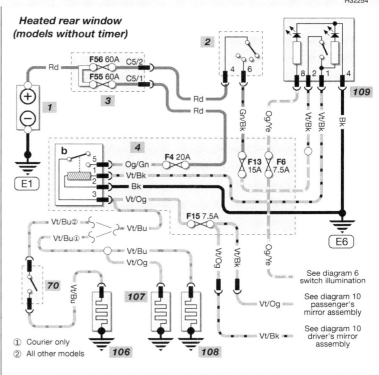

Heated rear window (models with timer)

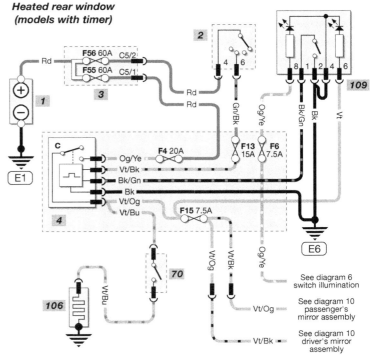

Wire colours

Bk	Black	**Na**	Natural
Bn	Brown	**Og**	Orange
Bu	Blue	**Rd**	Red
DG	Dark green	**Sr**	Silver
Gn	Green	**Vt**	Violet
Gy	Grey	**Wh**	White
LG	Light green	**Ye**	Yellow

Key to items

1 Battery
2 Ignition switch
3 Auxiliary fusebox
4 Central fusebox
   a = ignition relay
62 Multifunction switch
   c = front wiper
   d = front washer
   e = rear wash/wipe

70 Tailgate contact plate
115 Front wiper motor
116 Rear wiper motor
117 Front/rear washer pump
118 Driver's electric window switch
119 Passenger's electric window switch
120 Driver's electric window motor
121 Passenger's electric window motor
122 LH front seat heater switch

123 RH front seat heater switch
124 LH heated seat
125 RH heated seat

Diagram 11

H32255

Front and rear wash/wipe

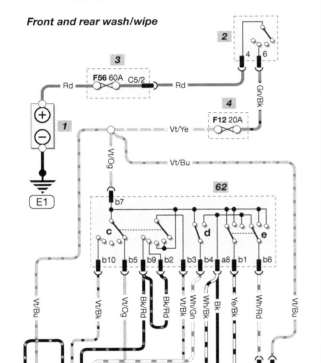

Electric windows

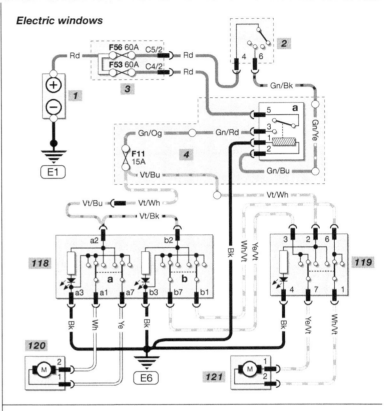

Heated seats

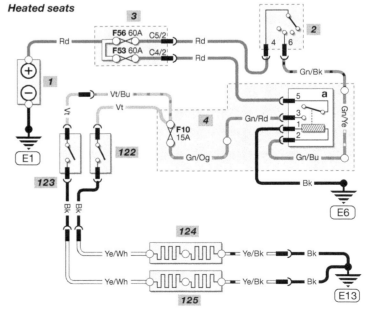

Wire colours

Bk	Black	**Na**	Natural
Bn	Brown	**Og**	Orange
Bu	Blue	**Rd**	Red
DG	Dark green	**Sr**	Silver
Gn	Green	**Vt**	Violet
Gy	Grey	**Wh**	White
LG	Light green	**Ye**	Yellow

Key to items

1 Battery
2 Ignition switch
3 Auxiliary fusebox
4 Central fusebox
62 Multifunction electronic module
67 RH front door switch
68 LH front door switch
130 Tailgate lock motor
131 Tailgate switch
132 LH rear door switch
133 RH rear door switch
134 Driver's door lock switch
135 Passenger's door lock switch
136 Driver's door lock
137 Passenger's door lock
138 LH rear door lock
139 RH rear door lock

Diagram 12

H32256

Central locking (multifunction electronic module) - models with double locking

Central locking - models without double locking

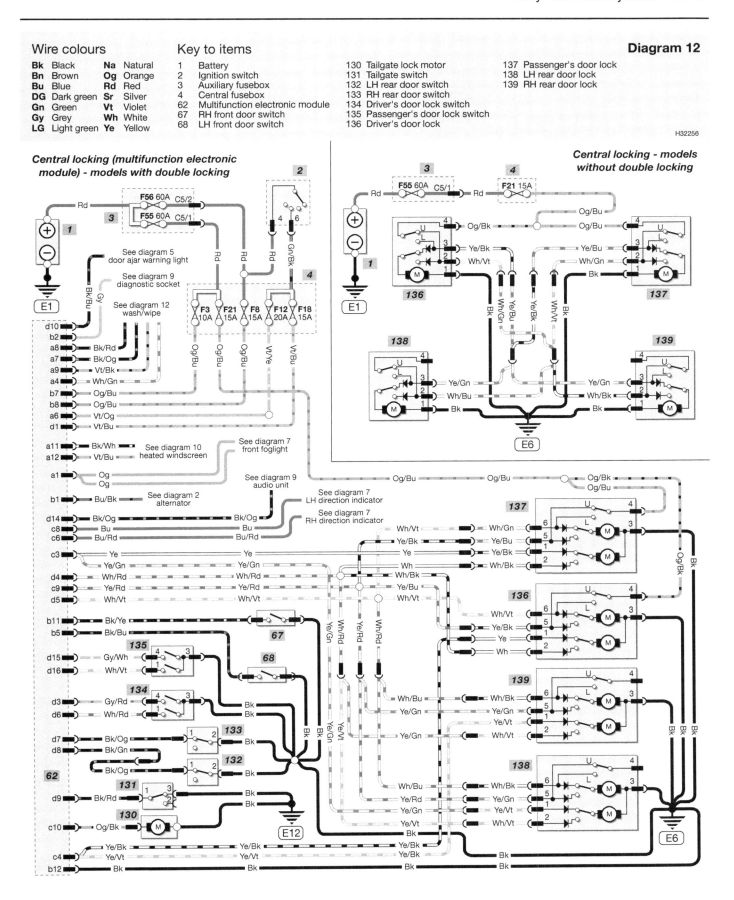

Wire colours

Bk	Black	**Na**	Natural
Bn	Brown	**Og**	Orange
Bu	Blue	**Rd**	Red
DG	Dark green	**Sr**	Silver
Gn	Green	**Vt**	Violet
Gy	Grey	**Wh**	White
LG	Light green	**Ye**	Yellow

Key to items

1 Battery
2 Ignition switch
3 Auxiliary fusebox
  c = power hold relay
  I = fuel pump relay
4 Central fusebox
145 Engine management control unit
146 Spark plug

147 Ignition coil
148 Inlet air temp sensor/
  MAP sensor
149 Throttle position sensor
150 Engine coolant temp. sensor
151 Power steering pressure switch
152 Oxygen sensor
153 Canister purge solenoid

154 Fuel injector
155 Idle speed control valve
156 Inertia switch
157 Camshaft position sensor
158 Crankshaft position sensor
159 Clutch switch

Diagram 13

H32257

Engine management 1.3L Endura E

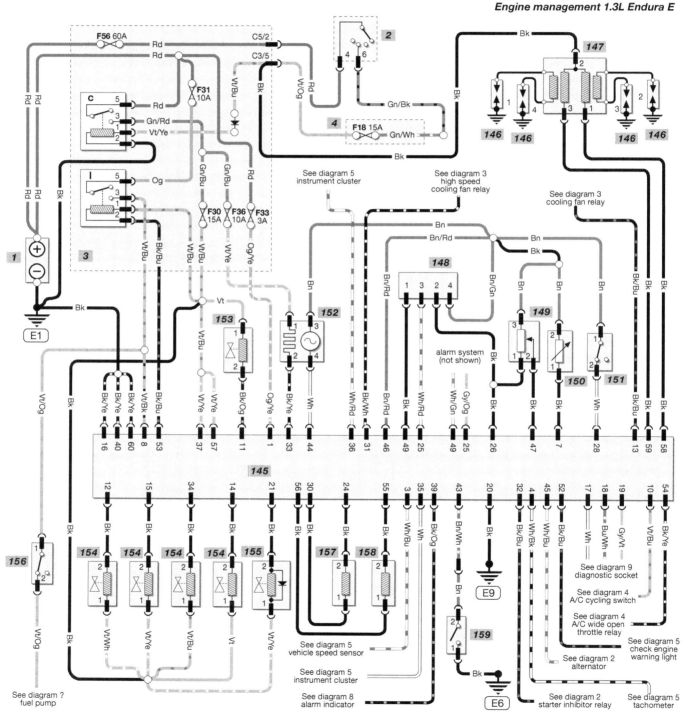

Wire colours

Bk	Black	**Na**	Natural
Bn	Brown	**Og**	Orange
Bu	Blue	**Rd**	Red
DG	Dark green	**Sr**	Silver
Gn	Green	**Vt**	Violet
Gy	Grey	**Wh**	White
LG	Light green	**Ye**	Yellow

Key to items

1   Battery
2   Ignition switch
3   Auxiliary fusebox
   c = power hold relay
   l = fuel pump relay
   f = auxiliary relay (with A/C only)
4   Central fusebox
48 Starter inhibitor/reversing light switch

145 Engine management control unit
146 Spark plug
147 Ignition coil
148 Inlet air temp sensor/
     MAP sensor
149 Throttle position sensor
150 Engine coolant temp. sensor
151 Power steering pressure switch

152 Oxygen sensor
153 Canister purge solenoid
154 Fuel injector
156 Inertia switch
157 Camshaft position sensor
158 Crankshaft position sensor
162 Idle speed control module

Diagram 14

H32258

Engine management 1.25L Zetec SE

① Models with air conditioning
② Models without air conditioning
③ Models with automatic transmission
④ Models without automatic transmission

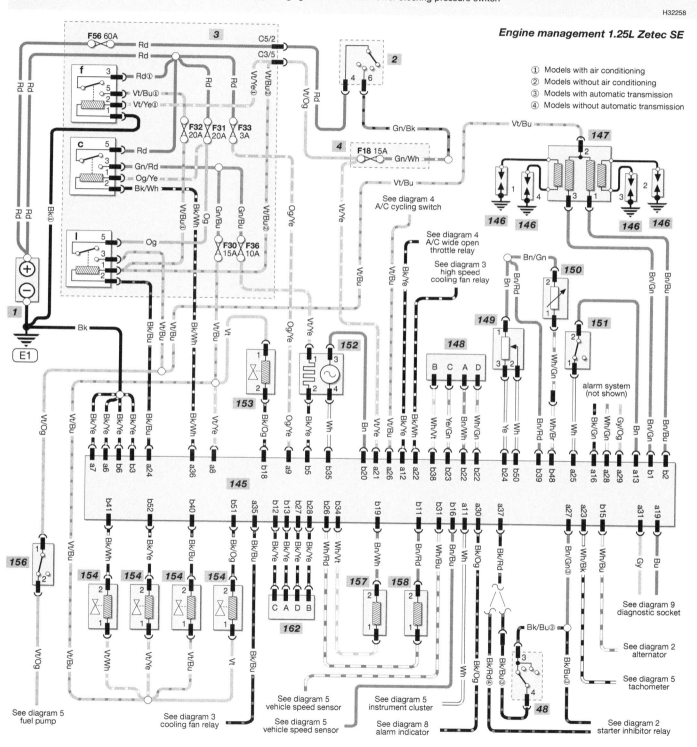

Wire colours

Bk	Black	**Na**	Natural
Bn	Brown	**Og**	Orange
Bu	Blue	**Rd**	Red
DG	Dark green	**Sr**	Silver
Gn	Green	**Vt**	Violet
Gy	Grey	**Wh**	White
LG	Light green	**Ye**	Yellow

Key to items

1 Battery
2 Ignition switch
3 Auxiliary fusebox
  c = power hold relay
  l = fuel pump relay
4 Central fusebox
145 Engine management control unit
146 Spark plug

147 Ignition coil
149 Throttle position sensor
150 Engine coolant temp. sensor
151 Power steering pressure switch
152 Oxygen sensor
153 Canister purge solenoid
154 Fuel injector
155 Idle speed control valve

156 Inertia switch
157 Camshaft position sensor
158 Crankshaft position sensor
159 Clutch switch
165 Inlet air temperature sensor
166 MAP sensor

Diagram 15

H32259

Engine management 1.4L Zetec SE

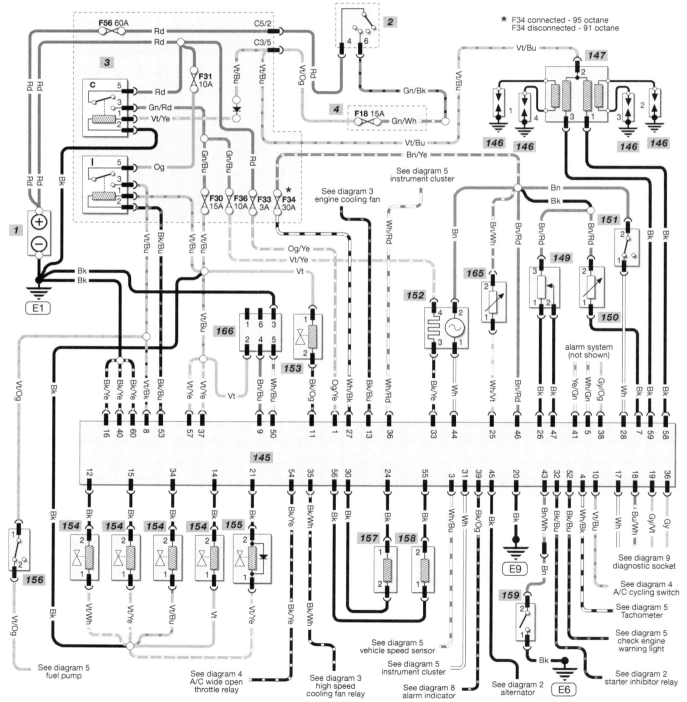

Wire colours

Bk	Black	**Na**	Natural
Bn	Brown	**Og**	Orange
Bu	Blue	**Rd**	Red
DG	Dark green	**Sr**	Silver
Gn	Green	**Vt**	Violet
Gy	Grey	**Wh**	White
LG	Light green	**Ye**	Yellow

Key to items

1 Battery
2 Ignition switch
3 Auxiliary fusebox
  c = power hold relay
  l = fuel pump relay
4 Central fusebox
145 Engine management control unit
146 Spark plug
147 Ignition coil

149 Throttle position sensor
151 Power steering pressure switch
152 Oxygen sensor
153 Canister purge solenoid
154 Fuel injector
155 Idle speed control valve
156 Inertia switch
157 Camshaft position sensor
158 Crankshaft position sensor

159 Clutch switch
165 Inlet air temperature sensor
166 MAP sensor
167 Cylinder head temperature sensor
168 Canister vent valve
169 Knock sensor

Diagram 16

H32260

Engine management 1.6L Zetec SE

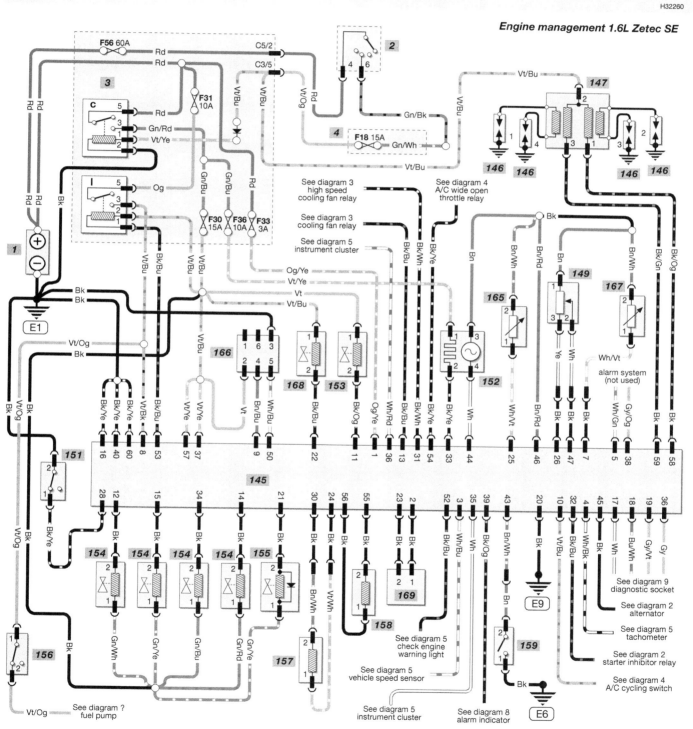

Wire colours

Bk	Black	**Na**	Natural
Bn	Brown	**Og**	Orange
Bu	Blue	**Rd**	Red
DG	Dark green	**Sr**	Silver
Gn	Green	**Vt**	Violet
Gy	Grey	**Wh**	White
LG	Light green	**Ye**	Yellow

Key to items

1 Battery
2 Ignition switch
3 Auxiliary fusebox
  b = fuel heater relay
  c = power hold relay
  m = glow plug relay
4 Central fusebox
145 Engine management control unit

150 Engine coolant temp. sensor
158 Crankshaft position sensor
175 Fuel heater
176 Glow plugs
177 EGR solenoid valve
178 Idle speed motor (models with
   air conditioning only)
179 EGR valve position sensor

180 Diesel pump unit
  a = partial load advance solenoid
  b = fuel lever variable resistor sensor
  c = cold start solenoid valve
  d = fuel shut-off solenoid

Diagram 17

H32261

Engine management
1.8L Diesel Endura DE

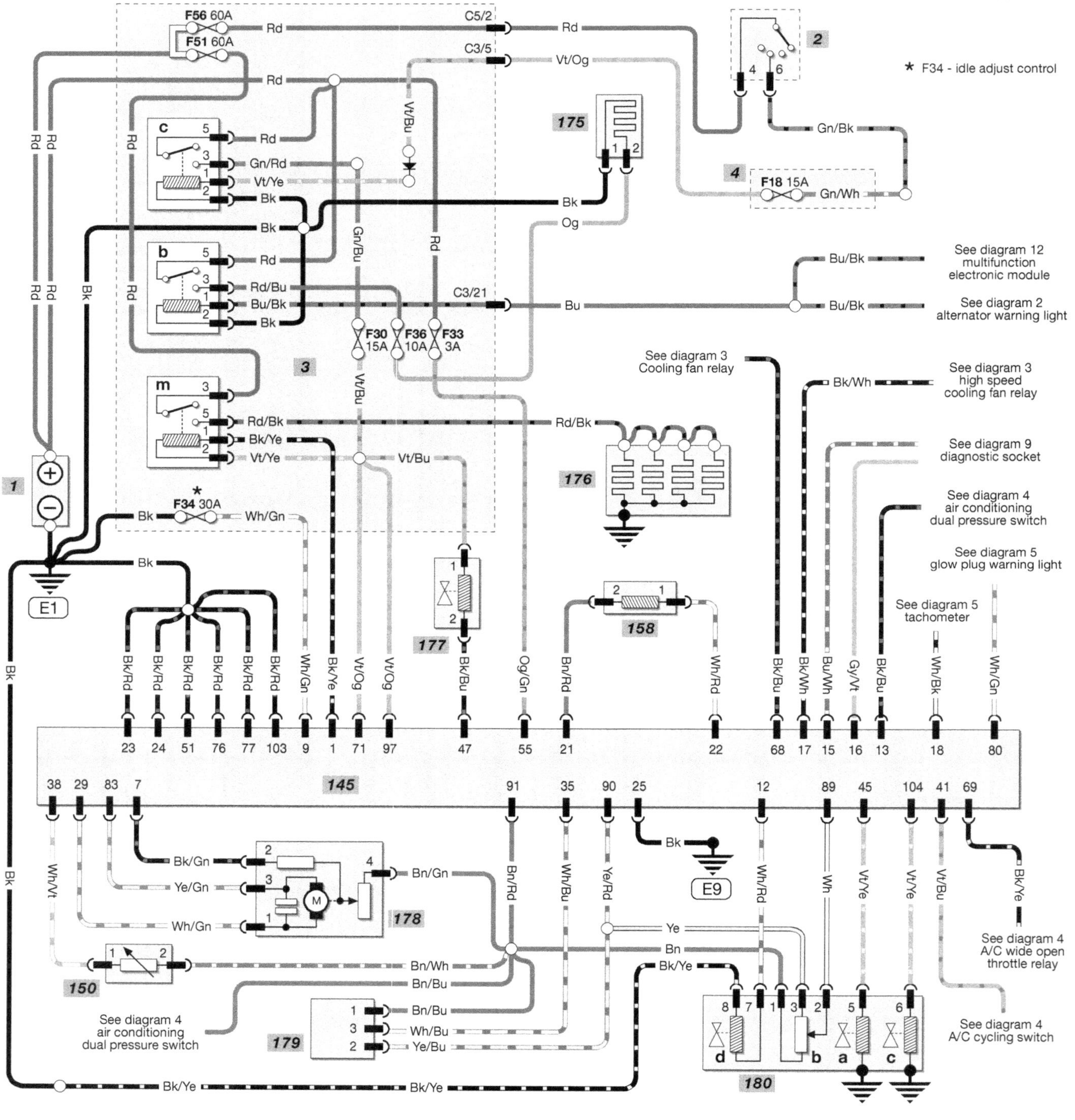

* F34 - idle adjust control

Wire colours

Bk	Black	**Na**	Natural
Bn	Brown	**Og**	Orange
Bu	Blue	**Rd**	Red
DG	Dark green	**Sr**	Silver
Gn	Green	**Vt**	Violet
Gy	Grey	**Wh**	White
LG	Light green	**Ye**	Yellow

Key to items

1   Battery
2   Ignition switch
3   Auxiliary fusebox
   c = power hold relay
   m = glow plug relay
   n = injector pump power relay
   o = auxiliary coolant heater relay 2

4   Central fusebox
145   Engine management control unit
158   Crankshaft position sensor
159   Clutch switch
165   Inlet air temperature sensor
166   MAP sensor
167   Cylinder head temperature sensor

176   Glow plugs
177   EGR solenoid valve
179   EGR valve position sensor
180   Diesel pump unit
185   Auxiliary coolant heater relay 1
186   Accelerator position sensor
187   Auxiliary coolant heater

Diagram 18

H32262

*Engine management
1.8L Diesel Endura DI*

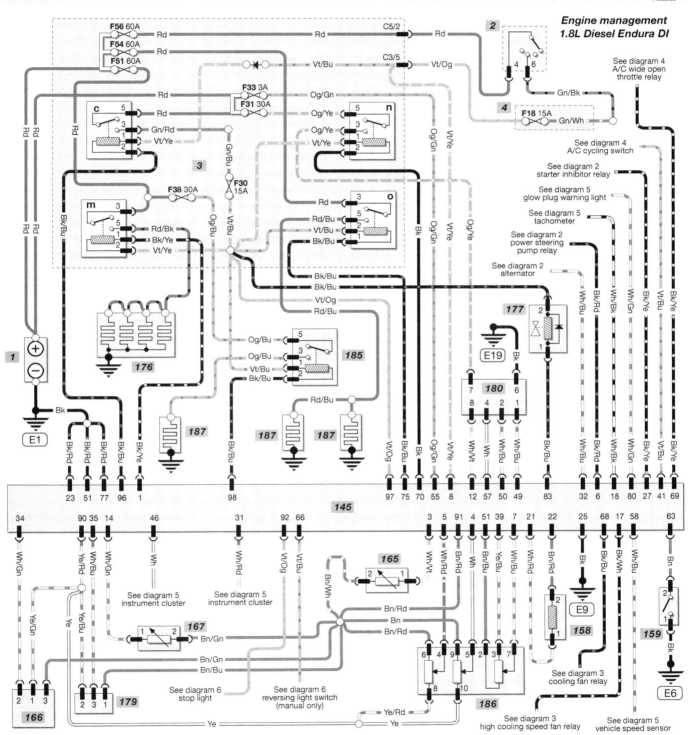

Reference REF•1

Dimensions and weights . . . .**REF•1**
Conversion factors . . . .**REF•2**
Buying spare parts . . . .**REF•3**
Vehicle identification numbers . . . .**REF•3**
General repair procedures . . . .**REF•4**
Jacking and vehicle support . . . .**REF•5**

Tools and working facilities . . . .**REF•6**
MOT test checks . . . .**REF•8**
Fault finding . . . .**REF•12**
Glossary of technical terms . . . .**REF•21**
Index . . . .**REF•26**

Dimensions and Weights

Note: *All figures are approximate, and may vary according to model. Refer to manufacturer's data for exact figures.*

Dimensions

Overall length:
  Hatchback and Van models . . . . .3828 mm
  Courier and Combi models . . . . .4115 mm
Overall width (excluding mirrors):
  Hatchback and Van models .1634 mm
  Courier and Combi models . . . . .1650 mm
Overall height (unladen):
  Hatchback models . . . . .1334 to 1409 mm
  Van models . . . . .1334 to 1377 mm
  Courier models . . . . .1804 to 1835 mm
  Combi models . . . . .1788 to 1819 mm
Wheelbase . . . . .2700 mm
  Hatchback and Van models .2446 mm
  Courier and Combi models . . . . .2700 mm

Weights

Kerb weight:
  Hatchback and Van models:
    Petrol models . . . . .1005 to 1159 kg
    Diesel models . . . . .1089 to 1218 kg
  Courier and Combi models:
    Petrol models . . . . .995 to 1215 kg
    Diesel models . . . . .1081 to 1301 kg
Maximum gross vehicle weight:
  Hatchback and Van models:
    Petrol models . . . . .1415 to 1485 kg
    Diesel models . . . . .1510 to 1550 kg
  Courier and Combi models:
    Petrol models . . . . .1310 to 1625 kg
    Diesel models . . . . .1400 to 1715 kg
Maximum towing weights . . . . .Refer to your Ford dealer
Maximum trailer nose weight . . . . .50 kg
Maximum roof rack load . . . . .75 kg

Conversion factors

Length (distance)

Inches (in)	x 25.4	= Millimetres (mm)	x 0.0394	= Inches (in)
Feet (ft)	x 0.305	= Metres (m)	x 3.281	= Feet (ft)
Miles	x 1.609	= Kilometres (km)	x 0.621	= Miles

Volume (capacity)

Cubic inches (cu in; in³)	x 16.387	= Cubic centimetres (cc; cm³)	x 0.061	= Cubic inches (cu in; in³)
Imperial pints (Imp pt)	x 0.568	= Litres (l)	x 1.76	= Imperial pints (Imp pt)
Imperial quarts (Imp qt)	x 1.137	= Litres (l)	x 0.88	= Imperial quarts (Imp qt)
Imperial quarts (Imp qt)	x 1.201	= US quarts (US qt)	x 0.833	= Imperial quarts (Imp qt)
US quarts (US qt)	x 0.946	= Litres (l)	x 1.057	= US quarts (US qt)
Imperial gallons (Imp gal)	x 4.546	= Litres (l)	x 0.22	= Imperial gallons (Imp gal)
Imperial gallons (Imp gal)	x 1.201	= US gallons (US gal)	x 0.833	= Imperial gallons (Imp gal)
US gallons (US gal)	x 3.785	= Litres (l)	x 0.264	= US gallons (US gal)

Mass (weight)

| Ounces (oz) | x 28.35 | = Grams (g) | x 0.035 | = Ounces (oz) |
| Pounds (lb) | x 0.454 | = Kilograms (kg) | x 2.205 | = Pounds (lb) |

Force

Ounces-force (ozf; oz)	x 0.278	= Newtons (N)	x 3.6	= Ounces-force (ozf; oz)
Pounds-force (lbf; lb)	x 4.448	= Newtons (N)	x 0.225	= Pounds-force (lbf; lb)
Newtons (N)	x 0.1	= Kilograms-force (kgf; kg)	x 9.81	= Newtons (N)

Pressure

Pounds-force per square inch (psi; lbf/in²; lb/in²)	x 0.070	= Kilograms-force per square centimetre (kgf/cm²; kg/cm²)	x 14.223	= Pounds-force per square inch (psi; lbf/in²; lb/in²)
Pounds-force per square inch (psi; lbf/in²; lb/in²)	x 0.068	= Atmospheres (atm)	x 14.696	= Pounds-force per square inch (psi; lbf/in²; lb/in²)
Pounds-force per square inch (psi; lbf/in²; lb/in²)	x 0.069	= Bars	x 14.5	= Pounds-force per square inch (psi; lbf/in²; lb/in²)
Pounds-force per square inch (psi; lbf/in²; lb/in²)	x 6.895	= Kilopascals (kPa)	x 0.145	= Pounds-force per square inch (psi; lbf/in²; lb/in²)
Kilopascals (kPa)	x 0.01	= Kilograms-force per square centimetre (kgf/cm²; kg/cm²)	x 98.1	= Kilopascals (kPa)
Millibar (mbar)	x 100	= Pascals (Pa)	x 0.01	= Millibar (mbar)
Millibar (mbar)	x 0.0145	= Pounds-force per square inch (psi; lbf/in²; lb/in²)	x 68.947	= Millibar (mbar)
Millibar (mbar)	x 0.75	= Millimetres of mercury (mmHg)	x 1.333	= Millibar (mbar)
Millibar (mbar)	x 0.401	= Inches of water (inH₂O)	x 2.491	= Millibar (mbar)
Millimetres of mercury (mmHg)	x 0.535	= Inches of water (inH₂O)	x 1.868	= Millimetres of mercury (mmHg)
Inches of water (inH₂O)	x 0.036	= Pounds-force per square inch (psi; lbf/in²; lb/in²)	x 27.68	= Inches of water (inH₂O)

Torque (moment of force)

Pounds-force inches (lbf in; lb in)	x 1.152	= Kilograms-force centimetre (kgf cm; kg cm)	x 0.868	= Pounds-force inches (lbf in; lb in)
Pounds-force inches (lbf in; lb in)	x 0.113	= Newton metres (Nm)	x 8.85	= Pounds-force inches (lbf in; lb in)
Pounds-force inches (lbf in; lb in)	x 0.083	= Pounds-force feet (lbf ft; lb ft)	x 12	= Pounds-force inches (lbf in; lb in)
Pounds-force feet (lbf ft; lb ft)	x 0.138	= Kilograms-force metres (kgf m; kg m)	x 7.233	= Pounds-force feet (lbf ft; lb ft)
Pounds-force feet (lbf ft; lb ft)	x 1.356	= Newton metres (Nm)	x 0.738	= Pounds-force feet (lbf ft; lb ft)
Newton metres (Nm)	x 0.102	= Kilograms-force metres (kgf m; kg m)	x 9.804	= Newton metres (Nm)

Power

| Horsepower (hp) | x 745.7 | = Watts (W) | x 0.0013 | = Horsepower (hp) |

Velocity (speed)

| Miles per hour (miles/hr; mph) | x 1.609 | = Kilometres per hour (km/hr; kph) | x 0.621 | = Miles per hour (miles/hr; mph) |

Fuel consumption*

| Miles per gallon, Imperial (mpg) | x 0.354 | = Kilometres per litre (km/l) | x 2.825 | = Miles per gallon, Imperial (mpg) |
| Miles per gallon, US (mpg) | x 0.425 | = Kilometres per litre (km/l) | x 2.352 | = Miles per gallon, US (mpg) |

Temperature

Degrees Fahrenheit = (°C x 1.8) + 32   Degrees Celsius (Degrees Centigrade; °C) = (°F - 32) x 0.56

It is common practice to convert from miles per gallon (mpg) to litres/100 kilometres (l/100km), where mpg x l/100 km = 282

Spare parts are available from many sources, including maker's appointed garages, accessory shops, and motor factors. To be sure of obtaining the correct parts, it will sometimes be necessary to quote the vehicle identification number. If possible, it can also be useful to take the old parts along for positive identification. Items such as starter motors and alternators may be available under a service exchange scheme – any parts returned should be clean.

Our advice regarding spare parts is as follows.

Officially appointed garages

This is the best source of parts which are peculiar to your car, and which are not otherwise generally available (eg, badges, interior trim, certain body panels, etc). It is also the only place at which you should buy parts if the vehicle is still under warranty.

Accessory shops

These are very good places to buy materials and components needed for the maintenance of your car (oil, air and fuel filters, light bulbs, drivebelts, greases, brake pads, touch-up paint, etc). Components of this nature sold by a reputable shop are usually of the same standard as those used by the car manufacturer.

Besides components, these shops also sell tools and general accessories, usually have convenient opening hours, charge lower prices, and can often be found close to home. Some accessory shops have parts counters where components needed for almost any repair job can be purchased or ordered.

Motor factors

Good factors will stock all the more important components which wear out comparatively quickly, and can sometimes supply individual components needed for the overhaul of a larger assembly (eg, brake seals and hydraulic parts, bearing shells, pistons, valves). They may also handle work such as cylinder block reboring, crankshaft regrinding, etc.

Tyre and exhaust specialists

These outlets may be independent, or members of a local or national chain. They frequently offer competitive prices when compared with a main dealer or local garage, but it will pay to obtain several quotes before making a decision. When researching prices, also ask what 'extras' may be added – for instance fitting a new valve and balancing the wheel are both commonly charged on top of the price of a new tyre.

Other sources

Beware of parts or materials obtained from market stalls, car boot sales or similar outlets. Such items are not invariably sub-standard, but there is little chance of compensation if they do prove unsatisfactory. in the case of safety-critical components such as brake pads, there is the risk not only of financial loss, but also of an accident causing injury or death.

Second-hand components or assemblies obtained from a car breaker can be a good buy in some circumstances, but this sort of purchase is best made by the experienced DIY mechanic.

Vehicle identification numbers

Modifications are a continuing and unpublicised process in vehicle manufacture, quite apart from major model changes. Spare parts manuals and lists are compiled upon a numerical basis, the individual vehicle identification numbers being essential to correct identification of the component concerned.

When ordering spare parts, always give as much information as possible. Quote the car model, year of manufacture and registration, chassis and engine numbers as appropriate.

The *Vehicle Identification Number (VIN)* plate is riveted to the bonnet lock crossmember and is visible once the bonnet has been opened. The vehicle identification (chassis) number is also stamped onto the floor of the passenger compartment, between the right-hand front seat and the door, and also onto the top left-hand corner of the facia assembly. The number on the floor can be viewed by lifting the flap in the carpet and the number on the facia is visible through the windscreen **(see illustrations)**.

The engine number can be found on the front of the cylinder block. On models fitted with the Zetec-SE petrol engine, the number is on the right-hand side whereas on all other models it can be found on the left-hand side of the block.

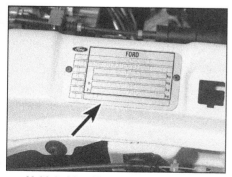

Vehicle identification plate location (arrowed)

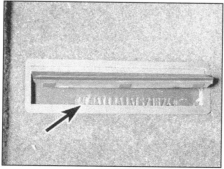

VIN number (arrowed) stamped on floor in passenger compartment

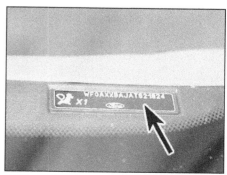

VIN number (arrowed) on facia assembly

Whenever servicing, repair or overhaul work is carried out on the car or its components, observe the following procedures and instructions. This will assist in carrying out the operation efficiently and to a professional standard of workmanship.

Joint mating faces and gaskets

When separating components at their mating faces, never insert screwdrivers or similar implements into the joint between the faces in order to prise them apart. This can cause severe damage which results in oil leaks, coolant leaks, etc upon reassembly. Separation is usually achieved by tapping along the joint with a soft-faced hammer in order to break the seal. However, note that this method may not be suitable where dowels are used for component location.

Where a gasket is used between the mating faces of two components, a new one must be fitted on reassembly; fit it dry unless otherwise stated in the repair procedure. Make sure that the mating faces are clean and dry, with all traces of old gasket removed. When cleaning a joint face, use a tool which is unlikely to score or damage the face, and remove any burrs or nicks with an oilstone or fine file.

Make sure that tapped holes are cleaned with a pipe cleaner, and keep them free of jointing compound, if this is being used, unless specifically instructed otherwise.

Ensure that all orifices, channels or pipes are clear, and blow through them, preferably using compressed air.

Oil seals

Oil seals can be removed by levering them out with a wide flat-bladed screwdriver or similar implement. Alternatively, a number of self-tapping screws may be screwed into the seal, and these used as a purchase for pliers or some similar device in order to pull the seal free.

Whenever an oil seal is removed from its working location, either individually or as part of an assembly, it should be renewed.

The very fine sealing lip of the seal is easily damaged, and will not seal if the surface it contacts is not completely clean and free from scratches, nicks or grooves. If the original sealing surface of the component cannot be restored, and the manufacturer has not made provision for slight relocation of the seal relative to the sealing surface, the component should be renewed.

Protect the lips of the seal from any surface which may damage them in the course of fitting. Use tape or a conical sleeve where possible. Lubricate the seal lips with oil before fitting and, on dual-lipped seals, fill the space between the lips with grease.

Unless otherwise stated, oil seals must be fitted with their sealing lips toward the lubricant to be sealed.

Use a tubular drift or block of wood of the appropriate size to install the seal and, if the seal housing is shouldered, drive the seal down to the shoulder. If the seal housing is unshouldered, the seal should be fitted with its face flush with the housing top face (unless otherwise instructed).

Screw threads and fastenings

Seized nuts, bolts and screws are quite a common occurrence where corrosion has set in, and the use of penetrating oil or releasing fluid will often overcome this problem if the offending item is soaked for a while before attempting to release it. The use of an impact driver may also provide a means of releasing such stubborn fastening devices, when used in conjunction with the appropriate screwdriver bit or socket. If none of these methods works, it may be necessary to resort to the careful application of heat, or the use of a hacksaw or nut splitter device.

Studs are usually removed by locking two nuts together on the threaded part, and then using a spanner on the lower nut to unscrew the stud. Studs or bolts which have broken off below the surface of the component in which they are mounted can sometimes be removed using a stud extractor. Always ensure that a blind tapped hole is completely free from oil, grease, water or other fluid before installing the bolt or stud. Failure to do this could cause the housing to crack due to the hydraulic action of the bolt or stud as it is screwed in.

When tightening a castellated nut to accept a split pin, tighten the nut to the specified torque, where applicable, and then tighten further to the next split pin hole. Never slacken the nut to align the split pin hole, unless stated in the repair procedure.

When checking or retightening a nut or bolt to a specified torque setting, slacken the nut or bolt by a quarter of a turn, and then retighten to the specified setting. However, this should not be attempted where angular tightening has been used.

For some screw fastenings, notably cylinder head bolts or nuts, torque wrench settings are no longer specified for the latter stages of tightening, "angle-tightening" being called up instead. Typically, a fairly low torque wrench setting will be applied to the bolts/nuts in the correct sequence, followed by one or more stages of tightening through specified angles.

Locknuts, locktabs and washers

Any fastening which will rotate against a component or housing during tightening should always have a washer between it and the relevant component or housing.

Spring or split washers should always be renewed when they are used to lock a critical component such as a big-end bearing retaining bolt or nut. Locktabs which are folded over to retain a nut or bolt should always be renewed.

Self-locking nuts can be re-used in non-critical areas, providing resistance can be felt when the locking portion passes over the bolt or stud thread. However, it should be noted that self-locking stiffnuts tend to lose their effectiveness after long periods of use, and should then be renewed as a matter of course.

Split pins must always be replaced with new ones of the correct size for the hole.

When thread-locking compound is found on the threads of a fastener which is to be re-used, it should be cleaned off with a wire brush and solvent, and fresh compound applied on reassembly.

Special tools

Some repair procedures in this manual entail the use of special tools such as a press, two or three-legged pullers, spring compressors, etc. Wherever possible, suitable readily-available alternatives to the manufacturer's special tools are described, and are shown in use. In some instances, where no alternative is possible, it has been necessary to resort to the use of a manufacturer's tool, and this has been done for reasons of safety as well as the efficient completion of the repair operation. Unless you are highly-skilled and have a thorough understanding of the procedures described, never attempt to bypass the use of any special tool when the procedure described specifies its use. Not only is there a very great risk of personal injury, but expensive damage could be caused to the components involved.

Environmental considerations

When disposing of used engine oil, brake fluid, antifreeze, etc, give due consideration to any detrimental environmental effects. Do not, for instance, pour any of the above liquids down drains into the general sewage system, or onto the ground to soak away. Many local council refuse tips provide a facility for waste oil disposal, as do some garages. If none of these facilities are available, consult your local Environmental Health Department, or the National Rivers Authority, for further advice.

With the universal tightening-up of legislation regarding the emission of environmentally-harmful substances from motor vehicles, most vehicles have tamperproof devices fitted to the main adjustment points of the fuel system. These devices are primarily designed to prevent unqualified persons from adjusting the fuel/air mixture, with the chance of a consequent increase in toxic emissions. If such devices are found during servicing or overhaul, they should, wherever possible, be renewed or refitted in accordance with the manufacturer's requirements or current legislation.

Note: It is antisocial and illegal to dump oil down the drain. To find the location of your local oil recycling bank, call this number free.

The jack supplied with the vehicle tool kit should only be used for changing the roadwheels – see *Wheel changing* at the front of this manual. When carrying out any other kind of work, raise the vehicle using a hydraulic (or 'trolley') jack, and always supplement the jack with axle stands positioned under the vehicle jacking points.

To raise the front of the vehicle, position the jack head underneath the reinforced sections of the body, next to the front jacking points for use with the vehicle jack **(see illustration)**. Support the vehicle with axle stands and slotted wooden blocks positioned under the reinforced sections of the body, just inboard of the sill panels.

To raise the rear of the vehicle, position the jack head under the reinforced sections of the sill panels (the same points as used for the wheelchanging jack). Lift the vehicle to the required height and support it on axle stands positioned underneath the rear suspension assembly mounting points.

The jack supplied with the vehicle locates with the jacking points on the sills. Ensure that the jack head is correctly engaged before attempting to raise the vehicle.

Never work under, around, or near a raised vehicle, unless it is adequately supported in at least two places with axle stands.

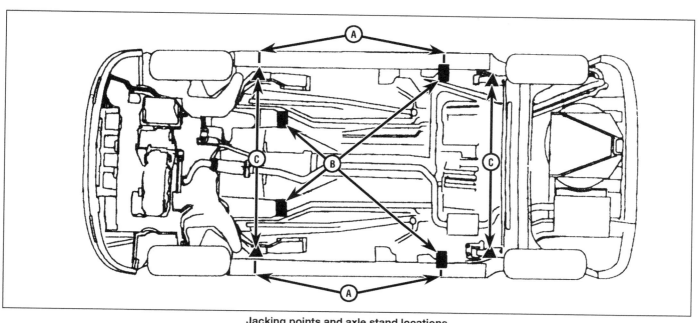

Jacking points and axle stand locations

A Jacking points for use with vehicle jack   *B Jacking points for use with hydraulic jack*   *C Axle stand locations*

Introduction

A selection of good tools is a fundamental requirement for anyone contemplating the maintenance and repair of a motor vehicle. For the owner who does not possess any, their purchase will prove a considerable expense, offsetting some of the savings made by doing-it-yourself. However, provided that the tools purchased meet the relevant national safety standards and are of good quality, they will last for many years and prove an extremely worthwhile investment.

To help the average owner to decide which tools are needed to carry out the various tasks detailed in this manual, we have compiled three lists of tools under the following headings: *Maintenance and minor repair, Repair and overhaul*, and *Special*. Newcomers to practical mechanics should start off with the *Maintenance and minor repair* tool kit, and confine themselves to the simpler jobs around the vehicle. Then, as confidence and experience grow, more difficult tasks can be undertaken, with extra tools being purchased as, and when, they are needed. In this way, a *Maintenance and minor repair* tool kit can be built up into a *Repair and overhaul* tool kit over a considerable period of time, without any major cash outlays. The experienced do-it-yourselfer will have a tool kit good enough for most repair and overhaul procedures, and will add tools from the *Special* category when it is felt that the expense is justified by the amount of use to which these tools will be put.

Maintenance and minor repair tool kit

The tools given in this list should be considered as a minimum requirement if routine maintenance, servicing and minor repair operations are to be undertaken. We recommend the purchase of combination spanners (ring one end, open-ended the other); although more expensive than open-ended ones, they do give the advantages of both types of spanner.

☐ *Combination spanners:*
  Metric - 8 to 19 mm inclusive
☐ *Adjustable spanner - 35 mm jaw (approx.)*
☐ *Spark plug spanner (with rubber insert) - petrol models*
☐ *Spark plug gap adjustment tool - petrol models*
☐ *Set of feeler gauges*
☐ *Brake bleed nipple spanner*
☐ *Screwdrivers:*
  Flat blade - 100 mm long x 6 mm dia
  Cross blade - 100 mm long x 6 mm dia
  Torx - various sizes (not all vehicles)
☐ *Combination pliers*
☐ *Hacksaw (junior)*
☐ *Tyre pump*
☐ *Tyre pressure gauge*
☐ *Oil can*
☐ *Oil filter removal tool*
☐ *Fine emery cloth*
☐ *Wire brush (small)*
☐ *Funnel (medium size)*
☐ *Sump drain plug key (not all vehicles)*

Repair and overhaul tool kit

These tools are virtually essential for anyone undertaking any major repairs to a motor vehicle, and are additional to those given in the *Maintenance and minor repair* list. Included in this list is a comprehensive set of sockets. Although these are expensive, they will be found invaluable as they are so versatile - particularly if various drives are included in the set. We recommend the half-inch square-drive type, as this can be used with most proprietary torque wrenches.

The tools in this list will sometimes need to be supplemented by tools from the *Special* list:

☐ *Sockets (or box spanners) to cover range in previous list (including Torx sockets)*
☐ *Reversible ratchet drive (for use with sockets)*
☐ *Extension piece, 250 mm (for use with sockets)*
☐ *Universal joint (for use with sockets)*
☐ *Flexible handle or sliding T "breaker bar" (for use with sockets)*
☐ *Torque wrench (for use with sockets)*
☐ *Self-locking grips*
☐ *Ball pein hammer*
☐ *Soft-faced mallet (plastic or rubber)*
☐ *Screwdrivers:*
  Flat blade - long & sturdy, short (chubby), and narrow (electrician's) types
  Cross blade - long & sturdy, and short (chubby) types
☐ *Pliers:*
  Long-nosed
  Side cutters (electrician's)
  Circlip (internal and external)
☐ *Cold chisel - 25 mm*
☐ *Scriber*
☐ *Scraper*
☐ *Centre-punch*
☐ *Pin punch*
☐ *Hacksaw*
☐ *Brake hose clamp*
☐ *Brake/clutch bleeding kit*
☐ *Selection of twist drills*
☐ *Steel rule/straight-edge*
☐ *Allen keys (inc. splined/Torx type)*
☐ *Selection of files*
☐ *Wire brush*
☐ *Axle stands*
☐ *Jack (strong trolley or hydraulic type)*
☐ *Light with extension lead*
☐ *Universal electrical multi-meter*

Sockets and reversible ratchet drive

Brake bleeding kit

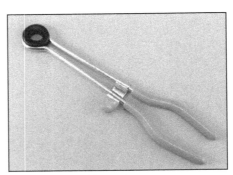

Torx key, socket and bit

Hose clamp

Angular-tightening gauge

Special tools

The tools in this list are those which are not used regularly, are expensive to buy, or which need to be used in accordance with their manufacturers' instructions. Unless relatively difficult mechanical jobs are undertaken frequently, it will not be economic to buy many of these tools. Where this is the case, you could consider clubbing together with friends (or joining a motorists' club) to make a joint purchase, or borrowing the tools against a deposit from a local garage or tool hire specialist. It is worth noting that many of the larger DIY superstores now carry a large range of special tools for hire at modest rates.

The following list contains only those tools and instruments freely available to the public, and not those special tools produced by the vehicle manufacturer specifically for its dealer network. You will find occasional references to these manufacturers' special tools in the text of this manual. Generally, an alternative method of doing the job without the vehicle manufacturers' special tool is given. However, sometimes there is no alternative to using them. Where this is the case and the relevant tool cannot be bought or borrowed, you will have to entrust the work to a dealer.

☐ Angular-tightening gauge
☐ Valve spring compressor
☐ Valve grinding tool
☐ Piston ring compressor
☐ Piston ring removal/installation tool
☐ Cylinder bore hone
☐ Balljoint separator
☐ Coil spring compressors (where applicable)
☐ Two/three-legged hub and bearing puller
☐ Impact screwdriver
☐ Micrometer and/or vernier calipers
☐ Dial gauge
☐ Stroboscopic timing light
☐ Dwell angle meter/tachometer
☐ Fault code reader
☐ Cylinder compression gauge
☐ Hand-operated vacuum pump and gauge
☐ Clutch plate alignment set
☐ Brake shoe steady spring cup removal tool
☐ Bush and bearing removal/installation set
☐ Stud extractors
☐ Tap and die set
☐ Lifting tackle
☐ Trolley jack

Buying tools

Reputable motor accessory shops and superstores often offer excellent quality tools at discount prices, so it pays to shop around.

Remember, you don't have to buy the most expensive items on the shelf, but it is always advisable to steer clear of the very cheap tools. Beware of 'bargains' offered on market stalls or at car boot sales. There are plenty of good tools around at reasonable prices, but always aim to purchase items which meet the relevant national safety standards. If in doubt, ask the proprietor or manager of the shop for advice before making a purchase.

Care and maintenance of tools

Having purchased a reasonable tool kit, it is necessary to keep the tools in a clean and serviceable condition. After use, always wipe off any dirt, grease and metal particles using a clean, dry cloth, before putting the tools away. Never leave them lying around after they have been used. A simple tool rack on the garage or workshop wall for items such as screwdrivers and pliers is a good idea. Store all normal spanners and sockets in a metal box. Any measuring instruments, gauges, meters, etc, must be carefully stored where they cannot be damaged or become rusty.

Take a little care when tools are used. Hammer heads inevitably become marked, and screwdrivers lose the keen edge on their blades from time to time. A little timely attention with emery cloth or a file will soon restore items like this to a good finish.

Working facilities

Not to be forgotten when discussing tools is the workshop itself. If anything more than routine maintenance is to be carried out, a suitable working area becomes essential.

It is appreciated that many an owner-mechanic is forced by circumstances to remove an engine or similar item without the benefit of a garage or workshop. Having done this, any repairs should always be done under the cover of a roof.

Wherever possible, any dismantling should be done on a clean, flat workbench or table at a suitable working height.

Any workbench needs a vice; one with a jaw opening of 100 mm is suitable for most jobs. As mentioned previously, some clean dry storage space is also required for tools, as well as for any lubricants, cleaning fluids, touch-up paints etc, which become necessary.

Another item which may be required, and which has a much more general usage, is an electric drill with a chuck capacity of at least 8 mm. This, together with a good range of twist drills, is virtually essential for fitting accessories.

Last, but not least, always keep a supply of old newspapers and clean, lint-free rags available, and try to keep any working area as clean as possible.

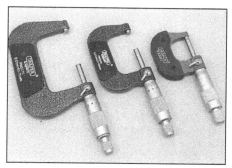

Micrometers

Dial test indicator ("dial gauge")

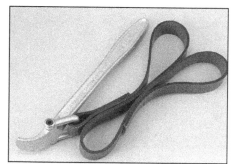

Strap wrench

Compression tester

Fault code reader

This is a guide to getting your vehicle through the MOT test. Obviously it will not be possible to examine the vehicle to the same standard as the professional MOT tester. However, working through the following checks will enable you to identify any problem areas before submitting the vehicle for the test.

Where a testable component is in borderline condition, the tester has discretion in deciding whether to pass or fail it. The basis of such discretion is whether the tester would be happy for a close relative or friend to use the vehicle with the component in that condition. If the vehicle presented is clean and evidently well cared for, the tester may be more inclined to pass a borderline component than if the vehicle is scruffy and apparently neglected.

It has only been possible to summarise the test requirements here, based on the regulations in force at the time of printing. Test standards are becoming increasingly stringent, although there are some exemptions for older vehicles.

An assistant will be needed to help carry out some of these checks.

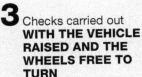

The checks have been sub-divided into four categories, as follows:

1 Checks carried out **FROM THE DRIVER'S SEAT**

2 Checks carried out **WITH THE VEHICLE ON THE GROUND**

3 Checks carried out **WITH THE VEHICLE RAISED AND THE WHEELS FREE TO TURN**

4 Checks carried out on **YOUR VEHICLE'S EXHAUST EMISSION SYSTEM**

---

1 Checks carried out **FROM THE DRIVER'S SEAT**

Handbrake

☐ Test the operation of the handbrake. Excessive travel (too many clicks) indicates incorrect brake or cable adjustment.
☐ Check that the handbrake cannot be released by tapping the lever sideways. Check the security of the lever mountings.

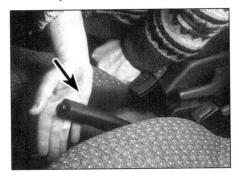

Footbrake

☐ Depress the brake pedal and check that it does not creep down to the floor, indicating a master cylinder fault. Release the pedal, wait a few seconds, then depress it again. If the pedal travels nearly to the floor before firm resistance is felt, brake adjustment or repair is necessary. If the pedal feels spongy, there is air in the hydraulic system which must be removed by bleeding.

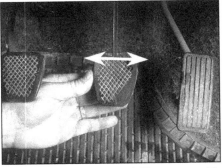

☐ Check that the brake pedal is secure and in good condition. Check also for signs of fluid leaks on the pedal, floor or carpets, which would indicate failed seals in the brake master cylinder.
☐ Check the servo unit (when applicable) by operating the brake pedal several times, then keeping the pedal depressed and starting the engine. As the engine starts, the pedal will move down slightly. If not, the vacuum hose or the servo itself may be faulty.

Steering wheel and column

☐ Examine the steering wheel for fractures or looseness of the hub, spokes or rim.
☐ Move the steering wheel from side to side and then up and down. Check that the steering wheel is not loose on the column, indicating wear or a loose retaining nut. Continue moving the steering wheel as before, but also turn it slightly from left to right.
☐ Check that the steering wheel is not loose on the column, and that there is no abnormal

movement of the steering wheel, indicating wear in the column support bearings or couplings.

Windscreen, mirrors and sunvisor

☐ The windscreen must be free of cracks or other significant damage within the driver's field of view. (Small stone chips are acceptable.) Rear view mirrors must be secure, intact, and capable of being adjusted.

290mm

☐ The driver's sunvisor must be capable of being stored in the "up" position.

Seat belts and seats

Note: *The following checks are applicable to all seat belts, front and rear.*

☐ Examine the webbing of all the belts (including rear belts if fitted) for cuts, serious fraying or deterioration. Fasten and unfasten each belt to check the buckles. If applicable, check the retracting mechanism. Check the security of all seat belt mountings accessible from inside the vehicle.

☐ Seat belts with pre-tensioners, once activated, have a "flag" or similar showing on the seat belt stalk. This, in itself, is not a reason for test failure.

☐ The front seats themselves must be securely attached and the backrests must lock in the upright position.

Doors

☐ Both front doors must be able to be opened and closed from outside and inside, and must latch securely when closed.

2 Checks carried out WITH THE VEHICLE ON THE GROUND

Vehicle identification

☐ Number plates must be in good condition, secure and legible, with letters and numbers correctly spaced – spacing at (A) should be at least twice that at (B).

☐ The VIN plate and/or homologation plate must be legible.

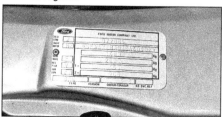

Electrical equipment

☐ Switch on the ignition and check the operation of the horn.

☐ Check the windscreen washers and wipers, examining the wiper blades; renew damaged or perished blades. Also check the operation of the stop-lights.

☐ Check the operation of the sidelights and number plate lights. The lenses and reflectors must be secure, clean and undamaged.

☐ Check the operation and alignment of the headlights. The headlight reflectors must not be tarnished and the lenses must be undamaged.

☐ Switch on the ignition and check the operation of the direction indicators (including the instrument panel tell-tale) and the hazard warning lights. Operation of the sidelights and stop-lights must not affect the indicators - if it does, the cause is usually a bad earth at the rear light cluster.

☐ Check the operation of the rear foglight(s), including the warning light on the instrument panel or in the switch.

☐ The ABS warning light must illuminate in accordance with the manufacturers' design. For most vehicles, the ABS warning light should illuminate when the ignition is switched on, and (if the system is operating properly) extinguish after a few seconds. Refer to the owner's handbook.

Footbrake

☐ Examine the master cylinder, brake pipes and servo unit for leaks, loose mountings, corrosion or other damage.

☐ The fluid reservoir must be secure and the fluid level must be between the upper (**A**) and lower (**B**) markings.

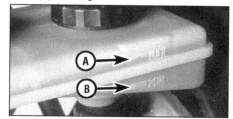

☐ Inspect both front brake flexible hoses for cracks or deterioration of the rubber. Turn the steering from lock to lock, and ensure that the hoses do not contact the wheel, tyre, or any part of the steering or suspension mechanism. With the brake pedal firmly depressed, check the hoses for bulges or leaks under pressure.

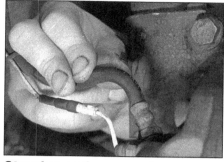

Steering and suspension

☐ Have your assistant turn the steering wheel from side to side slightly, up to the point where the steering gear just begins to transmit this movement to the roadwheels. Check for excessive free play between the steering wheel and the steering gear, indicating wear or insecurity of the steering column joints, the column-to-steering gear coupling, or the steering gear itself.

☐ Have your assistant turn the steering wheel more vigorously in each direction, so that the roadwheels just begin to turn. As this is done, examine all the steering joints, linkages, fittings and attachments. Renew any component that shows signs of wear or damage. On vehicles with power steering, check the security and condition of the steering pump, drivebelt and hoses.

☐ Check that the vehicle is standing level, and at approximately the correct ride height.

Shock absorbers

☐ Depress each corner of the vehicle in turn, then release it. The vehicle should rise and then settle in its normal position. If the vehicle continues to rise and fall, the shock absorber is defective. A shock absorber which has seized will also cause the vehicle to fail.

Exhaust system

☐ Start the engine. With your assistant holding a rag over the tailpipe, check the entire system for leaks. Repair or renew leaking sections.

3 Checks carried out **WITH THE VEHICLE RAISED AND THE WHEELS FREE TO TURN**

Jack up the front and rear of the vehicle, and securely support it on axle stands. Position the stands clear of the suspension assemblies. Ensure that the wheels are clear of the ground and that the steering can be turned from lock to lock.

Steering mechanism

☐ Have your assistant turn the steering from lock to lock. Check that the steering turns smoothly, and that no part of the steering mechanism, including a wheel or tyre, fouls any brake hose or pipe or any part of the body structure.
☐ Examine the steering rack rubber gaiters for damage or insecurity of the retaining clips. If power steering is fitted, check for signs of damage or leakage of the fluid hoses, pipes or connections. Also check for excessive stiffness or binding of the steering, a missing split pin or locking device, or severe corrosion of the body structure within 30 cm of any steering component attachment point.

Front and rear suspension and wheel bearings

☐ Starting at the front right-hand side, grasp the roadwheel at the 3 o'clock and 9 o'clock positions and rock gently but firmly. Check for free play or insecurity at the wheel bearings, suspension balljoints, or suspension mountings, pivots and attachments.
☐ Now grasp the wheel at the 12 o'clock and 6 o'clock positions and repeat the previous inspection. Spin the wheel, and check for roughness or tightness of the front wheel bearing.

☐ If excess free play is suspected at a component pivot point, this can be confirmed by using a large screwdriver or similar tool and levering between the mounting and the component attachment. This will confirm whether the wear is in the pivot bush, its retaining bolt, or in the mounting itself (the bolt holes can often become elongated).

☐ Carry out all the above checks at the other front wheel, and then at both rear wheels.

Springs and shock absorbers

☐ Examine the suspension struts (when applicable) for serious fluid leakage, corrosion, or damage to the casing. Also check the security of the mounting points.
☐ If coil springs are fitted, check that the spring ends locate in their seats, and that the spring is not corroded, cracked or broken.
☐ If leaf springs are fitted, check that all leaves are intact, that the axle is securely attached to each spring, and that there is no deterioration of the spring eye mountings, bushes, and shackles.

☐ The same general checks apply to vehicles fitted with other suspension types, such as torsion bars, hydraulic displacer units, etc. Ensure that all mountings and attachments are secure, that there are no signs of excessive wear, corrosion or damage, and (on hydraulic types) that there are no fluid leaks or damaged pipes.
☐ Inspect the shock absorbers for signs of serious fluid leakage. Check for wear of the mounting bushes or attachments, or damage to the body of the unit.

Driveshafts (fwd vehicles only)

☐ Rotate each front wheel in turn and inspect the constant velocity joint gaiters for splits or damage. Also check that each driveshaft is straight and undamaged.

Braking system

☐ If possible without dismantling, check brake pad wear and disc condition. Ensure that the friction lining material has not worn excessively, (A) and that the discs are not fractured, pitted, scored or badly worn (B).

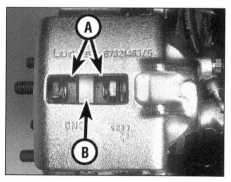

☐ Examine all the rigid brake pipes underneath the vehicle, and the flexible hose(s) at the rear. Look for corrosion, chafing or insecurity of the pipes, and for signs of bulging under pressure, chafing, splits or deterioration of the flexible hoses.
☐ Look for signs of fluid leaks at the brake calipers or on the brake backplates. Repair or renew leaking components.
☐ Slowly spin each wheel, while your assistant depresses and releases the footbrake. Ensure that each brake is operating and does not bind when the pedal is released.

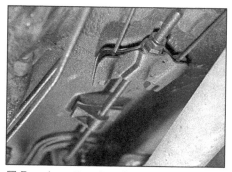

☐ Examine the handbrake mechanism, checking for frayed or broken cables, excessive corrosion, or wear or insecurity of the linkage. Check that the mechanism works on each relevant wheel, and releases fully, without binding.

☐ It is not possible to test brake efficiency without special equipment, but a road test can be carried out later to check that the vehicle pulls up in a straight line.

Fuel and exhaust systems

☐ Inspect the fuel tank (including the filler cap), fuel pipes, hoses and unions. All components must be secure and free from leaks.

☐ Examine the exhaust system over its entire length, checking for any damaged, broken or missing mountings, security of the retaining clamps and rust or corrosion.

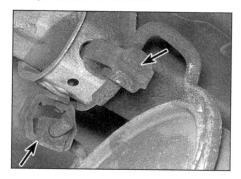

Wheels and tyres

☐ Examine the sidewalls and tread area of each tyre in turn. Check for cuts, tears, lumps, bulges, separation of the tread, and exposure of the ply or cord due to wear or damage. Check that the tyre bead is correctly seated on the wheel rim, that the valve is sound and properly seated, and that the wheel is not distorted or damaged.

☐ Check that the tyres are of the correct size for the vehicle, that they are of the same size and type on each axle, and that the pressures are correct.

☐ Check the tyre tread depth. The legal minimum at the time of writing is 1.6 mm over at least three-quarters of the tread width. Abnormal tread wear may indicate incorrect front wheel alignment.

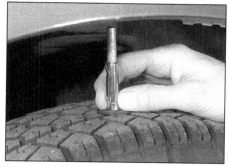

Body corrosion

☐ Check the condition of the entire vehicle structure for signs of corrosion in load-bearing areas. (These include chassis box sections, side sills, cross-members, pillars, and all suspension, steering, braking system and seat belt mountings and anchorages.) Any corrosion which has seriously reduced the thickness of a load-bearing area is likely to cause the vehicle to fail. In this case professional repairs are likely to be needed.

☐ Damage or corrosion which causes sharp or otherwise dangerous edges to be exposed will also cause the vehicle to fail.

4 Checks carried out on YOUR VEHICLE'S EXHAUST EMISSION SYSTEM

Petrol models

☐ Have the engine at normal operating temperature, and make sure that it is in good tune (ignition system in good order, air filter element clean, etc).

☐ Before any measurements are carried out, raise the engine speed to around 2500 rpm, and hold it at this speed for 20 seconds. Allow the engine speed to return to idle, and watch for smoke emissions from the exhaust tailpipe. If the idle speed is obviously much too high, or if dense blue or clearly-visible black smoke comes from the tailpipe for more than 5 seconds, the vehicle will fail. As a rule of thumb, blue smoke signifies oil being burnt (engine wear) while black smoke signifies unburnt fuel (dirty air cleaner element, or other carburettor or fuel system fault).

☐ An exhaust gas analyser capable of measuring carbon monoxide (CO) and hydrocarbons (HC) is now needed. If such an instrument cannot be hired or borrowed, a local garage may agree to perform the check for a small fee.

CO emissions (mixture)

☐ At the time of writing, for vehicles first used between 1st August 1975 and 31st July 1986 (P to C registration), the CO level must not exceed 4.5% by volume. For vehicles first used between 1st August 1986 and 31st July 1992 (D to J registration), the CO level must not exceed 3.5% by volume. Vehicles first

used after 1st August 1992 (K registration) must conform to the manufacturer's specification. The MOT tester has access to a DOT database or emissions handbook, which lists the CO and HC limits for each make and model of vehicle. The CO level is measured with the engine at idle speed, and at "fast idle". The following limits are given as a general guide:

> At idle speed -
> CO level no more than 0.5%
> At "fast idle" (2500 to 3000 rpm) -
> CO level no more than 0.3%
> (Minimum oil temperature 60°C)

☐ If the CO level cannot be reduced far enough to pass the test (and the fuel and ignition systems are otherwise in good condition) then the carburettor is badly worn, or there is some problem in the fuel injection system or catalytic converter (as applicable).

HC emissions

☐ With the CO within limits, HC emissions for vehicles first used between 1st August 1975 and 31st July 1992 (P to J registration) must not exceed 1200 ppm. Vehicles first used after 1st August 1992 (K registration) must conform to the manufacturer's specification. The MOT tester has access to a DOT database or emissions handbook, which lists the CO and HC limits for each make and model of vehicle. The HC level is measured with the engine at "fast idle". The following is given as a general guide:

> At "fast idle" (2500 to 3000 rpm) -
> HC level no more than 200 ppm
> (Minimum oil temperature 60°C)

☐ Excessive HC emissions are caused by incomplete combustion, the causes of which can include oil being burnt, mechanical wear and ignition/fuel system malfunction.

Diesel models

☐ The only emission test applicable to Diesel engines is the measuring of exhaust smoke density. The test involves accelerating the engine several times to its maximum unloaded speed.

Note: *It is of the utmost importance that the engine timing belt is in good condition before the test is carried out.*

☐ The limits for Diesel engine exhaust smoke, introduced in September 1995 are:

Vehicles first used before 1st August 1979:
Exempt from metered smoke testing, but must not emit "dense blue or clearly visible black smoke for a period of more than 5 seconds at idle" or "dense blue or clearly visible black smoke during acceleration which would obscure the view of other road users".

Non-turbocharged vehicles first used after 1st August 1979: 2.5m⁻¹

Turbocharged vehicles first used after 1st August 1979: 3.0m⁻¹

☐ Excessive smoke can be caused by a dirty air cleaner element. Otherwise, professional advice may be needed to find the cause.

Engine

☐ Engine fails to rotate when attempting to start
☐ Engine rotates, but will not start
☐ Engine difficult to start when cold
☐ Engine difficult to start when hot
☐ Starter motor noisy or excessively-rough in engagement
☐ Engine starts, but stops immediately
☐ Engine idles erratically
☐ Engine misfires at idle speed
☐ Engine misfires throughout the driving speed range
☐ Engine hesitates on acceleration
☐ Engine stalls
☐ Engine lacks power
☐ Engine backfires
☐ Oil pressure warning light illuminated with engine running
☐ Engine runs-on after switching off
☐ Engine noises

Cooling system

☐ Overheating
☐ Overcooling
☐ External coolant leakage
☐ Internal coolant leakage
☐ Corrosion

Fuel and exhaust systems

☐ Excessive fuel consumption
☐ Fuel leakage and/or fuel odour
☐ Excessive noise or fumes from exhaust system

Clutch

☐ Pedal travels to floor – no pressure or very little resistance
☐ Clutch fails to disengage (unable to select gears)
☐ Clutch slips (engine speed increases, with no increase in vehicle speed)
☐ Judder as clutch is engaged
☐ Noise when depressing or releasing clutch pedal

Manual transmission

☐ Noisy in neutral with engine running
☐ Noisy in one particular gear
☐ Difficulty engaging gears
☐ Jumps out of gear
☐ Vibration
☐ Lubricant leaks

Automatic transmission

☐ Fluid leakage
☐ Transmission fluid brown, or has burned smell
☐ General gear selection problems
☐ Transmission will not downshift (kickdown) with accelerator pedal fully depressed
☐ Engine will not start in any gear, or starts in gears other than Park or Neutral
☐ Transmission slips, shifts roughly, is noisy, or has no drive in forward or reverse gears

Driveshafts

☐ Vibration when accelerating or decelerating
☐ Clicking or knocking noise on turns (at slow speed on full-lock)

Braking system

☐ Vehicle pulls to one side under braking
☐ Noise (grinding or high-pitched squeal) when brakes applied
☐ Excessive brake pedal travel
☐ Brake pedal feels spongy when depressed
☐ Excessive brake pedal effort required to stop vehicle
☐ Judder felt through brake pedal or steering wheel when braking
☐ Brakes binding
☐ Rear wheels locking under normal braking

Suspension and steering

☐ Vehicle pulls to one side
☐ Wheel wobble and vibration
☐ Excessive pitching and/or rolling around corners, or during braking
☐ Wandering or general instability
☐ Excessively-stiff steering
☐ Excessive play in steering
☐ Lack of power assistance
☐ Tyre wear excessive

Electrical system

☐ Battery will not hold a charge for more than a few days
☐ Ignition/no-charge warning light remains illuminated with engine running
☐ Ignition/no-charge warning light fails to come on
☐ Lights inoperative
☐ Instrument readings inaccurate or erratic
☐ Horn inoperative, or unsatisfactory in operation
☐ Windscreen wipers inoperative, or unsatisfactory in operation
☐ Windscreen washers inoperative, or unsatisfactory in operation
☐ Electric windows inoperative, or unsatisfactory in operation
☐ Central locking system inoperative, or unsatisfactory in operation

Introduction

The vehicle owner who does his or her own maintenance according to the recommended service schedules should not have to use this section of the manual very often. Modern component reliability is such that, provided those items subject to wear or deterioration are inspected or renewed at the specified intervals, sudden failure is comparatively rare. Faults do not usually just happen as a result of sudden failure, but develop over a period of time. Major mechanical failures in particular are usually preceded by characteristic symptoms over hundreds or even thousands of miles. Those components which do occasionally fail without warning are often small and easily carried in the vehicle.

With any fault-finding, the first step is to decide where to begin investigations. Sometimes this is obvious, but on other occasions, a little detective work will be necessary. The owner who makes half a dozen haphazard adjustments or replacements may be successful in curing a fault (or its symptoms), but will be none the wiser if the fault recurs, and ultimately may have spent more time and money than was necessary. A calm and logical approach will be found to be more satisfactory in the long run. Always take into account any warning signs or abnormalities that may have been noticed in the period preceding the fault – power loss, high or low gauge readings, unusual smells, etc – and remember that failure of components such as fuses or spark plugs may only be pointers to some underlying fault.

The pages which follow provide an easy-reference guide to the more common problems which may occur during the operation of the vehicle. These problems and their possible causes are grouped under headings denoting various components or systems, such as Engine, Cooling system, etc. The Chapter which deals with the problem is shown in brackets, but in some instances it will be necessary to refer to the specific Chapter Part, depending on model or system, as applicable. Some problems may be more obvious, such as loose or disconnected wiring, and in these instances a Chapter reference may not be given as the problem can be simply overcome by dealing with the fault as it stands. Whatever the problem, certain basic principles apply. These are as follows:

Verify the fault. This is simply a matter of being sure that you know what the symptoms are before starting work. This is particularly important if you are investigating a fault for someone else, who may not have described it very accurately.

Don't overlook the obvious. For example, if the vehicle won't start, is there fuel in the tank? (Don't take anyone else's word on this particular point, and don't trust the fuel gauge either!) If an electrical fault is indicated, look for loose or broken wires before digging out the test gear.

Cure the disease, not the symptom. Substituting a flat battery with a fully-charged one will get you off the hard shoulder, but if the underlying cause is not attended to, the new battery will go the same way. Similarly, changing oil-fouled spark plugs for a new set will get you moving again, but remember that the reason for the fouling (if it wasn't simply an incorrect grade of plug) will have to be established and corrected.

Don't take anything for granted. Particularly, don't forget that a 'new' component may itself be defective (especially if it's been rattling around in the boot for months), and don't leave components out of a fault diagnosis sequence just because they are new or recently-fitted. When you do finally diagnose a difficult fault, you'll probably realise that all the evidence was there from the start.

Engine

Engine fails to rotate when attempting to start

☐ Battery terminal connections loose or corroded (see *Weekly checks*)
☐ Battery discharged or faulty (Chapter 5)
☐ Broken, loose or disconnected wiring in the starting circuit (Chapter 5)
☐ Defective starter solenoid or switch (Chapter 5)
☐ Defective starter motor (Chapter 5)
☐ Starter pinion or flywheel ring gear teeth loose or broken Chapters 2 and 5)
☐ Engine earth strap broken or disconnected (Chapter 5)

Engine rotates, but will not start

☐ Fuel cut-off switch energised (Chapter 4).
☐ Fuel tank empty
☐ Battery discharged (engine rotates slowly) (Chapter 5)
☐ Battery terminal connections loose or corroded (see *Weekly checks*)
☐ Ignition components damp or damaged – petrol models (Chapters 1 and 5)
☐ Broken, loose or disconnected wiring in the ignition circuit – petrol models (Chapters 1 and 5)
☐ Worn, faulty or incorrectly-gapped spark plugs – petrol models (Chapter 1)
☐ Preheating system faulty – diesel models (Chapter 5)
☐ Fuel injection system fault – petrol models (Chapter 4)
☐ Stop solenoid faulty – diesel models (Chapter 4)
☐ Air in fuel system – diesel models (Chapter 4)
☐ Major mechanical failure (eg camshaft drive) (Chapter 2)

Engine difficult to start when cold

☐ Battery discharged (Chapter 5)
☐ Battery terminal connections loose or corroded (see *Weekly checks*)
☐ Worn, faulty or incorrectly-gapped spark plugs – petrol models (Chapter 1)
☐ Preheating system faulty – diesel models (Chapter 5)
☐ Fuel injection system fault – petrol models (Chapter 4)
☐ Other ignition system fault – petrol models (Chapters 1 and 5)
☐ Low cylinder compressions (Chapter 2)

Engine difficult to start when hot

☐ Air filter element dirty or clogged (Chapter 1)
☐ Fuel injection system fault – petrol models (Chapter 4)
☐ Low cylinder compressions (Chapter 2)

Starter motor noisy or excessively-rough in engagement

☐ Starter pinion or flywheel ring gear teeth loose or broken (Chapters 2 and 5)
☐ Starter motor mounting bolts loose or missing (Chapter 5)
☐ Starter motor internal components worn or damaged (Chapter 5)

Engine starts, but stops immediately

☐ Loose or faulty electrical connections in the ignition circuit – petrol models (Chapters 1 and 5)
☐ Vacuum leak at the throttle body or inlet manifold – petrol models (Chapter 4)
☐ Blocked injector/fuel injection system fault – petrol models (Chapter 4)

Engine idles erratically

☐ Air filter element clogged (Chapter 1)
☐ Vacuum leak at the throttle body, inlet manifold or associated hoses – petrol models (Chapter 4)
☐ Worn, faulty or incorrectly-gapped spark plugs – petrol models (Chapter 1)
☐ Uneven or low cylinder compressions (Chapter 2)
☐ Camshaft lobes worn (Chapter 2)
☐ Timing belt/chain incorrectly fitted (Chapter 2)
☐ Blocked injector/fuel injection system fault – petrol models (Chapter 4)
☐ Faulty injector(s) – diesel models (Chapter 4)

Engine misfires at idle speed

☐ Worn, faulty or incorrectly-gapped spark plugs – petrol models (Chapter 1)
☐ Faulty spark plug HT leads (where fitted) – petrol models (Chapter 1)
☐ Vacuum leak at the throttle body, inlet manifold or associated hoses – petrol models (Chapter 4)
☐ Blocked injector/fuel injection system fault – petrol models (Chapter 4)
☐ Faulty injector(s) – diesel models (Chapter 4)
☐ Uneven or low cylinder compressions (Chapter 2)
☐ Disconnected, leaking, or perished crankcase ventilation hoses (Chapter 4)

Engine (continued)

Engine misfires throughout the driving speed range

☐ Fuel filter choked (Chapter 1)
☐ Fuel pump faulty, or delivery pressure low (Chapter 4)
☐ Fuel tank vent blocked, or fuel pipes restricted (Chapter 4)
☐ Vacuum leak at the throttle body, inlet manifold or associated hoses – petrol models (Chapter 4)
☐ Worn, faulty or incorrectly-gapped spark plugs – petrol models (Chapter 1)
☐ Faulty spark plug HT leads (where fitted) – petrol models (Chapter 1)
☐ Faulty injector(s) – diesel models (Chapter 4)
☐ Faulty ignition coil – petrol models (Chapter 5)
☐ Uneven or low cylinder compressions (Chapter 2)
☐ Blocked injector/fuel injection system fault – petrol models (Chapter 4)

Engine hesitates on acceleration

☐ Worn, faulty or incorrectly-gapped spark plugs – petrol models (Chapter 1)
☐ Vacuum leak at the throttle body, inlet manifold or associated hoses (Chapter 4)
☐ Blocked injector/fuel injection system fault – petrol models (Chapter 4)
☐ Faulty injector(s) – diesel models (Chapter 4)

Engine stalls

☐ Vacuum leak at the throttle body, inlet manifold or associated hoses – petrol models (Chapter 4)
☐ Fuel filter choked (Chapter 1)
☐ Fuel pump faulty, or delivery pressure low – petrol models (Chapter 4)
☐ Fuel tank vent blocked, or fuel pipes restricted (Chapter 4)
☐ Blocked injector/fuel injection system fault – petrol models (Chapter 4)
☐ Faulty injector(s) – diesel models (Chapter 4)

Engine lacks power

☐ Timing belt/chain incorrectly fitted (Chapter 2)
☐ Fuel filter choked (Chapter 1)
☐ Fuel pump faulty, or delivery pressure low (Chapter 4)
☐ Uneven or low cylinder compressions (Chapter 2)
☐ Worn, faulty or incorrectly-gapped spark plugs – petrol models (Chapter 1)
☐ Vacuum leak at the throttle body, inlet manifold or associated hoses – petrol models (Chapter 4)
☐ Blocked injector/fuel injection system fault – petrol models (Chapter 4)
☐ Faulty injector(s) – diesel models (Chapter 4)
☐ Injection pump timing incorrect – diesel models (Chapter 4)
☐ Brakes binding (Chapters 1 and 9)
☐ Clutch slipping (Chapter 6)

Engine backfires

☐ Timing belt incorrectly fitted (Chapter 2)
☐ Vacuum leak at the throttle body, inlet manifold or associated hoses – petrol models (Chapter 4)
☐ Blocked injector/fuel injection system fault – petrol models (Chapter 4)

Oil pressure warning light illuminated with engine running

☐ Low oil level, or incorrect oil grade (see *Weekly checks*)
☐ Faulty oil pressure sensor (Chapter 5)
☐ Worn engine bearings and/or oil pump (Chapter 2)
☐ High engine operating temperature (Chapter 3)
☐ Oil pressure relief valve defective (Chapter 2)
☐ Oil pick-up strainer clogged (Chapter 2)

Engine runs-on after switching off

☐ Excessive carbon build-up in engine (Chapter 2)
☐ High engine operating temperature (Chapter 3)
☐ Fuel injection system fault – petrol models (Chapter 4)
☐ Faulty stop solenoid – diesel models (Chapter 4)

Engine noises

Pre-ignition (pinking) or knocking during acceleration or under load

☐ Ignition timing incorrect/ignition system fault – petrol models (Chapters 1 and 5)
☐ Incorrect grade of spark plug – petrol models (Chapter 1)
☐ Incorrect grade of fuel (Chapter 4)
☐ Vacuum leak at the throttle body, inlet manifold or associated hoses – petrol models (Chapter 4)
☐ Excessive carbon build-up in engine (Chapter 2)
☐ Blocked injector/fuel injection system fault – petrol models (Chapter 4)

Whistling or wheezing noises

☐ Leaking inlet manifold or throttle body gasket – petrol models (Chapter 4)
☐ Leaking exhaust manifold gasket or pipe-to-manifold joint (Chapter 4)
☐ Leaking vacuum hose (Chapters 4, 5 and 9)
☐ Blowing cylinder head gasket (Chapter 2)

Tapping or rattling noises

☐ Worn valve gear or camshaft (Chapter 2)
☐ Ancillary component fault (coolant pump, alternator, etc) (Chapters 3, 5, etc)

Knocking or thumping noises

☐ Worn big-end bearings (regular heavy knocking, perhaps less under load) (Chapter 2)
☐ Worn main bearings (rumbling and knocking, perhaps worsening under load) (Chapter 2)
☐ Piston slap (most noticeable when cold) (Chapter 2)
☐ Ancillary component fault (coolant pump, alternator, etc) (Chapters 3, 5, etc)

Cooling system

Overheating

- ☐ Insufficient coolant in system (see *Weekly checks*)
- ☐ Thermostat faulty (Chapter 3)
- ☐ Radiator core blocked, or grille restricted (Chapter 3)
- ☐ Cooling fan faulty (Chapter 3)
- ☐ Inaccurate temperature gauge sender unit (Chapter 3)
- ☐ Airlock in cooling system (Chapter 3)
- ☐ Pressure cap faulty (Chapter 3)

Overcooling

- ☐ Thermostat faulty (Chapter 3)
- ☐ Inaccurate temperature gauge sender unit (Chapter 3)
- ☐ Cooling fan faulty (Chapter 3)

External coolant leakage

- ☐ Deteriorated or damaged hoses or hose clips (Chapter 1)

- ☐ Radiator core or heater matrix leaking (Chapter 3)
- ☐ Pressure cap faulty (Chapter 3)
- ☐ Coolant pump internal seal leaking (Chapter 3)
- ☐ Coolant pump-to-block seal leaking (Chapter 3)
- ☐ Boiling due to overheating (Chapter 3)
- ☐ Core plug leaking (Chapter 2)

Internal coolant leakage

- ☐ Leaking cylinder head gasket (Chapter 2)
- ☐ Cracked cylinder head or cylinder block (Chapter 2)

Corrosion

- ☐ Infrequent draining and flushing (Chapter 1)
- ☐ Incorrect coolant mixture or inappropriate coolant type (see *Weekly checks*)

Fuel and exhaust systems

Excessive fuel consumption

- ☐ Air filter element dirty or clogged (Chapter 1)
- ☐ Fuel injection system fault – petrol models (Chapter 4)
- ☐ Faulty injector(s) – diesel models (Chapter 4)
- ☐ Ignition timing incorrect/ignition system fault – petrol models (Chapters 1 and 5)
- ☐ Tyres under-inflated (see *Weekly checks*)

Fuel leakage and/or fuel odour

- ☐ Damaged or corroded fuel tank, pipes or connections (Chapter 4)

Excessive noise or fumes from exhaust system

- ☐ Leaking exhaust system or manifold joints (Chapters 1 and 4)
- ☐ Leaking, corroded or damaged silencers or pipe (Chapters 1 and 4)
- ☐ Broken mountings causing body or suspension contact (Chapter 1)

Clutch

Pedal travels to floor – no pressure or very little resistance
- [ ] Air in hydraulic system/faulty master or slave cylinder (Chapter 6)
- [ ] Faulty hydraulic release system (Chapter 6)
- [ ] Broken clutch release bearing or fork (Chapter 6)
- [ ] Broken diaphragm spring in clutch pressure plate (Chapter 6)

Clutch fails to disengage (unable to select gears)
- [ ] Air in hydraulic system/faulty master or slave cylinder (Chapter 6)
- [ ] Faulty hydraulic release system (Chapter 6)
- [ ] Clutch disc sticking on gearbox input shaft splines (Chapter 6)
- [ ] Clutch disc sticking to flywheel or pressure plate (Chapter 6)
- [ ] Faulty pressure plate assembly (Chapter 6)
- [ ] Clutch release mechanism worn or incorrectly assembled (Chapter 6)

Clutch slips (engine speed increases, with no increase in vehicle speed)
- [ ] Faulty hydraulic release system (Chapter 6)
- [ ] Clutch disc linings excessively worn (Chapter 6)
- [ ] Clutch disc linings contaminated with oil or grease (Chapter 6)
- [ ] Faulty pressure plate or weak diaphragm spring (Chapter 6)

Judder as clutch is engaged
- [ ] Clutch disc linings contaminated with oil or grease (Chapter 6)
- [ ] Clutch disc linings excessively worn (Chapter 6)
- [ ] Faulty or distorted pressure plate or diaphragm spring (Chapter 6).
- [ ] Worn or loose engine or gearbox mountings (Chapter 2)
- [ ] Clutch disc hub or gearbox input shaft splines worn (Chapter 6)

Noise when depressing or releasing clutch pedal
- [ ] Worn clutch release bearing (Chapter 6)
- [ ] Worn or dry clutch pedal bushes (Chapter 6)
- [ ] Faulty pressure plate assembly (Chapter 6)
- [ ] Pressure plate diaphragm spring broken (Chapter 6)
- [ ] Broken clutch disc cushioning springs (Chapter 6)

Manual transmission

Noisy in neutral with engine running
- [ ] Input shaft bearings worn (noise apparent with clutch pedal released, but not when depressed) (Chapter 7A)*
- [ ] Clutch release bearing worn (noise apparent with clutch pedal depressed, possibly less when released) (Chapter 6)

Noisy in one particular gear
- [ ] Worn, damaged or chipped gear teeth (Chapter 7A)*

Difficulty engaging gears
- [ ] Clutch fault (Chapter 6)
- [ ] Worn or damaged gearchange linkage/cable (Chapter 7A)
- [ ] Worn synchroniser units (Chapter 7A)*

Jumps out of gear
- [ ] Worn or damaged gearchange linkage/cable (Chapter 7A)
- [ ] Worn synchroniser units (Chapter 7A)*
- [ ] Worn selector forks (Chapter 7A)*

Vibration
- [ ] Lack of oil (Chapter 1)
- [ ] Worn bearings (Chapter 7A)*

Lubricant leaks
- [ ] Leaking differential output oil seal (Chapter 7A)
- [ ] Leaking housing joint (Chapter 7A)*
- [ ] Leaking input shaft oil seal (Chapter 7A)*

*Although the corrective action necessary to remedy the symptoms described is beyond the scope of the home mechanic, the above information should be helpful in isolating the cause of the condition, so that the owner can communicate clearly with a professional mechanic.

Automatic transmission

Note: *Due to the complexity of the automatic transmission, it is difficult for the home mechanic to properly diagnose and service this unit. For problems other than the following, the vehicle should be taken to a dealer service department or automatic transmission specialist. Do not be too hasty in removing the transmission if a fault is suspected, as most of the testing is carried out with the unit still fitted.*

Fluid leakage

☐ Automatic transmission fluid is usually dark in colour. Fluid leaks should not be confused with engine oil, which can easily be blown onto the transmission by airflow.

☐ To determine the source of a leak, first remove all built-up dirt and grime from the transmission housing and surrounding areas using a degreasing agent, or by steam-cleaning. Drive the vehicle at low speed, so airflow will not blow the leak far from its source. Raise and support the vehicle, and determine where the leak is coming from. The following are common areas of leakage:
   a) Oil pan (Chapter 1 and 7B)
   b) Dipstick tube (Chapter 1 and 7B)
   c) Transmission-to-fluid cooler unions (Chapter 7B)

Transmission fluid brown, or has burned smell

☐ Transmission fluid level low (Chapter 1)

General gear selection problems

☐ Chapter 7B deals with checking the selector cable on automatic transmissions. The following are common problems which may be caused by a faulty cable:
   a) Engine starting in gears other than Park or Neutral.
   b) Indicator panel indicating a gear other than the one actually being used.
   c) Vehicle moves when in Park or Neutral.
   d) Poor gear shift quality or erratic gear changes.

Engine will not start in any gear, or starts in gears other than Park or Neutral

☐ Incorrect starter/inhibitor (multi-function) switch adjustment (Chapter 7B)
☐ Incorrect selector cable adjustment (Chapter 7B)

Transmission slips, shifts roughly, is noisy, or has no drive in forward or reverse gears

☐ There are many probable causes for the above problems, but the home mechanic should be concerned with only one possibility – fluid level. Before taking the vehicle to a dealer or transmission specialist, check the fluid level and condition of the fluid as described in Chapter 1. Correct the fluid level as necessary, or change the fluid if needed. If the problem persists, professional help will be necessary.

Driveshafts

Vibration when accelerating or decelerating

☐ Worn inner constant velocity joint (Chapter 8)
☐ Bent or distorted driveshaft (Chapter 8)
☐ Worn intermediate bearing (Chapter 8)

Clicking or knocking noise on turns (at slow speed on full-lock)

☐ Worn outer constant velocity joint (Chapter 8)
☐ Lack of constant velocity joint lubricant, possibly due to damaged gaiter (Chapter 8)
☐ Worn intermediate bearing (Chapter 8)

Braking system

Note: *Before assuming that a brake problem exists, make sure that the tyres are in good condition and correctly inflated, that the front wheel alignment is correct, and that the vehicle is not loaded with weight in an unequal manner. Apart from checking the condition of all pipe and hose connections, any faults occurring on the anti-lock braking system should be referred to a Ford dealer for diagnosis.*

Vehicle pulls to one side under braking

- ☐ Worn, defective, damaged or contaminated brake pads/shoes on one side (Chapters 1 and 9)
- ☐ Seized or partially-seized brake caliper piston/wheel cylinder (Chapters 1 and 9)
- ☐ A mixture of brake pad/shoe lining materials fitted between sides (Chapters 1 and 9)
- ☐ Brake caliper/backplate mounting bolts loose (Chapter 9)
- ☐ Worn or damaged steering or suspension components (Chapters 1 and 10)

Noise (grinding or high-pitched squeal) when brakes applied

- ☐ Brake pad/shoe friction lining material worn down to metal backing (Chapters 1 and 9)
- ☐ Excessive corrosion of brake disc/drum (may be apparent after the vehicle has been standing for some time (Chapters 1 and 9)
- ☐ Foreign object (stone chipping, etc) trapped between brake disc and shield (Chapters 1 and 9)

Excessive brake pedal travel

- ☐ Faulty master cylinder (Chapter 9)
- ☐ Air in hydraulic system (Chapters 1 and 9)
- ☐ Faulty vacuum servo unit (Chapter 9)

Brake pedal feels spongy when depressed

- ☐ Air in hydraulic system (Chapters 1 and 9)
- ☐ Deteriorated flexible rubber brake hoses (Chapters 1 and 9)
- ☐ Master cylinder mounting nuts loose (Chapter 9)
- ☐ Faulty master cylinder (Chapter 9)

Excessive brake pedal effort required to stop vehicle

- ☐ Faulty vacuum servo unit (Chapter 9)
- ☐ Disconnected, damaged or insecure brake servo vacuum hose (Chapter 9)
- ☐ Primary or secondary hydraulic circuit failure (Chapter 9)
- ☐ Seized brake caliper/wheel cylinder piston (Chapter 9)
- ☐ Brake pads/shoes incorrectly fitted (Chapters 1 and 9)
- ☐ Incorrect grade of brake pads/shoes fitted (Chapters 1 and 9)
- ☐ Brake pad/shoe linings contaminated (Chapters 1 and 9)
- ☐ Faulty vacuum pump – diesel models (Chapter 9)

Judder felt through brake pedal or steering wheel when braking

- ☐ Excessive run-out or distortion of discs/drums (Chapters 1 and 9)
- ☐ Brake pad/shoe linings worn (Chapters 1 and 9)
- ☐ Brake caliper/backplate mounting bolts loose (Chapter 9)
- ☐ Wear in suspension or steering components or mountings (Chapters 1 and 10)

Brakes binding

- ☐ Seized brake caliper/wheel cylinder piston (Chapter 9)
- ☐ Incorrectly-adjusted handbrake mechanism (Chapter 9)
- ☐ Faulty master cylinder (Chapter 9)

Rear wheels locking under normal braking

- ☐ Rear brake shoe linings contaminated (Chapters 1 and 9)
- ☐ Rear brake drums warped (Chapters 1 and 9)

Suspension and steering

Note: *Before diagnosing suspension or steering faults, be sure that the trouble is not due to incorrect tyre pressures, mixtures of tyre types, or binding brakes.*

Vehicle pulls to one side

- [ ] Defective tyre (see *Weekly checks*)
- [ ] Excessive wear in suspension or steering components (Chapters 1 and 10)
- [ ] Incorrect front wheel alignment (Chapter 10)
- [ ] Accident damage to steering or suspension components (Chapter 1)

Wheel wobble and vibration

- [ ] Front roadwheels out of balance (vibration felt mainly through the steering wheel) (Chapters 1 and 10)
- [ ] Rear roadwheels out of balance (vibration felt throughout the vehicle) (see *Weekly checks* and Chapter 10)
- [ ] Roadwheels damaged or distorted (Chapters 1 and 10)
- [ ] Faulty or damaged tyre (see *Weekly checks*)
- [ ] Worn steering or suspension joints, bushes or components (Chapters 1 and 10)
- [ ] Wheel bolts loose (Chapters 1 and 10)

Excessive pitching and/or rolling around corners, or during braking

- [ ] Defective shock absorbers (Chapters 1 and 10)
- [ ] Broken or weak spring and/or suspension component (Chapters 1 and 10)
- [ ] Worn or damaged anti-roll bar or mountings (Chapter 10)

Wandering or general instability

- [ ] Incorrect front wheel alignment (Chapter 10)
- [ ] Worn steering or suspension joints, bushes or components (Chapters 1 and 10)
- [ ] Roadwheels out of balance (Chapters 1 and 10)
- [ ] Faulty or damaged tyre (see *Weekly checks*)
- [ ] Wheel bolts loose (Chapters 1 and 10)
- [ ] Defective shock absorbers (Chapters 1 and 10)

Excessively-stiff steering

- [ ] Seized steering linkage balljoint or suspension balljoint (Chapters 1 and 10)
- [ ] Broken or incorrectly-adjusted auxiliary drivebelt (Chapter 1)
- [ ] Incorrect front wheel alignment (Chapter 10)
- [ ] Steering gear damaged (Chapter 10)

Excessive play in steering

- [ ] Worn steering column/intermediate shaft joints (Chapter 10)
- [ ] Worn track rod balljoints (Chapters 1 and 10)
- [ ] Worn steering gear (Chapter 10)
- [ ] Worn steering or suspension joints, bushes or components (Chapters 1 and 10)

Lack of power assistance

- [ ] Broken or incorrectly-adjusted auxiliary drivebelt (Chapter 1)
- [ ] Incorrect power steering fluid level (see *Weekly checks*)
- [ ] Restriction in power steering fluid hoses (Chapter 1)
- [ ] Faulty power steering pump (Chapter 10)
- [ ] Faulty steering gear (Chapter 10)

Tyre wear excessive

Tyres worn on inside or outside edges

- [ ] Tyres under-inflated (wear on both edges) (see *Weekly checks*)
- [ ] Incorrect camber or castor angles (wear on one edge only) (Chapter 10)
- [ ] Worn steering or suspension joints, bushes or components (Chapters 1 and 10)
- [ ] Excessively-hard cornering
- [ ] Accident damage

Tyre treads exhibit feathered edges

- [ ] Incorrect toe-setting (Chapter 10)

Tyres worn in centre of tread

- [ ] Tyres over-inflated (see *Weekly checks*)

Tyres worn on inside and outside edges

- [ ] Tyres under-inflated (see *Weekly checks*)

Tyres worn unevenly

- [ ] Tyres/wheels out of balance (see *Weekly checks*)
- [ ] Excessive wheel or tyre run-out
- [ ] Worn shock absorbers (Chapters 1 and 10)
- [ ] Faulty tyre (see *Weekly checks*)

Electrical system

Note: *For problems associated with the starting system, refer to the faults listed under 'Engine' earlier in this Section.*

Battery will not hold a charge for more than a few days

- [ ] Battery defective internally (Chapter 5A)
- [ ] Battery terminal connections loose or corroded (see *Weekly checks*)
- [ ] Auxiliary drivebelt worn or incorrectly adjusted (Chapter 1)
- [ ] Alternator not charging at correct output (Chapter 5)
- [ ] Alternator or voltage regulator faulty (Chapter 5)
- [ ] Short-circuit causing continual battery drain (Chapters 5 and 12)

Ignition/no-charge warning light remains illuminated with engine running

- [ ] Auxiliary drivebelt broken, worn, or incorrectly adjusted (Chapter 1)
- [ ] Internal fault in alternator or voltage regulator (Chapter 5)
- [ ] Broken, disconnected, or loose wiring in charging circuit (Chapter 5)

Ignition/no-charge warning light fails to come on

- [ ] Warning light bulb blown (Chapter 12)
- [ ] Broken, disconnected, or loose wiring in warning light circuit (Chapter 12)
- [ ] Alternator faulty (Chapter 5)

Electrical system (continued)

Lights inoperative

- ☐ Bulb blown (Chapter 12)
- ☐ Corrosion of bulb or bulbholder contacts (Chapter 12)
- ☐ Blown fuse (Chapter 12)
- ☐ Faulty relay (Chapter 12)
- ☐ Broken, loose, or disconnected wiring (Chapter 12)
- ☐ Faulty switch (Chapter 12)

Instrument readings inaccurate or erratic

Instrument readings increase with engine speed

- ☐ Faulty voltage regulator (Chapter 12)

Fuel or temperature gauges give no reading

- ☐ Faulty gauge sender unit (Chapters 3 and 4)
- ☐ Wiring open-circuit (Chapter 12)
- ☐ Faulty gauge (Chapter 12)

Fuel or temperature gauges give continuous maximum reading

- ☐ Faulty gauge sender unit (Chapters 3 and 4)
- ☐ Wiring short-circuit (Chapter 12)
- ☐ Faulty gauge (Chapter 12)

Horn inoperative, or unsatisfactory in operation

Horn operates all the time

- ☐ Horn push either earthed or stuck down (Chapter 12)
- ☐ Horn cable-to-horn push earthed (Chapter 12)

Horn fails to operate

- ☐ Blown fuse (Chapter 12)
- ☐ Cable or cable connections loose, broken or disconnected (Chapter 12)
- ☐ Faulty horn (Chapter 12)

Horn emits intermittent or unsatisfactory sound

- ☐ Cable connections loose (Chapter 12)
- ☐ Horn mountings loose (Chapter 12)
- ☐ Faulty horn (Chapter 12)

Windscreen wipers inoperative, or unsatisfactory in operation

Wipers fail to operate, or operate very slowly

- ☐ Wiper blades stuck to screen, or linkage seized or binding (Chapter 12)
- ☐ Blown fuse (Chapter 12)
- ☐ Cable or cable connections loose, broken or disconnected (Chapter 12)
- ☐ Faulty relay (Chapter 12)
- ☐ Faulty wiper motor (Chapter 12)

Wiper blades sweep over too large or too small an area of the glass

- ☐ Wiper arms incorrectly positioned on spindles (Chapter 12)
- ☐ Excessive wear of wiper linkage (Chapter 12)
- ☐ Wiper motor or linkage mountings loose or insecure (Chapter 12)

Wiper blades fail to clean the glass effectively

- ☐ Wiper blade rubbers worn or perished (see *Weekly checks*)
- ☐ Wiper arm tension springs broken, or arm pivots seized (Chapter 12)
- ☐ Insufficient windscreen washer additive to adequately remove road film (see *Weekly checks*)

Windscreen washers inoperative, or unsatisfactory in operation

One or more washer jets inoperative

- ☐ Blocked washer jet
- ☐ Disconnected, kinked or restricted fluid hose (Chapter 12)
- ☐ Insufficient fluid in washer reservoir (see *Weekly checks*)

Washer pump fails to operate

- ☐ Broken or disconnected wiring or connections (Chapter 12)
- ☐ Blown fuse (Chapter 12)
- ☐ Faulty washer switch (Chapter 12)
- ☐ Faulty washer pump (Chapter 12)

Washer pump runs for some time before fluid is emitted from jets

- ☐ Faulty one-way valve in fluid supply hose (Chapter 12)

Electric windows inoperative, or unsatisfactory in operation

Window glass will only move in one direction

- ☐ Faulty switch (Chapter 12)

Window glass slow to move

- ☐ Regulator seized or damaged, or in need of lubrication (Chapter 11)
- ☐ Door internal components or trim fouling regulator (Chapter 11)
- ☐ Faulty motor (Chapter 11)

Window glass fails to move

- ☐ Blown fuse (Chapter 12)
- ☐ Faulty relay (Chapter 12)
- ☐ Broken or disconnected wiring or connections (Chapter 12)
- ☐ Faulty motor (Chapter 11)

Central locking system inoperative, or unsatisfactory in operation

Complete system failure

- ☐ Blown fuse (Chapter 12)
- ☐ Faulty relay (Chapter 12)
- ☐ Broken or disconnected wiring or connections (Chapter 12)
- ☐ Faulty motor (Chapter 11)

Latch locks but will not unlock, or unlocks but will not lock

- ☐ Faulty master switch (Chapter 12)
- ☐ Broken or disconnected latch operating rods or levers (Chapter 11)
- ☐ Faulty relay (Chapter 12)
- ☐ Faulty motor (Chapter 11)

One solenoid/motor fails to operate

- ☐ Broken or disconnected wiring or connections (Chapter 12)
- ☐ Faulty operating assembly (Chapter 11)
- ☐ Broken, binding or disconnected latch operating rods or levers (Chapter 11)
- ☐ Fault in door latch (Chapter 11)

A

ABS (Anti-lock brake system) A system, usually electronically controlled, that senses incipient wheel lockup during braking and relieves hydraulic pressure at wheels that are about to skid.

Air bag An inflatable bag hidden in the steering wheel (driver's side) or the dash or glovebox (passenger side). In a head-on collision, the bags inflate, preventing the driver and front passenger from being thrown forward into the steering wheel or windscreen.

Air cleaner A metal or plastic housing, containing a filter element, which removes dust and dirt from the air being drawn into the engine.

Air filter element The actual filter in an air cleaner system, usually manufactured from pleated paper and requiring renewal at regular intervals.

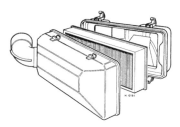

Air filter

Allen key A hexagonal wrench which fits into a recessed hexagonal hole.

Alligator clip A long-nosed spring-loaded metal clip with meshing teeth. Used to make temporary electrical connections.

Alternator A component in the electrical system which converts mechanical energy from a drivebelt into electrical energy to charge the battery and to operate the starting system, ignition system and electrical accessories.

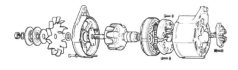

Alternator (exploded view)

Ampere (amp) A unit of measurement for the flow of electric current. One amp is the amount of current produced by one volt acting through a resistance of one ohm.

Anaerobic sealer A substance used to prevent bolts and screws from loosening. Anaerobic means that it does not require oxygen for activation. The Loctite brand is widely used.

Antifreeze A substance (usually ethylene glycol) mixed with water, and added to a vehicle's cooling system, to prevent freezing of the coolant in winter. Antifreeze also contains chemicals to inhibit corrosion and the formation of rust and other deposits that would tend to clog the radiator and coolant passages and reduce cooling efficiency.

Anti-seize compound A coating that reduces the risk of seizing on fasteners that are subjected to high temperatures, such as exhaust manifold bolts and nuts.

Anti-seize compound

Asbestos A natural fibrous mineral with great heat resistance, commonly used in the composition of brake friction materials. Asbestos is a health hazard and the dust created by brake systems should never be inhaled or ingested.

Axle A shaft on which a wheel revolves, or which revolves with a wheel. Also, a solid beam that connects the two wheels at one end of the vehicle. An axle which also transmits power to the wheels is known as a live axle.

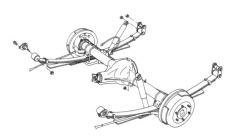

Axle assembly

Axleshaft A single rotating shaft, on either side of the differential, which delivers power from the final drive assembly to the drive wheels. Also called a driveshaft or a halfshaft.

B

Ball bearing An anti-friction bearing consisting of a hardened inner and outer race with hardened steel balls between two races.

Bearing

Bearing The curved surface on a shaft or in a bore, or the part assembled into either, that permits relative motion between them with minimum wear and friction.

Big-end bearing The bearing in the end of the connecting rod that's attached to the crankshaft.

Bleed nipple A valve on a brake wheel cylinder, caliper or other hydraulic component that is opened to purge the hydraulic system of air. Also called a bleed screw.

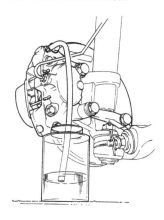

Brake bleeding

Brake bleeding Procedure for removing air from lines of a hydraulic brake system.

Brake disc The component of a disc brake that rotates with the wheels.

Brake drum The component of a drum brake that rotates with the wheels.

Brake linings The friction material which contacts the brake disc or drum to retard the vehicle's speed. The linings are bonded or riveted to the brake pads or shoes.

Brake pads The replaceable friction pads that pinch the brake disc when the brakes are applied. Brake pads consist of a friction material bonded or riveted to a rigid backing plate.

Brake shoe The crescent-shaped carrier to which the brake linings are mounted and which forces the lining against the rotating drum during braking.

Braking systems For more information on braking systems, consult the *Haynes Automotive Brake Manual*.

Breaker bar A long socket wrench handle providing greater leverage.

Bulkhead The insulated partition between the engine and the passenger compartment.

C

Caliper The non-rotating part of a disc-brake assembly that straddles the disc and carries the brake pads. The caliper also contains the hydraulic components that cause the pads to pinch the disc when the brakes are applied. A caliper is also a measuring tool that can be set to measure inside or outside dimensions of an object.

Camshaft A rotating shaft on which a series of cam lobes operate the valve mechanisms. The camshaft may be driven by gears, by sprockets and chain or by sprockets and a belt.

Canister A container in an evaporative emission control system; contains activated charcoal granules to trap vapours from the fuel system.

Canister

Carburettor A device which mixes fuel with air in the proper proportions to provide a desired power output from a spark ignition internal combustion engine.

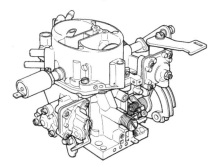

Carburettor

Castellated Resembling the parapets along the top of a castle wall. For example, a castellated balljoint stud nut.

Castellated nut

Castor In wheel alignment, the backward or forward tilt of the steering axis. Castor is positive when the steering axis is inclined rearward at the top.

Catalytic converter A silencer-like device in the exhaust system which converts certain pollutants in the exhaust gases into less harmful substances.

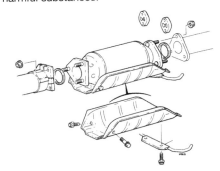

Catalytic converter

Circlip A ring-shaped clip used to prevent endwise movement of cylindrical parts and shafts. An internal circlip is installed in a groove in a housing; an external circlip fits into a groove on the outside of a cylindrical piece such as a shaft.

Clearance The amount of space between two parts. For example, between a piston and a cylinder, between a bearing and a journal, etc.

Coil spring A spiral of elastic steel found in various sizes throughout a vehicle, for example as a springing medium in the suspension and in the valve train.

Compression Reduction in volume, and increase in pressure and temperature, of a gas, caused by squeezing it into a smaller space.

Compression ratio The relationship between cylinder volume when the piston is at top dead centre and cylinder volume when the piston is at bottom dead centre.

Constant velocity (CV) joint A type of universal joint that cancels out vibrations caused by driving power being transmitted through an angle.

Core plug A disc or cup-shaped metal device inserted in a hole in a casting through which core was removed when the casting was formed. Also known as a freeze plug or expansion plug.

Crankcase The lower part of the engine block in which the crankshaft rotates.

Crankshaft The main rotating member, or shaft, running the length of the crankcase, with offset "throws" to which the connecting rods are attached.

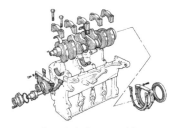

Crankshaft assembly

Crocodile clip See Alligator clip

D

Diagnostic code Code numbers obtained by accessing the diagnostic mode of an engine management computer. This code can be used to determine the area in the system where a malfunction may be located.

Disc brake A brake design incorporating a rotating disc onto which brake pads are squeezed. The resulting friction converts the energy of a moving vehicle into heat.

Double-overhead cam (DOHC) An engine that uses two overhead camshafts, usually one for the intake valves and one for the exhaust valves.

Drivebelt(s) The belt(s) used to drive accessories such as the alternator, water pump, power steering pump, air conditioning compressor, etc. off the crankshaft pulley.

Accessory drivebelts

Driveshaft Any shaft used to transmit motion. Commonly used when referring to the axleshafts on a front wheel drive vehicle.

Driveshaft

Drum brake A type of brake using a drum-shaped metal cylinder attached to the inner surface of the wheel. When the brake pedal is pressed, curved brake shoes with friction linings press against the inside of the drum to slow or stop the vehicle.

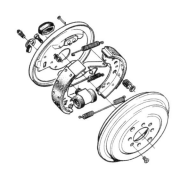

Drum brake assembly

E

EGR valve A valve used to introduce exhaust gases into the intake air stream.

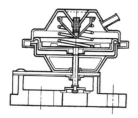

EGR valve

Electronic control unit (ECU) A computer which controls (for instance) ignition and fuel injection systems, or an anti-lock braking system. For more information refer to the *Haynes Automotive Electrical and Electronic Systems Manual*.

Electronic Fuel Injection (EFI) A computer controlled fuel system that distributes fuel through an injector located in each intake port of the engine.

Emergency brake A braking system, independent of the main hydraulic system, that can be used to slow or stop the vehicle if the primary brakes fail, or to hold the vehicle stationary even though the brake pedal isn't depressed. It usually consists of a hand lever that actuates either front or rear brakes mechanically through a series of cables and linkages. Also known as a handbrake or parking brake.

Endfloat The amount of lengthwise movement between two parts. As applied to a crankshaft, the distance that the crankshaft can move forward and back in the cylinder block.

Engine management system (EMS) A computer controlled system which manages the fuel injection and the ignition systems in an integrated fashion.

Exhaust manifold A part with several passages through which exhaust gases leave the engine combustion chambers and enter the exhaust pipe.

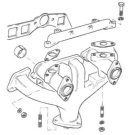

Exhaust manifold

F

Fan clutch A viscous (fluid) drive coupling device which permits variable engine fan speeds in relation to engine speeds.

Feeler blade A thin strip or blade of hardened steel, ground to an exact thickness, used to check or measure clearances between parts.

Feeler blade

Firing order The order in which the engine cylinders fire, or deliver their power strokes, beginning with the number one cylinder.

Flywheel A heavy spinning wheel in which energy is absorbed and stored by means of momentum. On cars, the flywheel is attached to the crankshaft to smooth out firing impulses.

Free play The amount of travel before any action takes place. The "looseness" in a linkage, or an assembly of parts, between the initial application of force and actual movement. For example, the distance the brake pedal moves before the pistons in the master cylinder are actuated.

Fuse An electrical device which protects a circuit against accidental overload. The typical fuse contains a soft piece of metal which is calibrated to melt at a predetermined current flow (expressed as amps) and break the circuit.

Fusible link A circuit protection device consisting of a conductor surrounded by heat-resistant insulation. The conductor is smaller than the wire it protects, so it acts as the weakest link in the circuit. Unlike a blown fuse, a failed fusible link must frequently be cut from the wire for replacement.

G

Gap The distance the spark must travel in jumping from the centre electrode to the side

Adjusting spark plug gap

electrode in a spark plug. Also refers to the spacing between the points in a contact breaker assembly in a conventional points-type ignition, or to the distance between the reluctor or rotor and the pickup coil in an electronic ignition.

Gasket Any thin, soft material - usually cork, cardboard, asbestos or soft metal - installed between two metal surfaces to ensure a good seal. For instance, the cylinder head gasket seals the joint between the block and the cylinder head.

Gasket

Gauge An instrument panel display used to monitor engine conditions. A gauge with a movable pointer on a dial or a fixed scale is an analogue gauge. A gauge with a numerical readout is called a digital gauge.

H

Halfshaft A rotating shaft that transmits power from the final drive unit to a drive wheel, usually when referring to a live rear axle.

Harmonic balancer A device designed to reduce torsion or twisting vibration in the crankshaft. May be incorporated in the crankshaft pulley. Also known as a vibration damper.

Hone An abrasive tool for correcting small irregularities or differences in diameter in an engine cylinder, brake cylinder, etc.

Hydraulic tappet A tappet that utilises hydraulic pressure from the engine's lubrication system to maintain zero clearance (constant contact with both camshaft and valve stem). Automatically adjusts to variation in valve stem length. Hydraulic tappets also reduce valve noise.

I

Ignition timing The moment at which the spark plug fires, usually expressed in the number of crankshaft degrees before the piston reaches the top of its stroke.

Inlet manifold A tube or housing with passages through which flows the air-fuel mixture (carburettor vehicles and vehicles with throttle body injection) or air only (port fuel-injected vehicles) to the port openings in the cylinder head.

J

Jump start Starting the engine of a vehicle with a discharged or weak battery by attaching jump leads from the weak battery to a charged or helper battery.

L

Load Sensing Proportioning Valve (LSPV) A brake hydraulic system control valve that works like a proportioning valve, but also takes into consideration the amount of weight carried by the rear axle.

Locknut A nut used to lock an adjustment nut, or other threaded component, in place. For example, a locknut is employed to keep the adjusting nut on the rocker arm in position.

Lockwasher A form of washer designed to prevent an attaching nut from working loose.

M

MacPherson strut A type of front suspension system devised by Earle MacPherson at Ford of England. In its original form, a simple lateral link with the anti-roll bar creates the lower control arm. A long strut - an integral coil spring and shock absorber - is mounted between the body and the steering knuckle. Many modern so-called MacPherson strut systems use a conventional lower A-arm and don't rely on the anti-roll bar for location.

Multimeter An electrical test instrument with the capability to measure voltage, current and resistance.

N

NOx Oxides of Nitrogen. A common toxic pollutant emitted by petrol and diesel engines at higher temperatures.

O

Ohm The unit of electrical resistance. One volt applied to a resistance of one ohm will produce a current of one amp.

Ohmmeter An instrument for measuring electrical resistance.

O-ring A type of sealing ring made of a special rubber-like material; in use, the O-ring is compressed into a groove to provide the sealing action.

O-ring

Overhead cam (ohc) engine An engine with the camshaft(s) located on top of the cylinder head(s).

Overhead valve (ohv) engine An engine with the valves located in the cylinder head, but with the camshaft located in the engine block.

Oxygen sensor A device installed in the engine exhaust manifold, which senses the oxygen content in the exhaust and converts this information into an electric current. Also called a Lambda sensor.

P

Phillips screw A type of screw head having a cross instead of a slot for a corresponding type of screwdriver.

Plastigage A thin strip of plastic thread, available in different sizes, used for measuring clearances. For example, a strip of Plastigage is laid across a bearing journal. The parts are assembled and dismantled; the width of the crushed strip indicates the clearance between journal and bearing.

Plastigage

Propeller shaft The long hollow tube with universal joints at both ends that carries power from the transmission to the differential on front-engined rear wheel drive vehicles.

Proportioning valve A hydraulic control valve which limits the amount of pressure to the rear brakes during panic stops to prevent wheel lock-up.

R

Rack-and-pinion steering A steering system with a pinion gear on the end of the steering shaft that mates with a rack (think of a geared wheel opened up and laid flat). When the steering wheel is turned, the pinion turns, moving the rack to the left or right. This movement is transmitted through the track rods to the steering arms at the wheels.

Radiator A liquid-to-air heat transfer device designed to reduce the temperature of the coolant in an internal combustion engine cooling system.

Refrigerant Any substance used as a heat transfer agent in an air-conditioning system. R-12 has been the principle refrigerant for many years; recently, however, manufacturers have begun using R-134a, a non-CFC substance that is considered less harmful to the ozone in the upper atmosphere.

Rocker arm A lever arm that rocks on a shaft or pivots on a stud. In an overhead valve engine, the rocker arm converts the upward movement of the pushrod into a downward movement to open a valve.

Rotor In a distributor, the rotating device inside the cap that connects the centre electrode and the outer terminals as it turns, distributing the high voltage from the coil secondary winding to the proper spark plug. Also, that part of an alternator which rotates inside the stator. Also, the rotating assembly of a turbocharger, including the compressor wheel, shaft and turbine wheel.

Runout The amount of wobble (in-and-out movement) of a gear or wheel as it's rotated. The amount a shaft rotates "out-of-true." The out-of-round condition of a rotating part.

S

Sealant A liquid or paste used to prevent leakage at a joint. Sometimes used in conjunction with a gasket.

Sealed beam lamp An older headlight design which integrates the reflector, lens and filaments into a hermetically-sealed one-piece unit. When a filament burns out or the lens cracks, the entire unit is simply replaced.

Serpentine drivebelt A single, long, wide accessory drivebelt that's used on some newer vehicles to drive all the accessories, instead of a series of smaller, shorter belts. Serpentine drivebelts are usually tensioned by an automatic tensioner.

Serpentine drivebelt

Shim Thin spacer, commonly used to adjust the clearance or relative positions between two parts. For example, shims inserted into or under bucket tappets control valve clearances. Clearance is adjusted by changing the thickness of the shim.

Slide hammer A special puller that screws into or hooks onto a component such as a shaft or bearing; a heavy sliding handle on the shaft bottoms against the end of the shaft to knock the component free.

Sprocket A tooth or projection on the periphery of a wheel, shaped to engage with a chain or drivebelt. Commonly used to refer to the sprocket wheel itself.

Starter inhibitor switch On vehicles with an automatic transmission, a switch that prevents starting if the vehicle is not in Neutral or Park.

Strut See MacPherson strut.

T

Tappet A cylindrical component which transmits motion from the cam to the valve stem, either directly or via a pushrod and rocker arm. Also called a cam follower.

Thermostat A heat-controlled valve that regulates the flow of coolant between the cylinder block and the radiator, so maintaining optimum engine operating temperature. A thermostat is also used in some air cleaners in which the temperature is regulated.

Thrust bearing The bearing in the clutch assembly that is moved in to the release levers by clutch pedal action to disengage the clutch. Also referred to as a release bearing.

Timing belt A toothed belt which drives the camshaft. Serious engine damage may result if it breaks in service.

Timing chain A chain which drives the camshaft.

Toe-in The amount the front wheels are closer together at the front than at the rear. On rear wheel drive vehicles, a slight amount of toe-in is usually specified to keep the front wheels running parallel on the road by offsetting other forces that tend to spread the wheels apart.

Toe-out The amount the front wheels are closer together at the rear than at the front. On front wheel drive vehicles, a slight amount of toe-out is usually specified.

Tools For full information on choosing and using tools, refer to the *Haynes Automotive Tools Manual*.

Tracer A stripe of a second colour applied to a wire insulator to distinguish that wire from another one with the same colour insulator.

Tune-up A process of accurate and careful adjustments and parts replacement to obtain the best possible engine performance.

Turbocharger A centrifugal device, driven by exhaust gases, that pressurises the intake air. Normally used to increase the power output from a given engine displacement, but can also be used primarily to reduce exhaust emissions (as on VW's "Umwelt" Diesel engine).

U

Universal joint or U-joint A double-pivoted connection for transmitting power from a driving to a driven shaft through an angle. A U-joint consists of two Y-shaped yokes and a cross-shaped member called the spider.

V

Valve A device through which the flow of liquid, gas, vacuum, or loose material in bulk may be started, stopped, or regulated by a movable part that opens, shuts, or partially obstructs one or more ports or passageways. A valve is also the movable part of such a device.

Valve clearance The clearance between the valve tip (the end of the valve stem) and the rocker arm or tappet. The valve clearance is measured when the valve is closed.

Vernier caliper A precision measuring instrument that measures inside and outside dimensions. Not quite as accurate as a micrometer, but more convenient.

Viscosity The thickness of a liquid or its resistance to flow.

Volt A unit for expressing electrical "pressure" in a circuit. One volt that will produce a current of one ampere through a resistance of one ohm.

W

Welding Various processes used to join metal items by heating the areas to be joined to a molten state and fusing them together. For more information refer to the *Haynes Automotive Welding Manual*.

Wiring diagram A drawing portraying the components and wires in a vehicle's electrical system, using standardised symbols. For more information refer to the *Haynes Automotive Electrical and Electronic Systems Manual*.

Note: *References throughout this index are in the form* **"Chapter number • Page number"**

A

Accelerator cable
Endura-DE engine – 4B•3
petrol engine – 4A•4
Accelerator pedal
Endura-DE engine – 4B•3
Endura-DI engine – 4C•3
petrol engine – 4A•4
Accelerator pedal sensor
Endura-DI engine – 4C•5
Accessory shops – REF•3
Acknowledgements – 0•6
Aerial – 12•17
Air cleaner assembly
Endura-DE engine – 4B•3
Endura-DI engine – 4C•3
petrol engine – 4A•3
Air conditioning system – 3•11, 3•12
Air filter
diesel engine – 1B•10
petrol engine – 1A•12
Air flow sensor
petrol engine – 4A•10
Air inlet components
Endura-DE engine – 4B•3
Endura-DI engine – 4C•3
petrol engine – 4A•3
Air recirculation control valve motor – 3•10
Air temperature sensor – 12•12
Endura-DI engine – 4C•5
petrol engine – 4A•11
Airbags – 0•5, 12•17
Alarm system and engine immobiliser – 12•17
Alternator – 5A•4, 5A•5
Antifreeze
diesel engine – 1B•12
petrol engine – 1A•16
Anti-lock braking system (ABS) – 9•14
Anti-roll bar
front – 10•6
Anti-theft alarm system and engine immobiliser – 12•17
Asbestos – 0•5
Automatic transmission – 2E•4, 7B•1 *et seq*
fault finding – REF•17
ATF – 0•20, 1A•9, 1A•12

Auxiliary drivebelt
diesel engine – 1B•7
petrol engine – 1A•7
Auxiliary shaft (Endura-DE engine) – 2E•9
oil seal – 2C•11
sprocket – 2C•10
Auxiliary warning system components – 12•12
Axle – 10•10, 10•11

B

Badges – 11•18
Battery – 0•5, 0•18, 5A•3
disconnection – 5A•2
Big-end bearings – 2E•15
clearance check – 2E•18
Bleeding
brakes – 9•2
clutch – 6•4
fuel system
Endura-DE engine – 4B•2
Endura-DI engine – 4C•3
power steering system – 10•17
Body corrosion – REF•11
Body electrical system – 12•1 *et seq*
Body exterior fittings – 11•17
Body trim strips and badges – 11•18
Bodywork and fittings – 11•1 *et seq*
Bonnet – 11•5
ajar switches – 12•12
lock – 11•6
release cable – 11•5
Brake and clutch fluid – 0•14, 0•20
diesel engine – 1B•11
petrol engine – 1A•15
Braking system – 9•1 *et seq*, REF•9, REF•10
diesel engine – 1B•9
fault finding – REF•18
petrol engine – 1A•10
Bulbs
exterior lights – 12•5
interior lights – 12•8
Bumpers – 11•4
Burning – 0•5
Buying spare parts – REF•3

C

Cables
  accelerator
    Endura-DE engine – 4B•3
    petrol engine – 4A•4
  bonnet release – 11•5
  speedometer – 12•13
  transmission selector
    petrol engine – 1A•7
  cold start
    Endura-DE engine – 4B•5
  handbrake – 9•12
Calipers – 9•8
Camshafts and tappets – 2E•11
    Endura-DE engine – 2C•11
    Endura-DI engine – 2D•10
    Zetec-SE engine – 2B•14
Camshaft oil seal
    Endura-DE engine – 2C•11
    Endura-DI engine – 2D•11
    Zetec-SE engine – 2B•13
Camshaft position sensor
    petrol engine – 4A•10
Camshaft sprocket
    Endura-DE engine – 2C•10
    Endura-DI engine – 2D•9
    Zetec-SE engine – 2B•12
Carpets – 11•2
Carpets – 11•21
Cassette player – 12•16
Catalytic converter – 4D•2, 4D•3
    Endura-DE engine – 4B•9
    Endura-DI engine – 4C•10
    petrol engine – 4A•13
Central locking system – 11•16
Centre console – 11•22
Centre pillar trim panel – 11•21
Charcoal canister renewal
    petrol engine – 4D•2
Charging – 5A•3, 5A•4
Cigarette lighter – 12•11
    illumination bulb – 12•8
Clock/temperature display – 12•11
    illumination bulb – 12•8
Clutch – 6•1 *et seq*
  fault finding – REF•16
  fluid – 0•14, 0•20
  pedal position switch
    Endura-DI engine – 4C•5
    petrol engine – 4A•11
Coil – 5B•2
Cold start cable
    Endura-DE engine – 4B•5
Compression test
    Endura-DE engine – 2C•4
    Endura-DI engine – 2D•4
    Endura-E engine – 2A•4
    Zetec-SE engine – 2B•4
Compressor – 3•12
Condenser – 3•12
Connecting rod assemblies – 2E•11, 2E•14, 2E•17
Console – 11•22
Contents – 0•2
Conversion factors – REF•2
Coolant – 0•15, 0•20
  diesel engine – 1B•11
  petrol engine – 1A•15

Coolant pump – 3•6
Coolant temperature sensor – 3•5
    petrol engine – 4A•10
Cooling, heating and air conditioning systems – 3•1 *et seq*
  fault finding – REF•15
Courtesy lights – 12•8
  switches – 12•5
Crankcase and bores – 2E•13
Crankcase emission control
    diesel engine – 4D•2, 4D•3
    petrol engine – 4D•1, 4D•2
Crankcase ventilation system
    petrol engine – 1A•12
Crankshaft – 2E•12, 2E•15, 2E•16
Crankshaft oil seals
    Endura-DE engine – 2C•16
    Endura-DI engine – 2D•18
    Endura-E engine – 2A•9, 2A•10
    Zetec-SE engine – 2B•21
Crankshaft position sensor – 5B•2
    Endura-DI engine – 4C•4
    petrol engine – 4A•10
Crankshaft pulley
    Endura-DE engine – 2C•7
    Endura-DI engine – 2D•7
    Endura-E engine – 2A•7
    Zetec-SE engine – 2B•7
Crankshaft sprocket
    Endura-DE engine – 2C•9
    Zetec-SE engine – 2B•13
Crossmember (front) – 10•7
Crushing – 0•5
Cylinder block/crankcase and bores – 2E•13
Cylinder head – 2E•6, 2E•8, 2E•9
    Endura-DE engine – 2C•13
    Endura-DI engine – 2D•12
    Endura-E engine – 2A•6
    Zetec-SE engine – 2B•16
Cylinder head cover
    Endura-DI engine – 2D•5
    Endura-E engine – 2A•5
    Zetec-SE engine – 2B•5
Cylinder head temperature sensor
    Endura-DI engine – 4C•4
    petrol engine – 4A•11

D

Dehydrator – 3•13
Dents in bodywork – 11•2
Depressurisation fuel system
    petrol engine – 4A•3
Diesel injection equipment – 0•5
    Endura-DI engine – 4C•4
Differential side gear oil seals – 7A•4, 7B•3
Dimensions and weights – REF•1
Direction indicator light – 12•6, 12•9
Discs – 9•6
  diesel engine – 1B•8
  petrol engine – 1A•8
Doors – 11•6, 11•14, 11•15, REF•9
  ajar switches – 12•12
  handles and lock components – 11•8, 11•15
  inner trim panel – 11•6
  lock – 11•16
  window glass and regulator – 11•11

Drivebelt
   diesel engine – 1B•7
   petrol engine – 1A•7
Driveplate
   Zetec-SE engine – 2B•22
Driveshafts – 8•1 *et seq*, REF•10
   fault finding – REF•17
   gaiter – 8•4, 8•5
    diesel engine – 1B•9
    petrol engine – 1A•9
Drivetrain
   diesel engine – 1B•9
   petrol engine – 1A•10
Drums – 9•7
   diesel engine – 1B•8
   petrol engine – 1A•9

E

Earth fault – 12•2
EGR valve
   Endura-DI engine – 4C•5
Electric shock – 0•5
Electrical equipment – REF•9
   diesel engine – 1B•9
   fault finding – 12•2, REF•19, REF•20
   petrol engine – 1A•10
Emission control systems – 4D•1 *et seq*, REF•11
Endura-DE diesel engine in-car repair procedures – 2C•1 *et seq*
Endura-DI diesel engine in-car repair procedures – 2D•1 *et seq*
Endura-E petrol engine in-car repair procedures – 2A•1 *et seq*
Engine fault finding – REF•13, REF•14
Engine immobiliser – 12•17
Engine oil – 0•13, 0•20
   diesel engine – 1B•6
   petrol engine – 1A•7
Engine removal and overhaul procedures – 2E•1 *et seq*
Environmental considerations – REF•4
Evaporative emission control
   petrol engine – 4D•2
Evaporator – 3•12
Exhaust emission control
   diesel engine – 4D•2, 4D•3
   petrol engine – 4D•1, 4D•3
Exhaust gas recirculation (EGR) system
   diesel engine – 4D•2, 4D•3
   petrol engine – 4D•3
Exhaust manifold
   Endura-DE engine – 4B•8
   Endura-DI engine – 4C•9
   petrol engine – 4A•12
Exhaust specialists – REF•3
Exhaust system – REF•10, REF•11
   Endura-DE engine – 4B•8
   Endura-DI engine – 4C•9
   petrol engine – 4A•13
Exterior fittings – 11•17
Exterior light units – 12•8

F

Facia – 11•22
   switches – 12•5
Fan – 3•4
   switch – 3•6

Fault Finding – REF•12 *et seq*
   automatic transmission – REF•17
   braking system – REF•18
   clutch – REF•16
   cooling system – REF•15
   driveshafts – REF•17
   electrical system – 12•2, REF•19, REF•20
   engine – REF•13, REF•14
   fuel and exhaust systems – REF•15
   manual transmission – REF•16
   suspension and steering – REF•19
Filling and respraying – 11•3
Filter
   air
    diesel engine – 1B•10
    petrol engine – 1A•12
   fuel
    diesel engine – 1B•10
    petrol engine – 1A•14
   oil
    diesel engine – 1B•6
    petrol engine – 1A•7
   pollen
    diesel engine – 1B•10
    petrol engine – 1A•10
Fire – 0•5
Fixed window glass – 11•17
Fluid leak
   diesel engine – 1B•8
   petrol engine – 1A•8
Flywheel
   Endura-DE engine – 2C•16
   Endura-DI engine – 2D•19
   Endura-E engine – 2A•10
   Zetec-SE engine – 2B•22
Foglight – 12•6, 12•9
Footbrake – REF•8
Front pillar trim panel – 11•21
Fuel and exhaust systems – Endura-DE diesel engine models – 4B•1 *et seq*, REF•11
Fuel and exhaust systems – Endura-DI diesel engine models – 4C•1 *et seq*, REF•11
Fuel and exhaust systems – petrol engine models – 4A•1 *et seq*, REF•11
Fuel and exhaust systems fault finding – REF•15
Fuel control valve
   Endura-DI engine – 4C•5
Fuel cut-off switch
   Endura-DE engine – 4B•7
   petrol engine – 4A•6
Fuel filler flap – 11•17
Fuel filter
   diesel engine – 1B•7, 1B•10
   petrol engine – 1A•14
Fuel gauge – 12•11
   sender unit
    Endura-DE engine – 4B•4
    Endura-DI engine – 4C•4
    petrol engine – 4A•6
Fuel heater – 5C•2
   Endura-DE engine – 4B•8
Fuel injection pump
   drive chain – 2E•10
   Endura-DE engine – 4B•6
   Endura-DI engine – 4C•5
   sprocket
    Endura-DI engine – 2D•9
   timing
    Endura-DE engine – 4B•5
    Endura-DI engine – 4C•5

Fuel injection system
  petrol engine – 4A•6, 4A•7
Fuel injectors
  Endura-DE engine – 4B•7
  Endura-DI engine – 4C•8
  petrol engine – 4A•7
Fuel lines
  petrol engine – 4A•3
Fuel pressure
  petrol engine – 4A•4
  regulator
    petrol engine – 4A•9
Fuel pump
  petrol engine – 4A•4
  petrol engine – 4A•6
Fuel rail and injectors
  petrol engine – 4A•7
Fuel shut-off solenoid
  Endura-DE engine – 4B•7
  petrol engine – 4A•6
Fuel tank
  Endura-DE engine – 4B•4
  Endura-DI engine – 4C•4
  petrol engine – 4A•5
Fuel tank filler pipe
  Endura-DE engine – 4B•4
  Endura-DI engine – 4C•4
  petrol engine – 4A•6
Fuel tank roll-over valve
  Endura-DE engine – 4B•4
  Endura-DI engine – 4C•4
  petrol engine – 4A•6
Fume or gas intoxication – 0•5
Fuses – 12•3

G

Gaiters
  driveshaft – 8•4, 8•5
  diesel engine – 1B•9
  petrol engine – 1A•9
  steering gear – 10•14
Gashes in bodywork – 11•2
Gaskets – REF•4
Gear selector mechanism
  automatic transmission – 7B•3
  manual transmission – 7A•2
General repair procedures – REF•4
Glossary of technical terms – REF•21 *et seq*
Glovebox light – 12•8
  switch – 12•5
Glow plugs – 5C•1
Grille panel – 11•5

H

Handbrake – 9•12, REF•8
  'on' warning light switch – 9•14
Handles
  door – 11•8, 11•15
Headlight – 12•5, 12•8
  adjustment switch – 12•5
  beam adjustment – 12•9
Headlining – 11•21

Heat shields
  Endura-DE engine – 4B•9
  Endura-DI engine – 4C•10
  petrol engine – 4A•14
Heating and ventilation system – 3•8
  blower motor – 3•9
    switch illumination bulb – 12•8
  control unit – 3•8
    illumination bulbs – 12•8
  heater assembly – 3•11
  matrix – 3•10
High-level stop-light – 12•8, 12•9
Hinge and lock lubrication
  diesel engine – 1B•9
  petrol engine – 1A•10
Horn – 12•13
Hose and fluid leak
  diesel engine – 1B•8
  petrol engine – 1A•8
Hoses – 3•2, 6•4, 9•3
HT coil – 5B•2
Hub
  front – 10•3, 10•4
  rear – 10•8
Hydrofluoric acid – 0•5

I

Identification numbers – REF•3
Idle air control valve
  petrol engine – 4A•9
Idle speed
  Endura-DE engine – 4B•4, 4B•5
Ignition switch – 12•4
Ignition system – petrol engine – 1A•11, 1A•14, 5B•1 *et seq*
Immobiliser – 12•17
Indicator light – 12•6, 12•9
Injection pipes
  Endura-DE engine – 4B•7
  Endura-DI engine – 4C•7
Injection pump
  belt
    diesel engine – 1B•11
    Endura-DE engine – 2C•7
  control unit
    Endura-DI engine – 4C•5
  sprocket
    Endura-DE engine – 2C•10
Injectors
  Endura-DE engine – 4B•7
  Endura-DI engine – 4C•8
  petrol engine – 4A•7
Inlet manifold
  Endura-DE engine – 4B•8
  Endura-DI engine – 4C•9
  petrol engine – 4A•11
Inner trim panel door – 11•6
Input shaft oil seal – 7A•5
Instrument panel – 12•9, 12•11
Instruments and electrical equipment
  diesel engine – 1B•9
  petrol engine – 1A•10
Interior trim – 11•20
Intermediate bearing (driveshaft) – 8•6

J

Jacking and vehicle support – REF•5
Joint mating faces – REF•4
Jump starting – 0•8

L

Leaks – 0•9
  diesel engine – 1B•8
  petrol engine – 1A•8
Leakdown test
  Endura-DE engine – 2C•5
  Endura-DI engine – 2D•4
Lights 'on' warning buzzer – 12•12
Limited Operation Strategy
  petrol engine – 4A•7
Load doors – 11•14, 11•15
Locks
  bonnet – 11•6
  central locking system – 11•16
  door – 11•8, 11•15
  lubrication
    diesel engine – 1B•9
    petrol engine – 1A•10
  steering column – 12•4
  tailgate – 11•14
Locknuts, locktabs and washers – REF•4
Loudspeakers – 12•16
Lower arm
  front – 10•7
Lubricants and fluids – 0•20
Luggage compartment
  light – 12•8
  switch – 12•5
  side trim panel – 11•21

M

Main bearings – 2E•15
  clearance check – 2E•16
Manifold absolute pressure sensor
  Endura-DI engine – 4C•5
  petrol engine – 4A•11
Manifolds
  Endura-DI engine – 4C•9
  Endura-DE engine – 4B•8
  petrol engine – 4A•11
Manual transmission – 2E•2, 2E•5, 7A•1 et seq
  fault finding – REF•16
  oil – 0•20
    diesel engine – 1B•11
    petrol engine – 1A•12
Map reading lights – 12•8
Mass air flow sensor
  petrol engine – 4A•10
Master cylinder
  brakes – 9•10
  clutch – 6•2
Maximum speed
  Endura-DE engine – 4B•5
Mirrors – 11•16, 11•17, REF•8
MOT test checks – REF•8 et seq

Motor factors – REF•3
Mountings
  Endura-DE engine – 2C•17
  Endura-DI engine – 2D•20
  Endura-E engine – 2A•11
  Zetec-SE engine – 2B•22
Multi-function switch – 7A•5

N

Number plate light – 12•7, 12•9

O

Officially appointed garages – REF•3
Oil cooler
  Endura-DI engine – 2D•17
Oil
  engine – 0•13, 0•20
    diesel engine – 1B•6
    petrol engine – 1A•7
  manual transmission – 0•20
    diesel engine – 1B•11
    petrol engine – 1A•12
Oil filler cap
  petrol engine – 1A•12
Oil filter
  diesel engine – 1B•6
  petrol engine – 1A•7
Oil pressure warning light switch – 5A•7
  Endura-DI engine – 2D•17
Oil pump
  Endura-DE engine – 2C•15
  Endura-DI engine – 2D•16
  Endura-E engine – 2A•9
  Zetec-SE engine – 2B•20
Oil seals – REF•4
  auxiliary shaft
    Endura-DE engine – 2C•11
  camshaft
    Endura-DE engine – 2C•11
    Endura-DI engine – 2D•11
    Zetec-SE engine – 2B•13
  crankshaft
    Endura-DE engine – 2C•16
    Endura-DI engine – 2D•18
    Endura-E engine – 2A•9, 2A•10
    Zetec-SE engine – 2B•21
  transmission – 7A•4, 7B•3
Open-circuit – 12•2
Oxygen (lambda) sensor
  petrol engine – 4D•3

P

Pads – 9•4
  diesel engine – 1B•8
  petrol engine – 1A•8
Parcel shelf support panel – 11•21

Pedal
  accelerator
    Endura-DE engine – 4B•3
    Endura-DI engine – 4C•3
    petrol engine – 4A•4
  brake – 9•10
  clutch – 6•5
    position switch – 4A•11, 4C•5
Pillar trim panel – 11•21
Pipes and hoses – 9•3
Piston/connecting rod assemblies – 2E•11, 2E•14, 2E•17
Plastic components – 11•3
Poisonous or irritant substances – 0•5
Pollen filter
  diesel engine – 1B•10
  petrol engine – 1A•10
Power steering fluid – 0•15, 0•20
  cooler – 10•16
  pressure switch – 10•17
Power steering pump – 10•15
Powertrain Control Module
  Endura-DI engine – 4C•5
  petrol engine – 4A•10
Pre-heating system – diesel engine – 5C•1 *et seq*
Pressure cap
  diesel engine – 1B•13
  petrol engine – 1A•16
Pressure-regulating valve – 9•13
Priming and bleeding fuel system
  Endura-DE engine – 4B•2
  Endura-DI engine – 4C•3
Puncture repair – 0•10
Purge valve
  petrol engine – 4D•2
Pushbutton switch illumination bulbs – 12•8

Q

Quarter windows – 11•13
Quick-release couplings
  petrol engine – 4A•3

R

Radiator – 3•2
  grille panel – 11•5
Radio/cassette player – 12•16
  aerial – 12•17
Rear axle – 10•10, 10•11
Rear lights – 12•6, 12•9
Relays – 12•3
Release bearing – 6•7
Remote control – 11•16
Remote tailgate release switch – 12•5
Repair procedures – REF•4
Respraying – 11•3
Reversing light switch – 7A•5, 7B•3
Ride height – 10•13
Road test
  diesel engine – 1B•9
  petrol engine – 1A•10
Roadside repairs – 0•7 *et seq*
Roadwheel nut tightness
  diesel engine – 1B•9
  petrol engine – 1A•10

Rocker arm components – 2E•8
Rocker cover
  Endura-E engine – 2A•5
Rocker gear
  Endura-E engine – 2A•5
Routine maintenance – bodywork and underframe – 11•1
Routine maintenance – upholstery and carpets – 11•2
Routine maintenance and servicing – diesel engine – 1B•1 *et seq*
Routine maintenance and servicing – petrol engine – 1A•1 *et seq*
Rust holes or gashes in bodywork – 11•2

S

Safety first! – 0•5, 0•14, 0•15
Scalding – 0•5
Scratches in bodywork – 11•2
Screw threads and fastenings – REF•4
Scuttle cover panel – 11•17
Seat belts – 11•19
Seats – 11•18
Selector cable
  automatic transmission – 1A•7, 7B•2
Servo unit – 9•11, 9•12
Shock absorbers – 10•11, REF•9, REF•10
  diesel engine – 1B•9
  petrol engine – 1A•9
Shoes – 9•5
  petrol engine – 1A•9
Short-circuit – 12•2
Sidelight – 12•6
Silencer
  Endura-DE engine – 4B•9
  petrol engine – 4A•14
Sill trim panels – 11•20
Slave cylinder
  clutch – 6•2
Sliding side windows – 11•13
Spare parts – REF•3
Spark plugs
  petrol engine – 1A•13
Speed sensor
  Endura-DI engine – 4C•5
  petrol engine – 4A•11
Speedometer – 12•11
  cable – 12•13
  drive – 7A•5, 7B•3
  drive pinion oil seal – 7A•5, 7B•3
Spoiler – 11•18
Springs – REF•10
Starting and charging systems – 5A•1 *et seq*
Start-up after overhaul – 2E•19
Steering – REF•9, REF•10
  diesel engine – 1B•8, 1B•9
  petrol engine – 1A•9, 1A•10
Steering angles – 10•18
Steering column – 10•13, REF•8
  combination switch – 12•4
  lock cylinder – 12•4
  shrouds – 11•20
Steering gear – 10•14
Steering wheel – 10•13, REF•8
Stop-light – 12•8
  switch – 9•14
Strut
  suspension
    front – 10•4
    rear – 10•9
  tailgate – 11•13

Sump
Endura-DE engine – 2C•14
Endura-DI engine – 2D•15
Endura-E engine – 2A•8
Zetec-SE engine – 2B•19
Sunroof – 11•17
switch – 12•5
Suspension and steering – 10•1 *et seq*, REF•9, REF•10
diesel engine – 1B•8, 1B•9
fault finding – REF•19
petrol engine – 1A•9, 1A•10
Switches – 12•4
fuel cut-off
petrol engine – 4A•6
heater blower motor – 3•8
clutch pedal position
Endura-DI engine – 4C•5
petrol engine – 4A•11
cooling system – 3•5
courtesy light – 12•5
door/tailgate/bonnet ajar – 12•12
electric window – 12•5
facia-mounted pushbutton – 12•5
glovebox light – 12•5
handbrake 'on' warning light – 9•14
headlight adjustment – 12•5
luggage compartment light – 12•5
mirror – 11•17
multi-function – 7A•5
oil pressure warning light – 5A•7
Endura-DI engine – 2D•17
remote tailgate release – 12•5
reversing light – 7A•5, 7B•3
steering column combination – 12•4
stop-light – 9•14
sunroof – 12•5

T

Tachometer – 12•11
Tailgate – 11•13
ajar switch – 12•12
glass – 11•17
lock – 11•14
release switch – 12•5
wiper motor – 12•14
Tappets – 2E•11
Endura-DE engine – 2C•11
Endura-DI engine – 2D•10
Zetec-SE engine – 2B•14
Temperature display – 12•11
illumination bulb – 12•8
Temperature gauge – 12•11
sender – 3•6
Temperature sensor – 12•12
Endura-DI engine – 4C•4, 4C•5
petrol engine – 4A•10, 4A•11
Thermostat – 3•3
Throttle body housing
petrol engine – 4A•7
Throttle position sensor
petrol engine – 4A•11
Timing belt
diesel engine – 1B•11
Endura-DE engine – 2C•7
Endura-DI engine – 2D•8
petrol engine – 1A•14
Zetec-SE engine – 2B•9

Timing belt covers
Endura-DE engine – 2C•7
Zetec-SE engine – 2B•8
Timing belt tensioner
Endura-DE engine – 2C•4, 2C•9
Endura-DI engine – 2D•9
Zetec-SE engine – 2B•11
Timing chain cover
Endura-E engine – 2A•7, 2A•8
Timing
fuel injection pump
Endura-DE engine – 4B•5
Endura-DI engine – 4C•5
ignition – 5B•3
Tools and working facilities – REF•4, REF•6 *et seq*
Top Dead Centre (TDC) for No 1 cylinder location
Endura-DE engine – 2C•5
Endura-DI engine – 2D•4
Endura-E engine – 2A•4
Zetec-SE engine – 2B•5
Towing – 0•9
Track rod end – 10•17
Transmission mountings
Endura-DE engine – 2C•17
Endura-DI engine – 2D•20
Endura-E engine – 2A•11
Zetec-SE engine – 2B•22
Transmission selector shaft oil seal – 7A•4
Trim strips and badges – 11•18, 11•20
Turbocharger
Endura-DI engine – 4C•8
Tyres – 0•16, REF•11
pressures – 0•21
specialists – REF•3

U

Underbonnet check points – 0•12
Underframe – 11•1
Undershield – 11•18
Unleaded petrol – 4A•3
Upholstery and carpets – 11•2

V

Vacuum pump (braking system) – 9•15, 9•16
Vacuum servo unit – 9•11, 9•12
Valve clearances
diesel engine – 1B•10
Endura-DE engine – 2C•6
Endura-DI engine – 2D•6
Endura-E engine – 2A•5
petrol engine – 1A•7, 1A•14
Zetec-SE engine – 2B•7
Valve stem oil seals – 2E•9
Valves – 2E•8
Vehicle identification numbers – REF•3, REF•9
Vehicle speed sensor
Endura-DI engine – 4C•5
petrol engine – 4A•11
Vehicle support – REF•5
Vibration damper
Endura-DE engine – 2C•7
Zetec-SE engine – 2B•7

W

Warning light bulbs – 12•11
   handbrake 'on' – 9•14
   oil pressure – 5A•7
Washer fluid – 0•17
   level sensor – 12•12
Washer system – 12•15
Weekly checks – 0•12 *et seq*
Weights – REF•1
Wheels – REF•11
   alignment and steering angles – 10•18
   bearings – REF•10
    front – 10•3, 10•4
    rear – 10•8
   changing – 0•10
Wheel cylinders – 9•9
Wheel sensor – 9•15
Wheelarch liners and engine undershield – 11•18
Windows
   door – 11•11
   electric – 11•16
   fixed glass – 11•17
   motors – 11•16
   quarter – 11•13
   sliding – 11•13
   switches – 12•5
   windscreen, tailgate and fixed window glass – 11•17
Windscreen – REF•8
   wiper motor and linkage – 12•13
Wiper arm – 12•13
Wiper blades – 0•17
Wiper motor and linkage – 12•13, 12•14
Wiring diagrams – 12•20 *et seq*
Working facilities – REF•6

Y

Your Ford Fiesta Manual – 0•6

Z

Zetec-SE petrol engine in-car repair procedures – 2B•1 *et seq*

Preserving Our Motoring Heritage

< The Model J Duesenberg Derham Tourster. Only eight of these magnificent cars were ever built – this is the only example to be found outside the United States of America

Almost every car you've ever loved, loathed or desired is gathered under one roof at the Haynes Motor Museum. Over 300 immaculately presented cars and motorbikes represent every aspect of our motoring heritage, from elegant reminders of bygone days, such as the superb Model J Duesenberg to curiosities like the bug-eyed BMW Isetta. There are also many old friends and flames. Perhaps you remember the 1959 Ford Popular that you did your courting in? The magnificent 'Red Collection' is a spectacle of classic sports cars including AC, Alfa Romeo, Austin Healey, Ferrari, Lamborghini, Maserati, MG, Riley, Porsche and Triumph.

A Perfect Day Out

Each and every vehicle at the Haynes Motor Museum has played its part in the history and culture of Motoring. Today, they make a wonderful spectacle and a great day out for all the family. Bring the kids, bring Mum and Dad, but above all bring your camera to capture those golden memories for ever. You will also find an impressive array of motoring memorabilia, a comfortable 70 seat video cinema and one of the most extensive transport book shops in Britain. The Pit Stop Cafe serves everything from a cup of tea to wholesome, home-made meals or, if you prefer, you can enjoy the large picnic area nestled in the beautiful rural surroundings of Somerset.

> John Haynes O.B.E., Founder and Chairman of the museum at the wheel of a Haynes Light 12.

< Graham Hill's Lola Cosworth Formula 1 car next to a 1934 Riley Sports.

The Museum is situated on the A359 Yeovil to Frome road at Sparkford, just off the A303 in Somerset. It is about 40 miles south of Bristol, and 25 minutes drive from the M5 intersection at Taunton.
Open 9.30am - 5.30pm (10.00am - 4.00pm Winter) 7 days a week, *except Christmas Day, Boxing Day and New Years Day*
Special rates available for schools, coach parties and outings Charitable Trust No. 292048